RADIOCARBON DATES

from samples funded by E
between 1988 an

RADIOCARBON DATES

*from samples funded by English Heritage
between 1988 and 1993*

Alex Bayliss, Christopher Bronk Ramsey, Gordon Cook,
Gerry McCormac, Robert Otlet, and Jill Walker

ENGLISH HERITAGE

Published by English Heritage, The Engine House, Fire Fly Avenue, Swindon SN2 2EH
www.english-heritage.org.uk

English Heritage is the Government's statutory adviser on all aspects of the historic
environment.

First published 2013

10 9 8 7 6 5 4 3 2 1

ISBN 978-1-84802-229-4

Product Code 51780

British Library Cataloguing in Publication Data
A CIP catalogue record for this book is available from the British Library.

The National Monuments Record is the public archive of English Heritage.
For more information, contact NMR Enquiry and Research Services, National
Monuments Record Centre, The Engine House, Fire Fly Avenue, Swindon SN2 2EH;
telephone (01793) 414600.

Edited and brought to publication by David M Jones, Publishing, English Heritage,
The Engine House, Fire Fly Avenue, Swindon SN2 2EH.

Cover design and page layout by www.farbott.com
Indexed by Alan Rutter
Printed by 4edge Ltd, Hockley. www.4edge.co.uk

Contents

Radiocarbon Dates funded by English Heritage between 1988 and 1993

Introduction

This volume presents a detailed catalogue of the radiocarbon dates funded by English Heritage between April 1988 and March 1993. In total, details of 881 determinations are provided.

Only samples from sites in which English Heritage had a formal interest were eligible for dating through the Ancient Monuments Laboratory. Often samples came from archaeological excavations funded, wholly or in part, by English Heritage. Some samples were from sites excavated by the in-house archaeological team or on sites in guardianship (Fig 1), but many were from excavations undertaken by others with funding from the English Heritage Archaeology Commissions Programme. Many of these sites were excavated in advance of development. This volume covers a period of transition in English archaeology when funding from developers first became widely available, following the adoption of new planning guidance in the early 1990s (PPG16 1990). Inevitably, post-excavation analysis and publication follows on from excavation, however, and so most of the sites included in this volume were excavated before the implementation of PPG16.

Samples were also submitted from the large-scale archaeological surveys of wetlands which were undertaken at this time, and from excavations of sites under threat (Fig 2). Work also continued on the publication of sites that had been excavated with public funding over previous decades. Other samples were submitted from archaeological research programmes undertaken by the staff of the Ancient Monuments Laboratory and their university-based contractors. For example, research to investigate whether a series of plant macrofossils from Leicester: Shires and Worcester: Deansway (see below, 103 and 231–5), which were neither carbonised, mineralised, or waterlogged, were ancient and preserved by some other means.

This datelist also covers a period of transition in the radiocarbon dating programme funded by English Heritage. The last samples were submitted to AERE Harwell in March 1989, although processing of these samples and the completion of summary datelists for the journal *Radiocarbon* continued until the closure of the laboratory in 1990 (Hardiman *et al* 1992; Walker *et al* 1990; 1991a–b). During 1989 and 1990, conventional radiocarbon dates, measured by liquid scintillation spectrometry, were provided by The Queen's University, Belfast Radiocarbon Dating Laboratory, including 16 that were dated using the high-precision facility. From 1990, conventional radiocarbon measurements were increasingly undertaken by the Scottish Universities Research and Reactor Centre at East Kilbride, with only high-precision work being undertaken in Belfast (Fig 3).

During this time the availability of accelerator mass spectrometry increased, from only the handful of samples that could be dated each year in the late 1980s to around

Fig 1. *Excavations at Beeston Castle, Cheshire in 1980 and 1983. (© English Heritage)*

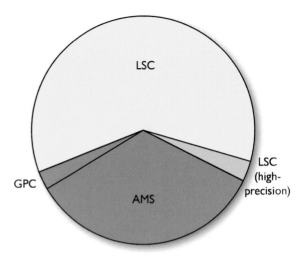

 appears here as the large photograph in the upper left.

Fig 4. *Techniques of radiocarbon dating used for the measurements reported in this volume (LSC, liquid scintillation counting; GPC, gas-proportional counting; LSC (high-precision), high-precision liquid scintillation counting; AMS, accelerator mass spectrometry).*

Fig 2. *Bronze Age barrows on Snail Down, Wiltshire showing the evidence of erosion by military exercises. (© Crown Copyright. NMR)*

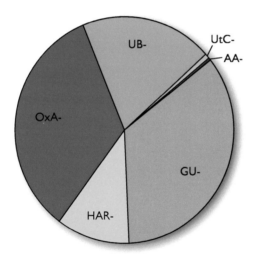

Fig 3. *Proportion of radiocarbon measurements included in this volume processed by each collaborating facility (AA-, Arizona Accelerator Mass Spectrometer Laboratory; GU-, Scottish Universities Research and Reactor Centre; HAR-, AERE Harwell; OxA-, Oxford Radiocarbon Accelerator Unit; UB-, The Queen's University, Belfast Radiocarbon Dating Laboratory; UtC-, Utrecht van der Graaf Laboratorium).*

50 each year in the early 1990s. Occasionally, samples that were submitted for conventional dating failed to produce sufficient carbon dioxide for liquid scintillation counting and so the gas was sent for dating by accelerator mass spectrometry (Fig 3).

Figure 4 shows the number of radiocarbon determinations reported in this volume made by each measurement technique. Overall, even though capacity was still limited, 34% of measurements were made by accelerator mass

spectrometry. This new technique met the demand for the dating of small samples, which had previously been addressed by the miniature gas-proportional counting system at Harwell (2%). Most samples (64%) were dated using liquid scintillation counting, with 16 being dated by high-precision facilities (2%). A general introduction to methods of measuring the radiocarbon content of archaeological samples is provided by Bayliss *et al* (2004b).

History of this volume

The compilation of this datelist began in 1994.

The majority of the radiocarbon dates included in this volume have not been published previously in datelist form, although many appear in archaeological publications on specific sites. Summary datelists in the journals *Radiocarbon* and *Archaeometry* are available for many of the measurements made at the Harwell Laboratory (Walker *et al* 1990; 1991a–b; Hardiman *et al* 1992) and the Oxford Radiocarbon Accelerator Unit (Hedges *et al* 1990; 1991a–b; 1992; 1993; 1994; 1995; 1996; 1997).

In this volume, we have provided as much information as possible about the character and provenance of each sample. In some cases, additional information has become available since the original publication of the results. This is the case, for example, for samples of wood and charcoal which were dated at AERE Harwell, where excess material was retrieved from the laboratory on its demolition in 1995 that has subsequently been identified to age and species (Bayliss *et al* 2012, xxvi–xl). Further interpretation may also have been possible in cases where the radiocarbon dates have subsequently been incorporated in formal chronological models (see below).

The data published here were gathered by collating information from the archives of both the Ancient Monuments Laboratory and the dating laboratories concerned, and reconciling this as far as possible with information in published sources. Submitters were asked to check the draft publication entries for their sites, and to provide interpretative comments on the overall utility of the suite of radiocarbon dates and on each individual measurement.

The date when final comments were made is stated in the catalogue. This is important because, although almost all the comments were made on calibrated dates, the sophistication of the statistical techniques available for their interpretation has changed markedly since these radiocarbon dates were first reported. No effort has been made to amend the submitters' interpretation of their radiocarbon dates.

Consequently, the reader is warned that some treatments of results and views about them may be inaccurate and reflect misunderstandings about radiocarbon dating, statistics, and calibration. Sometimes, scientific understanding has simply moved on in the period since the comments were originally drafted.

Archaeological interpretation and scientific understanding develop through time, and so too will the interpretation of the radiocarbon dates presented in this volume. The key objective in the publication of this catalogue is to ensure that the basic data are available in sufficient detail to allow new interpretations and chronological models to be constructed.

Sample selection and characterisation

Two-thirds of the samples included in this volume were dated by the detection of radiocarbon decay events using either liquid scintillation or gas-proportional counting (Fig 4). The size of the samples necessary for the available measurement techniques (Table 1) was often the limiting factor in the selection of samples for dating.

Table 1. Typical quantities of material required for different radiocarbon measurement techniques in 1988–93.

Material	LSC	miniature GPC	AMS
Charcoal	15g	0.5g	30mg
Wood (wet)	100g	2g	200mg+
Peat (wet)	200g	6g	2g+
Bone and antler	300g+	10g	2g–

Whilst a wide range of organic materials could be dated (Fig 5), bone and antler (21%), charcoal and other charred plant remains (39%), peat and other sediments (24%), and waterlogged plant remains (15%) constituted the majority of samples, whilst chitin, skin, land snails, and unspecified organic matter were dated only occasionally.

During the period when these measurements were undertaken, calcined bone could not be dated reliably using radiocarbon. Robust protocols for dating the structural carbonate in such samples were far in the future (Lanting *et al* 2001), and the cremation process either destroys the protein component of the bone entirely or denatures it to the point that contaminating exogenous carbon from the burial environment cannot be removed reliably during laboratory

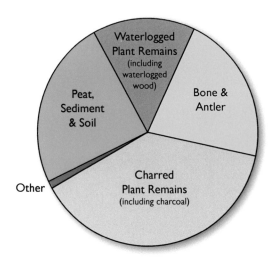

Fig 5. *Types of material dated.*

processing (making the resultant date unreliable). As part of early attempts to determine whether reliable radiocarbon dates could be obtained from charred bone using accelerator mass spectrometry, seven experimental measurements were made on the surviving protein fraction of charred human bones. Six samples were from cremations at Radley: Barrow Hills, Oxfordshire. Of these measurements, three (OxA-1872–3 and OxA-1879, see 145–7) gave dates which appear consistent with the stratigraphic position of these cremations and the associated ceramic types, and three (OxA-1876–8, see p146) gave dates which appear anomalous. The seventh measurement (OxA-1834 from a mortuary deposit at Hardendale Nab, Cumbria, see p87) also gave a date which was consistent with archaeological expectation.

The sample size requirements for conventional radiocarbon dating and accelerator mass spectrometry at this time meant that, in the majority of cases (53%), material which originally derived from different living organisms had to be bulked together to make up a sample of sufficient size for dating (Fig 6). It is often unclear, for example, whether a single charred cereal grain was dated, or whether several were bulked together for processing. As highlighted by

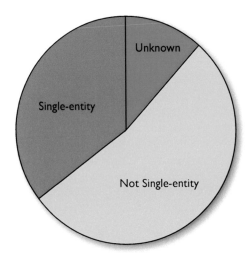

Fig 6. *Single-entity and bulk samples.*

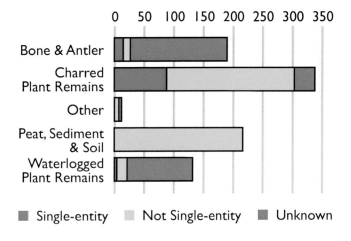

Fig 7. *Single-entity and bulk samples by material type.*

Ashmore (1999), this runs the risk that the sample will include fragments of various ages, giving a radiocarbon measurement that is the mean of all and the age of none. On the premise that a sample will always date to the latest material within it, however, such samples should at the very least provide reliable *termini post quos* for the contexts from which they were recovered.

It is clear, however, that some types of material produced single-entity samples that were sufficiently large for dating more frequently than other materials (Fig 7). This variation ranges from 100% of peat and sediment samples, which by definition are bulk materials, to bone and antler, where 86% of the dates reported in this volume derive from a single animal. In contrast, charred plant remains usually had to be bulked together to provide the required weight for analysis, although occasionally timbers charred *in situ* or single cereal grains were large enough for dating on their own. These instances, however, only provide 10% of the samples of charred plant remains dated.

Charred plant remains provided the largest group of dates reported in this volume (Fig 5), although 87% of these were charcoal. Of these, 47% were identified before submission for dating, and Rowena Gale has been able to identify a further 8% of these samples from excess material which remained in

the archive at AERE Harwell. These retrospective identifications have not, of course, been undertaken on the actual charcoal that was combusted and dated, but it is reasonable to suggest that the excess material constitutes a random sample from the charcoal originally submitted for dating. This assumption is, of course, far more reliable when a relatively large sub-sample can be identified than if the amount of surviving material is very small.

Identification of charcoal samples to age and species before dating is critical for interpreting the resultant radiocarbon date, because of the old-wood effect (Bowman 1990, 51). The carbon in tree-rings is fixed from the atmosphere during the year in which the tree-ring formed. Consequently, the carbon in a twig is only a few years old when the twig is burnt and enters the archaeological record, but the rings at the centre of a long-lived tree can contain carbon that is several centuries older than the burning event. If this age-at-death offset is unknown, the radiocarbon date may be much older than archaeological activity with which the sample is associated.

Of the 49% of charcoal samples included in this volume that have been identified, 39% were probably composed of species of tree and shrub (eg hazel or birch) that are relatively short-lived. The age-at-death of these samples is therefore unlikely to have been more than a few decades. The other 61% of the identified charcoal samples either consisted of a species of tree which lives to some age (eg oak or ash), or contained a component of such a species. These samples could have an old-wood offset of several centuries, if wood from the centre of a mature tree was sampled. Not all such samples will have an appreciable offset, however, as a sapling or branch or sapwood may have been dated. For conventional samples, even when a mature tree was dated, the majority of the wood would have derived from the later rings, rather than the centre pith[1]. In these circumstances, old-wood offsets of more than a century or two are probably rare, although, as with unidentified samples, the potential for an age-at-death offset in such samples means that they can only strictly be interpreted as *termini post quos* for the deposits from which they were recovered. Overall, 78% of the measurements reported on charcoal samples in this volume fall into this category (Fig 8).

Bone and antler samples form the next most numerous type of material dated (Fig 5). Over half of these samples were of human bone (Fig 9). Overall, 78% of animal bone samples were identified to species, and only one sample (OxA-3045

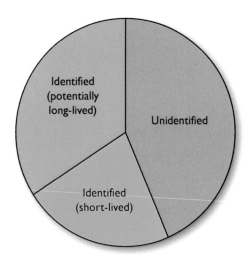

Fig 8. *Identification of charcoal samples.*

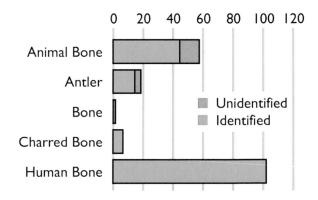

Fig 9. *Identification of bone and antler samples.*

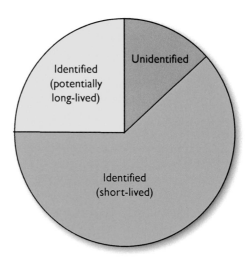

Fig 10. *(left) Soil profile from A66 Stainmore Pass: Vale House Farm, dated by UB-3347. (© English Heritage, photography by Dr Maureen McHugh)*

Fig 11. *(above) Identification of waterlogged wood samples.*

Fig 12. *(below) Brushwood (HAR-8765) preserved in the primary fill of the Haddenham V enclosure ditch, Cambridgeshire. (© C Evans)*

from Wessex Linear Ditches: Brigmerston Down linear ditch, see p208) is only recorded as bone. Of the 19 antler samples included in this volume, 15 were identified as red deer (and the other four were unidentified).

Peat, sediment, and soil constitute another frequently dated type of sample (Fig 10). These samples are rarely described more specifically. Generally the term used to describe the deposit submitted for dating appears to reflect its perceived organic content, rather than any more technical definition.

Of the waterlogged plant macrofossils submitted for dating, only 12 samples were short-lived herbaceous plant remains and not waterlogged wood. All but one of these (OxA-4816 from Yarnton Iron Age and Roman: floodplain section B, see p237) were identified before dating. Overall, 87% of the waterlogged wood samples reported in this volume have been identified (Fig 11): 82% before submission of the material for dating, and 5% from excess material which remained in the archive at AERE Harwell. These retrospective identifications have also been undertaken by Rowena Gale. Of the dated waterlogged wood samples that have been identified, 71% consisted of relatively short-lived material with an age-at-death of no more than a few decades (Fig 12), and 29% consisted of longer-lived material, which could potentially have an old-wood offset of several centuries.

The character of the sample material is only one criterion by which the association between a radiocarbon date and the target event that is of archaeological interest can be assessed. The importance of considering the taphonomy of dated material has been long known (Waterbolk 1971), although during the period covered by this volume the sample size requirement was a major restriction on sample choice (see again, Table 1). Often, it simply was not possible to date a single seed or a single fragment of charcoal.

The types of context which provided the samples considered here are shown in Figure 13. The largest group of samples is provided by sedimentary units. In the majority of

cases (80%), the bulk organic content of a deposit, usually peat, was itself dated. The sample is therefore composed of the unit that is of interest. In other cases, however, fragments of waterlogged plant remains or charcoal were isolated from a deposit and dated (Fig 14). Even when dating sediment itself, however, the relationship between the dated material and the archaeological event that is of interest has to be considered. All the material within a sediment does not necessarily date to the time when it formed. It could contain reworked material, for example if already waterlogged material was washed into a forming deposit, or it could contain a component of more recent rootlets that grew down into an existing layer. Such issues can only be assessed on a case-by-case basis by consideration of the characteristics of particular deposits and by assessing the compatibility of groups of related dates (see below).

Pits and ditches make up just over 20% of sampled contexts (Fig 13), with most samples being composed of charcoal or disarticulated animal bone (Fig 14). Although the concentration of material can sometimes indicate a discrete disposal event in the context (eg GU-5307 from Westhampnett, West Sussex, see below p216–7), in other cases all the material from a fill or feature had to be bulked together to provide the required sample weight (eg HAR-2906 from Christchurch: Bargates, Site X17, Dorset which was 'a combined sample from various locations in the ring ditch', see below p53–4). In these circumstances, material of diverse ages may have been present in the sample. Similar taphonomic considerations apply to samples from occupation deposits, such as middens, which make up another 10% of samples included in this datelist.

Almost all radiocarbon dates on human bone reported in this datelist come from graves containing articulated human skeletons (Fig 14). Here the articulation of the bones provides good evidence that the individual had recently died when their

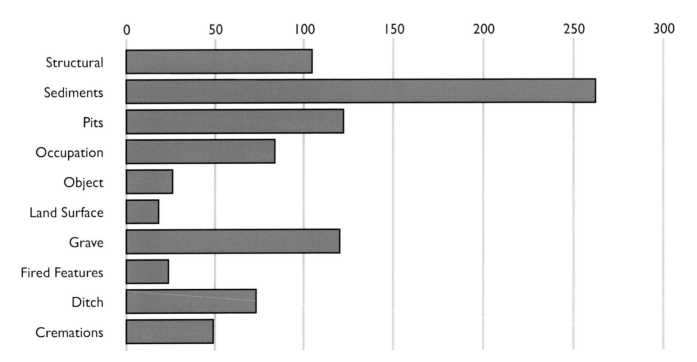

Fig 13. *Contexts of dated samples.*

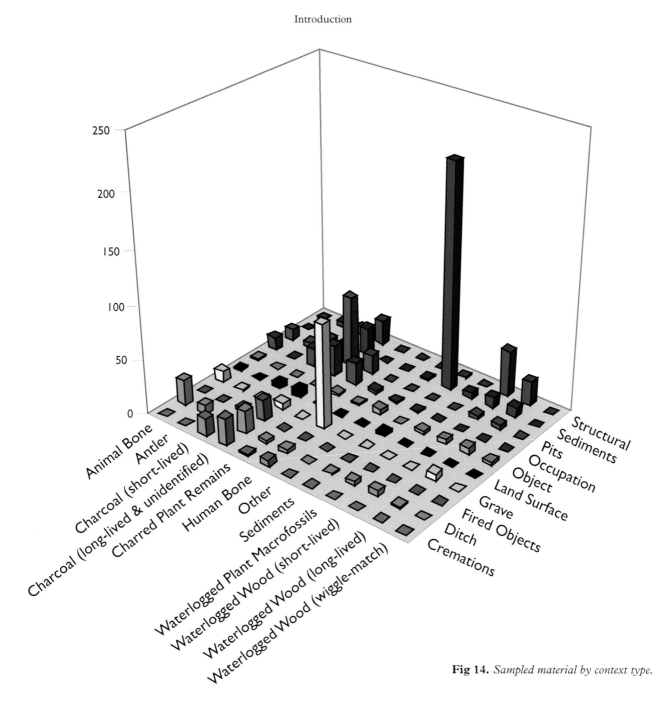

Fig 14. *Sampled material by context type.*

body was buried, and so the radiocarbon date should be close in age to that of the burial. A number of groups of articulated animal bones were also dated (eg GU-5012, a burial of an articulated horse from Worcester: Deansway, see p232–3).

Experimental attempts to date the protein fraction of charred bone by accelerator mass spectrometry have already been noted. Otherwise, only charred plant remains, usually charcoal (Fig 14), could be dated from cremation deposits. Although the dated material in these contexts was probably derived from fuel used in the cremation process, the old-wood effect can make the resultant radiocarbon dates older than the time when the deposits formed. Similar concerns relate to fired features, such as hearths and kilns.

Structural contexts provide 12% of the deposits sampled for radiocarbon dating in the period covered by this datelist (Fig 13). Here, there is a direct functional relationship between the dated material and the archaeological structure that is of interest. Almost all samples from structural contexts are of

wood or charcoal (Fig 14) and so dates from such material are disproportionately subject to the old-wood effect. Even in the absence of identification of the dated material, however, sometimes detailed consideration of a context can give an indication of the scale of such a potential offset. For example, unidentified wood from a waterlogged hurdle (eg GU-5053 from Wootton Creek, Isle of Wight, see p229–30) is likely to have been roundwood, whereas an unidentified charred post (eg HAR-10520 from Haddenham: Upper Delphs causewayed enclosure, Cambridgeshire, see p49–50) was probably of larger scantling and so older. Further complications can arise with structural timbers. Although in the past most wood was not seasoned before use, as this makes it much harder to work, building timber was a valuable resource which could, and was, reused. Such reuse would again make a radiocarbon date older than the structure from which it was recovered. This potential issue highlights the advantages of obtaining dates from more than one timber in a structure.

A smaller number of samples were dated from old land surfaces (Fig 13). Here the objective was usually to provide a *terminus post quem* for the construction of an overlying feature (eg OxA-3621–2 from A30: Sourton Down, occupation, Devon, see p2–3), rather than to date the activity on the old land surface itself. Most samples from this type of context were of charcoal (Fig 14), and so may incorporate an old-wood offset.

The final class of material that was submitted for dating comprises those samples which are of intrinsic interest. In these cases, the context of the find is irrelevant. Such material includes finds such as the Bronze Age sewn-plank boat discovered in Dover, Kent (GU-5291–2, see p59), and Roman spruce cones (GU-5268, see p75) from Godmanchester: Rectory Farm, Cambridgeshire, which demonstrate that this species was present in Britain before the seventeenth century AD (Fig 15). It also includes Saxon finds such as a wicker basket from Anslow's Cottages, Berkshire (OxA-2126, see p14), and a stone anchor from Hemington Fields, Leicestershire (OxA-3028, see p92). A number of samples from bog oaks, which were dated as part of a research programme to construct a prehistoric master tree-ring sequence for England, also fall into this category (eg UB-3271–4 from Wootton Creek B, Isle of Wight, see p230–1).

Laboratory methods

Details of the methods used for the preparation and radiocarbon dating of the samples included in this volume are provided in the references cited in this section. It is important that these technical details can be traced for each measurement, as scientific methods are continuously evolving. This information is essential in assessing the reliability of each measurement in any future analysis.

Samples dated at the Scottish Universities Research and Reactor Centre (GU-) were prepared as described by Stenhouse and Baxter (1983), combusted to carbon dioxide, converted to benzene using a chromium-activated catalyst (Fig 16), and dated by liquid scintillation spectrometry (Noakes *et al* 1965).

The gelatin fraction of antler and bone samples was extracted and dated (Longin 1971). All other samples underwent an acid-alkali-alkali-acid pretreatment protocol (Olsson 1979). For charred and waterlogged plant remains, the alkali- and acid-insoluble fraction was dated. Wood samples underwent an additional stage of bleaching with a hypochlorite solution before combustion. For peats, different fractions could be selected for dating: the alkali-soluble 'humic acid' fraction after either the first or second alkali pretreatment (or both together if the sample was small), the acid- and alkali-insoluble 'humin' fraction, or all three of these fractions combined (the 'acid-washed' fraction). Occasionally,

Fig 15. *Waterlogged cones of* Picea abies *(spruce) (GU-5268) from a Roman feature at Godmanchester: Rectory Farm, Cambridgeshire. (© English Heritage, photography by Peter Murphy)*

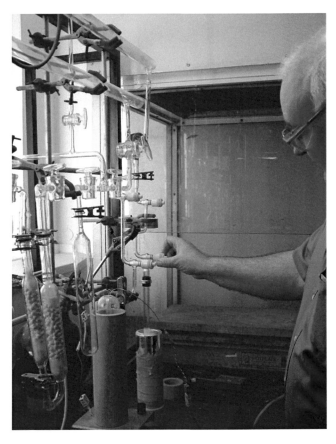

Fig 16. *Robert Anderson collecting benzene at the Scottish Universities Research and Reactor Centre. (© English Heritage, photography by Amanda Grieve)*

the acid-soluble fraction from the first acid pretreatment (the 'fulvic acid' fraction) was dated, although by the time the dates in this volume were made, this fraction was known often to produce anomalous ages (Dresser 1970). The chemical fraction selected for dating for each peat sample dated at the Scottish Research and Reactor Centre is noted in the datelist.

A small number of samples, following pre-treatment and combustion for conventional dating, produced insufficient carbon dioxide for benzene synthesis. Sub-samples of carbon dioxide were sent either to the Arizona Accelerator Mass Spectrometer Laboratory (AA-9568–9 and AA-12598, see p74 and p14 respectively), where they were graphitised and dated by accelerator mass spectrometry as described by Slota et al (1987) and Linick et al (1986), or to the Utrecht van der Graaf Laboratorium (UtC-1702–3 and UtC-2098–9, see p221 and p113 respectively), where they were graphitised and dated by accelerator mass spectrometry as described by van der Borg et al (1987).

At the Oxford Radiocarbon Accelerator Unit, samples of charred material (mostly charcoal and carbonised plant macrofossils, but also some charred bone) were pretreated using the acid-alkali-acid protocol described by Hedges et al (1989, and see Brock et al 2010, table 1 (ZR)). Occasionally, a sample was so fragile that it would not withstand the alkali step, and so it was simply treated with acid and multiple water rinses[2]. One charred waterlogged twig (OxA-2297 from the Hullbridge Survey: Blackwater 28, The Stumble, see p93) was processed as if it was a waterlogged wood sample.

Unburnt bone and antler samples in this datelist with laboratory numbers below OxA-2100 were pretreated as described by Gillespie et al (1984; 1986). Samples of fleece and hoof from waterlogged animal carcasses found in a peat deposit on the Solway Plain (OxA-3640 and OxA-4215, see p133 and p135 respectively) were also processed using this method. The extracted protein from other bone and antler samples dated at Oxford and included in this volume was purified using the ion exchange protocol outlined in Hedges and Law (1989) and Law and Hedges (1989).

Waterlogged wood, plant remains, and peat were pretreated using an acid-alkali-acid protocol, followed by a bleaching step using sodium hypochlorite (Hedges et al 1989, and see Brock et al 2010, table 1 (UW)[3]). The plant macrofossils from Leicester: Shires and Worcester: Deansway (see above) were also pretreated in this way. For some fragile samples, the strength of the bleach used in the final stage of pretreatment was reduced (Hedges et al 1989, and see Brock et al 2010, table 1 (UV)), or even entirely omitted (Hedges et al 1989, and see Brock et al 2010, table 1 (VV or WW)[4]). Occasionally, the alkali-soluble fraction of a peat was extracted for dating (Hedges et al 1989, 113)[5].

Soils were pretreated using an acid-alkali-acid protocol, with a solvent extraction (acetone or chloroform) after the first acid step. Either the acid- and alkali-insoluble, 'humin', fraction or the alkali-soluble, 'humic acid' fraction could be selected for dating[6].

The sample of skin dated from the waterlogged cow carcass found in a peat deposit on the Solway Plain (OxA-3642, see p133) was pretreated using acid-alkali-acid steps at room temperature, followed by a bleaching step using sodium

Fig 17. *Robert Hedges undertaking maintenance on the first accelerator mass spectrometer at the Oxford Radiocarbon Accelerator Unit. (© ORAU)*

hypochlorite. The protein was then dissolved in (6 molar) hydrochloric acid, dried, redissolved in water at a pH of 3 and purified using the ion exchange protocol outlined in Gillespie et al (1984). The single sample of land snails (OxA-3041, p189) was pretreated as described by Hedges et al (1989, 113).

Samples were then combusted to carbon dioxide (Hedges et al 1992). Those with laboratory numbers below OxA-2095 were then graphitised as described by Wand et al (1984) and Gillespie et al (1984), and dated by accelerator mass spectrometry (Gillespie et al 1983; Hedges 1981; Fig 17). Those with laboratory numbers greater than OxA-2095 were measured by accelerator mass spectrometry using the carbon dioxide ion-source (Bronk and Hedges 1990).

At the Belfast Radiocarbon Dating Laboratory (Fig 18) samples of charred and waterlogged plant remains, peat, and soil were pretreated using an acid-alkali-acid protocol (Mook and Waterbolk 1985). The acid- and alkali-insoluble, 'humin', fraction was selected for dating. In a few cases, this protocol was varied. Where this is the case, this is noted in the datelist.

Samples of waterlogged wood were either pretreated using the acid-alkali-acid protocol outlined above, or were bleached to de-lignify and extract cellulose. The samples were either planed into wood shavings or, if very soft, cut into small pieces with a knife. They were placed in a bleaching solution consisting of three litres of de-ionised water, 110ml of 1 molar hydrochloric acid, and 80g of sodium chlorite in the fume cupboard. Further aliquots of hydrochloric acid (55ml) and sodium chlorite (40g) might be added if necessary to complete the bleaching. The mixture was then gently heated to drive off chlorine gas and strained. The bleached wood was then placed in three litres of 1 molar hydrochloric acid at 80°C for an hour to consume any unreacted bleach. The sample was then washed in de-ionised water three times, before it was dried for combustion. For some samples it is not clear which pretreatment protocol was used. The methods applied to particular samples of waterlogged wood are noted in the datelist entries.

The method of pretreatment used for bone and antler samples at Belfast was essentially that described by Longin (1971). The sample was demineralised in 2% hydrochloric

Fig 18. *Mike Baillie, Jonathan Pilcher, and Gordon Pearson outside the Queen's University Belfast Radiocarbon Dating Laboratory. (© Queen's University Belfast)*

age tree-ring samples of the expected age of the unknown samples prior to their conversion. High-precision measurements were produced by extended counting times in a dedicated liquid scintillation spectrometer. Typically 250,000 counts were accumulated before age calculation.

Samples dated at AERE Harwell were pretreated using the standard acid-base-acid protocol (Otlet and Slade 1974). Once roots and other obviously intrusive material had been physically removed, samples were placed in (3 molar) hydrochloric acid and heated for 30 minutes, thus removing carbonates. Contamination by humic acids was removed by heating samples in (1 molar) sodium hydroxide for 30 minutes. After this the material was washed to neutral pH and then given a final cold wash in (3 molar) hydrochloric acid to remove any carbonate that might have been present in the washing water or produced by absorption of atmospheric carbon dioxide. The sample was finally rinsed to neutral pH with distilled water and oven-dried. The solid acid- and alkali-insoluble residue was then combusted and dated.

For bone samples, the collagen fraction was isolated and dated. Bones were washed and cut into small pieces, then put into (1 molar) hydrochloric acid. The acid was changed daily until titration showed there was no further reaction. A cold (0.08 molar) sodium hydroxide wash was used to remove any humic acid contamination and a final rinse in (1 molar) hydrochloric acid was then given. The sample was then washed in distilled water until neutral pH and oven-dried.

acid until the bone had softened and the pH remained stable. The acid was replaced if necessary. The sample was then washed in demineralised water to remove calcium humates, and placed in slightly acid (pH 2) demineralised water, heated to 90°C for 5–18 hours, and the supernatant vacuum filtered. The sample was then evaporated dry, re-dissolved in de-ionised water and filtered again. The supernatant was then evaporated dry before combustion.

Samples were then combusted to carbon dioxide in a positive pressure combustion stream of oxygen, converted to benzene using a chromium-based catalyst as described by Noakes *et al* (1965), and dated by liquid scintillation spectrometry (Pearson 1979; 1984).

Larger samples were needed for high-precision dating. Pretreatment and combustion protocols were as described above, but samples were synthesised to benzene on a dedicated high-precision conversion line. This had the capacity to process larger samples (up to 40 litre atmospheres of carbon dioxide), so that the amount of benzene produced would exceed the target counting volume of 15ml. Sample-to-sample memory effects were minimised by running known-

Fig 19. *Geoff Bradburn loading counting vials into a Packard model 337 Liquid Scintillation Spectrometer at AERE Harwell. (© NDA, reproduced with permission from the NDA)*

For samples dated by liquid scintillation spectrometry, the sample was then combusted to carbon dioxide (Switsur 1972; Switsur et al 1974) and synthesised to benzene using a method similar to that initially described by Tamers (1965) and a vanadium-based catalyst (Otlet 1977). Procedures for liquid scintillation counting (Fig 19) and error calculation are described by Otlet (1979) and Otlet and Warchal (1978). All samples processed at Harwell were dated using these methods, unless there is a laboratory comment in the datelist specifying otherwise.

Six samples were dated using the higher precision liquid scintillation system described by Otlet and Polach (1990), and 20 samples were dated in the miniature gas proportional counter. These samples were also pretreated and combusted to carbon dioxide as outlined by Otlet and Slade (1974). Procedures for gas purification, counter filling, and gas proportional counting are described by Otlet and Evans (1983) and Otlet et al (1983; 1986). Where a sample was dated using either of these systems, this is noted in the datelist entry.

Fractionation and radiocarbon ages

The conventions for quoting radiocarbon dates and supporting information used here conform to the international standard known as the Trondheim Convention (Stuiver and Kra 1986).

The uncalibrated results are given as radiocarbon years before present (BP), where present has been fixed at AD 1950. These results are conventional radiocarbon ages (Stuiver and Polach 1977), and so have been corrected for fractionation. One sample (OxA-3035 from Chigborough Farm, Essex, see p53) dates to after AD 1950. The radiocarbon content of this sample is expressed as a fraction of modern carbon (Mook and van der Plicht 1999).

Most of the radiocarbon ages contained in this datelist have been calculated using measured $\delta^{13}C$ values. At the Oxford Radiocarbon Accelerator Unit, measured $\delta^{13}C$ values could not be obtained until a conventional mass spectrometer was acquired during 1989. Samples dated before this time, and a number of others samples where there was insufficient carbon dioxide for both radiocarbon dating and stable isotopic measurement, had radiocarbon ages calculated using estimated values. These were -19.0‰ for antler and bone samples, and -26.0‰ for charred and waterlogged plant remains and peat. It was also not possible to obtain a measured $\delta^{13}C$ value for one sample dated at AERE Harwell (HAR-9410, see p69). This radiocarbon age, on a charcoal sample, was calculated using an assumed value of -25.0‰.

Results which are, or may be, of the same actual radiocarbon age have been tested for statistical consistency using methods described by Ward and Wilson (1978).

Calibration

Radiocarbon results are not true calendar ages, but have to be converted to calendar time using a calibration curve (Pearson 1987). This is made up of radiocarbon measurements on samples whose age is known through other methods. High-precision data are currently available back to 10,600 BC, based on tree-ring samples which have been dated by dendrochronology. Beyond this, a variety of archives now provide calibration back to 50,000 cal BP, although the uncertainties in this period are much greater. Reimer et al (2009) present the calibration curves which are presently agreed by the international radiocarbon community, and provide a discussion of current understanding of the subject.

Calibrated date ranges provided in this datelist have been calculated using the maximum intercept method (Stuiver and Reimer 1986), OxCal v4.1 (Bronk Ramsey 1995; 1998; 2001; 2009), and the dataset for terrestrial samples from the Northern hemisphere published by Reimer et al (2004). This is identical to the currently internationally agreed atmospheric dataset for the Northern hemisphere (Reimer et al 2009) back to 10,050 cal BC. For samples which calibrate before this date, the updated IntCal09 has been used[7].

Two classes of measurements have not been calibrated using these atmospheric datasets. The first is the single sample where the radiocarbon measurement is more recent than AD 1950[8]. This result may show the effect of the radiocarbon produced by the atmospheric testing of nuclear weapons between AD 1945 and AD 1980, and so it has been calibrated using the atmospheric data of Kueppers et al (2004). The second is OxA-3490, from Godmanchester: Rectory Farm, Cambridgeshire, which has a reported radiocarbon age of >50,000 BP, and so is beyond calibration (see p76).

Calibrated date ranges are quoted in this volume in the form recommended by Mook (1986) with the end points rounded outwards to 10 years (or five years when error terms are less than ±25 BP). The date ranges for measurements which calibrate before 10,600 cal BC have been rounded outwards to 100 years to reflect the greater uncertainty in the calibration data for this early period. For the modern result, date ranges have been rounded outwards to the nearest year. Ranges in the datelist itself are quoted at 68% and 95% confidence; the calibrated date ranges referred to in the commentaries are those for 95% confidence unless otherwise specified.

At the time the measurements reported in this datelist were produced, the calibration of the radiocarbon timescale was much less well understood. The need for calibration had become apparent during the 1960s (Willis et al 1960; Suess 1967), and a variety of calibration curves were proposed during the 1970s (eg Ralph et al 1973; Clark 1975). The first internationally agreed consensus calibration data were issued in 1986. These data covered the period from AD 1950 to 2500 BC. They comprised replicate high-precision radiocarbon measurements from laboratories in Belfast and Seattle on bi-decadal or decadal samples of wood which had been independently dated by dendrochronology (Stuiver and Pearson 1986; Pearson and Stuiver 1986). Beyond this period the calendar timescale was covered by measurements from Belfast between 2500 BC and 5210 BC (Pearson et al 1986), and from various laboratories between 5210 BC and 7210 BC (Linick et al 1985; Stuiver et al 1986; Kromer et al 1986).

Along with the consensus calibration curve, came user-friendly personal computer software for the calibration of

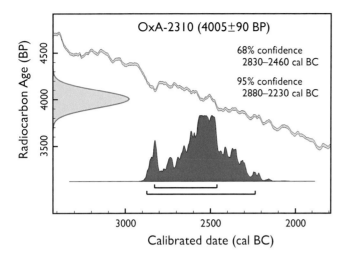

Fig 20. *Calibrated radiocarbon date for OxA-2310.*

radiocarbon results (Stuiver and Reimer 1986). This software employed the maximum intercept method of calibration, which included the uncertainty on the radiocarbon age in the calculation of the calibrated date range. This program (CALIB v1.3) meant that calibrated dates became widely available to archaeologists. In 1993, tree-ring calibration of the radiocarbon timescale was extended from 7210 BC to 9440 BC (Pearson *et al* 1993; Kromer and Becker 1993).

The maximum intercept method has been used for the calibrated dates provided in this datelist and, whilst it is hoped that readers will find the calibrations provided in this volume helpful, it is necessary to recognise their limitations. First, the intercept method itself is best regarded as a 'quick and simple' way of providing an indication of the calendar date of a sample. The full complexity of the calendar age is only apparent from the probability distribution of the calibrated date. This can be illustrated by considering the calibration of OxA-2310, a determination on a cattle mandible from a pit containing Grooved Ware at Hunstanton: Redgate Hill, Norfolk (see below p95–6). This measurement (4005±90 BP) calibrates to 2880–2230 cal BC (at 95% confidence) and 2830–2460 cal BC (at 68% confidence) using the maximum intercept method. The calibration of this sample using the probability method (Stuiver and Reimer 1993) is shown in Figure 20. It can be seen that some parts of the calibrated range are more probable than others: it is, for example, much more probable that this sample dates to the 26th century cal BC than that it dates to the 28th century cal BC. It is not so much that the intercept calibration is wrong, but it does not necessarily convey the full complexity of the scientific information available.

The second limitation of the calibrated dates provided in this volume is that they are not definitive. Radiocarbon calibration is continually being refined, with updated and internationally agreed calibration curves being issued periodically (eg Stuiver and Pearson 1986; Pearson and Stuiver 1986; Stuiver *et al* 1998b; Reimer *et al* 2004, and currently Reimer *et al* 2009). It is thus certain that the calibrated dates quoted here will become outdated, and that the measurements listed here will need to be recalibrated. It is one of the major objectives of this datelist to provide easy

access to the information needed for such re-calibration, so that these data can be used in future research. It is for this reason that it is so important that users cite both the unique laboratory identifier for each measurement and the uncalibrated radiocarbon age when citing the results listed in this volume. This is a courtesy and convenience to the readers of your publications who will themselves need to recalibrate the results in due course!

Quality assurance

Radiocarbon dating laboratories have been attentive to the accuracy and reproducibility of their measurements since the early years of the method. Groups of radiocarbon laboratories were exchanging and dating known-age materials in the 1950s (eg Willis *et al* 1960), and much effort went into the establishment of internationally agreed standard materials (Olsson 1970; Polach 1972; Mann 1983).

In the late 1970s, the British laboratories then in operation participated in a formal inter-comparison study in which samples of benzene of known activities were distributed and dated (Otlet *et al* 1980). The conventional radiocarbon laboratories at AERE Harwell, The Queen's University, Belfast, and Glasgow University all contributed to this study, which demonstrated excellent reproducibility in the counting and combustion stages of the dating process.

The early international inter-comparison studies, undertaken during the 1980s, present a rather different picture. The first, in which the laboratories at The Queen's University, Belfast and Glasgow University participated, was based on the dating of a series of decadal tree-ring samples from a waterlogged bog oak. This study suggested that error estimates based on counting statistics alone were in many cases too low to account for the total error on the measurements, although for high-precision laboratories there was evidence that quoted errors might in fact be overly conservative. There was also clear evidence of systematic laboratory bias in some facilities (International Study Group 1982).

Further analysis of these data, along with published radiocarbon dates on timbers, which had been subsequently dated by dendrochronology during the initiative to establish a prehistoric tree-ring chronology for England (Hillam *et al* 1990), supported the conclusions of this study (Baillie 1990).

A larger, three-stage, study undertaken between 1986 and 1990, provided a more detailed assessment of the variability between laboratories in different stages of the dating process (Scott *et al* 1990). Generally, quoted errors were seen to adequately describe the precision of a result internally within a laboratory, but to underestimate the total inter-laboratory variation. Again, there was evidence of systematic bias within some laboratories. Of the laboratories whose dates are listed in this volume, only the Scottish Universities Research and Reactor Centre participated in this study.

Following the introduction of a set of six new reference materials by the International Atomic Energy Agency in 1990 (Rozanski *et al* 1992; Table 2), a third, two-stage, international inter-comparison study was carried out between 1991 and 1994 (Scott 2003).

Table 2. Reference materials and their consensus radiocarbon values in the IAEA study.

Sample	Material	¹⁴C (pMC)[9]
C-1	Carrara marble	0.02±0.02
C-2	Fresh water travertine	41.14±0.03
C-3	Wood cellulose	129.41±0.06
C-4	Subfossil kauri wood	0.02–0.44[10]
C-5	Subfossil wood	23.05±0.02
C-6	Sucrose	150.61±0.11

All the facilities whose dates are included in this volume, which were operational in 1991 (the radiocarbon dating laboratory at AERE Harwell had closed in 1990), participated in this inter-comparison (Table 3).

Table 3. Radiocarbon values for the IAEA reference materials reported before February 1991 by laboratories who provided measurements detailed in this volume (Rozanski 1991).

Laboratory	Sample	¹⁴C (pMC)
GU-	C-1	−0.14±0.10
AA-	C-1	0.00±0.12
OxA-	C-1	0.10±0.15
UtC-	C-1	0.00±0.88
UB-	C-2	41.42±0.13
UB-	C-2	41.10±0.13
UB-	C-2	40.93±0.13
UB-	C-2	41.45±0.13
UB-	C-2	41.08±0.13
UB-	C-2	40.88±0.13
GU-	C-2	41.22±0.22
AA-	C-2	40.8±0.4
OxA-	C-2	42.47±1.0
UtC-	C-2	41.1±0.2
UB-	C-3	129.43±0.20
UB-	C-3	129.20±0.20
UB-	C-3	129.11±0.20
UB-	C-3	129.40±0.18
UB-	C-3	129.02±0.18
UB-	C-3	129.02±0.18
GU-	C-3	130.76±0.45
AA-	C-3	130.6±0.4
OxA-	C-3	129.6±0.9
UtC-	C-3	129.9±0.6
UB-	C-4	0.198±0.016
GU-	C-4	0.18±0.11
AA-	C-4	0.28±0.12
OxA-	C-4	0.12±0.15
UtC-	C-4	0.12±0.08
UB-	C-5	23.28±0.35
GU-	C-5	23.18±0.18
AA-	C-5	23.03±0.14
OxA-	C-5	23.39±1.25
UtC-	C-5	23.10±0.13
UB-	C-6	149.39±0.35
GU-	C-6	150.78±0.46
AA-	C-6	150.0±0.4
OxA-	C-6	151.5±1.0

These tests indicate no laboratory offsets and demonstrate the validity of the precision quoted (Fig 21).

Periodic, formal international inter-comparison exercises are only one strand in the protocols radiocarbon laboratories adopt to ensure the accuracy of the measurements they report. All the laboratories whose results are included in this datelist also maintained a continual programme of internal laboratory quality assurance procedures during the time when the reported measurements were made.

One of the principal methods for assessing the reproducibility of a dating laboratory is to consider the variation in replicate measurements made on the same material. All sets of replicate measurements relevant to dated samples reported in this volume are listed in Table 4. Some of these replicate measurements were undertaken at the time the original results were produced as part of these internal quality assurance procedures, but most were undertaken either to explore the dating of different chemical fractions of a sample or to validate results which were unexpected. Some are replicate measurements that have been undertaken on these samples subsequently, as part of later studies. The differences between groups of measurements on the same material are illustrated in Figure 22.

Of the 36 samples for which replicate measurements are available, in 17 cases the groups of repeat measurements are statistically significantly different at 95% confidence (Table 4; Ward and Wilson 1978). This is far more than the 1 in 20 cases that would be expected simply on statistical grounds, if this was a random set of replicate measurements on identical material. This is clearly not the case, as neither was the selection of samples for replication random nor was the material dated always exactly the same.

Of the 12 groups of measurements including bone samples, six were selected for replication because the original measurements produced dates that were archaeologically unexpected. In one case (OxA-3362, see p40), the original result was successfully replicated and the archaeological provenance of the sample proved to be at fault, but in the other five cases the original measurements proved to be inaccurate for a variety of technical reasons[11]. One sample (GU-5269, see p38) was replicated because the original measurement had a δ¹³C value outside the usual range for bone samples, and indeed proved to be anomalously recent. The three groups that were undertaken for experimental reasons (OxA-3140, OxA-3640, and OxA-4215, see p203, p133, and p135 respectively), because a variety of materials or chemical fractions from the same organism were dated, all produced statistically consistent sets of measurements, as did the only two samples selected for replication randomly (GU-5112 and OxA-1918; Table 4, see p11 and p15 respectively).

Two replicate sets of measurements are available on samples of waterlogged wood. The wicker basket from Anslow's Cottages, Berkshire, originally dated in 1989 (OxA-2126, see p14) was re-dated in 2010 to determine whether accurate radiocarbon dates could be obtained on material which had been in cold storage for more than 20 years. One of the recent measurements (SUERC-28984) is clearly anomalously early (Table 4), although the other three measurements are statistically consistent (T'=0.6;

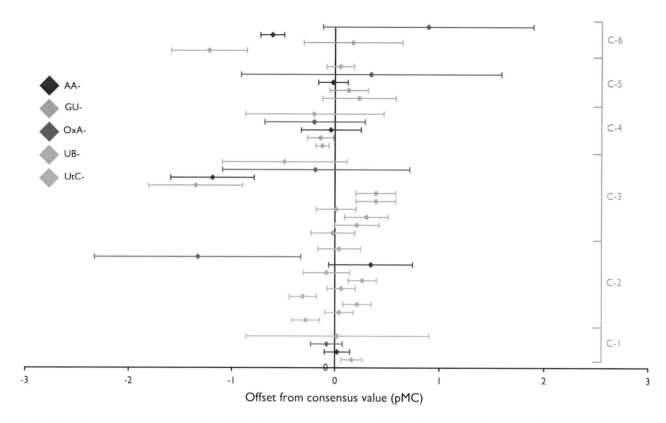

Fig 21. *Offsets between the consensus values (Table 2) and measurements on IAEA reference materials undertaken as part of the 1991 inter-comparison study by facilities whose dates are reported in this volume (Table 3).*

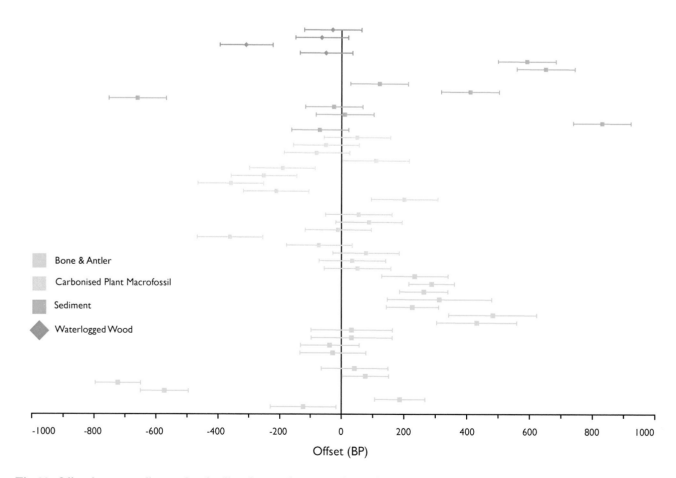

Fig 22. *Offsets between replicate pairs of radiocarbon results on samples considered in this study (where there are more than two measurements, the first measurement listed in Table 4 is compared with each succeeding measurement).*

Table 4. Replicate radiocarbon measurements for samples included in this datelist; entries in red are statistically significantly different at 95% confidence (Ward and Wilson 1978). LSC = liquid scintillation spectrometry; AMS = accelerator mass spectrometry; GPC = miniature gas-proportional counting; HP = higher precision liquid scintillation spectrometry.

Site	Material	Laboratory Number	Radiocarbon Age (BP)	Method	Ward and Wilson (1978)
Addingham Church	human bone	GU-5112	990±70	LSC	T'=1.9; T'(5%)=3.8; ν=1
		GU-5112B	1110±50	LSC	
Addingham Church	human bone	GU-5113	1460±50	LSC	T'=7.2; T'(5%)=3.8; ν=1
		GU-5113B	1270±50	LSC	
Anslow's Cottages	waterlogged wood	OxA-2126	1060±80	AMS	T'=51.9; T'(5%)=7.8; ν=3
		OxA-22480	1111±28	AMS	
		SUERC-28983	1370±30	AMS	
		SUERC-28984	1125±30	AMS	
Aylesbury: Prebendal	human bone	OxA-1918	2350±60	AMS	T'=0.3; T'(5%)=3.8; ν=1
		SUERC-18212	2315±35	AMS	
	triticum sp. (free-threshing species)	OxA-1923	1005±70	AMS	
	triticum æstivum	OxA-23361	952±22	AMS	T'=0.7;T'(5%)=6.0; ν=2
	triticum æstivum	OxA-23362	969±23		
Barford: Park Farm	charcoal	GU-5043	2160±70	LSC	T'=0.6; T'(5%)=3.8; ν=1
		GU-5044	2080±80	LSC	
Beverley: Long Lane	peat (humic acid)	GU-5107	2020±60	LSC	T'=0.3; T'(5%)=3.8; ν=1
	peat (humin)	GU-5108	2090±120	LSC	
Brighton Bypass: Mile Oak	human bone	GU-5269	2240±70	LSC	T'=51.9; T'(5%)=6; ν=2
		GU-5675	2810±70	LSC	
		GU-5691	2960±100	LSC	
Brighton Bypass: Mile Oak	animal bone	OxA-3362	270±60	AMS	T'=0.7; T'(5%)=3.8; ν=1
		OxA-3386	190±75	AMS	
Castledyke: Barton-on-Humber	human bone (collagen)	OxA-3140	1065±70	AMS	T'=0.2; T'(5%)=3.8; ν=1
	human bone (amino acids)	OxA-3672	1020±75	AMS	
Eckweek	carbonised plant macrofossils	UB-3204	891±42	LSC	T'=1.1; T'(5%)=3.8; ν=1
		UB-3205	962±53	LSC	
Etton Landscape: Maxey	peat (humic acid)	GU-5123	10900±120	LSC	T'=13.0; T'(5%)=3.8; ν=1
	peat (humin)	GU-5124	10070±190	LSC	
Ferrybridge Henge	charcoal	GU-5216	3900±80	LSC	T'=11.4; T'(5%)=3.8; ν=1
		GU-5217	4260±70	LSC	
Godmanchester: Rectory Farm	charcoal and coal	OxA-3483	15200±140	AMS	n/a
	charcoal (coal fraction)	OxA-3490	>50,000	AMS	
	charcoal (charcoal fraction)	OxA-3491	4360±75	AMS	
Ipswich: St Stephen's Lane	charcoal	GU-5270	1210±50	LSC	T'=0.0; T'(5%)=3.8; ν=1
		GU-5674	1220±80	LSC	
Lichfield: Cathedral	human bone	GU-5281	2410±50	LSC	T'=329.4; T'(5%)=3.8; ν=1
		GU-5434	960±60	LSC	
Lismore Fields: Buxton	charcoal	UB-3290	5024±126	LSC	T'=0.9; T'(5%)=6.0; ν=2
		SUERC-24131	4935±30	AMS	
		OxA-20743	4968±33	AMS	
Lismore Fields: Buxton	charcoal	UB-3294	7042±124	LSC	T'=534.6; T'(5%)=6.0; ν=2
	hazelnut shell	SUERC-31289	5455±30	AMS	
		OxA-23368	6840±65	AMS	
Lismore Fields: Buxton	charcoal	UB-3295	4703±75	LSC	T'=6.3; T'(5%)=3.8; ν=1
		OxA-23585	4914±37	AMS	
Lismore Fields: Buxton	charcoal	UB-3297	4567±164	LSC	T'=4.4; T'(5%)=3.8; ν=1
		SUERC-32293	4925±30	AMS	
Lismore Fields: Buxton	charcoal	UB-3377	4709±66	LSC	T'=10.4; T'(5%)=6.0; ν=2
	hazelnut shell	SUERC-32535	4960±40	AMS	
		OxA-23545	4900±30	AMS	
Mancetter	carbonised plant macrofossils	UtC-2098	2100±80	AMS	T'=1.1; T'(5%)=3.8; ν=1
		UtC-2099	1990±70	AMS	

Site	Material	Laboratory Number	Radiocarbon Age (BP)	Method	Ward and Wilson (1978)
Market Lavington	peat (cellulose)	OxA-2999	2110±70	AMS	T'=0.0; T'(5%)=3.8; ν=1
	peat (humic acid)	OxA-3000	2100±70	AMS	
North West Wetlands Survey: Bonds Farm	waterlogged wood	GU-5063	3120±60	LSC	T'=0.1; T'(5%)=3.8; ν=1
		GU-5064	3150±70	LSC	
North West Wetlands Survey: Knowsley Park	peat (humic acid)	GU-5246	9280±80	LSC	T'=0.0; T'(5%)=3.8; ν=1
	peat (acid-washed)	SRR-4515	9305±80	LSC	
North West Wetlands Survey: Solway Cow	hoof	OxA-3640	1185±70	AMS	T'=0.1; T'(5%)=6.0; ν=2
	animal bone	OxA-3641	1210±80	AMS	
	skin	OxA-3642	1220±75	AMS	
North West Wetlands Survey: Solway Sheep	fleece	OxA-4215	265±95	AMS	T'=0.1; T'(5%)=3.8; ν=1
	animal bone	OxA-4216	230±75	AMS	
Somerset Levels: Claylands, Cripps River	peat (humin)	HAR-9188	2900±90	LSC	T'=36.0; T'(5%)=3.8; ν=1
		HAR-9189	3560±60	LSC	
West Heslerton: Yedingham	peat (2nd humic acid)	GU-5002	11420±80	LSC	T'=13.1; T'(5%)=3.8; ν=1
		GU-5006	11010±80	LSC	
West Heslerton: Yedingham	peat (2nd humic acid)	GU-5003	10480±80	LSC	T'=506.2; T'(5%)=7.8; ν=3
		GU-5004	10360±60	LSC	
	peat (fulvic acid)	GU-5020	8390±70	LSC	
	peat (1st humic acid)	GU-5021	9830±80	LSC	
Westhampnett	soil (humic acid)	GU-5310	9210±90	LSC	T'=18.0; T'(5%)=3.8; ν=1
		AA-11770	8620±105	LSC	
Wharram Percy: South Manor	carbonised plant macrofossils	GU-5119	1030±60	LSC	T'=0.8; T'(5%)=3.8; ν=1
		GU-5120	1110±70	LSC	
Wharram Percy: The Dam	carbonised plant macrofossils	GU-5183	1250±60	LSC	T'=0.8; T'(5%)=6.0; ν=2
		HAR-1329	1300±80	LSC	
		HAR-1337	1200±80	LSC	
Whitwell Quarry Long Cairn (pilot)	human bone	OxA-4176	5380±90	AMS	T'=25.8; T'(5%)=6.0; ν=2
		OxA-14493	4946±32	AMS	
		GrA-27519	4895±40	AMS	
Whitwell Quarry Long Cairn (pilot)	human bone	OxA-4177	5190±100	AMS	T'=9.6; T'(5%)=7.8; ν=3
		OxA-14494	4961±33	AMS	
		GrA-27513	4875±40		
		OxA-12763	4925±38	AMS	
Whitwell Quarry Long Cairn (pilot)	human bone	OxA-4326	5115±70	AMS	T'=13.4; T'(5%)=6.0; ν=2
		GrA-27515	4825±40	AMS	
		OxA-14495	4879±32	AMS	

T'(5%)=6.0; ν=2). The pair of replicate measurements from a wooden stake in a channel from the North West Wetlands Survey at Bonds Farm (see p00) are also statistically consistent (Table 4).

Interpretation of the suite of replicate measurements on samples of carbonised plant remains is more complicated. Seven replicate groups consist of bulk samples, which were divided and dated more than once. In these cases, it is a reasonable assumption that the dated samples on average consisted of very similar material. Six sets of measurements in this class are statistically consistent, with only the pair of results from Ferrybridge Henge (see p120) being inconsistent (Table 4). The replicate measurements from Mancetter (see p113) were from two separate samples of charcoal which were pretreated and combusted at Glasgow, but which produced insufficient carbon dioxide for liquid scintillation spectrometry and so were graphitised and dated at Utrecht. Five replicate groups from Lismore Fields: Buxton (see p112–3) consist of an original measurement on a bulk sample, replicated by one or more measurements on single-entity samples of short-lived carbonised plant remains from the same deposit. In these circumstances, it is unclear whether the differences between measurements arise from inhomogeneity in the material dated or from inter-laboratory differences (Table 4). A further pair of measurements on single grains of *Triticum æstivum* wheat from a layer of charred grain within a pit at Aylesbury: Prebendal are statistically consistent with the result on a bulk sample of grain previously undertaken (Table 4). The final set of replicate measurements on carbonised plant material was made on a sample from Godmanchester: Rectory Farm (see p74–7), where a successful attempt was made to isolate the charcoal component of the sample (OxA-3491) from contamination by coal (OxA-3483 and OxA-3490).

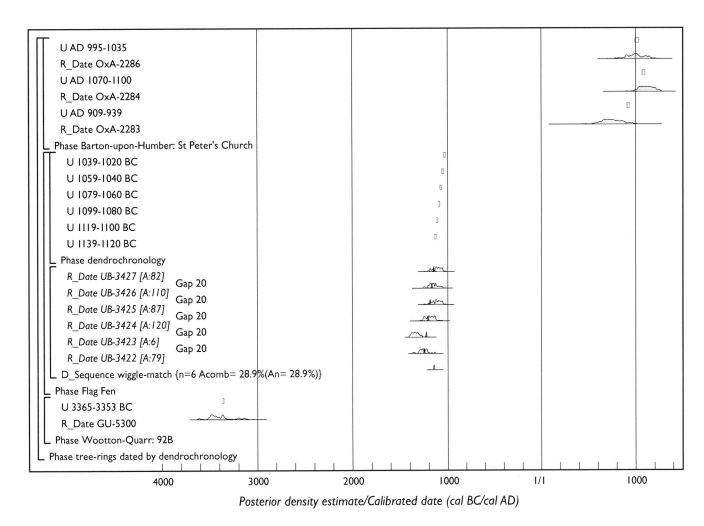

Posterior density estimate/Calibrated date (cal BC/cal AD)

Fig 23. *Calibrated radiocarbon dates from samples dated by dendrochronology.*

Finally, eight sets of replicate measurements are available on a variety of chemical fractions of organic sediment. Three of these sets of measurements are statistically consistent, but five are statistically inconsistent (Table 4). One humic acid/humin pair, from Beverley: Long Lane (see p25–7), is statistically consistent, but another, older, pair from Etton Landscape: Maxey (see p69–70) are not. A cellulose/humic acid pair from Market Lavington (see p113–4) are statistically consistent, but repeated humin fractions from Somerset Levels: Claylands, Cripps River (see p179) are not. Three further sets of measurements on various humic acid fractions from West Heslerton: Yedingham (see p214–6) and Westhampnett (see p216–8) are also not consistent (Table 4). Overall, it may be no accident that four out of the five samples that produced statistically inconsistent sets of measurements dated to before 9000 BP. For such old samples, a very small amount of contamination from recent mobile compounds could make an observable difference to the reported ages.

From this discussion, it is apparent that, during the period covered by this datelist, replication was largely a trouble-shooting mechanism. It was used to resolve issues arising from samples which produced dates that were archaeologically unexpected, and also to investigate alternative chemical protocols for dating certain sample types. There was an element of random replication for quality control purposes, but both sample availability and cost limited this strategy.

The accuracy of a small number of the radiocarbon dates listed in this volume, however, can be assessed in relation to independent dating information. The power of this test crucially depends on the association between the material that was sent for radiocarbon dating and the independent dating evidence.

Most reliable are samples of wood where we know which tree-rings were sampled for radiocarbon dating, and where a dendrochronological date is now available for these rings. Four single measurements fall into this category, in each case producing calibrated radiocarbon dates which include the actual years spanned by the dated material (Fig 23).

A series of six samples taken from the dendrochronological master sequence from Flag Fen, Cambridgeshire (see p71–2) is, however, problematic. Wiggle-matching of this sequence using the methodology of Christen and Litton (1995), produces an estimated date for the last ring of this sequence of *1195–1180 cal BC (8% probability)* or *1160–1130 cal BC (85% probability*; Fig 23). This is not compatible with the date of this ring of 1020 BC provided by dendrochronology (Neve 1999). Although some refinements to calibration data in the first and second millennia BC

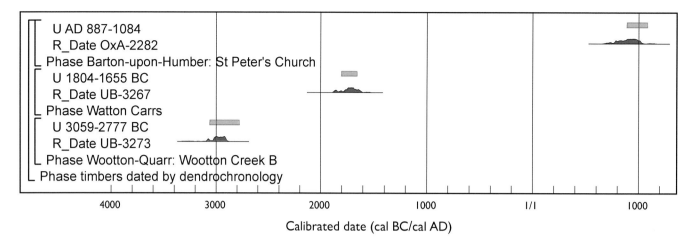

U AD 887-1084
R_Date OxA-2282
Phase Barton-upon-Humber: St Peter's Church
U 1804-1655 BC
R_Date UB-3267
Phase Watton Carrs
U 3059-2777 BC
R_Date UB-3273
Phase Wootton-Quarr: Wootton Creek B
Phase timbers dated by dendrochronology

4000   3000   2000   1000   1/1   1000

Calibrated date (cal BC/cal AD)

Fig 24. *Calibrated radiocarbon dates from timbers dated by dendrochronology.*

have subsequently been proposed (Kromer *et al* 2001; 2010), a shift of this scale is unlikely. With the exception of UB-3423, which has poor individual agreement and is older than would be expected from its relative position in the ring sequence, the other radiocarbon dates in this series are in good agreement with the relative order provided by the dendrochronological sequence. This means that if there was a measurement problem in the laboratory at this time, it led to a systematic bias for this whole group of measurements. Alternatively, there may have been an administrative error with sample labelling at some time, although we have been unable to trace such a mistake.

Three more samples come from timbers which now have dendrochronological dates, although the exact tree-rings that were included in the radiocarbon samples are unclear. All of these samples produced calibrated radiocarbon dates which include the dates of the sampled timbers known from dendrochronology (Fig 24).

Finally, two statistically consistent measurements on hazel charcoal from layers of burnt debris close to the base of cellared building (2140) at Ipswich: St Stephen's Lane (Table 4; and see below p97–8) provide a calibrated radiocarbon date which has poor agreement (A: 19; Bronk Ramsey 1995, 429) with a date of *c*. AD 925 for a group of coins recovered from a stratigraphically earlier building. Further post-excavation analysis is required to investigate this discrepancy.

Statistical modelling

During the period in which the radiocarbon dates reported in this volume were measured, statistical techniques for the analysis of results were limited. The statistical consistency of groups of measurements could be assessed using the chi-squared test (Ward and Wilson 1978), and the wiggle-matching of floating tree-ring sequences was possible using the methodology of Pearson (1986). At this time the first papers, outling a new statistical approach for the interpretation of radiocarbon dates and archaeological information together were presented (Naylor and Smith 1988;

Buck *et al* 1991; 1992), but accessible computer software allowing its wide-scale implementation was in the future (Bronk Ramsey 1995).

Weighted means of replicate radiocarbon measurements should be taken before calibration for samples which ceased exchanging carbon with the biosphere at exactly the same time. Most commonly these are replicate samples from the same living organism. For example, the weighted mean of the three measurements on the Solway cow (OxA-3640–2; Table 4, see also below p133) is 1204 ±44 BP, which calibrates to cal AD 680–970 (95% confidence).

Measurements which derive from bulk samples made up of material from more than one organism are more problematic. In a sample of bulk charcoal, for example, it is extremely unlikely that all the dated fragments derive from tree-rings which were laid down in exactly the same year. Even if composed entirely of short-lived wood species, it is likely that brushwood which formed over several years, or even several decades, may be represented in the sample. In these circumstances, the (probably incorrect) assumption that all the dated material died in the same year has already been made when submitting a bulk sample for radiocarbon dating. At the time the samples listed in this volume were submitted for dating, such assumptions were largely unavoidable. For this reason, weighted means of replicate measurements from bulk samples have also been taken before calibration, as the assumption of the statistical approach is consistent with that made in the submission of the samples for dating.

The first type of application where statistical manipulation of radiocarbon dates in relation to the calibration curve was attempted was for the wiggle-matching of floating tree-ring sequences (Pearson 1986). Here, the relative calendrical position of the samples was known from tree-ring analysis, but their absolute position on the calendar scale had to be determined through radiocarbon dating. Such an exercise was undertaken, for example, for dating the waterlogged and charred wooden mortuary chamber in the Haddenham long barrow (Evans and Hodder 2006a, 185–7).

This brings us to the subsequent use that has been made of the radiocarbon dates detailed in this volume in formal,

Fig 25. *Excavation of a Bronze Age sewn-plank boat from Dover, Kent in 1992. (© Canterbury Archaeological Trust Ltd)*

Bayesian chronological models (Buck *et al* 1996). Formal statistical modelling of archaeological chronologies has been a major, if not revolutionary, development in our ability to interpret radiocarbon dates over the past twenty years, and has become widely used in English archaeology (Bayliss and Bronk Ramsey 2004; Bayliss 2009)[12].

Post-excavation analysis and publication of many of the sites and radiocarbon dates listed in this volume occurred before this methodology was developed and widely implemented (eg Buck *et al* 1991; 1992; 1994a–b; Bronk Ramsey 1995). The samples were also selected before Bayesian simulation models became an integral part of the sampling procedure (Bayliss and Bronk Ramsey 2004, fig 2). Some of the sites included in this volume, however, were the subject of some of the first attempts to apply this methodology to English archaeology and, over the succeeding decades, many of the measurements included in this volume have been incorporated in sophisticated chronological models for individual sites and, more recently, in wider synthetic studies.

Pioneering application include various models for sites excavated in advance of the Brighton Bypass, East Sussex (Bayliss *et al* 2002) and for a series of earthen dykes in Cambridgeshire (Bayliss *et al* 1996). Early studies also include a synthesis of the chronology of the Flag Fen basin (Bayliss and Pryor 2001), an attempt to model the chronology of the Easterton Brook at Market Lavington, Wiltshire (Wiltshire and Bayliss 2006), and models for the chronology of Stonea Camp, Cambridgeshire (Bayliss 2005) and a series of barrows on Snail Down, Wiltshire (Ashbee with Bayliss 2005).

Further site-based Bayesian models include those presented for Barton-upon-Humber: St Peter's Church, Humberside (Bayliss and Atkins 2011), Drayton: Cursus, Oxfordshire (Bayliss *et al* 2003a), the Dover Boat (Bayliss *et al* 2003; Fig 25), Iron Age sites at Haddenham, Cambridgeshire (Marshall 2006), Hambledon Hill, Dorset (Bayliss *et al* 2008), a series of prehistoric monuments at Raunds, Northamptonshire (Healy *et al* 2007), Trethurgy Round, Cornwall (Marshall 2004), Whitwell long cairn, Derbyshire (Marshall *et al* 2011), and Saxon and Iron Age activity at Yarnton, Oxfordshire (Bayliss and Hey 2004; Hey *et al* 1999; Bayliss and Hey 2011).

In wider synthetic studies of radiocarbon dates associated with earlier Neolithic material culture, Whittle *et al* (2011) and Griffiths (2011) present a number of additional site-based models and a series of more interpretative models for aspects of early Neolithic 'things and practices' across England.

Further chronological models are under construction, both for particular sites, and for analysis of wider archaeological questions. Of particular relevance to many of the dates reported in this volume are current developments in producing deposition models for peat sequences (Blaauw and Christen 2005; Bronk Ramsey 2008; Christen *et al* 1995; Haslett and Parnell 2008; Parnell *et al* 2008).

Already published models in due course will be reinterpreted and remodelled. It is in the creation of new models that the detailed information contained in this datelist will prove invaluable. It will allow the necessary critical assessment of sample character and taphonomy, and measurement accuracy, to be made. This will allow informed decisions to be made about how each radiocarbon date is most realistically incorporated into a particular model.

Using the Datelist

Radiocarbon determinations are identified by a unique laboratory code. So, for example, OxA is the code for the Oxford Radiocarbon Accelerator Unit, and OxA-2578 was the 2,578th measurement produced by the laboratory. This code is the internationally agreed identifier by which every radiocarbon determination can be traced. OxA-2578 refers to the result produced on a sample of human mandible from a crouched inhumation at Oakham, Leicestershire, and only to that measurement. An index of these codes is therefore provided to enable further details of dates cited elsewhere to be easily traced.

A more traditional index of key terms is also provided. This enables dates from particular sites, or of particular materials, of with particular archaeological associations to be traced (eg dates relating to the elm decline or Collared Urns).

Acknowledgments

This datelist has be compiled and edited successively by Amanda Grieve and Kate Cullen, on the basis of information provided by the submitters of the samples dated and by the radiocarbon laboratories. The mammoth task of cataloguing the paper and material archive from AERE Harwell, which was retrieved by English Heritage on the demolition of the laboratory building in 1995, was undertaken with exemplary patience and care by Sarah Hill. We are all grateful to all the submitters of the samples included in this datelist, who have generously responded to our requests for information and comments on their dates often many years after the initial submission of the samples.

Design has been the responsibility of Mark Simmons, and the overall production of the volume has been overseen by David Jones. The information has been output from the English Heritage Radiocarbon Database. This has been developed over many years, successively by Paul Cheetham, Sarah Hill, Manuela Lopez, Marcos Guillen, Mike Gratton, David Head, Carlton Carver, and Gordon Mackay. Henriette Granlund Marsden and John Meadows kindly proof-read this volume.

I am particularly indebted to Christopher Bronk Ramsey, Gordon Cook, Bob Otlet, Gerry McCormac, Stephen Hoper, and Jill Walker, who have all checked through the datelist and contributed materially to the accuracy of the information in this introduction. Radiocarbon dating is a complex and labour-intensive process which takes time. It would be impossible without the dedicated attention of the laboratory staff to each and every sample. We are grateful to Stephen Hoper, Gordon Pearson, Florence Qua, and Fiona Sharpe for processing and dating the samples at the Queen's University, Belfast, to Robert Anderson and Philip Naysmith for similarly processing and dating samples dated at the Scottish Universities Research and Reactor Centre, and to Geoff Bradburn, John Fairchild, and Curly Humphries for processing and dating the samples dated at AERE Harwell. Our thanks also go to Angela Bowles, Angie Bryan (née Stoker), John Foreman, John Gowlett, Teddy Hall, Robert Hedges, Evelyn Hendy, Rupert Housley, Martin Humm, Ian Law, Philip Leach, Clare Owen, Colin Perry, and Gert Jaap van Klinken for undertaking the measurements at the Oxford Radiocarbon Accelerator Unit. David Haddon-Reece and David Jordan ran the radiocarbon dating programme for the Ancient Monuments Laboratory of English Heritage during the period when the samples listed in this volume were submitted for dating.

Alex Bayliss
English Heritage, 1 Waterhouse Square,
138–142 Holborn, London, EC1N 2ST

1 *It should be noted that most charcoal samples submitted to AERE Harwell for dating were divided at the Ancient Monuments Laboratory into short-lived material and longer-lived material, and that the longer-lived charcoal was only included in the dating sample if more material was needed to make up the necessary sample weight.*

2 *OxA-3393, OxA-3653, and OxA-3972.*

3 *OxA-2996–9, OxA-3001–2, OxA-4816, and OxA-4819.*

4 *OxA-1976–8, OxA-2072, OxA-3644, OxA-4079, and OxA-4186–8.*

5 *OxA-3000 and OxA-4185.*

6 *OxA-3492 and OxA-3152 respectively.*

7 *GU-5002–4, GU-5006, GU-5011, GU-5021, GU-5042, GU-5086, GU-5123–4, GU-5202, OxA-3393, OxA-3483, OxA-3492, and OxA-4166–7.*

8 *OxA-3035.*

9 *This sample is considered to be a background sample, having no measurable ¹⁴C. Its activity is thus 0.00pMC.*

10 *This sample exhibited the widest spread of results, and is the only samples where mean values determined by the different measurement techniques differed. The 95% confidence interval for the median was therefore reported as the most appropriate consensus value.*

11 *GU-5113 appears to be slightly too old for reasons that are unexplained; GU-5281 was contaminated by dead carbon from a faulty oxygen cylinder; and OxA-4176–7 and OxA-4326, which all had low yields of collagen, seem to have been contaminated during the ion exchange process.*

12 *Lindley (1985) provides a user-friendly introduction to the principles of Bayesian statistics, and Bayliss et al (2007) provide an introduction to the practice of chronological modelling for archaeological problems.*

A30: Sourton Down, Devon

Location: SX 546919
Lat. 50.42.29 N; Long. 04.03.36 W

Project manager: S Reed and B Kerr (Exeter City Museum and Central Archaeology Service), 1986 and 1991

Description: excavation, field survey, and palaeoenvironmental sampling were carried out at Sourton Down, near Okehampton in 1986 and 1991, in advance of improvements to the A30 Trunk Road between the Okehampton Bypass and Launceston Bypass. Excavations in 1986 focussed on a suspected prehistoric enclosure, a section of Roman road or trackway, a Scheduled Ancient Monument identified as a possible Roman signal station or Civil War fortification, and a deserted medieval settlement.

Objectives: to provide a chronological framework for the sites in the absence of other dating evidence, and for the peat sequence recorded outside the proposed route corridor. The radiocarbon dating of the peat sequence was intended to allow the correlation between the excavated sites and environmental changes to be determined.

References: Balkwill and Silvester 1976, 86–9
Weddell and Reed 1997, 39–48

A30: Sourton Down, occupation, Devon

Location: SX 546919 to SX 542914
Lat. 50.42.32 N; Long. 04.03.36 W, to 50.42.16 N, 04.03.55 W

Project manager: S Reed (Exeter Museums Archaeological Field Unit) B Kerr (Central Archaeology Service), 1987 and 1991

Archival body: Plymouth Museum

Description: in 1990 and 1991, environmental sampling was carried out alongside the archaeological excavations. Samples for pollen analysis were taken from the fills of a quarry, two soil profiles beneath the Roman road, and two beneath the bank of the medieval settlement. The suspected prehistoric enclosure, located at SX 54649189, measured 11–12m by 21m, and was enclosed by a low rubble bank. Seven small pits or postholes were excavated within the enclosure, but no relationship between them and the enclosure was identified (GU-5193–6). The pits contained similar dark, charcoal-rich fills, and may have had a ritual purpose. The Roman road/trackway, located at SX 54579207, had been mainly built directly on the silty clay subsoil, and partially on a layer of redeposited natural clay. A sample was submitted for dating from a buried soil deposit located on the southern side of the road (OxA-3390). The 7m-wide road surface consisted of a well-laid, single layer of rounded cobbles. A further section of the Roman road was excavated (area 3), located at SX 54199161, where a medieval culvert cut across it. Here, the primary road surface comprised a layer of tightly-packed stones set into clay. This sealed a buried soil, beneath which were flecks of charcoal from root holes cut into the natural subsoil. Samples of this charcoal were also submitted for radiocarbon dating (OxA-3621–2). The surviving road surface was 4.4m wide and was flanked by ditches 5.6m apart. After the ditches had silted up, a second surface was laid on top of the first. Before the establishment of the early medieval settlement, the road was raised by a series of layers, upon which was laid a surface of local stone. Quarry pits associated with this phase were also excavated. A cobbled trackway leading from the settlement seemed to lead to the road.

Objectives: to provide a chronology of occupation in the absence of other dating evidence, using material collected as part of the environmental record. The environmental analysis was considered to be of particular importance as it was hoped that it would allow a correlation between the Exeter Museums Archaeological Field Unit's excavations of the 1990s, and those of the Central Excavation Service's investigations of the mid-1980s.

References: Hedges *et al* 1994, 360
Weddell and Reed 1997, 86–9, 39–148

GU–5193 3590 ±50 BP

$\delta^{13}C$: -26.3‰

Sample: 4161-914, submitted in February 1991 by T Pearson

Material: charcoal: *Quercus* sp.; *Betula* sp. (C Dickson)

Initial comment: the four samples GU-5193–6 came from flat-bottomed circular pits, with undercut edges. The fills were of uniform black soil, occasionally with fire-crazed stones, sealed in some cases with a packing of stone rubble, similar to the stones of the enclosure bank. One of the pits (cut 1193), also produced calcined bone. GU-5193 (sample 1923) was from the lower fill of pit 1193, context 1226. The pit also contained burnt bone.

Objectives: to date the features. The closest parallels to these features are Bronze Age funerary pits found by Frances Griffith under cairns at Colliford in Cornwall (Griffith 1984, 49–139).

Calibrated date: 1σ: 2030–1880 cal BC
2σ: 2130–1770 cal BC

Final comment: B Kerr (1994), radiocarbon dating of the wood charcoal contained in the fill of 1193 produced a late Neolithic–early Bronze Age date. Although the skeletal material contained in the fill was insufficient to support a funerary interpretation for this feature, it is possible it had a ritual purpose.

Laboratory comment: Ancient Monuments Laboratory (2003), note that Weddell and Reed (1997) misidentify the dated material as *Betula* and *Corylus* spp., whereas in fact fragments of *Betula* and *Quercus* spp. were dated.

References: Griffith 1984, 49–139

GU–5194 3710 ±110 BP

$\delta^{13}C$: -24.0‰

Sample: 4161-921, submitted in February 1991 by T Pearson

Material: charcoal: *Quercus* sp.; *Corylus* sp.; *Betula* sp. (C Dickson)

Initial comment: obtained from sample 1921: from the fill of pit 1191, context 1192. The charcoal appears to be mature wood. *See* also GU-5193.

Objectives: as GU-5193

Calibrated date: 1σ: 2290–1940 cal BC
                     2σ: 2470–1770 cal BC

Final comment: B Kerr (1994), radiocarbon dating of wood charcoal contained in the fill of pit 1191 produced a late Neolithic–early Bronze Age date. It is possible the pit had a ritual purpose.

GU–5195 3570 ±100 BP

δ¹³C: -24.5‰

Sample: 4161-915, submitted in February 1991 by T Pearson

Material: charcoal: *Quercus* sp.; *Betula* sp. (C Dickson)

Initial comment: obtained from sample 1915: from the fill of pit 1186, context 1187. The charcoal appears to be mature wood although fairly fragmented. *See* also GU-5193.

Objectives: as GU-5193

Calibrated date: 1σ: 2040–1760 cal BC
                     2σ: 2200–1680 cal BC

Final comment: B Kerr (1994), radiocarbon dating of wood charcoal contained in the fill of pit 1186 produced a late Neolithic–early Bronze Age date. It is possible the pit had a ritual purpose.

GU–5196 3570 ±70 BP

δ¹³C: -25.2‰

Sample: 4161-912, submitted in February 1991 by T Pearson

Material: charcoal: *Quercus* sp.; *Corylus* sp. (C Dickson)

Initial comment: obtained from sample 1912: from the fill of pit 1197, context 1198/1199. The sample appears to be of mature wood. *See* also GU-5193.

Objectives: as GU-5193

Calibrated date: 1σ: 2030–1780 cal BC
                     2σ: 2140–1740 cal BC

Final comment: B Kerr (1994), radiocarbon dating of the wood charcoal contained in the fill of the pit produced a late Neolithic-early Bronze Age date. It is possible the pit had a ritual purpose.

OxA–3390 3340 ±70 BP

δ¹³C: -29.7‰

Sample: 416-1910, submitted on 22 February 1992 by T Pearson

Material: charcoal: *Corylus avellana* (N Balaam 1991)

Initial comment: taken during the excavation of the Sourton Trackway, recovered from layer 1095, a dark humic soil immediately below the metalled surface. This sample contains fragments of bark, which have been separated out for radiocarbon analysis. The dark humic layer 1095 was extensive and appeared to be well-sealed and undisturbed.

Objectives: to date the trackway in the absence of any other dating evidence. The trackway has been shown to be one of the earliest elements in this extensive relict landscape, and it has determined the layout of subsequent field systems. Its dating is thus critical to our understanding of the development of this landscape.

Calibrated date: 1σ: 1740–1520 cal BC
                     2σ: 1870–1450 cal BC

Final comment: B Kerr (1994), the burial soil deposit was radiocarbon dated to the early Bronze Age, this shows that Bronze Age activity continued outside the excavated area.

OxA–3621 7290 ±90 BP

δ¹³C: -26.5‰

Sample: 554348, submitted on 3 April 1992 by C G Henderson

Material: charcoal: *Acer* sp./Pomoideae, two fragments; *Quercus* sp., mainly (V Straker 1991)

Initial comment: OxA-3621 and OxA-3622 are from the same sample: from the top 0.04m of the B horizon below a buried soil beneath an agger. The depth below the surface was 0.6m. The charcoal was mainly concentrated within collapsed root channels, which predate the agger's construction, which is itself sealed beneath a medieval road. The B horizon had occasional intrusive small rootlets. The area is subject to seasonal waterlogging.

Objectives: stratigraphic evidence suggests the charcoal derives from vegetation clearance prior to road construction. A date from this sample would give a *terminus post quem* for the road construction. The form and alignment suggest a Roman date for the road's construction, and indeed it pre-dates the nearby thirteenth- to fifteenth-century settlement.

Calibrated date: 1σ: 6240–6050 cal BC
                     2σ: 6380–5990 cal BC

Final comment: S Reed (2 February 1994), the dates obtained from OxA-3621 and OxA-3622 indicate an episode of burning in the early Mesolithic period, and, if anthropogenic in origin, are much earlier than any other dates obtained for Mesolithic clearance activity in the south-west of England. It is possible that, due to the small area the sample was taken from, the dates do relate to localised Mesolithic activity in the area. However, the dates do not relate in any way to the archaeology encountered on the A30 Sourton Down excavations.

Laboratory comment: Ancient Monuments Laboratory (1997), the two results on charcoal from a buried soil horizon beneath the road (OxA-3621 and OxA-3622) are not statistically significantly different at 95% confidence (T'=1; T'(5%)=3.8; ν=1; Ward and Wilson 1978).

References: Hedges *et al* 1994, 360
                Ward and Wilson 1978

OxA–3622 7255 ±75 BP

δ¹³C: -26.7‰

Sample: 554348, submitted on 4 March 1992 by C G Henderson

Material: charcoal: *Acer* sp./Pomoideae, two fragments; *Quercus* sp., mainly (V Straker 1991)

Initial comment: as OxA-3621

Objectives: as OxA-3621

Calibrated date: *1σ:* 6230–6030 cal BC
                       2σ: 6250–5990 cal BC

Final comment: see OxA-3621

References: Hedges *et al* 1994, 360

A66 Stainmore Pass, Durham

Location: NY 995137
                Lat. 54.31.06 N; Long. 02.00.28 W

Project manager: B Vyner (Tees Archaeology and Durham County Council), 1989–91

Description: a second carriageway for the A66 was proposed over the 7km section between Bowes, on the east, and Rey Cross, on the summit of the Stainmore Pass. This provided an opportunity to build on the field examination of the putative Roman monuments through the survey and excavation of sites threatened with damage or destruction. Further field survey was undertaken and an assessment made of the nature of early settlement and land-use in the Pennine uplands. Among the excavated sites are the extensive Roman earthwork enclosure at Rey Cross, at the summit of Stainmore, as well as a Roman 'signal' station on Bowes Moor, both of which have been at the centre of speculation concerning the date and extent of the first Roman advance into northern England and south-west Scotland.

Objectives: to establish chronology of vegetational change/development to aid archaeological interpretation of the Stainmore landscape and to contribute to the development of the regional overview.

Final comment: B Vyner (2001), fine resolution pollen and charcoal analysis from a series of sites shows that at the end of the Mesolithic blanket peat began to replace woodland on the gently undulating plateau and that there was also some small-scale woodland clearance at about this time. The woodland on the slopes of the valley gave way to blanket peat in the early Bronze Age and there is evidence for arable cultivation. There does not appear to have been any further cultivation until the Middle Ages. Despite the abundance of archaeological sites the Romans appear to have had little impact upon the environment of this upland landscape, although it was a group of Roman sites that was immediately threatened by road construction. The palynological and radiocarbon evidence shows that the area north of the present A66 on Stainmore has always been marginal for agriculture. There have been four main episodes of land utilisation: 1. sixth millennium cal BC - vegetation manipulation. 2. elm decline, early fourth millennium cal BC

- but not necessarily anthropogenic? 3. limited arable agriculture, early second millennium cal BC, largely inferred. 4. activity extending into Roman-British period.

References: Crompton 1953
                  Edwards and Hirons 1982
                  Gear and Turner 1992
                  Simmons and Innes 1987
                  Turner and Hodgson 1981
                  Vyner 2001
                  Welch 1984

A66 Stainmore Pass: Bowes Moor field system, section B, Durham

Location: NY 906124
                Lat. 54.30.26 N; Long. 02.08.45 W

Project manager: B Vyner (Consultant), 1989–91

Archival body: Tees Archaeology and Durham County Council

Description: about half-way between the farmhouse of Old Spital and the eastern rampart of the Rey Cross marching camp stands an area of earth and stone banks. They are spread over roughly 17.5ha, both on the moor and in the fields to the south of the road, and straddle a low but steep natural ridge which runs north-south near the north side of the road. One of the banks appeared to underlie the Roman road and for this reason the complex has been identified as a prehistoric field system.

Objectives: to establish the chronology of vegetational change/development to aid archaeological interpretation of the Stainmore landscape and to contribute to the development of the regional overview.

References: Gear and Turner 1992
                  Turner and Hodgson 1981
                  Welch 1984

UB–3413 979 ±26 BP

δ¹³C: -29.0 ±0.2‰

Sample: A66 FB2, submitted on 8 March 1991 by M McHugh

Material: peat (M McHugh)

Initial comment: from Bowes Moor field system, section B: the sample was taken from the upper *in situ* peat.

Objectives: to date the transition between the basal mor-type humus form and overlying humified peat.

Calibrated date: *1σ:* cal AD 1020–1040
                       2σ: cal AD 1010–1160

Final comment: B Vyner (12 October 1998), increasingly wet soil surface conditions subsequently culminated in the accumulation of a second organic topsoil throughout the area of the now abandoned arable area. The transition between the basal mor-type humus form and overlying humified peat is thought primarily to reflect vegetation change and equates with the general rise in wild grasses prior to *c* AD 1285 (Gear and Turner 1992). While this change might be climatically and edaphically driven, corresponding with the close of the Iron Age/Roman British climatic optimum, around the fifth century AD (Turner and Hodgson 1981). It might also reflect renewed activity in the area with perhaps increased grazing pressures leading to the suppression of *Calluna* and allowing grasses such as *Deschampsia, Molinia,* or *Nardus* to invade (Welch 1984). This suggestion is supported by soil morphological indicators of local disturbance, a simultaneous decline in woodland (Gear and Turner 1992), and the radiocarbon dating of the upper *in situ* peat which provides a very broad tenth-century timescale for the enclosure.

UB–3415 1876 ±41 BP

δ¹³C: -28.2 ±0.2‰

Sample: A66 FBZ, submitted on 8 March 1991 by M McHugh

Material: soil (buried) (M McHugh)

Initial comment: from Bowes Moor field system, section B. Suggests an Iron Age/Romano-British horizon for the ending of soil activity.

Objectives: to date the soil horizon.

Calibrated date:　1σ: cal AD 70–220
　　　　　　　　　2σ: cal AD 30–240

Final comment: B Vyner (12 October 1998), a thin organic topsoil accumulated throughout the area of the Bowes Moor field system reflecting vegetation change and increasing surface soil wetness. Although acidification and podzolic-type processes were active prior to this, subsoil morphology indicates a biologically active and largely aerobic soil environment, topsoil development was therefore rapid. While the precise timescale is uncertain, such humified organic topsoils may develop in as little as 100 years in deserted pasture land (Crompton 1953). This radiocarbon date thus provides a fairly accurate Iron Age/Romano-British timescale for environmental change. Peat developed some 1750 years earlier only 100m to the east, over soils essentially similar in terms of parent material and drainage. This suggests that the field system was in use for some considerable time after *c* 1990 BC, although cultivations are thought to have ceased well before *c* AD 110.

References:　Crompton 1953

UB–3416 1083 ±26 BP

δ¹³C: -30.4 ±0.2‰

Sample: A66 FBI, submitted on 8 March 1991 by M McHugh

Material: peat (M McHugh)

Initial comment: from Bowes Moor field system, section B (*see* UB-3415).

Objectives: to date the soil horizon.

Calibrated date:　1σ: cal AD 900–1000
　　　　　　　　　2σ: cal AD 890–1020

Final comment: B Vyner (12 October 1998), no comment in A Gear report.

A66 Stainmore Pass: Bowes Moor field system, section N, Durham

Location:　　　　NY 906124
　　　　　　　　Lat. 54.30.26 N; Long. 02.08.45 W

Project manager:　B Vyner (Consultant), 1989–91

Archival body:　Tees Archaeology and Durham County Council

Description: about half-way between the farmhouse of Old Spital and the eastern rampart of the Rey Cross marching camp stands an area of earth and stone banks. They are spread over roughly 17.5ha, both on the moor and in the fields to the south of the road, and straddle a low but steep natural ridge which runs north-south near the north side of the road. One of the banks appeared to underlie the Roman road and for this reason the complex has been identified as a prehistoric field system.

Objectives: to establish chronology of vegetational change/development to aid archaeological interpretation of the Stainmore landscape and to contribute to the development of the regional overview.

UB–3414 1413 ±26 BP

δ¹³C: -28.9 ±0.2‰

Sample: A66 FBN, submitted on 8 March 1991 by M McHugh

Material: peat (A Gear)

Initial comment: from Bowes Moor field system, section N.

Objectives: to date the soil horizon.

Calibrated date:　1σ: cal AD 610–660
　　　　　　　　　2σ: cal AD 590–660

Final comment: B Vyner (12 October 1998), no comment in A Gear report.

A66 Stainmore Pass: Bowes Moor Tower site, Durham

Location:　　　　NY 929124
　　　　　　　　Lat. 54.30.26 N; Long. 02.06.37 W

Project manager:　B Vyner (Consultant), 1989–91

Archival body:　Tees Archaeology and Durham County Council

Description: the Bowes Moor earthwork stands on the level crest of a slight spur, close to the modern road. The well-marked ramparts enclose a rectangular area measuring 10m by 6.5m with a single ditch on the north and east sides.

Objectives: to establish chronology of vegetational change/development to aid archaeological interpretation of the Stainmore landscape and to contribute to the development of the regional overview.

UB–3406 2209 ±27 BP

$\delta^{13}C$: -29.2 ±0.2‰

Sample: A66 SS, submitted on 14 February 1991 by M McHugh

Material: soil (buried) (M McHugh)

Initial comment: from Bowes Moor Tower site (NY 929124).

Objectives: to establish chronology of vegetational change/development on this site.

Calibrated date: 1σ: 370–200 cal BC
                     2σ: 390–190 cal BC

Final comment: B Vyner (12 October 1998), dates a horizon indicating correlated soil development and sealing disturbed subsoil levels, both of which had taken place well before the construction of the Roman signal station.

A66 Stainmore Pass: Coach and Horses earthwork, Durham

Location: NY 935125
                     Lat. 54.30.30 N; Long. 02.06.04 W

Project manager: B Vyner (Consultant), 1989–91

Archival body: Tees Archaeology and Durham County Council

Description: the Coach and Horses site was 0.75km east of Bowes Moor Hotel. Traces of apparent cord rig cultivation were found under later blanket bog. After the removal of a small post-medieval earthwork, site A, a group of parallel gullies was discovered. These ran east-west, alongside the modern road, and were also seen in a smaller trench, site B, 30m to the east.

Objectives: to establish chronology of vegetational change/development to aid archaeological interpretation of the Stainmore landscape and to contribute to the development of the regional overview.

UB–3346 2216 ±53 BP

$\delta^{13}C$: -29.6 ±0.2‰

Sample: CH1, submitted on 21 February 1990 by M McHugh

Material: peat (A Gear)

Initial comment: Coach and Horses samples 1 and 2 were taken from site 2, area A. The Coach and Horses earthwork comprises a platform of unknown date and function. The samples were taken from a thin buried peat, context 15. It was sealed by a homogeneous silty mineral horizon and shallow peat, ie <40cm.

Objectives: in the absence of archaeological evidence, dating provides a rationale for current soils and pollen work. The latter are important regardless of earthwork function since the buried peat overlies possible cord rigg and is sealed by mineral soil predating regional peat development. It is therefore associated with a phase of human activity and subsequently, a period of instability and possibly erosion. The soils are currently under investigation.

Calibrated date: 1σ: 390–200 cal BC
                     2σ: 400–120 cal BC

Final comment: B Vyner (12 October 1998), the date provides a *terminus ante quem* for seemingly limited (chronologically and spatially) cord rigg cultivation.

UB–3369 1877 ±28 BP

$\delta^{13}C$: -29.3 ±0.2‰

Sample: CHC, submitted on 19 October 1990 by M McHugh

Material: peat (A Gear)

Initial comment: from the Coach and Horses site (*see* UB-3346).

Objectives: provision for upper (most recent) limit for agricultural interference.

Calibrated date: 1σ: cal AD 80–140
                     2σ: cal AD 60–230

Final comment: B Vyner (12 October 1998), seals a buried organic soil and suggests cessation of soil development before the Romano-British period.

A66 Stainmore Pass: Deepdale Aqueduct, Durham

Location: NY 961148
                     Lat. 54.31.44 N; Long. 02.03.40 W

Project manager: B Vyner (Consultant), 1989–91

Archival body: Tees Archaeology and Durham County Council

Description: over 200 years ago Hutchinson remarked upon a shallow water channel running through the Deepdale Valley to the north of Stainmore, which had been noted during excavation in 1772–3 (Tomalin 1973, 182). He interpreted this feature as the remains of an aqueduct which had fed Bowes fort in the Roman period. The watercourse survives as a shallow channel and upcast bank running along the contours of the hillside, beginning at the beck at the west end of Deepdale, and running east to the field walls of West Stoney Keld.

Objectives: to establish the chronology of vegetational change/development to aid archaeological interpretation of the Stainmore landscape, and to contribute to the development of the regional overview.

References: Tomalin 1973

UB–3481 443 ±18 BP

$\delta^{13}C$: -28.6 ±0.2‰

Sample: A14 (sample 10), submitted on 2 September 1991 by M McHugh

Material: soil (organic lens) (A Gear)

Initial comment: from Deepdale aqueduct.

Objectives: to date the aqueduct of possible Roman construction.

Calibrated date: 1σ: cal AD 1435–1450
2σ: cal AD 1430–1455

Final comment: B Vyner (12 October 1998), the date suggests that the aqueduct was maintained and refurbished in the medieval period.

Laboratory comment: University of Belfast (26 July 2012), it is unclear whether the alkali soluble or insoluble fraction was extracted for dating.

A66 Stainmore Pass: Marching Camp, Durham

Location: NY 995137
Lat. 54.31.06 N; Long. 02.00.28 W

Project manager: B Vyner (Consultant), 1989–91

Archival body: Tees Archaeology and Durham County Council

Description: the remains of a temporary camp of Roman date, situated at the highest point of the Stainmore Pass. The camp is also situated astride the main Roman road from York to Carlisle which, locally, linked the forts of Brough and Bowes. The Roman camp, which is roughly rectangular in shape, encloses an area of 8.1ha. Excavation at the monument in AD 1990 prior to the road widening confirmed the existence of an outer ditch on the east and west sides of the camp. The camp is thought to have been constructed during the first century AD. Use of the camp continued for some time as late third- and fourth-century pottery was found during the excavations.

Objectives: to establish the chronology of vegetational change/development, to aid archaeological interpretation of the Stainmore landscape, and to contribute to the development of the regional overview.

UB–3405 2625 ±34 BP

$\delta^{13}C$: -28.0 ±0.2‰

Sample: A66 MC, submitted on 14 February 1991 by M McHugh

Material: soil (buried) (M McHugh)

Initial comment: from the marching camp.

Objectives: to date the deposit.

Calibrated date: 1σ: 820–790 cal BC
2σ: 840–770 cal BC

Final comment: B Vyner (12 October 1998), dating evidence from the excavation includes a few pieces of pottery from the construction deposits of the camp, which have been dated to the first to second century. This radiocarbon result is probably dating residual material within the layer. Whilst the date is not very useful in confirming a first-century date, they do not dispute it.

A66 Stainmore Pass: pollen site 1, Durham

Location: NY 907124
Lat. 54.30.26 N; Long. 02.08.40 W

Project manager: B Vyner (Consultant), 1989–90

Archival body: Tees Archaeology/Durham County Council

Description: the A66 Project represented the first opportunity to undertake detailed soils analysis in conjunction with a rescue archaeology project. During the academic year 1989-90 three peat profiles from Bowes were examined. Pollen, charcoal, and humification analyses were made on samples taken from an area of deep peat, pollen site 1, on the gently sloping plateau approximately 20m to the west of a small stream. The peat stratigraphy is more or less uniform throughout except that below 1.5m there is a small amount of mineral material in most samples.

Objectives: to establish the chronology of vegetational change/development, to aid archaeological interpretation of the Stainmore landscape, and to contribute to the development of the regional overview.

UB–3283 1471 ±43 BP

$\delta^{13}C$: -28.0 ±0.2‰

Sample: F1/001 49-50cm, submitted on 5 March 1990 by A J Gear

Material: peat (A Gear)

Initial comment: from pollen site 1, located in an area of deep peat on the gently sloping plateau approximately 20m to the west of a small stream.

Objectives: to establish a chronology of vegetational change/development of the Stainmore landscape.

Calibrated date: 1σ: cal AD 550–640
2σ: cal AD 530–660

Final comment: B Vyner (12 October 1998), no comments in A Gear report.

UB–3284 5117 ±68 BP

$\delta^{13}C$: -25.8 ±0.2‰

Sample: F1/002 214-218cm, submitted on 5 March 1990 by A J Gear

Material: peat (A Gear)

Initial comment: from pollen site 1 (*see* UB-3283): taken at a depth of 214–218cm.

Objectives: to establish a chronology of vegetational change/development of the Stainmore landscape.

Calibrated date: 1σ: 3980–3800 cal BC
2σ: 4050–3710 cal BC

Final comment: B Vyner (12 October 1998), this result indicates a return to the former moorland pollen values following earlier reductions, perhaps by clearance.

UB–3285 5336 ±60 BP

δ¹³C: -28.2 ±0.2‰

Sample: F1/003 224-228cm, submitted on 5 March 1990 by A J Gear

Material: peat (A Gear)

Initial comment: from pollen site 1 (*see* UB-3823): taken at a depth of 224–228cm.

Objectives: to establish a chronology of vegetational change/development of the Stainmore landscape.

Calibrated date: 1σ: 4320–4040 cal BC
   2σ: 4340–3990 cal BC

Final comment: B Vyner (12 October 1998), the radiocarbon and palynological evidence from site 1 indicates that the deep peat deposits began to develop in this area *c* 4150 cal BC (UB-3285).

UB–3286 2198 ±59 BP

δ¹³C: -27.5 ±0.2‰

Sample: F1/004 81-82cm, submitted on 23 March 1990 by A J Gear

Material: peat (A Gear)

Initial comment: from pollen site 1 (*see* UB-3823): taken at a depth of 81–82 cm.

Objectives: to establish a chronology of vegetational change/development of the Stainmore landscape.

Calibrated date: 1σ: 380–170 cal BC
   2σ: 400–60 cal BC

Final comment: B Vyner (12 October 1998), by *c* 280 BC, the immediately pre-Roman period, the area had become almost totally treeless and has remained so until the present day.

UB–3287 2420 ±46 BP

δ¹³C: -27.8 ±0.2‰

Sample: F1/005 107-108cm, submitted on 23 March 1990 by A J Gear

Material: peat (A Gear)

Initial comment: from pollen site 1 (*see* UB-3283): taken at a depth of 107–108cm.

Objectives: to establish a chronology of vegetational change/development of the Stainmore landscape.

Calibrated date: 1σ: 740–400 cal BC
   2σ: 770–390 cal BC

Final comment: B Vyner (12 October 1998), no comment in A Gear report.

UB–3288 3232 ±50 BP

δ¹³C: -27.6 ±0.2‰

Sample: F1/006 132-133cm, submitted on 23 March 1990 by A J Gear

Material: peat (A Gear)

Initial comment: from pollen site 1 (*see* UB-3283): taken at a depth of 132–133cm.

Objectives: to establish a chronology of vegetational change/development of the Stainmore landscape.

Calibrated date: 1σ: 1530–1440 cal BC
   2σ: 1630–1410 cal BC

Final comment: B Vyner (12 October 1998), evidence from site 1 in the form of a single grain of *Secale cereale* dated to *c* 1515 BC (UB-3288), indicates arable agriculture was being practised about that time, but probably not at this location, which has one of developing peat.

UB–3340 3652 ±45 BP

δ¹³C: -27.8 ±0.2‰

Sample: F1/001 154-158cm, submitted on 23 March 1990 by A J Gear

Material: peat (A Gear)

Initial comment: from pollen site 1 (*see* UB-3823): taken at a depth of 154–158cm.

Objectives: to establish a chronology of vegetational change/development of the Stainmore landscape.

Calibrated date: 1σ: 2130–1950 cal BC
   2σ: 2200–1890 cal BC

Final comment: B Vyner (12 October 1998), no comments in A Gear report.

UB–3341 4728 ±52 BP

δ¹³C: -27.5 ±0.2‰

Sample: F1/008 185-189cm, submitted on 23 March 1990 by A J Gear

Material: peat (A Gear)

Initial comment: from pollen site 1 (*see* UB-3283): taken at a depth of 185–189cm.

Objectives: to date the *Ulmus* decline.

Calibrated date: 1σ: 3640–3370 cal BC
   2σ: 3640–3360 cal BC

Final comment: B Vyner (12 October 1998), this date for the *Ulmus* decline falls within the range of dates previously recorded in the Pennines (Simmons and Innes 1987). It also suggests mixed woodlands were growing on the better-drained slopes until this period.

References: Simmons and Innes 1987

A66 Stainmore Pass: pollen site 2, Durham

Location: NY 908123
      Lat. 54.30.23 N; Long. 02.08.34 W

Project manager: B Vyner (Consultant), 1989–90

Archival body: Tees Archaeology and Durham County Council

Description: the A66 Project represented the first opportunity to undertake detailed soils analysis in conjunction with a rescue archaeology project. During the academic year 1989–90 three peat profiles from Bowes were examined. Pollen site 2 was around 150m from pollen site 1 and is centred within an area of shallow peaty soil which was once enclosed by a field wall. The remains of this wall is partly buried by blanket peat.

Objectives: to establish the chronology of vegetational change/development, to aid archaeological interpretation of the Stainmore landscape, and to contribute to the development of the regional overview.

UB–3342 3620 ±47 BP

δ¹³C: -27.9 ±0.2‰

Sample: F2/009 28-29cm, submitted on 16 May 1990 by A Gear

Material: peat (A Gear)

Initial comment: from pollen site 2, approximately 150m from site 1, centred within an area of shallow peaty soil which was enclosed by a field wall (NY 908123). The sample was taken from a depth of 28–29cm.

Objectives: to date a period of early arable cultivation.

Calibrated date: *1σ:* 2040–1910 cal BC
                2σ: 2140–1880 cal BC

Final comment: B Vyner (12 October 1998), early arable cultivation in the area is indicated by a single grain of *Avena-Triticum* group pollen at 1.80m, although it must be emphasised that there is no collaborative evidence in the form of the suite of herbaceous pollen taxa often associated with cereal cultivation. The earliest more convincing evidence is found in the bottom 1cm of peat at site 2, UB-3342, where there is a total of three *Avena-Triticum* group and three *Hordeum* group pollen grains were found within a 6mm span of peat.

UB–3343 676 ±49 BP

δ¹³C: -28.6 ±0.2‰

Sample: F2/010 7-8cm, submitted on 16 May 1990 by A Gear

Material: peat (A Gear)

Initial comment: from pollen site 2 (*see* UB-3342): taken at a depth of 7–8cm.

Objectives: to date a period of renewed arable activity.

Calibrated date: *1σ:* cal AD 1270–1390
                2σ: cal AD 1260–1400

Final comment: B Vyner (12 October 1998), it was not until medieval times that there is pollen evidence for renewed cultivation in the area around site 2. This takes the form of *Secale cereale* at *c* 1285 BC, together with rises in the wild grass group and the *Potentilla* type curves. The palynological evidence presented here strongly suggests the local area was being used for pasture. This is consistent with the fact that some peat was accumulating.

A66 Stainmore Pass: pollen site 3, Durham

Location: NY 929124
          Lat. 54.30.26 N; Long. 02.06.37 W

Project manager: B Vyner (Consultant), 1989–90

Archival body: Tees Archaeology and Durham County Council

Description: the A66 Project represented the first opportunity to undertake detailed soils analysis in conjunction with a rescue archaeology project. During the academic year 1989–90 three peat profiles from Bowes were examined. Pollen site 3 lies in an area of shallow peat on a gently sloping hillside around 2.2km east of pollen site 2. A shallow peat deposit near the Roman earthwork on Bowes Moor, pollen site 3, was analysed in detail using fine-resolution techniques at the base.

Objectives: to establish a chronology of vegetational change/development, to aid archaeological interpretation of the Stainmore landscape, and to contribute to the development of the regional overview.

UB–3344 1055 ±43 BP

δ¹³C: -29.2 ±0.2‰

Sample: SS/011 22-24, submitted on 6 August 1990 by A Gear

Material: peat (A Gear)

Initial comment: from pollen site 3, an area of shallow peat overlaying shale on a gently sloping hillside around 2.2km east of site 2 (NZ 929124). The monolith was collected about 15m from the western boundary of the Roman tower site. The sample was taken from a peat monolith at a depth of 22–24cm.

Objectives: to establish the chronology of vegetational change/development of the Stainmore landscape.

Calibrated date: *1σ:* cal AD 900–1030
                2σ: cal AD 890–1040

Final comment: B Vyner (12 October 1998), despite the late post-Roman date provided by the base of the adjacent control peat, organic soils within the upper central rampart indicate that peat was developing locally by the fourth century, probably over adjacent flatter plateau areas just to the north. Humified wood detritus within this peat suggests that *Alnus* sp. or *Betula* sp. had been present at some time.

UB–3345 145 ±49 BP

δ¹³C: -28.7 ±0.2‰

Sample: SS/012 7-8cm, submitted on 6 August 1990 by A Gear

Material: peat (A Gear)

Initial comment: from pollen site 3 (*see* UB-3344): taken at a depth of 7–8cm.

Objectives: to establish a chronology of vegetational change/development of the Stainmore landscape.

Calibrated date: 1σ: cal AD 1660–1950
2σ: cal AD 1650–1955*

Final comment: B Vyner (12 October 1998), no comment in A Gear report.

A66 Stainmore Pass: Ravock, field system, site B, Durham

Location: NY 96301465
Lat. 54.31.38 N; Long. 02.03.31 W

Project manager: B Vyner (Consultant), 1989–91

Archival body: Tees Archaeology and Durham County Council

Description: the Ravock field system can be described as coaxial, there being one major alignment of straight boundaries running south-west to north-east down the north-facing slope of the Deepdale Valley. The boundaries at Ravock are constructed of stones heaped to form a ridge. Only the larger stones are visible through the heather, but where they are crossed by the track at the bottom of the hillside it can be seen that the banks consist mainly of smaller angular stones.

Objectives: to establish a chronology of vegetational change/development to aid archaeological interpretation of the Stainmore landscape and to contribute to the development of the regional overview.

UB–3482 239 ±17 BP

δ¹³C: -28.6 ±0.2‰

Sample: B07, submitted on 2 September 1991 by M McHugh

Material: soil (organic lens) (J Innes)

Initial comment: from Ravock field system, site B.

Objectives: date provision for associated material to the possible Bronze Age field boundary.

Calibrated date: 1σ: cal AD 1645–1665
2σ: cal AD 1645–1800

Final comment: B Vyner (12 October 1998), this result suggests that it may apply to only a small sample of walling, analogy suggests is likely to be more ancient.

Laboratory comment: University of Belfast (26 July 2012), it is unclear whether the alkali soluble or insoluble fraction was extracted for dating.

A66 Stainmore Pass: Ravock, field system, site D, Durham

Location: NY 995137
Lat. 54.31.06 N; Long. 02.00.28 W

Project manager: B Vyner (Consultant), 1989–91

Archival body: Tees Archaeology and Durham County Council

Description: the Ravock field system can be described as coaxial, there being one major alignment of straight boundaries running south-west to north-east down the north-facing slope of the Deepdale Valley. The boundaries at Ravock are constructed of stones heaped to form a ridge. Only the larger stones are visible through the heather, but where they are crossed by the track at the bottom of the hillside it can be seen that the banks consist mainly of smaller angular stones.

Objectives: to establish a chronology of vegetational change/development, to aid archaeological interpretation of the Stainmore landscape, and to contribute to the development of the regional overview.

UB–3483 442 ±18 BP

δ¹³C: -29.5 ±0.2‰

Sample: D23 (sample 4), submitted on 2 September 1991 by J Innes

Material: peat (basal) (J Innes)

Initial comment: from Ravock field system, site D: basal peat sealing the field wall of feature D.

Objectives: to provide a minimum date for a field boundary wall (feature D), and check the age of peat initiation across the site.

Calibrated date: 1σ: cal AD 1435–1450
2σ: cal AD 1430–1455

Final comment: B Vyner (12 October 1998), this late date suggests that peat formation occurred much later in some parts of the site than in others. Very different dates for peat initiation across a hill slope are quite reasonable, however, as local micro-topography may be the critical factor (Edwards and Hirons 1982). The enclosure lies in a lower and flatter area than the steeper slope of feature D, where peat formation would logically have been later. The field wall itself is, however, perhaps much older than the minimum date of *c* AD 1450. Unfortunately, no sediment suitable for analysis could be recovered from below the wall which could have assisted its dating. *See* also UB–3481.

References: Edwards and Hirons 1982

A66 Stainmore Pass: Ravock, oval enclosure, Durham

Location: NY 963148
Lat. 54.31.44 N; Long. 02.03.28 W

Project manager: B Vyner (Consultant), 1989–91

Archival body: Tees Archaeology and Durham County Council

Description: on the slopes of the hillside to the south of the field system, is an oval enclosure, which may be a settlement site, although the only structural feature to be found within it is a dividing wall running across the upper, south-western, quarter.

Objectives: to establish the chronology of vegetational change/development, to aid archaeological interpretation of the Stainmore landscape, and to contribute to the development of the regional overview.

UB–3480 929 ±18 BP

δ*¹³C:* -29.6 ±0.2‰

Sample: E18, submitted on 2 September 1991 by
M McHugh

Material: peat (J Innes)

Initial comment: from an oval enclosure at Ravock.

Objectives: dating basal peat sealing the boundary wall of a
late prehistoric enclosure.

Calibrated date: *1σ:* cal AD 1040–1160
   2σ: cal AD 1030–1165

Final comment: B Vyner (12 October 1998), it forms a
minimum age for the oval enclosure, which may have been
constructed before *c* AD 1000, and may be the oldest feature
sampled from this part of the study. It is much more likely
that a major time period elapsed between the construction of
the enclosure and its burial by later peat growth, than
between the upper soil horizon and its burial by the
enclosure wall. The enclosure is thus much more likely to be
of Iron Age or Romano-British date than much later.

A66 Stainmore Pass: Vale House Farm, Durham

Location: NY 94771276
                     Lat. 54.30.37 N; Long. 02.04.56 W

Project manager: B Vyner (Consultant), 1989–91

Archival body: Tees Archaeology and Durham County
                     Council

Description: this was a large enclosure with low-banks and, in
places, an external ditch, which runs northwards from the
road for 35km and turns to the east at the top of the slope,
where it is disturbed by a later quarry track.

Objectives: to establish the chronology of vegetational
change/development, to aid archaeological interpretation of
the Stainmore landscape, and to contribute to the
development of the regional overview.

UB–3347 1604 ±53 BP

δ*¹³C:* -28.7 ±0.2‰

Sample: A66VH89 A, 23, submitted in January 1990 by
M McHugh

Material: organic matter (buried turf material and organic
topsoil) (A Gear)

Initial comment: from Vale House, site 4, section A, context
23 (NY 948124). The Vale House earthwork comprises a
turf bank forming an enclosure of unknown function. The
horizon sampled lies at the base of the turf bank and directly
over the *in situ* soil profile. It is thought to comprise an
organic horizon associated with an inverted turf.

Objectives: in the absence of any archaeological evidence,
dating is a prerequisite for both soils and pollen work. The
request for dating is viewed in the context of human activity,
soil degradation, vegetation change, and peat initiation. This
work is part of a larger study which includes detailed pollen
work (associated deep peat) and a series of excavations.

Ideally the project will allow environmental
(landuse/soil/vegetation) reconstruction during varied
periods, Bronze Age to Roman and possibly earlier.

Calibrated date: *1σ:* cal AD 400–540
                     2σ: cal AD 330–580

Final comment: B Vyner (12 October 1998), the date
confirms the association of the turf bank with the
construction of the nearby Roman signal tower.

Laboratory comment: University of Belfast (26 July 2021), no
record survives of the pretreatment protocol undertaken on
this sample, and it is not clear whether the alkakli soluble or
the insoluble fraction was dated.

UB–3370 681 ±27 BP

δ*¹³C:* -30.1 ±0.2‰

Sample: VHC, submitted on 19 October 1990 by
M McHugh

Material: peat (A Gear)

Initial comment: from Vale House Farm (*see* UB-3347).

Objectives: provision of an upper date limit for the
construction of the enclosure boundary.

Calibrated date: *1σ:* cal AD 1280–1300
                     2σ: cal AD 1270–1390

Final comment: B Vyner (12 October 1998), the dating of the
basal peat corresponds with the worsening of the climate
(Lamb 1977).

References: Lamb 1977

Addingham Church Hall, Yorkshire (West Riding)

Location: SE 08464972
                     Lat. 53.56.36 N; Long. 01.52.16 W

Project manager: R Turner (West Yorkshire Archaeological
                     Service), 1990

Archival body: West Yorkshire Archive Service

Description: excavations in the environs of Addingham
Church were funded by English Heritage and West Yorkshire
Archaeology Service in advance of building works on the
Church Hall. Following a successful evaluation in 1989, an
area of *c* 150m² was fully excavated in order to confirm the
archaeological potential of this part of the scheduled
site. The site lies within an undeveloped area surrounding the
medieval and 18th-century church, but there are several
indications of Anglo-Saxon activity: the '-ingham' part of the
name Addingham; the oval cemetery; two Anglo-Saxon stone
crosses; an Anglo-Scandinavian bone comb case; and
historical references, amongst others to a ninth-century
archbishop's residence.

Objectives: the primary intention is to expose any Anglo-
Saxon or medieval activity on this part of the site. In this
area it is clear that a number of graves exist, the dating of
which will be crucial. The inhumations will, despite the poor
survival of the small bones, allow the recovery of at least
some social and anatomical data.

Final comment: S Wrathmell (10 January 1995), the series of samples was taken from human skeletons uncovered some distance outside the medieval and modern churchyard. Addingham is known to have been a residence of the Archbishop of York in the mid-ninth century, and the samples were submitted to determine whether the otherwise undated burials could be assigned to that period. Most of the graves, including those sampled, had been laid out uniformly in rows and were expected to mark a relatively cohesive period of interment. After the resubmission of two samples, all four now provide relatively coherent results, which compare well with the documented history of the site.

References: Adams 1996

GU–5112 990 ±70 BP

δ¹³C: -20.8‰

Sample: ACH90/A93, submitted on 13 February 1991 by R Turner

Material: human bone

Initial comment: from within a well-defined, undisturbed grave. There is a small amount of root and worm disturbance.

Objectives: to date the use of the cemetery. The sample is thought to be pre-twelfth or thirteenth century AD. There was no alternative dating evidence for the graves.

Calibrated date: *1σ:* cal AD 980–1160
                      2σ: cal AD 890–1220

Final comment: S Wrathmell (10 January 1995), the dating of this sample was so far removed from that of the adjacent grave sample (GU-5113) that it was resubmitted (*see* GU-5112B).

Laboratory comment: see GU-5112 B

GU–5112 B 1110 ±50 BP

δ¹³C: -22.3‰

Sample: ACH90/A93, submitted in September 1991 by R Turner

Material: human bone

Initial comment: a replicate sample of GU-5112.

Objectives: as GU-5112

Calibrated date: *1σ:* cal AD 0–0
                      2σ: 1 cal BC–cal AD 1

Final comment: S Wrathmell (10 January 1995), the dating of this resubmitted sample conforms well to that of the other two samples from a cohesive set of interments, expected on historical grounds to date from the middle to late Saxon periods.

Laboratory comment: English Heritage (25 January 2012), the two results from this skeleton are statistically consistent (T'=1.9; T'(5%)=3.8; v=1; Ward and Wilson 1978). The weighted mean of these measurements (1070 ±41 BP) calibrates to cal AD 880–1030 (at 95% confidence; Reimer *et al* 2004), or to cal AD 900–1020 (at 68% confidence).

References: Reimer *et al* 2004
                    Ward and Wilson 1978

GU–5113 1460 ±50 BP

δ¹³C: -20.7‰

Sample: ACH90/A104, submitted on 13 February 1991 by R Turner

Material: human bone

Initial comment: as GU-5112

Objectives: as GU-5112

Calibrated date: *1σ:* cal AD 550–650
                      2σ: cal AD 470–660

Final comment: S Wrathmell (10 January 1995), the dating of this sample was outside the expected range, given the spatial relationship of this grave to the other sampled interments, and given the putatively Christian attribution of this cemetery. It was therefore resubmitted (*see* GU-5113 B).

Laboratory comment: English Heritage (25 January 2012), the two results from the skeleton are statistically significantly different (T'=7.2; T'(5%)=3.8; v=1; Ward and Wilson 1978).

GU–5113 B 1270 ±50 BP

δ¹³C: -20.6‰

Sample: ACH90/A104, submitted in September 1991 by R Turner

Material: human bone

Initial comment: a replicate sample of GU-5113.

Objectives: as GU-5112

Calibrated date: *1σ:* cal AD 670–780
                      2σ: cal AD 650–890

Final comment: S Wrathmell (10 January 1995), the dating of this resubmitted sample conforms well to that of two other samples from a cohesive set of interments expected to date from the middle to late Saxon periods on historical grounds.

Laboratory comment: see GU-5113

References: Ward and Wilson 1978

GU–5114 1250 ±60 BP

δ¹³C: -20.6‰

Sample: ACH90/A120, submitted on 13 February 1991 by R Turner

Material: human bone

Initial comment: as GU-5112

Objectives: as GU-5112

Calibrated date: *1σ:* cal AD 670–880
                      2σ: cal AD 650–940

Final comment: S Wrathmell (10 January 1995), the dating of this sample conforms well to that of two other samples from a cohesive set of human interments, which was expected on historical grounds to date from the middle to late Saxon periods.

GU–5115 1200 ±60 BP

δ¹³C: -20.8‰

Sample: ACH90/A182, submitted on 13 February 1991 by R Turner

Material: human bone

Initial comment: as GU-5112

Objectives: as GU-5112

Calibrated date: *1σ:* cal AD 710–900
            2σ: cal AD 670–990

Final comment: see GU-5114

Alcester: Gas House Lane, AL23, Warwickshire

Location: SP 093574
          Lat. 52.12.52 N; Long. 01.51.50 W

Project manager: J Greig (University of Birmingham), 1990

Description: excavations at Gas House Lane revealed parts of the Alcester Roman town defences and buildings within the defended area, in addition to a large collection of Roman pottery, one of the most significant assemblages from the town.

Objectives: to date any deposits which may have accumulated prior to the construction of the first defences at Alcester.

References: Cracknell 1996

GU–5137 2150 ±50 BP

δ¹³C: -28.7‰

Sample: 346/0/8, submitted on 14 March 1991 by J Greig

Material: waterlogged plant macrofossil: *Prunus/Crataegus* sp., twigs (J Greig)

Initial comment: from a channel, which could be a ditch, associated with the Roman defences of Alcester or an earlier, perhaps more natural feature (although the flora includes weeds of a cultivated ground, *Valerianella* and *Aphanes*).

Objectives: the sample came from a layer below ones with dateable pottery. A date would ascertain if the sample relates to Roman Alcester or its Iron Age predecessor, and establish its chronological relationship to other organic deposits elsewhere in Alcester.

Calibrated date: *1σ:* 360–110 cal BC
            2σ: 380–40 cal BC

Final comment: J Greig (8 August 1993), this date is in contrast to most of the archaeological evidence from Alcester which is Roman. The environmental importance is the evidence of a well-developed hedge flora, which is a rare and interesting find.

Alfriston, East Sussex

Location: TQ 509036
          Lat. 50.48.42 N; Long. 00.08.32 E

Project manager: P Drewett (Institute of Archaeology, London), 1974

Archival body: Sussex Past, Barbican House

Description: a small, ploughed out, Bronze Age, oval barrow comprising a single dump of material derived from the two flanking ditches and containing a single central crouched inhumation; this is one of only 12 known third-millennium burial sites in East Sussex.

Objectives: to clarify a possible anomaly with the previous result on similar material.

Final comment: P Drewett (19 December 1994), sample HAR-940 from the primary silts of the flanking ditch is consistent with the material culture and barrow morphology. The remaining three dates suggest a later Bronze Age modification to the barrow and that the central crouched burial may be a secondary burial of later Bronze Age date.

Laboratory comment: Ancient Monuments Laboratory (19 December 1994), three further dates (HAR-940 (ALF1), HAR-942 (ALF4), and HAR-1811 (ALF12)) from this site were funded prior to 1981 and were published in the first volume of *Radiocarbon Dates* (Jordan *et al* 1994, 4).

References: Hardiman *et al* 1992, 47
         Jordan *et al* 1994, 4

HAR–941 2540 ±70 BP

δ¹³C: -23.3‰

Sample: ALF 2, submitted on 10 March 74 by P L Drewett

Material: antler

Initial comment: from the north-west quadrant mound, layer 2.

Objectives: to clarify a possible anomaly with the previous result on similar material.

Calibrated date: *1σ:* 800–540 cal BC
            2σ: 830–410 cal BC

Final comment: P L Drewett (19 December 1994), this date is similar to HAR-942 so may represent later Bronze Age additions to the Neolithic oval barrow.

Laboratory comment: AERE Harwell (11 May 1989), this sample was measured in the miniature gas proportional counter (Otlet *et al* 1983).

References: Otlet *et al* 1983

Amesbury: New Barn Down, Wiltshire

Location: SU 17834237
          Lat. 51.10.47 N; Long. 01.44.42 W

Project manager: P Ashbee (Archaeology Centre of East Anglian Studies, University of East Anglia), July to September 1956

Archival body: Salisbury and South Wiltshire Museum

Description: four barrows on New Barn Down were selected for excavation because of sustained plough damage (Amesbury 58, 61a, 61, and 72).

Objectives: to provide absolute dating for the construction and use of a bell barrow (Amesbury 58), a bowl barrow (Amesbury 61), and a saucer barrow (Amesbury 72), and the associated Beaker and Wessex cultures.

Laboratory comment: English Heritage (2012), one further measurement (HAR-1237) was published in the first volume of *Radiocarbon Dates* (Jordan *et al* 1994, 5), and three in the second (HAR-6225–7; Bayliss *et al* 2012, 5–6).

References: Ashbee 1978
                   Ashbee 1979–80
                   Ashbee 1984
                   Ashbee 1992
                   Bayliss *et al* 2012
                   Hardiman *et al* 1992, 64
                   Jordan *et al* 1994
                   Piggott 1973a
                   Piggott 1973b

HAR–10514 3290 ±80 BP

δ¹³C: -24.7‰

Sample: NEWB49, submitted in February 1990 by D Jordon

Material: charcoal: *Fraxinus* sp.

Initial comment: charcoal from cremation grave 2 beneath barrow 61.

Objectives: to provide a more refined date for barrow 61.

Calibrated date: *1σ:* 1690–1460 cal BC
                        2σ: 1750–1410 cal BC

Final comment: P Ashbee (1992), the date yielded is significantly different from the previous ones from the same source (HAR-6225), the dates were amalgamated with HAR-6227 and when calibrated with the R M Clark (1975) curve they gave 1σ 2035–1865 cal BC, 2σ 2110–1790 cal BC. Calibration has also shown a significant difference between the dates from the barrow 61 samples, which could be accounted for by the ancient wood upon the cremation pyre, by contamination, or by chance.

References: Ashbee 1992
                   Clark 1975

HAR–10515 3610 ±90 BP

δ¹³C: -25.8‰

Sample: NEWB8, submitted in February 1990 by D Jordon

Material: charcoal: *Quercus* sp.

Initial comment: charcoal from base of the middle ditch at New Barn (B4), lower humus (1) - part of the larger saucer barrow 72.

Objectives: to provide a more refined date for barrow 72.

Calibrated date: *1σ:* 2130–1880 cal BC
                        2σ: 2210–1740 cal BC

Final comment: P Ashbee (1992), the dates from barrow 72 particularly HAR-10515, provide indirectly, a date for the Collared Urn interred beneath the initial bowl barrow. This is not out of place when set beside those, which have accumulated for the series (Longworth 1984, 140).

References: Ashbee 1992
                   Longworth 1984

HAR–10516 4070 ±90 BP

δ¹³C: -24.6‰

Sample: NEWB10, submitted in February 1990 by D Jordon

Material: charcoal: *Fraxinus* sp.

Initial comment: charcoal from the filling of a horseshoe pit at New Barn (B4), which was stratified beneath the larger saucer barrow 72.

Objectives: as HAR-10515

Calibrated date: *1σ:* 2870–2470 cal BC
                        2σ: 2890–2350 cal BC

Final comment: see HAR-10515

References: Ashbee 1992

Anslow's Cottages, Berkshire

Location: SU 693710
                     Lat. 51.26.00 N; Long. 01.00.11 W

Project manager: S Lobb (Wessex Archaeology), 1985–6

Archival body: Reading Museum

Description: a later Bronze Age settlement adjacent to an old river channel, within which were revealed several timber structures. The site lies on the floodplain of the river Kennet about 150m from the present course of the river, although the excavated river channel joins an abandoned loop of the river only 40m to the east. The site was excavated prior to sand and gravel extraction.

Objectives: to establish a chronology for the site.

Final comment: J Gardiner (18 October 1993), the samples sent for dating were all from wood taken from a series of waterfront and river channel structures associated with a former channel of the River Kennet. A series of structures were apparent on excavation but there was no means of dating them. Dates confirm waterside activity contemporary with nearby Bronze Age settlement and elucidate a lengthy sequence of revetment and water channel management during the Saxon period culminating in the construction of possible fish weir and the presence of a wicker fish trap.

Laboratory comment: English Heritage (20 January 2012), eight further dates (HAR-9179–86) from this site were funded prior to 1988 and are published in Bayliss *et al* 2012 (6–8).

References: Bayliss *et al* 2012
                   Butterworth and Lobb 1992
                   Hedges *et al* 1994, 365

OxA–2126 1060 ±80 BP

$\delta^{13}C$: -28.4‰

Sample: wicker basket; special find 1073, submitted in January 1987 by J Watson

Material: wood (waterlogged) (J Watson)

Initial comment: a wicker basket, or possible eel trap, found within a Saxon river channel close to a timber structure thought to be part of a fish weir or similar structure. The warp and weft is made up of *Corylus* sp., and the post/plug, *Alnus* sp.

Objectives: to demonstrate the chronological relationship between the eel trap and the Bronze Age silted up water channel in which it was found. Two alternative hypotheses exist; that it is Bronze Age or medieval. In either event this object, which cannot be dated on style alone as the style is continuous, is of such value the date is sought.

Calibrated date: 1σ: cal AD 890–1030
                     2σ: cal AD 770–1160

Final comment: J Gardiner (1994), radiocarbon dating was the only means of dating what is an unusual find, thought more or less to be *in situ*. The date is statistically identical to those from the fish weir indicating late Saxon water channel management and fishing.

Laboratory comment: English Heritage (25 January 2012), in 2010 three further radiocarbon measurements were obtained from this basket (OxA-22480, 1111 ±28 BP; SUERC-28983, 1370 ±30 BP; and SUERC-28984, 1125 ±30 BP). The four measurements are not statistically consistent (T'=51.9; T'(5%)=7.8; ν=3; Ward and Wilson 1978), although, once SUERC-28984 (which is clearly anomalously early) is removed, the remaining three measurements are statistically consistent (T'=0.6; T'(5%)=6.0; ν=2; Ward and Wilson 1978). The weighted mean of these three results (1114 ±20 BP) provides the best estimate for the age of the basket, which calibrates to cal AD 885–990 (at 95% confidence; Reimer *et al* 2004).

References: Reimer *et al* 2004
                     Ward and Wilson 1978

Axminster Bypass, Devon

Location: SY 28159797
                     Lat. 50.46.35 N; Long. 03.01.09 W

Project manager: S Reed (Exeter City Museum), 1990–2

Archival body: Royal Albert Memorial Museum

Description: a series of excavations and watching briefs took place along the line of the Axminster bypass. The 1.6km route passes from the Roman road to the west of the town across the Axe/Yarty floodplain to the south, and then turns eastward to rejoin the Roman road at Burrowshot Cross. The site close to the junction of two major Roman roads, and to Axminster itself was one of the earliest Saxon foundations in Devon (Hoskins 1972, 324). Nevertheless, these excavations were the first large-scale systematic archaeological investigations to be undertaken in the area.

Objectives: to provide a chronology for pollen analysis from a column sealed beneath a Roman road.

References: Hoskins 1972
                     Weddell *et al* 1993

AA–12598 3255 ±65 BP

$\delta^{13}C$: -25.3‰

Sample: 418309A, submitted on 18 January 1993 by S Reed

Material: wood (waterlogged): *Alnus* sp.; *Quercus* sp. (V Straker)

Initial comment: taken at a depth of 1.48m, from the top 0.02m of a silted watercourse. This context was sealed beneath an alluvial soil upon which a Roman road was constructed. The context was undisturbed and contained no intrusive roots. The situation of the deposit would suggest it was waterlogged for most of the year.

Objectives: AA-12598 and GU-5289 would provide a chronology for the pollen analysis currently being undertaken on a column taken through this context, up to the base of the Roman road. The dating of these deposits would also enhance the understanding of the prehistoric alluvial sequences of the River Yarty which were exposed during excavations.

Calibrated date: 1σ: 1620–1440 cal BC
                     2σ: 1690–1410 cal BC

Final comment: V Straker and J Jones (1993), the calibrated range for this result overlaps with that of the basal sample (GU-5289), which may suggest that the sediments accumulated rapidly or that these waterlogged deposits span more than 200 years. They place the entire sediment sequence in trench 6 into the mid-second millennium cal BC. Environmental evidence suggests that the Yarty floodplain was largely open at this period, supporting a herbaceous grassland flora with arable agriculture in the vicinity.

Laboratory comment: SURRC Radiocarbon Dating Laboratory (1993), this was a poor quality sample which produced insufficient carbon dioxide for conventional dating.

GU–5289 3230 ±90 BP

$\delta^{13}C$: -28.7‰

Sample: 418309B, submitted on 18 January 1993 by S Reed

Material: wood (waterlogged): *Alnus* sp.; *Quercus* sp. (V Straker)

Initial comment: taken at a depth of 1.79–1.82m, from the basal 0.02m of a silted watercourse (*see also* AA-12598).

Objectives: as AA-12598

Calibrated date: 1σ: 1620–1410 cal BC
                     2σ: 1740–1310 cal BC

Final comment: see AA-12598

Laboratory comment: see AA-12598

Aylesbury Prebendal, Buckinghamshire

Location: SP 81631394
Lat. 51.49.02 N; Long. 00.48.57 W

Project manager: M Farley (Buckinghamshire County Museum), 1985

Archival body: Buckinghamshire County Museum

Description: a multi-period site excavated prior to development, lay just west of the church and was to be developed for offices with an underground car park. The principal discovery was a deep ditch, which had been recut, and belonged to the ditch of an early to middle Iron Age hillfort. Clay slingshots, animal bone, and pottery fragments were recovered from the ditch fill. On the base of the the first phase of the ditch lay a human skull deliberately placed and packed around with limestone blocks. The interior of the hillfort contained two pits with deposits of human skulls and animal bones. Parts of four human burials were also discovered, two of which were accompanied by animal skeletons. No evidence for late Iron Age activity was encountered, but Romano-British artefacts, a middle Saxon ditch, medieval and later pits, wells, and buildings were also excavated. Renewed activity in the later sixteenth to seventeenth centuries was also identified and continued through to the nineteenth century.

Objectives: these samples were intended to date the ritual Iron Age deposits, and to date possible Saxon occupation.

Final comment: M E Farley (1990), samples OxA-1918–20 come from a discrete ritual deposit dated on ceramic grounds to the early Iron Age. The deposit, which lies within a hillfort and beneath the modern town, contained plentiful animal bone, much of it disarticulated. Human remains, also articulated, were recovered, in some cases accompanied by animals. The dates satisfactorily confirm the prediction based on ceramic typology.

Laboratory comment: English Heritage (2009), in 1998, a sample of bone from the Iron Age head burial in the enclosure ditch, which could not be dated in 1988 (from feature 4002, fill 734, cut 620), was successfully dated (OxA-18629; 2226 ±24 BP, and a previous measurement: OxA-8066; 2180 ±40 BP; together gave a weighted mean (T'=1.0, T'(5%)=3.8, ν=1; Ward and Wilson 1978) of 2214 ±21 BP; and a *posterior density estimate at 95% probability of 390–300 cal BC*). In 2008, a new programme of radiocarbon dating was undertaken, following a reassessment of the site's Iron Age chronology using Bayesian modelling (Meadows *et al* in prep).

Laboratory comment: Oxford Radiocarbon Accelerator Unit (12 October 1989), one further sample (human bone from feature 4002, fill 734, cut 620) was submitted for dating but failed to produce a result. The bone was pretreated and a date was made on the resulting graphite target. The result was approximately 12,000–13,000 BP, very different to the expected late Bronze Age/early Iron Age. Subsequent visual examination of the bone surface revealed a shiny appearance with some of the pores filled with a resin looking material. The chemical analysis indicated that the product yield was abnormally high - many times higher than was found on all the other bones on the site - and this would tend to

confirm the microscopic observation that the bone had been conserved. The contaminant would appear to be a petroleum based product, the effect of which had been to make the date too old.

References: Farley and Jones 2012
Farley 1986
Hedges *et al* 1990, 222–3
Ward and Wilson 1978

OxA–1918 2350 ±60 BP

$\delta^{13}C$: -21.0‰ (assumed)

Sample: 3040 630 975, submitted in November 1988 by M E Farley

Material: human bone (left femur head) (C Osborne 1985)

Initial comment: from articulated human skeleton of young person buried with a goat on the right and an ovicaprid partly beneath on their left. Both upper and lower trunk were cut away by later pits. The whole was found beneath later cultivation and occupation levels. From feature 3040, fill 630, cut 975.

Objectives: one of three samples (OxA-1918, OxA-1919, and OxA-1920) intended to date the ritual deposit.

Calibrated date: *1σ:* 420–380 cal BC
                    2σ: 740–230 cal BC

Final comment: see series comments

Final comment: J Meadows (2009), a further radiocarbon dating result (SUERC-18212) was obtained for this burial in 2008 (burial 3040; human 1; 2315 ±35 BP) which together gives a weighted mean of 2324 ±31 BP (T'=0.3; T'(5%)=3.8; ν=1; Ward and Wilson 1978), and a *posterior density estimate at 95% probability of 400–360 cal BC*.

References: Ward and Wilson 1978

OxA–1919 2330 ±60 BP

$\delta^{13}C$: -21.0‰ (assumed)

Sample: 3018 630 975, submitted in November 1988 by M E Farley

Material: animal bone: *Ovis* sp., left horn core and parietal of sheep (G Jones 1985)

Initial comment: from intact sheep skull wedged between incomplete but articulated skeleton of adult person and an underlying human humerus. Part removed by later disturbances. The whole lay beneath later cultivation and occupation layers. From feature 3149, fill 630, cut 975.

Objectives: as OxA-1918

Calibrated date: *1σ:* 410–380 cal BC
                    2σ: 710–210 cal BC

Final comment: see series comments

OxA–1920 2340 ±70 BP

$\delta^{13}C$: -21.0‰ (assumed)

Sample: 3149 630 975, submitted in November 1988 by M E Farley

Material: animal bone: *Ovis* sp., or caprid; two lumbar vertebrae (G Jones 1985)

Initial comment: from articulated group of ovicaprid vertebrae, which was part of a substantial deposit of animal and human bone. The whole was beneath the later cultivation and occupation layers. From feature 3149, fill 630, cut 975.

Objectives: as OxA-1918

Calibrated date: 1σ: 420–380 cal BC
2σ: 750–200 cal BC

Final comment: see series comments

OxA–1921 1310 ±60 BP

δ¹³C: -21.0‰ (assumed)

Sample: 474 513, submitted in November 1988 by M E Farley

Material: animal bone: *Sus* sp., mastoid process (G Jones 1985)

Initial comment: part of an immature pig skull incorporated in the lower fill of a ditch along with much other animal bone. From fill 474, cut 513.

Objectives: to date the infill and use of the ditch, expected to be Saxon.

Calibrated date: 1σ: cal AD 650–780
2σ: cal AD 630–880

Final comment: M E Farley (1990), this confirms the artefactual dating of a middle Saxon presence.

OxA–1922 2180 ±70 BP

δ¹³C: -21.0‰ (assumed)

Sample: 164 296, submitted in November 1988 by M E Farley

Material: human bone (L Moffett)

Initial comment: one of many pieces of human bone from post-Iron Age contexts.

Objectives: to date the human bone and establish how long the inhabitants were using this area as a burial site.

Calibrated date: 1σ: 380–120 cal BC
2σ: 400–40 cal BC

Final comment: M E Farley (1990), the date suggests a more extensive ritual landscape than that represented by the deposit, and may have been disturbed by later on-site activities.

OxA–1923 1005 ±70 BP

δ¹³C: -26.0‰ (assumed)

Sample: 2006 480 400, submitted in November 1988 by M E Farley

Material: grain: *Triticum* sp., free threshing species (L Moffett)

Initial comment: from a layer of charred grain within a large pit, fill 2006, cut 400.

Objectives: the result will be relevant to crop purity discussions and to the market economy of the town.

Calibrated date: 1σ: cal AD 980–1150
2σ: cal AD 890–1190

Final comment: M Farley (1990), it fits well with the sparse ceramic evidence suggesting substantial Saxon-Norman grain deposit.

Final comment: (J Meadows 2011): two further measurements on single grains of wheat were subsequently obtained from this deposit (OxA-23361; 952 +/- 22 BP and OxA-23362; 969 +/- 23 BP). The three results are statistically consistent (T'=0.7; T'(5%)=6.0; ν=2; Ward and Wilson 1978). Their weighted mean (962 +/- 16 BP) calibrates to cal AD 1020-1155 (95% confidence; Reimer et al 2004). It appears more likely that the grain deposit dates to the first century of the Norman period, but an early eleventh-century date is certainly possible.

References: Reimer et al 2004
Ward and Wilson 1978

Bancroft Mausoleum, Buckinghamshire

Location: SP 825406
Lat. 52.03.26 N; Long. 00.47.48 W

Project manager: R J Williams (Milton Keynes Archaeology Unit), 1983–4

Archival body: Buckinghamshire Museum

Description: Bancroft Mausoleum and villa lies in Wolverton parish, 0.75km north of Bradwell village and 1km south-east of Wolverton. It is a multi-phased site, including early Iron Age structures and a late-Roman mausoleum.

Objectives: to estimate the date when the Iron Age building construction occurred on the site, which is without closely associated datable artefacts. Also to date with greater accuracy two burials associated with the latter phases of the site use.

References: Williams and Zeepvat 1994

UB–3233 2339 ±42 BP

δ¹³C: -25.8 ±0.2‰

Sample: MK360 380, submitted in November 1989 by R J Williams

Material: charcoal: *Quercus* sp., heartwood (C Cartwright)

Initial comment: from the fill of a substantial posthole of a triple-ringed circular building.

Objectives: UB-3233 and UB-3234 should give a date to the construction of this very substantial and rare triple-ringed late Bronze Age/early Iron Age building. The associated pottery is of a very rare type for which few, if any, independent dates are available. Also sites of this period are rare in this region.

Calibrated date: 1σ: 410–390 cal BC
2σ: 510–370 cal BC

Final comment: C Cartwright (1994), the dates were expected to be slightly older than the construction of the building. Curiously this is at odds with the ceramic evidence which, whilst consisting of many unusual vessel types, invites close comparison with later Bronze Age and earlier Iron Age assemblages from southern England. Following a detailed assessment of the incidence and distribution of the earliest diagnostic pottery sherds from the building, it is thought that radiocarbon determinations, which suggest a fifth- or sixth-century date for the building are correct and that the early pottery sherds are mainly residual, derived from an earlier midden.

UB–3234 2382 ±42 BP

δ¹³C: -25.2 ±0.2‰

Sample: MK360 570, submitted in November 1989 by R J Williams

Material: charcoal: *Fraxinus* sp., heartwood (C Cartwright)

Initial comment: part of carbonised stump within a posthole of triple-ringed circular building.

Objectives: as UB-3233

Calibrated date: 1σ: 510–390 cal BC
 2σ: 740–390 cal BC

Final comment: see UB-3233

UB–3235 1656 ±29 BP

δ¹³C: -20.9 ±0.2‰

Sample: MK360 145, submitted in November 1989 by R J Williams

Material: human bone (male, aged 35–45) (A Stirland)

Initial comment: found as part of a complete inhumation within a stone-lined grave (grave 2).

Objectives: UB-3235 and UB-3236 are part of a small cemetery of eight inhumations. The graves had been lined with stone plundered from the adjacent fourth-century Roman Mausoleum. There were no associated grave goods to date, though the burials must be contemporary with the demolition of the Mausoleum. The burials are thought to be immediately post-Roman, but some doubt remains.

Calibrated date: 1σ: cal AD 380–430
 2σ: cal AD 260–440

Final comment: C Cartwright (1994), the calibrated dates are considered to be a very accurate reflection of the dates of burial. Whilst there is no independent dating evidence, it is possible that the line of eight burials slightly overlaps with the shrine, and which from the coin evidence may have continued in use into the first quarter of the fifth century. On balance, it is likely that the graves are of early fifth-century date, and represent burials of some of the final inhabitants of the villa before its ultimate desertion.

Laboratory comment: University of Belfast (16 March 1990), some of the bones were glued together, the pieces nearest to the glue and indian ink were removed before pretreatment.

UB–3236 1606 ±34 BP

δ¹³C: -24.0 ±0.2‰

Sample: MK360 114, submitted in November 1989 by R J Williams

Material: human bone (male, aged 35–45) (A Stirland)

Initial comment: found as a complete inhumation within a deep waterlogged grave (grave 4) dug into clay.

Objectives: as UB-3235

Calibrated date: 1σ: cal AD 410–540
 2σ: cal AD 380–550

Final comment: see UB-3235

Laboratory comment: University of Belfast (27 March 1990), some of the bones were glued together, the pieces nearest to the glue and indian ink were removed before pretreatment.

Bar Brook, Peak District, Derbyshire

Location: SK 27287551
 Lat. 53.16.32 N; Long. 01.35.27 W

Project manager: J Barnatt (Peak National Park), 1983

Archival body: Sheffield City Museum

Description: a trench at a junction of two earthen field boundary banks. The trench was at the heart of the Big Moor field system on the gritstone upland, and above the Swine Sty settlement (Richardson and Preston 1969; Machin 1971; Machin and Beswick 1975) excavated by the Hunter Archaeological Society in the late 1960s and 1970s.

Objectives: to provide a chronology for the site; there are currently no dates available for field systems in the Peak District.

Final comment: J Barnatt (8 July 1991), four of the dates (OxA-2292, OxA-2293, OxA-2294, and OxA-2356) are from charcoal scattered through the two field boundaries investigated, two samples per bank, and probably confirm a later Bronze Age date. Although on stratigraphic grounds one excavated bank is earlier than the other, the radiocarbon dates are statistically inseparable. All four dates are later than that previously obtained from Swine Sty (HAR-1233; 3560 ±80 BP; which calibrates to cal BC 2140–1690 at 95% confidence; Reimer *et al* 2004). This difference supports the hypotheses that the field system was in use over a relatively long period, as suggested by frequent indicators of complex horizontal stratigraphy and modifications to the layout. A fifth dated sample, OxA-2295, was from charcoal found in a pit underlying the earlier of the two banks. The radiocarbon date shows the pit belongs to a separate episode of use, in the Mesolithic period. There was also a hearth associated with this early activity, and a microlith of later Mesolithic type was found in the bank. The presence of the Mesolithic sample raises the possibility that charcoal of this date existed across much of the site and thus could have contaminated the other four samples. This would make the results of radiocarbon counting somewhat earlier than the actual dates of the two features. However, this seems unlikely given the consistency of the four results, and the predicted Bronze Age date for the site.

References: Hedges *et al* 1991a, 126
Machin 1971
Machin and Beswick 1975
Reimer *et al* 2004
Richardson and Preston 1969

OxA–2292 3070 ±70 BP

$\delta^{13}C$: -26.1‰

Sample: BB83S1, submitted in August 1989 by K Smith

Material: charcoal: unidentified

Initial comment: a composite sample from the north-south bank (layers 8, 9, and 10) taken in both sample areas A and B and combined to give a suitably sized sample.

Objectives: this sample is similar to OxA-2356; a date could be compared with the pre-bank dates for samples OxA-2294 and OxA-2295 as well as the later bank, sample OxA-2293. It should date the field bank, roughly, and act as a potential control on OxA-2356.

Calibrated date: 1σ: 1430–1260 cal BC
2σ: 1500–1120 cal BC

Final comment: J Barnatt (July 1991), this date, for the earlier of the two banks, is consistent with the other taken, OxA-2356.

OxA–2293 2990 ±70 BP

$\delta^{13}C$: -26.7‰

Sample: BB83S2, submitted in August 1989 by K Smith

Material: charcoal: unidentified

Initial comment: a composite sample from layer 8 in the eastern bank, sample area C.

Objectives: the sample relates to the bank which stratigraphically was the later of the two. Analysis might demonstrate whether the two features are broadly contemporary or whether there was a longer time lapse between them.

Calibrated date: 1σ: 1380–1120 cal BC
2σ: 1420–1000 cal BC

Final comment: J Barnatt (July 1991), this date, for the later of the two banks, is consistent with the other taken from below it, OxA-2294.

OxA–2294 2820 ±70 BP

$\delta^{13}C$: -26.8‰

Sample: BB83S3, submitted in August 1989 by K Smith

Material: charcoal: unidentified

Initial comment: composite sample from the top 1–5cm of layer 20, a natural variation in the subsoil surface. This sample was sealed by the eastern bank, layer 8.

Objectives: the sample relates to the bank which stratigraphically was the later of the two. Analysis might demonstrate whether the two features are broadly contemporary or whether there was a longer time lapse between them.

Calibrated date: 1σ: 1060–900 cal BC
2σ: 1210–810 cal BC

Final comment: J Barnatt (July 1991), this date, from below the later of the two banks, is consistent with the other taken from the bank itself, OxA-2293.

OxA–2295 8130 ±90 BP

$\delta^{13}C$: -27.2‰

Sample: BB83S4, submitted in August 1989 by K Smith

Material: charcoal: unidentified

Initial comment: from the fill of F13 found sealed within layer 25.

Objectives: the feature within which the charcoal was found was sealed by the spread from the bank. It could therefore relate either to activity broadly contemporary with the bank or pre-date them both, perhaps by many years. Contrast will be possible with OxA-2294. Together OxA-2295 and OxA-2294 should give an insight into the date of pre-bank activity.

Calibrated date: 1σ: 7300–7040 cal BC
2σ: 7450–6820 cal BC

Final comment: J Barnatt (July 1991), this date was something of a surprise, but was not inconsistent with the stratigraphy demonstrated during excavation. While the pit was earlier than the field banks, it had been assumed to still be a Bronze Age feature; the radiocarbon date shows that it relates to unsuspected Mesolithic activity.

OxA–2356 3190 ±60 BP

$\delta^{13}C$: -25.7‰

Sample: BB83S5, submitted in August 1989 by K Smith

Material: charcoal: unidentified

Initial comment: a composite sample from the lower portion of layer 9 in the southern bank, sample area B.

Objectives: to compare with the pre-bank dates OxA-2294 and OxA-2295 and the later bank, OxA-2293. It will give an indication of the date of construction of the field bank.

Calibrated date: 1σ: 1520–1410 cal BC
2σ: 1620–1320 cal BC

Final comment: J Barnatt (July 1991), this date, for the earlier of the two banks, is consistent with the other taken, OxA-2292.

Bar Brook II, Peak District, Derbyshire

Location: SK 27757581
Lat. 53.16.42 N; Long. 01.35.02 W

Project manager: J Barnatt (Peak District National Park), August 1989

Archival body: Sheffield City Museum

Description: a re-excavation and restoration of an embanked stone circle, sited within an eastern extension of the Big Moor cairnfields. The site was extensively excavated in the 1960s by G D Lewis.

Objectives: to dismantle the monument, take appropriate samples (pollen, soil, and radiocarbon) and rebuild the monument to its pre-excavation state.

Final comment: J Barnatt (July 1991), the earlier excavation produced one date, BM-179 (3450 ±150 BP; cal BC 2200–1430 at 95% confidence; Reimer *et al* 2004), from a cremation pit under an internal cairn (Lewis 1966). This accords well with one of the dates, OxA-2440, obtained from charcoal recovered in 1989 from under the bank of the stone circle itself. A second sample, OxA-2439, from charcoal within one of the stoneholes, gave an early medieval date that is inconsistent with what is known of the site and stone circles in general. In retrospect this sample is either contaminated, or more likely the charcoal relates to a time when the orthostat fell and has subsequently migrated down the soil profile within the stonehole.

References: Hedges *et al* 1991a, 126–7
                   Lewis 1966
                   Reimer *et al* 2004

OxA–2439 960 ±60 BP

δ¹³C: -28.1‰

Sample: BBII89, submitted in February 1990 by K Smith

Material: charcoal: *Fraxinus* sp. (3g) (C Cartwright)

Initial comment: from the undisturbed fill of a stonehole, a pale grey-brown sandy loam, from an area near the base of the hole, under the original position of the orthostat. This stone fell before the 1960s and the upper parts of the stratigraphy were truncated by excavation in the 1960s. Only the fill of the stonehole remained by the 1989 re-excavation of the site. The only possible sources of contamination were a small quantity of rootlets, and perhaps the proximity to the surface (but the fallen orthostat covered the feature until 1988 and the pale colour of the stonehole fill, which contrasted with the peaty humus above, suggests there was little downward movement of material).

Objectives: the 1960s excavation produced BM-179 (3450 ±150 BP; cal BC 2200–1430 at 95% confidence; Reimer *et al* 2004) from an internal burial. OxA-2439 and OxA-2440 will hopefully, in combination, give a firmer date for the monument itself rather than a feature which may post-date the ring cairn by some time. This sample should relate directly to the date of the building of the orthostats and ring cairn (which is structurally integrated with the orthostats which are unlikely to have been able to stand without the supporting bank).

Calibrated date: *1σ:* cal AD 1010–1160
                        2σ: cal AD 980–1220

Final comment: J Barnatt (July 1991), in retrospect this sample was either contaminated or, more likely, the charcoal relates to a moorland burning episode at some time before the orthostat fell. On entering the disturbance created when the stone fell, it appears to have subsequently migrated a short distance down the soil profile within the stonehole.

References: Reimer *et al* 2004

OxA–2440 3535 ±70 BP

δ¹³C: -26.8‰

Sample: BBII90 sample 2, submitted in February 1990 by K Smith

Material: charcoal: *Corylus* sp. (C Cartwright)

Initial comment: from a buried soil below the ring cairn bank from within a narrow baulk left from the 1960s excavation. The buried soil (context 43) was a pale yellow-brown loamy sand, sealed by an iron pan and the ring cairn bank above this. The sample was obtained by flotation and all material from layer 43 that was well-sealed under the undisturbed bank and not contaminated by humic material associated with roots. The only obvious source of possible contamination was a small number of rootlets through the layer as a whole.

Objectives: see OxA-2439. This sample should also give a date for clearance of the site prior to the ring cairn being built.

Calibrated date: *1σ:* 1960–1750 cal BC
                        2σ: 2120–1690 cal BC

Final comment: J Barnatt (July 1991), this sample provides a good *terminus post quem* for the construction of the monument, which is derived from charcoal that may well have been deposited at the time the land was cleared to build the site. It is consistent with what was expected and complements the date from the site obtained during the 1960s excavation.

Barford: Park Farm, Warwickshire

Location: SP 292616
                      Lat. 52.15.05 N; Long. 01.34.20 W

Project manager: S Cracknell (Warwickshire County
                      Council), July 1988

Archival body: Warwickshire Museum

Description: a multi-period site with the most intensive occupation in the Iron Age. Major features were a linear boundary ditch, which was followed by an enclosure containing two hut circles and a penannular gully.

Objectives: the main purpose of the project was to clarify details of the structure of Iron Age settlement in Warwickshire. In contrast to the sprawling site at Wasperton nearby, Park Farm was isolated and it was thought that it could have played a different role. The dating programme aimed to determine the overall period of occupation of the site in order to relate contemporary features within this settlement and beyond.

Final comment: S Cracknell (6 June 1995), initially, four sets of charred plant remains recovered from soil samples were submitted to the Oxford Radiocarbon Accelerator Unit (OxA-2303–6). These samples covered a range of features and were all expected to yield similar results as the site was initially thought to be largely single period. However, the dates proved to be widely separated and as a result a second series was submitted, this time to the Scottish Universities Research and Reactor Centre. The aim of the new series was to provide a date for the digging of the enclosure ditch. Although it was thought that all three dates should be the same, the two from below the working hollow (GU–5043–4) are significantly later than the one from elsewhere in the circuit (GU–5045). The first two dates are statistically indistinguishable from those associated with the working hollow that lay above the sampled soil. It may therefore be that the working hollow, as represented by the dark soils and broken pots, was not the full extent of the reuse of the enclosure ditch. On this basis GU–5045 is the only radiocarbon date which can be taken to represent the original cutting of the enclosure ditch but this cannot be relied upon; it is safer to consider the ditch as broadly fourth to first century BC. (It should be noted that the two samples from below the working hollow, GU–5043 and GU–5044, which were submitted from a single sample and split by size of fragments, gave similar results suggesting minimal contamination).

References: Cracknell and Hingley 1993–4

GU–5043 2160 ±70 BP

δ¹³C: -26.2‰

Sample: 2/4 subsample 1, submitted on 12 November 1990 by S Cracknell

Material: charcoal: unidentified

Initial comment: from fill of enclosure ditch segment 2f, well below level of already dated working hollow, 160mm approx. above side of ditch. No associated pottery.

Objectives: previous dates from this site did not date the main occupation. This series from the lowest fills of the enclosure ditch should relate to the main occupation.

Calibrated date: *1σ:* 360–100 cal BC
                     2σ: 400 cal BC–cal AD 1

Final comment: S Cracknell (6 June 1995), this result confirms an Iron Age date for the enclosure ditch. The result is close enough to that for GU–5044 to be considered uncontaminated (both from a single sample) however, both are statistically indistinguishable in date from those samples that lay above the sampled soil, which brings into question the extent of the reuse of the ditch.

GU–5044 2080 ±80 BP

δ¹³C: -25.4‰

Sample: 2/4 subsample 2, submitted on 12 November 1990 by S Cracknell

Material: charcoal: unidentified, stem or young branch

Initial comment: as GU-5043

Objectives: as GU-5043

Calibrated date: *1σ:* 200 cal BC–cal AD 10
                     2σ: 370 cal BC–cal AD 80

Final comment: see GU-5043

Laboratory comment: Ancient Monuments Laboratory (2003), the results from the two sub-samples are statistically consistent (T′=0.6; T′(5%)=3.8; ν=1; Ward and Wilson 1978).

References: Ward and Wilson 1978

GU–5045 2500 ±90 BP

δ¹³C: -25.2‰

Sample: 2/4, submitted on 12 November 1990 by S Cracknell

Material: charcoal: unidentified

Initial comment: from lowest fill of enclosure ditch, segment 2K. One sherd of ceramic phase C was associated.

Objectives: as GU-5043

Calibrated date: *1σ:* 800–410 cal BC
                     2σ: 830–390 cal BC

Final comment: S Cracknell (6 June 1995), *see* GU-5043 and GU-5044, this result confirms Iron Age dating for the enclosure ditch, GU-5045 exclusively possibly represents the original cutting of the enclosure ditch, but it is safer to date this event more broadly to the first to fourth centuries BC.

OxA–2303 2085 ±70 BP

δ¹³C: -26.1‰

Sample: PF88 480, submitted on 14 December 1988 by S Cracknell

Material: carbonised plant macrofossil

Initial comment: from a small hole in a working hollow in the top of the enclosure ditch. This sample should be contemporary with OxA-2304 and date to towards the end of the life of the site.

Objectives: one of a series designed to give the overall date of the site and if possible, some idea of how contemporary the features are.

Calibrated date: *1σ:* 200 cal BC–cal AD 1
                     2σ: 360 cal BC–cal AD 70

Final comment: S Cracknell (6 June 1995), this sample was expected to produce a similar date to others of this series (OxA-2303 to 2306), which produced widely separated results. It is close to OxA-2304. These two samples produced results closest to expectation.

References: Hedges *et al* 1993, 161

OxA–2304 2060 ±70 BP

δ¹³C: -26.5‰

Sample: PF88 222, submitted on 14 December 1988 by S Cracknell

Material: carbonised plant macrofossil

Initial comment: from a small posthole in the east of the enclosure, fill of 52. This posthole is contemporary with the main use of the area.

Objectives: as OxA-2303

Calibrated date: *1σ:* 180 cal BC–cal AD 20
                     2σ: 360 cal BC–cal AD 80

Final comment: S Cracknell (6 June 1995), this sample should have produced a result close to others in the series (OxA-2303 to 2306) but is only similar to OxA-2303; the others though have variation much wider than expected.

References: Hedges *et al* 1993, 161

OxA–2305 3555 ±70 BP

δ¹³C: -26.0‰ (assumed)

Sample: PF88 53, submitted on 14 December 1988 by S Cracknell

Material: carbonised plant macrofossil

Initial comment: as OxA-2304

Objectives: as OxA-2303

Calibrated date: *1σ:* 2020–1770 cal BC
                 2σ: 2130–1690 cal BC

Final comment: S Cracknell (6 June 1995), this result is the most extreme of the series, which had been expected to provide close results. Perhaps it (with OxA-2306) represents earlier, temporary use of the site, prior to the major phase of use during the Iron Age.

References: Hedges *et al* 1993, 161

OxA–2306 2910 ±70 BP

δ¹³C: -26.2‰

Sample: PF88 434, submitted on 14 December 1988 by S Cracknell

Material: carbonised plant macrofossil

Initial comment: from a small hole in a working area in the north west of the site. The hole is contemporary with the main use of the site.

Objectives: as OxA-2303

Calibrated date: *1σ:* 1260–1000 cal BC
                 2σ: 1380–910 cal BC

Final comment: S Cracknell (6 June 1995), like OxA-2305, this result unexpectedly widely ranges from the series (OxA-2303–6) and likewise possibly represents earlier temporary use of the site pre-dating the major Iron Age phase of occupation.

References: Hedges *et al* 1993, 161

Barnard Castle: Moss Mire, Durham

Location:	NZ 0516 approximately Lat. 54.32.21 N; Long. 01.55.22 W
Project manager:	A Donaldson (University of Durham), 1978
Archival body:	University of Durham

Description: a peat bog. The site is important since it lies between the lowlands and uplands in Teesdale, both of which have a number of pollen diagrams, and at the moment is a unique site in a fairly rich agricultural region in the valley of the Middle Tees Basin.

Objectives: the three samples (MM192, HAR-6804; MM260, HAR-6805, and MM220, HAR-9028) represent the early forest clearance phases in the diagram and are extremely important for fixing a chronology onto the extension of agricultural activities into the valley bottom in this area. As a guide to the vegetation changes and agriculture in the area these samples will be invaluable to regional archaeologists.

Final comment: G Campbell (3 September 2007), it appears that the work on this pollen diagram was never completed and no physical archive has survived at Durham University (September 2007). As such the value of these dates is greatly reduced. The date for initial clearance (HAR-6804) agrees well with other sites from Lowland Durham.

Laboratory comment: Ancient Monuments Laboratory (1994), three dates from this site (HAR-3073, HAR-3074, and HAR-3075) were funded prior to 1981 and were published in the first volume of *Radiocarbon Dates* (Jordan *et al* 1994, 9–10). A further two dates (HAR-6804 and HAR-6805) were published in Bayliss *et al* (2012, 16–7). HAR-4747, HAR-4748, and HAR-6845 were held in the small sample queue and later abandoned.

References: Austin 1980
                    Bayliss *et al* 2012
                    Hardiman *et al* 1992, 58
                    Jordan *et al* 1994, 9–10
                    Reimer *et al* 2004

HAR–9028 3070 ±90 BP

δ¹³C: -29.1‰

Sample: MM220, submitted on 11 January 1979 by A M Donaldson

Material: peat

Initial comment: from the forested period preceding the first major clearance.

Objectives: to provide a chronology for a pollen diagram.

Calibrated date: *1σ:* 1440–1210 cal BC
                 2σ: 1520–1050 cal BC

Final comment: G Campbell (3 September 2007), this date presumably provides a date for a change in pollen spectra or stratigraphy or possibly just a half way point (*see* series comments).

Laboratory comment: AERE Harwell (11 May 1989), this sample was measured in the miniature gas proportional counter (Otlet *et al* 1983).

References: Otlet *et al* 1983

Barton-on-Humber, Castledyke, Humberside

Location:	TA 032217 Lat. 53.40.53 N; Long. 00.26.14 W
Project manager:	M Foreman (Humberside Archaeology Unit), 1990
Archival body:	North Lincolnshire Museum

Description: a total of *c* 106 skeletons were excavated, some 60% of which had grave goods (jewellery, weapons etc). Associated with some of the burials, were postholes, perhaps signifying burial structures. Observed were a variety of burial depths (shallow, poorer, deeper with richer grave goods) and evidence of the individuals' gender and age groupings (more women than men, more men than small children and infants).

Objectives: to establish the date of the pre-cemetery activity.

Final comment: M Foreman (July 1994), whereas from the evidence of dateable finds there is little from Castledyke which can firmly be dated to the fifth century, and an early date cannot be assumed for the solitary cremation (a continued practice into the sixth century); Radiocarbon dating has extended the chronology of this site. Additionally this and associated nearby (contemporaneous?) excavated sites (new Vicarage Gardens, 1981 and Birketts Garage, 1990), where evidence of the occupation from the Saxon period was also recovered, provides an overview of Saxon activity in this area.

Laboratory comment: Ancient Monuments Laboratory (24 July 1992), these two results are not statistically significantly different (T'=0.2; T'(5%)=3.8; ν=1) Ward and Wilson 1978).

Laboratory comment: (24 July 1992), OxA-3140 was obtained from the ion-exchanged gelatin extracted from the dentine. OxA-3672 is based on two specific amino-acids, GlyProHyp and GlyProAla, which came from the <10kD peptides in the >10kD gelatin (Hedges and Van Klinken 1992).

References: Drinkall and Foreman 1998
Gillespie *et al* 1985, 422
Hedges and Van Klinken 1992
Ward and Wilson 1978
Whitwell 1990

OxA–3140 1065 ±70 BP

$\delta^{13}C$: -21.3‰

Sample: RC4, site context 928L, submitted on 12 March 1991 by G Watkins

Material: human bone (tooth)

Initial comment: from the loose chalk rubble fill of a ditch. The ditch fill was cut by a cremation burial (likely to be no later than seventh century AD). In addition, the bank associated with the ditch is held to have limited the extent of Anglian burial of the sixth and seventh centuries AD.

Objectives: to confirm that the ditch pre-dates (and may have defined) the area used for the cemetery. Datable artefacts are absent from the lower ditch fills. It is hoped to determine whether, as at Wetwang and elsewhere, prehistoric features retained or acquired significance into the Anglian period.

Calibrated date: 1σ: cal AD 890–1030
2σ: cal AD 780–1160

Final comment: M Foreman (July 1994), the tooth is considered to be intrusive. The most likely explanation is movement between chalk rubble elements of the fill promoted by animal action, or by the flow of water down through this loose material.

OxA–3672 1020 ±75 BP

$\delta^{13}C$: -18.9‰

Sample: RC4, site context 928L, submitted on 12 March 1991 by G Watkins

Material: human bone (tooth)

Initial comment: a repeat of OxA-3140 using Gly-Pro-Hyp fraction.

Objectives: as OxA-3140

Calibrated date: 1σ: cal AD 970–1120
2σ: cal AD 880–1180

Final comment: see OxA-3140

Barton-upon-Humber: St Peter's Church, Humberside

Location: TA 035219
Lat. 53.40.59 N; Long. 00.25.58 W

Project manager: W Rodwell (Consultant), 1978 and 1981

Archival body: English Heritage

Description: an Anglo-Saxon and medieval church and cemetery.

Objectives: to refine the dating of the cemetery sequence and clarify the chronology of the surviving church fabric.

Final comment: W Rodwell (9 March 1995), two samples concern the dating of the late Saxon tower, and its subsequent alterations (*see also* HAR-2865, HAR-2863, HAR-2864, and HAR-3106), giving precision to art-historical conclusions. The other samples all relate to two areas of late Saxon and Norman cemetery to the east of the tenth century church; they confirm that the preserved timber coffins here belong to a tenth–twelfth century sequence, and that there is likely to have been a phase of pre-church burial in one area.

Laboratory comment: Ancient Monuments Laboratory (1995), four further dates from this site (HAR-2863, HAR-2864, HAR-2865, and HAR-3106) were funded prior to 1981 and were published in Jordan *et al* (1994, 11), and four more samples were dated between 1981 and 1988 and published in Bayliss *et al* (2012, 17–8; HAR-5655, -6476, -6501, and -6838).

References: Bayliss *et al* 2012
Hedges *et al* 1991a, 127–8
Jordan *et al* 1994, 11
Rodwell and Atkins 2011
Rodwell and Rodwell 1982

OxA–2282 1120 ±80 BP

$\delta^{13}C$: -24.6‰

Sample: BH09 F1753, submitted in July 1989 by W Rodwell

Material: wood (waterlogged): *Quercus* sp. (D Haddon-Reece)

Initial comment: part of a series of well-preserved early timber coffins in a cemetery dominated by an important Anglo-Saxon church.

Objectives: there are complex stratigraphic relationships between the graves and structures; there is an observable development of the cemetery and a variety of coffin types. Radiocarbon dating is the principal means of establishing the chronology of the cemetery.

Calibrated date: 1σ: cal AD 780–1020
2σ: cal AD 680–1040

Final comment: W Rodwell (9 March 1995), from an exceptionally well-preserved timber coffin in the third generation of burials in the cemetery north-east of the late Saxon church. The result confirms suspicions that this cemetery contains burials that are likely to ante-date the known church.

Final comment: A Bayliss (20 July 2007), there is some doubt as to whether this sample actually came from coffin F1753, or from a timber subsequently assigned to another coffin. No drill holes were present on any of the surviving boards from this coffin similar to those identified for the other AMS samples. The calibrated date is, however, sufficiently imprecise to be consistent with the dates of all the rings present in this coffin (AD 887–1084 inclusive; Tyers 2001b, 10–11).

References:　　Tyers 2001b, 10–1

OxA–2283 1300 ±110 BP

δ¹³C: -25.5‰

Sample: BH10 F1790 side, submitted in July 1989 by W Rodwell

Material: wood (waterlogged): *Quercus* sp.

Initial comment: as OxA-2282

Objectives: as OxA-2282

Calibrated date:　　*1σ:* cal AD 640–870
　　　　　　　　　　　　2σ: cal AD 540–990

Final comment: W Rodwell (9 March 1995), a preserved timber from the same horizon as OxA-2282, and assignable stratigraphically to the late Saxon period. The two dates agree well, but *see* OxA-2284.

Final comment: A Bayliss (20 July 2007), tree-ring analysis later demonstrated that OxA-2283 consisted of a 30-year block of rings from the north-side board of coffin F1790, the centre of which dates to AD 924 on the basis of dendrochronology (Tyers 2001b, 13–4). The measurement is demonstrably accurate, as it is statistically consistent with the weighted mean of the measurements of this age available from the calibration curve (T'=2.6; T'(5%)=3.8; ν=1; Reimer *et al* 2004; Ward and Wilson 1978).

References:　　Reimer *et al* 2004
　　　　　　　　　Tyers 2001b, 13–4
　　　　　　　　　Ward and Wilson 1978

OxA–2284 915 ±80 BP

δ¹³C: -26.2‰

Sample: BH10 F1790 other, submitted in July 1989 by W Rodwell

Material: wood (waterlogged): *Quercus* sp.

Initial comment: as OxA-2282

Objectives: as OxA-2282

Calibrated date:　　*1σ:* cal AD 1020–1220
　　　　　　　　　　　　2σ: cal AD 980–1270

Final comment: W Rodwell (9 March 1995), the sample was taken from the same coffin as OxA-2283, but from a different plank. It is disconcerting that the dates for the two samples are

mutually exclusive. This sample suggests a fully Norman date. There is no evidence for reused timber in this coffin.

Final comment: A Bayliss (20 July 2007), tree-ring analysis later demonstrated that OxA-2284 consisted of a 30-year block of rings from the lid of coffin F1790, the centre of which dates to AD 1085 on the basis of dendrochronology (Tyers 2001b, 13–14). The measurement is demonstrably accurate, as it is statistically consistent with the weighted mean of the measurements of this age available from the calibration curve (T'=0.0; T'(5%)=3.8; ν=1; Reimer *et al* 2004; Ward and Wilson 1978).

References:　　Reimer *et al* 2004
　　　　　　　　　Tyers 2001b, 13–4
　　　　　　　　　Ward and Wilson 1978

OxA–2285 820 ±80 BP

δ¹³C: -25.2‰

Sample: BH11 F3946, submitted in July 1989 by W Rodwell

Material: wood (waterlogged): *Quercus* sp.

Initial comment: as OxA-2282

Objectives: as OxA-2282

Calibrated date:　　*1σ:* cal AD 1150–1280
　　　　　　　　　　　　2σ: cal AD 1020–1300

Final comment: W Rodwell (9 March 1995), this coffin was made, at least in part, from recycled planks, and belongs to a later phase in the cemetery north-east of the late Saxon church. The result suggests a Norman or slightly later date, which is consistent with the stratigraphic evidence.

Final comment: A Bayliss (20 July 2007), subsequent tree-ring analysis confirmed that this sample consisted of a decadal block of rings, the centre of which is 57–91 years earlier than the felling date of the tree. Incorporating this offset allows a revised calibration of cal AD 1100–1390 (at 95% confidence; Reimer *et al* 2004) or cal AD 1160–1330 (at 68% confidence) to be proposed. This timber remains undated by dendrochronology (Tyers 2001b, 28).

References:　　Reimer *et al* 2004
　　　　　　　　　Tyers 2001b, 28

OxA–2286 1035 ±80 BP

δ¹³C: -25.0‰

Sample: BH12 F5045, submitted in July 1989 by W Rodwell

Material: wood (waterlogged): *Quercus* sp.

Initial comment: as OxA-2282

Objectives: as OxA-2282

Calibrated date:　　*1σ:* cal AD 890–1040
　　　　　　　　　　　　2σ: cal AD 780–1170

Final comment: W Rodwell (9 March 1995), this coffin included some recycled timbers in its construction. It came from an early horizon in the cemetery north-east of the late Saxon church, where it should belong stratigraphically to the tenth century. The result confirms the stratigraphic deduction.

Final comment: A Bayliss (20 July 2007), tree-ring analysis later demonstrated that OxA-2286 consisted of a 40-year block of rings from the lid of coffin F5045, the centre of which dates to AD 1015 on the basis of dendrochronology (Tyers 2001b, 45–6). The measurement is demonstrably accurate, as it is statistically consistent with the weighted mean of the measurements of this age available from the calibration curve (T′=0.1; T′(5%)=3.8; ν=1; Reimer *et al* 2004; Ward and Wilson 1978).

References: Reimer *et al* 2004
Tyers 2001b, 45–6
Ward and Wilson 1978

OxA–2287 970 ±80 BP

δ¹³C: -25.5‰

Sample: BH13 F5474, submitted in July 1989 by W Rodwell

Material: wood (waterlogged): *Pinus* sp.

Initial comment: as OxA-2282

Objectives: as OxA-2282

Calibrated date: 1σ: cal AD 990–1170
2σ: cal AD 890–1230

Final comment: W Rodwell (9 March 1995), this child's coffin, made entirely of *Pinus* sp., is unique at Barton, and is suspected of being a Scandinavian import. Found in the late Saxon cemetery north-east of the church, stratigraphically it is thought to belong to the tenth or eleventh century. The result is consistent with the putative association of the coffin with Danish activity in eastern England in the early eleventh century.

Final comment: A Bayliss (20 July 2007), subsequent tree-ring analysis confirmed that the sample consisted of a 60-year block of rings from board 841089, the centre of which was 69 years earlier than the felling date of the timber. Incorporating this offset allows a revised calibration of cal AD 960–1300 (at 95% confidence; Reimer *et al* 2004), or cal AD 1060–1230 (at 68% confidence) to be proposed. This coffin currently remains undated by dendrochronology (Tyers 2001b, 60–1).

References: Reimer *et al* 2004
Tyers 2001b, 60–1

Battle Abbey, East Sussex

Location: TQ 748157
Lat. 50.54.49 N; Long. 00.29.13 E

Project manager: G Beresford (English Heritage), 1988

Archival body: English Heritage

Description: a Benedictine abbey which stands on the site of the Battle of Hastings in AD 1066. It was built by William the Conqueror to commemorate his victory and to atone for the dead. The high altar was placed on the spot where Harold was thought to have fallen.

Objectives: to provide dating evidence for the timber trench sealed beneath the Gatehouse walls.

References: Bronk Ramsey *et al* 2000a, 471–2

OxA–2253 360 ±60 BP

δ¹³C: -25.1‰

Sample: BA26 SF24, submitted in August 1989 by G Beresford

Material: charcoal (remaining subsample identified): Salicaceae (R Gale 1998)

Initial comment: sealed in a timber trench below medieval floor levels. The trench ran under late eleventh-/early twelfth-century walls.

Objectives: to distinguish between possible Roman, 'pagan Saxon', or late Saxon periods for construction of the trench.

Calibrated date: 1σ: cal AD 1440–1640
2σ: cal AD 1430–1660

Final comment: G Beresford (4 May 2000), the sample was found in a timber trench which ran under the late eleventh/twelfth-century gatehouse walls, and was sealed beneath the medieval floor levels. However, this result shows that it was an intrusion.

Beeston Castle, Cheshire

Location: SJ 538593
Lat. 53.07.43 N; Long. 02.41.26 W

Project manager: P J Hough, 1980, 1983

Archival body: English Heritage

Description: a medieval fortress. The thirteenth-century ruin of Beeston Castle is located on a rocky summit 500ft above the Cheshire plain with views of the Pennines in the east and the Welsh mountains in the west.

Objectives: to establish a series of dates for successive phases of defence.

Final comment: P Ellis (3 January 1995), the chief group of dates (HAR-4402 (2380 ±100 BP), HAR-4405, HAR-5609, HAR-5610 (1890 ±120 BP), HAR-6459, HAR-6464, HAR-6465, HAR-6468, HAR-6469, HAR-6503, and HAR-6504) is from the rampart found beneath the outer curtain of the medieval castle or from its collapse downslope. The earliest date (HAR-4405) ought to be compatible with that of the Ewart Park bronzes suggested to be a foundation deposit. The latest (HAR-5610; 1890 ±120 BP) could be argued to carry the sequence up to the Roman period. The long date range is compatible with the stratigraphic evidence. The outer ward dates (HAR-4401 and HAR-4406) suggest that a prehistoric settlement there spanned the first millennium BC. Radiocarbon dating of the plant remains might provide a clearer chronology. The Neolithic dates (HAR-6461 and HAR-6462) are supported by early to middle Neolithic pottery finds. Two date (HAR-8101 and HAR-8102) were taken in conjunction with pollen sampling.

Laboratory comment: Ancient Monuments Laboratory (2 October 2003), four samples BCOWC05 (HAR-9021), 0657/621 (HAR-6463 and HAR-9020), BC0519 (HAR-6460 and HAR-9098), and HAR-4497 were submitted for dating but failed to produce results. Fourteen further samples were published in Bayliss *et al* (2012, 20–3; HAR-4401, -4405–6, -5609, -6459, -6462, -6464–5, -6468–9, -6503–4, and -8101–2).

References: Bayliss *et al* 2012
Ellis 1993
Hough 1984
Otlet *et al* 1983

HAR–4402 2380 ±100 BP

$\delta^{13}C$: -28.0‰

Sample: BCOGRC03, submitted in October 1980 by P R Hough

Material: charcoal: unidentified

Initial comment: from the fill of a cylindrical posthole at the top of a ditch in the outer ward. The posthole is one of three forming part of a tentative palisade with an ambiguous relationship with a supposed bank deposit. The sample contains two elements: BC0212 was collected from higher in the posthole than BC0214.

Objectives: to date the palisade.

Calibrated date: 1σ: 750–380 cal BC
2σ: 800–200 cal BC

Final comment: P Ellis (3 January 1995), the stratigraphic position of posthole F213 was unclear. It might be associated with period 2A palisade features. However, the date suggests a feature associated with the period 3B rampart.

Laboratory comment: AERE Harwell (4 July 1989), this sample was measured in the miniature gas proportional counter (Otlet *et al* 1983).

References: Otlet *et al* 1983
Walker *et al* 1990, 166

HAR–5610 1890 ±120 BP

$\delta^{13}C$: -26.4‰

Sample: BCOGRC07, submitted in June 1983 by P R Hough

Material: charcoal (remaining subsample identified): unidentified (1.03g); *Corylus* sp. (2.04g, 100%) (R Gale 1999)

Initial comment: from an *in situ* timber in a stone rampart below foundation level; context BCO375A.

Objectives: to date the stone rampart.

Calibrated date: 1σ: 20 cal BC–cal AD 250
2σ: 180 cal BC–cal AD 410

Final comment: P Ellis (3 January 1995), a displaced fragment of wood. If this is from rampart material then the date carries the sequence to the Romano-British period. Alternatively the timber may derive from Romano-British use of the entranceway.

Laboratory comment: AERE Harwell (28 July 1989), this sample was measured in the miniature gas proportional counter (Otlet *et al* 1983).

References: Hardiman *et al* 1992, 60
Otlet *et al* 1983

HAR–6461 5330 ±110 BP

$\delta^{13}C$: -27.2‰

Sample: BCO542, submitted in July 1984 by P R Hough

Material: charcoal: *Quercus* sp., heartwood (<0.01g, 100%) (R Gale 1999)

Initial comment: sample 84; from the base of a scoop/hollow on the north side of the main route onto the hill. Sealed by the colluvial sand it is perhaps the earliest trace of a ditch and/or quarry scoop on the line of the outer defences.

Objectives: to give the earliest date for the defences.

Calibrated date: 1σ: 4330–3990 cal BC
2σ: 4370–3950 cal BC

Final comment: P Ellis (3 January 1995), from an area of amorphous occupation evidence with early to middle Neolithic pottery. The date is compatible with HAR-6462.

Laboratory comment: AERE Harwell (4 July 1989), this sample was measured in the miniature gas proportional counter (Otlet *et al* 1983).

References: Hardiman *et al* 1992, 61
Otlet *et al* 1983

Beverley: Long Lane, Humberside

Location: TA 047378
Lat. 53.49.32 N; Long. 00.24.33 W

Project manager: M McHugh (University of Newcastle upon Tyne), 1989

Archival body: Hull and East Riding Museum

Description: a small eutrophic basin mire, some 1.5km south of Beverley. Excavation of the mire by Humberside County Council Archaeological Unit had revealed a number of distinctive sand 'intrusions' or cones rising from the underlying (late Devensian) till to penetrate the peat.

Objectives: these 'intrusions' are now thought to represent former spring orifices which had served as foci for groundwater discharge from the regional chalk aquifer (Younger and McHugh 1995). Timbers partially lodged with the sub-peat till, dated dendrochronologically to *c* 4750 BC had probably subsided via a quicksand effect during an early phase of vigorous groundwater discharge. This is thought to equate with the peak in precipitation and rising sea levels of late Atlantic times. Subsequent peat accumulation and humification are thought to be intimately linked with variations in spring flow. Dating was undertaken in order to relate these variations to Holocene water table fluctuations and thus to climatic and sea-level change.

Final comment: M McHugh (10 February 1995), dating of the humic fraction of the basal peat (GU-5108) at around 1.3m depth suggests that organic matter began to accumulate during early sub-Atlantic times. Any peat accumulating prior to this was probably lost via vigorous groundwater discharge during the increasingly wet conditions of the late sub-Boreal. The date provided by the humic acid fraction of the basal peat (GU-5107) shows that peat accumulation and humification were probably almost contemporaneous. Subsequent climatic amelioration combined with the rising sea levels of the 'Roman Transgressions' allowed humified peat to accumulate under the influence of the water table. The presence of a sand interlayer contiguous with the sand cone suggests that these hydrologically 'quiet' conditions were interrupted by a period of vigorous groundwater discharge. Dating of peat from directly above this interlayer (at around 1.07m depth, GU-5152) suggests that this peak in precipitation may correlate with the increasingly wet and unsettled conditions following the Roman occupation (possible *circa* the sixth century AD). Peat accumulation then resumed under the influence of the water table (though it was rising more rapidly than before) until accumulation outstripped the water table in *c* the eighth–tenth centuries AD and a Carr-type peat was able to develop (GU-5071). This may correlate with the onset of warm dry conditions in the British Isles (Lamb 1977).

References: Lamb 1977
Younger and McHugh 1995

GU–5071 1170 ±50 BP

δ¹³C: -23.5‰

Sample: Upper peat, submitted on 24 January 1991 by M McHugh

Material: peat (humic acid fraction)

Initial comment: semi-fibrous peat overlying humified organic material which itself lies within a spring fed basin; taken from a depth of 0.75m below the present ground surface.

Objectives: to provide a *terminus ante quem* for spring activity within the mire. It may be linked with dates from organic material below and dendrochronological dates. Together these may provide important palaeoclimatic and environmental information of particular relevance to the forthcoming Humber Wetlands Project as well as the development of the site itself.

Calibrated date: 1σ: cal AD 770–950
2σ: cal AD 690–990

Final comment: M McHugh (10 February 1995), dating of the upper peat shows that peat development outstripped the water table in the eighth–tenth centuries AD. The development of this debris-rich Carr-type peat may be linked with times of warmth and dryness in Britain following the ninth century AD.

GU–5107 2020 ±60 BP

δ¹³C: -28.8‰

Sample: Lower peat 1, submitted on 24 January 1991 by M McHugh

Material: peat (humic acid fraction, highly humified mineralogenic peat of markedly low bulk density) (M McHugh)

Initial comment: lower peat (humic acid fraction): from the base of the mire *c* 1.3m below the present ground surface.

Objectives: a date for this sample will be the latest by which the underlying gravels had accumulated and marks the beginning of the overlying peat growth.

Calibrated date: 1σ: 100 cal BC–cal AD 60
2σ: 200 cal BC–cal AD 120

Final comment: M McHugh (10 February 1995), dating of the humic acid fraction of the basal peat suggests that peat began to accumulate in the late Iron Age to the Iron Age/Romano-British transition. Comparison with the date provided by the humin fraction (GU-5108) suggests that organic matter accumulation and humification were almost contemporaneous.

Laboratory comment: see GU-5108

GU–5108 2090 ±120 BP

δ¹³C: -29.5‰

Sample: Lower peat 2, submitted on 24 January 1991 by M McHugh

Material: peat (humin fraction, highly humified mineralogenic peat of markedley low bulk density) (M McHugh)

Initial comment: lower peat (humin fraction); *see* GU-5107.

Objectives: as GU-5107

Calibrated date: 1σ: 360 cal BC–cal AD 50
2σ: 400 cal BC–cal AD 140

Final comment: M McHugh (10 August 1995), dating of the humin fraction of the basal peat suggests that erosive spring activity may have resumed/peaked during the extremely wet conditions of early Iron Age times and links peat accumulation with the continued wetness of the Iron Age and/or the rising sea levels of the 'Roman Transgressions'.

Laboratory comment: English Heritage (25 January 2012), the results on the humic acid and humin fractions are statistically consistent (T'=0.3; T'(5%)=3.8; ν=1; Ward and Wilson 1978), and the weighted mean (2034 ±54 BP) calibrates to 200 cal BC–cal AD 80 (95% confidence; Reimer *et al* 2004), or 110 cal BC–cal AD 30 (68% confidence).

References: Reimer *et al* 2004
Ward and Wilson 1978

GU–5152 1310 ±50 BP

δ¹³C: -28.8‰

Sample: Middle peat, submitted on 30 April 1991 by M McHugh

Material: peat (humic acid fraction)

Initial comment: from directly above a sand and silt interlayer at 1.07m depth below the present ground surface. The sand and silt deposit below was known to be related to artesian spring activity.

Objectives: the third date in a series of four, this date is intended to provide a *terminus ante quem* for vigorous spring activity and therefore provide palaeoclimatic data which will be related to the onset of peat formation and subsequent declining artesian activity.

Calibrated date: 1σ: cal AD 650–770
2σ: cal AD 640–810

Final comment: M McHugh (10 February 1995), dating of the middle peat provides a broad *terminus ante quem* for a surge in spring flow. It seems probable that this peak in precipitation reflects the increasingly wet and unsettled conditions which followed the Roman occupation (possibly in the sixth century AD).

UB–3275 4523 ±39 BP

δ¹³C: -25.3 ±0.2‰

Sample: BPGA6, submitted in January 1990 by C Groves

Material: wood (waterlogged): *Quercus* sp.

Initial comment: from timber resting on river gravels and a thin layer of clay.

Objectives: to aid dendrochronological dating.

Calibrated date: 1σ: 3360–3100 cal BC
2σ: 3370–3090 cal BC

Final comment: C Groves (20 December 1993), UB-3275 was one of several samples to be submitted for dendrochronological analysis. Two of the other timbers were dendrochronologically dated to the Neolithic period. Stratigraphic evidence indicated a pre-Iron Age date for UB-3275. As no dendrochronological date could be obtained, a sample was submitted for radiocarbon dating to provide more precise dating evidence. The radiocarbon results indicate that UB-3275 is slightly younger than the dendrochronologically dated samples.

Laboratory comment: University of Belfast (3 April 1990), this sample was pretreated using the acid based acid protocol.

Bigbury Camp, Kent

Location: TR 114576
Lat. 51.16.40 N; Long. 01.01.53 E

Project manager: P Blockley (Canterbury Archaeological Trust), 1982

Archival body: Canterbury Archaeological Trust

Description: samples were taken from a sequence of carbon-rich layers resting between the base of a slighted rampart and the inner ditch of the defences (Blockey and Blockley 1989).

Objectives: it was hoped that the dating of these deposits might provide supporting evidence for a conflagration following Caesar's attack on Bigbury in 54 BC. Only the uppermost layer in the sequence provided enough carbon for dating purposes.

Final comment: P Bennett (30 December 1994), whilst analysis of ceramics indicated construction of the defences in the second century BC and the slighting of the rampart in the mid first century BC, the calibrated radiocarbon dates at 1 and 2 sigma covered too wide a date range to assist with further chronological definition of the rampart destruction.

Laboratory comment: Ancient Monuments Laboratory, two further samples LAYER14 (HAR-5031) and LAYER15 (HAR-5032) were submitted for dating but did not produce results.

References: Blockley and Blockley 1989

HAR–5030 1930 ±70 BP

δ¹³C: -27.5‰

Sample: LAYER9-1, submitted on 28 May 1982 by P Blockley

Material: charcoal (in soil matrix)

Initial comment: from layer 9.

Objectives: it was hoped that the dating of the deposits might provide supporting evidence for a conflagration following Caesar's attack on Bigbury in 54 BC. Only the uppermost layer in the sequence provided enough carbon for dating purposes.

Calibrated date: 1σ: cal AD 1–140
2σ: 90 cal BC–cal AD 240

Final comment: P Bennett (30 December 1994), whilst analysis of ceramics indicated construction of the defences in the second century BC and the slighting of the rampart in the mid first century BC, the calibrated radiocarbon dates at 1 and 2 sigma covered too wide a date range to assist with further chronological definition of the rampart destruction.

Laboratory comment: AERE Harwell (27 February 1989), this sample was measured in the miniature gas proportional counter (Otlet *et al* 1983).

References: Otlet *et al* 1983

Bincombe: Round Barrow, Dorset

Location: SY 67268580
Lat. 54.40.13 N; Long. 02.27.48 W

Project manager: R Robertson-Mackay (Unknown), 1963

Archival body: English Heritage

Description: one of three barrows (Grinsell No. 12; Scheduled Ancient Monument DO205), which form part of the very important Dorset Ridgeway cemetery.

Objectives: the central burial is missing and hence the initial construction date is unknown. It is hoped to obtain a *terminus ante quem* for the construction of the barrow, which also relates to dates for adjacent barrows in the cemetery.

References: Best 1964
Calkin 1967

UB–3299 3801 ±60 BP

δ¹³C: -25.8 ±0.2‰

Sample: MPBW205B, submitted on 6 September 1989 by R Robertson-Mackay

Material: charred wood: unidentified

Initial comment: from posts possibly used as grave markers on top of the mound which was subsequently denuded, and found in the barrow ditch, stratified in an early position above primary siltings. They were found in layer 16 of the North Ditch, a compact chalk silting derived from the barrow mound.

Objectives: to give a *terminus ante quem* for the barrow mound construction and initial denudation.

Calibrated date: 1σ: 2340–2140 cal BC
2σ: 2470–2030 cal BC

Laboratory comment: University of Belfast (4 September 1990), the surface layer was scraped off before processing due to suspected contamination with polyvinyl acetate in toluene.

UB–3382 3979 ±51 BP

$\delta^{13}C$: -26.3 ±0.2‰

Sample: MPBW205E, submitted on 6 September 1989 by R Robertson-Mackay

Material: charred wood: unidentified

Initial comment: from one of a series of secondary burials, higher up in the mound. The wooden slat was placed immediately on top of a flexed burial, probably of later Wessex, early Bronze Age date.

Objectives: to provide confirmation of the date of related inhumation, in the absence of grave goods.

Calibrated date: 1σ: 2570–2460 cal BC
2σ: 2620–2340 cal BC

Binsey, Oxfordshire

Location: SP 486079
Lat. 51.46.02 N; Long. 01.17.44 W

Project manager: J Blair (The Queen's College, Oxford), 1987–8

Description: a large sub-oval enclosure associated with St Margaret's chapel and its graveyard. The excavations identified a series of boundary features.

Objectives: to date the site.

Final comment: J Blair (19 January 1995), the one substantially useful date, though unfortunately in isolation, is HAR-8921, which provides the only solid dating evidence for the use of the site. The other three dates, which do form a sequence, were unfortunately almost useless, since the stratigraphically earliest (HAR-8922) proved to be modern. It remains uncertain whether the original enclosure is of Iron Age or post-Roman date; it may possibly belong to the series of small Iron Age forts on the terrace-edge and island sites on the Thames gravels.

Laboratory comment: Ancient Monuments Laboratory (2003), four further samples BYC39 (HAR-8932), BYC96 (HAR-8933), BYC7 (HAR-8934), and BYC06 (HAR-6234) were submitted for dating but failed to produce results.

References: Blair 1988

HAR–8921 1740 ±90 BP

$\delta^{13}C$: -23.7‰

Sample: BYC32, submitted on 5 January 1988 by W J Blair

Material: animal bone: *Equus* sp. (B Leverton)

Initial comment: from the secondary silting of the first defensive ditch, pre-dating the construction of the wall which produced sample 39 (undated). Site ref: L32.

Objectives: to determine the date of the fortified enclosure and the sequence of the boundary features.

Calibrated date: 1σ: cal AD 170–410
2σ: cal AD 70–540

Final comment: J Blair (19 January 1995), this date from animal bone was crucial, since it is the only dating evidence from the earlier phases of the site, and indicates activity within or near the earthwork in the Romano-British or early historic period.

HAR–8922 220 ±60 BP

$\delta^{13}C$: -22.8‰

Sample: BYC10c, submitted on 5 January 1988 by W J Blair

Material: animal bone: *Equus* sp.; *Bos* sp. (B Leverton)

Initial comment: from the floor of the third ditch in the earliest part of its primary fill. The sample is certainly later than 9b (undated); probably later than HAR-8923; and certainly earlier than samples 7 (undated) or 3 (HAR-8935 below). Site ref: L10C.

Objectives: as HAR-8921

Calibrated date: 1σ: cal AD 1640–1955*
2σ: cal AD 1510–1955*

Final comment: J Blair (19 January 1995), this was completely unexpected: unless it was a rogue result, it shows that the re-cutting of the ditch on the south-east side of the site (where, perhaps significantly, it forms a field boundary) continued into recent times. From this it follows that samples HAR-8923 and HAR-8935, which produced central and late medieval dates, were redeposited, or they come from overlying layers.

HAR–8923 960 ±70 BP

$\delta^{13}C$: -23.0‰

Sample: BYC5e, submitted on 5 January 1988 by W J Blair

Material: animal bone: *Equus* sp.; *Bos* sp. (B Leverton)

Initial comment: over the fill of the second ditch; probably but not certainly contemporary with the digging of the third ditch. The context is certainly later than sample 9e (undated), certainly earlier than samples 7 or 3 (HAR-8935 below). Site ref: L5a.

Objectives: as HAR-8921

Calibrated date: 1σ: cal AD 1010–1170
2σ: cal AD 900–1220

Final comment: J Blair (19 January 1995), this central medieval date was unexpected, but in the event not surprising since the date from HAR-8922 shows that the sample must have been redeposited in recent times.

HAR–8935 590 ±90 BP

$\delta^{13}C$: -22.8‰

Sample: BYC3, submitted on 5 January 1988 by W J Blair

Material: animal bone: *Canis* sp.; *Ovis* sp. (B Leverton)

Initial comment: from a gravel bank overlying the fill of the whole sequence of major ditches. Site ref: L3.

Objectives: as HAR-8921

Calibrated date: *1σ:* cal AD 1280–1430
                       2σ: cal AD 1260–1460

Final comment: see HAR-8923

References: Walker *et al* 1991a, 112

Birdlip Bypass: site 3, Gloucestershire

Location: SO 932143
                      Lat. 51.49.37 N; Long. 02.05.55 W

Project manager: C Parry (Gloucestershire County Council Archaeology Service), 1987–8

Archival body: Corinium Museum Cirencester

Description: site 3 was occupied during the late Iron Age and Romano-British period. The earlier settlement appears to have been concentrated within a complex of two enclosures revealed by cropmarks, the westernmost being partially excavated. The excavation concentrated mostly on the late Iron Age features, and at least two phases within this were defined in area C.

Objectives: dating would contribute towards our understanding of the construction of phase I, as well as providing a date for the introduction of the wheelthrown pottery (or at least a date before which this was not present).

References: Parry 1998
                      Parry and Rawes 1989

OxA–2544 2700 ±100 BP

δ¹³C: -27.1‰

δ¹³C: $\delta^{13}C$: -27.1‰

Sample: context 13, area A, submitted on 30 January 1990 by C Parry

Material: charcoal (23.56g submitted, the bulk of 21.34g comprises): *Fagus* sp.; *Crataegus* sp.; *Prunus* sp.; *Betula* sp.; *Corylus* sp. (C Cartwright 1990)

Initial comment: incorporated within the fill of pit 12 preserved as a shallow hollow within bedrock, and revealed by hand cleaning after machine removal of topsoil which lay directly above the fill. The pit lay on the exterior circumference of a penannular feature (truncated by cultivation) which produced no finds, but is probably contemporary. The charcoal was extracted from the fill by wet sieving.

Objectives: few early Bronze Age sites have been recently excavated on the Gloucestershire Cotswolds, and no local radiocarbon dates for this period are available. The date will clarify the period of this early phase on site 3, at present postulated from a limited pottery assemblage.

Calibrated date: *1σ:* 970–790 cal BC
                      2σ: 1120–590 cal BC

Final comment: C Parry (18 March 1991), the date obtained is in accord with a tentative middle Bronze Age dating of

grog-tempered pottery (of Collared or Biconical form) from the same deposit, although it does fall at the end of the date range for this period. At two sigma, the calibrated date range overlaps with the middle Bronze Age dates for pottery from Chapeltump II (Locock *et al* 2000) and coincides well with the calibrated date ranges for the Biconical and Trevisker-related assemblages from Brean Down (Bell 1990, 110, fig. 82, units 6 and 56).

References: Bell 1990
                      Hedges *et al* 1991b, 289
                      Locock *et al* 2000

UB–3301 2270 ±30 BP

δ¹³C: $\delta^{13}C$: -23.1 ±0.2‰

Sample: context 452, area C, submitted on 30 January 1990 by C Parry

Material: animal bone (unidentified) (K Dobney)

Initial comment: collected during excavation of the lower fills (contexts 453, 456, 457) of storage pit 429. These fills represent a quickly accumulated, possibly backfilled, deposit of redeposited limestone subsoil, sealed by a later fill, context 451.

Objectives: site 3 was a settlement of two major phases. Phase I, from which HAR-3301, HAR-3302 and HAR-3303 were collected, can be assigned to the latter part of the Iron Age, although its ceramic tradition was essentially middle Iron Age in character. Phase II saw the settlement's expansion, and also the introduction of wheelthrown pottery. Phase I therefore dates to a transitional period before major spatial and technological changes occurred. In Gloucestershire, no comparable sequence from recent excavation is known, and no radiocarbon date for the later Iron Age is available.

Calibrated date: *1σ:* 400–260 cal BC
                      2σ: 400–210 cal BC

Final comment: C Parry (18 March 1991), the date is in accord with finds of Iron Age pottery from the context. The sample was removed from the lower fill of a storage pit, and was one of three such samples (UB-3301, UB-3302, and UB-3303) to be submitted from a group of 19 pits; the dates obtained were closely comparable, and suggest that occupation of a small farmstead began during the middle Iron Age.

UB–3302 2222 ±44 BP

δ¹³C: $\delta^{13}C$: -23.8 ±0.2‰

Sample: context 560, area C, submitted on 30 January 1990 by C Parry

Material: animal bone (unidentified)

Initial comment: collected during excavation of the lower fill of storage pit 561, where it lay above a thin, charred organic layer at the base of the pit, and below a similar deposit, 559.

Objectives: as UB-3301

Calibrated date: *1σ:* 390–200 cal BC
                      2σ: 400–170 cal BC

Final comment: see UB-3301

UB–3303 2198 ±37 BP

δ¹³C: -22.0 ±0.2‰

Sample: context 533, area C, submitted on 30 January 1990 by C Parry

Material: animal bone (unidentified)

Initial comment: collected during excavation of the lower fills (contexts 535-541, *see* UB-3301) of storage pit 384.

Objectives: as UB-3301

Calibrated date: 1σ: 370–190 cal BC
                     2σ: 390–160 cal BC

Final comment: see UB-3301

Birdoswald: Midgeholme Moss, Cumbria

Location: NY 613665
                     Lat. 54.59.29 N; Long. 02.36.18 W

Project manager: J B Innes (University of Durham), 1988

Archival body: English Heritage

Description: a valley mire about 200m by 100m in extent which lies close to major archaeological sites of Roman and later date at Birdoswald.

Objectives: to provide a dating framework for pollen analysis being carried out on the peat sequence at Midgeholme Moss. Pollen and soil studies are being carried out to provide information of the environmental history of the site in the pre-Roman and Romano-British occupation phases. These studies should provide valuable information on the landscape history of the Hadrian's Wall area, in particular, information regarding pre- and post-wall agriculture.

References: Hedges *et al* 1991b, 286–7
                     Innes 1988

OxA–2324 1410 ±80 BP

δ¹³C: -28.3‰

Sample: MM-3, submitted on 11 October 1989 by J B Innes

Material: peat (detrital clayey)

Initial comment: from a depth of 37cm below the surface, corresponding with the start of pollen zone MM-i.

Objectives: to date the start of a phase of agricultural activity, which includes cereal cultivation and represents the most intensive episode of forest clearance and land-use at the site. The archaeological period is not known, but the position between elm decline suggests perhaps mid or late Flandrian III.

Calibrated date: 1σ: cal AD 570–670
                     2σ: cal AD 430–780

Final comment: J Innes (1991), this sample dates the start of a phase of agricultural activity which includes cereal cultivation and is the most intensive episode of forest clearance at the site. It is shown to be early post-Roman, which is in agreement with similar evidence of land-use history in Northumberland.

OxA–2325 2040 ±80 BP

δ¹³C: -28.9‰

Sample: MM-2, submitted on 11 October 1989 by J B Innes

Material: peat (detrital peat/Gyttja)

Initial comment: from a depth of 100cm below the surface.

Objectives: to date a phase of forest clearance including cereal grains which occurs in mid pollen zone MM-g, and which forms the first major episode of forest disturbance at the site. The archaeological period is not known, but the distance above elm decline suggests it must be post-Neolithic.

Calibrated date: 1σ: 170 cal BC–cal AD 60
                     2σ: 360 cal BC–cal AD 130

Final comment: J Innes (1991), this sample was intended to date a phase of forest clearance including cereal pollen which forms the first major episode of deforestation at the site. The date shows this agricultural phase to be of late Iron Age to early Romano-British age, which accords well with the nearby archaeological sites.

OxA–2326 5270 ±90 BP

δ¹³C: -30.7‰

Sample: MM-1, submitted on 11 October 1989 by J B Innes

Material: peat (detrital peat/Gyttja)

Initial comment: from a depth of 205cm from the surface, and from the boundary between zones MM-3 and MM-f.

Objectives: to date the elm decline (Flandrian II/III transition) which is the most recent pollen stratigraphic marker horizon present within the pollen diagram, and will thus confirm the correspondence of the timing of early and mid-Flandrian vegetational history at Midgeholme Moss with other dated pollen stratigraphies in the area. It will permit a relative date to be assigned to pollen fluctuations in levels assumed at present to be of early Flandrian III. It is expected that the date of this horizon will be *c* 3800 cal BC (5000 BP).

Calibrated date: 1σ: 4240–3970 cal BC
                     2σ: 4340–3940 cal BC

Final comment: J Innes (1991), this date is highly satisfactory as it compares very closely with the great majority of previous dates for the elm decline in north-west England, which cluster a little before 5000 BP. It establishes the Flandrian II/III transition and dates the earliest indications of forest clearance at the site.

Birdoswald: Midgeholme Moss 1, Cumbria

Location: NY 616667
                     Lat. 54.59.36 N; Long. 02.36.01 W

Project manager: P Wiltshire (Consultant), 1990

Archival body: English Heritage

Description: a valley mire about 200m by 100m in extent which lies close to major archaeological sites of Roman and later date at Birdoswald.

Objectives: to provide a dating framework for pollen analysis being carried out on the peat sequence at Midgeholme Moss. Pollen and soil analysis are being carried out to provide information on the environmental history of the site in the pre-Roman and Romano-British occupation phases. These studies should provide valuable information on the landscape history of the Hadrian's Wall area in particular information regarding pre- and post-wall agriculture.

Final comment: T Wilmott (1997), radiocarbon dates led to the re-interpretation of the pollen analysis, which produce some broad preliminary chronological comparison. The radiocarbon data has provided a clearer understanding of the regional landscape immediately prior to, during, and just after the building of the Wall and the fort of Birdoswald.

References: Wilmott 1997

GU–5072 1730 ±60 BP

δ¹³C: -29.4‰

Sample: 420-BIRD1, submitted in February 1991 by P Wiltshire

Material: peat

Initial comment: unhumified, fibrous peat sampled from monolith tin II (*see* also GU-5073 and GU-5074). A series of monoliths, I, II, and III, were obtained from a soil section dug in the eastern end of Midgeholme Moss. The sample was taken from a depth of 48–50cm, approximately 1.20m above the water table; directly above a thin layer of fine silty clay at the base of the unhumified peat. Fine to medium roots were present.

Objectives: this sample forms part of a series taken to provide a dating framework for pollen analysis being carried out on the peat sequence at Midgeholme Moss.

Calibrated date: *1σ:* cal AD 230–400
                       2σ: cal AD 130–430

Final comment: see series comments

GU–5073 2440 ±60 BP

δ¹³C: -29.3‰

Sample: 420-BIRD2, submitted in February 1991 by P Wiltshire

Material: peat

Initial comment: from monolith tin II (*see* also GU-5072 and GU-5074.) The sample was taken from a depth of 56–58cm, and was taken directly below a thin layer of fine silty clay at the top of a transition between the unhumified and the humified peat.

Objectives: as GU-5072

Calibrated date: *1σ:* 760–400 cal BC
                       2σ: 790–390 cal BC

Final comment: see series comments

GU–5074 3540 ±70 BP

δ¹³C: -30.3‰

Sample: 420-BIRD3, submitted in February 1991 by P Wiltshire

Material: peat

Initial comment: slightly humified, semi-fibrous peat sampled from monolith tin II (*see* also GU-5072 and GU-5073). The sample was taken from a depth of 74–76cm, in the transition between unhumified and humified peat.

Objectives: as GU-5072

Calibrated date: *1σ:* 1960–1760 cal BC
                       2σ: 2120–1690 cal BC

Final comment: see series comments

GU–5075 4410 ±60 BP

δ¹³C: -29.6‰

Sample: 420-BIRD4, submitted in February 1991 by P Wiltshire

Material: peat

Initial comment: humified fibrous peat sampled from monolith tin III, from a depth of 86–88cm, in the transition between unhumified and humified fibrous peat.

Objectives: as GU-5072

Calibrated date: *1σ:* 3270–2920 cal BC
                       2σ: 3350–2900 cal BC

Final comment: see series comments

GU–5076 4610 ±60 BP

δ¹³C: -29.7‰

Sample: 420-BIRD5, submitted in February 1991 by P Wiltshire

Material: peat

Initial comment: humified fibrous to semi-fibrous peat sampled from monolith tin III, from a depth of 104–106cm, from a layer of well humified peat.

Objectives: as GU-5072

Calibrated date: *1σ:* 3500–3350 cal BC
                       2σ: 3630–3110 cal BC

Final comment: see series comments

GU–5077 4820 ±70 BP

δ¹³C: -29.6‰

Sample: 420-BIRD6, submitted in February 1991 by P Wiltshire

Material: peat

Initial comment: well humified, semi-fibrous peat sampled from monolith tin III, from a depth of 116–118cm, taken within well humified peat.

Objectives: as GU-5072

Calibrated date: *1σ:* 3660–3520 cal BC
                       2σ: 3720–3370 cal BC

Final comment: see series comments

Birdoswald: Midgeholme Moss 2, Cumbria

Location: NY 616667
Lat. 54.59.36 N; Long. 02.36.01 W

Project manager: P Wiltshire (Consultant), 1990

Description: a valley mire about 200m by 100m in extent which lies close to major archaeological sites of Roman and later date at Birdoswald.

Objectives: to provide a dating framework for pollen analysis being carried out on the peat sequence at Midgeholme Moss. Pollen and soil studies are being carried out to provide information of the environmental history of the site in the pre-Roman and Romano-British occupation phases. These studies should provide valuable information on the landscape history of the Hadrian's Wall area, in particular, information regarding pre- and post-wall agriculture.

Final comment: T Wilmott (1997), radiocarbon dates led to the re-interpretation of the pollen analysis, which produce some broad preliminary chronological comparison. The radiocarbon data has provided a clearer understanding of the regional landscape immediately prior to, during, and just after the building of the Wall and the fort of Birdoswald.

References: Wilmott 1997

GU–5078 1240 ±50 BP

$\delta^{13}C$: -28.7‰

Sample: 420-PIIA1, submitted in February 1991 by P Wiltshire

Material: peat

Initial comment: from very fibrous, unhumified, phragmites peat with visible wood fragments, seeds, and a few coarse roots. The sample was taken from peat core A, at a depth of 100–104cm, obtained using 9cm Russian auger; and was located west of the possible Roman road and west of the samples from Midgeholme 1 (GU-5072 to GU-5076, 420-BIRD1-6).

Objectives: this sample forms part of a series taken to provide a dating framework for pollen analysis being carried out on the peat sequence at Midgeholme Moss.

Calibrated date: 1σ: cal AD 680–880
2σ: cal AD 660–900

Final comment: see series comments

GU–5079 1400 ±50 BP

$\delta^{13}C$: -29.0‰

Sample: 420-PIIA2, submitted in February 1991 by P Wiltshire

Material: peat

Initial comment: from a very fibrous, unhumified, phragmites peat with visible wood fragments, seeds, and a few coarse roots. The sample was taken from peat core A, at a depth of 120–124 cm.

Objectives: as GU-5078

Calibrated date: 1σ: cal AD 600–670
2σ: cal AD 560–690

Final comment: see series comments

GU–5080 1470 ±50 BP

$\delta^{13}C$: -28.1‰

Sample: 420-PIIA3, submitted in February 1991 by P Wiltshire

Material: peat

Initial comment: from fibrous, unhumified, phragmites peat, with visible wood fragments, seeds, and a few coarse roots. The sample was taken from peat core A at a depth of 140–144cm.

Objectives: as GU-5078

Calibrated date: 1σ: cal AD 540–650
2σ: cal AD 430–660

Final comment: see series comments

GU–5081 2100 ±60 BP

$\delta^{13}C$: -29.3‰

Sample: 420-PIIA5, submitted in February 1991 by P Wiltshire

Material: peat

Initial comment: from slightly humified fibrous peat with some mineral inclusions. The sample was taken at a depth of 175-179cm, within the transition between unhumified and humified peat, at the base of the unhumified peat.

Objectives: as GU-5078

Calibrated date: 1σ: 200–40 cal BC
2σ: 360 cal BC–cal AD 30

Final comment: see series comments

Final comment: T Wilmott (1997), this radiocarbon date indicates along with pollen analysis that there was a relatively rapid peat growth here and, in spite of trees actually growing on the pollen site, woodland clearance appears to have been in progress.

GU–5082 2100 ±60 BP

$\delta^{13}C$: -29.3‰

Sample: 420-PIIA5, submitted in February 1991 by P Wiltshire

Material: peat

Initial comment: from humified, phragmites peat with mineral inclusions, but less consolidated than GU-5081 above. The sample was taken at a depth of 190–194cm.

Objectives: as GU-5078

Calibrated date: 1σ: 200–40 cal BC
2σ: 360 cal BC–cal AD 30

Final comment: T Wilmott (1997), this date suggests strongly that this woodland clearance was made in the late Iron Age and was not related to the Wall.

GU–5083 2800 ±70 BP

$\delta^{13}C$: -29.7‰

Sample: 420-PIIA6, submitted in February 1991 by P Wiltshire

Material: peat

Initial comment: from well humified, unconsolidated peat, with apparent phragmites and a few medium roots. The sample was taken from a depth of 215–219cm.

Objectives: as GU-5078

Calibrated date: 1σ: 1030–840 cal BC
2σ: 1190–810 cal BC

Final comment: see series comments

GU–5084 2680 ±70 BP

$\delta^{13}C$: -29.7‰

Sample: 420-PIIA7, submitted in February 1991 by P Wiltshire

Material: peat

Initial comment: from well humified, unconsolidated peat with phragmites apparent, and a few medium roots. The sample was obtained from a depth of 250–254cm.

Objectives: as GU-5078

Calibrated date: 1σ: 910–790 cal BC
2σ: 1000–770 cal BC

Final comment: see series comments

Birdoswald: Midgeholme Moss 7/91, Cumbria

Location: NY 616667
Lat. 54.59.36 N; Long. 02.36.01 W

Project manager: P Wiltshire (Consultant), 1990

Description: a valley mire about 200m by 100m in extent which lies close to major archaeological sites of Roman and later date at Birdoswald.

Objectives: to provide a dating framework for pollen analysis being carried out on the peat sequence at Midgeholme Moss. Pollen and soil analysis are being carried out to provide information on the environmental history of the site in the pre-Roman and Romano-British occupation phases. These studies should provide valuable information on the landscape history of the Hadrian's Wall area in particular information regarding pre- and post-Wall agriculture.

Final comment: T Wilmott (1997), radiocarbon dates led to the re-interpretation of the pollen analysis, which produce some broad preliminary chronological comparison. The radiocarbon data has provided a clearer understanding of the

regional landscape immediately prior to, during, and just after the building of the Wall and the fort of Birdoswald.

References: Wilmott 1997

GU–5175 1850 ±60 BP

$\delta^{13}C$: -26.3‰

Sample: MM1/40-44, submitted on 17 May 1991 by P Wiltshire

Material: peat

Initial comment: from monolith tin I from the eastern edge of Midgeholme Moss, at a depth of 40–44cm.

Objectives: to expand the dating framework for the pollen analysis.

Calibrated date: 1σ: cal AD 80–240
2σ: cal AD 20–330

Final comment: see series comments

GU–5176 1960 ±50 BP

$\delta^{13}C$: -29.1‰

Sample: MM1/52-56, submitted on 17 May 1991 by P Wiltshire

Material: peat

Initial comment: from monolith tin I from the eastern edge of Midgeholme Moss, at a depth of 52–56cm.

Objectives: to expand the dating framework for the pollen analysis.

Calibrated date: 1σ: 20 cal BC–cal AD 90
2σ: 60 cal BC–cal AD 140

Final comment: see series comments

GU–5177 1660 ±80 BP

$\delta^{13}C$: -28.5‰

Sample: MMA/II/130-134, submitted on 17 May 1991 by P Wiltshire

Material: peat

Initial comment: from core A (II) at the east end of Midgeholme Moss, at a depth of 130–134cm.

Objectives: to supplement the dating of the pollen sequence.

Calibrated date: 1σ: cal AD 250–530
2σ: cal AD 210–570

Final comment: see series comments

GU–5179 1740 ±90 BP

$\delta^{13}C$: -29.2‰

Sample: MMA/II/158-162, submitted on 17 May 1991 by P Wiltshire

Material: peat

Initial comment: from core A (II) at the east end of Midgeholme Moss, at a depth of 158–162cm.

Objectives: as GU-5177

Calibrated date: 1σ: cal AD 170–410
                      2σ: cal AD 70–540

Final comment: T Wilmott (1997), this date indicates when there was a change from wood peat to unhumified grass/sedge peat.

Brampton: A1-M1 Link Road, Cambridgeshire

Location: TL 204716
                         Lat. 52.19.44 N; Long. 00.13.59 W

Project manager: T Malim (English Heritage), 1991

Description: excavations in advance of construction of a trunk road at a known cropmark complex (Scheduled Ancient Monument Cambridgeshire 121) gave a complete plan for a discrete Neolithic monument, interpreted as a mortuary enclosure at the eastern end of a cursus.

Objectives: the site consists of a linear ditched enclosure which in morphology resembles a Neolithic mortuary enclosure. It lies at the end of a cursus, and has several hengiform and barrow monuments (all ploughed flat) in the immediate vicinity. Virtually no dating evidence from pottery or bone has been found, and thus radiocarbon dating is the only method to verify or disprove our interpreted dates for the monument.

Final comment: T Malim (18 August 1993), very little dating evidence was recovered for establishing the period of construction of the ditched enclosure under excavation. This monument occurs at the end of a cursus, in a landscape with henges and barrows, and it has been interpreted on morphological grounds as a Neolithic mortuary enclosure. The dates obtained from two pits which stratigraphically post-date the infilling of the original ditches give a late Neolithic–Bronze Age transition date. A firm *terminus ante quem* for the monument has therefore been established, and evidence for continuity of use over a long time-period demonstrated.

GU–5264 3910 ±70 BP

$\delta^{13}C$: -26.2‰

Sample: A1M1-91 28C, submitted in August 1992 by T Malim and P Murphy

Material: charcoal: *Quercus* sp. (P Murphy)

Initial comment: from the primary fills of a pit sealed by *c* 20cm of secondary fills within the pit. The feature was sealed by *c* 80cm of topsoil/subsoil complex.

Objectives: GU-5264 comes from a pit immediately outside of the western ditch terminals, and is provisionally interpreted as a postpit for a totem or part of the facade of a monument; but it could be a post terminal for a series of antennae ditches which seem to pre-date the monument.

Calibrated date: 1σ: 2480–2290 cal BC
                      2σ: 2580–2150 cal BC

Final comment: T Malim (18 August 1993), the date represents activity related to the monument during the period of Neolithic/Bronze Age transition, and probably shows continuity of use of the ceremonial monuments, between which the pit is situated, during a period a long time after their construction.

GU–5265 4140 ±140 BP

$\delta^{13}C$: -25.2‰

Sample: A1M1-91 36.3, submitted in August 1992 by T Malim and P Murphy

Material: charcoal: *Quercus* sp. (P Murphy)

Initial comment: from a feature which appears to be a pit, and reused on several occasions. It is paired with another, both of which are ditch terminals, or late cuts into previous ditch terminals of the enclosure, with a very narrow causeway between. This causeway does not seem to represent a main entrance to the monument, however the nature of the deposits filling these pits suggest that they were used for burning material rather than as postpits in which the posts had burnt *in situ*. They definitely appear to represent a period of use of the monument. The sample was sealed beneath later fills (24.1) in this pit, and the feature itself was sealed beneath *c* 80cm of topsoil/subsoil complex.

Objectives: very few datable artefacts were recovered from secure contexts and fills from other features were mostly sterile and homogeneous. This sample appears to belong to the 'in use' phase of the monument and in the absence of artefacts, it is hoped radiocarbon dating will provide a date for this phase.

Calibrated date: 1σ: 2900–2490 cal BC
                      2σ: 3090–2300 cal BC

Final comment: T Malim (18 August 1993), this date gives a late Neolithic date for a feature that post-dates the infilling of the original monument, confirming a Neolithic date for the mortuary enclosure itself.

OxA–3972 600 ±55 BP

$\delta^{13}C$: -20.5‰

Sample: A1M1-91 26.3, submitted in August 1992 by T Malim and P Murphy

Material: grain: *Triticum* sp., four charred grains (P Murphy)

Initial comment: a bulked sample from the lower primary fills of the enclosure ditch terminal; the charcoal was gathered from flotation. The feature was sealed beneath *c* 0.8m of topsoil and alluvial subsoil, and this sample was sealed further by *c* 0.2m of secondary ditch fill. The sample comes from the north-western ditch terminal, which may have been an entrance to the interior. Deep pan-busting is known throughout the site, but great care was taken to avoid taking samples from near such marks.

Objectives: to establish a firm date for the monument's use/abandonment. This sample is also associated with part of a Neolithic leaf-shaped arrowhead.

Calibrated date: 1σ: cal AD 1290–1410
                      2σ: cal AD 1280–1440

Final comment: T Malim (18 August 1993), this result shows that the carbonized grains of wheat are intrusive and thus represent contamination of the ditch terminal fill probably by dessication cracking or pan-busting.

References: Hedges *et al* 1994, 365–6

Brandon: Staunch Meadow, Suffolk

Location: TL 778864
Lat. 52.26.46 N; Long. 00.36.59 E

Project manager: A Tester (Suffolk Archaeological Unit), 1981–2, 1984–5

Description: a middle Saxon settlement including buildings, an industrial area, church, and attendant cemeteries all concentrated within a readily defined island. The occupation of the bulk of the site is restricted to the middle Saxon period. The settlement sits beside a 1km wide arm of the Fenland which follows the valley of the Little Ouse river *c* 6km inland from Hockwold Fen; Brandon was probably the lowest crossing point of the river Ouse until recent times. The site occupies a sand ridge surrounded by peat, and stands as an island in time of flood. The river is some 50m north of the 'island' while the southern margin of the peat deposits (i.e. the edge of the flood plain) is *c* 80m to the south. The island is *c* 350m east-west by 150m north-south at its widest point with an area of some 4.75ha; of this *c* 1.5ha at the west end appears to have been unoccupied and a further *c* 1.25ha at the east end of the island has been Scheduled as an Ancient Monument.

Objectives: the samples submitted were from valley sediments, charcoal layers of wooden structures on floodplain adjacent to site. The intention was to date palaeoecological results and to establish dates for the structures.

References: Carr *et al* 1988

Brandon: Staunch Meadow, wooden structures, Suffolk

Location: TL 778864
Lat. 52.26.46 N; Long. 00.36.59 E

Project manager: R Carr (Suffolk Archaeological Unit), 1982 and 1985

Archival body: Suffolk County Council Archaeological Service

Description: posts comprising components of a timber causeway on the floodplain of the River Little Ouse.

Objectives: to date the causeway.

Final comment: P Murphy (6 June 2003), these dates establish an Anglo-Saxon date for the causeway.

Laboratory comment: Ancient Monuments Laboratory (1995), two further dates from Brandon (HAR-4086 and HAR-4087) were published in Jordan *et al* 1994, 26). Three further dates were published in Bayliss *et al* (2012, 36; HAR-9273–5).

References: Bayliss *et al* 2012
Carr *et al* 1988
Carr 1992
Jordan *et al* 1994, 26

GU–5046 1360 ±30 BP

$\delta^{13}C$: -24.7‰

Sample: BRD 018 1051, submitted in September 1990 by P Murphy

Material: wood (waterlogged): *Quercus* sp., quartered tree probably with a flat base but the outside surfaces were not present, 360x150x80mm (P Murphy)

Initial comment: from the base of a posthole along a wall of a building (1094). The sample was at a depth of *c* 0.6m and was preserved in wet sand, which was overlain by a peaty topsoil.

Objectives: building 1094 had exceptionally well-preserved remains revealing a detailed plan; the plan is unusual within the context of the site and for the period generally. This has implications for the use of the buildings and their development, which requires dating.

Calibrated date: 1σ: cal AD 650–670
2σ: cal AD 640–690

Final comment: see series comments

GU–5047 1360 ±50 BP

$\delta^{13}C$: -24.9‰

Sample: BRD 018 1235, submitted in September 1990 by P Murphy

Material: wood (waterlogged): *Quercus* sp., 65 rings including 1-4 sapwood (P Murphy)

Initial comment: located in wet sand and peat under a peaty topsoil. It is one sample from a sequence of four piles and was 45 cm below the topsoil.

Objectives: this pile was probably from a bridge linking the island to the surrounding farmland. It is significant in locating the direction of further occupation but it cannot be stratigraphically dated to the Saxon period. It could be medieval.

Calibrated date: 1σ: cal AD 640–680
2σ: cal AD 600–770

Final comment: see series comments

GU–5048 1440 ±50 BP

$\delta^{13}C$: -23.9‰

Sample: BRD 018 1982, submitted in September 1990 by P Murphy

Material: wood (waterlogged): *Quercus* sp., a small stake, 30cm long and 5.5cm wide (P Murphy)

Initial comment: from part of a causeway. It was located at least 0.5m below the turf in wet sand below peat and a peaty topsoil.

Objectives: this sample is from the primary phase of a causeway and dates the expansion of the settlement to the surrounding higher ground. It precedes a late Saxon bridge and is phased with the construction of the church and building 1094 (*see* GU–5046) for which radiocarbon offers the main source of dating.

Calibrated date: 1σ: cal AD 570–660
                      2σ: cal AD 540–670

Final comment: see series comments

Brightlingsea: Moverons Pit, Essex

Location: TM 06971831
               Lat. 51.49.28 N; Long. 01.00.13 E

Project manager: C P Clarke (Essex County Council), 1989–90

Archival body: Essex County Council

Description: a Deverel-Rimbury cemetery, on the eastern side of the Colne estuary excavated in advance of gravel extraction. In all 43 burial pits were identified containing 46 individual cremations. Nearly three-quarters of them were buried in urns, all of which are Deverel-Rimbury urns of the Ardleigh type. The burials can be sub-divided according to type and orientation - 13 cremations were un-urned, 30 in single vessels, and 3 with two vessels each. Sixteen vessels were buried in an upright position, 15 were inverted, one was buried on its side, and one was uncertain. The cremation tended to cluster in groups of up to eight, usually placed between the ring ditches (of which there were 31 within the excavated area).

Objectives: to test a model for spatial development of the middle Bronze Age cemetery; and to identify any chronological grouping of the three burial types encounter (upright urns, inverted urns, un-urned).

Final comment: N Brown (1995), these results suggest that there maybe a developmental sequence within the pottery of the Ardleigh group away from profuse decoration, horseshoe handles, and grog tempering with the later pottery becoming increasingly similar to the material from central and southern Essex.

Final comment: C P Clarke (3 March 1995), the results support a model of
a) 28 ring ditches without surviving burial remains probably spreading east-west;
b) a transitional phase of one ring ditch containing urned cremations; and
c) a final phase of cremation groups placed between the earlier ring ditches.
The dates were too close to identify chronological grouping for burial types. In addition the dates provide a valuable series of dates for the Ardleigh group of Deverel-Rimbury ceramics. They confirm the early dating of this distinctive, highly decorative pottery, previously suggested on typological grounds.

References: Brown and Kinnes 1995
                 Clarke 1991

GU–5099 3180 ±50 BP

δ¹³C: -24.2‰

Sample: 1018/521, submitted on 28 February 1991 by C P Clarke

Material: charcoal: *Quercus* sp. (P Murphy)

Initial comment: from feature 1018, context 521: one of three inverted urns (Brown and Kinnes 1995, table 12.3, 359), together with GU-5100 and GU-5101. The matrices of all fills in this series surrounding cremation vessels, and of fills inside the vessels were similar, ranging from sandy silt loam to loamy sand. The subsoil was coarse sandy fluvial glacial drift with overlying horizons of silty loessic material. Pebbles were common within the drift.

Objectives: to establish if there is any broad indication of phasing according to type of burial, in this case in an inverted urn.

Calibrated date: 1σ: 1500–1410 cal BC
                      2σ: 1540–1320 cal BC

Final comment: C P Clarke (3 March 1995), cremation burial in inverted vessel.

References: Brown and Kinnes 1995, 359

GU–5100 3180 ±50 BP

δ¹³C: -24.2‰

Sample: 1098/716, submitted on 28 February 1991 by C P Clarke

Material: charcoal: *Quercus* sp. (P Murphy)

Initial comment: as GU-5099 (Brown and Kinnes 1995, table 12.3, 374).

Objectives: to establish the longevity of inverted urn burials. *See* also GU-5099.

Calibrated date: 1σ: 1500–1410 cal BC
                      2σ: 1540–1320 cal BC

Final comment: C P Clarke (3 March 1995), cremation burial in inverted vessel. In the same age group as GU-5101 and GU-5105.

GU–5101 3210 ±80 BP

δ¹³C: -23.5‰

Sample: 1100/717, submitted on 28 February 1991 by C P Clarke

Material: charcoal: *Quercus* sp. (P Murphy)

Initial comment: associated with Brown 1995 (table 12.3, 325). *See* GU-5099.

Objectives: to establish the longevity of inverted urn burials. *See* also GU-5099.

Calibrated date: 1σ: 1610–1410 cal BC
                      2σ: 1690–1310 cal BC

Final comment: C P Clarke (3 March 1995), cremation burial in inverted vessel. In the same group as GU-5100 and GU-5105.

GU–5102 3490 ±140 BP

$\delta^{13}C$: -23.7‰

Sample: 1001/514, submitted on 28 February 1991 by C P Clarke

Material: charcoal: *Quercus* sp. (P Murphy)

Initial comment: one of two upright urns together with GU-5103 (Bown and Kinnes 1995, table 12.3, 345–6). *See* also GU-5099.

Objectives: to establish if there is any broad indication of phasing according to type of burial, in the case of GU-5102 and GU-5103, in upright burial urns.

Calibrated date: *1σ*: 2020–1630 cal BC
                      2σ: 2210–1490 cal BC

Final comment: C P Clarke (3 March 1995), the earliest date in the series confirming a transitional stage in the development of the cemetery.

GU–5103 3240 ±70 BP

$\delta^{13}C$: -25.6‰

Sample: 1025/530, submitted on 28 February 1991 by C P Clarke

Material: charcoal: *Quercus* sp. (P Murphy)

Initial comment: one of two upright urns (Brown and Kinnes 1995, table 12.3, 364), together with GU-5102.

Objectives: as GU-5102

Calibrated date: *1σ*: 1610–1430 cal BC
                      2σ: 1690–1390 cal BC

Final comment: C P Clarke (3 March 1995), cremation burial in an upright vessel.

GU–5104 3450 ±50 BP

$\delta^{13}C$: -24.4‰

Sample: 1024/531, submitted on 28 February 1991 by C P Clarke

Material: charcoal: *Quercus* sp. (P Murphy)

Initial comment: one of two un-urned cremations together with GU-5105. This sample was from the northern edge of the cemetery. *See* also GU-5099.

Objectives: to establish if there is any broad indication of phasing according to type of burial, in the case of GU-5104 and GU-5105, un-urned cremations.

Calibrated date: *1σ*: 1880–1690 cal BC
                      2σ: 1900–1630 cal BC

Final comment: C P Clarke (3 March 1995), one of the two earliest dates in the sequence, again suggesting that the earliest cremation burials occur in one part of the cemetery before spreading back between the ring ditches to the south east.

GU–5105 3080 ±60 BP

$\delta^{13}C$: -25.0‰

Sample: 1130/919, submitted on 28 February 1991 by C P Clarke

Material: charcoal: *Quercus* sp. (P Murphy)

Initial comment: one of two un-urned cremations together with GU-5104. *See* also GU-5099.

Objectives: as GU-5104

Calibrated date: *1σ*: 1430–1260 cal BC
                      2σ: 1500–1130 cal BC

Final comment: C P Clarke (3 March 1995), un-urned cremation burial. In the same group as GU-5100 and GU-5101.

GU–5106 1530 ±50 BP

$\delta^{13}C$: -25.9‰

Sample: 1142/798, 796, 795, submitted on 28 February 1991 by C P Clarke

Material: charcoal: *Quercus* sp. (P Murphy)

Initial comment: from the fill of the firepit.

Objectives: there is evidence from Deverel-Rimbury sites elsewhere for ritual activity involving the use of fire. Brightlingsea had a number of firepits near to the ring ditches, and a date for GU-5106 is designed to establish whether this activity represents ritual burning of some kind at the place of burial; no pyre locations were located.

Calibrated date: *1σ*: cal AD 430–600
                      2σ: cal AD 410–640

Final comment: C P Clarke (3 March 1995), an unexpected result, and the only evidence of Saxon activity on the site.

Brighton Bypass, East Sussex

Location: TQ 340084 central point
                   Lat. 50.51.31 N; Long. 00.05.47 W

Project manager: M Bennell (English Heritage), 1989–90

Description: forty-one radiocarbon age determinations were obtained on samples from the archaeological investigations along the line of the Brighton Bypass. Thirty samples were processed by the Oxford Radiocarbon Accelerator Unit between 1991 and 1995, four by the Queen's University of Belfast Radiocarbon Laboratory in 1994, and seven by the Scottish Universities Research and Reactor Centre at East Kilbride in 1993–4 and 1997 (Rudling 2002).

Objectives: six sites along the route of the bypass were subject to a programme of radiocarbon dating that was specific to each one: Downsview, Mile Oak, Redhill, Sweetpatch Bottom, Toadeshole Bottom East, and Toadeshole Bottom West.

Final comment: A Bayliss, G T Cook, F G McCormac and P Pettitt (2002), the Bronze Age settlement at Downsview probably starts rather earlier than the site at Mile Oak (84% confidence), but finishes slightly earlier too (75% confidence). However, there is almost certainly a substantial period of overlap when both sites were occupied, and so they can be regarded as, at least broadly, contemporary. Parts of the environmental sequences at Sweetpatch Valley Bottom and Toadeshole Bottom East also appear to be broadly contemporary with the settlement activity, although the dated part of the sequence at Toadeshole Bottom West appears to be slightly later. It is unclear whether any of the dated environmental sequences cover the earlier period represented by the activity at Redhill.

Laboratory comment: English Heritage (25 January 2012), eight further samples from Mile Oak, and eleven samples from Downsview, were submitted and dated after March 1993 (Rudling 2002, table 9.1).

References: Rudling 2002

Brighton Bypass: Mile Oak, East Sussex

Location: TQ 24450795 to TQ 25140788
Lat. 50.51.26 N; Long. 00.13.54 W, to
50.51.23 N; 00.13.19 W

Project manager: M Russell (Archaeology South East), 1988–90

Archival body: Brighton Museum

Description: excavations in advance of the proposed Brighton Bypass at Mile Oak Farm revealed a double-entranced oval enclosure, interpreted as a late Neolithic/early Bronze Age Class II henge monument, two areas of middle Bronze Age settlement, and an area of late Bronze Age activity associated with metalworking. The area investigated occupied a position on the southern margin of the South Downs, overlooking Mile Oak, Southwick, and Portslade.

Objectives: the dating programme for Mile Oak was conceived in 1990–1, before formal statistical modelling of chronological problems using radiocarbon dating and other information together was possible. For this reason, and because of the very partial nature of excavation which was possible on the site, the dating strategy was designed to address more limited aims than was the case at Downsview. In particular it was hoped that the construction of the ditched enclosure (243/245/1557) could be dated, along with the burial thought to be associated with it (2707). The aim was to provide dates spanning the use of middle Bronze Age settlement, not to attempt to elucidate the sequence of the huts. In addition the chronology of the late Bronze Age metalworking activity and mounds in area K were to be explored.

Final comment: M Russell (4 October 1995), thirteen samples were taken from the Mile Oak excavations. OxA-3153 represents material retrieved from the late Neolithic/early Bronze Age henge monument. Samples OxA-5106 to OxA-5109 all relate to the disuse of the henge and the establishment of a middle Bronze Age settlement. Samples OxA-3154, OxA-3155, and OxA-5110 relate to late Bronze Age settlement/industrial activity within trench K. GU-5269 and OxA-5105 relate to later prehistoric and post-medieval burials. OxA-3361, OxA-3362, and OxA-3386 are invalidated due to finds contamination.

Laboratory comment: English Heritage (25 January 2012), eight further samples were submitted and dated after March 1993 (Rudling 2002, table 9.1).

References: Harding and Lee 1987
Rudling 2002

GU–5269 2240 ±70 BP

$\delta^{13}C$: -26.4‰

Sample: MO4, submitted on 29 May 1992 by M Russell

Material: human bone (left and right femur) (S Browne)

Initial comment: context 2707; from a contracted male burial lying just within the north–north-west entrance of a probable henge monument, and sealed beneath a hut terrace dated to the late Bronze Age. The upper portion of the grave cut was disturbed by a later hut, but the skeleton remained undisturbed.

Objectives: to establish whether the burial is contemporary with the henge enclosure or a later addition; and to establish how much earlier the burial was in relation to the late Bronze Age hut structures.

Calibrated date: 1σ: 400–200 cal BC
2σ: 410–110 cal BC

Final comment: M Russell (4 October 1995), the determination indicates a date in the Iron Age, suggesting that observed the stratigraphic relationship (ie that the middle Bronze Age hut terrace cut the burial pit) was incorrect.

Laboratory comment: SUERC Radiocarbon Dating Laboratory (AMS) (7 August 1997), the $\delta^{13}C$ value for this sample is very light for a bone and would normally indicate incomplete combustion or substantial contamination of the sample. Two replicate measurements were therefore obtained, GU-5675 (2810 ±70 BP) on new bone from this individual, and GU-5691 (2960 ±100 BP) on a small amount of collagen remaining from the original submission. These replicate measurements are statistically consistent with each other (T'=1.5; T'(5%)=6.0; ν=2; Ward and Wilson 1978), but statistically significantly different from GU-5269 (T'=47.7; T'(5%)=6.0; ν=2). GU-5269 must therefore be considered anomalous.

Laboratory comment: English Heritage (25 January 2012), the most accurate radiocarbon date for this burial is provided by the mean of GU-5675 and GU-5691 (2628 ±45 BP), which calibrates to 890–760 cal BC (at 95% confidence; Reimer *et al* 2004), or 820–790 cal BC (at 68% confidence).

References: Reimer *et al* 2004
Ward and Wilson 1978

GU–5675 2810 ±70 BP

$\delta^{13}C$: -20.5‰

Sample: MO4-II, submitted on 25 November 1996 by M Russell

Material: human bone (left arm and left lower leg) (S Browne)

Initial comment: a replicate of GU-5269.

Objectives: as GU-5269

Calibrated date: *1σ:* 1050–890 cal BC
                    2σ: 1200–810 cal BC

Final comment: see GU-5269

GU–5691 2960 ±100 BP

δ¹³C: -22.9‰

Sample: MO4, submitted on 25 November 1996 by M Russell

Material: human bone (left and right femur) (S Browne)

Initial comment: a repeat of the original sample GU-5269.

Objectives: as GU-5269

Calibrated date: *1σ:* 1380–1010 cal BC
                    2σ: 1440–900 cal BC

Final comment: see GU-5269

OxA–3153 3480 ±80 BP

δ¹³C: -21.4‰

Sample: MO2, submitted on 7 March 1991 by M Russell

Material: animal bone: *Cervus* sp., left femur (R O'Shea)

Initial comment: from the primary silt of the henge ditch, layer 2642, overlying isolated solution deposit 2642; the silt was fine and sandy, 5cm wide, and formed a continuous deposit (possibly deliberate) around the length of the ditch. The bone was *c* 70cm below the ground surface.

Objectives: the ditch did not appear to be recut or cleaned out. Layer 2642 could be a deliberate deposit of fertile soil set down shortly after the construction of the monument, and therefore may have a similar date to MO1 (OxA-3361, OxA-3362, and OxA-3386). As with MO1, it is important to place the first recorded Sussex henge within the known chronology of ritual sites.

Calibrated date: *1σ:* 1910–1690 cal BC
                    2σ: 2030–1610 cal BC

Final comment: M Russell (4 November 1995), this sample was recovered from the primary silt of a prehistoric enclosure interpreted as the possible remains of a Class II henge monument. The date range is consistent with the constructional date ranges of 'classic' henge monuments as noted by Harding and Lee (1987, 11–56).

References: Harding and Lee 1987, 11–56
                      Hedges *et al* 1997, 254

OxA–3154 3050 ±80 BP

δ¹³C: -21.5‰

Sample: MO3, submitted on 7 March 1991 by M Russell

Material: animal bone: *Cervus* sp. (R O'Shea)

Initial comment: from the top of a posthole forming an eight ?post structure within a middle Bronze Age metalworking complex; sealed by a late Bronze Age mound.

Objectives: to provide a date for the dismantling of metalworking activity. There are few metalworking sites (and

none in Sussex) of Bronze Age date recorded or provided with radiocarbon dates.

Calibrated date: *1σ:* 1420–1210 cal BC
                    2σ: 1500–1050 cal BC

Final comment: M Russell (4 October 1995), this sample was dated to ascertain whether the structure in question was broadly contemporary with the middle Bronze Age settlement and the henge 400m to the east. The results suggest a date in the later Bronze Age and that structural components within trench K are all broadly contemporary.

References: Hedges *et al* 1997

OxA–3155 2950 ±100 BP

δ¹³C: -20.8‰

Sample: MO4, submitted on 7 March 1991 by M Russell

Material: animal bone: *Ovis* sp., tooth and bones; *Bos* sp., tooth and bones (R O'Shea)

Initial comment: from the centre of a pit fill of fine silt with medium to large flint and chalk fragments. The bone was recovered 18cm from the base of the ploughsoil (the field had not been ploughed since 1924 so there is a slight possibility of contamination from modern fertilizer). The pit cut through the middle chalk.

Objectives: the bone was from a pit inside a roundhouse, partially overlain by a middle Bronze Age roundhouse. Pottery suggests an early Bronze Age/middle Bronze date. Very few hut plans of this date are recorded, especially in Sussex. As recent ploughing has been particularly damaging, the hut may be connected with the phase of metalworking and therefore with OxA-3154.

Calibrated date: *1σ:* 1370–1000 cal BC
                    2σ: 1430–900 cal BC

Final comment: M Russell (4 October 1995), the determination suggests a late Bronze Age date and that all structural components within trench K are broadly contemporary.

References: Hedges *et al* 1997, 254

OxA–3361 310 ±60 BP

δ¹³C: -22.1‰

Sample: MO1, submitted on 7 March 1991 by M Russell

Material: animal bone: *Ovis* sp., right radius and left humerus (R O'Shea)

Initial comment: from the base of the henge ditch, 70cm below the ground surface, from layer 2708, in a chalk isolated solution deposit sealed by layer 2642 (brown loam).

Objectives: the ditch did not appear to have been recut or periodically cleaned. Layer 2708 represents a primary weathering deposit forming at an early stage of ditch exposure. No other finds were available for dating. This is the first recorded henge from Sussex and therefore it is important to place the site within the suggested chronology of henge monuments.

Calibrated date: *1σ:* cal AD 1480–1660
                    2σ: cal AD 1440–1950

Final comment: M Russell (4 October 1995), OxA-3361 and OxA-3362 were thought to have been retrieved from an undisturbed primary context at the base of a prehistoric enclosure ditch. Context 2708 has unfortunately become conflated with topsoil clearance layer 2708 containing Roman, medieval and post-medieval pottery and modern plastics. The samples are therefore invalidated.

References: Hedges *et al* 1997, 254

OxA–3362 270 ±60 BP

δ¹³C: -21.2‰

Sample: MO1, submitted on 7 March 1991 by M Russell

Material: animal bone: *Ovis* sp., right radius and left humerus (R O'Shea)

Initial comment: as OxA-3361

Objectives: as OxA-3361

Calibrated date: *1σ:* cal AD 1520–1800
                       2σ: cal AD 1460–1955*

Final comment: see OxA-3361

References: Hedges *et al* 1997, 254–5

OxA–3386 190 ±75 BP

δ¹³C: -22.1‰

Sample: MO1, submitted on 7 March 1991 by M Russell

Material: animal bone: *Ovis* sp., right radius and left humerus (R O'Shea)

Initial comment: a replicate measurement on the same bone as OxA-3361.

Objectives: as OxA-3361

Calibrated date: *1σ:* cal AD 1640–1955*
                       2σ: cal AD 1510–1955*

Final comment: see OxA-3361

Laboratory comment: English Heritage (25 January 2012), the two measurements on this bone are statistically consistent (T'=1.6; T'(5%)=3.8; ν=1; Ward and Wilson 1978). The weighted mean (264 ±47 BP) calibrates to cal AD 1480–1955* (at 95% confidence; Reimer *et al* 2004), or to cal AD 1520–1800 (at 68% confidence).

References: Reimer *et al* 2004
                       Ward and Wilson 1978

Brighton Bypass: Red Hill, East Sussex

Location: TQ 285084
                     Lat. 50.51.37 N; Long. 00.10.26 W

Project manager: M Bennell (Field Archaeology Unit, Institute of Archaeology), 1989

Archival body: Brighton Museum

Description: the site at Red Hill lies at the north west edge of Brighton. The geology of the area is Upper Chalk with an undulating but extensive capping of clay-with-flints. The area of the excavations consists of a relatively level tract of high ground either side of the original western end of Mill Road. To the north and west the ground drops steeply into two dry valleys: the valley to the west was investigated by the Toadhole Bottom East valley transect. To the east and south the land drops more gently and is occupied by residential development while to the north west is a narrow strip of relatively level high ground, along which the Devil's Dyke Road runs, which links Red Hill with further high ground to the north-west. The site was the first on the A27 project to be investigated. It was initially chosen for excavation because the flintwork assemblage collected by Toms suggested the site had potential for establishing the nature of Downland settlement during the Mesolithic and Neolithic periods.

Objectives: to provide dates for the few features excavated on this site and see whether they tie in with the flintwork found.

Final comment: M Bennell and L Barber (30 September 1993), the samples submitted show that the few features located during the excavations cover the late Neolithic/early Bronze Age. This agrees well with the unstratified flintwork from the site and shows that early features can often still survive on clay-with-flints, even if the area has been intensively ploughed. Unfortunately, the substantial Mesolithic flintwork assemblage has no corresponding features or AMS dates.

References: Hedges *et al* 1994, 362

OxA–3246 4060 ±80 BP

δ¹³C: -24.8‰

Sample: 210861/110, submitted in 1991 by M Bennell

Material: charcoal: unidentified

Initial comment: from a charcoal-rich leached horizon just below a fire-cracked flint filled hearth. The sample was 250mm below the surface.

Objectives: the hearth was partly over an earlier ditch. Dating the hearth will give a terminal date for the ditch and establish whether the hearth is contemporary with the fire pit to the west. There is no diagnostic pottery, in fact no pottery at all, from the hearth or ditch.

Calibrated date: *1σ:* 2860–2470 cal BC
                       2σ: 2890–2410 cal BC

Final comment: M Bennell and L Barber (30 September 1993), this result gives the feature a late Neolithic date. Unfortunately no other associated dating material was present for the feature. The date does, however, suggest the sample from the ditch (OxA-3247), which the hearth overlay, is residual. The heart date correlates well with the bulk of the unstratified flintwork from the excavations.

OxA–3247 3700 ±80 BP

δ¹³C: -26.0‰ (assumed)

Sample: 210861/116, submitted in 1991 by M Bennell

Material: charcoal: unidentified

Initial comment: from a shallow amorphous ditch. It was below the level of intrusion by rootlets, and there was no tree disturbance in this area. The sample was 350mm below the surface.

Objectives: the ditch pre-dates the hearth, charcoal from which is also being dated. The two dates will corroborate each other and give an idea of the time difference between them. This could be considerable, as the site was a Mesolithic camp. There is no other dateable material from the ditch.

Calibrated date: 1σ: 2210–1970 cal BC
2σ: 2340–1880 cal BC

Final comment: M Bennell and L Barber (30 September 1993), the upper fill of this was root-disturbed in places and it seems likely that the sample, giving a late Neolithic-early Bronze Age date, was intrusive considering the hearth (OxA-3246) was stratigraphically later. The date range is not out of place, however, as OxA-3248 and the flintwork from the site show activity during this period.

OxA–3248 3810 ±70 BP

δ¹³C: -25.3‰

Sample: 210861/160, submitted in 1991 by M Bennell

Material: charcoal: *Pinus* sp. (J Hather)

Initial comment: from the base of a small pit, the lower layer of which was fire-cracked flints and charcoal. The sample was 470mm below the surface.

Objectives: the sample comes from the only feature in the part of the site west of the road. There is no other archaeological material within the feature which can be dated (except some fire-cracked flints) and no other diagnostic material associated with it. Dating the fire pit would help to define the length of continuing activities here on a known Mesolithic and early Bronze Age camp site.

Calibrated date: 1σ: 2400–2140 cal BC
2σ: 2480–2030 cal BC

Final comment: M Bennell and L Barber (30 September 1993), the late Neolithic/early Bronze Age date obtained from this isolated pit correlates well with the bulk of the flintwork from the ploughsoil over the site and shows this area to have been utilized at roughly the same period as that to the north-west, which produced OxA-3246–7.

Brighton Bypass: Sweetpatch Bottom, East Sussex

Location: TQ 304096
Lat. 50.52.14 N; Long. 00.08.48 W

Project manager: K Wilkinson (Institute of Archaeology, London), 1990

Archival body: Brighton Museum

Description: a sediment infilled dry valley situated north of Brighton, 0.5km east of the A23, in the Patcham area. The site is a 'bowl' at a height of *c* 50m OD, surrounded on its east, west, and north by the south scarp of the South

Downs, and on the south by the coastal plain. Over a period of approximately 10,000 years, and through various mechanisms, sediment has moved from the chalk escarpment and filled the 'bowl'.

Objectives: the overall aim of this series of samples was to date the associated environmental sequence, especially the adjacent snail sequence. Programmes of magnetic susceptibility measurements, flotation for charred macrofossils, and excavation for artefact recovery were also carried out (Wilkinson in Rudling 2002, 203–38).

Final comment: A Bayliss (1996), all samples were of small pieces of charcoal from discrete concentrations within the colluvium. OxA-2991–4 were from a single flotation column and were directly stratigraphically related (from the earliest OxA-2994, OxA-2993, OxA-2992, and OxA-2991). OxA-2995 was from the same archaeological sequence and section and was found at a lower level, although it was also 5m distant from the other samples. The taphonomy of material found within colluvium is always difficult to assess reliably. In this case it was hoped that the submission of material from charcoal concentrations would minimise the possibility that the material derived from substantially older deposits which had been reworked. Unfortunately, all of the charcoal was too small for identification to age or species to be possible. Analysis of the results from Sweetpatch Bottom demonstrates that both the stratigraphic sequence and the height sequence recording during excavation are statistically consistent with the radiocarbon results. This gives support to our use of these results to date the associated colluviation and environmental evidence. However, the lack of charcoal identification, and so the possibility of wood age offsets, and the uncertainties of the taphonomy of material from colluvium, mean that it is probably stretching the evidence too far to use this sequence to constrain the calibration of the results. Nevertheless, the simple calibrations of these results below are probably reasonably reliable indications of the date of the sequence from the site, showing that the lower portions at least are broadly contemporary with the nearby settlement evidence excavated at Downsview and Mile Oak.

Laboratory comment: Oxford Radiocarbon Accelerator Unit (1991), a further sample was submitted, SP90 samp 3, which consisted mostly of soil matrix with a limited amount of wood charcoal in the form of very small fragments. Despite picking out as much of the charcoal as was possible, we were unable to get a sufficient quantity to successfully pretreat and combust the sample. We were therefore not able to date it.

References: Bell 1983
Evans 1971
Hedges *et al* 1992, 146–7
Wilkinson *et al* 2002, 203–38

OxA–2991 2270 ±80 BP

δ¹³C: -25.1‰

Sample: SP90 samp 7, submitted on 2 January 1991 by K Wilkinson

Material: charcoal (unidentified)

Initial comment: from context 6, a calcareous, moderately compacted colluvial sediment, moderately stony with medium to very small flint pieces. This sample was situated 6cm above OxA-2992, and taken at a depth of 59.31m OD.

Objectives: the sample is associated with pottery of Bronze Age date, and also with a blip in the magnetic susceptibility curve, which it will be used to date. This blip could indicate burning or soil development. The sample is also immediately adjacent to a snail column and so can be directly used to date the column. Finally it will act as a check on the residuality of the pottery.

Calibrated date: 1σ: 410–200 cal BC
2σ: 520–120 cal BC

Final comment: K Wilkinson (1992), OxA-2991 to OxA-2994 are from the lowest layers of the sequence in the dry valley. They also give some indication as to the speed of accumulation of these colluvial deposits, the results showing that this was at a very slow rate in the Bronze Age and early Iron Age. However, other data show that accumulation in the historic period was at a greater rate. The consistency with which charcoal appears in contexts 6 and 7 nevertheless argues for considerable activity (probably agricultural) in the Bronze and Iron Ages.

OxA–2992 2410 ±80 BP

δ¹³C: -25.1‰

Sample: SP90 samp 8, submitted on 2 January 1991 by K Wilkinson

Material: charcoal: unidentified

Initial comment: one of three samples from context 7 (*see* also OxA-2993 and OxA-2994). Context 7 was a loosely compacted brown calcareous sediment, very stony with large to small sub angular flint. The sample was taken at a depth of 59.187m OD, 12cm below OxA-2994 and 6cm below OxA-2993.

Objectives: OxA-2992, OxA-2993, and OxA-2994 cover the range at which the deepest ceramics were found, hence radiocarbon dating is the only method of dating the sediments below which I believe to be a sort of clearance horizon (as evidenced by the large quantity of charcoal) which is particularly important to Sussex. The dating of these three samples will also act as a test on residuality on the pottery, which is early Bronze Age. The samples were taken at 6cm intervals from each other and like OxA-2991, are adjacent to a snail column. The dates produced can also be applied directly to the snail samples.

Calibrated date: 1σ: 750–390 cal BC
2σ: 790–360 cal BC

Final comment: see OxA-2991.

OxA–2993 2680 ±80 BP

δ¹³C: -26.4‰

Sample: SP90 samp 9, submitted on 2 January 1991 by K Wilkinson

Material: charcoal: unidentified

Initial comment: from context 7 (see also OxA-2992 and OxA-2994); taken at a depth of 59.127m OD, 6cm below OxA-2994 and 6cm above OxA-2992.

Objectives: as OxA-2992

Calibrated date: 1σ: 910–790 cal BC
2σ: 1010–670 cal BC

Final comment: see OxA-2991

OxA–2994 3560 ±80 BP

δ¹³C: -24.1‰

Sample: SP90 samp 10, submitted on 2 January 1991 by K Wilkinson

Material: charcoal: unidentified

Initial comment: from context 7 (see also OxA-2992 and OxA-2993); from a depth of 59.067m OD, 6cm above OxA-2993 and 12cm above OxA-2992.

Objectives: as OxA-2992

Calibrated date: 1σ: 2030–1770 cal BC
2σ: 2140–1690 cal BC

Final comment: K Wilkinson (1992), OxA-2994 effectively dates the onset of colluviation, and therefore probably the onset of intensive agriculture (the mollusc evidence shows open conditions throughout), to the middle Bronze Age period, tying in well with other colluvial deposits in Sussex (eg Bell 1983). *See* also OxA-2991.

References: Bell 1983

OxA–2995 3560 ±80 BP

δ¹³C: -24.8‰

Sample: SP90 samp 5, submitted on 2 January 1991 by K Wilkinson

Material: charcoal (unidentified)

Initial comment: from context 14, a subsoil hollow in the chalk fill, moderately stony, compact and clay rich. It appears to be less calcareous than the other sediments. The sample was taken from a depth of 59.322m OD.

Objectives: dating of this context is very important as it is of a pre-pottery period. All similar subsoil hollows have proven to be Mesolithic. Snail samples were taken adjacent to where this sample was found, and the dates could have implications for the colonisation of snails after the last Glacial. Thus it is vital to know when in the Mesolithic this deposit came from. If later than the Mesolithic there are implications as to the cause of deposition.

Calibrated date: 1σ: 2030–1770 cal BC
2σ: 2140–1690 cal BC

Final comment: K Wilkinson (1992), OxA-2995 is from a hollow in the chalk bedrock, at the very base of the section. Such hollows have been interpreted as being Mesolithic in origin (eg BM-1544; 6820 ±85 BP; 5890–5560 cal BC at 95% confidence; Reimer *et al* 2004; Bell 1983), having been caused by tree throw (Evans 1971). This result shows that this process was not confined to the Mesolithic, and the similarity with OxA-2994 suggests it could be associated with increased agricultural activity.

References: Bell 1983
Evans 1971
Reimer *et al* 2004

Brighton Bypass: Toadhole Bottom East, East Sussex

Location: TQ 278077
Lat. 50.51.15 N; Long. 00.11.03 W

Project manager: K Wilkinson (Institute of Archaeology, London), 1989

Archival body: Brighton Museum

Description: Toadhole Bottom East and West are branches of the same dry valley system, which merge a little to the east of where the trenches were cut.

Objectives: this sequence of samples relates to snail assemblages studied from the site. Interest particularly focused on the dates of tree clearance and colluviation and on the possibility that, in conjunction with the sequence from Toadhole Bottom West, a complete environmental sequence running from the late glacial to the present day could be studied.

Final comment: A Bayliss (1996), the radiocarbon dates from this site are statistically significantly inconsistent in relation to the stratigraphic sequence (A=7.5%; Bronk Ramsey 1995; *see* archive). This is because OxA-3077 is significantly too old. This difference is probably too large to be accounted for by the 'old-wood effect' (Bowman 1990, 15), since few native trees grow to be a thousand years old. It is more likely that the charcoal was residual in the buried soil. The two measurements from the subsoil hollow, OxA-3078 and OxA-3079, are not significantly different at 95% confidence (T'=0.0; T'(5%)=3.8; ν=1; Ward and Wilson 1978). This does not contradict the contention that the charcoal from this hollow relates to the event of tree clearance. Excluding OxA-3077, the three remaining determinations are consistent with the stratigraphy (A=99.2%; Bronk Ramsey 1995; *see* archive), although again the lack of charcoal identification and the uncertainties of the taphonomy of material from colluvium, mean that it is probably stretching the evidence too far to use this sequence to constrain the calibration of the results. Nevertheless, the consistency of the radiocarbon measurements supports the case for these results reliably dating the environmental sequence at this site, suggesting that this dates to the first half of the second millennium BC.

References: Bell 1983
Bowman 1990
Bronk Ramsey 1995
Evans 1972
Hedges *et al* 1992, 146
Kerney 1977
Thorley 1981
Ward and Wilson 1978

OxA-3077 4020 ±90 BP

δ¹³C: -25.7‰

Sample: THBE 1038, submitted on 4 February 1991 by K Wilkinson

Material: charcoal (unidentified)

Initial comment: from context 1038, a buried soil consisting of dark red brown clay silt and containing a small amount of charcoal; it is very silt/clay rich with only a few stones, and is

decalcified as there were few snails. The context starts at 176cm and finishes at 186cm below the ground surface. The layer does seem truncated in some places, but the sample was taken where the context is at its thickest. Below the context are late glacial solifluxion deposits.

Objectives: this sample is important to date as it represents the only early postglacial soil (probably Neolithic) found on any of the sites. As such it represents a standstill phase before initial colluviation with context 1035. This sample together with that from 1035 (OxA-3080) will give some indication as to a hiatus (if present) between these contexts and therefore give some idea as to the period of stability. One piece of Neolithic pottery has come from 1038, although there is a possibility this may be residual. This sample will also allow correlation with samples from Toadhole Bottom West.

Calibrated date: 1σ: 2840–2460 cal BC
2σ: 2880–2290 cal BC

Final comment: K Wilkinson (1992), the date produced, and the relatively open nature of the mollusc fauna, suggests that forest clearance had already occurred by the late Neolithic, although the absence of colluvium could suggest that this clearance was relatively local in extent.

OxA-3078 3560 ±80 BP

δ¹³C: -23.8‰

Sample: THBE 1029(i), submitted on 4 February 1991 by K Wilkinson

Material: charcoal: *Pinus* sp. (J G Hather)

Initial comment: from context 1029; from the fill of a subsoil hollow. These have been interpreted by Evans (1972) as tree throw hollows. The context is a mid brown silty clay with a rich snail fauna, much charcoal and worked flint, and the layer is very well defined. The context is *c* 0.04m thick and has 1038 above it, and chalk bedrock below. There are large numbers of molluscs so it should be quite calcareous.

Objectives: the sample should be dated as it has several implications. Firstly, it is the earliest context on any of my sites with human activity. Secondly, the snail fauna is very interesting, indicating some period Atlantic, Mollusc zone D² (Kerney 1977). Thirdly, Bell had a similar fauna from a subsoil hollow with a date of cal BC 8020-7540 at 95% confidence (BM-1544, 8770 ±90 BP; Bell 1983, 135; Burleigh *et al* 1981, 16). This is interesting as one species, *Pomatias elegans*, also present in this sample, has not been known before this date. The sample is half of a half-section of the hollow, the other half being OxA-3079. The two together could act as a check for this most important date.

Calibrated date: 1σ: 2030–1770 cal BC
2σ: 2140–1690 cal BC

Final comment: K Wilkinson (1992), OxA-3078 and OxA-3079 come from opposite sides of a subsoil hollow. The shade-loving molluscan fauna from this hollow suggests a pre-Neolithic date, ie very similar to Kerney's zone D² dating to 7500 ±100 BP (St-3410; 6560–6110 cal BC at 95% confidence; Reimer *et al* 2004; Kerney 1977). However, both OxA-3078 and OxA-3079 show early to mid-Bronze Age dates, suggesting that the tree throw creating this hollow occurred during this period. If this is the case it would suggest that (local) clearance in the Neolithic was not maintained in the Bronze Age, large scale clearance only occurring in the middle Bronze Age (OxA-3080).

References: Bell 1983, 135
Evans 1972
Kerney 1977
Reimer *et al* 2004

OxA–3079 3550 ±90 BP

δ¹³C: -27.7‰

Sample: THBE 1029 (ii), submitted on 4 February 1991 by K Wilkinson

Material: charcoal: *Pinus* sp. (J G Hather)

Initial comment: as OxA-3078

Objectives: as OxA-3078

Calibrated date: 1σ: 2030–1750 cal BC
2σ: 2140–1680 cal BC

Final comment: see OxA-3078

OxA–3080 3260 ±70 BP

δ¹³C: -27.7‰

Sample: THBE 1035, submitted on 4 February 1991 by K Wilkinson

Material: charcoal (unidentified)

Initial comment: from context 1035, a mid dark brown clay silt. The context contained considerable quantities of charcoal, but of a very small size thus only a small amount was recovered. The layer starts at 162cm and finishes at 176cm below the ground surface. This layer is not calcareous as no snails were present. Below this context is the probable buried soil 1038, and above is the first colluvial layer 1034.

Objectives: this context probably represents a clearance horizon, as there is a great deal of charcoal, and magnetic susceptibility shows a peak here. Clearance is probably Bronze Age, but this is no means certain. The snail fauna certainly changes after this point to become one typical of colluvial cleared ground (above) and below is a woodland type of fauna. This sample would allow comparison with OxA-3077, to see if there is a hiatus between the buried soil (OxA-3077) and the supposed clearance horizon (this sample, OxA-3080).

Calibrated date: 1σ: 1620–1440 cal BC
2σ: 1740–1410 cal BC

Final comment: K Wilkinsin (1992), OxA-3080 is from the layer immediately above OxA-3077, and is from the first colluvial deposit, and thus probably marks the onset of large-scale agriculture. A further argument for this is the almost total absence of any shade-loving mollusc species in this layer. The middle Bronze date for this clearance ties in well with other work in Sussex, where forest clearance in the Bronze Age has been hypothesised (eg Bell 1983; Thorley 1981).

References: Bell 1983
Thorley 1981

Brighton Bypass: Toadhole Bottom West, East Sussex

Location: TQ 277077
Lat. 50.51.15 N; Long. 00.11.08 W

Project manager: K Wilkinson (Institute of Archaeology, London), 1990

Archival body: Brighton Museum

Description: Toadhole Bottom East and West are branches of the same dry valley system, which merge a little to the east of where the trenches were cut.

Objectives: the upper part of the environmental sequence at this site was dated to complement the programme of work at Toadhole Bottom East, and to produce a complete sequence from the late glacial to the present date.

Final comment: A Bayliss (1996), OxA-3081 and OxA-3083 are from the same layer of colluvium, 1045, and are not statistically significantly different at 95% confidence (T'=0.1; T'(5%)-3.8; v=1; Ward and Wilson 1978). This suggests that the measurements should provide a reliable indication of the date of the layer. However, like OxA-3077 from Toadhole Bottom East, OxA-3082 is far too early to be consistent with the stratigraphic sequence (A=0.0%; Bronk Ramsey 1995; *see* archive). Again this anomaly is of such a magnitude that the reworking of old material in the deposits seems the most likely explanation. The two dates from 1045 do support the contention that colluviation occurred slightly later here than at Toadhole Bottom East, although the two sequences do not provide an environmental record for the whole of the Holocene.

References: Bronk Ramsey 1995
Hedges *et al* 1992, 146
Ward and Wilson 1978

OxA–3081 2700 ±90 BP

δ¹³C: -28.5‰

Sample: THBW 260, submitted on 4 March 1991 by K Wilkinson

Material: charcoal (unidentified)

Initial comment: from the bottom of context 1045, a silty dark brown clay loam. The layer is calcareous to a certain extent, but there is no rootlet activity. The context begins at 134cm below the ground surface and finishes at 152cm. It immediately overlay a layer of large flint nodules (1047) and underlies 1044.

Objectives: this sample represents the initiation of colluviation in this dry valley, and thus it is important to date. The snail information shows an open landscape so a hypothesis of the initial colluviation being caused by ploughing seems probable. This result could date the onset of ploughing in this valley; and also determine how long a period of time this layer accumulated over (together with OxA-3083 from the top of the layer). The date will also be compared to that for the clearance at Toadhole Bottom East to see if they correlate.

Calibrated date: 1σ: 930–790 cal BC
2σ: 1050–670 cal BC

Final comment: K Wilkinson (1992), Toadhole Bottom West seems to have a later history of colluviation than Toadhole Bottom East. OxA-3081 and OxA-3083 come from the deepest large-scale colluvial layer (the layers below were devoid of charcoal). The late Bronze Age/early Iron Age dates indicate an increase in (possibly agricultural) activity in this period.

OxA–3082 3520 ±90 BP

δ¹³C: -25.5‰

Sample: THBW 3, submitted on 4 March 1991 by K Wilkinson

Material: charcoal (unidentified)

Initial comment: a collection of fragments of wood charcoal from context 1044, a medium dark brown silty clay loam. The sample was taken as a discrete spot sample. There are no sign of rootlets. The layer is colluvial in nature, probably being formed by plough action and gravity in unison. The context starts at 98cm below the modern ground level and finishes at 134cm. Pottery in the layer is mostly East Sussex Ware (Iron Age and Romano-British). There was no visible disturbance, and the environment is reasonably calcareous as snail preservation is good.

Objectives: although pottery in the layer was Roman/Iron Age, this context could be medieval (ie pottery residuality). It is important to know the date as this context marks an impoverishment of the snail fauna to one of a very open nature demonstrating increased cultivation. Thus it is important to demonstrate when this intensification took place. Dates have also been submitted for the context below (1045) which has the first fauna present on the site and shows the first clearance. Samples have also been submitted from the sister site at Toadhole Bottom East and it is important to correlate the two.

Calibrated date: 1σ: 1960–1740 cal BC
2σ: 2140–1620 cal BC

Final comment: K Wilkinson (1992), OxA-3082 is from the layer stratigraphically above OxA-3081 and OxA-3083, and therefore its early/middle Bronze Age date must suggest the reworking of a previously laid deposit, illustrating the problem of dating colluvial contexts.

OxA–3083 2660 ±70 BP

δ¹³C: -24.2‰

Sample: THBW 2, submitted on 4 March 1991 by K Wilkinson

Material: charcoal (unidentified)

Initial comment: from the same context (1045) as OxA-3081, *see* above. The sample comes from the top of the context.

Objectives: this sample represents the period in the biostratigraphy just prior to reduction in the fauna in 1044. It is thus important to know if there is a hiatus of deposition as represented by the dates OxA-3082 and OxA-3083. This hiatus could represent a cessation of agriculture (if it is present at all). Pottery from the context is again East Sussex Ware, but there are no medieval sherds. This date, together with OxA-3081, will allow the period of deposition of this layer to be attained.

Calibrated date: 1σ: 900–790 cal BC
2σ: 980–670 cal BC

Final comment: see OxA-3081

Bromfield, Shropshire

Location: SO 485775
Lat. 52.23.34 N; Long. 02.45.25 W

Project manager: S Stanford and G Hughes (University of Birmingham), 1978–9, 1981, and 1991

Archival body: Shropshire County Museum

Description: Neolithic and Beaker occupation, and a mid-late Bronze Age cemetery.

Objectives: to provide a chronology for the site.

Final comment: G Hughes (16 August 1995), the early date provided by OxA-4207 provides additional evidence of Neolithic activity at Bromfield. However, it is of little assistance in refining the date of the ring ditch B10. The date from the primary fill at the central feature (OxA-4210) and from the cremation pit (OxA-4208) suggest an early Bronze Age date for the monument associated with ring ditch B9. The two dates from the central feature appear to support the suggestion made by the soil micro-morphological analysis that the later stages of infilling was a slow gradual process perhaps taking several hundred years.

Laboratory comment: English Heritage (8 March 2012), one further date from this site was funded prior to 1981 and published in Jordan *et al* (1994, 27; HAR-3968), and seven further dates were funded between 1981 and 1988 and published in Bayliss *et al* (2012, 42–4; HAR-6544–7, -6560–1, and -6566).

References: Bayliss *et al* 2012
Hedges *et al* 1994, 361
Jordan *et al* 1994, 27
Stanford 1982
Stanford 1985
Stanford 1995

OxA–4207 4570 ±95 BP

δ¹³C: -24.2‰

Sample: 55-F6(1009), submitted in January 1993 by E G Hughes

Material: charcoal: *Quercus* sp., one fragment; *Corylus* sp., 18 fragments and one fragment of nut shell (R Gale 1991)

Initial comment: from a sandy silt and gravel deposit (1009) near the bottom of a bowl-shaped pit (F6), cut by a ring ditch thought to be Iron Age in date (B10, F2). The sample comprised of a scatter of charcoal fragments approximately 0.8m below the surface and 0.5m below the top of the pit. A larger charcoal sample was collected from overlying context (1008) but it was felt that the context was too secondary to be of use in dating the feature.

Objectives: no other dating evidence or artefacts were obtained from this feature. It is hoped that the radiocarbon date will assist in placing this enigmatic feature within the overall sequence being developed at Bromfield. The date will also provide a *terminus post quem* for the construction of the ring ditch itself. This information will be particularly useful in the light of the unusual find of Iron Age artefacts from the associated inhumation burial (F4).

Calibrated date: 1σ: 3500–3100 cal BC
2σ: 3630–2940 cal BC

Final comment: G Hughes (16 August 1995), the date has provided a *terminus post quem* for the ring ditch B10. While not very informative in this respect it does provide further evidence for earlier Neolithic activity at Bromfield. Previous evidence was recorded by Stan Stanford underlying a nearby barrow (B15) and from a group of pits containing Neolithic pottery.

OxA–4208 3510 ±90 BP

δ¹³C: -25.9‰

Sample: 57-F8(2003), submitted in January 1993 by E G Hughes

Material: charcoal: *Salix/Populus sp.* (R Gale 1993)

Initial comment: from a concentration of charcoal fragments associated with fragments of cremated bone within a small cremation pit (F8); approximately 0.4m below the surface. The pit was a small feature located near the inner edge of the northern part of ring ditch (F3).

Objectives: to assist in the establishment of both a relative and an absolute chronology for the monument (BG). No datable artefacts were collected from the cremation pit or any of the associated features and no stratigraphic relationships existed.

Calibrated date: 1σ: 1950–1690 cal BC
2σ: 2130–1610 cal BC

Final comment: G Hughes (16 August 1995), the result is considered to be a fairly reliable date indicator for the deposition of the cremation. It suggests approximate contemporaneity with the construction of the central pit (OxA-4210) and with previously dated cremations from a nearby barrow (B15).

OxA–4209 2970 ±100 BP

δ¹³C: -25.4‰

Sample: 58-F22 (2016), submitted in January 1993 by E G Hughes

Material: charcoal: unidentified

Initial comment: from a localised concentration of charcoal (2016) within a clayey silt fill (2015) of large feature (F22), at the centre of ring ditch (F3, barrow B9). The sample was collected approximately 0.9m below the surface.

Objectives: no datable artefacts were collected from this feature. A date should assist in providing an absolute and relative chronology for the monument (B9). In particular the chronological relationship between this central feature and the surrounding ring ditch is unclear. This date will also assist (together with a date from the primary fill, OxA-4210) and the soil micromorphological analysis) with determining the manner in which the feature has silted up.

Calibrated date: 1σ: 1380–1020 cal BC
2σ: 1440–910 cal BC

Final comment: G Hughes (16 August 1995), the apparent difference between this result and that for sample OxA-4210 supports the suggestion made by the soil micromorphological analysis that the later stages of infilling of the central feature was a slow, gradual process, possibly taking several hundred years.

OxA–4210 3535 ±105 BP

δ¹³C: -24.2‰

Sample: 59-F22 (2034), submitted in January 1993 by E G Hughes

Material: charcoal: unidentified

Initial comment: from the primary fill (2034) of feature (F22) at the centre of ring ditch F3 (B9). The fill consisted of silt and gravel suggesting a rapid infilling of the feature soon after its construction. It seems likely that charcoal was deposited within this fill early in the history of the feature. The sample was collected approximately 1.2m below the surface.

Objectives: to provide an approximate date for the establishment of the feature. This information will assist in the placing of the feature and the associated ring ditch within the overall sequence at Bromfield.

Calibrated date: 1σ: 2030–1740 cal BC
2σ: 2200–1610 cal BC

Final comment: G Hughes (16 August 1995), the result has assisted in the interpretation of the infilling processes relating to the central feature (*see also* OxA-4209). The result is also comparable to that from the nearby cremation pit, OxA-4208, suggesting approximate contemporaneity. Together, the two features suggest an early Bronze Age date for the monument.

Burton Dassett, Warwickshire

Location: SP 38715203
Lat. 52.09.53 N; Long. 01.26.02 W

Project manager: N Palmer (Warwickshire Museum), 1987

Archival body: Warwickshire Museum

Description: a deserted medieval market town, which prospered during the fourteenth and fifteenth centuries AD, but was abandoned by AD 1500. Excavations were carried out in advance of the construction of the M40 motorway.

Objectives: to provide dating evidence for the programme of sampling for charred and cereal remains carried out, and to establish whether spelt wheat was being cultivated in the medieval period.

References: Gaimster *et al* 1989
Hedges *et al* 1990, 223
Moffett 1991

OxA–2226 1530 ±70 BP

δ¹³C: -24.4‰

Sample: BD86 B 679/1/2, submitted on 4 February 1988 by N Palmer

Material: carbonised plant macrofossil (*Triticum spelta,* chaff) (L Moffett)

Initial comment: from pit 679, a large shallow subcircular pit (1.8m × 1.6m × 0.2m deep) with a sloping, rounded profile and a single fill layer (679/1) of olive (Munsell 5Y4/4) clay loam with occasional small pieces of limestone (1%). The sample has been extracted from a 25 litre soil sample taken from the centre of the pit. The pit was cut into the natural subsoil and overlaid by topsoil.

Objectives: to establish whether the spelt wheat was medieval rather than residual Romano-British material.

Calibrated date: 1σ: cal AD 420–610
2σ: cal AD 390–660

Final comment: L Moffett (1990), the cultivation of spelt wheat in Britain is believed to have declined at the end of the Roman period, although it continued on the continent into the twentieth century. Spelt has occasionally been found in medieval contexts in Britain. These finds have not previously been radiocarbon dated, and it is possible that either they represent residual early material, or that spelt continued to be cultivated in Britain as on the continent. This date shows that spelt from Burton Dassett is residual from the late Roman/Dark Age and thus derives from the end of the period in which spelt is known to have been cultivated in Britain.

Cambridgeshire Dykes, Cambridgeshire

Location: TL 51454753 and TL 548541
Lat. 52.06.18 N; Long. 00.12.42 E, and
Lat. 52.09.47 N; Long. 00.15.48 E

Project manager: B Robinson (Cambridge Archaeological Unit), 1991–92

Description: a series of four linear earthworks (Devil's, Fleam, Brent, and Bran), which traverse the chalk plain of south Cambridgeshire. Each of the earthworks is comprised of a single bank and ditch running in a north-westerly to south-easterly direction. Traditionally, they were thought to be East Anglian defences built as a response to Mercian aggression in the mid seventh century.

Objectives: to establish a firm chronological framework for these monuments, presumed to be of Anglo-Saxon date.

Final comment: T Malim (1995), a sequence of well-stratified radiocarbon dates has established that the first phase of Fleam Dyke was most probably constructed in the fifth century AD. Ensuing phases, which produced the typical profile of the monument as it survives today, were sixth century or later in date, and, by analogy, the other three Cambridgeshire Dykes (Bran Ditch, Brent Ditch, Devils Dyke) are assumed to be of similar date (Malim 1996).

References: Malim 1996

Cambridgeshire Dykes: Brent Ditch, Cambridgeshire

Location: TL 51454753
Lat. 52.06.18 N; Long. 00.12.42 E

Project manager: B Robinson (Cambridge Archaeological Unit), 1992

Archival body: Cambridgeshire County Council

Description: Brent Ditch survives as an earthwork for nearly 4km. The northern end at 30m OD has been cut through the glacial sands and gravels which cap the middle chalk. It crosses a band of middle chalk before rising up to 80m at its northern terminal at Abington Park. There it abuts a spur of boulder clay. Two sections were excavated at Brent Ditch in advance of the destruction of a considerable segment due to road-widening activities. At this point the monument, presumed to be Anglo-Saxon, survives as a shallow linear depression running across cultivated land. Excavation revealed that the monument was much more substantial than previously thought. No bank has survived in this area though the ditch is well preserved. Its original profile was similar to those of Devil's Dyke and Fleam Dyke: exceptionally steep-sided and flat-bottomed.

Objectives: Fleam Dyke, Devil's Dyke, and Brent Ditch have been dated by artefacts in the buried soil beneath their banks to the later or post-Roman period. None can be dated closer than AD 350–905. Brent Ditch has not yet been dated at all, but is assumed to fit into this range.

Final comment: T Malim (13 August 1993), the present dating of human bone from Brent Ditch has been interpreted as residual surface material included in ditch fill. The date formed part of a series of samples collected during excavations through the Cambridgeshire Dykes in an endeavour to gain scientific dates for these monuments independent of the generally subjective dating, which has assigned them to the later pagan Anglo-Saxon period.

References: Hedges *et al* 1994, 364
Robinson 1992

OxA–4065 2105 ±55 BP

δ¹³C: -18.5‰

Sample: PAMBD92/16, submitted on 5 January 1993 by T Malim

Material: human bone (pelvis fragment) (C Duhig)

Initial comment: the find was recovered from the base of Brent Ditch, 2.5m from the ground surface, and sealed by rapidly accumulating weathering in fills of almost pure chalk. The find must have been washed into the ditch within the first few months of its life. There was no root or earthworm activity at this depth and no recutting or other disturbance.

Objectives: the bone, from secure deposits within the ditch, can potentially provide a much tighter date than other artefacts as it must be expected to survive less well on the surface (in a ploughsoil) than pottery or coins. Therefore it probably represents the date of deposition closer to the cutting of the ditch.

Calibrated date: 1σ: 200–40 cal BC
2σ: 360 cal BC–cal AD 20

Final comment: T Malim (26 July 1993), this sample, from basal fills of the ditch, has given an anomalous date of the first century BC from deposits that also contained second century AD Roman coins. The sample is therefore interpreted as having come from residual material.

Cambridgeshire Dykes: Fleam Dyke, Cambridgeshire

Location: TL 548541
Lat. 52.09.47 N; Long. 00.15.48 E

Project manager: G Wait (Cambridge Archaeological Unit), 1991

Archival body: Cambridgeshire County Council

Description: a section across the Cambridgeshire Fleam Dyke Scheduled Ancient Monument (Cambridgeshire 6) was undertaken prior to the duelling of the A11 trunk road. The Fleam Dyke extends from the Fen edge between Fulbourn and Little Wilbraham towards the south-east, for a distance of about five miles. Thereafter, for a further two miles it is greatly diminished in size, appearing only as a large embanked hedge.

Objectives: to establish whether more than one construction phase could be identified and to date the dyke more accurately than post-third century to pre-tenth century.

Final comment: T Malim (1995), the seven dates received firmly establish an early Anglo-Saxon date for construction and use of the Fleam Dyke, mostly within the fifth and sixth centuries AD. The dates also demonstrate the longevity of the monument commensurate with its complex stratigraphic sequence and its division into at least three phases of construction; a period of between 130–340 years can be calculated for this use with a 95% probability. These results move debate on the origins and purpose of the Fleam, and other Cambridgeshire Dykes, to a more defined period, and one that is earlier than generally believed by scholars in the past. The dates emphasise the importance of establishing chronological sequences through our major monuments by use of absolute dating methods.

Laboratory comment: English Heritage (26 January 2012), six further samples were submitted for dating after March 1993 (OxA-5349-54).

References: Hedges *et al* 1994, 364
Wait 1991

OxA–4066 1580 ±55 BP

δ¹³C: -21.8‰

Sample: BALFD91 (22)SA1, submitted on 8 February 1993 by P Spoerry

Material: animal bone (unidentified)

Initial comment: from context 22, one of the phase 1 bank deposits of the Dyke itself; from a layer of silt with chalk fragments, well above the water table at a depth of 1.5m from the current ground surface. It is believed that context 22 represents the surface of the phase 1 bank. The subsoil is chalk-derived. There is a slight possibility of animal burrow disturbance.

Objectives: no dating evidence is currently available from within the bank phases. Buried soil beneath the banks produced residual Roman material, but no better information is currently available. The monument is traditionally believed to date to the mid-seventh century AD, however, at present it can only be dated within the bracket of the fourth to tenth centuries AD.

Calibrated date: 1σ: cal AD 410–550
2σ: cal AD 350–610

Final comment: P Spoerry (1994), a very useful date indeed, and the first radiocarbon date from any of the four Cambridgeshire Dykes. The Dykes have been assigned a middle Saxon date in the past reflecting on Anglian response to Penda's Mercia in the seventh century. The fifth-century date established by this sample from a stabilization layer capping the first phase bank, gives Fleam Dyke an initial construction date more in keeping with the earlier period of British-Saxon tension and conflict. It emphasises the importance of obtaining further radiocarbon dates from the other two major episodes of bank construction, and primary ditch fills.

Cannington, Somerset

Location: ST 252406
Lat. 51.09.33 N; Long. 03.04.11 W

Project manager: S Hirst (University College London), 1962–3

Archival body: Somerset County Council Museum Service

Description: the site is on the northern rim of Cannington Park Quarry, which exploits limestone of Carboniferous age. Cannington is an important period cemetery with a possible Roman or even earlier origin. This is of interest as an exposition of mortuary behaviour in one of the most challenging periods of British history and as providing physical details of the large sample of a population in the area over several centuries.

Objectives: it is hoped that radiocarbon dating can be used to answer general questions concerning chronology and spatial development and to provide a date range for individual graves. It could help define limits before and after which the cemetery was not used; to suggest peaks or troughs of burial intensity and to define a minimum period of use.

Final comment: S Hirst (13 July 1994), dating for the Cannington cemetery, of several hundred graves, is based on radiocarbon, and on a small number of dated objects found in graves; most graves have no finds. The series of radiocarbon determinations are fundamental in providing an overall likely range for burial, from the mid fourth to the late seventh centuries AD; and in providing date ranges for individual graves, which have given a basis for the study of the spatial and temporal development of the cemetery. OxA-3446 (2020 ±75 BP; 210 cal BC–cal AD 130 at 95% confidence; Reimer *et al* 2004) is of animal bones and shows they are much earlier than the cemetery.

Laboratory comment: English Heritage (17 January 2012), twenty-five dates from this site were published in Bayliss *et al* (2012, 52–7; HAR-5483–9, -6255–6, -6259, -6269–70, -7097–8, -8049–53, -8806–7, and -9135–8).

References: Hedges *et al* 1993, 162
Rahtz *et al* 2000
Reimer *et al* 2004

OxA–3446 2020 ±75 BP

δ¹³C: -21.2‰

Sample: CAN FT 17, submitted on 15 February 1991 by S M Hirst

Material: animal bone: *Ovis* sp., astragali (nine left, eight right) (S Payne 1991)

Initial comment: from the remains of at least 18 sheep aged between 15 and 18 months, buried in pit FT17 dug into limestone bedrock. The pitfill contains Roman and prehistoric sherds, but these may be residual. Many of the other bones were damaged by rootlets despite the depth of the pit (*c* 1m).

Objectives: to date the sheep skeletons for zooarchaeological interest and to establish whether they are contemporary with the cemetery and occupation or later.

Calibrated date: 1σ: 160 cal BC–cal AD 70
2σ: 210 cal BC–cal AD 130

Final comment: S Hirst (13 July 1994), thought by the excavators to be either of the period of the cemetery or modern. So the date ranges are a considerable surprise and the only evidence for late Iron Age/early Roman use of the site. The purpose of the pit is not known.

Causewayed enclosures: Haddenham, Upper Delphs, Cambridgeshire

Location: TL 412737
Lat. 52.20.34 N; Long. 00.04.23 E

Project manager: C Evans (Cambridge Archaeological Unit) and I Hodder (University of Cambridge), 1985

Archival body: Cambridgeshire County Council

Description: from the structural sequence of the Upper Delphs causewayed enclosure.

Objectives: to date the period of construction and use of the causewayed enclosure.

Final comment: C Evans and I Hodder (2004), generally these results are not helpful in clarifying the chronology of the enclosure, and further dates should have been obtained. Based on these results, and those from comparable early Neolithic assemblages in the region, in all likelihood the primary usage of the enclosure occurred between *c* 3750–3400 cal BC.

Laboratory comment: English Heritage (17 January 2012), four further dates from this site were published in Bayliss *et al* (2012, 131; HAR-8092–4, and HAR-8096).

References: Bayliss *et al* 2012
Evans and Hodder 2006a
Hardiman *et al* 1992, 64–5
Whittle *et al* 2011, 271–8

HAR–10512 4490 ±140 BP

δ¹³C: -25.2‰

Sample: HAD87CE, submitted in July 1988 by C Evans

Material: peat

Initial comment: peat from [3992] in ditch segment O from the causewayed enclosure.

Objectives: to date late recutting of the enclosure.

Calibrated date: 1σ: 3490–2920 cal BC
2σ: 3640–2870 cal BC

Final comment: C Evans (20 July 2004), as far as could be ascertained (there being some slight doubt of the exact provenance of this sample) it dates the later Neolithic (terminal) recutting of causewayed enclosure ditch O, and it is therefore considered reasonable.

HAR–10518 4020 ±110 BP

δ¹³C: -26.8‰

Sample: 3911, submitted in July 1988 by C Evans

Material: charcoal: unidentified

Initial comment: from the fill of a small pit located in the middle of the causewayed enclosure, immediately exterior to the HAD VIII enclosure. The pit contained domestic rubbish, worked flint, and plain ware bowls.

Objectives: to date an important assemblage of plain late Neolithic bowls and to ascertain whether the material is contemporary with the later (terminal) usage of the causewayed enclosure, or the HAD VIII enclosure (second millennium BC).

Calibrated date: 1σ: 2840–2460 cal BC
2σ: 2890–2200 cal BC

Final comment: C Evans (2004), this result cannot provide a reliable date for this pit given the assemblages of artefacts, and is probably 500–1000 years too late.

HAR–10520 4690 ±90 BP

δ¹³C: -24.7‰

Sample: 0632, submitted in July 1988 by C Evans

Material: charcoal: unidentified

Initial comment: from a burnt post in the secondary fills of the east side of the butt end of the causewayed enclosure ditch (segment C).

Objectives: to date the later phase of activity and usage in the eastern side of the Upper Delphs causewayed enclosure.

Calibrated date: 1σ: 3640–3360 cal BC
2σ: 3660–3130 cal BC

Final comment: C Evans and I Hodder (2004), this result is consistent with those from the primary fills of the enclosure (HAR-8093 and HAR-8096), and fits well with the later part of the range of dates for Mildenhall ceramics.

Causewayed enclosures: Staines (interior), Surrey

Location:	TQ 0241072610
	Lat. 51.26.33 N; Long. 00.31.35 W
Project manager:	R Robertson-Mackay (English Heritage), 1961–63
Archival body:	English Heritage, Natural History Museum, and British Museum

Description: a Neolithic causewayed enclosure covering a total area of approximately 2.4ha, defined by double concentric interrupted ditches, which were for the most part naturally filled. There were many traces of activity within the interior, presumed to be contemporary with the ditches, including pits, gullies, post and stakeholes, and varying concentrations of struck and burnt flint, and pottery. Human burials were found. There is little Ebbsfleet pottery in secondary contexts and there are later prehistoric, Roman, and medieval finds.

Objectives: the threat of destruction of the site for gravel extraction led to rescue excavations. The excavations developed gradually and in accordance with the progress of gravel extraction.

Final comment: R Robertson-Mackay (1987), insufficient charcoal came from early Neolithic contexts for a reliable date. The bone samples produced dates which were too recent, possibly due to humic acids in the ground water.

References:	Robertson-Mackay 1987
	Whittle *et al* 2011, 388–93

HAR–8439 1440 ±80 BP

$\delta^{13}C$: -28.3‰

Sample: 16F53, submitted in 1982 by L Blackmore

Material: charcoal: unidentified

Initial comment: from a small pit *c* 0.25m deep, within the interior of the neolithic enclosure. No other finds were obtained from this feature, which would appear to be associated with a number of other sterile features possibly representing the remains of a timber structure.

Objectives: to confirm the date of the enclosure.

Calibrated date:	*1σ:* cal AD 540–660
	2σ: cal AD 420–770

Final comment: R Robertson-Mackay (1987), associated with a complex of postholes. Once again the date would be too recent.

HAR–9023 1520 ±70 BP

$\delta^{13}C$: -25.3‰

Sample: 50F1423, submitted in July 1982 by L Blackmore

Material: charcoal (remaining subsample identified): unidentified (0.92g); *Betula* sp. (0.46g, 100%)

Initial comment: from a large pit 0.69m deep, within the interior of the Neolithic enclosure (layer 3). Other finds include Neolithic flint and pottery, and 24 fragments of daub. Romano-British pottery was found in the uppermost fill (layer 1).

Objectives: to confirm the date of the enclosure.

Calibrated date:	*1σ:* cal AD 430–620
	2σ: cal AD 390–660

Final comment: F Healy (2008), this date was unexpected as this feature was thought to be Neolithic on submission of the sample.

References:	Hardiman *et al* 1992, 59

HAR–9025 1290 ±80 BP

$\delta^{13}C$: -28.0‰

Sample: 34F1542, submitted in October 1988 by L Blackmore

Material: charcoal (charcoal, remaining sparse subsample identified): unidentified (0.12g); *Quercus* sp. (0.01g, 50%); *Betula* sp. (0.01g, 50%) (R Gale 2000)

Initial comment: from the lower fill of a posthole of probable Neolithic date, within the interior of the Neolithic enclosure. This feature forms one of a complex of eight postholes possibly representing a timber structure.

Objectives: as HAR-9023

Calibrated date:	*1σ:* cal AD 650–810
	2σ: cal AD 600–940

Final comment: see HAR-9023

HAR–9026 1380 ±80 BP

$\delta^{13}C$: -25.6‰

Sample: 12F332, submitted in October 1988 by L Blackmore

Material: charcoal: unidentified

Initial comment: from a gully within the interior of the Neolithic enclosure. This feature cuts the pit which cuts that producing sample 12F342 (AML 822662, no result). It may be related to a complex of sterile features including that producing sample 16F53 (HAR-8439). Both Iron Age and Saxon pottery were found in the upper fill of this feature.

Objectives: to establish the date of the enclosure and to confirm/support the date of HAR-8439.

Calibrated date:	*1σ:* cal AD 600–690
	2σ: cal AD 540–780

Final comment: F Healy (2008), this date confirms the unexpected Saxon activity within the Neolithic enclosure.

References:	Hardiman *et al* 1992, 59

Causewayed enclosures: Staines (trench 49), Surrey

Location: TQ 024726
Lat. 51.26.33 N; Long. 00.31.35 W

Project manager: R Robertson-Mackay (English Heritage), 1961–3

Archival body: English Heritage, British Museum

Description: a Neolithic causewayed enclosure covering a total area of approximately 2.4ha, defined by double concentric interrupted ditches, which were for the most part naturally filled. There were many traces of activity within the interior, presumed to be contemporary with the ditches, including pits, gullies, postholes and stakeholes, and varying concentrations of struck and burnt flint, and pottery. Human burials were found. There is little Ebbsfleet pottery in secondary contexts and there are later prehistoric, Roman, and medieval finds.

Objectives: the threat of destruction of the site for gravel extraction led to rescue excavations. The excavations developed gradually and in accordance with the progress of gravel extraction.

Final comment: R Robertson-Mackay (1987), insufficient charcoal came from early Neolithic contexts for a reliable date. The bone samples produced dates which were too recent, possibly due to humic acids in the ground water.

References: Whittle *et al* 2011, 388–93

HAR–8440 2260 ±70 BP

$\delta^{13}C$: -29.0‰

Sample: 4928A (STAINES 8), submitted on 16 November 1982 by L Blackmore

Material: wood (waterlogged): unidentified

Initial comment: from a peaty layer in filled-in watercourse in Valley of County Ditch, above HAR-9024.

Objectives: to provide dates for an environmental sequence adjacent to the Neolithic causewayed enclosure at Staines.

Calibrated date: 1σ: 400-200 cal BC
410-160 cal BC
2σ: 1 cal BC–cal AD 1

Final comment: A Bayliss (26 January 2012), these samples were originally submitted in 1982, but do not seem to have been dated until 1989. Records of the environmental evidence associated with these dates has not been traced.

HAR–8441 4150 ±70 BP

$\delta^{13}C$: -30.7‰

Sample: ST308, submitted on 11 October 1988 by R Robertson-Mackay

Material: peat

Initial comment: from trench 49.

Objectives: as HAR-8440

Calibrated date: 1σ: 2880-2580 cal BC
2910-2490 cal BC
2σ: 1 cal BC–cal AD 1

Final comment: see HAR-8440

HAR–9024 3950 ±70 BP

$\delta^{13}C$: -27.4‰

Sample: SEC30B (STAINES 9), submitted in October 1988 by L Blackmore

Material: charcoal (bark, previously waterlogged, remaining subsample now dry and structurally collapsed): unidentified (0.04g); bark, conifer (1.05g, 100%) (R Gale 2000)

Initial comment: from a shell-marl layer in the filled-in watercourse in Valley of County Ditch, below HAR-8440.

Objectives: as HAR-8440.

Calibrated date: 1σ: 2570–2340 cal BC
2σ: 2630–2210 cal BC

Final comment: see HAR-8440.

References: Hardiman *et al* 1992, 59

Chanctonbury Ring, West Sussex

Location: TQ 139121
Lat. 50.53.48 N; Long. 00.22.49 W

Project manager: D Rudling (Institute of Archaeology, London), 1987

Archival body: Horsham Museum

Description: the latest analysis (2001) suggests an earlier, late Bronze Age date for the construction of the univallate hillfort. In the Roman period the prehistoric enclosure earthworks provided a boundary for the Romano-British temples.

Objectives: these are the first articulated human remains recovered from Chanctonbury Ring, a late Bronze Age hillfort and Romano-Celtic temple site. The site had previously yielded disarticulated prehistoric human bones, and excavations (trench V) in 1990 recovered several residual (prehistoric) or Romano-British cranial fragments and four fibula fragments. Dating the bones found in 1987 might help to identify one of the functions of this multi-period site.

References: Rudling 2001

GU–5116 900 ±200 BP

$\delta^{13}C$: -23.7‰

Sample: 1987, submitted on 6 March 1991 by D Rudling

Material: human bone (femur) (D Brothwell)

Initial comment: bone fragments from two articulated legs were found in the shallow chalky soil forming part of the root ball of a tree, which fell in October 1987.

Objectives: as series objectives.

Calibrated date: 1σ: cal AD 900–1290
2σ: cal AD 670–1430

Final comment: D Rudling (2001), the tenth–thirteenth century dating of the submitted bones was unexpected and provides the only date for activity within the former hillfort and Roman temple complex at this period. The precise nature of this activity (burial, murder, execution, etc) remains unknown.

Laboratory comment: SURRC Radiocarbon Dating Laboratory (1991), the collagen yield from this sample was very low, hence the large error term. The date does, however, define the sample within the medieval period rather than early Iron Age or Roman periods.

Chesters bridge abutment, Northumberland

Location:	NY 915701
	Lat. 55.01.31 N; Long. 02.07.59 W
Project manager:	P Bidwell (South Shields Roman Fort Museum), 1983
Archival body:	English Heritage

Description: a Roman bridge crossing the North Tyne. Bridge 2 consists of three piers 4.9m in width, 9.3m in length, and spaced 10.8m apart.

Objectives: to see if dating can support the interpretation of the construction of the bridge between AD 205–207.

Final comment: P Marshall (2001), the dating evidence for the bridge is far from satisfactory because none of it can be indisputably linked with its construction. But the weight of the evidence, such as it is, favours a late second or early third century AD date, during Severus' reign during the governorship of Alfenus Senecio (*c* AD 205–207).

Laboratory comment: University of Belfast (26 July 2012), these samples were processed using the high-precision dating facility.

References:	Bidwell and Holbrook 1989

UB–3131 1919 ±16 BP

$\delta^{13}C$: -26.8 ±0.2‰

Sample: crane post from bridge 2, submitted in March 1989 by P T Bidwell

Material: wood (waterlogged): *Quercus* sp.

Initial comment: from the inner ten rings of wood taken from a crane post.

Objectives: to ascertain whether the dating can support the interpretation of construction between AD 205–207.

Calibrated date: *1σ:* cal AD 65–120
                 2σ: cal AD 30–130

Final comment: P Marshall (2001), the result does not disprove the interpretation of construction between AD 205–7 given the possibility that the timber is reused.

Laboratory comment: University of Belfast (27 July 2012), no record survives of whether this sample was pretreated using the acid based alkali protocol or was bleached.

UB–3132 1960 ±16 BP

$\delta^{13}C$: -26.2 ±0.2‰

Sample: crane post from bridge 2, submitted in March 1989 by P T Bidwell

Material: wood (waterlogged): *Quercus* sp.

Initial comment: from the outer ten rings of wood taken from a crane post.

Objectives: as UB-3131

Calibrated date: *1σ:* cal AD 20–70
                 2σ: cal AD 1–80

Final comment: see UB-3131

Laboratory comment: see UB-3131

Chetwynd Aston, Shropshire

Location:	SJ 756164
	Lat. 52.44.40 N; Long. 02.21.41 W
Project manager:	G Smith (Central Excavation Service), 1990
Archival body:	English Heritage

Description: a low-lying, irregular, triple-ditched enclosure, presumed to be of mid-to-late Iron Age date by comparison with other similar sites in Shropshire.

Objectives: to give a chronological setting for the site, which lacked any artefactual evidence, and to provide a chronological setting for macrobotanical remains found nearby in the same ditch.

References:	Smith 1991

GU–5197 2100 ±70 BP

$\delta^{13}C$: -26.7‰

Sample: 455-4020, submitted on 17 October 1991 by G H Smith

Material: wood (waterlogged): unidentified

Initial comment: from the primary silt at the base of a deep ditch (2m) below the level of any root contamination and probably continually below the watertable since deposition. The sample came from layer 1048, a sandy clay containing lenses of organic material interpreted as vegetation contemporary with the settlement.

Objectives: this is a major settlement amongst those known in the Upper Severn Valley although mostly undated. Limited excavation has produced considerable archaeobotanical material but no cultural artefacts. A radiocarbon date will assign a general period to the site and in turn make it worthwhile to analyse the botanical material for environmental information.

Calibrated date: *1σ:* 210–40 cal BC
                 2σ: 370 cal BC–cal AD 60

Final comment: G Smith (29 March 1995), the sample of immature wood from near the base of one of the main enclosure ditches should provide a closely primary date for the monument. There was no supporting artefactual evidence but the calibrated date range agreed well with the expected later first millennium BC date by comparison with other similar low-lying, multiple-ditched enclosures in Shropshire. The dating has therefore fulfilled the objectives of the enquiry.

Chigborough Farm, Essex

Location: TL 87950815
Lat. 51.44.24 N; Long. 00.43.21 E

Project manager: O Bedwin (Essex County Council), 1988–9

Archival body: Essex County Council

Description: a prehistoric settlement on the north edge of the Blackwater estuary. Chigborough Farm is being examined by Essex County Council Archaeology Section prior to gravel extraction as part of a broad programme to study settlement patterns in the lower Blackwater valley.

Objectives: the radiocarbon dates will help clarify the interpretation of the features.

References: Wallis and Waughman 1998
Waughman 1989

HAR–10199 2980 ±80 BP

δ¹³C: -29.3‰

Sample: 10.88971, submitted on 5 December 1988 by P Murphy

Material: wood (waterlogged): unidentified

Initial comment: from the bottom of a waterlogged deposit at the bottom of a Bronze Age well or watering hole. The context was a black organic loam, virtually stone free and was sealed by successive fills of gravelly clays and silts. Immediately above the waterlogged material and extending into the top stony part of it was a complete Deverel Rimbury Bucket Urn, broken *in situ* at the edge of the feature. The bottom of the waterlogged material was 2.65m OD beneath the sample and the top 3.10m OD; the sample was taken from the bottom 0.15m.

Objectives: to obtain a radiocarbon date for use in conjunction with Deverel Rimbury urn. The date will be included in a pottery study and also date the feature, as no other ceramic material was recovered from the lower fills.

Calibrated date: *1σ:* 1380–1050 cal BC
2σ: 1430–940 cal BC

Final comment: O Bedwin (21 October 1994), this confirms the suspected date of a Bronze Age well, and helps to fill out the picture of the late Bronze Age landscape.

References: Hardiman *et al* 1992, 56

OxA–3035 1.135 ±0.0012 fM

δ¹³C: -27.1‰

Sample: CHIG2138, submitted on 3 August 1990 by P Murphy

Material: grain: *Triticum dicoccum* (P Murphy 1990)

Initial comment: from the single fill of a posthole within a sub-rectangular building surrounded by a group of postholes of similar fill. The context was uncontaminated by other archaeological layers but there was evidence for a small amount of modern rootlet action.

Objectives: it is important to obtain a date for this building which, if Neolithic or early Bronze Age, is without parallel in Essex. Ceramic dating for many earlier features on the site is poor and the date obtained may clarify the interpretation of the early prehistoric features.

Calibrated date: *1σ:* cal AD 1957–1958
2σ: cal AD 1957–1958

Final comment: O Bedwin (21 October 1994), the context was shallow and directly under the modern topsoil. Evidently some intrusive material (from stubble burning?) was present.

Laboratory comment: English Heritage (25 January 2012), this measurement has been calibrated using the data of Kueppers *et al* (2004), with the constraint that this sample must date to before its excavation in AD 1988/9.

References: Hedges *et al* 1992, 148
Kueppers *et al* 2004

Christchurch: Bargates, site X17, Dorset

Location: SZ 15759305
Lat. 50.44.11 N; Long. 01.46.36 W

Project manager: K Jarvis (Guildhall Museum, Poole), 1969–80

Archival body: Guildhall Museum, Poole

Description: traces of late Neolithic occupation with Grooved Ware pottery, two Bronze Age ring ditches, early Iron Age occupation, and a seventh-century AD pagan Saxon cemetery with 30 graves.

Objectives: to date the late Neolithic Grooved Ware occupation.

Laboratory comment: Ancient Monuments Laboratory (2003), one further date from this site, HAR-2907, was published in Jordan *et al* (1994, 36–7).

References: Jarvis 1982
Jordan *et al* 1994, 36–7

HAR–2906 3510 ±70 BP

δ¹³C: -25.2‰

Sample: X17-100, submitted on 31 October 1978 by K Jarvis

Material: charcoal: *Quercus* sp., from mature timbers (C A Keepax 1978)

Initial comment: a combined sample from various locations in the ring ditch. There was no stratigraphy in the ditch, the fill being fine sand. However, all samples were located *c* 10–15cm from the bottom of the ditch in the primary silt.

The depth of the ditch is *c* 60cm. Most of the fragments are large suggesting we are dealing with contemporary charcoal.

Objectives: to date the ring ditch. There are very few radiocarbon dates for Wessex ring ditches and pottery.

Calibrated date: 1σ: 1940–1740 cal BC
  2σ: 2030–1660 cal BC

Final comment: K Jarvis (16 February 1995), the date obtained is consistent with stratigraphy and finds evidence for the ring ditch.

Laboratory comment: AERE Harwell (15 May 1990), this sample was measured in the miniature gas proportional counter (Otlet *et al* 1983).

References: Hardiman *et al* 1992, 58
  Otlet *et al* 1983

Danby Rigg, North Yorkshire

Location: NZ 70460549 to NZ 70780658
 Lat. 54.26.23 N; Long. 00.54.49 W, to
 54.26.58 N; 00.54.30 W

Project manager: A F Harding (University of Durham), 1986–9

Archival body: Dorman Museum

Description: a stretch of moorland on the south side of the valley of the river Esk. Excavation and survey produced evidence of activity on the site ranging from the early Bronze Age to the Viking period.

Objectives: to date the site. No dates are currently available for the cross-dyke sites of the North York Moors. Danby Rigg is especially appropriate in view of its proximity to a cairnfield.

Final comment: A Harding (21 August 1995), HAR-8908 (1140 ±60 BP, cal AD 710–1020 at 95% confidence; Reimer *et al* 2004) and HAR-8911 (990 ±60 BP, cal AD 900–1180 at 95% confidence; Reimer *et al* 2004) indicate an early medieval date for the Danby Rigg Triple Dykes, where a Bronze Age date had been assumed. There is no associated artefactual evidence. HAR-8909 (1510 ±80 BP, cal AD 390–670 at 95% confidence; Reimer *et al* 2004) is significantly earlier than the other three dates, which form an overlapping sequence. No obvious explanation is apparent. UB-3192 and UB-3193 indicate the expected Bronze Age date for the cremation pit with Collared Urns in ring cairn 235. There is no artefactual material to corroborate the later date of UB-3193.

Laboratory comment: English Heritage (17 January 2012), four further dates from this site were published in Bayliss *et al* (2012, 74–5; HAR-8908–11).

References: Bayliss *et al* 2012
  Harding and Ostoja-Zagorski 1994
  Reimer *et al* 2004

UB–3192 3394 ±39 BP

δ¹³C: -26.1 ±0.2‰

Sample: 1989/4B, submitted on 4 August 1989 by A F Harding

Material: charcoal: unidentified

Initial comment: from a small pit (451), apparently undisturbed, close to the large central pit from which Collared Urns with cremated bone were extracted in the nineteenth century AD. It is presumed to date the use of the ring cairn, though its exact relationship to the construction of the ring and digging of the central pit is unknown. There is no evidence of disturbance by the nineteenth-century diggers.

Objectives: the ring cairn is one of the earliest monuments on Danby Rigg and probably precedes the creation of the cairnfield, which is one of the most extensive in Britain. The date should provide a *terminus post quem* for the cairnfield and thus, by implication, for the onset of soil degradation.

Calibrated date: 1σ: 1750–1630 cal BC
  2σ: 1870–1610 cal BC

Final comment: A Harding (21 August 1995), this result agrees with the archaeological dating of the ring cairn to the early Bronze Age, but is at variance with UB-3193 from the same context.

Laboratory comment: English Heritage (26 January 2012), these two measurements from the same context are statistically significantly different (T'=108.8; T'(5%)=3.8; ν=1; Ward and Wilson 1978), suggesting that the earlier result on unidentified charcoal may have contained a substantial component of long-lived material.

References: Ward and Wilson 1978

UB–3193 2826 ±38 BP

δ¹³C: -26.7 ±0.2‰

Sample: 1989/4A, submitted on 4 August 1989 by A F Harding

Material: grain (carbonised)

Initial comment: as UB-3194

Objectives: as UB-3194

Calibrated date: 1σ: 1020–920 cal BC
  2σ: 1120–890 cal BC

Final comment: A Harding (21 August 1995), this result indicates a late Bronze Age date, for which there is no archaeological corroboration from this ring cairn. It is at variance with UB-3192 from the same context.

Devil's Quoits, Oxfordshire

Location: SP 71120475
 Lat. 51.44.22 N; Long. 01.24.16 W

Project manager: G Lambrick (Oxford Archaeological Unit), 1972–3 and 1988

Archival body: Oxford Archaeology

Description: the site lies south of the village of Stanton Harcourt. Excavations here have revealed a large henge, around 160m in diameter. The bank has been nearly entirely eroded and the ditch filled in. Excavations have also revealed stones and stone sockets within the henge. Only one megalith remains partially buried near its stonehole.

There are other stones piled up at the edge of the site. At least some of these stones do appear to be the missing megaliths from within the henge. The stoneholes are set out in a ring roughly 80m in diameter within the henge and it is thought that there could have been as many as 24 in the circle. At the centre of the henge a series of postholes have been found, which appear to form a loose spiral pattern.

Objectives: primarily to date the sequence and construction of the henge and stone circle, to date the ditch deposits contemporary with the henge use and indirectly, landuse and cultivation close to the henge.

Final comment: F Healy (10 January 1994), the henge ditch: OxA-3686 and OxA-3688 combine with the earlier of two determinations made on bulked bone samples from the basal fills of the ditch in the 1970s (HAR-1887; 4010 ±120 BP) to form a sequence which conforms to the ditch stratigraphy and confirms the later Neolithic origin of the monument and its continued use into the early Bronze Age. The perhaps slightly anomalous age of OxA-3687 may reflect the redeposition of the sample on which it was made.

Stone Circle: OxA-3690 and OxA-3689 indicate a later Neolithic construction date for the stone circle. The relation between this and the construction of the surrounding henge remains unclear, although the two events were clearly close in time. If conglomerate fragments and antler picks from layer G derive from the building of the stone circle, then this took place when the henge was already in existence. If so, OxA-3689 would give a truer indication of the construction date of the stone circle than OxA-3690.

Laboratory comment: English Heritage (8 March 2012), two further radiocarbon dates from this site were not funded by English Heritage (HAR-1887; 4010 ±120 BP, which calibrates to 2890–2150 cal BC at 95% confidence; Reimer *et al* 2004, and HAR-1888; 3590 ±70 BP, which calibrates to 2140–1740 cal BC at 95% confidence; Reimer *et al* 2004), and are published in Barclay *et al* 1995, 46).

References: Barclay *et al* 1995
                       Hedges *et al* 1994, 361
                       Reimer *et al* 2004

OxA–3686 3745 ±60 BP

$\delta^{13}C$: -22.3‰

Sample: DQSH CA/1, submitted in 1992 by G Lambrick and A Barclay

Material: antler: *Cervus elaphus* (B Levitan)

Initial comment: from the upper most layer (Fa), which immediately underlay a horizon of stabilization and *in situ* soil formation (layer F). It was unaffected by Roman ploughing in the henge ditch. The layer represents a phase of slower silting.

Objectives: to date the final phase of the ditch silting.

Calibrated date: *1σ:* 2280–2030 cal BC
                        2σ: 2350–1970 cal BC

Final comment: F Healy (10 January 1994), it suggests that the henge ditch was being allowed to silt up by the late third millennium cal BC.

OxA–3687 3995 ±60 BP

$\delta^{13}C$: -24.4‰

Sample: DQSH CA/2, submitted in 1992 by G Lambrick and A Barclay

Material: animal bone: *Bos* sp., ulna (B Levitan)

Initial comment: from layer G, a gradual soil silt overlying the primary gravel fill of the ditch bottom. This layer was associated with Beaker pottery and flintwork and should be contemporary with the site's occupation. Layer G may have derived from cultivation close to the henge ditch.

Objectives: the sample forms part of a sequence through the ditch silts and will date a period associated with the use of Beakers.

Calibrated date: *1σ:* 2580–2460 cal BC
                        2σ: 2840–2340 cal BC

Final comment: F Healy (10 January 1994), if the sample was not redeposited (*see* comments on series) its age should relate to the use of the monument, since layer G contained *in situ* hearths, Beaker and Bronze Age pottery and struck flint and animal bone.

OxA–3688 3845 ±45 BP

$\delta^{13}C$: -24.2‰

Sample: DQSH CA/3, submitted in 1992 by G Lambrick and A Barclay

Material: animal bone (Bovid or Cervid) (B Levitan)

Initial comment: from layer H, immediately underlying layer G, which produced the sample for OxA-3687. Little artefactual material other than residual flintwork was recovered at this level.

Objectives: the sample forms part of a sequence, which should date the occupation of the site.

Calibrated date: *1σ:* 2460–2200 cal BC
                        2σ: 2470–2140 cal BC

Final comment: F Healy (10 January 1994), it is younger than OxA-3687, overlapping with it only at 95% confidence.

OxA–3689 3955 ±65 BP

$\delta^{13}C$: -22.1‰

Sample: DQSH CA/6, submitted in 1992 by G Lambrick and A Barclay

Material: antler: *Cervus elaphus* (B Levitan)

Initial comment: from the original packing material in stonehole F17, part of the Devil's Quoits stone circle. Although the standing stone had been removed disturbance of the packing material was minimal.

Objectives: to date the circle construction and determine its phasing with the henge. Very few stone circles have radiocarbon dates and therefore the association within a henge is of great importance nationally.

Calibrated date: *1σ:* 2570–2340 cal BC
                        2σ: 2630–2230 cal BC

Final comment: F Healy (10 January 1994), the pick is likely to date from the original excavation of the stonehole despite the fact that the feature had been disturbed when the stone was removed, probably in the medieval period.

OxA–3690 4165 ±70 BP

δ¹³C: -26.3‰

Sample: DQSH CA/7, submitted in 1992 by G Lambrick and A Barclay

Material: charcoal: *Quercus* sp. (M Robinson)

Initial comment: from the original stonehole fill, F227, from the Devil's Quoits stone circle. The standing stone had been removed but the disturbance was minimal.

Objectives: as OxA-3689

Calibrated date: 1σ: 2890–2620 cal BC
2σ: 2910–2490 cal BC

Final comment: F Healy (10 January 1994), OxA-3690 was made on charcoal from the basal fill of the socket of stonehole 227 and must thus be contemporary with or earlier than, the erection of the stone.

Dorchester Bypass: Flagstones, Dorset

Location: SY 70408995
Lat. 50.25.28 N; Long. 02.25.09 W

Project manager: P Woodward (Wessex Archaeology), 1987

Archival body: Dorset County Museum

Description: site 4 of the survey and excavation along the route of the southern Dorchester Bypass: the western portion of a Neolithic causewayed enclosure with an inner ring ditch and central burial pit.

Objectives: to date the activity of the site.

Laboratory comment: English Heritage (17 January 2012), four further dates from this site were published in Bayliss *et al* (2012, 77–8; HAR-8578, -9158–61).

References: Hedges *et al* 1991b, 288
Smith 1997
Woodward 1988
Woodward and Smith 1987

OxA–2321 4210 ±110 BP

δ¹³C: -23.0‰

Sample: W183.364.76, submitted in June 1989 by P J Woodward

Material: human bone (right femur, 10–12 years old infant) (J Rogers)

Initial comment: from an infant crouched burial inserted into the chalk primary fill of a ditch segment of the causewayed enclosure.

Objectives: to date the burial and its insertion into the primary ditch fills and thus to date the general use of the monument. This can be compared with antler (HAR-8578) and burials in the ditch (HAR-9158). The date of use and occupation of the monument is crucial for understanding the Neolithic sequence.

Calibrated date: 1σ: 2920–2620 cal BC
2σ: 3090–2480 cal BC

Final comment: F Healy (19 July 1991), HAR-9158 (4490 ±70 BP; 3490–2920 cal BC at 95% confidence; Reimer *et al* 2004), OxA-2322, and OxA-2321, form a sequence consistent with the stratigraphy, suggesting that the enclosure was constructed during the middle Neolithic, with the burial which provided the sample for OxA-2321 cut into the primary fill at a later date.

OxA–2322 4450 ±90 BP

δ¹³C: -24.1‰

Sample: W183.581.92, submitted in June 1989 by P J Woodward

Material: antler: *Cervus elaphus* (M Maltby)

Initial comment: from the base of a ditch segment of causewayed enclosure, sealed by the immediate collapse of the adjacent bank and buried by coarse chalk rubble.

Objectives: to provide a construction date for the causewayed enclosure and compare with HAR-8578 and HAR-9158.

Calibrated date: 1σ: 3350–2920 cal BC
2σ: 3490–2890 cal BC

Final comment: see OxA-2321

OxA–2380 205 ±60 BP

δ¹³C: -24.6‰

Sample: FGP1/88, submitted in November 1989 by V Straker

Material: carbonised plant macrofossil (*Vitis vinifera*, pip) (V Straker 1989)

Initial comment: from the Bronze Age fill of a Neolithic causewayed enclosure ditch. There are five sherds of early Neolithic pottery, so it is possible that the pip could be earlier than the Bronze Age.

Objectives: no evidence existed for the cultivation or use of the grape in early prehistoric Britain until the radiocarbon date OxA-931 (4660 ±80 BP; 3640–3100 cal BC at 95% confidence; Pearson *et al* 1986) obtained by G Jones and A Legge from a grape seed from the Stepleton spur of Hambledon Hill, Dorset. Without further securely dated examples it will not be possible to ascertain the status of this crop in Britain.

Calibrated date: 1σ: cal AD 1640–1955*
2σ: cal AD 1520–1955*

Final comment: V Staker (1991), the seeds (OxA-2380 and OxA-2381) were from well sealed and apparently uncontaminated Bronze Age deposits, which were over a metre below the present ground surface. It can only be assumed that they were taken down by earthworm activity.

References: Pearson *et al* 1986

OxA–2381 160 ±60 BP

$\delta^{13}C$: -24.1‰

Sample: FGP2/92, submitted in November 1989 by V Straker

Material: carbonised plant macrofossil (*Vitis vinifera*, pip) (V Straker 1989)

Initial comment: as OxA-2380

Objectives: as OxA-2380

Calibrated date: *1σ:* cal AD 1660–1955★
                     2σ: cal AD 1640–1955★

Final comment: see OxA-2380

Dorchester Bypass: Middle Farm, Dorset

Location: SP 67298995
                     Lat. 50.42.28 N; Long. 02.27.48 W

Project manager: P Woodward (Wessex Archaeology), 1987

Archival body: Dorset County Museum

Description: a sub-divided early to middle Bronze Age enclosure: south-west of Middle Farm the Dorchester Bypass route crosses a north-south shallow coombe and then rises over a spur projecting from one of the east-west ridges north of and parallel to Maiden Castle.

Objectives: to refine the dating of the Bronze Age landscape around Maiden Castle.

Laboratory comment: English Heritage (17 January 2012), one further date from this site was published in Bayliss *et al* (2012, 78; HAR-9160).

References: Bayliss *et al* 2012
                     Hedges *et al* 1991b, 288
                     Smith 1997
                     Woodward and Smith 1987

OxA–2382 4800 ±70 BP

$\delta^{13}C$: -25.4‰

Sample: W186.3062, submitted in June 1989 by P J Woodward

Material: charcoal: *Quercus* sp. (M Allen)

Initial comment: from soil samples taken from postholes cut into chalk and chalk with clay with flints. The postholes form a hut circle. They are shallow and contained modern rootlets and some intrusive burrowing mollusca (*Cecilioides acicula*), but were well-sealed, thus the charcoal is probably not contaminated.

Objectives: to date the destruction, *terminus post quem*, of the building for which no other absolute dating evidence is available, and no direct stratigraphic relationships between other archaeological features survive.

Calibrated date: *1σ:* 3650–3520 cal BC
                     2σ: 3710–3370 cal BC

Final comment: F Healy (19 July 1991), OxA-2382 is likely to relate to earlier Neolithic activity, attested on the site by residual artefacts. The presence of charcoal of this age in the postholes of the round house, one of which contained a grogged Bronze Age sherd, may perhaps be accounted for by its having been built on a topsoil rich in earlier Neolithic charcoal, which could have entered the postholes as the timbers rotted *in situ* or were removed.

Dorchester: Allington Avenue, Dorset

Location: SY 702899
                     Lat. 50.42.27 N; Long. 02.25.19 W

Project manager: S Davies (Wessex Archaeology), 1984–5

Archival body: Dorset County Museum

Description: plans for a substantial housing development of *c* 16ha on the south-eastern outskirts of Dorchester, about a kilometre outside the Roman town of *Durnovaria*, offered the opportunity to examine in detail a very large area of rural landscape, which had already produced evidence of use from the Neolithic period onwards. The site lies on a gentle east-west ridge between the town and Mount Pleasant. Excavations in the 1970s defined the latter as an important centre in the late Neolithic and Bronze Age, subsequently farmed in the later prehistoric period (Wainwright 1979).

Objectives: to clarify the chronological sequence of the site.

Laboratory comment: English Heritage (17 January 2012), one further date from this site was published in Bayliss *et al* (2012, 78–9; HAR-8579).

References: Bayliss *et al* 2012
                     Davies *et al* 1986
                     Davies *et al* 2002
                     Wainwright 1979
                     Walker *et al* 1991a, 102

HAR–9661 2160 ±70 BP

$\delta^{13}C$: -22.5‰

Sample: W984434, submitted on 17 February 1988 by S M Davies

Material: human bone (left femur, skeleton 305, male 45 years+)

Initial comment: from a middle Iron Age pit burial in the centre of a round barrow.

Objectives: to establish the presence/absence of earlier and/or middle Iron Age activity on the site.

Calibrated date: *1σ:* 360–100 cal BC
                     2σ: 400 cal BC–cal AD 1

Final comment: S Davies, P Bellamy, M Heaton and P Woodward (2002), this date suggests that the pit burials were a middle to late Iron Age insertion into monument 2300. This date lends support to the fragmentary iron pin being a deliberate grave good.

HAR–9662 3810 ±120 BP

δ¹³C: -23.1‰

Sample: W984434, submitted on 17 February 1988 by
S M Davies

Material: human bone (right femur, skeleton 126, male
25–35 years)

Initial comment: from an undated trussed inhumation
inserted into a Bronze Age barrow ditch and sealed by
Romano-British plough soils.

Objectives: to establish the timespan of active monument use.

Calibrated date: 1σ: 2470–2040 cal BC
                      2σ: 2580–1920 cal BC

Final comment: S Davies, P Bellamy, M Heaton and
P Woodward (2002), this date from a burial in grave 127,
indicates that by 2580–1920 cal BC the enclosure ditches
were at least half filled up.

Dover Boat, Kent

Location: TR 32014128
                    Lat. 51.07.22 N; Long. 01.18.54 E

Project manager: M Bates (Canterbury Archaeological
                    Trust), 1992

Description: the Bronze Age wooden boat was discovered in
September 1992 while a major new road and sewer system
was being developed in the old town of Dover. A team from
Canterbury Archaeological Trust (CAT), funded by English
Heritage, identified some timbers in a construction pit.

An inspection revealed boat timbers and associated peats
suggesting it could be prehistoric. The timbers extended for
some 6m and were of a plank-sewn boat similiar to the
prehistoric vessels found at North Ferriby. The vessel was
recorded *in situ* and then cut into ten sections which were
lifted in early October 1992. The contractors then discovered
a further 3.5m of the craft including either the stern or bow.
This in turn was similiarly lifted in the middle of October.
A total of 9.5m of vessel were lifted which was about a half
to two thirds of the original vessel. The boat had four bottom
planks, the long central plank being replaced by two planks.
Initial investigations revealed that she was a sea-going vessel
that had been abandoned up a freshwater creek and was of
middle Bronze Age date. The remains were shaped like a
modern punt with a flat bottom, vertical sides, and a flat
sloping south end. The lowest side plank was stitched with
withies of yew to the outer edge of each bottom plank and
curved upwards. The planks were initially made watertight
with a cauking of moss laid on the inboard face of each
seam. Tool marks indicate the vessel was fashioned using
axes with curved blades.

Objectives: accurate dating is essential to realise the potential
of the discovery for the history of early water transport in
North West Europe, and its social and economic
implications.

References: Clark 1992
                    Clark 2004a
                    Clark 2004b
                    Clark and Keeley 1997

Corfield 1993
Corfield 1994
King 1993
Lawrence 1993
Owen and Frost 2000
Parfitt 1993a
Parfitt 1993b
Parfitt and Bates 1993
Slack 1993

Dover Boat: wiggle-matching, Kent

Location: TR 320415
                    Lat. 51.07.30 N; Long. 01.18.57 E

Project manager: P Clark (Canterbury Archaeological
                    Trust), 1992

Archival body: Dover Museum

Description: the Dover boat was deposited within a laminated
sequence of tufa and silt, overlying peat and underlying thick
bedded silts, which had been cut into by an *in situ* Roman
timber harbour revetment. It was recovered from a depth of
7m below the present ground level, and regularly inundated
with fresh river water.

Objectives: technological similarities with the Ferriby boats
suggest a date around the middle Bronze Age, though the
construction of the boat is unparalleled in the ancient world.
Its size and geographical position strongly suggests it was a
sea-going vessel, if so one of the earliest examples in the
world. Accurate dating is essential to realise the potential of
the discovery for the history of early water transport in
North West Europe and its social and economic implications.

Final comment: A Bayliss (2004), the combined analysis of
the tree-ring and radiocarbon data demonstrates that the
wigglematch sequence dates to 1742–1589 BC, adding the
distribution of an appropriate sapwood estimate (Hillam *et al*
1987) to this sequence provides a *terminus post quem* for the
boat as the tree-ring sequence has no heartwood-sapwood
boundary. The weighted mean of the reliable measurements
on the short-lived yew stitches and moss caulking (UB-4164;
3323 ±18 BP and Q-3242; 3205 ±60 BP) can then be
constrained by this *terminus post quem* to provide an estimate
for the date of the boat of *cal BC 1575–1520* (at 95%
confidence).

Laboratory comment: English Heritage (26 January 2012),
three further dates were funded by the University of
Cambridge, Q-3240 (3285 ±50 BP; cal BC 1690–1440 at
95% confidence; Reimer *et al* 2004) and Q-3241 (3225 ±80
BP; cal BC 1690–1310 at 95% confidence; Reimer *et al*
2004), both on oak planking from the boat, and Q-3242
(3205 ±60 BP; cal BC 1620–1380 at 95% confidence;
Reimer *et al* 2004) on moss caulking. Six further samples
were submitted and dated after March 1993 (UB-4142–6,
and UB-4164).

References: Bayliss *et al* 2004a
                    Bayliss and Orton 1994
                    Hillam *et al* 1987
                    Reimer *et al* 2004
                    Ward and Wilson 1978

GU–5291 3490 ±50 BP

δ¹³C: -26.3‰

Sample: DB92/1, submitted on 27 January 1993 by D Jordan

Material: waterlogged plant macrofossil (moss)

Initial comment: from Dover 6 east piece 5, V403, V402 and V401, below 166N cut. The moss was found under the boat and had been used as sealant. The environment is calcarious and there may be some danger of contamination or hard water error.

Objectives: the moss is probably contemporary with the latest use of the boat which is, itself, an important archaeological find. The moss is short-lived and a date from it should be reliable if contamination or hard water error is not a problem.

Calibrated date: *1σ:* 1890–1740 cal BC
                   2σ: 1950–1680 cal BC

Final comment: see series comments.

Laboratory comment: Ancient Monuments Laboratory (2003), the result is statistically significantly different from a replicate sample of moss caulking (Q-3242) (T'=13.3; T'(5%)=3.8; ν=1; Ward and Wilson 1978). The moss must be later than the structure of the boat (after 1589 BC), however the model is in poor agreement if this constraint is included (A=4.5%). GU-5291 cannot be regarded as an accurate radiocarbon measurement, but is significantly too old.

References: Ward and Wilson 1978

GU–5292 3830 ±70 BP

δ¹³C: -25.5‰

Sample: DB92/2, submitted on 27 January 1993 by D Jordan

Material: wood (waterlogged): *Taxus* sp. (J Watson)

Initial comment: piece N, stitch 135, 404; the sample is part of a yew strap used to hold the planks of boat together.

Objectives: the strapping should closely date the latest use of the boat. Even if the planks had been reused several times, the strapping should be the last part to be replaced. The strapping is unlikely to represent more than a few years of growth and is likely to be a reliable dating material.

Calibrated date: *1σ:* 2460–2140 cal BC
                   2σ: 2480–2040 cal BC

Final comment: see series comments.

Laboratory comment: Ancient Monuments Laboratory (2003), the result is statistically significantly different from a replicate sample of yew withies which were used to stitch the boat together (UB-4164) (T'=49.0; T'(5%)=3.8; ν=1; Ward and Wilson 1978). The withies must be later than the structure of the boat (after 1589 BC), however, the model is in poor agreement if this constraint is included (A=0.0%). GU-5292 cannot be regarded as an accurate radiocarbon measurement, but is significantly too old.

References: Ward and Wilson 1978

Dover sediments: group 1, Kent

Location: TR 3196341252, TR 31990 41278, and TR 3199041252
                     Lat. 51.07.22 N; Long. 01.18.54 E, Lat. 51.07.23 N; Long. 01.18.56 E, and Lat. 51.07.22 N; Long. 01.18.56 E

Project manager: M Bates (Canterbury Archaeological Trust), 1992

Description: the Dover A20 road and sewerage scheme.

Objectives: to provide a chronological framework for reconstructing sea-level change and the relationship of archaeological structures to the marine environment.

Final comment: M Bates (1994), this series of samples all derive from sandy peats outcropping at similar elevations, relative to OD, overlying silts (infill of the Roman harbour) and below marine sands and gravels. All age estimates indicate a later Roman or post-Roman date for the peats. They suggest rapid infilling of the basin contrary to previous ideas, and the broad contemporaneity of the regression episode as indicated by the presence of the peats. The dates provide maximum age estimates for the re-establishment of marine conditions.

GU–5324 1640 ±60 BP

δ¹³C: -27.2‰

Sample: GSF 18, unit D, submitted on 16 March 1993 by M Bates

Material: wood (waterlogged): *Salix* sp. (J Hather)

Initial comment: from organic silts immediately below the medieval town wall. The unit lies above sediments of sand and silt relating to the infill of the estuary in post-Roman times. The upper surface of the unit is unconformably overlain by marine gravel and town wall.

Objectives: to date sediments for which no direct archaeological data (at this spatial location) is available. The unit is critical both for topographic reconstruction (and correct chronstratigraphic assignment) and to aid calibration of relative land-sea level/archaeological structure relationships.

Calibrated date: *1σ:* cal AD 340–530
                   2σ: cal AD 250–560

Final comment: M Bates (1994), this sample adequately dates the sediments below the town wall and demonstrates broad contemporaneity with other outcrops of freshwater sediments at similar elevations in the area (eg OxA-4184 and OxA-4185). No field stratigraphic data could provide this link.

OxA–4183 1545 ±65 BP

δ¹³C: -25.6‰

Sample: GSF21, 0.00–0.30m, submitted on 16 March 1993 by M Bates

Material: wood (waterlogged): *Corylus* sp., one fragment identified (J Hather)

Initial comment: from organic silts *c* 0.5m below a post-medieval concrete floor. The unit grades into organic silt below and unconformably overlain by beach gravels, *c* 0.5m thick.

Objectives: this sample forms a pair with OxA-4184. It will provide an estimate for the sedimentation rate for harbour fill and give a maximum age for the onset of the second marine phase. It is necessary for the topographic mapping of the units.

Calibrated date: *1σ:* cal AD 420–600
                      2σ: cal AD 380–650

Final comment: M Bates (1994), the age estimate confirms a late or post-Roman age for the sequence consistent with the stratigraphic position overlying fill of the Roman harbour. The date is stratigraphically consistent with that for OxA-4184. This age estimate suggests rapid infill of the harbour basin and provides a maximum age for the commencement of deposition of sands and gravels of the final marine phase.

References: Hedges *et al* 1994, 362–3

OxA–4184 1670 ±65 BP

δ¹³C: -25.1‰

Sample: GSF21, 0.30–0.40m, submitted on 16 March 1993 by M Bates

Material: waterlogged plant macrofossil: *Equisetum* sp., stem tissue (J Hather)

Initial comment: from organic silts *c* 0.8-0.9m below the base of the concrete floor. The unit grades into the sand unit below and highly organic silt with freshwater molluscs above.

Objectives: to date the final phase of the first marine infill in the lower Dour and represents the temporary establishment of freshwater conditions. It will date an important unit to aid topographic reconstruction, and aid in determining sedimentation rates and tectonic rates for the Dour valley. It forms a pair with OxA-4183.

Calibrated date: *1σ:* cal AD 260–430
                      2σ: cal AD 230–550

Final comment: M Bates (1994), the age estimate is consistent with that from the overlying sample OxA-4183. The date confirms the rapid infill of the harbour basin.

References: Hedges *et al* 1994, 362–3

OxA–4185 1740 ±70 BP

δ¹³C: -27.6‰

Sample: DSC-2, 4.99–5.01m, submitted on 16 March 1993 by M Bates

Material: peat

Initial comment: from 5.0m below the ground surface. Peat has eroded and oxidised the upper contact onto sand at *c* 4cm above the sample datum. Sharp significant amounts of sand could be seen in the peat at the basal contact.

Objectives: peat lies above the harbour infill deposits and represents a temporary regression prior to the final marine episode in the area. A date will help establish the rate of

harbour infill and provide a means of correlation of the sequence with other potentially chronologically identical units, therefore aiding topographic mapping of the surfaces.

Calibrated date: *1σ:* cal AD 220–400
                      2σ: cal AD 120–430

Final comment: M Bates (1994), this age estimate provides additional confirmation for the broad contemporaneity of the temporary marine regression above the harbour fill in the lower Dour valley. The estimate compares well with those from GU-5324 and OxA-4183.

References: Hedges *et al* 1994, 362–3

Dover sediments: group 2, Kent

Location: TR 3201442268, TR 3199041252, and
                TR 3201442268
                Lat. 51.07.22 N; Long. 01.18.54 E,
                Lat. 51.07.23 N; Long. 01.18.56 E, and
                Lat. 51.07.22 N; Long. 01.18.56 E

Project manager: M Bates (Canterbury Archaeological Trust), 1992

Description: the Dover A20 road and sewage scheme.

Objectives: to provide a chronological framework for interpreting the sedimentary sequences.

Final comment: M Bates (1994), the peat samples in this series all lie unconformably below Roman harbour deposits and are inter-stratified with tufa-rich sediments. The dates indicate prehistoric ages for these sediments with considerable time depth present within borehole TWS-5. The age estimates suggest the existence of possible unconformity and/or slow rates of deposition. The AMS determinations produced stratigraphically consistent age estimates, however the conventional date, GU-5323, produced an apparent inversion in the sequence when compared with the AMS measurements.

GU–5323 5120 ±80 BP

δ¹³C: -25.6‰

Sample: TWS-5, 6.39–6.41m, submitted on 16 March 1993 by M Bates

Material: wood (waterlogged): *Quercus* sp. (J Hather)

Initial comment: from organic silt in a borehole adjacent to the pit containing the Dover Boat; at a depth of 6.39-6.41m from the ground surface. The sequence consists of inter-stratified peats and tufa pellet gravels and is below a major unconformity at 5.72m, above which rounded beach gravels occur.

Objectives: the five samples in this group, GU-5323, OxA-4186, OxA-4187, OxA-4188, and OxA-4189, will answer questions relating to rates of sedimentation in the pre-harbour sequences and a cross check between conventional and AMS dates will be possible. Comparison with OxA-4186 will enable an assessment of contemporaneity/diachronism in these sediments.

Calibrated date: *1σ:* 3990–3800 cal BC
                      2σ: 4060–3710 cal BC

Final comment: M Bates (1994), this age estimate is anomalous when compared to the AMS dates from the same core. The prehistoric age is confirmed but the age order is inverted. It is noted that this may be a function of differing substrates. Careful consideration to materials used for future dating is indicated.

OxA–4186 4810 ±95 BP

δ¹³C: -27.4‰

Sample: DSC-2, 7.09–7.11m, submitted on 16 March 1993 by M Bates

Material: peat

Initial comment: from 7.0m below the surface water table. Peat has eroded the upper surface (c 4cm above the sample) and graded lower contact into organic tufa pellet gravels. The peat is firm and black.

Objectives: peat represents terrestrial deposits formed prior to marine transgression culminating in Roman harbour development. The peat/tufa sequence is lithologically similar to that in association with the Dover Boat. A date will provide evidence on synchroneity or the diachronous nature of this sequence commonly found at the base of the valley.

Calibrated date: *1σ:* 3700–3510 cal BC
                2σ: 3790–3360 cal BC

Final comment: M Bates (1994), this confirms the prehistoric/pre-Roman date for the sediments (tufa and peat) immediately below the assumed harbour deposits.

References: Hedges *et al* 1994, 362–3

OxA–4187 4340 ±85 BP

δ¹³C: -25.8‰

Sample: TWS-5, 6.72–6.74m, submitted on 16 March 1993 by M Bates

Material: peat

Initial comment: as GU-5323, but from a depth of 6.39–6.41m from the ground surface.

Objectives: as GU-5323

Calibrated date: *1σ:* 3090–2890 cal BC
                2σ: 3340–2760 cal BC

Final comment: M Bates (1994), this age estimate demonstrates a correct stratigraphic relationship with the other accelerator dates from the same core. A prehistoric age for the sequence is demonstrated. Problems are noted when the accelerator dates are compared with conventional dates from the same core. The age estimate confirms a significant time-depth to the sequence and the probability that major unconformities exist in the sequence.

References: Hedges *et al* 1994, 362–3

OxA–4188 6315 ±85 BP

δ¹³C: -26.1‰

Sample: TWS-5, 6.80–6.82m, submitted on 16 March 1993 by M Bates

Material: peat

Initial comment: as GU-5323, but from a depth of 6.80–6.82m from the ground surface.

Objectives: as GU-5323

Calibrated date: *1σ:* 5370–5210 cal BC
                2σ: 5480–5050 cal BC

Final comment: M Bates (1994), this age estimate is consistent with its stratigraphic position within the core and within the AMS date sequence.

References: Hedges *et al* 1994, 362–3

OxA–4189 8380 ±110 BP

δ¹³C: -26.4‰

Sample: TWS-5, 6.90–6.92m, submitted on 16 March 1993 by M Bates

Material: peat

Initial comment: as GU-5323, but from a depth of 6.90–6.92m from the ground surface.

Objectives: as GU-5323

Calibrated date: *1σ:* 7570–7330 cal BC
                2σ: 7600–7080 cal BC

Final comment: M Bates (1994), this age estimate is consistent with its stratigraphic position within the core and within the AMS date sequence.

References: Hedges *et al* 1994, 362–3

Drayton: cursus, Oxfordshire

Location: SU 490944
                Lat. 51.38.45 N; Long. 01.17.30 W

Project manager: G Lambrick and A Barclay (Oxford Archaeological Unit), 1982

Archival body: Oxfordshire Museum

Description: a cursus monument on the Thames floodplain.

Objectives: to date the cursus and associated pottery.

Final comment: A Barclay, A Bayliss, G Lambrick, and M Robinson (1997), four samples from the cursus ditch are from the primary fill, HAR-6477, HAR-6478, OxA-2071 (4810 ±70 BP; 3710–3370 cal BC at 95% confidence; Reimer *et al* 2004), and OxA-2072 (3630 ±80 BP; 2210 -1760 cal BC at 95% confidence; Reimer *et al* 2004). However, the four measurements are statistically very significantly different (T'=169.7; T'(5%)=7.3; ν=3; Ward and Wilson 1978), and span at least a thousand calendar years. This suggests that all the dated material does not date to the period in which the primary fill accumulated. The statistical model provides an estimate for the date of the construction of the cursus of *3600–3530 cal BC or 3500–3420 cal BC (68% probability)* or *3620–3390 cal BC (95% probability)*. Perhaps the most convincing argument for its validity is the consistency of results from the earliest cursus contexts, and the consistency of five of the results with the recorded stratigraphy. The date range would be consistent with the hypothesis that the Drayton long barrow aligns on the northern end of the cursus, given that this monument was itself probably constructed some time in the mid fourth millennium cal BC. The recovery of mostly plain sherds and a decorated neck sherd of Peterborough Ware from the base of the ditch is also consistent with this date range, especially now that a development for this ceramic style within the later fourth millennium cal BC can be demonstrated (Gibson and Kinnes 1997).

Laboratory comment: English Heritage (17 January 2012), two further dates from this site were published in Bayliss *et al* (2012, 82–3; HAR-6477–8).

References: Ainslie and Wallis 1987
Barclay *et al* 2003
Bayliss *et al* 2012
Gibson and Kinnes 1997
Hedges *et al* 1990, 221–2
Reimer *et al* 2004
Ward and Wilson 1978

OxA–2071 4810 ±70 BP

δ¹³C: -26.0‰ (assumed)

Sample: ABDC7, submitted in October 1988 by G Lambrick

Material: waterlogged plant macrofossil: bark, unidentified (M Robinson)

Initial comment: sealed by alluvium from the base of the cursus ditch.

Objectives: to check earlier dates (HAR-6477 and HAR-6478) obtained on bone from the same context, which represent by some way the earliest dates for a Neolithic cursus. The context also produced Peterborough ware pottery including a Mortlake style rim for which the bone dates are surprisingly early. It is possible, though somewhat unlikely, that those two samples of bones collected from along the base of the cursus ditch are derived from earlier activity. This sample being preserved largely by waterlogging is much less likely to be derived material, and is therefore much more reliable. It is conceivable that the cursus was cleaned out after it's original construction and that this sample provides only a *terminus ante quem.*

Calibrated date: *1σ:* 3660–3520 cal BC
2σ: 3710–3370 cal BC

Final comment: A Barclay, A Bayliss, G Lambrick, and M Robinson (1997), some doubt surrounds this sample (*see* HAR-6477) as well as others from the same context (HAR-6477, HAR-6478, and OxA-2072) because none are from articulated material or material with a demonstrably functional relationship to the cursus. OxA-2071 was obtained from a piece of slightly singed waterlogged bark from the base of the ditch. Although the fragile nature of this material suggests that there cannot be a long gap before it was sealed in the primary silt, the possibility that this sample relates to tree clearance activity before the monument construction cannot be excluded. However, it is also possible that its deposition relates to the early use of the monument.

OxA–2072 3630 ±80 BP

δ¹³C: -24.7‰

Sample: ABDC8, submitted in October 1988 by G Lambrick

Material: waterlogged plant macrofossil: *Prunus spinosa*, seed (M Robinson)

Initial comment: preserved by possible singeing and waterlogging. This sample is of a material preserved in such a way that there is less likelihood of redeposition being a factor, though other seeds from the context were more obviously singed and this could be a factor in the preservation of this item.

Objectives: to act as a check against HAR-6477 and HAR-6478, which gave the earliest dates for a cursus in Britain.

Calibrated date: *1σ:* 2140–1890 cal BC
2σ: 2210–1760 cal BC

Final comment: A Barclay, A Bayliss, G Lambrick, and M Robinson (1997), *see* HAR-6477. Although stratified above the level of the bark (OxA-2071), this sample was still recorded as within the primary fill and from near the bottom of the cursus ditch. This result is considerably later than the other material from this context, and perhaps suggests that the ditch had been cleaned out or recuts during the period of secondary, Beaker related activity associated with the cursus. Alternatively all the other measurements from this context may be residual, and OxA-2072 may represent the true date of the construction of the cursus. Although this is possible, the consistency of the other measurements and the existence of known secondary activity on the site suggest that it is more likely that evidence of recutting was missed in excavation. An alternative explanation is that the recording is in error and the material was actually from the secondary silt, which we know from the archaeomagnetic evidence, took many centuries to accumulate.

Drayton: cursus, tree-throw holes, Oxfordshire

Location: SU 490944
Lat. 51.38.45 N; Long. 01.17.30 W

Project manager: G Lambrick (and) A Barclay (Oxford Archaeological Unit), 1982

Archival body: Oxfordshire Museum

Description: a cursus monument and other activity on the Thames floodplain.

Objectives: to date charcoal from tree throw holes containing cultural material thought likely to be associated with clearance; to date a possible sunken-featured building suspected of being Saxon in origin, but devoid of cultural material except a few animal bones; and to provide a chronological framework for the environmental sequence.

Final comment: A Barclay, A Bayliss, G Lambrick and M Robinson (1997), the radiocarbon dates submitted to date the tree-throw holes suggest at least two possible phases of tree clearance, on and around the area of the cursus. The dates obtained for samples OxA-2073 (4800 ±100 BP; 3790–3360 cal BC; Reimer *et al* 2004), and OxA-2075

(4940 ±80 BP; 3960–3530 cal BC; Reimer *et al* 2004), combined with the stratigraphic relationship of OxA-2073 to the cursus bank, suggest that some tree clearance occurred prior to the construction of the monument.

Laboratory comment: English Heritage (17 January 2012), one further date from this site was published in Bayliss *et al* (2012, 83; HAR-9163).

References: Ainslie and Wallis 1987
                  Barclay *et al* 2003
                  Bayliss *et al* 2012
                  Hedges *et al* 1990, 221–2
                  Reimer *et al* 2004

OxA–2073 4800 ±100 BP

δ¹³C: -26.5‰

Sample: ABDC9, submitted in October 1988 by G Lambrick

Material: charcoal: *Fraxinus* sp.; *Corylus* sp. (M Robinson)

Initial comment: sealed beneath Roman and later alluvium soil in the top of a tree-throw hold beneath the cursus bank; a similar stratigraphic position to OxA-2074. This soil horizon is in the top of the soil fill of the tree hole and since the lower fill contained little charcoal the sample may well post date the tree-throw rather than being derived from charcoal already in the soil where the tree was growing. The sample will provide a *terminus post quem* for construction of the cursus since it underlies the associated internal gravel bank, which was clearly undisturbed at this point. As such it provides a possible check on the early dates HAR-6477 and HAR-6478. This sample is one of a series related to tree-throw holes with associated worked flints.

Objectives: to provide a *terminus post quem* for the construction of the cursus and a *terminus ante quem* for the tree-throw hole in relation to other similar features, which may be related to one or more clearance episodes including clearance for the cursus.

Calibrated date: *1σ:* 3660–3380 cal BC
                       2σ: 3790–3360 cal BC

Final comment: A Barclay, A Bayliss, G Lambrick, and M Robinson (1997), in estimating the construction date of the cursus we are fortunate to have measurements on stratigraphically related samples. OxA-2073 was from a tree-throw hole and OxA-2074 from the soil, both sealed beneath the cursus bank. This means that these two measurements should provide reliable *termini post quem* for the construction of the monument. Both samples appear to have contained a majority of short-lived material, although OxA-2073 did contain some fragments of *Fraxinus* sp., which can be quite long-lived. It should be noted however that if this material does contain an age off-set, it is too old and so would still provide an accurate *terminus post quem* for the cursus. *See* also HAR-6477 and OxA-2075.

OxA–2074 4620 ±80 BP

δ¹³C: -28.8‰

Sample: ABDC10, submitted in October 1988 by G Lambrick

Material: charcoal: Pomoideae (M Robinson)

Initial comment: sealed beneath Romano-British alluvium. The soil horizon is being studied for micromorphology and overlies a tree throw hole possibly associated with clearance prior to construction of the cursus. Worked flints came from this context, and the stratigraphy is similar to OxA-2073.

Objectives: as OxA-2073

Calibrated date: *1σ:* 3520–3340 cal BC
                       2σ: 3640–3090 cal BC

Final comment: see OxA-2073

OxA–2075 4940 ±80 BP

δ¹³C: -24.8‰

Sample: ABDC11, submitted in October 1988 by G Lambrick

Material: charcoal: *Quercus* sp., roots (M Robinson)

Initial comment: from the upper fill of a tree-throw hole, which also contained flints and bone, sealed beneath alluvium.

Objectives: to provide a date for the possible clearance activity on the site relating to many tree-throw holes exhibiting evidence of burning. Together with OxA-2073, OxA-2074, and OxA-2076, it should become clear whether one or more episodes of clearance are represented.

Calibrated date: *1σ:* 3800–3640 cal BC
                       2σ: 3960–3530 cal BC

Final comment: A Barclay, A Bayliss, G Lambrick, and M Robinson (1997), OxA-2075 is on charcoal identified as *Quercus* sp. (including root wood) from a tree-throw hole. This sample has an unknown age-offset, although this may pre-date the creation of the tree-throw hole and the removal of the tree by anything up to 500 years. If this variable is considered to be a small age-offset then there is possible evidence for tree clearance as a separate phase and at some time, may be centuries, before the construction of the cursus. Alternatively a large age-offset would support clearance immediately prior to the cursus construction. On the whole, when allowance is made for the age of the trees at death, it is perfectly possible that the burning of these two trees was part of the same episode as the building of the cursus.

OxA–2076 4220 ±80 BP

δ¹³C: -26.6‰

Sample: ABDC12, submitted in October 1988 by G Lambrick

Material: charcoal: Pomoideae; *Quercus* sp., roots (M Robinson)

Initial comment: from the soil fill of a tree-throw hole sealed by alluvium, which also contained bone and fragmentary pottery.

Objectives: as OxA-2075

Calibrated date: *1σ:* 2910–2690 cal BC
                       2σ: 3020–2570 cal BC

Final comment: A Barclay, A Bayliss, G Lambrick, and M Robinson (1997), the determinations obtained for samples OxA-2076 and OxA-2078 indicate that there was at least one later episode of tree clearance on the site. Again both samples have unknown age-offsets (see OxA-2075) that could be as much as 500 years. OxA-2078 is from tree-throw hole 178, which was found to contain sherds of Beaker and Grooved ware. Given that the overlap between these two ceramic styles is likely to fall within the later third millennium cal BC, then this date appears to be broadly consistent with the pottery. Likewise OxA-2076 may be consistent with the Grooved Ware and Beaker pottery recovered from the preserved ground surface in area 1.

OxA–2077 400 ±70 BP

δ¹³C: -21.0‰

Sample: ABDC13, submitted in October 1988 by G Lambrick

Material: animal bone: *Equus* sp. (B Levitan)

Initial comment: near the base of a circular feature, possibly a Saxon *Grubenhaus.*

Objectives: to establish whether three circular *Grubenhäuser* type features and two possible rectangular buildings represent Saxon activity. The circular features are not sufficiently similar to typical *Grubenhäuser* to be sure of their date on morphological grounds.

Calibrated date: *1σ:* cal AD 1430–1630
                     2σ: cal AD 1410–1650

Final comment: A Barclay, A Bayliss, G Lambrick, and M Robinson (1997), this feature was thought to be of early medieval date. However, OxA-2077, the single determination obtained from animal bone within its fill, indicates a probable later medieval date.

OxA–2078 3880 ±70 BP

δ¹³C: -27.1‰

Sample: ABDC14, submitted in October 1988 by G Lambrick

Material: charcoal: *Quercus* sp. (M Robinson)

Initial comment: from a pocket or hollow in the soil fill of a tree-throw hole, associated with Peterborough ware, Grooved ware, and Beaker pottery. The best interpretation of this hollow, which contained over 50 fragments of *Quercus* sp. root, is that it is a hole left by the upper part of a large root or buttress, which partly burnt and partly rotted after soil had accumulated around it when the tree had fallen.

Objectives: to contribute to the dating of tree-throw holes possibly associated with clearance. Together with OxA-2073, OxA-2074, and OxA-2076 there should be some indication of whether more than one episode of clearance is represented.

Calibrated date: *1σ:* 2470–2210 cal BC
                     2σ: 2570–2140 cal BC

Final comment: see OxA-2076

Eaglestone Flat, Derbyshire

Location: SK 26657406
                     Lat. 53.15.45 N; Long. 01.36.02 W

Project manager: J Barnatt (Peak National Park), 1989–90

Archival body: Peak District National Park

Description: a complex palimpsest of small cairns, platforms, clearance features and vestigial walls, all sited on an upland gritstone shelf that was utilised for agricultural purposes in later prehistory (Barnatt 1986). Associated with these remains is an open cemetery of cremations in pits, some with cordoned urns.

Objectives: Eaglestone Flat is of particular regional importance in that it is the first excavated site in the Peak District with a direct relationship between funerary structures and prehistoric field boundaries. It also contains the first cremation cemetery to be scientifically excavated in the region. The site therefore offers the first opportunity to obtain a sequence of radiocarbon dates, which includes samples relating to agricultural features and from burial contexts.

Final comment: J Barnatt (1994), nine samples (GU-5127 to GU-5130, OxA-3090, OxA-3091, OxA-3245, OxA-3349, and OxA-3350) derive from the second season and form a series when combined with the four dates from the first series (OxA-2422 to OxA-2425). They form a useful set primarily because they confirm that the complex palimpsest of clearance and ritual features were built over at least 200 years and possibly considerably longer than this. The dates, in combination with stratigraphic considerations, show that the site was used for cremation burial throughout the same period.

References: Barnatt 1986
                     Barnatt 1987
                     Barnatt 1994

GU–5127 3450 ±70 BP

δ¹³C: -25.5‰

Sample: EF90A, submitted in March 1991 by J Barnatt

Material: charcoal: *Betula* sp. (C Dixon)

Initial comment: from a single discrete scatter of charcoal (EF90 samples 1098/1099) sealed immediately under a stone bank (120) at its eastern end. The charcoal is likely to have been deposited immediately before the construction of the feature. The feature is one in a long linear arrangement and is approximately in the middle of the chronological sequence. The feature was undisturbed and there is little or no chance of contamination.

Objectives: this sample will have a direct bearing on the stratigraphic sequence of stone structures. The submitted date should contrast with the dates already obtained for early feature 22 (OxA-2422, OxA-2423, and OxA-2422), and for a later one, 273 (OxA-3090).

Calibrated date: *1σ:* 1890–1680 cal BC
                     2σ: 1950–1600 cal BC

Final comment: J Barnatt (1992), the date derived from this sample is consistent with that expected. It is earlier than the date for cairn 273, as predicted from the horizontal stratigraphy. However, it is also unexpectedly earlier than the three dates from cairn 22. This demonstrates that the phasing of the site, as derived from horizontal stratigraphy, is probably more complex than first postulated.

GU–5128 3530 ±50 BP

δ¹³C: -26.2‰

Sample: EF90E, submitted in March 1991 by J Barnatt

Material: charcoal: *Betula* sp. (C Dixon)

Initial comment: from a large amount of charcoal of bark with curvature retained, found well sealed within a cremation pit containing burnt bone. The feature was undisturbed and there is little or no chance of contamination.

Objectives: this sample is one of two submitted (*see* also GU-5129) to give representative dates for the eight samples excavated of simple cremations within pits with burnt sides. This sample has the added advantage that pit 227 underlies a stone platform (204) and thus provides indirect dating evidence for this as well.

Calibrated date: *1σ:* 1940–1770 cal BC
                  2σ: 2020–1740 cal BC

Final comment: J Barnatt (1992), the date derived from this sample is consistent with the others from cremations on site (GU-5129, GU-5130, OxA-3091, and OxA-3245). The position of the cremation pit, under platform 240, adds confirmation that this stone feature is early in the site sequence.

GU–5129 3520 ±70 BP

δ¹³C: -26.3‰

Sample: EF90G, submitted in March 1991 by J Barnatt

Material: charcoal: *Betula* sp. (C Dixon)

Initial comment: found well sealed within the lower fill of cremation pit 231, containing a mixture of burnt bone and the charcoal submitted. The feature was undisturbed and there is little or no chance of contamination.

Objectives: this sample, together with GU-5128, is submitted to give representative dates for the eight samples excavated of simple cremations within pits with burnt sides.

Calibrated date: *1σ:* 1950–1740 cal BC
                  2σ: 2040–1680 cal BC

Final comment: J Barnatt (1992), the date derived from this sample is consistent with the others from cremations on site (GU-5128, GU-5130, OxA-3091, and OxA-3245).

GU–5130 3480 ±70 BP

δ¹³C: -26.5‰

Sample: EF90K, submitted in March 1991 by J Barnatt

Material: charcoal: *Betula* sp. (C Dixon)

Initial comment: found within a large cordoned urn associated with a cremation, all within pit 35. Although the fill was disturbed by vole runs there seems little chance of contamination as there are no trees near the site, thus

modern *Betula* sp. is unlikely to have entered the feature. Equally, burnt heather was not identified which is the one indicator of contamination to be expected.

Objectives: this sample is one of two submitted to give representative dates for the six examples excavated of cremations in urns.

Calibrated date: *1σ:* 1900–1690 cal BC
                  2σ: 2020–1620 cal BC

Final comment: J Barnatt (1992), the date derived from this sample is consistent with the others from cremations on site (GU-5128, GU-5129, OxA-3091, and OxA-3245). It is a little earlier than would have been predicted for a cordoned urn, but not unduly so.

OxA–2422 3155 ±80 BP

δ¹³C: -25.1‰

Sample: EF89/C22/238Q, submitted in December 1989 by K Smith

Material: charcoal: *Quercus* sp., branch or stem material (R Gale)

Initial comment: the four samples, OxA-2422, OxA-2423, OxA-2424, and OxA-2425, all came from within a *c* 2.0m × 1.5m patch of soil (36) adjacent to, and later than, a prehistoric wall (16). Soil 36 comprised a mottled sandy loam containing scattered pieces of charcoal, calcined bone, and burnt gritstones. Under one end of 36 was a small pit with burnt sides (40) containing further charcoal and a cremation. The upper portions of this had been disturbed by clearance of surrounding stones in prehistory (39) (probably subsequent to the pit). Thus it was difficult to demonstrate with certainty the stratigraphic relationship between the pit (40) and the pyre (39). To avoid this problem the charcoal has been divided in two and a preferred sample of pieces found well away from 39/40 should be dated independently. 36 as a whole was sealed by a thin prehistoric soil (18), covered in turn by a gritty sand (10) left after an intense peat fire in the 1940s. However, the intervening layer was unbroken except by small numbers of rootlets.

Objectives: this sample will have a direct bearing on the date of funerary activity on site, which in this case can be demonstrated stratigraphically to be late in the sequence in so far as it relates to the structures excavated. Thus this date, in combination with the other sample submitted which appertains to a feature early in the sequence, will elucidate the chronological range.

Calibrated date: *1σ:* 1510–1320 cal BC
                  2σ: 1620–1260 cal BC

Final comment: J Barnatt (1991), the three samples of charcoal, (OxA-2422 to OxA-2424), from sealed contexts below the cairn are consistent with the expected date of the feature, and consistent with each other. OxA-2422, together with OxA-2424, were analysed to test the reliability of using *Quercus* sp. twigs and young branches for radiocarbon dating, as compared with samples of *Betula* sp.

References: Hedges *et al* 1991a, 127

OxA–2423 3220 ±70 BP

δ¹³C: -26.4‰

Sample: EF89/C22/238B, submitted in December 1989 by K Smith

Material: charcoal: *Betula* sp. (R Gale)

Initial comment: as OxA-2422

Objectives: as OxA-2422

Calibrated date: *1σ:* 1610–1420 cal BC
                      2σ: 1670–1320 cal BC

Final comment: J Barnatt (1991), this sample, of exclusively *Betula* sp. charcoal, was used as a control to compare with OxA-2422 and OxA-2424 from *Quercus* sp. twigs and young branches. *See also* OxA-2422.

References: Hedges *et al* 1991a, 127

OxA–2424 3105 ±80 BP

δ¹³C: -26.8‰

Sample: EF89/C36B, submitted in December 1989 by K Smith

Material: charcoal: *Quercus* sp., stem or young branch (R Gale)

Initial comment: as OxA-2422

Objectives: as OxA-2422

Calibrated date: *1σ:* 1450–1290 cal BC
                      2σ: 1530–1130 cal BC

Final comment: see OxA-2422

References: Hedges *et al* 1991a, 127

OxA–2425 3105 ±80 BP

δ¹³C: -26.8‰

Sample: EF89/C36B, submitted in December 1989 by K Smith

Material: charcoal: *Betula* sp. (R Gale)

Initial comment: as OxA-2422

Objectives: this sample should have a direct bearing on the date of the cairn. Stratigraphically this cairn is the earliest identifiable structure on the site.

Calibrated date: *1σ:* 1450–1290 cal BC
                      2σ: 1530–1130 cal BC

Final comment: J Barnatt (1991), the charcoal from this cremation pyre is consistent with the expected date, both for the site as a whole, and the stratigraphic position of the feature.

References: Hedges *et al* 1991a, 127

OxA–3090 3250 ±80 BP

δ¹³C: -26.0‰ (assumed)

Sample: EF90B, submitted in March 1991 by J Barnatt

Material: charcoal: *Betula* sp. (C Dixon)

Initial comment: a scatter of charcoal combined to make a single sample (comprising samples 1023/1029/1032) derived from a small area under a small cairn containing a cremation and an enlarged food vessel on a slab. The charcoal was directly under three of the stones of the feature and should relate directly to its construction. The feature was undisturbed and there is little or no chance of contamination.

Objectives: this sample will have a direct bearing on the stratigraphic sequence of stone structures. It should contrast with two others, one for the stone bank, 120 (GU-5127), which cairn 173 abuts and earlier feature 22 (OxA-2422 to OxA-2424) dated last year. This sample is also useful in that it dates an enlarged food vessel for which few dates are available.

Calibrated date: *1σ:* 1620–1430 cal BC
                      2σ: 1740–1390 cal BC

Final comment: J Barnatt (1992), the date derived from this sample is consistent with that expected. It is later than the date for bank 120, as predicted from the horizontal stratigraphy. However, it is unexpectedly no later than the three dates from cairn 22. This demonstrates that the phasing of the site as derived from horizontal stratigraphy is probably more complex than first postulated.

References: Hedges *et al* 1992, 147

OxA–3091 3420 ±120 BP

δ¹³C: -26.0‰ (assumed)

Sample: EF90H, submitted on 13 May 1991 by J Barnatt

Material: charcoal: *Betula* sp. (C Dixon)

Initial comment: sealed within the upper fill (context 684) of cremation pit 173. It was associated with only a few cremated bones and *Quercus* sp. charcoal. The lower fill had much of the cremation with exclusively *Quercus* sp. charcoal. The upper fill was placed in the pit immediately after the lower as part of the same event. There was no obvious disturbance except for small numbers of small rootlets.

Objectives: as part of the series for the site it will provide one of three dates for cremations in pits with burnt sides. The other two are at the other end of the site and hence this sample will examine the spatial shift through time.

Calibrated date: *1σ:* 1890–1530 cal BC
                      2σ: 2040–1440 cal BC

Final comment: J Barnatt (1992), this date is consistent with the others from cremations on the site (GU-5129, GU-5130, OxA-3245, and GU-5128).

References: Hedges *et al* 1992, 147

OxA–3245 3430 ±90 BP

δ¹³C: -24.9‰

Sample: EF90J, submitted in March 1991 by J Barnatt

Material: charcoal: *Betula* sp. (C Dixon)

Initial comment: sealed within a small cordoned urn associated with a cremation, a bone whistle, and lithics; all within a small pit (21). Although the edge of the pit was clipped by a modern drain this did not affect the fill of the urn significantly. There is little chance of contamination.

Objectives: this sample is one of two submitted to give representative dates for the six examples excavated of cremations in urns.

Calibrated date: *1σ:* 1890–1620 cal BC
                    2σ: 1960–1510 cal BC

Final comment: J Barnatt (1992), the date derived from this sample is consistent with the others from cremations on the site (GU-5128, GU-5129, GU-5130, and OxA-3091). It is a little earlier than would have been predicted for a cordoned urn, but not unduly so.

References: Hedges *et al* 1992, 147

OxA–3549 3480 ±75 BP

δ¹³C: -24.9‰

Sample: EF90C, submitted on 16 January 1992 by J Barnatt

Material: charcoal: *Betula* sp.

Initial comment: from charcoal sealed immediately under a stone bank.

Objectives: to provide a date for the stone bank and to determine whether it is contemporary with the early cremations.

Calibrated date: *1σ:* 1900–1690 cal BC
                    2σ: 2020–1610 cal BC

Final comment: J Barnatt (1993), the date derived from this sample is comparable with five early dates for cremations analysed previously, and confirms that some of the stone structures on the site are equally as early.

References: Hedges *et al* 1993, 159

OxA–3550 3360 ±75 BP

δ¹³C: -25.2‰

Sample: EF90M, submitted on 16 January 1992 by J Barnatt

Material: charcoal: *Betula* sp. (R Gale)

Initial comment: sealed within a cordoned urn associated with a smashed second cordoned urn and two faience beads; all within small pit 218, covered by a gritstone slab, all under cairn 217. There were no signs of disturbance, so the sample is highly unlikely to be contaminated. The urn was opened under controlled conditions in a museum and therefore unlikely to be contaminated at this stage.

Objectives: this sample supplements the dates already obtained from the site. It has been submitted to resolve the date of feature 217 and thus help resolve the relative sequence of features in the eastern part of the site.

Calibrated date: *1σ:* 1750–1530 cal BC
                    2σ: 1880–1460 cal BC

Final comment: J Barnatt (1993), this sample is consistent with that expected. It provides a second example of a burial dated somewhat later than the majority of the dated cremations on site. It is later than stone feature 120, as the horizontal stratigraphy would suggest.

References: Hedges *et al* 1993, 159

Eckweek, Avon

Location: ST 712578
                   Lat. 51.19.05 N; Long. 20.24.48 W

Project manager: A Kidd (Avon County Council), 1989

Archival body: Roman Baths Museum, Bath

Description: a deserted settlement some five miles south-west of Bath, near the modern village of Peasedown St John; it is mentioned in the Domesday survey. Excavation revealed the presence of timber and stone buildings of a farmstead occupied during late Saxon and medieval periods (*c* AD 950–1400).

Objectives: to establish a chronology for the site.

Final comment: A Kidd (31 January 1990), overall, in the absence of artefactual dating prior to the thirteenth century, the dates have proved useful in refining the chronology of the local medieval pottery sequence which had previously been rather poorly defined.

UB–3203 1019 ±58 BP

δ¹³C: -24.4 ±0.2‰

Sample: 340, submitted on 12 October 1989 by A Kidd

Material: grain (charred cereal grain, wheat, barley, weed seeds, small charcoal and shell fragments) (V Straker)

Initial comment: from the charcoal-rich lower fill of a pit cut into natural: one of a group of cascading pits linked by gullies. The pit contained earlier medieval pottery and was sealed by a greenish clayey soil containing somewhat later pottery; above this lay thick loamy topsoil. The sample was collected from at least 70cm below the modern ground surface.

Objectives: to help date the complex of cascading pits and thus relate them to the features underlying the later medieval farmhouse.

Calibrated date: *1σ:* cal AD 980–1040
                    2σ: cal AD 890–1160

Final comment: A Kidd (31 January 1990), although an early twelfth century AD date is possible from the calibrated date range and would agree with the ceramic phasing which would date the context to cal AD 1100–1250, it is possible that the date is slightly too early and that the sample consisted of old carbon since it was obtained by floatation of a large soil sample containing dispersed charcoal.

UB–3204 891 ±42 BP

δ¹³C: -23.3 ±0.2‰

Sample: 359A, submitted on 12 October 1989 by A Kidd

Material: grain (charred cereal grain, free-threshing wheat, oats, chaff, hulled barley, corn cockle seeds) (V Straker)

Initial comment: from a dense loam/charcoal mix forming the primary fill of a pit cut *c* 60cm into natural. It was sealed by a grey loamy upper fill and, above that, by a rubbly layer. The sample was collected *c* 70cm below the modern ground level.

Objectives: the large quantity of charred grain recovered from this context has allowed two samples to be dated (see also UB-3205). The samples are from a sealed primary pit fill associated with excellent environmental evidence and much early pottery. An accurate date would greatly aid the phasing and dating of the earlier features: a late Saxon date is possible. This pit is adjacent to the cascading pits from whence came UB-3203.

Calibrated date: 1σ: cal AD 1040–1220
2σ: cal AD 1020–1230

Final comment: A Kidd (31 January 1990), UB-3204 and UB-3205 are from the same deposit, and on the basis of the ceramic phasing it is unlikely that the context is later than the early twelfth century AD. The date range at 95% confidence gives the most acceptable dates; and these dates proved useful in defining the chronological development of the previously poorly understood local early medieval pottery.

Laboratory comment: English Heritage (25 January 2012), the two measurements on short-life bulk samples from this deposit are statistically consistent (T'=1; T'(5%)=3.8; ν=1; Ward and Wilson 1978), so a weighted mean may be taken (919 ±33 BP), which calibrates to cal AD 1020–1220 (at 95% confidence; Reimer *et al* 2004), or cal AD 1030–1170 (at 68% confidence).

References: Reimer *et al* 2004
Ward and Wilson 1978

UB–3205 962 ±53 BP

δ¹³C: -23.3 ±0.2‰

Sample: 359B, submitted on 12 October 1989 by A Kidd

Material: grain: Cereal indet (V Straker)

Initial comment: as UB-3204

Objectives: as UB-3204

Calibrated date: 1σ: cal AD 1020–1160
2σ: cal AD 980–1210

Final comment: see UB-3204

Laboratory comment: see UB-3204

UB–3206 830 ±41 BP

δ¹³C: -23.9 ±0.2‰

Sample: 170, submitted on 12 October 1989 by A Kidd

Material: charcoal: unidentified (V Straker)

Initial comment: samples were taken all along the secondary fill of a gully, which partially underlay a late medieval limestone walled farmhouse. This gully was one of a group of related and broadly contemporary pits and gullies cut into the natural. Below 170 was a clean brown silt forming the primary fill 207; above was a loamy soil with dispersed charcoal 155 filling a recut and then an extensive soil horizon of grey/brown loam 114, which sealed the entire gully and was itself covered by the later building's floor and destruction levels. All samples were at least 70cm below modern ground level.

Objectives: to help date the complex of pits and gullies underneath the later medieval farmhouse. Ceramic dating of these features is inadequate and a late Saxon date is considered possible. Comparison with the other samples submitted will be essential to site phasing.

Calibrated date: 1σ: cal AD 1170–1260
2σ: cal AD 1050–1280

Final comment: A Kidd (31 January 1990), in view of the attribution of this context to ceramic phase 4 (AD 1100–1250), UB-3206 accords well. It is likely that this was a destruction deposit associated with the changeover from timber to stone buildings.

UB–3298 990 ±64 BP

δ¹³C: -23.3 ±0.2‰

Sample: 237, submitted on 15 February 1989 by A Young

Material: grain (charred cereal grains, free threshing wheat, rachis fragments, and weed seeds) (V Straker)

Initial comment: from a charcoal layer forming the lowest fill of a pit *c* 40cm deep cut into natural clay; it is possibly the cellar/sunken floor of a late Saxon/Norman timber building. The pit was sealed, but not disturbed by a late medieval stone farmhouse.

Objectives: to date phase III, the earliest phase of medieval occupation on the site. Medieval pottery is still inadequately dated in Avon and Eckweek provides a valuable stratified sequence, which can be dated by coins for the later occupation but requires radiocarbon dates for the earlier possibly tenth- to twelfth-century AD phase.

Calibrated date: 1σ: cal AD 990–1160
2σ: cal AD 890–1210

Final comment: A Kidd (31 January 1990), a difficult date to interpret since the bulk of the fill of this pit dated to AD 1250–1300 on ceramic grounds. The charcoal layer may have formed a lining of a *grubenhaus* pit where it cut an earlier such pit dated AD 1050–1100. The calibrated ranges would allow an early twelfth-century date and it is possible that the pit remained open for 150 years.

Ellacott, Stow-on-the-Wold, Gloucestershire

Location: SP 19412595
Lat. 51.55.53 N; Long. 01.43.04 W

Project manager: C Parry (Gloucestershire County Council), 1992

Archival body: Corinium Museum, Cirencester

Description: a ditch of defensive dimensions aligned upon the postulated defences of an Iron Age hillfort (Crawford 1933).

Objectives: to establish whether the ditch is Iron Age or not.

Final comment: C Parry (3 May 1994), the two samples submitted yielded closely comparable dates to indicate that the suspected Iron Age ditch belonged to the middle Bronze Age. The ditch is reinterpreted as the defences of a hilltop enclosure, possibly of Rams Hill type. The presence of an Iron Age hillfort at Stow-on-the-Wold has yet to be proved.

References: Crawford 1933
Hedges *et al* 1994, 363

OxA–3652 2955 ±65 BP

δ¹³C: -21.2‰

Sample: 11905/29/1, submitted on 23 April 1992 by C Parry

Material: animal bone

Initial comment: from the fill (context 29) of a ditch (context 30) which appears to represent one of a pair of ditches forming a defensive system. Context 29, a friable-compact brown silty clay, contained up to 80% limestone fragments, and is interpreted as slumped (or backfilled) rampart material. This context yielded a single sherd of non-diagnostic prehistoric pottery.

Objectives: to indicate an approximate date for the deposit in which it lay and, in addition, suggest a date for the construction of the ditch. The ditch is interpreted as a portion of the defences of an Iron Age hillfort, which has long been postulated at Stow but never proved.

Calibrated date: *1σ:* 1300–1050 cal BC
2σ: 1400–970 cal BC

Final comment: C Parry (3 May 1994), the date was earlier than expected, suggesting that the suspected Iron Age ditch was, in fact, middle Bronze Age.

OxA–3801 2960 ±65 BP

δ¹³C: -20.9‰

Sample: 11905/29/2, submitted on 23 April 1992 by C Parry

Material: animal bone

Initial comment: as OxA-3652

Objectives: as OxA-3652

Calibrated date: *1σ:* 1300–1050 cal BC
2σ: 1400–990 cal BC

Final comment: see OxA-3652

Enderby: Grove Farm, Leicestershire

Location: SK 551002
Lat. 52.35.47 N; Long. 01.11.11 W

Project manager: P Clay (Leicestershire Museums Archaeological Unit), 1984

Archival body: Leicestershire Museums

Description: a late Iron Age enclosure situated on a boulder clay ridge, 5km south-west of Leicester and 1.5km north-east of Enderby, overlooking the confluence of Lubbesthorpe Brook and other tributary streams flowing into the River Soar. Excavations revealed several phases of activity including circular buildings. Environmental information suggests the practice of a mixed economy during the first century BC and the first century AD.

Objectives: to establish a chronology for the site.

Laboratory comment: Ancient Monuments Laboratory (2003), one further sample A30 83C2 (HAR-9279) was submitted for dating but failed to produce a result.

References: Clay 1992a
Hardiman *et al* 1992, 59

HAR–9410 1870 ±90 BP

δ¹³C: -25.0‰ (assumed)

Sample: A30 83C1, submitted on 9 January 1988 by P Clay

Material: charcoal: *Sorbus aucuparia* L.; *Acer campestre* L.; *Populus* sp.; *Fraxinus* sp.; *Quercus* sp. (N Field)

Initial comment: from an eaves drip trench surrounding a first phase Iron Age building. This may derive from the destruction of the building and therefore provide a terminal date for its use.

Objectives: to provide a date for the first phase of the building and to date associated pottery.

Calibrated date: *1σ:* cal AD 30–250
2σ: 50 cal BC–cal AD 390

Final comment: P Clay (18 April 1995), Iron Age dates are notoriously difficult to calibrate bearing in mind the twists on the curve. Our stratigraphical information would suggest the context is within the calibrated range at 95% confidence rather than at 68% unless insular Iron Age settlements carried on into the late first century AD with virtually no contact with the Roman invaders, which is unlikely. We are at present having more Iron Age dates processed (both radiocarbon and thermoluminescence), which may help our interpretation.

Etton Landscape, Maxey, Cambridgeshire

Location: TF 51453075
Lat. 52.51.09 N; Long. 00.14.58 E

Project manager: C French (Fenland Archaeological Unit), 1987

Archival body: The British Museum

Description: a Neolithic/early Bronze Age settlement and ceremonial complex on meandering streams and the fen edge on the River Welland first terrace gravels, on the route of the A15 Bypass near Glinton and Northborough villages.

Objectives: this series of dates was chosen to set a relative chronology for the main phases of activity at the Etton Landscape/A15 bypass site. The site was in fact a series of superimposed landscapes, ranging in date from the Neolithic to the Roman period, all partially buried by river alluvial deposits.

Final comment: C French (19 July 1994), in general, the radiocarbon dates (Q-3093 to Q-3100 and Q-3147 to Q3150) obtained served to reinforce the dating opinions arrived at on site from artefacts and stratigraphic relationships. It also provided an excellent landscape context for the adjacent ceremonial sites, such as the Etton causewayed enclosure and both Etton Landscape hengiform sites (EL2 and EL4).

Laboratory comment: English Heritage (21 January 2012), eleven further dates from this site were published in Bayliss *et al* (2012, 89–91; Q-3093–3100, and Q-3147–50). The humic acid fraction of peat sample ELRT6/1/1 (GU–5125) failed.

References: French and Pryor 2005, 97
                      Taylor and French 1985

GU–5123 10900 ±120 BP

δ¹³C: -29.4‰

Sample: ELRT4, submitted on 15 March 1991 by M Macklin

Material: peat

Initial comment: peat from a palaeochannel base.

Objectives: to date the channel abandonment.

Calibrated date: *1σ:* 11000–10600 cal BC
                       2σ: 11200–10600 cal BC

Final comment: C French (15 November 2006), this dates the base of a very late glacial river channel to the east of the Etton causewayed enclosure associated with pollen data for a cold climate, sparse, and open vegetation.

Laboratory comment: SURRC Radiocarbon Dating Laboratory (20 June 1991), the second humic acid fraction dated.

References: French and Pryor 2005

GU–5124 10070 ±190 BP

δ¹³C: -19.3‰

Sample: ELRT4/2, submitted on 15 March 1991 by M Macklin

Material: peat

Initial comment: peat from a palaeochannel base.

Objectives: as GU-5123

Calibrated date: *1σ:* 10100–9300 cal BC
                       2σ: 10470–9220 cal BC

Final comment: C French (15 November 2006), this dates the base of a very late glacial river channel to the east of the Etton causewayed enclosure associated with pollen data for a cold climate, sparse and open vegetation.

Final comment: A Bayliss (22 October 2007), the radiocarbon results from the base of the river channel are not statistically consistent (T'=13.0; T'(5%)=3.8; ν=1; Ward and Wilson 1978). The acid and alkali insoluble (humin) fraction is significantly younger.

Laboratory comment: SURRC Radiocarbon Dating Laboratory (20 June 1991), the humin fraction was dated.

References: French and Pryor 2005
                      Ward and Wilson 1978

GU–5126 7380 ±90 BP

δ¹³C: -21.0‰

Sample: ELRT6/1/2, submitted on 15 March 1991 by M Macklin

Material: peat

Initial comment: peat from a palaeochannel base.

Objectives: as GU-5123

Calibrated date: *1σ:* 6380–6100 cal BC
                       2σ: 6440–6050 cal BC

Final comment: C French (15 November 2006), this dates the base of another channel belt to the south of the Etton causewayed enclosure to Mesolithic times and is associated with pollen data for a fully wooded landscape.

Laboratory comment: SURRC Radiocarbon Dating Laboratory (20 June 1991), the humin fraction was dated.

References: French and Pryor 2005

Ferrybridge Henge, Yorkshire (West Riding)

Location: SE 47482424
                     Lat. 53.42.44 N; Long. 01.16.50 W

Project manager: J D Hedges (West Yorkshire Archaeological Service), 1991

Archival body: British Museum and Wakefield Museum

Description: a henge monument with a large bank and inner ditch with two entrances opposite each other.

Objectives: due to extensive ploughing in the area, it has meant the erosion of the earthwork, so any datable information from the henge is very important.

Final comment: I Roberts (15 October 2008), these samples were to date the phase 2 henge bank. Subsequently, a charred grain sample from the phase 1 bank has been dated by the University of Arizona to cal BC 3360–2870 at 95% confidence (4390 ±95 BP; AA-40923; Reimer *et al* 2004). This compares well with the phase 2 dates and together broadly suggest that the inner ditch and phase 1 bank were probably constructed around 3000 BC, with the outer ditch and the second phase of bank being constructed in the mid-third millennium BC (Roberts *et al* 2005, 235).

Laboratory comment: English Heritage (26 January 2012), the two measurements on different size fractions of bulk charcoal from this deposit are statistically significantly different (T'=11.4; T'(5%)=3.8; ν=1; Ward and Wilson 1978), the latest measurement therefore provides a *terminus post quem* for the henge bank.

References: Brown *et al* 2007
                      Reimer *et al* 2004
                      Roberts *et al* 2005, 223–35
                      Ward and Wilson 1978

GU–5216 3900 ±80 BP

$\delta^{13}C$: -24.9‰

Sample: FB91 A - Fine, submitted on 12 March 1992 by J D Hedges

Material: charcoal: *Quercus* sp. (Allan Hall 1991)

Initial comment: recovered between two layers from the bank of the henge, which was constructed from redeposited magnesian limestone; lenses of charcoal could be seen over *c* 5m, and were immediately below plough soil approximately 30cm deep.

Objectives: the sample was sealed within the bank during one phase of construction and will give a *terminus post quem* for the date of this use of the henge.

Calibrated date: 1σ: 2480–2210 cal BC
2σ: 2580–2140 cal BC

Final comment: see series comments.

GU–5217 4260 ±70 BP

$\delta^{13}C$: -24.8‰

Sample: FB91 B Large, submitted on 12 March 1992 by J D Hedges

Material: charcoal: *Quercus* sp. (Allan Hall 1991)

Initial comment: a replicate sample of GU-5216.

Objectives: as GU-5216

Calibrated date: 1σ: 2920–2870 cal BC
2σ: 3030–2630 cal BC

Final comment: see series comments.

Flag Fen, Cambridgeshire

Location: TL 227989
Lat. 52.34.25 N; Long. 00.11.21 W

Project manager: M Macklin (Fenland Archaeological Trust), 1990

Description: Flag Fen is on the south eastern limits of the city of Peterborough. The landscape is very low-lying, and prior to drainage of the seventeenth century, was characterised by large areas of freshwater to slightly, brackish wetland surrounded by dried, flood-free, fen-edge plain. At present Flag Fen has yet to unearth any datable artefact that pre-dates the middle Bronze Age.

Objectives: radiocarbon dating remains the only method of dating local environmental sequences.

References: Pryor 1992
Pryor 2001

Flag Fen: wiggle-matching, Cambridgeshire

Location: TL 227989
Lat. 52.34.25 N; Long. 00.11.21 W

Project manager: M Macklin (Fenland Archaeological Trust), 1990

Archival body: Fenland Archaeological Trust

Description: six samples of waterlogged wood from the floating tree-ring sequence at Flag Fen were submitted for high precision radiocarbon measurement.

Objectives: to date the floating tree-ring sequence.

Final comment: A Bayliss and F Pryor (1999), the dates for the tree-rings estimated by the wiggle-matching do not correspond precisely to the dates provided by dendrochron-ology (Bayliss and Pryor 2001; table 16.3). The reasons for this difference are not fully understood, although some discussion of possible contributory factors is provided by Kromer *et al* (1996). Furthermore recent work (McCormac *et al* 1995; Kromer *et al* 1996) has highlighted the need for refinements to the present calibration data set. Here we have used the calibration data adopted internationally in 1986 (Pearson and Stuiver 1986), although it was revised in 1993 (Stuiver and Pearson 1993) and a new internationally accepted revision is due to be published in 1998 (Stuiver *et al* 1998a).

Laboratory comment: University of Belfast (26 July 2012), these samples were processed using the high-precision dating facility.

Laboratory comment: English Heritage (27 January 2012), recalculated using the calibration data of Reimer *et al* (2004), this wiggle-match model still has poor overall agreement (n=6 A$_{comb}$ =28.9 (A$_n$ =28.9); Fig. 23 this volume), although only *UB-3423* has poor individual agreement (A:6). This model suggests that the last ring of the wiggle-match sequence dates to *1195–1180 cal BC (8% probability)*, or *1160–1130 cal BC (85% probability)*, or *1125–1115 cal BC (2% probability)*. This is not compatible with the date of this ring of 1020 BC known from dendrochronology.

References: Bayliss and Pryor 2001
Kromer *et al* 1996
McCormac *et al* 1995
Pearson and Stuiver 1986
Reimer *et al* 2004
Stuiver *et al* 1998a
Stuiver and Reimer 1993

UB–3422 3004 ±19 BP

$\delta^{13}C$: -27.5 ±0.2‰

Sample: B9/2, Q8315, Block 2, submitted on 14 March 1991 by J Neve

Material: wood (waterlogged): *Quercus* sp.

Initial comment: this sample forms part of a series of six to be taken from two pieces of wood, with overlapping ring-series. The samples are taken to provide six high-precision dates for a wigglematch date on the timbers.

Objectives: will allow the whole Flag Fen ring-sequence to be tied down to its correct date with confidence.

Calibrated date: 1σ: 1300–1215 cal BC
2σ: 1375–1130 cal BC

Final comment: J Neve (1999), this sample was subsequently dated by dendrochronology to 1139–1120 BC.

Laboratory comment: University of Belfast (10 April 1991), this sample was bleached.

UB–3423 3061 ±21 BP

$\delta^{13}C$: -27.7 ±0.2‰

Sample: B9/2, Q8315, Block 3, submitted on 14 March 1991 by J Neve

Material: wood (waterlogged): *Quercus* sp. (J Neve)

Initial comment: as UB-3422

Objectives: as UB-3422

Calibrated date: 1σ: 1390–1305 cal BC
                     2σ: 1410–1265 cal BC

Final comment: J Neve (1999), this sample was subsequently dated by dendrochronology to 1119–1110 BC.

Laboratory comment: English Heritage (2001), this measurement has poor individual agreement in the wiggle-match model (A:19.8).

Laboratory comment: see UB-3422

UB–3424 2960 ±22 BP

$\delta^{13}C$: -28.5 ±0.2‰

Sample: B9/2, Q8315, Block 4, submitted on 14 March 1991 by J Neve

Material: wood (waterlogged): *Quercus* sp.

Initial comment: as UB-3422

Objectives: as UB-3422

Calibrated date: 1σ: 1260–1125 cal BC
                     2σ: 1270–1115 cal BC

Final comment: J Neve (1999), this sample was subsequently dated by dendrochronology to 1099–1080 BC.

Laboratory comment: see UB-3422

UB–3425 2921 ±17 BP

$\delta^{13}C$: -28.3 ±0.2‰

Sample: B9/2, Block 5 and A1895, submitted on 14 March 1991 by J Neve

Material: wood (waterlogged): *Quercus* sp.

Initial comment: as UB-3422

Objectives: as UB-3422

Calibrated date: 1σ: 1190–1055 cal BC
                     2σ: 1210–1045 cal BC

Final comment: J Neve (1999), this sample was subsequently dated by dendrochronology to 1079–1060 BC.

Laboratory comment: English Heritage (2001), this measurement has poor individual agreement in the wiggle-match model (A:19.8).

Laboratory comment: see UB-3422

UB–3426 2935 ±17 BP

$\delta^{13}C$: -27.8 ±0.2‰

Sample: B9/2, Block 6 and A1895, Block 2, submitted on 14 March 1991 by J Neve

Material: wood (waterlogged): *Quercus* sp.

Initial comment: as UB-3422

Objectives: as UB-3422

Calibrated date: 1σ: 1195–1115 cal BC
                     2σ: 1260–1050 cal BC

Final comment: J Neve (1999), this sample was subsequently dated by dendrochronology to 1059–1040 BC.

Laboratory comment: see UB-3422

UB–3427 2918 ±17 BP

$\delta^{13}C$: -28.6 ±0.2‰

Sample: B9/2, Block 7 and A1895, Block 3, submitted on 14 March 1991 by J Neve

Material: wood (waterlogged): *Quercus* sp.

Initial comment: as UB-3422

Objectives: as UB-3422

Calibrated date: 1σ: 1190–1055 cal BC
                     2σ: 1210–1030 cal BC

Final comment: J Neve (1999), this sample was subsequently dated by dendrochronology to 1039–1020 BC.

Laboratory comment: see UB-3422

Fordington Farm: round barrow, Dorset

Location: SY 69898989
                   Lat. 50.42.26 N; Long. 02.25.35 W

Project manager: M J Allen (Wessex Archaeology), 1988

Archival body: Dorset County Museum

Description: this round barrow, visible as slight mound in a field of scrub pasture was excavated as a result of the intended conversion of the site into sports pitches. Four constructional and three surviving burial phases were identified.

Objectives: to determine the date of the burials and whether they are late Neolithic or early Bronze Age.

References: Bellamy 1991
                   Chowne and Copson 1989

UB–3304 3715 ±54 BP

$\delta^{13}C$: -23.9 ±0.2‰

Sample: bone - burial 70, submitted on 15 January 1990 by M J Allen

Material: human bone (left and right femuri) (V Jenkins 1988)

Initial comment: this is one of two graves in an inner segmented ditched barrow. The form is typical of a late Neolithic/early Bronze Age date but examples are rare.

Objectives: to determine whether it is late Neolithic or early Bronze Age.

Calibrated date: 1σ: 2200–2030 cal BC
                      2σ: 2290–1950 cal BC

Final comment: F Healy (19 July 1991), this date and UB-3305 date burials unaccompanied by artefacts from two rectangular pits cut into the pre-barrow land surface, surrounded by a discontinuous circular ditch covered by a small mound. Each burial had apparently been contained within a timber structure and consisted of the disarticulated, but separate bones of an adult male, an adult female and a foetal or neonatal child in grave 70, and an adult male and child in grave 59. The closely similar determinations are consistent with the identical stratigraphic position and rite of the two burials.

UB–3305 3767 ±47 BP

δ¹³C: -21.6 ±0.2‰

Sample: bone - burial 59, submitted on 15 January 1990 by M J Allen

Material: human bone (left and right humeri) (V Jenkins 1988)

Initial comment: this is the second grave in an inner segmented ditched barrow, primary burial 59, grave fill 60. The form is typical of a late Neolithic/early Bronze Age date but examples are rare.

Objectives: to determine whether it is late Neolithic or early Bronze Age.

Calibrated date: 1σ: 2280–2130 cal BC
                      2σ: 2340–2030 cal BC

Final comment: see UB-3304

UB–3306 3844 ±30 BP

δ¹³C: -22.5 ±0.2‰

Sample: bone - burial 61, submitted on 15 January 1990 by M J Allen

Material: human bone (left and right femora) (V Jenkins 1988)

Initial comment: this is one of two graves in an inner segmented ditched barrow, burial 61, grave fill 62. The form is typical of a late Neolithic/early Bronze Age date but examples are rare.

Objectives: to determine whether it is late Neolithic or early Bronze Age.

Calibrated date: 1σ: 2390–2210 cal BC
                      2σ: 2470–2200 cal BC

Final comment: F Healy (19 July 1991), the earliest determination of the three, dates the articulated skeleton of a young adult male found with cattle bones and a barbed and tanged arrowhead in a grave cut through the primary mound into the pre-barrow land surface and itself cut by a pit containing an inverted Collared Urn containing a cremation accompanied by a copper alloy knife dagger. The inversion of stratigraphic sequence among the radiocarbon determinations maybe attributable to a confusion of samples or to a short time span for the whole sequence.

Gloucester: St Oswald's Priory, Gloucestershire

Location: SO 830190
                    Lat. 51.52.08 N; Long. 02.14.49 W

Project manager: C M Heighway (Gloucester Excavation Unit), 1978

Archival body: Gloucester City Museum

Description: the minster of St Oswald was, according to William of Malmesbury, founded at Gloucester c AD 900 by Æthelred, Ealdorman of Mercia and his wife Æthelflæd. Excavations 1974–9 and 1983 established the plan and sequence of a Saxon church, some of which survives as a ruin.

Objectives: the radiocarbon dates were expected to provide evidence for the foundation date of the excavated church, which has produced structural evidence but no closely-datable artefacts.

Final comment: C M Heighway (21 April 1995), these samples date the foundation of the church, which is pre-AD 1086 on architectural grounds, and which is said by William of Malmesbury to date from the time of Alfred. Burials began when the church was built. The two samples HAR-8357 and HAR-8358 appear to confirm the late ninth-century date for the church's construction.

Laboratory comment: Ancient Monuments Laboratory (2003), two further samples 4175B348 (HAR-9698) and 4175B525 (HAR-9699) were submitted for dating but failed to produce results.

Laboratory comment: English Heritage (17 January 2012), two further dates from this site were published in Bayliss *et al* (2012, 129; HAR-8357-8).

References: Bayliss *et al* 2012
                    Hardiman *et al* 1992, 51
                    Heighway 1978
                    Heighway 1980
                    Heighway and Bryant 1999

HAR–9700 1170 ±60 BP

δ¹³C: -21.4‰

Sample: 4175B464, submitted in November 1988 by C Heighway

Material: human bone

Initial comment: from B464, the only burial found which pre-dated the foundation of the church, since it was cut by the foundations of the north porticus.

Objectives: to provide evidence for the foundation date of the church, but also to establish whether or not this burial was Roman.

Calibrated date: 1σ: cal AD 770–970
                      2σ: cal AD 680–1000

Final comment: C Heighway (21 April 1995), this date shows that B464 was not Roman, but was part of a pre-church cemetery of eighth- to ninth-century date of which nothing else is known. Such a cemetery is also suggested by the presence in the first church fabric of broken eighth–ninth-century cross-shafts.

Laboratory comment: AERE Harwell (6 October 1989), this sample was processed using the larger sample, higher precision liquid scintillation system.

Godmanchester: Rectory Farm, Cambridgeshire

Location:	TL 258710 Lat. 52.19.21 N; Long. 00.09.20 W
Project manager:	F McAvoy (Central Excavation Service), 1988–92
Archival body:	English Heritage

Description: multi-period cropmarks, covering *c* 40ha in the Lower Ouse Valley, investigated prior to mineral extraction.

Objectives: to establish a chronological framework through scientific dating for the origin and development of a new form of Neolithic 'enclosure' and its associated monuments and structures.

Laboratory comment: English Heritage (3 February 2012), three further bone samples 432-3530, 432-8501, and 432-8502 were submitted for dating but failed due to low collagen yield.

References:	McAvoy 1991 Whittle *et al* 2011, 278–93

AA–9568 1865 ±55 BP

δ¹³C: -20.8‰

Sample: 432-8503, submitted on 12 February 1992 by K Izard

Material: human bone (F McAvoy 1989)

Initial comment: from a human skeleton found in a shallow grave cut into a turf mound, which was enclosed by a large ?Neolithic ring ditch. The burial is not in a central position, but is next to the terminal of an ?enclosure ditch, which also cuts the mound.

Objectives: there was no associated artefactual evidence and a date was required in order to establish when this feature was considered to be a suitable place for burial.

Calibrated date: 1σ: cal AD 70–240
2σ: cal AD 20–320

Final comment: F McAvoy (19 July 1994), this showed that the burial on the mound was taking place within the Roman period.

Laboratory comment: SUERC Radiocarbon Dating Laboratory (AMS) (1 April 1993), this sample produced too little carbon dioxide for conventional dating and so was sent for graphitisation and dating at the Arizona AMS laboratory.

AA–9569 3740 ±55 BP

δ¹³C: -26.0‰

Sample: 432-3018, submitted on 12 February 1992 by K Izard

Material: animal bone: *Bos* sp. (F McAvoy 1989)

Initial comment: from two cattle mandibles (left and right) found just above the primary fill of one of the two entrance ditch terminals of the Neolithic 'enclosure'. In the other ditch terminal there was an upper ox skull placed on the base of the ditch and it is possible that these are from one animal.

Objectives: there were no dates from the ditch, as opposed to the posts, which form part of this unique monument. This sample, although not in itself from an absolute primary context, may be related to a skull which is, but this cannot be dated.

Calibrated date: 1σ: 2270–2030 cal BC
2σ: 2300–1970 cal BC

Final comment: F Healy (2008), this measurement is statistically inconsistent with a second result from disarticulated animal bone from the primary silts of the enclosure (OxA-4360; 4360 ±100 BP; 3360-2700 cal BC at 95% probability; Reimer *et al* 2004). For both measurements to be accurate, the surface of the primary silts would have had to have remained stable and exposed for a thousand years or so. This is implausible, especially on the gravels in which the ditch was cut. This suggests that collagen preservation may have been variable to poor on this site, as elsewhere in the Valley of the Great Ouse. On the basis of the disagreement between this result and the reliable charcoal dates from this monument, this date is probably anomalously recent, and OxA-4360 is to be preferred.

Final comment: F McAvoy (19 July 1994), this result can be compared with OxA-4360 obtained from the animal bone found in a similar position within the other entrance ditch terminal and with the results of the determinations from samples of charcoal recovered from a series of posts, which were located around the interior of the 'enclosure'. They provide confirmation of the early prehistoric origins of this structure.

Laboratory comment: see AA-9568

GU–5213 3240 ±50 BP

δ¹³C: -24.8‰

Sample: 432-8206, submitted on 4 November 1991 by K Izard

Material: wood (waterlogged): unidentified

Initial comment: from a length of wattle fence or lining present along the side of one of a group of pits similar size and form. These were all cut into a junction between the ditches of the Neolithic 'enclosure' and a later cursus.

Objectives: these pits all have similar fills and contain relatively large amounts of animal bone and unburnt wood. There is, however, no ceramic material and the dating is too heavily dependent upon a few flints - in particular a barbed and tanged arrowhead.

Calibrated date: *1σ*: 1610–1440 cal BC
                             2σ: 1630–1410 cal BC

Final comment: F McAvoy (19 July 1994), this result can be compared with GU–5266 and GU–5267 and indicates that this is one of the latest pits in the group. These determinations anchor, chronologically, a suggested sequence of environmental change.

GU–5266 4000 ±60 BP

δ¹³C: -27.6‰

Sample: 432-9941, submitted on 4 November 1991 by F McAvoy

Material: wood (waterlogged): unidentified

Initial comment: from small twigs within the base fills of one of a group of pits of similar size and form. These were all cut into a junction between the ditches of the Neolithic 'enclosure' and a later cursus.

Objectives: these pits cut through a cursus ditch at a focal point for an earlier Neolithic 'enclosure'. Botanical evidence suggests that two of the pits have far more woodland/scrub species than the others. This sample is from one of the pits (9963) with the highest proportion of woodland. The twigs may be associated with 'placed' deposits and the pits appear to have been rapidly backfilled.

Calibrated date: *1σ*: 2580–2460 cal BC
                             2σ: 2840–2340 cal BC

Final comment: F McAvoy (19 July 1994), this result can be compared with GU–5213 and GU–5267 and indicates that this is one of the earliest pits in the group. The result also provides a *terminus ante quem* for the infilling of the cursus ditch at this point.

GU–5267 3830 ±60 BP

δ¹³C: -27.2‰

Sample: 432-9975, submitted on 4 November 1991 by F McAvoy

Material: wood (waterlogged): twig

Initial comment: as GU–5266

Objectives: as GU–5266

Calibrated date: *1σ*: 2460–2150 cal BC
                             2σ: 2480–2050 cal BC

Final comment: F McAvoy (19 July 1994), this result can be compared with GU–5213 and GU–5266 and indicates that this is one of the earliest pits in the group.

GU–5268 1950 ±60 BP

δ¹³C: -23.8‰

Sample: 432-8244, submitted on 4 November 1991 by F McAvoy

Material: waterlogged plant macrofossil: *Picea abies* sp., spruce cones (P Murphy 1992)

Initial comment: cones from the basal waterlogged gravel fill of a 'pond', well sealed under organic fills and demolition rubble, which is associated with the Romano-British complex.

Objectives: spruce is an alien tree, usually supposed to have been introduced from the seventeenth-century. This record (with leaves and shoots) establishes its presence in the Roman period may have wider implications for interpretation of pollen data of other sites.

Calibrated date: *1σ*: 20 cal BC–cal AD 130
                             2σ: 90 cal BC–cal AD 220

Final comment: P Murphy (21 March 2012), cones of *Picea abies* (spruce) from Roman contexts at Godmanchester, Cambridgeshire. Spruce is not a native post-glacial tree in the UK, and it had been assumed that it was first introduced in the post-medieval period for forestry. The confirmation of a Roman date for these cones, which were found with other remains of the tree and occurred with other garden plants, suggests that spruce first came to England as part of a hardy planting for a garden - replacing the Mediterranean conifers that characterised contemporary gardens in Italy.

OxA–2323 4220 ±90 BP

δ¹³C: -23.3‰

Sample: 432-3611, submitted in November 1989 by T Pearson

Material: antler

Initial comment: antler found in the fill of one of the postholes within the Neolithic 'enclosure'.

Objectives: to date the antler and possibly the posthole.

Calibrated date: *1σ*: 2910–2670 cal BC
                             2σ: 3030–2500 cal BC

Final comment: F Healy (2008), this sample may have suffered the same problem of contamination as AA-9569.

Final comment: F McAvoy (19 July 1994), this date is much later in comparison with others from the post series. The antler may be evidence for later activity within this post-setting as the post could not have been present at its time of deposition.

References: Hedges *et al* 1991b, 289

OxA–3366 3390 ±75 BP

δ¹³C: -26.9‰

Sample: 432-8001, submitted on 1 August 1991 by F McAvoy

Material: charcoal: unidentified

Initial comment: charcoal from a cremation (9265) of a young adult, cut into the upper fill of a transverse ditch, within the interior of the Neolithic enclosure. The western end of the ditch curved around a posthole, part of a series located within the enclosure and the eastern end was cut through a small square enclosure ditch.

Objectives: the sparse nature of the material evidence and the contextual relationships with other features provided the justification for seeking a radiocarbon date.

Calibrated date: 1σ: 1760–1610 cal BC
                     2σ: 1890–1500 cal BC

Final comment: F McAvoy (19 July 1994), this result will inform comment on the nature of activity and structural development within the Neolithic 'enclosure'.

References: Hedges *et al* 1993, 157

OxA–3367 4950 ±80 BP

δ¹³C: -25.9‰

Sample: 432-8017/8, submitted in 1991 by F McAvoy

Material: charcoal: unidentified

Initial comment: the charred post (9349) found in posthole (9349) part of a series of 24, which form part of a 'new' type of Neolithic monument. The sample was taken from the bottom of the post, which in this case was severely truncated by machining.

Objectives: it is of vital importance to date this new form of monument. We have proved its relationship with a later 'cursus' but artefact recovery from both structures was sparse and undiagnostic. The posts all show signs of burning indicating deliberate destruction.

Calibrated date: 1σ: 3900–3650 cal BC
                     2σ: 3960–3540 cal BC

Final comment: F McAvoy (19 July 1994), this result may be compared with others from the posthole series.

References: Hedges *et al* 1993, 157

OxA–3369 4850 ±80 BP

δ¹³C: -24.0‰

Sample: 432-8047, submitted in 1991 by F McAvoy

Material: charcoal: unidentified

Initial comment: charcoal found in the post pipe (9802) of one of a series of postholes 9801, located around the interior of the Neolithic enclosure.

Objectives: as OxA-3367

Calibrated date: 1σ: 3710–3530 cal BC
                     2σ: 3800–3380 cal BC

Final comment: F McAvoy (19 July 1994), there is an apparent anomaly here when this result is compared with OxA-3491, which is from the postpit of the same feature.

References: Hedges *et al* 1993, 157

OxA–3370 5050 ±80 BP

δ¹³C: -25.2‰

Sample: 432-8094, submitted in 1991 by F McAvoy

Material: charcoal: unidentified

Initial comment: from the post pipe (9829) of posthole 9827, one of a series of 24, which form part of a new type of Neolithic monument.

Objectives: as OxA-3367

Calibrated date: 1σ: 3960–3710 cal BC
                     2σ: 4040–3650 cal BC

Final comment: F McAvoy (19 July 1994), this result may be compared with others from the posthole series.

References: Hedges *et al* 1993, 157

OxA–3483 15200 ±140 BP

δ¹³C: -34.9‰

Sample: 432-8094/51, submitted in 1991 by F McAvoy

Material: charcoal: unidentified

Initial comment: from the postpit (9805) of posthole 9801, part of a series of 24, which form part of a new type of Neolithic monument.

Objectives: as OxA-3367

Calibrated date: 1σ: 16700–16200 cal BC
                     2σ: 16800–16000 cal BC

Laboratory comment: Oxford Radiocarbon Accelerator Unit (1993), when the samples from posthole 9801 were dated, it was noted that a 'coal-like' material was mixed in with the wood charcoal. The initial date from the postpit contents (OxA-3483) on a mixture of charcoal and 'coal' indicated there must be a problem. Subsequent microscope separate of the two materials produced OxA-3491 for the charcoal alone, and OxA-3490 for the coal, thus clearly confirming the presence of a ¹⁴C-dead contaminant. The δ¹³C values of the two substances were very different, -33.7‰ for the 'coal' and -26.4‰ for the wood charcoal.

References: Hedges *et al* 1993, 157

OxA–3490 >50000 BP

δ¹³C: -33.7‰

Sample: 432-8049/8051, submitted in 1991 by F McAvoy

Material: charcoal (coal)

Initial comment: as OxA-3483

Objectives: as OxA-3367

Laboratory comment: see OxA-3483

References: Hedges *et al* 1993, 157

OxA–3491 4360 ±75 BP

δ¹³C: -26.4‰

Sample: 432-8094/51, submitted in 1991 by F McAvoy

Material: charcoal: unidentified

Initial comment: charcoal separated out from sample OxA-3483.

Objectives: as OxA-3367

Calibrated date: 1σ: 3100–2900 cal BC
                     2σ: 3340–2870 cal BC

Final comment: F McAvoy (19 July 1994), this result can be compared with those obtained from the other postholes in the series located around the interior of the Neolithic enclosure.

Laboratory comment: see OxA–3483

References:　　　Hedges *et al* 1993, 157

OxA–3646 5035 ±70 BP

δ¹³C: -23.7‰

Sample: 432-8008, submitted on 12 February 1992 by K Izard

Material: charcoal: unidentified

Initial comment: charcoal recovered from the fill 4342 of the post pipe of posthole 9783. This is one of the series of postholes, which form part of a new type of Neolithic monument.

Objectives: this is a unique monument and this sample will give validity to the dates obtained from three other postholes in the series (OxA–3367, OxA–3369, and OxA–3370).

Calibrated date:　　1σ: 3960–3710 cal BC
　　　　　　　　　　2σ: 3980–3650 cal BC

Final comment: F McAvoy (19 July 1994), this result may be compared with others from the posthole series.

References:　　　Hedges *et al* 1993, 157

Gravelly Guy, Oxfordshire

Location:　　　　SP 401051
　　　　　　　　　Lat. 51.44.34 N; Long. 01.25.09 W

Project manager:　G Lambrick (Oxford Archaeological Unit), 1984

Archival body:　　Oxford Archaeology

Description: detailed excavation has taken place on a Neolithic to Bronze Age settlement and ritual complex on the gravel terrace adjacent to this site, which is made up of two shallow gullies on the pre-alluvial ground surface on the Windrush floodplain at Gravelly Guy.

Objectives: to date the two shallow gullies and place them within the chronological sequence in this area.

Final comment: F Healy (30 March 1995), GU–5097 and GU–5098 confirm the established chronology of intensified cultivation and alluviation in the Upper Thames Basin (Lambrick 1992a, 218–20; Lambrick 1992b, 88–9).

References:　　　Lambrick 1992a
　　　　　　　　　Lambrick 1992b

GU–5097 3740 ±50 BP

δ¹³C: -28.9‰

Sample: SHGG35, submitted on 30 January 1991 by G Lambrick

Material: wood (waterlogged): *Alnus* sp., mostly (M Robinson)

Initial comment: the sample was well stratified in an organic layer within channel sediments below the permanent watertable. Some calcareous gravel was present in the deposit.

Objectives: detailed excavation has taken place on a Neolithic to Bronze Age settlement and ritual complex on the gravel terrace adjacent to this section (*see* UB-3122, UB-3123, UB-3125 to UB-3128, UB-3130, and OxA-2296). The biological remains from this deposit are of Neolithic/Bronze Age character and offer the only potential waterlogged evidence for the site which itself is well-dated.

Calibrated date:　　1σ: 2210–2040 cal BC
　　　　　　　　　　2σ: 2300–1980 cal BC

Final comment: F Healy (30 March 1995), the sample on which GU-5097 was made came from the lower of two waterlogged gullies on the edge of the Windrush floodplain at the foot of the second gravel terrace. It was stratified beneath the gully which provided the sample for GU-5098 and both were sealed by successive Iron Age and Roman colluvial deposits interdigitated with alluvial floodplain deposits. GU-5097 places the high tree and shrub values of the associated pollen sample (Scaife 2004) in the early Bronze Age. The early Bronze Age date for this lower deposit may relate it to contemporary activity on the terrace, represented by ring ditches and pits in Gravelly Guy field and others in the wider complex surrounding the Devil's Quoits circle henge, of which the Gravelly Guy features form a part (Barclay *et al* 1995).

References:　　　Barclay *et al* 1995
　　　　　　　　　Scaife 2004

GU–5098 2660 ±50 BP

δ¹³C: -27.5‰

Sample: SHGG38, submitted on 30 January 1991 by G Lambrick

Material: waterlogged plant macrofossil: Pomoideae, waterlogged twigs; *Prunus* sp., waterlogged twigs (M Robinson)

Initial comment: well-stratified in the bottom layer of a waterlogged ditch, which superseded the channel.

Objectives: to enable the environmental evidence from the ditch to be related to the Iron Age and Roman settlement and fields on the gravel terrace. It would also provide a date on the alluvial/ploughwash sequence.

Calibrated date:　　1σ: 840–790 cal BC
　　　　　　　　　　2σ: 910–780 cal BC

Final comment: F Healy (30 March 1995), the sample on which GU-5098 was made came from the upper of two waterlogged gullies on the edge of the Windrush floodplain at the foot of the second gravel terrace. It was stratified beneath the gully which provided the sample for GU-5097 and both were sealed by successive Iron Age and Roman colluvial deposits interdigitated with alluvial floodplain deposits. GU-5098 provides a *terminus post quem* for local alluviation and colluviation. The associated pollen sample indicates that by this time the immediate vegetation was increasingly a wetland one and the adjoining terrace was in cultivation with few trees remaining (Scaife 2004). The late

Bronze/early Iron Age date for this upper deposit relates it to the beginnings of a long-lived, permanent settlement on the adjoining terrace and of others spaced along the terrace edge (Lambrick 1992b, figs 30–1).

References: Lambrick 1992b
                    Scaife 2004

Gravelly Guy: Stanton Harcourt, Oxfordshire

Location: SP 405052
                    Lat. 51.44.37 N; Long. 01.24.48 W

Project manager: G Lambrick (Oxford Archaeological Unit), 1984

Archival body: Oxford Archaeology

Description: a multi-period settlement site, which can be divided into two broad periods of significance. The late Neolithic and Bronze Age landscape was dominated by the funerary and ceremonial monuments with occasional domestic features; the Iron Age and early Roman period saw a mixed agricultural landscape which incorporated a shift of settlement activity across a common basic land division persisting through both periods.

Objectives: to provide a chronology for the site.

Final comment: F Healy (30 March 1995), *later Neolithic and early Bronze Age:* UB-3122, UB-3123, UB-3125, and UB-3126 clarify the chronology of the wider ritual-funerary complex centred on the Devil's Quoits circle henge (Barclay *et al* 1995). The near indistinguishability of UB-3122, UB-3123, and UB-3125 corresponds to stratigraphic evidence that all three successive burials were made over a very short span of time. *Early Iron Age occupation:* OxA-2296 and UB-3130 go some way to confirm the earlier part of the ceramic sequence for the Iron Age settlement.

References: Barclay *et al* 1995

OxA–2296 2440 ±80 BP

$\delta^{13}C$: -22.9‰

Sample: SHGG8, submitted on 27 February 1989 by G Lambrick

Material: animal bone (mixed domestic species) (B Levitan)

Initial comment: from context 2219, a smallish pit with a distinctive group of probably late Bronze Age pottery within the area of a possibly contemporary house.

Objectives: the ceramic evidence suggests that this is one of the earliest features belonging to the fully excavated complete Iron Age settlement, and is the most securely attributable feature of this period. In view of problems with radiocarbon calibration, and for later features redepositions, it is not considered worth obtaining a sequence of dates, especially given the limited stratigraphy. It is important however to gain if possible some indication of the date of the settlement's origin.

Calibrated date: *1σ*: 770–400 cal BC
                    2σ: 800–380 cal BC

Final comment: G Lambrick (1990), the width of the ranges reflects the problems of calibration in this period. The result is on a sample of domestic animal bone from a small pit with a fairly distinctive group of pottery of late Bronze Age or early Iron Age style, which includes forms and decoration compatible with J Barrett's 'decorated' phase of the late Bronze Age. It is thought to be one of the earliest of over 800 pits in a fully excavated Iron Age settlement. It is one of only three contexts with distinctively early groups, the other two are less reliably attributable to this phase. Despite the very wide age range when calibrated, the result is useful in broadly confirming the expected period, and may be compared with a conventional date, UB-3130, on a charateristically 'early Iron Age' type of assemblage which is much commoner on the site. These two samples support the expectation that the problems of calibration would make it difficult to use radiocarbon dating to give a more accurate idea of the date of its origins than can be obtained from the pottery. The limited sampling has nevertheless proved useful in confirming the broad ceramic dating.

References: Hedges *et al* 1990, 222

UB–3122 3709 ±35 BP

$\delta^{13}C$: -24.3 ±0.2‰

Sample: SHGG1, submitted on 27 February 1989 by G Lambrick

Material: human bone (male) (M Harman)

Initial comment: from context 4013/12, a Beaker burial with significant and rich grave goods. The earliest in a stratified sequence of burial deposits within a multiple ring ditch, which is part of the major ceremonial/funerary complex surrounding the Devil's Quoits stone circle henge.

Objectives: to help establish the chronology of a sequence of burials, within a complex ring ditch. This sample is also associated with an important group of Beaker grave goods.

Calibrated date: *1σ*: 2200–2030 cal BC
                    2σ: 2210–1980 cal BC

Final comment: F Healy (30 March 1995), UB-3122 dates the skeleton of a middle-aged man buried at the centre of a barrow represented by ring ditch 4013. The burial was contained in a wooden chamber which a particularly rich grave assemblage comprising a Beaker of Clarke's (1970) Late Southern group, an antler-pommelled bronze dagger of Gerloff's (1975) type Butterwick with three copper rivets and an antler pommel, a fragmentary copper alloy awl or pin, a slate wristguard, a 'sponge finger' whetstone, a polished antler spatula, a flint scraper, and two flakes. This grave was the second of a series of central burials, the first of which was almost completely removed by its excavation. The third and fourth are dated by UB-3123 and UB-3125. The date is well within the known range for the type of burial and the associated artefacts.

References: Clarke 1970
                    Gerloff 1975

UB–3123 3666 ±35 BP

$\delta^{13}C$: -23.5 ±0.2‰

Sample: SHGG2, submitted on 27 February 1989 by
G Lambrick

Material: human bone (male) (M Harman)

Initial comment: from context 4013/9, a Beaker burial
stratified immediately above the burial context 4013/2
(UB-3122), and associated with a fine handled Beaker.
The stratigraphy suggests that a wooden chamber for burial
4013/2 collapsed after the burial of 4013/9, so a similar
date might be expected.

Objectives: to help establish the chronology of a sequence of
burials, within a complex ring ditch. This sample is also
associated with a complete handled Beaker.

Calibrated date: 1σ: 2140–1970 cal BC
                       2σ: 2190–1940 cal BC

Final comment: F Healy (30 March 1995), UB-3123 dates
the skeleton of a young woman buried above the grave dated
by UB-3122 and accompanied by a large handled Beaker, a
copper alloy awl, and a flint flake.

UB–3125 3677 ±53 BP

$\delta^{13}C$: -26.5 ±0.2‰

Sample: SHGG3 and SHGG4, submitted on 27 February
1989 by G Lambrick

Material: charcoal: *Quercus* sp. (R Gale)

Initial comment: from context 4014/3, a cremation deposit
stratified later than 4013/2 (UB-3122) and 4013/9 (UB-3123).

Objectives: to help establish the chronology of a sequence of
burials, within a complex ring ditch.

Calibrated date: 1σ: 2140–1970 cal BC
                       2σ: 2210–1910 cal BC

Final comment: F Healy (30 March 1995), UB-3125 dates
charcoal from one of two unaccompanied cremation deposits
stratified above the burial dated by UB-3123.

UB–3126 3379 ±40 BP

$\delta^{13}C$: -26.4 ±0.2‰

Sample: SHGG5, submitted on 27 February 1989 by
G Lambrick

Material: charcoal: Pomoideae; *Corylus* sp. (R Gale)

Initial comment: from context 1/F/1-2, the stabilised fill of an
unusual hengiform ring trench. The sample is not from
slumped topsoil but part of a more extensive patchy spread
of charcoal from this level in the ditch.

Objectives: to provide a *terminus ante quem* for the feature and
a date for its ceasing to be maintained in its original form.

Calibrated date: 1σ: 1740–1620 cal BC
                       2σ: 1760–1530 cal BC

Final comment: F Healy (30 March 1995), this date provides a
terminus ante quem for the construction of an unusual hengiform
monument some 10m in diameter, the ditch of which seems to
have been revetted. By the time the charcoal which yielded this

Bronze Age date was deposited over the stabilised silt of the ditch
the monument had been built, remodelled and gone out of use.
There is no unambiguous artefactual dating evidence. A late
Neolithic origin seems likely on morphological grounds.

UB–3127 3760 ±40 BP

$\delta^{13}C$: -25.6 ±0.2‰

Sample: SHGG6, submitted on 27 February 1989 by
G Lambrick

Material: charcoal: *Quercus* sp.; *Corylus* sp., nuts; *Prunus* sp.,
nuts (R Gale)

Initial comment: from context 2961/A/3, the lower levels of a
pit occurring within a small cluster of pits. The sample is
associated with charred plant remains, flints, and Beaker
pottery. The context is part of a domestic Beaker settlement
close to contemporary burial monuments.

Objectives: to date this domestic activity, which is adjacent to
contemporary burials.

Calibrated date: 1σ: 2280–2130 cal BC
                       2σ: 2300–2030 cal BC

Final comment: F Healy (30 March 1995), UB-3128 is older
than UB-3127, barely overlapping with it at the two sigma
range, despite being made on charcoal from the topmost
layer of the same pit. This may perhaps reflect the presence
of redeposited charcoal in the upper part of the pit. Both
measurements fall within the range for Beaker pottery
(Kinnes *et al* 1991).

References: Kinnes *et al* 1991

UB–3128 3922 ±45 BP

$\delta^{13}C$: -25.9 ±0.2‰

Sample: SHGG7, submitted on 27 February 1989 by
G Lambrick

Material: charcoal: *Quercus* sp.; *Corylus* sp., nuts; *Prunus* sp.,
nuts (R Gale)

Initial comment: from context 2961/A/1, the upper levels of a
pit occurring within a small cluster of such pits. Compare
with UB-3127 from lower levels of the same pit.

Objectives: as UB-3127

Calibrated date: 1σ: 2480–2340 cal BC
                       2σ: 2570–2280 cal BC

Final comment: see UB-3127

UB–3130 2270 ±55 BP

$\delta^{13}C$: -23.6 ±0.2‰

Sample: SHGG9, submitted on 27 February 1989 by
G Lambrick

Material: animal bone (mixed domestic species) (B Levitan)

Initial comment: from pit 269, a subcircular, cylindrical-
profiled 'storage' pit in the main settlement area. The pit also
contained an early Iron Age pottery assemblage of angular
jars and fineware bowls, a fragment of a shale bracelet or
armlet, and a dog burial.

Objectives: to help elucidate the origin of the Iron Age settlement at Gravelly Guy.

Calibrated date: *1σ:* 400–210 cal BC
                     2σ: 410–190 cal BC

Final comment: F Healy (30 March 1995), the wide calibrated age range limits the value of the measurement. *See* also OxA-2296.

Haddenham: IX, Cambridgeshire

Location: TL 410734
            Lat. 52.20.24 N; Long. 00.04.12 E

Project manager: C Evans (Cambridge Archaeological Unit) and I Hodder (University of Cambridge), 1987

Archival body: Cambridgeshrie County Council

Description: a circular feature set within a sub-square ditched enclosure whose sides ran south to conjoin the causewayed enclosure.

Objectives: given its plan and configuration, the circular enclosure was expected to be of late Neolithic/early Bronze Age date and probably a ring ditch. The main features did, however, seem to be Iron Age. A radiocarbon determination was submitted to confirm the archaeological interpretation.

Final comment: C Evans (20 July 2004), the date confirms the middle/later Iron Age attribution of the HAD IX enclosure.

References: Evans and Hodder 2006b
              Hardiman *et al* 1992, 65

HAR–10513 2110 ±90 BP

$\delta^{13}C$: -28.0‰

Sample: HAD IX87, F.507/528, submitted in July 1988 by C Evans

Material: wood (desiccated, previously waterlogged, remaining subsample identified): unidentified (0.72g); cf *Alnus/Corylus* sp. (0.07g, 3%); bark, unidentified (2.26g, 97%) (R Gale 1999)

Initial comment: from F507/528, ditch circuit 1.3–2.25m wide and deepest along its northern side and at the southern junction with the interior north/south ditch. Its relatively homogenous fills would suggest that it was regularly maintained.

Objectives: to establish the date of the ditch and ascertain whether it is Iron Age in date and if it is contemporary with the early phases of the HAD V enclosure.

Calibrated date: *1σ:* 360 cal BC–cal AD 1
                     2σ: 390 cal BC–cal AD 80

Final comment: C Evans and I Hodder (2000), the date suggests that despite its predominantly sandy ware assemblage, the HAD IX enclosure was essentially contemporary with the HAD V sequence at least in its period I.

References: Hardiman *et al* 1992, 64–5

Haddenham: V, Cambridgeshire

Location: TL 411733
            Lat. 52.20.21 N; Long. 00.04.17 E

Project manager: C Evans (Cambridge Archaeological Unit) and I Hodder (University of Cambridge), 1985–6

Archival body: Cambridgeshire County Council

Description: a distinct sub-square cropmark located on the south side of the Upper Delphs Terrace. Alluvial cover of the site meant survival was excellent, with floor surfaces and banks intact and deeper cut features waterlogged.

Objectives: to test the hypothesis that the shared orientation (and presumed contemporaniety) with another very similar sub-square enclosure and field boundary situated some 200m to the north-west (HAD VI and VII), would allow dating of a major phase of landscape organisation on the Upper Delphs Terrace.

Final comment: C Evans (20 July 2004), this series of dates, confirms well the later Iron Age attribution and attests to its usage during the last two centuries BC and first century AD.

References: Evans and Hodder 2006b
              Walker *et al* 1991a, 92–3

HAR–8764 2110 ±70 BP

$\delta^{13}C$: -27.1‰

Sample: HV 2655, submitted in May 1987 by C Evans

Material: charcoal (remaining subsample identified): unidentified (4.98g); *Alnus* sp. (0.05g, 2.7%); *Quercus* sp., heartwood (1.79g, 97.3%) (R Gale 1999)

Initial comment: from a pit found in association with pre-enclosure building A, sealed by the main roundhouse C.

Objectives: to date pre-enclosure occupation on the site (probably early Iron Age) and associated ard patterns. It is the first time such patterns have been found in a prehistoric Fenland context.

Calibrated date: *1σ:* 350–40 cal BC
                     2σ: 380 cal BC–cal AD 50

Final comment: C Evans and I Hodder (2000), the date suggests that building 3 probably dates to the first half/middle of the second century cal BC and this would support Hill's attribution of the Iron Age pottery from the site to the last two centuries of the first millennium BC.

HAR–8765 1990 ±60 BP

$\delta^{13}C$: -27.3‰

Sample: HV 2289, submitted in May 1987 by C Evans

Material: waterlogged plant macrofossil: twig, large

Initial comment: from brushwood in the base of the main enclosure ditch, sealed by a dumped secondary gravel causeway.

Objectives: to date the construction of the ditched yard enclosure.

Calibrated date: 1σ: 50 cal BC–cal AD 80
         2σ: 170 cal BC–cal AD 130

Final comment: C Evans and I Hodder (2000), the date is virtually indistinguishable from HAR-8766 for the end of building 4, suggesting an approximate correspondence between the demise of the building and alteration of the enclosure's entrance.

Laboratory comment: Ancient Monuments Laboratory (2000), HAR-8765 and HAR-8766 are statistically consistent (T'=0.0;T'(5%)=3.8; ν=1; Ward and Wilson 1978). However, HAR-8766 is possibly affected by an unknown age offset because it is oak heartwood.

References: Ward and Wilson 1978

HAR–8766 2000 ±60 BP

$\delta^{13}C$: -25.4‰

Sample: HV 2735, submitted in May 1987 by C Evans

Material: charcoal (remaining subsample identified): unidentified (57.85g); *Quercus* sp., heartwood (23.79g, 100%) (R Gale 1999)

Initial comment: from a burnt post from the destruction of main roundhouse C.

Objectives: to date the destruction of the main roundhouse building.

Calibrated date: 1σ: 60 cal BC–cal AD 70
         2σ: 180 cal BC–cal AD 130

Final comment: C Evans and I Hodder (2000), the date for the end of building 4 is virtually indistinguishable from HAR-8765 suggesting an approximate correspondence between the demise of the building and alterations to the enclosure entrance.

HAR–8767 1970 ±60 BP

$\delta^{13}C$: -28.5‰

Sample: 1635/1679, submitted in May 1987 by C Evans

Material: waterlogged plant macrofossil: twig, large

Initial comment: from the uppermost organic fill of main enclosure ditch F.95, in direct association with an articulated skeleton of a juvenile common crane.

Objectives: to date the final usage/abandonment of the ditch enclosure and the on-set of freshwater flooding. Also of importance is that it will directly date the skeleton of the common crane. This has great zoological value as it throws light on crane breeding areas in prehistory.

Calibrated date: 1σ: 50 cal BC–cal AD 90
         2σ: 110 cal BC–cal AD 140

Final comment: C Evans and I Hodder (2000), the date for the primary F.95 fills beneath the entrance causeway is somewhat later than might be expected given the V-shaped profile of the ditch at this point (locally surviving due to its causeway sealing) suggesting that it had undergone little maintenance/mucking out.

Haddenham: VI, Cambridgeshire

Location: TL 411733
           Lat. 52.20.21 N; Long. 00.04.17 E

Project manager: C Evans (Cambridge Archaeological Unit) and I Hodder (University of Cambridge), 1986

Archival body: Cambridgeshire County Council

Description: a sub-square enclosure enclosing an area 30m by 30m, with a possible entrance in the south-west corner and a circular gully in the north-east corner lay at the terminus of ditch F100, which continued north-west from the HAD V enclosure. Another ditch ran from the north-west corner of HAD VI towards site VII.

Objectives: to establish the date of the enclosure and ascertain whether it was contemporary and an interrelated component of a larger Iron Age landscape.

Final comment: C Evans (20 July 2004), although one or two centuries earlier than anticipated, the date does confirm the middle/later Iron Age attribution of the HAD VI enclosure ('matching' with HAD V).

References: Evans and Hodder 2006b
           Hardiman *et al* 1992, 65

HAR–10519 2240 ±80 BP

$\delta^{13}C$: -27.4‰

Sample: 3806, submitted in July 1988 by C Evans

Material: wood (waterlogged): unidentified

Initial comment: from the primary fill of the north ditch of a south-lying enclosure (HAD VI). The ditch was sealed by the upcast bank of the north enclosure. The south enclosure was not excavated as such apart from this single slot.

Objectives: to establish the date of the south-lying HAD VI enclosure and ascertain whether it is Iron Age in date and if it is contemporary with the early phases of the HAD V enclosure.

Calibrated date: 1σ: 400–190 cal BC
         2σ: 420–60 cal BC

Final comment: C Evans and I Hodder (2000), a surprisingly early date when compared to that of building 3 from HAD V. If the feature does relate to an earlier form of HAD VI, then its foundation may actually have pre-dated the construction of the HAD V enclosure itself.

Haddenham: VI, long barrow, Cambridgeshire

Location: TL 419767
           Lat. 52.20.10 N; Long. 00.05.04 E

Project manager: C Evans (Cambridge Archaeological Unit) and I Hodder (University of Cambridge), 1986

Archival body: Cambridgeshire County Council

Description: a series of wood, charcoal, and (unsuccessfully dated) bone samples from a partially waterlogged Neolithic long barrow. The mound was surrounded by a slight revetment, on the outside of which were set banks. Surrounding the barrow was a ditch. The north-eastern end of the mound was revetted by a timber facade, consisting of a line of posts set into a construction trench. Behind this was a wooden mortuary structure, surrounded by a ring bank which formed part of the mound. The mortuary structure had three axial posts, which divided the space into sub-chambers. In the proximal section was found a turf mound. In front of the facade was a gravel forecourt and a fore-structure consisting of a hornwork entranceway, the latter revetting fore-banks on either side. Set above these and across the hornwork entrance was a 'facade-bank' (the status of which is extremely problematic).

Objectives: to date the construction and use of the long barrow.

Final comment: C Evans and I Hodder (2004), given the tree-ring correlations between the timbers of the mortuary structure, by normative archaeological logic the dating of the monument is essentially a matter of pegging an 'event'. To this extent the *c* 3600 cal BC attribution based on the wiggle-matching generally seems a reasonable 'fixing' of the timbers' felling. That this date is later than the majority of the other radiocarbon assays can presumably be credited to the fact that it must have been the heartwood rather than the outer sapwood which was dated. By this, and the size/age of the timbers involved, a 3600 cal BC date could directly coincide with three of the original samples (HAR-9172, HAR-9174, and HAR-9175). This attribution is furthermore generally appropriate to what comparative local dates are available for the monument's material culture (eg Evans *et al* 1999).

References:　　Evans *et al* 1999
　　　　　　　　Evans and Hodder 2006a
　　　　　　　　Whittle *et al* 2011, 278–93

HAR–9171 4660 ±50 BP

δ¹³C: -26.3‰

Sample: HAD6LB25, submitted in March 1988 by C Evans

Material: charcoal: *Quercus* sp. (R Morgan 1988)

Initial comment: from a cremation within the pre-barrow Neolithic ground surface, sealed by the mortuary structure and the long barrow (F. 710).

Objectives: to date the pre-mortuary structure and pre-barrow activity.

Calibrated date:　　*1σ:* 3520–3360 cal BC
　　　　　　　　　　2σ: 3630–3350 cal BC

Final comment: R Morgan (1990), this result seems to be one to three centuries too late in relation to its stratigraphic position beneath the mortuary structure.

HAR–9172 4960 ±90 BP

δ¹³C: -26.4‰

Sample: HAD6LB17, submitted in March 1988 by C Evans

Material: wood (waterlogged): *Quercus* sp., charred (R Morgan 1988)

Initial comment: from part of the mortuary structure wall from the front chamber, within the long barrow (F. 724).

Objectives: to date the front chamber and establish whether it is the same date as the back chamber or a later addition to the structure. HAR-9177 dates the roof, and HAR-9175 the floor of the back chamber.

Calibrated date:　　*1σ:* 3920–3650 cal BC
　　　　　　　　　　2σ: 3970–3530 cal BC

Final comment: R Morgan (1990), apart from HAR-9173 (which is significantly later), the dates from the timber structure show strong concordance, all falling between *c* 3900–3600 cal BC.

References:　　Hardiman *et al* 1992, 64–5

HAR–9173 4730 ±80 BP

δ¹³C: -26.0‰

Sample: HAD6LB14, submitted in March 1988 by C Evans

Material: wood: *Quercus* sp., burnt (R Morgan 1988)

Initial comment: from a facade timber (F. 720) found within lenses of gravel, which form the forecourt pavement.

Objectives: several lenses of gravel in the forecourt suggest a long period of use and the signs of burning may suggest much activity. This sample would provide a good date for the use of the forecourt in comparison to HAR-9174, which shows when this activity ended.

Calibrated date:　　*1σ:* 3640–3370 cal BC
　　　　　　　　　　2σ: 3660–3350 cal BC

Final comment: see HAR-9172

HAR–9174 4930 ±60 BP

δ¹³C: -26.3‰

Sample: HAD6LB22, submitted in March 1988 by C Evans

Material: charcoal: *Quercus* sp. (R Morgan 1988)

Initial comment: from a timber from the facade bank (F. 739), found within one of various areas of burning, which occur on the surface of the long barrow at its east end, above the filled-in forecourt. The burning on the barrow occurs after 1m of deposits have accumulated in the forecourt. The burning is therefore a late phase of activity.

Objectives: to date this late phase of activity.

Calibrated date:　　*1σ:* 3780–3650 cal BC
　　　　　　　　　　2σ: 3930–3630 cal BC

Final comment: see HAR-9172

HAR–9175 4950 ±70 BP

δ¹³C: -26.4‰

Sample: HAD6LB26, submitted in March 1988 by C Evans

Material: wood (waterlogged): *Quercus* sp., charred (R Morgan 1988)

Initial comment: from the floor of the mortuary structure (F. 78).

Objectives: to establish the date of the floor of the structure. It is not clear how long the structure was open and the floor could have been laid at any stage. The nature of the planking suggests that dendrochronology will not be useful here.

Calibrated date: 1σ: 3800–3650 cal BC
2σ: 3950–3630 cal BC

Final comment: see HAR-9172

HAR–9176 5050 ±60 BP

δ¹³C: -26.9‰

Sample: HAD6LB11, submitted in March 1988 by C Evans

Material: wood (waterlogged): *Quercus* sp., charred (R Morgan 1988)

Initial comment: from a facade post (F. 714). The facade was a free standing timber structure pre-dating the construction of the mound.

Objectives: to establish the date of the facade in order to calculate how much earlier it is than the final mound construction.

Calibrated date: 1σ: 3960–3770 cal BC
2σ: 3980–3700 cal BC

Final comment: see HAR-9172

HAR–9177 5140 ±70 BP

δ¹³C: -26.4‰

Sample: HAD6LB07, submitted in March 1988 by C Evans

Material: wood (waterlogged): *Quercus* sp., charred (R Morgan 1988)

Initial comment: from the roof of the mortuary structure (F. 727).

Objectives: to date the roof of the mortuary structure. The roof could well be a final act in the history of the structure and it cannot be assumed that all the elements are contemporary (*see also* HAR-9172 and HAR-9175).

Calibrated date: 1σ: 4040–3810 cal BC
2σ: 4060–3780 cal BC

Final comment: see HAR-9172

HAR–9178 5770 ±140 BP

δ¹³C: -21.3‰

Sample: HAD LAURA, submitted in March 1988 by C Evans

Material: human bone (teeth)

Initial comment: from the secondary inhumation (F. 742) in the top of the barrow mound.

Objectives: to date the secondary use of the long mound for burial.

Calibrated date: 1σ: 4790–4450 cal BC
2σ: 4960–4340 cal BC

Final comment: R Morgan (1990), this result must be one to two millennia too early in relation to the stratigraphic position of this burial within the long barrow sequence.

Laboratory comment: Ancient Monuments Laboratory (2004), although the δ¹³C value is within the expected range for uncharred human bone, this result may be anomalous because of poor collagen preservation. An attempt to date the other secondary burial in the long mound (F. 743) recently demonstrated that this burial does not contain sufficient collagen for dating.

UB–3167 4947 ±20 BP

δ¹³C: -26.2 ±0.2‰

Sample: sample 1 [3642/3645], submitted in 1989 by R Morgan

Material: wood (waterlogged): *Quercus* sp. (R Morgan 1989)

Initial comment: from feature 709, the floor timber of the proximal sub-chamber, rings 140–160 of the floating tree-ring sequence.

Objectives: to provide an absolute date by wiggle-matching for the floating tree-ring series from Haddenham long barrow.

Calibrated date: 1σ: 3760–3695 cal BC
2σ: 3780–3655 cal BC

Final comment: R Morgan (1990), the pattern shown by the series of dates were readily matched against the curve of Pearson *et al* (1986), producing an end date for the chronology of 3628 ±21 BC (at 68% confidence). Since no sapwood was traced, an allowance of at least 10–55 rings must be added (Hillam *et al* 1987), and there is in addition an unknown amount of missing heartwood. Felling could have taken place after 3618 BC, 3573 ±21 BC, if the sapwood estimate is added to the date span.

Laboratory comment: University of Belfast (26 July 2012), no record survives of whether this sample was pretreated using the acid based alkali protocol or was bleached, but it was dated in the high-precision facility.

Laboratory comment: English Heritage (28 January 2012), this wiggle-matching calculated using the calibration data of Reimer *et al* (2004), provides an estimate for the date of the final ring of this tree-ring sequence of *3630–3580 cal BC (95% probability; Whittle et al 2011, fig 6.17)*.

References: Hillam *et al* 1987
Pearson *et al* 1986
Reimer *et al* 2004
Whittle *et al* 2011, fig 6.17

UB–3168 4900 ±18 BP

δ¹³C: -27.2 ±0.2‰

Sample: sample 2 [3642/3645], submitted in 1989 by R Morgan

Material: wood (waterlogged): *Quercus* sp. (R Morgan 1989)

Initial comment: from feature 709, the floor timber of the proximal sub-chamber, rings 160–180 of the floating tree-ring sequence.

Objectives: as UB-3167.

Calibrated date: 1σ: 3700–3650 cal BC
2σ: 3710–3645 cal BC

Final comment: see UB-3167

Laboratory comment: see UB-3167

Laboratory comment: see UB-3167

UB–3169 4891 ±18 BP

δ¹³C: -25.8 ±0.2‰

Sample: sample 3 [3642/3645], submitted in 1989 by R Morgan

Material: wood (waterlogged): *Quercus* sp. (R Morgan 1989)

Initial comment: from feature 709, the floor timber of the proximal sub-chamber, rings 180–200 of the floating tree-ring sequence.

Objectives: as UB-3167.

Calibrated date: 1σ: 3695–3650 cal BC
2σ: 3705–3640 cal BC

Final comment: see UB-3167

Laboratory comment: see UB-3167

Laboratory comment: see UB-3167

UB–3170 4893 ±18 BP

δ¹³C: -26.1 ±0.2‰

Sample: sample 4 [3642/3645], submitted in 1989 by R Morgan

Material: wood (waterlogged): *Quercus* sp. (R Morgan 1989)

Initial comment: from feature 709, the floor timber of the proximal sub-chamber, rings 200–220 of the floating tree-ring sequence.

Objectives: as UB-3167

Calibrated date: 1σ: 3695–3650 cal BC
2σ: 3705–3640 cal BC

Final comment: see UB-3167

Laboratory comment: see UB-3167

Laboratory comment: see UB-3167

UB–3171 4874 ±20 BP

δ¹³C: -24.9 ±0.2‰

Sample: sample 5 [3642/3645], submitted in 1989 by R Morgan

Material: wood (waterlogged): *Quercus* sp., charred (R Morgan 1989)

Initial comment: from feature 709, the floor timber of the proximal sub-chamber, rings 220–240 of the floating tree-ring sequence.

Objectives: as UB-3167

Calibrated date: 1σ: 3660–3640 cal BC
2σ: 3700–3640 cal BC

Final comment: see UB-3167

Laboratory comment: see UB-3167

Laboratory comment: see UB-3167

Hambledon Hill, Dorset

Location: ST 84921226
Lat. 50.54.31 N; Long. 02.12.52 W

Project manager: R J Mercer (University of Edinburgh), 1974–86

Description: the hill lies off the south-west edge of Cranborne Chase, immediately north of Hod Hill in the confluence of the rivers Iwerne and Stour. It consists of a central dome of Upper Chalk with radiating spurs, largely of Lower Chalk. The central dome is occupied by a large causewayed enclosure of 8.3ha and a smaller causewayed enclosure of just under 1ha occupies the southern (Stepleton) spur. There are two long barrows and numerous pits. The two enclosures and all or most of the hill are surrounded by outworks. The extent of Neolithic earthworks on the north spur is obscured by an Iron Age hillfort. The investigations of 1974–86 followed on from trial excavations by Sieveking and Erskine in 1951 and by Bonney in 1958–60. By the end of 1986 it was clear that the hill had been the site of an early-middle Neolithic earthwork complex up to 100ha in extent, and that Neolithic earthworks extended to the north spur. In 1996 a new earthwork survey by the RCHME confirmed the possibility of a Neolithic date for the outworks around the north spur, under the Iron Age defences. Equally important, the survey has advanced understanding of the development of the Iron Age hillfort and the later landscape and provided a baseline for its future management.

Objectives: to define the form, function, extent, use, and development of the complex and their implications for contemporary social organisation.

References: Bayliss *et al* 2008
Farrar 1951
Healy 2004
Mercer 1980
Mercer 1985
Mercer 1988
Mercer 1999
Mercer and Healy 2008
Oswald *et al* 2001
Palmer 1976a
RCHME 1970

Hambledon Hill: discrete features in central area, Dorset

Location: ST 852123
Lat. 50.54.34 N; Long. 02.12.38 W

Project manager: R J Mercer (University of Edinburgh), 1974–7, 1982

Archival body: Dorset County Museum

Description: extensive area excavation within the main causewayed enclosure (about 15% of its interior) and on a smaller scale outside it revealed at least 70 pits, often in clusters, most of them containing early Neolithic artefacts.

Objectives: the dates were obtained to relate the pits to the adjacent earthworks and in some cases to date their contents, notably Gabbroic pottery and a group XVI axehead in one pit.

Laboratory comment: Ancient Monuments Laboratory (2003), two further dates from this site were funded prior to 1981 and were published in the first volume of *Radiocarbon Dates*, HAR-2041 and HAR-3061 (Jordan *et al* 1994, 69–70).

References: Jordan *et al* 1994, 69–70

HAR–9166 4920 ±70 BP

δ¹³C: -27.5‰

Sample: HH75/556, submitted on 25 February 1976 by R Mercer

Material: charcoal: *Quercus* sp., a few fragments; *?Quercus sp*, a fragment (C A Keepax)

Initial comment: site B, feature 57, layer 1: from a pit with a fill of rich-black loam, orange-brown loam with orange pea chalk and chalk lumps, and chalk wash. Layer 1, in particular, contained a rich assemblage of material including antler deposits, pot, bone, and stone rubber fragments. This sample is comparable with HAR-2041 (4110 ±80 BP; cal BC 2900–2470 at 95% confidence; Reimer *et al* 2004).

Objectives: to determine the age of the pit and its contents.

Calibrated date: 1σ: 3780–3640 cal BC
2σ: 3940–3530 cal BC

Final comment: F Healy (26 November 2006), the bulked charcoal sample means that date may be older than the pit. It is, however, within the span of early Neolithic activity on the hill and is compatible with the associated Neolithic Bowl pottery and other artefacts.

Laboratory comment: AERE Harwell (28 February 1989), this sample was measured in the miniature gas proportional counter (Otlet *et al* 1983).

References: Otlet *et al* 1983
Reimer *et al* 2004

HAR–9167 4830 ±80 BP

δ¹³C: -25.9‰

Sample: HH75/559, submitted on 25 February 1976 by R Mercer

Material: charcoal (*c* 50% identified): hawthorn type, possibly; *Quercus* sp.; *Corylus* sp. (C A Keepax)

Initial comment: site B, feature 14, layer 3; from a steep-sided, flat-bottomed pit with a rich assemblage of pottery and other finds including a large greenstone axe. Layer 3 consisted of black soil, gravel and chalk lumps, and produced the main finds.

Objectives: to date the pit and its contents.

Calibrated date: 1σ: 3700–3520 cal BC
2σ: 3780–3370 cal BC

Final comment: F Healy (26 November 2006), the remainder of the charcoal subsequently identified by P Austin as *Corylus avellana*, *Quercus* sp, and *Maloideae*, from pit with group XVI stone axe and three Neolithic Bowls, including two vessels in gabbroic fabric. The bulked charcoal sample means that date may be older than the pit. It is, however, within the span of early Neolithic activity on the hill and is compatible with the associated artefacts.

Laboratory comment: AERE Harwell (9 November 1988), this sample was measured in the miniature gas proportional counter (Otlet *et al* 1983).

References: Otlet *et al* 1983

Hambledon Hill: inner east cross dyke, Dorset

Location: ST 849122
Lat. 50.54.31 N; Long. 02.12.53 W

Project manager: R Mercer (Edinburgh University), 1975

Archival body: Dorset County Museum

Description: the inner of two segmented bank-and-ditch earthworks, parallel to each other and to the east side of the main enclosure, running the width of the neck of land between the main enclosure and the Shroton spur.

Objectives: to refine the date of the earthwork.

Final comment: F Healy (2005), formal modelling of the chronology of Hambledon Hill suggests that the inner east cross dyke was constructed in *3690–3620 cal BC (95% probability*; Bayliss *et al* 2008; table 4.2).

Laboratory comment: (28 January 2012), six further samples were submitted and dated after March 1993.

References: Bayliss *et al* 2008
Hardiman *et al* 1992, 53

HAR–9168 4660 ±100 BP

δ¹³C: -26.1‰

Sample: HH75/1535, submitted on 25 February 1976 by R Mercer

Material: charcoal (*c* 50% identified): *?Quercus sp* (C A Keepax 1989)

Initial comment: site D2, cross ditch 1, layer 11; from the primary chalk wash overlying the solid chalk bottom of the ditch. The silt deposit contains some chalk and flint lumps and incorporates a few finds of bone and antler.

Objectives: to define the place of the cross-dykes in the development of the complex.

Calibrated date: 1σ: 3630–3350 cal BC
2σ: 3650–3090 cal BC

Final comment: F Healy (January 2005), two single entity samples of *Corylus* charcoal (OxA-8863–4) from a discrete spread in the primary silt in segment 4 yielded measurements which are statistically consistent with the pre-existing measurement on part of the bulk sample from which they were extracted (HAR-9168; T'=4.3; $T'(5\%)$=6.0; v=2; Ward and Wilson 1978), suggesting that it was homogenous.

Laboratory comment: AERE Harwell (11 April 1989), this sample was measured in the miniature gas proportional counter (Otlet *et al* 1983).

| *References:* | Otlet *et al* 1983 |
| | Ward and Wilson 1978 |

Hambledon Hill: main enclosure, Dorset

Location:	ST 84921226
	Lat. 50.54.31 N; Long. 02.12.53 W
Project manager:	R Mercer (University of Edinburgh), 1976
Archival body:	Dorset County Museum

Description: causewayed enclosure ditch.

Objectives: to date this part of the enclosure as a step towards establishing the chronology of the whole.

Final comment: F Healy (2005), formal modelling of the chronology of Hambledon Hill suggests that the main enclosure was constructed in *3680–3630 cal BC (95% probability*; Bayliss *et al* 2008; table 4.2).

Laboratory comment: English Heritage (28 January 2012), a total of 47 radiocarbon measurements have been obtained from the main enclosure at Hambledon Hill (Bayliss *et al* 2008, table 4.1).

| *References:* | Bayliss *et al* 2008 |
| | Walker *et al* 1991a, 88 |

HAR–2370 5220 ±110 BP

$\delta^{13}C$: -24.9‰

Sample: HH7640, submitted in November 1977 by R Mercer

Material: charcoal: *Quercus* sp. (C A Keepax 1977)

Initial comment: site G, causewayed enclosure ditch, segment 3, layer 10: from the chalk and flint vacuous rubble fill of the ditch interrupted by layers of pinkish or brown silt. The deposit lies directly on the solid chalk floor of the ditch.

Objectives: as series comments.

| *Calibrated date:* | *1σ:* 4240–3950 cal BC |
| | *2σ:* 4340–3780 cal BC |

Final comment: F Healy (26 November 2006), provides a *terminus post quem* for that context.

Laboratory comment: AERE Harwell (April 1989), this sample was measured in the miniature gas proportional counter (Otlet *et al* 1983).

| *References:* | Otlet *et al* 1983 |

Hambledon Hill: main enclosure 3, Dorset

Location:	ST 84921226
	Lat. 50.54.31 N; Long. 02.12.53 W
Project manager:	R Mercer (University of Edinburgh), 1975–6
Archival body:	Dorset County Museum

Description: main causewayed enclosure segments 5, 6, and 7. A row of three contiguous segments in the south-east of the circuit.

Objectives: to date this part of the enclosure as a step towards establishing the chronology of the whole.

| *References:* | Hardiman *et al* 1992, 53 |

HAR–9169 4140 ±100 BP

$\delta^{13}C$: -26.4‰

Sample: HH751498, submitted on 25 February 1976 by R Mercer

Material: charcoal (not twiggy, 50% identified): *Quercus* sp.; *Crataegus* sp., possibly; *Corylus* sp. (C A Keepax 1976)

Initial comment: site F, causewayed enclosure ditch layer 6; this layer consists of dark brown soil, chalk lumps and large flint nodules which fills a variable but roughly V-shaped slot recut into the ditch fill at a point when the secondary silts had accumulated almost to the brim. This deposit is a regular feature of the causewayed enclosure ditch and is consistently associated with dumps of organic remains and cultural material (flint work, pot, axe fragments). On archaeological grounds the accumulation of the secondary silts might be expected to have taken a considerable period of time, *c* 200–300 years.

Objectives: to date this deposit.

| *Calibrated date:* | *1σ:* 2890–2500 cal BC |
| | *2σ:* 2920–2460 cal BC |

Final comment: F Healy (26 November 2006), segment 8, layer 6. From a concentration of stylistically late Beaker pottery *above* the slot rather than in it. Since the measurement pre-dates the currency of Beaker pottery in Britain, the sample may have included Neolithic charcoal.

Laboratory comment: AERE Harwell (12 May 1989), this sample was measured in the miniature gas proportional counter (Otlet *et al* 1983).

| *References:* | Otlet *et al* 1983 |

Hardendale Nab, Cumbria

Location:	NY 58141401
	Lat. 54.31.10 N; Long. 02.38.48 W
Project manager:	J Williams (Cumbria and Lancaster Archaeological Unit), May to June 1986
Archival body:	Lancaster University Archaeological Unit

Description: excavations were undertaken on a cairn at Hardendale Quarry, Shap, Cumbria. The site lies on level ground just below the top of an escarpment of Lower Carboniferous Limestone and has extensive views over the Lowther valley to the south, west, and north.

Objectives: the only dating evidence is provided by the urns and a sherd of Roman pottery and a copper-alloy belt fitting of Roman or later date. Therefore further dating is essential to establish a more precise chronology for the cairn.

Final comment: J Williams (19 December 1993), the dates provide confirmation of an early Bronze Age sequence for the site, as further demonstrated by Collared Urns from phase 3, but do not allow refinement of the sequences within the Bronze Age. OxA-1834–5 and OxA-2127 appear to be consistent as a group but OxA-1836 would have been expected to be contemporary with OxA-1835. If the sequence was to be demonstrated OxA-1835–6 and possibly OxA-2127 would be roughly contemporary with OxA-1834, possibly a little later. There would be no reason to stop all the dates falling within a time bracket indistinguishable in radiocarbon terms.

References: Hedges *et al* 1994, 362

OxA–1834 3360 ±60 BP

δ¹³C: -21.0‰ (assumed)

Sample: HARDQ 009, submitted on 8 May 1987 by J Williams

Material: human bone (charred) (J Henderson)

Initial comment: collection of human bone essentially disarticulated but possibly partly articulated when buried at the base of, and mixed in with, the latest stone spread of the cairn. The burial would appear to have been cut through this latest level.

Objectives: to provide dating for phase 4 of a four-phase sequence. Phase 4 perhaps belongs to the possible reuse of the cairn in the Anglo-Saxon period.

Calibrated date: 1σ: 1740–1530 cal BC
                        2σ: 1870–1500 cal BC

Final comment: J Williams (19 December 1993), OxA-1835, OxA-1834, and OxA-2127 appear to be consistent as a group but OxA-1836 would have been expected to be contemporary with OxA-1834, possibly a little later.

OxA–1835 3290 ±100 BP

δ¹³C: -21.0‰ (assumed)

Sample: 303 (Layer 16), submitted on 8 May 1987 by J Williams

Material: animal bone: *Aricola terrestris*, tibia (S Stallibrass)

Initial comment: the faunal assemblage is remarkable for both the quality and quantity of it microfauna. Because of the stony structure of the cairn, it is possible that at least some of the microfauna are post cairn intrusions.

Objectives: it is important to be able to say whether or not this assemblage is contemporaneous with the human usage of the monument, since it has the potential to give us very valuable information regarding the local environment in the Bronze Age.

Calibrated date: 1σ: 1690–1450 cal BC
                        2σ: 1880–1390 cal BC

Final comment: S Stallibrass (8 October 1993), this result showed conclusively that the accumulation of microfauna-rich layer in the Bronze Age cairn was contemporaneous with its use as a human burial monument. The absolute date on the watervoles, recovered from the habitat no longer used by the species in Britain, is in the second millennium cal BC.

OxA–1836 4190 ±90 BP

δ¹³C: -21.0‰ (assumed)

Sample: 316 (Layer 19), submitted in December 1988 by J Williams

Material: animal bone: Anurans (S Stallibrass)

Initial comment: the faunal assemblage is remarkable for both the quality and quantity of it microfauna. Because of the stony structure of the cairn, it is possible that at least some of the microfauna are post cairn intrusions.

Objectives: it is important to be able to say whether or not this assemblage is contemporaneous with the human usage of the monument, since it has the potential to give us very valuable information regarding the local environment in the Bronze Age.

Calibrated date: 1σ: 2900–2620 cal BC
                        2σ: 3010–2490 cal BC

Final comment: S Stallibrass (8 October 1993), stratigraphically, it was possible for the microfauna-rich layer to include younger material that had percolated down through the limestone rubble, but this radiocarbon date is 1000 years too old. Residuality is highly unlikely. The standard error on the radiocarbon date appears to be no larger than 'normal' and so discrepancy between expectation and result remain unresolved.

Laboratory comment: Oxford Radiocarbon Accelerator Unit (27 January 2009), this sample was in a batch tested for amino acid content. It had 87.19mg/g of powdered bone, which suggests that it was sufficiently well-preserved for reliable analysis. After gelatinisation, some solid residue remained, which is usually a sign of cross-linked/unreacted protein. Of the 180mg of sample used, 16.1mg of collagen was yielded, which is again sufficient for reliable analysis.

OxA–2127 3430 ±80 BP

δ¹³C: -22.6‰

Sample: HARDQ 010, submitted in December 1988 by J Williams

Material: human bone (inhumation aged 6-8 years) (J Henderson)

Initial comment: from a collection of human bones, with no real articulation apart perhaps from part of the rib cage, set into limestone natural. Below the kerb of the phase 2 ring cairn. The site lies on limestone with the cairn primarily constructed out of limestone, some pink granite, and basalt. Excavations took place at the time of the Chernobyl disaster, although the sample was excavated within a day of being uncovered, so contamination is unlikely.

Objectives: the sample is intended to establish a date for phase 1.

Calibrated date: 1σ: 1880–1630 cal BC
2σ: 1950–1520 cal BC

Final comment: see OxA–1834

Harston: Manor Farm, Cambridgeshire

Location: TL 418498
Lat. 52.07.40 N; Long. 00.04.18 E

Project manager: T Malim (Cambridge Archaeological Unit), 1991

Description: multi-period cropmark site, which is nine miles south-west of Cambridge.

Objectives: the dates were designed to confirm a Bronze Age date for the ring ditches and the cremated bone, and to ascertain whether Anglo-Saxon reuse of one of the barrows occurred.

Final comment: T Malim (18 August 1993), charcoal associated with cremated human bone confirmed an early Bronze Age date for one ring ditch and burial pyre. A second ring ditch had structural details that included a *Grubenhaus* and postholes external to it, within the area of the flattened mound. Charcoal from the *Grubenhaus* pit confirmed a pagan Saxon date, whilst charcoal from one of the post pipes gave an early Bronze Age date. Therefore, showing that there was an original timber structure contemporary with the ring ditch.

References: Hedges *et al* 1993, 159
Malim 1993

OxA–3637 1485 ±75 BP

δ¹³C: -25.5‰

Sample: HARMF 91 16.0, submitted on 16 January 1992 by T Malim

Material: charcoal: *?Quercus sp* (P Murphy 1991)

Initial comment: pit fill (16) sealed by orange-brown sandy gravelly silt (2) through which pit (15) had been dug. The total depth of overburden from the top of (16) to the top of the plough soil was 0.4m. The sample taken from the upper fills of pit (16).

Objectives: radiocarbon dating of this sample will help to confirm the interpretation that intrusive Saxon pits, resembling *Grubenhäuser* have been dug into the centre of a Bronze Age ring ditch. If the date is prehistoric, then we must look for other reasons why a small amount of objects, dated to the Roman and Saxon periods, have been inserted into a presumed barrow.

Calibrated date: 1σ: cal AD 530–650
2σ: cal AD 410–670

Final comment: T Malim (18 August 1993), dating successfully confirmed a Saxon date for this pit in the centre of a ring ditch. It was presumed the feature represented a *Grubenhaus*, reusing the centre of a barrow, and the radiocarbon date confirmed this.

OxA–3638 3420 ±90 BP

δ¹³C: -22.7‰

Sample: HARMF 91 13.2, submitted on 16 January 1992 by T Malim

Material: charcoal: unidentified

Initial comment: appears to be the contents of a post pipe within a posthole, sealed by ploughsoil and subsoil approximately 0.4m deep.

Objectives: the sample comes from a posthole within a ring ditch. As such it may represent part of an original structure built whilst constructing the barrow. However, possible Saxon intrusion in the form of a presumed *Grubenhaus* makes the period to which the posthole in question (and related postholes) can be dated very uncertain. Are these postholes part of the original structure, or are they part of Saxon reuse of the area?

Calibrated date: 1σ: 1880–1610 cal BC
2σ: 1960–1500 cal BC

Final comment: T Malim (18 August 1993), this date confirmed the posthole was an original structural feature of the Bronze Age barrow and not associated with the later use of the ring ditch during the Dark Ages.

OxA–3639 3460 ±80 BP

δ¹³C: -21.2‰

Sample: HARMF 91 7.1, submitted on 16 January 1992 by T Malim

Material: charcoal: *Quercus* sp. (P Murphy 1991)

Initial comment: from a charcoal spread (7.1), whose thickest depth was 0.05m sealed by ploughsoil. The charcoal layer seals and fills stakeholes cut into burnt chalk-marl (7.0), and partly seals a cremation pit. This deposit is therefore seen as part of the burial phase and has been truncated by recent ploughing. The thickness of the ploughsoil was only 0.10–0.15m above the charcoal layer.

Objectives: cremated human bone from an adjoining pit would appear to be unfit in its own right for carbon dating. The present sample comes from charcoal spread that possibley partly seals the cremation, and is assumed to be associated with the burial ritual. Both features are in the centre of a ring ditch and stakeholes suggesting a structure has been cut into the chalk-marl subsoil, which shows evidence of high temperature. All of which are sealed by the charcoal layer.

Calibrated date: 1σ: 1890–1680 cal BC
2σ: 2020–1530 cal BC

Final comment: T Malim (18 August 1993), the date confirmed that this charcoal associated with cremated human bones is from the Bronze Age. The pit and bones were found in the centre of a ring ditch. The evidence suggests a funeral pyre dating to the Bronze Age was positioned in the centre of the ring ditch.

Haughmond Abbey, Shropshire

Location:	SJ 542152 Lat. 52.43.55 N; Long. 02.40.42 W
Project manager:	N J Palmer (Warwickshire Museum), 1979
Archival body:	Warwickshire Museum

Description: in its first phase the church consisted of a single cell with square *porticus*-like trancepts. Immediately to the west was a graveyard containing at least 25 graves. The addition of a cloister and the west extension of the nave reflect an expansion and regularisation of the community in the second quarter of the twelfth century.

Objectives: to help establish a date for the earliest monastic occupation on the site.

Laboratory comment: University of Belfast (1 February 1990), one further sample (UB-3191; HA4, grave fill 4221/1) was lost, and subsequently replaced by two further samples of human bone from other graves (UB-3228 and UB-3229).

Laboratory comment: Ancient Monuments Laboratory (7 February 2002), the three bone samples (HA3, HA5 and HA6; UB-3190, UB-3228, and UB-3229 respectively) are all statistically consistent (T'=0.0; ν=2; T'(5%)=6.0; Ward and Wilson 1978) and thus could all be of the same age. The calibrated results are therefore not inconsistent with the expected dates.

References:	Pearson 2003 Pearson and McCormac 2003, 360 Ward and Wilson 1978 Webster and Cherry 1980, 240–1

UB–3188 983 ±34 BP

δ¹³C: -26.4 ±0.2‰

Sample: HA1: layer 4219/1, submitted on 10 June 1989 by N J Palmer

Material: charcoal: unidentified

Initial comment: context 4219 was a patch of red loamy sand, ash, and charcoal, 1.20 × 0.30m across. It overlay 4226, a layer of dark yellowish brown sandy clay, interpreted as the original ground surface of the west of the original abbey church. It was sealed by layer 4210, a greyish brown sandy loam, a make-up under the floor of the later extension to the nave of the early church. It was cut by 4143, the construction trench for the south wall of the later abbey church of *c* AD 1200.

Objectives: to help establish a date for the earliest monastic occupation on the site in conjunction with somewhat limited ceramics, architectural, and documentary evidence. For later phases the other sources of evidence are felt to be sufficient.

Calibrated date:	*1σ:* cal AD 1010–1120 *2σ:* cal AD 990–1160

Final comment: N J Palmer (9 July 1991), this date centres on a pre-Conquest date, although rather earlier than expected, this date range would not be impossible however, given the possibility that it may be considerably older than its context and affected by an unknown age at death off-set.

UB–3189 1156 ±35 BP

δ¹³C: -26.6 ±0.2‰

Sample: HA2: layer 4259/1, submitted on 10 June 1989 by N J Palmer

Material: charcoal: unidentified

Initial comment: context 4259 was a patch of ash and charcoal, probably the result of a fire, 1.10m × 0.65m across. It overlay 4226, a layer of dark yellowish brown sand-clay, interpreted as the original ground surface and the west of the original abbey church. It was sealed by 4210, a greyish brown sandy loam, a make-up layer under the floor of the later extension and the nave of the early church. Context 4259 was at *c* 90.9m OD.

Objectives: as UB-3188

Calibrated date:	*1σ:* cal AD 820–950 *2σ:* cal AD 770–990

Final comment: N J Palmer (9 July 1991), this sample was significantly earlier as well as UB-3188, although it is possible that this represents an earlier clearance episode, but it is more likely that this charcoal came from wood of a greater age.

UB–3190 886 ±47 BP

δ¹³C: -20.3 ±0.2‰

Sample: HA3: grave fill 4220/1, submitted on 4 August 1989 by N J Palmer

Material: human bone (C Osborne 1989)

Initial comment: this sample came from articulated skeleton in bottom of grave 4220, 2.40m x. 0.80m × 0.60m deep, filled with yellowish brown sandy loam. The grave cut layer 4222, a yellowish brown loamy sand with blotches of pale yellow sand, which itself overlaid the original ground surface (4226) of dark yellowish brown sandy clay loam: a layer of make-up below the floor of the second phase extension to the early yard.

Objectives: it is hoped that this sample, in conjunction with the others submitted will provide a date for the construction and use of the earliest monastic church. As this grave is immediately adjacent to the church it is likely to be one of the earliest in the graveyard.

Calibrated date:	*1σ:* cal AD 1040–1220 *2σ:* cal AD 1020–1260

Final comment: N J Palmer (9 July 1991), the three bone samples (UB-3190, UB-3228, and UB-3229) were all statistically consistent and could all be the same age. The calibrated results are therefore not inconsistent with the expected dates.

UB–3228 888 ±47 BP

δ¹³C: -20.2 ±0.2‰

Sample: HA5 Grave 4231, submitted on 29 November 1989 by N J Palmer

Material: human bone (C Osborne 1989)

Initial comment: this sample came from an articulated skeleton placed within the lining of sandstone slabs at the bottom of grave 4231. The lining was covered at the head and feet ends with broken sandstone slabs and in the middle by stains of a wooden plank. The grave was filled with yellowish brown loamy sand and measured 2.42m × 0.95m at 0.85m deep. Grave 4231 cuts grave 4253 and was cut by grave 4233. It was sealed by make-up layers (4211, a dark yellowish brown sandy loam) beneath floor of the phase 2 extension to the early church.

Objectives: it is hoped that this sample, in conjunction with the others submitted, will provide a date for the construction and use of the earliest monastic church. Grave 4231 is a secondary one in the earliest phase 1 graveyard. It was some distance form the west end of the church and presumably therefore quite late in the sequence.

Calibrated date: *1σ:* cal AD 1040–1220
                     2σ: cal AD 1020–1260

Final comment: see UB-3190

UB–3229 881 ±37 BP

δ¹³C: -20.2 ±0.2‰

Sample: HA-6 Grave 4245, submitted on 29 November 1989 by N J Palmer

Material: human bone (C Osborne 1989)

Initial comment: this sample came from an articulated skeleton placed within a lining of sandstone slabs at the bottom of grave 4245, 2.2m × 0.84m × 0.4m deep and filled with yellowish brown sandy loam. The grave was adjacent to the west end of the early church, but cut by an earlier grave (4246), as well as the original ground surface (4226). The grave was sealed by 4232 (a yellowish brown sandy loam), a make-up layer below the floor of the phase 2 extension of the early church.

Objectives: it is hoped that this sample, in conjunction with the others submitted, will provide a date for the construction and use of the earliest monastic church. Grave 4245 is a secondary one in the earliest phase 1 graveyard.

Calibrated date: *1σ:* cal AD 1050–1220
                     2σ: cal AD 1030–1230

Final comment: see UB-3190

Hemington Fields, Leicestershire

Location: SK 4530
                     Lat. 52.51.55 N; Long. 01.19.53 W

Project manager: C R Salisbury (Independent), 1985–94

Archival body: Dr C Salisbury, Nottingham

Description: a palaeochannel in the vicinity of the confluence of the Rivers Derwent and Trent.

Objectives: to date the structures and their period of use.

Final comment: C Salisbury (11 January 1998), all these samples come from structures built into the river bed during the formation of a meander core in the Trent floodplain bounded by a thirteenth- to fourteenth-century AD

palaeochannel. It is hoped to establish a sequence of channels, which are associated with and modified by a twelfth-century mill dam, a series of bridges from the eleventh to thirteenth century AD, and many fish weirs. Combined with dendrochronological evidence, the dates suggest that the core did not expand regularly but was formed by a shifting pattern of anastomotic channels with the survival of untouched 'parcels' of gravel, one of which incorporates a thirteenth-century BC palaeochannel.

Laboratory comment: English Heritage (17 January 2012), five further dates from this site were published in Bayliss *et al* 2012 (146–7; HAR-8223–4 and HAR-8507–9).

References: Bayliss *et al* 2012
                      Clay 1986
                      Clay 1992b
                      Clay and Salisbury 1991
                      Losco-Bradley and Salisbury 1988
                      Salisbury 1980
                      Salisbury 1984
                      Salisbury 1991
                      Salisbury 1992

GU–5065 1230 ±50 BP

δ¹³C: -27.9‰

Sample: PL FW 19, submitted on 29 January 1991 by C R Salisbury

Material: wood (waterlogged): *Alnus* sp., outer 8 rings (C R Salisbury 1991)

Initial comment: from round section posts B and C, part of a fish weir or revetment. This sample, together with GU-5066 to GU-5070, and OxA-3028, was found *in situ* on the beds of a palaeochannels in the Trent floodplain. These channels are 3-4m deep and form part of a braided system at the confluence of the Trent and Derwent. The samples were 3–4m below the water table and surrounded by clean metamorphic derived gravel, which would have rapidly filled the channels in antiquity. Below is Devensian gravel and above is open country pasture.

Objectives: an area of palaeochannels near the confluence of the Trent and Derwent. These were controlled by weirs and perhaps stone revetments or causeways. Associated with a Norman mill, it is probably the site of an important fishing industry using unique fishing tackle anchors. Dating will establish its duration.

Calibrated date: *1σ:* cal AD 690–890
                     2σ: cal AD 660–940

Final comment: C R Salisbury (11 January 1998), the estimate on this fish weir post, set in the ancient river bed of an expanding meander core, together with all the other fish weir posts (GU-5465–70), helps to explain the development of this core. There was no steady expansion but a complex of changing braided and anastomotic channels caused partly by the natural development of sand bars but also by the presence of the fish weirs.

References: Salisbury 1995, 34–5
                      Salisbury 1996, 24–32

GU–5066 1180 ±100 BP

δ¹³C: -26.6‰

Sample: PL FW 21, submitted on 29 January 1991 by
C R Salisbury

Material: wood (waterlogged): *Corylus* sp. (C R Salisbury
1989)

Initial comment: as GU-5065

Objectives: as GU-5065

Calibrated date: *1σ:* cal AD 690–990
                        2σ: cal AD 650–1030

Final comment: see GU-5065

GU–5067 1160 ±100 BP

δ¹³C: -27.4‰

Sample: PL FW 22, submitted on 29 January 1991 by
C R Salisbury

Material: wood (waterlogged): *Alnus* sp., 5 rings only
(C R Salisbury 1989)

Initial comment: as GU-5065

Objectives: as GU-5065

Calibrated date: *1σ:* cal AD 710–990
                        2σ: cal AD 650–1040

Final comment: see GU-5065

GU–5068 1240 ±70 BP

δ¹³C: -27.0‰

Sample: PL FW 25, submitted on 29 January 1991 by
C R Salisbury

Material: wood (waterlogged; round section posts - willow,
alder, maple, hawthorn): *Fraxinus* sp.; *Alnus* sp.; *Salix* sp.;
Acer sp. (C R Salisbury 1989)

Initial comment: from the five posts A, B, D, E, and F. *See*
GU-5065.

Objectives: as GU-5065

Calibrated date: *1σ:* cal AD 670–890
                        2σ: cal AD 650–980

Final comment: see GU-5065

GU–5069 1090 ±110 BP

δ¹³C: -25.6‰

Sample: PL FW 28, submitted on 29 January 1991 by
C R Salisbury

Material: wood (waterlogged; *Ilex* sp.; 5 outer rings of round
section posts): *Alnus* sp.; *Corylus* sp. (C R Salisbury 1990)

Initial comment: from posts 4, 14, 19, and 20. *See* GU-5065

Objectives: as GU-5065

Calibrated date: *1σ:* cal AD 780–1030
                        2σ: cal AD 670–1180

Final comment: see GU-5065

GU–5070 1070 ±60 BP

δ¹³C: -27.7‰

Sample: PL FW 32, submitted on 29 January 1991 by
C R Salisbury

Material: wood (waterlogged): ? *Corylus* sp. (C R Salisbury
1990)

Initial comment: as GU-5065

Objectives: as GU-5065

Calibrated date: *1σ:* cal AD 890–1030
                        2σ: cal AD 820–1120

Final comment: see GU-5065

OxA–2288 1175 ±80 BP

δ¹³C: -28.4‰

Sample: PL17T231, submitted on 1 August 1989 by
C R Salisbury

Material: wood (waterlogged): *Corylus* sp., 50 rings with bark
edge (C R Salisbury 1989)

Initial comment: from a post forming part of a fish trap or
revetment. The post was set into the same river bed on
which anchor stone 18 lay (*see* OxA-2289).

Objectives: to give a precise date for the river bed when it
contained flowing water.

Calibrated date: *1σ:* cal AD 720–980
                        2σ: cal AD 660–1020

Final comment: see GU-5065

References: Hedges *et al* 1990, 223

OxA–2289 690 ±80 BP

δ¹³C: -27.8‰

Sample: PL15AN18, submitted on 1 August 1989 by
C R Salisbury

Material: wood (round section post): *Salix* sp. (C R Salisbury
1988)

Initial comment: from a twisted willow rod found in the
groove of a stone anchor (no. 18). Staining on the stone
suggests that the band extended round the anchor and
would probably have been used to hold a fishing basket. The
channel was rapidly filled in antiquity by clean gravel and its
bed is about 4m below the watertable.

Objectives: the site is an infilled ancient river channel near the
confluence of the Trent and Derwent. It is probably part of a
braided system including a mill dam (dated by
dendrochronology to cal AD 1120). The sample will give a
precise date for the river bed when it contained flowing
water and for the use of the anchor stones which are a
unique feature of this site.

Calibrated date: *1σ:* cal AD 1260–1390
                 2σ: cal AD 1210–1420

Final comment: C R Salisbury (11 January 1998), this sample from within the meander belt of the River Derwent is at least three centuries later than the OxA-3028 from an anchor withy in the nearby Trent meander core, even though they are of the same style. OxA-2289 was 75m from OxA-2288 and is approximately 400 years later, which suggests lateral river meandering.

References: Hedges *et al* 1990, 223

OxA–3028 1240 ±90 BP

δ¹³C: -25.7‰

Sample: PL AN 42, submitted on 29 January 1991 by C R Salisbury

Material: wood (waterlogged): *Salix* sp., 1-year-old withy

Initial comment: a twisted withy band encircling a stone fishing tackle anchor found *in situ* on the bed of a palaeochannel in the Trent Flood Plain, together with GU-5065–5070. These channels are 3–4m deep and form part of a braided system at the confluence of the Trent and Derwent. *See* GU-5065.

Objectives: as GU-5065

Calibrated date: *1σ:* cal AD 660–900
                 2σ: cal AD 640–990

Final comment: C R Salisbury (11 January 1998), the date range of this withy is almost identical with the surrounding fish weirs (GU-5065–8) confirming the impression that these anchors are used to hold fishing gear. 126 examples of this unique site artefact type have been recovered from this meander core.

References: Hedges *et al* 1992, 148

Hullbridge Survey, Essex

Location: TQ 8194 centred on
             Lat. 51.36.53 N; Long. 00.36.50 E

Project manager: T J Wilkinson (Essex County Council), 1982–7

Description: a series of samples were submitted from naturally-forming peats and other biogenic deposits and from archaeological deposits at intertidal sites on the Essex Coast.

Objectives: primarily to establish a chronology for transgressive and regressive overlaps and to relate human activity to this sequence.

References: Wilkinson and Murphy 1995

Hullbridge Survey: Blackwater 28, The Stumble, Essex

Location: TL 09140725
             Lat. 51.43.52 N; Long. 00.45.13 E

Project manager: P Murphy (University of East Anglia), 1985–8

Archival body: Essex County Council

Description: a multi-period complex comprising both dry and wet-land sites extending over intertidal mudflats between Osea Island and the north bank of the Blackwater. The site consists of a Neolithic dry land habitation site on the old land surface to the east and a complex of Iron Age and later wooden structures preserved in estuarine clays and infilled creeks towards the west.

Objectives: to provide dating of the wooden structures.

Final comment: P Murphy (18 September 1995), dates on wooden structures show that construction extended between *c* 400 cal BC (HAR-8880) and the post-medieval period.

Laboratory comment: English Heritage (17 January 2012), nine further dates from this site were published in Bayliss *et al* 2012 (158–60; HAR-7057–8, -8457–61, and -8880–1).

References: Bayliss *et al* 2012

HAR–9644 1900 ±70 BP

δ¹³C: -30.1‰

Sample: B28/244, submitted in August 1988 by P Murphy

Material: wood (waterlogged; roundwood)

Initial comment: wooden hurdle structure exposed on foreshore.

Objectives: previously obtained dates on wooden structures at this site are mainly Iron Age, though later dates have also been obtained. This is the best-preserved hurdle structure from the site and needs to be fitted into the sequence.

Calibrated date: *1σ:* cal AD 20–220
                 2σ: 50 cal BC–cal AD 320

Final comment: P Murphy (18 September 1995), an Iron Age structure.

References: Hardiman *et al* 1992, 56

OxA–1914 4020 ±70 BP

δ¹³C: -26.0‰ (assumed)

Sample: BL28A138, submitted on 4 November 1988 by P Murphy

Material: grain: *Triticum* sp., carbonised (P Murphy 1988)

Initial comment: from a posthole 18cm in diameter and 13cm deep, forming part of a Neolithic structure. The site is located on an intertidal mud-flat and is thus submerged twice daily by water of varying salinity. The archaeological deposits are somewhat disturbed by burrowing invertebrates which have introduced some intrusive biological material.

Objectives: to provide a date for cereal production at the site, believed to be early for this area and by association to date the artefacts and structures.

Calibrated date: *1σ:* 2630–2470 cal BC
                     2σ: 2870–2340 cal BC

Final comment: P Murphy (18 September 1995), this is a significant date as it establishes continuation of cereal production in this area in the late Neolithic.

References: Hedges *et al* 1991a, 125
                     Murphy 1988

OxA–1915 4060 ±80 BP

δ¹³C: -26.0‰ (assumed)

Sample: BL28D215, submitted on 4 November 1988 by P Murphy

Material: carbonised plant macrofossil (*Corylus avellana* nutshell fragments) (P Murphy 1988)

Initial comment: from a shallow depression (less than 5cm deep) containing a clay 10cm fill with charcoal, burnt flint, and Grooved Ware sherds.

Objectives: to date latest phase of activity at site, pre-dating local marine transgression.

Calibrated date: *1σ:* 2860–2470 cal BC
                     2σ: 2890–2410 cal BC

Final comment: P Murphy (18 September 1995), the result demonstrates a late Neolithic date for a feature in this area of the site.

References: Hedges *et al* 1991a, 125

OxA–2297 3885 ±70 BP

δ¹³C: -25.3‰

Sample: 28 279, submitted in 1989 by P Murphy

Material: wood: twig

Initial comment: from a deposit of heat-shattered flints and charcoal forming a burnt flint mound on the pre-transgression palaeosol, subsequently sealed by estuarine clays. It came from an intertidal site and the deposit was subject to some burrowing by annelids and molluscs.

Objectives: the function and date of 'burnt mounds' has been hotly discussed recently, but in general they appear to represent a phenomenon of Bronze Age date. The examples from The Stumble must, on stratigraphic grounds, be of late Neolithic or earlier date, however. They are thus unusually early examples, but cannot be dated artefactually. A radiocarbon determination would be the only way of establishing their position in the archaeological sequence of the site.

Calibrated date: *1σ:* 2480–2210 cal BC
                     2σ: 2570–2140 cal BC

Final comment: P Murphy (18 September 1995), the date indicates that this burnt flint mound immediately pre-dates the Thames III transgression, in which the Neolithic surface

was submerged. The mound was in use at a time when conditions were becoming wetter due to deteriorating freshwater drainage and the area was no longer suitable for settlement.

References: Hedges *et al* 1991a, 125

OxA–2298 4780 ±70 BP

δ¹³C: -27.5‰

Sample: 28C270, submitted in September 1989 by P Murphy

Material: carbonised plant macrofossil (*Corylus avellana* nutshell) (P Murphy 1989)

Initial comment: from the fill of pit 279. This is an intertidal site. Shallow features are subject to bioturbation, but the sample came from a deep undisturbed feature.

Objectives: despite abundant early-middle Neolithic artefacts, dates so far received (OxA-1914 and OxA-1915) proved to relate to later Neolithic activity. This sample and also OxA-2299 were taken from clearly-defined pits containing early–middle Neolithic pottery. They should thus give dates for settlement and agriculture at this site, which, given its geographical location, may well be unusually early.

Calibrated date: *1σ:* 3650–3380 cal BC
                     2σ: 3700–3370 cal BC

Final comment: P Murphy (18 September 1995), the date on *Corylus* nutshell from this pit confirms that the nutshells and cereals from the site are indeed penecontemporaneous and relate to an economy based partly on foraging, partly on farming (*see* OxA-2299).

References: Hedges *et al* 1991a, 125
                     Murphy 1989

OxA–2299 4675 ±70 BP

δ¹³C: -24.8‰

Sample: 28C266, submitted in September 1989 by P Murphy

Material: grain: *Triticum dicoccum*, carbonised (P Murphy 1989)

Initial comment: from the fill of pit 265, which had been dug through a palaeosol, infilled and then subsequently sealed by estuarine clays (*see* also HAR-2298).

Objectives: as HAR-2298

Calibrated date: *1σ:* 3630–3360 cal BC
                     2σ: 3640–3340 cal BC

Final comment: P Murphy (18 September 1995), this is the earliest date so far obtained on charred cereals from Essex. See also OxA-2298 for a date on *Corylus* nutshell from an adjacent feature.

References: Hedges *et al* 1991a, 125
                     Murphy 1989

Hullbridge Survey: Bradwell Power Station, Essex

Location: TM 024093
Lat. 51.44.43 N; Long. 00.55.56 E

Project manager: P Murphy (University of East Anglia), February 1987

Archival body: Essex County Council

Description: test boring undertaken as a preliminary to the then-proposed storage of nuclear waste in an area to the east of Bradwell Power Station provided bore logs and delft cores, which have given useful data on the stratigraphy of the outer Blackwater Estuary at the north-east corner of the Dengie Peninsula.

Objectives: to provide dating for the pollen analysis.

References: Hardiman *et al* 1992, 56
Wilkinson 1987
Wilkinson and Murphy 1988

HAR–9643 6670 ±130 BP

$\delta^{13}C$: -28.6‰

Sample: BCORE553, submitted in August 1988 by P Murphy

Material: peat (peaty clay)

Initial comment: contractor's borehole 553 revealed this biogenic deposit of presumed early Flandrian date at a depth of 6.11–6.22m beneath estuarine clay.

Objectives: as part of the Hullbridge Survey project all biogenic deposits exposed in the estuary have been dated and sampled for palaeoecological study. This borehole provides samples of the only early Flandrian organic sediments available. Pollen analysis by R Scaife will provide information on contemporary vegetation but independent dating is needed.

Calibrated date: 1σ: 5710–5480 cal BC
2σ: 5840–5370 cal BC

Final comment: P Murphy (18 September 1995), the sediment was formed in estuarine conditions with woodland dominated by *Tilia* nearby. The date is the earliest available from the project.

Hunsbury Hillfort, Northamptonshire

Location: SP 748584
Lat. 52.13.21 N; Long. 01.38.13 W

Project manager: D A Jackson (Northamptonshire County Council Archaeological Unit), 1988

Archival body: Northamptonshire County Council Archaeological Unit

Description: one trench was excavated across an eroded section of the north rampart.

Objectives: to date the construction of the rampart.

Final comment: D A Jackson (9 August 1994), the radiocarbon dates come from the charred remains of timbers associated with box rampart. They suggest that this was constructed in the early Iron Age period.

References: Jackson 1994

HAR–10568 2390 ±70 BP

$\delta^{13}C$: -25.3‰

Sample: HHG, submitted on 28 June 1988 by D A Jackson

Material: charcoal: *Quercus* sp.

Initial comment: charred wood from post, found *in situ* within the rampart.

Objectives: to date the construction of the rampart.

Calibrated date: 1σ: 730–390 cal BC
2σ: 770–360 cal BC

Final comment: D A Jackson (9 August 1994), from a charred post found within the core of the rampart; presumably contemporary with the earliest structure.

Laboratory comment: AERE Harwell (17 June 1990), this sample was processed using the larger sample, high-precision liquid scintillation system.

HAR–10569 2420 ±100 BP

$\delta^{13}C$: -29.8‰

Sample: HHB, submitted on 28 June 1988 by D A Jackson

Material: charcoal: unidentified, not oak

Initial comment: possibly from a plank used to support the rampart (not *in situ*).

Objectives: to date the construction of the rampart.

Calibrated date: 1σ: 770–390 cal BC
2σ: 810–230 cal BC

Final comment: D A Jackson (9 August 1994), from a plank-like timber probably associated with the burnt box structure. The date conforms well with HAR-10568).

Laboratory comment: AERE Harwell (17 June 1990), this sample was processed using the larger sample, high-precision liquid scintillation system.

HAR–10570 2310 ±70 BP

$\delta^{13}C$: -25.2‰

Sample: HHH, submitted on 28 June 1988 by D A Jackson

Material: charcoal: *Quercus* sp.

Initial comment: charred wood from post forming wall at the rear of the rampart (found *in situ*).

Objectives: to date the construction of the rampart.

Calibrated date: 1σ: 410–260 cal BC
2σ: 710–200 cal BC

Final comment: D A Jackson (9 August 1994), later than the other two dates. This may suggest that some of the timbers in the rear revetment were replaced.

Laboratory comment: AERE Harwell (17 June 1990), this sample was processed using the larger sample, high-precision liquid scintillation system.

Hunstanton: Redgate Hill, Norfolk

Location:	TF 67803980 Lat. 52.55.44 N; Long. 00.29.47 E
Project manager:	P Murphy (Centre for East Anglian Studies, University of East Anglia), 1970–1
Archival body:	Norwich Castle Museum

Description: a complex of prehistoric pits and postholes dating from the late Neolithic and early Bronze Age.

Objectives: excavations in 1971 revealed postholes of a unique complex of structures most of which, including a large trapezoid enclosure, were without satisfactory dating evidence. A small quantity of bone recovered from structure E would serve to date not only the structure itself, but the main enclosure, with which the structure was integral. This would be the most important contribution which radiocarbon dating could make to the understanding of the excavated area.

Final comment: F Healy (9 June 1995), all postholes on Redgate Hill were severely eroded and there were few datable finds from them, leaving their age uncertain. OxA-2307–9 were all made on extremely small animal bone samples. Within their limitations they suggest that the structures were built, used, and decayed, in the course of the Bronze Age. This would not conflict with the range of temper, form, and decoration among the small collection of pottery from structural contexts. The similarity of OxA-2310 and OxA-2311 corresponds to the homogeneity in style and fabric of the later Neolithic Grooved Ware from the site. Both fall well within the range of dates for southern British Grooved Ware (Garwood 1999). This suggests that a date of 2290–1890 cal BC (BM-704; 3685 ±65 BP; Reimer *et al* 2004), obtained on animal bone from a now unidentified pit described as containing Grooved Ware, may in fact have been made on a sample from pit 34 which contained a Collared Urn.

References:	Bradley *et al* 1992 Garwood 1999 Hedges *et al* 1991a, 126 Reimer *et al* 2004

OxA–2307 2720 ±80 BP

$\delta^{13}C$: -23.4‰

Sample: HUN 302 (1), submitted in March 1989 by P Murphy

Material: animal bone (includes pig) (G Jones)

Initial comment: from a posthole of a small structure (E) incorporated into a large trapezoid enclosure. The feature was very shallow and cut into chalk.

Objectives: to date the so far unique complex of which the structure forms a part, and for which artefactual dating evidence is inconclusive.

Calibrated date:	*1σ:* 970–800 cal BC
	2σ: 1050–780 cal BC

Final comment: F Healy (9 June 1995), the sample came from layer 1 of double posthole 302. It is likely to date from after the decay of a post-built structure (E) integral to a large post-built trapezoid enclosure.

OxA–2308 3370 ±70 BP

$\delta^{13}C$: -22.6‰

Sample: HUN 309 (4), submitted in March 1989 by P Murphy

Material: animal bone (including cattle) (G Jones)

Initial comment: from a posthole common to the north side of a large trapezoid enclosure and small structure (E). Other details are as OxA-2307.

Objectives: as OxA-2307

Calibrated date:	*1σ:* 1750–1530 cal BC
	2σ: 1880–1490 cal BC

Final comment: F Healy (9 June 1995), the sample came from layer 4 of double posthole 309, which formed part of a large trapezoid enclosure and of a post-built structure (E) which was integral to it. It is likely to relate to the construction and use of the structures.

OxA–2309 3810 ±80 BP

$\delta^{13}C$: -22.4‰

Sample: HUN 303 (2), submitted in March 1989 by P Murphy

Material: animal bone (including pig) (G Jones)

Initial comment: as OxA-2307

Objectives: as OxA-2307

Calibrated date:	*1σ:* 2460–2130 cal BC
	2σ: 2480–2020 cal BC

Final comment: F Healy (9 June 1995), the sample came from layer 2 of slot and double posthole 303 (not 302, as published due to a typing error in Hedges *et al* (1991a, 122). It is likely to relate to the construction and use of the structure.

References:	Hedges *et al* 1991a, 122

OxA–2310 4005 ±90 BP

$\delta^{13}C$: -23.0‰

Sample: HUN 12, submitted in March 1989 by P Murphy

Material: animal bone: *Bos* sp., cattle mandible fragment (G Jones)

Initial comment: from the fill of pit 12, containing struck flint and Grooved Ware. The pit was shallow, cut into chalk, and penetrated to some extent by roots.

Objectives: to date the deposition of artefacts in the pit. A single radiocarbon determination of 2290–1890 cal BC at 95% confidence (BM-704; 3685 ±65 BP; Reimer *et al* 2004) was made in the 1970s, but it is now impossible to determine from which pit the sample came. This date is also anomalously late.

Calibrated date: *1σ:* 2630–2460 cal BC
                          2σ: 2880–2240 cal BC

Final comment: F Healy (9 June 1995), OxA-2310, like OxA-2311, dates one of nine pits containing Grooved Ware in the Clacton substyle, struck flint, animal bone, and sea shells.

References: Reimer *et al* 2004

OxA–2311 4170 ±90 BP

δ¹³C: -22.6‰

Sample: HUN 22, submitted in March 1989 by P Murphy

Material: animal bone

Initial comment: as OxA-2310

Objectives: as OxA-2310

Calibrated date: *1σ:* 2900–2580 cal BC
                          2σ: 2930–2480 cal BC

Final comment: see OxA-2310

Ipswich, Blackfriars (School Street), Suffolk

Location: TM 192425
                         Lat. 52.02.12 N; Long. 01.11.44 E

Project manager: K Wade (Suffolk Archaeological Unit), 1984

Archival body: Suffolk Archaeological Unit

Description: 250 burials (148 male adults, 64 female adults, 14 unsexed adults, and 24 juveniles), interred between AD 1263 and AD 1538 were examined. The burials represent interments within the friary complex.

Objectives: to determine whether the syphilis burial pre-dates AD 1493.

References: Mays 1991

UB–3202 380 ±18 BP

δ¹³C: -19.4 ±0.2‰
δ¹³C (diet): -19.3 ±0.1‰
δ¹⁵N (diet): +16.1 ±0.3‰

Sample: 895549; skeleton 1965, submitted on 16 October 1989 by S Mays

Material: human bone (S Mays 1989)

Initial comment: inhumation in a single grave - burial beneath floor of church.

Objectives: this skeleton shows signs of syphilis, a current theory is that syphilis was spread to Europe from the New World on Columbus' return from America in AD 1493. No convincing evidence exists for syphilis in Europe prior to this date. Documentary evidence dates the burial to between AD 1263 and AD 1537; the aim of radiocarbon dating is to determine whether the burial pre-dates AD 1493, and hence is the first evidence for syphilis in Europe prior to AD 1493.

Calibrated date: *1σ:* cal AD 1455–1610
                          2σ: cal AD 1445–1620

Final comment: S Mays (2001), although this date ranges over AD 1440–1620, the range can be narrowed since it is known that the friary ceased to be used for burial in AD 1538. Combining the information that the burial must pre-date AD 1539 with the radiocarbon result using a Bayesian approach (Gelfand and Smith 1990) and the OxCal calibration programme (Bronk-Ramsey 1995), allows us to revise the probability distribution for the date of this individual. This procedure permits the 95% probability range to be recalculated as *cal AD 1445–1520*, and indicates that the probability that this burial pre-dates AD 1493 is 73%.

Laboratory comment: University of Belfast (27 July 2012), this sample was measured in the high-precision facility.

References: Bronk Ramsey 1995
                         Gelfand and Smith 1990
                         Mays *et al* 2002

Ipswich: Foundation Street, Suffolk

Location: TM 165442
                         Lat. 52.03.11 N; Long. 01.09.27 E

Project manager: T Loader (Suffolk Archaeological Unit), 1985

Archival body: Suffolk Archaeological Unit

Description: the sample came from building 677, which was a burnt down cellared building.

Objectives: to provide a date for the burning of the building, which may signify a major decline in the fortunes of the town during the middle and late tenth century, as is suggested from other sites in Ipswich. This suggestion remains mainly hypothetical as the ceramic dating is so limited. There is little doubt that radiocarbon dating would go a long way to providing an answer as to whether such a postulated decline (perhaps following the English re-conquest of East Anglia from the Danes) is reality or simply an artefact of the inadequacy of the archaeological record.

Final comment: T Loader (17 May 1994), samples of carbonised grain were selected from the contents of burnt down buildings from Foundation Street. Radiocarbon results have indicated a range from the late seventh to late tenth century AD; all of which have been persistently at odds with ceramic and stratigraphic evidence for eleventh- or twelfth-century dates.

GU–5218 1240 ±50 BP

δ¹³C: -23.2‰

Sample: IAS 4601 0741, submitted on 3 April 1992 by

T Loader

Material: grain: *Avenena* sp., carbonised (P Murphy 1992)

Initial comment: the sample is from one of the eight separate heaps of grain, lying above the clay floor of a cellared building. The grain was sealed by the carbonised remnants of the building (677) and a further grain sample (0754) some 0.6m below the surface of the natural. No obvious contaminants were recorded.

Objectives: the context is one of six roughly contemporary burnt-down buildings from various sites in Ipswich. By dating the contents of more than one building there may be an indication of a single catastrophe, possibly the one that more than halved the number of burgesses between AD 1066 and AD 1086.

Calibrated date: *1σ:* cal AD 680–880
                   2σ: cal AD 660–900

Final comment: T Loader (17 May 1994), the sample of carbonised grain stored in the cellar of a building should provide a fairly close date for when the building was burnt down. The radiocarbon result is at odds with the ceramic and stratigraphic evidence, which indicates a significantly later date range.

GU–5219 1170 ±50 BP

δ¹³C: -22.6‰

Sample: IAS 4601 0760, submitted on 3 April 1992 by T Loader

Material: grain: *Avenena* sp., carbonised (P Murphy 1992)

Initial comment: as GU-5218

Objectives: as GU-5218

Calibrated date: *1σ:* cal AD 770–950
                   2σ: cal AD 690–990

Final comment: see GU-5218

Ipswich: St Stephen's Lane, Suffolk

Location: TM 164444
               Lat. 52.03.18 N; Long. 01.09.22 E

Project manager: T Loader (Suffolk Archaeological Unit), 1988

Archival body: Suffolk Sites and Monuments Record, Suffolk Archaeological Unit

Description: the samples were taken from a two-phase rectangular cellared structure, lying end on to and some 14m back from the St Stephen's Lane frontage, and forming one of a group of similar contemporary buildings with structures 29 and 2140.

Objectives: to provide a date for the burning of the structure, which may signify a major decline in the fortunes of the town during the middle and late tenth century is suggested from other sites in Ipswich. This suggestion remains mainly hypothetical as the ceramic dating is so limited. There is little doubt that radiocarbon dating would go a long way to providing an answer as to whether such a decline (perhaps following the English re-conquest of East Anglia from the Danes) is reality or simply an artefact of the inadequacy of the archaeological record.

Final comment: T Loader (17 May 1994), samples of carbonised grain were selected from the contents of burnt down buildings from St Stephen's Lane. Radiocarbon results

have indicated a range from late seventh to late tenth century AD, all of which have been persistently at odds with ceramic and stratigraphic evidence for eleventh- or twelfth-century dates.

GU–5220 1160 ±50 BP

δ¹³C: -23.8‰

Sample: IAS 3104 2476, submitted on 3 April 1992 by T Loader

Material: grain: *Avenena* sp., carbonised (P Murphy 1992)

Initial comment: the grain was situated towards the base of burnt layer 2081, at the base of the infilled building, and was sealed below a layer of burned clay. Lying some 1.2m below the surface of the natural, there is no indication of any possible contaminants in building 2022.

Objectives: as GU-5218

Calibrated date: *1σ:* cal AD 770–970
                   2σ: cal AD 710–990

Final comment: T Loader (17 May 1994), the sample of carbonised grain stored in the cellar of a building should provide a fairly close date for when the building was burnt down. The radiocarbon result is at odds with the ceramic and stratigraphic evidence, which indicates a significantly later date range.

GU–5221 1150 ±50 BP

δ¹³C: -22.7‰

Sample: IAS 3104 2388, submitted on 3 April 1992 by T Loader

Material: grain (charred bread): *Secale cereale*, carbonised; *Triticum* sp., carbonised (P Murphy 1992)

Initial comment: carbonised bread rolls were found lying directly above wicker structure 2252 at the base of layer 2081 directly above the floor of the cellar. No obvious contaminants were recorded in building 2202.

Objectives: as GU-5218

Calibrated date: *1σ:* cal AD 780–980
                   2σ: cal AD 720–1000

Final comment: see GU-5220

GU–5270 1210 ±50 BP

δ¹³C: -26.0‰

Sample: IAS 3104 2604, submitted on 3 November 1992 by T Loader

Material: charcoal: *Corylus* sp. (P Murphy 1992)

Initial comment: this sample was located within layers of burnt debris close to the base of a cellared building (2140) - derived from collapse of the structure following fire damage. This building cuts an earlier infilled cellared structure containing a coin group dated to *c* AD 925. Early medieval coarse-wares were found in the infilling.

Objectives: earlier radiocarbon work in grain samples (GU-5218 to GU-5221) from contemporary contexts from Ipswich suggest an eighth- to ninth-century dating, which is not consistent with ceramic dates. This sample provides an independent test on an alternative short-life sample.

Calibrated date: 1σ: cal AD 710–890
2σ: cal AD 670–970

Final comment: T Loader (17 May 1994), the radiocarbon date range for the sample is not consistent with the stratigraphic and ceramic evidence. As such it has failed to provide any closer dating of the structure from which it was removed.

GU–5674 1220 ±80 BP

δ¹³C: -25.9‰

Sample: IAS 3104 2604, submitted on 3 April 1992 by T Loader

Material: charcoal: *Corylus* sp. (P Murphy 1992)

Initial comment: a replicate of GU-5270.

Objectives: as GU-5270

Calibrated date: 1σ: cal AD 680–900
2σ: cal AD 650–990

Final comment: see GU-5270

Laboratory comment: English Heritage (28 January 2012), the two results from this deposit are statistically consistent (T'=0.0; T'(5%)=3.8; v=1; Ward and Wilson 1978). Their weighted mean (1213 ±43 BP) calibrates to cal AD 680–950 (95% confidence; Reimer *et al* 2004), or to cal AD 720–890 (68% confidence).

References: Reimer *et al* 2004
Ward and Wilson 1978

Isles of Scilly Project

Location: SV 9214 centred on
Lat. 49.56.48 N; Long. 06.17.41 W

Project manager: J Ratcliffe and V Straker (Cornwall Archaeology Unit and Bristol University), 1989–93

Description: between 1985 and 1993 a small-scale recording and sampling programme was undertaken to assess the palaeoenvironmental potential of early coastal sites around the Isles of Scilly.

Objectives: for intertidal peat deposits, the aim was to test their potential for enhancing understanding of the vegetational history of Scilly and past sea-level change; for cliff-face sites, the aim was to assess their potential for understanding the diet and economy of early Scillonians.

Final comment: J Ratcliffe and V Straker (1995), the radiocarbon dates have provided a chronological framework for the palaeoenvironmental evidence.

References: Ratcliffe and Straker 1996

Isles of Scilly Project: St Agnes, Porth Killier

Location: SV 88100848
Lat. 49.53.39 N; Long. 06.20.36 W

Project manager: V Straker (University of Bristol), 1989

Archival body: Isles of Scilly Museum

Description: part of the Isles of Scilly project which involves coastal monitoring and recording due to erosion, by the Cornwall Archaeology Unit.

Objectives: to refine the pottery and feature chronology with which these samples were associated.

Final comment: J Ratcliffe (1994), these determinations are extremely useful representing as they do the first dates obtained for this settlement. Scilly's most extensive prehistoric cliff-face site, which has been recorded since the 1930s and has yielded substantial quantities of pottery (and other artefacts). A Bronze Age date range was expected and, as well as confirming the date of the structural remains, it can be used to refine Scilly's Prehistoric pottery sequence (still largely floating).

References: Hedges *et al* 1994, 363
Ratcliffe and Straker 1996

OxA–3647 3220 ±70 BP

δ¹³C: -20.3‰

Sample: AGNPK1, submitted in March 1992 by V Straker

Material: grain (carbonised) (V Straker 1989)

Initial comment: from the top of the midden associated with prehistoric huts exposed in section (layer 14). A bulk sample collected, sieved in water, and plant animal remains extracted. The midden also contained bone (only 10g non-marine species) and shell.

Objectives: to date archaeological features and refine the pottery chronology, which is very insecure for the prehistoric period on Scilly.

Calibrated date: 1σ: 1610–1420 cal BC
2σ: 1670–1320 cal BC

Final comment: J Ratcliffe (1994), the dates for samples OxA-3647 and OxA-3648 are the wrong way round by overlap, but when calibrated are useful because they show that the midden they were taken from was deposited during the middle to late Bronze Age. Since other features and layers both pre- and post-date this midden it can be assumed that the occupation at the settlement both began before and continued after its deposition.

OxA–3648 3170 ±65 BP

δ¹³C: -22.6‰

Sample: AGNPK2, submitted in March 1992 by V Straker

Material: grain: *Hordeum* sp., charred (V Straker 1989)

Initial comment: base of midden associated with prehistoric huts exposed in section (Layer 14). Bulk sample collected,

Isles of Scilly Project: St Martin's, Higher Town Beach

sieved in water and plant animal remains extracted. Also contained bone (42g) from non-marine species.

Objectives: to date archaeological features and refine pottery chronology is very insecure for prehistoric period on Scilly.

Calibrated date: 1σ: 1510–1400 cal BC
2σ: 1610–1300 cal BC

Final comment: see OxA-3647

Isles of Scilly Project: St Martins, Higher Town Beach

Location: SV 93481530
Lat. 49.57.29 N; Long. 06.16.26 W

Project manager: V Straker (University of Bristol), 1990

Archival body: Isles of Scilly Museum

Description: part of the continuing programme in the monitoring, recording, and conservation of archaeological remains exposed in the cliff-face around the islands, many of which are suffering rapid coastal erosion.

Objectives: the peat in this area was thinner and contained a higher sand component, the dates will show its association with the probable stone row on the Higher Town Beach.

Final comment: J Ratcliffe (1994), these are really exciting dates since they have made possible the identification of three separate phases of early 'peat' formation in an area, which is now part of Scilly's intertidal zone. The samples were taken from three different locations and it would have been difficult, if not impossible, to phase them without the use of radiocarbon dating.

References: Ratcliffe and Straker 1996

GU–5060 4510 ±60 BP

δ¹³C: -27.4‰

Sample: MARHTB 1, submitted on 15 November 1990 by V Straker

Material: peat

Initial comment: from the basal 5cm of peat. This overlies grey sand. The peat has a high silt component and a thinner horizontal sample would have contained little organic material.

Objectives: dating of the peat samples will give precise information on when peat started to develop and whether it does post-date many archaeological monuments which are exposed on the beach today. This will refine considerably our knowledge of sea level rise on Scilly, which is vital to the understanding of the prehistoric landscape, the chronology of the reduction in the area of dry land, and the development of the present landscape.

Calibrated date: 1σ: 3360–3090 cal BC
2σ: 3490–3010 cal BC

Final comment: J Ratcliffe (1994), the late Neolithic date obtained for the base of this 'peat' exposure is very exciting and will be used not only to place the pollen data obtained in a chronological sequence but also to help test the present model for sea-level change in Scilly.

GU–5061 5210 ±60 BP

δ¹³C: -27.3‰

Sample: MARHTB 2, submitted on 22 November 1990 by V Straker

Material: peat

Initial comment: sample of peat 1cm thick from a monolith collected at low spring tide. This is the only location where peat overlay dark grey silts.

Objectives: as GU-5060

Calibrated date: 1σ: 4050–3960 cal BC
2σ: 4240–3940 cal BC

Final comment: J Ratcliffe (1994), the early Neolithic date for the base of this 'peat' exposure is the earliest secure date obtained for an intertidal peat deposit in Scilly. It will prove very valuable in testing the current model for sea-level change and placing the pollen data in a chronological sequence.

GU–5062 1570 ±50 BP

δ¹³C: -28.3‰

Sample: MARHTB 3, submitted on 22 November 1990 by V Straker

Material: peat

Initial comment: peat from adjacent to the middle standing stone. Higher up the beach than MARHTB 1 and 2, but still submerged at low tide.

Objectives: as GU-5060

Calibrated date: 1σ: cal AD 420–560
2σ: cal AD 390–610

Final comment: J Ratcliffe (1994), this was a surprising result because this peat deposit had been assured in the field to be an inland extension of MARHTB 1 (GU-5060). In fact it is much later (beginning in the late Romano-British or early medieval period). Romano-British remains were excavated on the beach earlier this century. This date will also be used to check the sea-level model and provide a chronological context for the pollen data.

Isles of Scilly Project: St Martins, Higher Town Beach Par

Location: SV 93481530
Lat. 49.57.29 N; Long. 06.16.26 W

Project manager: V Straker (University of Bristol), 1991

Archival body: Isles of Scilly Museum

Description: part of the continuing programme in the monitoring, recording, and conservation of archaeological remains exposed in the cliff-face around the islands, many of which are suffering rapid coastal erosion.

Objectives: continuing the programme in providing a dating sequence for the peat deposits.

Final comment: J Ratcliffe (1994), with the exception of PAR1 (GU-5222) these dates are disappointing. Power augering to a depth of 2m provided the opportunity to take

99

radiocarbon samples from three successive 'peat' deposits, the top one already dated to the early Neolithic (*see* MARHTB2; GU-5061). Unfortunately, the dates are muddled and unreliable (when judged in relation to each other and those obtained previously). This may be the result of the type of auger used.

References: Ratcliffe and Straker 1996

GU–5222 5410 ±70 BP

δ¹³C: -26.1‰

Sample: PAR1, submitted in March 1992 by V Straker

Material: wood (waterlogged): *Quercus* sp. (V Straker 1991)

Initial comment: the sample is from the outermost rings of a piece of mature oak embedded in the top of an intertidal peat bed. Its surface was exposed at low tide. It is the first piece of mature wood to be recovered from the peat, and may relate to the woodland cover. The peat from this area was dated by GU-5061.

Objectives: dating of the peat samples will give precise information on when peat started to develop and whether it does post-date many archaeological monuments which are exposed on the beach today. This will refine considerably our knowledge of sea-level rise on Scilly, which is vital to the understanding of the prehistoric landscape, the chronology of the reduction in the area of dry land, and the development of the present landscape.

Calibrated date: *1σ:* 4340–4170 cal BC
                       2σ: 4370–4040 cal BC

Final comment: J Ratcliffe (1994), this early Neolithic date was the one hoped for - the piece of oak just pre-dating the formation of the 'peat' it was embedded in. The date certainly disproves local theories that the wood was from an eighteenth-century wreck. Unfortunately, its surface is too eroded to tell whether or not it was worked.

GU–5223 4040 ±60 BP

δ¹³C: -26.5‰

Sample: PAR2, submitted in March 1992 by V Straker

Material: peat

Initial comment: column 1, top 2cms upper peat.

Objectives: as GU-5222

Calibrated date: *1σ:* 2830–2470 cal BC
                       2σ: 2870–2460 cal BC

Final comment: J Ratcliffe (1994), the dates for PAR 2–4 (samples from the top, middle and base of the upper 'peat') may be reliable since they are in the right order. However, PAR 4 is the equivalent of sample MARHTB 2 but its date is more than 500 years later. This suggests that the whole sequence of dates for the upper 'peat' deposit may be too late.

GU–5224 4190 ±50 BP

δ¹³C: -27.2‰

Sample: PAR3, submitted in March 1992 by V Straker

Material: peat

Initial comment: column 1, middle 2cm upper peat.

Objectives: as GU-5222

Calibrated date: *1σ:* 2890–2680 cal BC
                       2σ: 2910–2620 cal BC

Final comment: see GU-5223

GU–5225 4770 ±50 BP

δ¹³C: -27.2‰

Sample: PAR4, submitted in March 1992 by V Straker

Material: peat

Initial comment: column 1, basal 2cm upper peat.

Objectives: as GU-5222

Calibrated date: *1σ:* 3640–3520 cal BC
                       2σ: 3660–3370 cal BC

Final comment: see GU-5223

GU–5226 3880 ±50 BP

δ¹³C: -27.5‰

Sample: PAR5, submitted in 1992 by V Straker

Material: peat

Initial comment: column 1, top 2cm middle peat.

Objectives: as GU-5222

Calibrated date: *1σ:* 2470–2280 cal BC
                       2σ: 2480–2200 cal BC

Final comment: J Ratcliffe (1994), this date, for the top of the middle 'peat', is in the correct order in the sense that it is later than that for the middle of this deposit (PAR 6). However, it is later in relation to the overlying 'peat' being of early Bronze Age date, while the base of the latter is early Neolithic (MARHTB 2 and PAR 4).

GU–5227 4110 ±50 BP

δ¹³C: -27.5‰

Sample: PAR6, submitted in March 1992 by V Straker

Material: peat

Initial comment: column 1, middle 2cm middle peat.

Objectives: as GU-5222

Calibrated date: *1σ:* 2870–2570 cal BC
                       2σ: 2880–2490 cal BC

Final comment: J Ratcliffe (1994), this date, for the middle of the middle 'peat' is ok in relation to the date for PAR 5, the top of this deposit, but is too recent in relation to the upper peat phase (PAR 4 and MARHTB 2) - it should be at least Mesolithic in date.

GU–5228 4030 ±60 BP

$\delta^{13}C$: -27.5‰

Sample: PAR7, submitted in March 1992 by V Straker

Material: peat

Initial comment: column 1, all of the lowest peat (2cm band).

Objectives: as GU-5222

Calibrated date: *1σ:* 2630–2470 cal BC
                   2σ: 2860–2460 cal BC

Final comment: J Ratcliffe (1994), being the sample of the base of the lowest 'peat' this should be the earliest date in the sequence but in fact it is one of the most recent (late Neolithic–early Bronze Age). Definitely not a reliable date.

Isles of Scilly Project: Tresco, Crab's Ledge

Location: SV 89751370
                 Lat. 49.56.31 N; Long. 06.19.28 W

Project manager: V Straker (University of Bristol), 1990

Archival body: Isles of Scilly Museum

Description: part of the continuing programme in the monitoring, recording and conservation of archaeological remains exposed in the cliff face around the islands, many of which are suffering rapid coastal erosion. At Crab's Ledge on Tresco, the peat appears to overlie a field wall.

Objectives: continuing the programme in providing a dating sequence for the peat deposits.

Final comment: J Ratcliffe (1994), there is quite a bit of discrepancy between the two pairs of dates - TRESCL 1 and 2 versus TRESCL 3 and 4, which is surprising because they are samples of the same general deposit. However, the results give a broad indication of when the 'peat' began forming (late Iron Age/early Romano-British) and this date confirms the impression gained during the field survey that the peat post-dated the laying out of the boulder-walled field system, which extends further down the beach and is prehistoric in character.

References: Ratcliffe and Straker 1996

GU–5056 1880 ±100 BP

$\delta^{13}C$: -26.5‰

Sample: TRESCL 1, submitted on 15 November 1990 by V Straker

Material: peat

Initial comment: surviving top of peat (0–1cm).

Objectives: dating of the peat samples will give precise information on when peat started to develop and whether it does post-date many archaeological monuments which are exposed on the beach today. This will refine considerably our knowledge of sea level rise on Scilly, which is vital to the understanding of the prehistoric landscape, the chronology of the reduction in the area of dry land, and the development of the present landscape.

Calibrated date: *1σ:* cal AD 20–250
                   2σ: 100 cal BC–cal AD 390

Final comment: J Ratcliffe (1994), this date for the top of the 'peat' is at odds with TRESCL 3, a sample of the top of the 'peat' taken at another location. The difference is 400 years. Is this the result of the samples having low organic content, or varying degrees of truncation?

Laboratory comment: English Heritage (30 January 2012), the two radiocarbon determinations from the top of this peat deposit are statistically significantly different (T′=9.9; T′(5%)=3.8; ν=1; Ward and Wilson 1978).

References: Ward and Wilson 1978

GU–5057 1980 ±90 BP

$\delta^{13}C$: -25.6‰

Sample: TRESCL 2, submitted on 15 November 1990 by V Straker

Material: peat

Initial comment: from the base of the peat (19–20cm), with a high mineral component.

Objectives: as GU-5056

Calibrated date: *1σ:* 90 cal BC–cal AD 130
                   2σ: 210 cal BC–cal AD 240

Final comment: J Ratcliffe, this date for the base of the 'peat' is 200 years later than that for TRESCL 4, a sample of the base taken at a different location. Presumably this has to be the result of the low organic content of the samples making them less reliable as dating material.

Laboratory comment: English Heritage (30 January 2012), the two results from the base of this peat deposit are statistically indistinguishable (T′=2.2; T′(5%)=3.8; ν=1; Ward and Wilson 1978).

References: Ward and Wilson 1978

GU–5058 1480 ±80 BP

$\delta^{13}C$: -25.3‰

Sample: TRESCL 3, submitted on 15 November 1990 by V Straker

Material: peat

Initial comment: top of peat adjacent to field wall.

Objectives: as GU-5056

Calibrated date: *1σ:* cal AD 530–650
                   2σ: cal AD 410–680

Final comment: see GU-5056

Laboratory comment: see GU-5056

GU–5059 2180 ±100 BP

$\delta^{13}C$: -24.9‰

Sample: TRESCL 4, submitted on 15 November 1990 by V Straker

Material: peat

Initial comment: from the base of the peat adjacent to the field wall (9–10cm). This was underlain by dark grey silty sand.

Objectives: as GU-5056

Calibrated date: 1σ: 390–60 cal BC
                        2σ: 410 cal BC–cal AD 30

Final comment: see GU-5057

Laboratory comment: see GU-5057

Isles of Scilly Project: Tresco, Crab's Ledge, Crab

Location: SV 89711375
                     Lat. 49.56.36 N; Long. 06.19.35 W

Project manager: V Straker (University of Bristol), 1991

Archival body: Isle of Scilly Museum

Description: part of the continuing programme in the monitoring, recording, and conservation of archaeological remains exposed in the cliff-face around the islands, many of which are suffering rapid coastal erosion. At Crab's Ledge on Tresco, the peat appears to overlie a field wall.

Objectives: continuing the programme in providing a dating sequence for the peat deposits.

Final comment: J Ratcliffe (17 June 1994), CRAB 1 was not within an expected date range, and even if this is ignored the other three dates in this sequence are too early when compared with TRESCL1–4. This is disappointing since it was hoped that such sub-samples from a power auger column could be used to date such buried intertidal 'peats'. If cross-contamination is the problem a different auger may solve it.

References: Ratcliffe and Straker 1996

GU–5229 8250 ±70 BP

δ¹³C: -27.5‰

Sample: CRAB1, submitted in March 1992 by V Straker

Material: peat

Initial comment: top 2cm, upper peat: column VI.

Objectives: the intertidal 'peats' (including humic silty clays and loams) are important not only because the upper bands are suffering severe erosion and are therefore a rapidly diminishing resource. They clearly preserve considerable information on the environmental history of the Isles of Scilly; most particularly sea-level change, vegetation, and the impact of human activity on the landscape.

Calibrated date: 1σ: 7460–7140 cal BC
                      2σ: 7500–7060 cal BC

Final comment: J Ratcliffe (17 June 1994), a Roman or early medieval date was expected.

GU–5230 1600 ±60 BP

δ¹³C: -24.9‰

Sample: CRAB2, submitted in March 1992 by V Straker

Material: peat

Initial comment: from the basal 2cm, the upper peat: column VI.

Objectives: as GU-5229

Calibrated date: 1σ: cal AD 400–550
                      2σ: cal AD 260–600

Final comment: J Ratcliffe (17 June 1994), this date is 400–600 years later than the two dates obtained for the base of the upper 'peat' (*see* TRESCL2 and 4; GU-5057 and GU-5059).

GU–5231 1830 ±90 BP

δ¹³C: -25.6‰

Sample: CRAB3, submitted in March 1992 by V Straker

Material: peat

Initial comment: from the top 2cm, the middle peat: Column VI, really a humic sandy loam.

Objectives: as GU-5229

Calibrated date: 1σ: cal AD 70–330
                      2σ: 40 cal BC–cal AD 410

Final comment: J Ratcliffe (17 June 1994), this date for the top of the lower 'peat' is surely too late, since it is later than the two previous dates obtained for the base of the upper 'peat' (TRESCL2 and 4). Though it is acceptable in terms of its relation to CRAB 2 (GU-5230).

GU–5232 2140 ±60 BP

δ¹³C: -25.9‰

Sample: CRAB4, submitted in March 1992 by V Straker

Material: peat

Initial comment: from the basal 2cm, the lowest peat: column VI, really a humic silty clay loam.

Objectives: as GU-5229

Calibrated date: 1σ: 360–60 cal BC
                      2σ: 380 cal BC–cal AD 1

Final comment: J Ratcliffe (17 June 1994), though acceptable in relation to CRAB 3, this date for the base of the lower peat appears to be too late in relation to previous dates for the base of the upper 'peat' (TRESCL 1–4; GU-5056–9).

Isles of Scilly: St Mary's, Halangy Porth

Location: SV 9012
                     Lat. 49.55.39 N; Long. 06.19.15 W

Project manager: P Ashbee (Independent), 1975

Archival body: Isles of Scilly Museum

Description: a circular building exposed in the cliff.

Objectives: the dates from Halangy are required in order to date the features exposed in the eroding cliff section.

References: Walker *et al* 1990, 165

HAR–1313 2260 ±90 BP

δ¹³C: -24.1‰

Sample: SCILLY01, submitted in 1975 by P Ashbee

Material: charcoal (twig): *Ulex* sp., or possibly *Sarothamnus scoparius* (C A Keepax 1975)

Initial comment: collected during the excavation of the possible entrance to a stone-built hut exposed in the seacliff and beneath a fossil sand dune. The entrance was infilled to a depth of *c* 1m with hillwash: fragments were scattered with pottery in this fill. The estimated archaeological date is 2000 BC.

Objectives: to date the structure.

Calibrated date: 1σ: 410–200 cal BC
2σ: 520–60 cal BC

Final comment: K Cullen (12 January 2010), the stone-built hut appears to be of Iron Age rather than Bronze Age date as anticipated.

Laboratory comment: AERE Harwell (3 March 1988), this sample was measured in the miniature gas proportional counter (Otlet *et al* 1983).

References: Otlet *et al* 1983

Leicester: Shires, Leicestershire

Location: SK 58580464
Lat. 52.38.10 N; Long. 01.08.03 W

Project manager: J Lucas (University of Birmingham), 1988

Archival body: University of Birmingham

Description: two sites were sampled: Leicester and Worcester. The samples consist of seed material which is not charred, waterlogged, or visibly mineralised, and therefore the seeds were visually indistinguishable from modern seeds. The soil conditions were neither desiccated nor anaerobic and there was no obvious mechanism by which the seeds could have been preserved. The seeds came from contexts which were chosen to be archaeologically well-sealed and well-dated. The Leicester sample was from a medieval pit.

Objectives: since the seeds were of the common disturbed-ground species (*Sambucus nigra*), one possible and likely explanation was that the seeds were modern intrusions. This would have had implications for the integrity of the archaeological contexts despite their well-sealed appearance. Another possible explanation was that the seeds were archaeological but preserved by some unexplained means. The possibility that some seeds might survive many centuries without an obvious means of preservation has been suspected by archaeobotanists but dating confirmation is needed.

References: Hedges *et al* 1993, 162–3

OxA–3067 1190 ±60 BP

δ¹³C: -24.1‰

Sample: 399, submitted on 1 March 1991 by L Moffett

Material: plant macrofossils (*Sambucus nigra* seeds) (L Moffett 1991)

Initial comment: from a shallow loam-filled medieval pit. Residuality within the pit was very small. The pit cut an earlier feature but was otherwise isolated from the surrounding pits. No other possible contaminants were noted. The pit was 1m deep and sealed by 1.75m of medieval to post-medieval cultivated horizons.

Objectives: to determine whether the seeds are archaeological.

Calibrated date: 1σ: cal AD 720–940
2σ: cal AD 670–990

Final comment: L Moffett (1993), the samples dated from this site (OxA-3067 and OxA-3068) and those from Worcester: Deansway (OxA-3064, OxA-3065, and OxA-3066) are either well-correlated with the archaeological dates, or are earlier than the archaeological dates, confirming that the seeds in these samples are indeed archaeological and have survived in some cases probably over a thousand years of burial.

OxA–3068 1340 ±70 BP

δ¹³C: -22.3‰

Sample: 246, submitted on 1 March 1991 by L Moffett

Material: plant macrofossils (*Sambucus* seeds) (L Moffett 1991)

Initial comment: from the bottom cess layer of a large, predominantly loam-filled feature with cess deposits at the bottom. It was selected as it cut 1.25m deep into the natural sand and gravel, and was isolated from any intercutting pits. The only possible contamination was from the loam fill that seals this cess layer. The pit was sealed by 1.75m of medieval to post-medieval cultivated horizons.

Objectives: to determine whether the seeds are archaeological.

Calibrated date: 1σ: cal AD 640–770
2σ: cal AD 590–860

Final comment: see OxA-3067

Lichfield Cathedral, Staffordshire

Location: SK 116098
Lat. 52.41.08 N; Long. 01.49.42 W

Project manager: W Rodwell (Independent), 1992

Archival body: Dean and Chapter, Lichfield Cathedral

Description: the cathedral has a long and distinguished ecclesiastical history in the Anglo-Saxon period, which has hitherto been unsupported by archaeological evidence. The foundation of the cathedral dates from no later than 669 cal AD.

Objectives: to provide a chronology for burials at the cathedral.

Laboratory comment: English Heritage (30 January 2012), two further samples were submitted and dated after March 1993.

GU–5281 2410 ±50 BP

$\delta^{13}C$: -20.6‰

Sample: LC01, submitted on 1 September 1993 by W Rodwell

Material: human bone (J Rogers 1992)

Initial comment: part of skeleton 16 from one of the primary graves in the Anglo-Saxon cemetery, east of the original cathedral, and sealed below the floor of the thirteenth-century quire aisle extension. It was also sealed by the construction levels for the late eleventh-century sanctuary apse.

Objectives: to confirm a date for this primary grave. The grave had side-ledges and a head recess, and is of the type likely to be middle Saxon.

Calibrated date: 1σ: 730–400 cal BC
                      2σ: 760–390 cal BC

Final comment: W Rodwell (14 March 1994), this is an inexplicable result. It implies an early Iron Age date. It is consistent with the result for LC 02 (GU-5282), but that is no help. I still believe the cemetery under Lichfield Cathedral to be Anglo-Saxon, not prehistoric. Laboratory error seems the most likely explanation (cf. LC 03 (GU-5283) and LC 07 (GU-5354)).

Laboratory comment: SURRC Radiocarbon Dating Laboratory (1994), the inexplicable result was caused by the addition of dead carbon from a contaminated oxygen cylinder.

Laboratory comment: English Heritage (30 January 2012), a replicate measurement was subsequently obtained for this burial (cal AD 980–1220 (95% confidence)); GU-5434; 960 ±60 BP; Reimer *et al* 2004).

References: Reimer *et al* 2004

GU–5282 2560 ±100 BP

$\delta^{13}C$: -26.0‰

Sample: LC02, submitted in February 1993 by W Rodwell

Material: human bone

Initial comment: from skeleton 19, *see* GU-5281.

Objectives: as GU-5281

Calibrated date: 1σ: 820–540 cal BC
                      2σ: 910–400 cal BC

Final comment: W Rodwell (14 March 1994), an inexplicable result. *See* GU-5281.

Laboratory comment: SURRC Radiocarbon Dating Laboratory (1994), again the inexplicable result was caused by the addition of dead carbon from a contaminated oxygen cylinder.

GU–5283 1650 ±50 BP

$\delta^{13}C$: -22.8‰

Sample: LC03, submitted in February 1993 by W Rodwell

Material: human bone

Initial comment: from skeleton 28 from the west end of the south quire aisle where the grave was sealed and cut by the foundation of the late eleventh-century cathedral. There is ample charcoal from this burial to provide a check on the date obtained from the bone sample if required.

Objectives: this was a charcoal-filled grave, sandwiched in a sequence of four generations of burial, apparently inside part of the Anglo-Saxon cathedral. It is stratigraphically later than samples LC 04, 05, and 06, (GU-5284, GU-5285, and GU-5286), but earlier than the late eleventh-century wall that cut the grave.

Calibrated date: 1σ: cal AD 340–430
                      2σ: cal AD 250–540

Final comment: W Rodwell (14 March 1994), a curious result suggesting a Roman date for what is unquestionably a middle or late Saxon grave (cf the early dates yielded by HAR-5281 and HAR-5282, but note that they are from a different part of the site). A subsequent dating of charcoal (GU-5354) associated with LC 03 yielded an acceptable result, showing that the problem lay with the bone from the grave, or with the laboratory.

GU–5284 1030 ±50 BP

$\delta^{13}C$: -22.9‰

Sample: LC04, submitted in February 1993 by W Rodwell

Material: human bone

Initial comment: from skeleton 30, and as GU-5283 from the west end of the south quire aisle where the grave was sealed and cut by the foundation of the late eleventh-century cathedral. The burial was accompanied by two Anglo-Saxon glass beads, probably belonging to an early stage in the Christian archaeology of Lichfield, potentially seventh century. The grave was part of a sequence of high-ranking graves, apparently inside the Anglo-Saxon Cathedral.

Objectives: to establish a date for the burial which stratigraphically is later than LC 05 (GU-5285) and LC 06 (GU-5286), but earlier than LC 03 (GU-5283).

Calibrated date: 1σ: cal AD 980–1030
                      2σ: cal AD 890–1160

Final comment: W Rodwell (14 March 1994), a middle rather than late Saxon date was expected on grounds of site stratigraphy, finds from the grave, and other radiocarbon dates from the burial sequence.

GU–5285 1210 ±50 BP

$\delta^{13}C$: -21.1‰

Sample: LC05, submitted in February 1993 by W Rodwell

Material: human bone

Initial comment: from skeleton 35; from one of the two earliest graves (*see* also GU-5283) in the Anglo-Saxon cathedral (and perhaps earlier).

Objectives: to establish a date for the burial. This date will be comparable with LC 06 (GU-5286), and earlier than LC 03 and LC 04 (GU-5283 and GU-5284). It should be no later than the middle Saxon period, and is crucial to establishing the beginning of the burial sequence in the cathedral.

Calibrated date: *1σ:* cal AD 710–890
                   2σ: cal AD 670–970

Final comment: W Rodwell (14 March 1994), the middle Saxon date yielded is entirely consistent with expectations and, when taken together with LC 06 and 07 (GU-5286 and GU-5354) provides valuable evidence for the beginning of the burial sequence inside the Anglo-Saxon cathedral.

GU–5286 1200 ±50 BP

δ¹³C: -22.0‰

Sample: LC06, submitted in February 1993 by W Rodwell

Material: human bone

Initial comment: from skeleton 34, and as GU-5283, from the west end of the south quire aisle where the grave was sealed and cut by the foundation of the late eleventh-century cathedral.

Objectives: to establish a date for the burial. The date should be similar to LC 05 (GU-5285) being the second of the earliest pair of graves in the cathedral, as so far excavated.

Calibrated date: *1σ:* cal AD 720–900
                   2σ: cal AD 680–980

Final comment: W Rodwell (14 March 1994), the similarity of this result to LC 05 (GU-5285) is gratifying, since the two burials were contemporaneous in stratigraphic terms, and believed to be middle Saxon.

Liffs Low, Derbyshire

Location: SK 15145764
                   Lat. 53.03.56 N; Long. 01.46.26 W

Project manager: J Barnatt (Peak National Park), 1984

Archival body: Peak Park Joint Planning Board, Buxton Museum and Art Gallery

Description: a Scheduled barrow, sited on the limestone plateau in Derbyshire.

Objectives: the excavations were undertaken to elucidate illicit and poorly documented work in the 1930s when a S3 Beaker, a polished pendant, and at least three skeletons were unearthed.

Final comment: J Barnatt (8 July 1991), the 1984 excavation demonstrated that the barrow comprised a complex multi-phased structure which also had signs of pre-barrow activity in the form of stakeholes and pits. One such pit gave an earlier Neolithic date (OxA-2290).

References: Barnatt 1989
                 Barnatt 1995
                 Barnatt and Collis 1996
                 Hedges *et al* 1991a, 127

OxA–2290 5000 ±80 BP

δ¹³C: -26.6‰

Sample: LL84SF50, submitted in July 1989 by K Smith

Material: charcoal: unidentified

Initial comment: a sample from a small pit beneath and central to the barrow. The pit was surrounded by concentric arcs and stakeholes, suggesting contemporary features immediately predating the construction of the primary mound.

Objectives: the barrow appears to be much more complex than previously realised, with probably both late Neolithic and earlier Bronze Age phases. The phase of activity represented by this feature appears to pre-date the earliest mound but to be part of the ceremonial leading to its construction. The date should indicate this link as well as the period of activity.

Calibrated date: *1σ:* 3950–3690 cal BC
                   2σ: 3970–3640 cal BC

Final comment: J Barnatt (8 July 1991), the charcoal, within a pit under the primary barrow, confirms that the feature and probably others nearby are associated with activity in the earlier Neolithic, as opposed to being ritual features made immediately prior to the barrow being built.

OxA–2291 4850 ±80 BP

δ¹³C: -25.7‰

Sample: LL84SF48, submitted in July 1989 by K Smith

Material: charcoal: unidentified

Initial comment: a sample from a layer that is either the capping of the primary mound or the basal layer of the south enlargement of the barrow. The uncertainty lies more with the limits on excavation than difficulties of interpretation.

Objectives: this date is required either to date the phase of final use of the primary mound or to date the enhancement of the monument. It is important for demonstrating the sequential use of the monument.

Calibrated date: *1σ:* 3710–3530 cal BC
                   2σ: 3800–3380 cal BC

Final comment: J Barnatt (8 July 1991), in retrospect this sample of charcoal, from directly under the primary barrow, is not contemporary with the mound but lies in the buried soil and is residual from pre-barrow activity in the earlier Neolithic.

OxA–2354 4960 ±70 BP

δ¹³C: -31.2‰

Sample: LL84SF28, submitted in July 1989 by K Smith

Material: charcoal: unidentified

Initial comment: a sample from the top layer of a small pit below the northern addition to the monument. This pit should be the primary interment feature for this addition. The sample comprises two concentrations of charcoal found in close proximity.

Objectives: the date provide a *terminus post quem* for the addition to the mound and a *terminus ante quem* for the primary mound. It should also provide one of a sequence of dates for the monument.

Calibrated date: *1σ:* 3900–3650 cal BC
                   2σ: 3960–3630 cal BC

Final comment: J Barnatt (8 July 1991), in retrospect this sample of charcoal, from within the mound, does not date from one of its construction phases, but is residual from earlier Neolithic pre-barrow activity.

OxA–2355 5270 ±70 BP

δ¹³C: -31.9‰

Sample: LL84SF35, submitted in July 1989 by K Smith

Material: charcoal: unidentified

Initial comment: a sample from the upper layer of the northern addition to the monument, beneath the stone rosette.

Objectives: the latest date in the sequence, this should indicate the date of the final activity concerned with additions to this monuments.

Calibrated date: *1σ:* 4240–3980 cal BC
                      2σ: 4330–3950 cal BC

Final comment: J Barnatt (8 July 1991), in retrospect this sample of charcoal, from within the mound, does not date from one of its construction phases, but is residual from the earlier Neolithic pre-barrow activity.

Lindow Moss: pollen sequence, Cheshire

Location: SJ 82168072
               Lat. 53.19.22 N; Long. 02.16.04 W

Project manager: R Scaife (University of Southampton), 1989

Description: the discovery of the first part of another well-preserved human body at Lindow Moss in February 1987, led to another chapter in the story of archaeological work on this site.

Objectives: to provide a chronological framework for an environmental sequence through Lindow Moss, taken by a Russian/Jowesey corer, in the vicinity of the find spot of the bog body.

Final comment: A Bayliss (31 January 2012), no environmental analysis appears to have been undertaken on these sediments.

References: Branch 1988

UB–3237 1488 ±44 BP

δ¹³C: -28.1 ±0.2‰

Sample: LM1/20-22, submitted on 1 December 1989 by D Jordan

Material: peat

Initial comment: taken from a depth of 20–22cm in Lindow Moss as part of a pollen core.

Objectives: to date part of an important pollen sequence associated with the Lindow Moss body.

Calibrated date: *1σ:* cal AD 540–620
                      2σ: cal AD 430–650

UB–3238 1764 ±48 BP

δ¹³C: -26.8 ±0.2‰

Sample: LM2/55-57, submitted on 1 December 1989 by D Jordan

Material: peat

Initial comment: this sample is taken from a depth of 55–57cm in the Lindow Moss as part of a pollen core.

Objectives: as UB-3237

Calibrated date: *1σ:* cal AD 220–340
                      2σ: cal AD 130–400

UB–3239 2345 ±45 BP

δ¹³C: -27.4 ±0.2‰

Sample: LM3/117-119, submitted on 1 December 1989 by D Jordan

Material: peat

Initial comment: this sample is taken from a depth of 117–119cm in the Lindow Moss as part of pollen core.

Objectives: as UB-3237

Calibrated date: *1σ:* 410–390 cal BC
                      2σ: 520–370 cal BC

UB–3240 2447 ±43 BP

δ¹³C: -28.3 ±0.2‰

Sample: LM4/119-121, submitted on 1 December 1989 by D Jordan

Material: peat

Initial comment: this sample is taken from a depth of 119–121cm in the Lindow Moss as part of a pollen core.

Objectives: as UB-3237

Calibrated date: *1σ:* 750–410 cal BC
                      2σ: 770–400 cal BC

UB–3241 3724 ±55 BP

δ¹³C: -29.2 ±0.2‰

Sample: LM5/188-190, submitted on 1 December 1989 by D Jordan

Material: peat

Initial comment: this sample is taken from a depth of 188–190cm in the Lindow Moss as part of a pollen core.

Objectives: as UB-3237

Calibrated date: *1σ:* 2210–2030 cal BC
                      2σ: 2290–1950 cal BC

Ling Howe, Humberside

Location: SE 964357
               Lat. 53.48.30 N; Long. 00.32.09 W

Project manager: J Dent (Humberside County Council Archaeology Unit), 1984

Archival body: Humberside Archaeological Unit

Description: a Neolithic long barrow, excavation carried out in advance of road widening.

Objectives: to establish the date for the construction for the long barrow.

References: Hardiman *et al* 1992, 52

HAR–9248 5220 ±100 BP

δ¹³C: -25.9‰

Sample: LIN84024, submitted in June 1989 by J Dent

Material: charcoal: unidentified

Initial comment: from old soil beneath the chalk mound material of a Neolithic long barrow.

Objectives: to establish a *terminus post quem* for the construction of the mound.

Calibrated date: 1σ: 4230–3950 cal BC
2σ: 4330–3790 cal BC

Final comment: J Dent, the date provides a *terminus post quem* for the mound construction.

Laboratory comment: AERE Harwell (30 November 1989), this sample was measured in the miniature gas proportional counter (Otlet *et al* 1983).

References: Otlet *et al* 1983

Lismore Fields, Buxton, Derbyshire

Location: SK 050731
Lat. 53.15.17 N; Long. 01.55.30 W

Project manager: D Garton (Trent and Peak Archaeological Trust), 1984–6

Archival body: Trent and Peak Archaeological Trust

Description: in 1984 work prompted by a housing development and funded by Derbyshire County Council, English Heritage, and the Trustees of the Chatsworth Settlement sought to investigate the supposed line of a Roman road at Lismore Fields in Buxton. What emerged, in place of the resoundingly absent Roman road, after some three seasons of excavation, was an earlier Neolithic settlement consisting of a lithic and pottery assemblage associated with a group features including sub-rectangular buildings with preserved floors, postholes, and pits (Garton 1991). Analysis of the ground plans has suggested that three similar structures are present. Charred plant remains from the buildings included emmer grains and chaff, flax seeds, hazelnuts, and crab apple fruits and seeds. Taken together with a series of five dates from buildings, ranging between 3950 and 3340 cal BC (OxA-2434–8) at 95% confidence (Reimer *et al* 2004; Garton 1991, 19) this site arguably challenges previous views of the earlier Neolithic in the Peak and asks us to test our ideas on how settlement of varying levels of permanency or seasonality might be expected to appear. The location of the site, within an upland basin formed by the Wye Valley at 300m OD and surrounded on all sides by hills, challenges the models with which so much has already been achieved. Quite incidentally, the spatially

coincident but quite distinct later Mesolithic assemblage and possible features at Lismore Fields also reinforce the emergent picture gained from the surface collection surveys. The dated charcoal from a posthole associated with a ring-slot feature perhaps places the assemblage around the late fifth or early fourth millennium (calibrated) BC. The character of the later Mesolithic to earlier Neolithic transition is perhaps a subject worthy of further research in its own right.

Objectives: diagnostic artefacts of only later Mesolithic and Neolithic date have been recovered from some 3800m² of excavations. The features are widely spread and intercutting sequences of features are rare - only two periods of activity may be represented. This contrasts with the evidence from the pollen analysis, which shows clearance and disturbance of the vegetation throughout the sampled profiles, so it might just be the lack of artefacts that gives this minimal impression of the periods of occupation.

Laboratory comment: English Heritage (17 January 2012), one further date (HAR-6500) from this site was published in Bayliss *et al* (2012, 187). Forty-seven additional samples were submitted and dated in 2008–10.

References: Bayliss *et al* 2012
Garton 1987
Garton 1991
Reimer *et al* 2004

OxA–1976 3540 ±70 BP

δ¹³C: -26.0‰ (assumed)

Sample: LF47-48, submitted on 1 February 1989 by D Jordan

Material: peat

Initial comment: Buxton 2: 47–48cm.

Objectives: to date the pollen column.

Calibrated date: 1σ: 1960–1760 cal BC
2σ: 2120–1690 cal BC

Final comment: P Wiltshire (1991), this core was taken by R S Scaife, the relationship between this core and Buxton 1, 4, and 5 is complex. But if one interpolates from the radiocarbon dates it would appear that Buxton covers the older part of the sequence (*c* 7250–3050 BP), Buxton 4 the middle section (*c* 3990–1990 BP), whilst Buxton 1 takes in the upper sequence (*c* 3990 BP at the base, no estimate for the top). Alder carr vegetation seems to have dominated the pollen sampling locality for much of the period under question, although extra-local and regional vegetational changes can also be discerned. On the basis of the AMS dates and the palynology, there is good evidence at Lismore Fields for late Mesolithic woodland disturbance, probably through the use of fire since microscopic charcoal was abundant in the peat. The presence of Mesolithic artefacts on the adjoining site demonstrates that hunter/gatherer communities were exploiting the area. Higher in the profile there is more evidence of woodland clearance, with a continuous record of cereal pollen. The interpolated date for what must be the beginning of Neolithic cereal agriculture is remarkably early, *c* 6000 BP. Woodland regeneration follows however further Neolithic activity is observed in the peat between *c* 5000–4680 BP thus reflecting the building activity on the adjacent archaeological site. Further vegetational changes in the later prehistoric period suggest the area continued to be occupied and exploited (except perhaps for a partial abandonment in the late Bronze Age). After the Neolithic though no more archaeological remains were found.

References: Hedges *et al* 1991b, 287–8

OxA–1977 4460 ±100 BP

δ¹³C: -26.0‰ (assumed)

Sample: LF76-77, submitted on 1 February 1989 by D Jordan

Material: peat

Initial comment: Buxton 2: 76–77cm.

Objectives: pollen column dating.

Calibrated date: 1σ: 3360–2920 cal BC
                     2σ: 3500–2890 cal BC

Final comment: see OxA-1976

Final comment: J Meadows (27 November 2011), single fragments of bark and a twig isolated from the peat sample remaining from this analysis has been dated subsequently (OxA-20828, 4116 ±38 BP; 2880–2500 cal BC; Reimer *et al* 2004; SUERC-24606, 4065 ±35 BP; 2860–2480 cal BC).

References: Hedges *et al* 1991b, 287–8
                     Reimer *et al* 2004

OxA–1978 6630 ±80 BP

δ¹³C: -26.0‰ (assumed)

Sample: LF126-127, submitted on 1 February 1989 by D Jordan

Material: peat

Initial comment: Buxton 2: 126–127cm.

Objectives: pollen column dating.

Calibrated date: 1σ: 5630–5480 cal BC
                     2σ: 5710–5470 cal BC

Final comment: see OxA-1976

Final comment: J Meadows (27 November 2011), two twigs isolated from the peat sample remaining from this analysis have been subsequently dated, providing dates of 4050–3950 cal BC (OxA-20829; 5178 ±35 BP) and 3970–3790 cal BC (SUERC-24605; 5090 ±35 BP; Reimer *et al* 2004).

References: Hedges *et al* 1991b, 287–8
                     Reimer *et al* 2004

OxA–2433 5270 ±100 BP

δ¹³C: -27.4‰

Sample: BLF 55a, submitted on 13 February 1990 by D Garton

Material: charcoal (4.50g): *Sorbus* sp., est. min age 25; *Prunus spinosa*, est. min age 10; *Crataegus* sp., est. min age 7; *Corylus* sp., est. min age 7, and 15 (G Morgan).

Initial comment: the soil sampled formed a circular shape in plan in the centre of the posthole; it is interpreted as a postpipe. The charcoal and burnt cobbles are presumed to have fallen into the void when the post was withdrawn. Though slow-grown, only young wood has been identified; it may be derived from the structure, or a hearth/fire nearby.

Objectives: the post-rings (2) and ring-slots (7) are of one of two sizes (the larger one is also found as a half-ring) and constructed in segments; they are thought to be contemporaneous structures although their date and function are unknown. Posthole 0055 formed part of a structure with ring-slot 0054 and posthole 0064. Posthole 0055 was linked to slot 0054 by the limit of a darker basal soil which is interpreted as the edge of the wall line of the former structure. The structure formed by ring-slot 0054 and postholes 0055 plus 0064 apparently contained a late Mesolithic knapping episode, but burnt flint excluded from the interior of the structure appears to be Neolithic. The burnt flint spreads from building I and may be contemporaneous with its demise.

Calibrated date: 1σ: 4240–3970 cal BC
                     2σ: 4340–3810 cal BC

Final comment: D Garton and J Kenworthy (1992), the date for the posthole associated with the ring-slot is surprisingly early. Two typologically similar ring-slots cut large postholes set in a line.

Final comment: J Meadows (27 November 2011), this sample probably contained a component of residual charcoal.

References: Hedges *et al* 1991b, 287–8

OxA–2434 4930 ±70 BP

δ¹³C: -23.8‰

Sample: BLF 89e, submitted on 13 February 1990 by D Garton

Material: grain (0.70g) (carbonised): Cereal indet; *Triticum* sp. (G Jones)

Initial comment: from the postpipe of a stone packed posthole from the centre-line of building I; it cannot be assigned to either unit, so cannot be used in the first instance for dating the building. The quantity of grain suggests that it was charred at a single event, either at or soon before, the demise of the building.

Objectives: it contains probably breadwheat grains (no rachis fragments are present which are required for conclusive identification). The breadwheat is too rare to be dated directly, and new techniques may allow confirmation in the future, so the emmer/spelt and indeterminate grains from the same sample are submitted for dating.

Calibrated date: 1σ: 3790–3640 cal BC
                     2σ: 3940–3540 cal BC

Final comment: D Garton and J B Kenworthy (1992), the dates from building I, OxA-2434, OxA-2436, OxA-2437, and OxA-2438, are statistically coherent (and with UB-3290 from the same building) and given an overall pooled weighted mean of 4923 ±35 BP which calibrates to 3780–3640 cal BC at 95% confidence (Reimer *et al* 2004). The similarity of the charcoal and seed dates show that there is no old wood effect. *See* also OxA-2435.

References: Hedges *et al* 1991b, 287–8
                     Reimer *et al* 2004

OxA–2435 4680 ±70 BP

δ¹³C: -26.5‰

Sample: BLF 238a/g, submitted on 13 February 1990 by D Garton

Material: charcoal (5g): Pomoideae, est. min age 4; *Corylus* sp., est. min age 5, 10, and 12 (G Morgan).

Initial comment: this sample could have been building material or represent other activities conducted within the area. The concentration of charred material within this deposit suggests that it originates from a single event, probably the demise of the building. Only species with an estimated minimum age of <30 years are included in the sample for radiocarbon.

Objectives: the posthole forms part of building II. The sampled material was from the postpipe below stones interpreted as deliberate backfill of the hole after the post had been removed. The sample, together with UB-3289, dates the construction, or demise, of the building.

Calibrated date: *1σ:* 3630–3360 cal BC
                       2σ: 3640–3340 cal BC

Final comment: D Garton and JB Kenworthy (1992), this date for building II is coherent with UB-3289; together they give a pooled mean date of 4705 ±55 BP, which calibrates to 3640–3360 cal BC at 95% confidence (Reimer *et al* 2004). A comparison between both the complete data sets and the pooled means suggest building I is earlier than building II, although the similarity of the ground-plans suggest that they are closely related in form, and by implication, in time.

References: Hedges *et al* 1991b, 287–8
                      Reimer *et al* 2004

OxA–2436 4970 ±70 BP

δ¹³C: -25.9‰

Sample: BLF 110h/k, submitted on 13 February 1990 by D Garton

Material: carbonised plant macrofossil (charred flax seeds (*Linus usitatissimum*)) (G Jones)

Initial comment: from the two fillings of the postpipe; the flax seeds occurred both singly and as a fused lump.

Objectives: the posthole forms part of the eastern unit of building I. The presence of so many flax seeds and their fusion into a lump, would suggest that they were a single deposit, burnt at the demise of the building, which fell into the void created by the removal of the post. Together with OxA-2438 this sample should date the demise of the eastern unit of the building and the use of flax in a Neolithic context in the Peak District.

Calibrated date: *1σ:* 3910–3650 cal BC
                       2σ: 3960–3640 cal BC

Final comment: see OxA-2434

References: Hedges *et al* 1991b, 287–8

OxA–2437 4840 ±70 BP

δ¹³C: -25.9‰

Sample: BLF 15a, submitted on 13 February 1990 by D Garton

Material: charcoal (4g): *Corylus* sp., est. min age 4, and 40+ (fragments) (G Morgan)

Initial comment: the sample consisted of *Corylus* sp. charcoal only, *Quercus* sp. has been excluded because of its great age (100+ years). The concentration of charred material within this deposit suggests that it originates from a single event, probably the demise of the building.

Objectives: the posthole forms part of the western unit of building I. The sampled material was from the post pipe; it may therefore represent building materials or activities conducted within the area. Together with UB-3290, the sample should date the construction of the western unit of the building or its demise (the time gap is probably too small to be determined by radiocarbon).

Calibrated date: *1σ:* 3700–3530 cal BC
                       2σ: 3770–3380 cal BC

Final comment: see OxA-2434

References: Hedges *et al* 1991b, 287–8

OxA–2438 4920 ±80 BP

δ¹³C: -23.4‰

Sample: BLF 103q, submitted on 13 February 1990 by D Garton

Material: charcoal (1.50g) (or grain (emmer/spelt + indet. wheat *c* 0.1g)): *Corylus* sp., est. min age 5, and 10 (G Morgan/G Jones)

Initial comment: the sample derived from building I, it could comprise either the hazel charcoal or the grain. The hazel charcoal could represent actual building material or other activities conducted within its confines; the grain must have been charred at, or soon before, the demise of the building.

Objectives: the posthole forms part of the eastern unit of building I. The sampled material was from the subsidence below stones interpreted as collapsed post-packing, ie the material fell into the void immediately on post-withdrawal before the surrounding packing stones fell in. The sample therefore represents material charred at, or soon before, the demise of the building. In the same layer a substantial sherd of a Plain, Carinated, Neolithic Bowl was recovered. The radiocarbon date, together with OxA-2436, dates the demise of the eastern unit of the building and the use of this pottery type.

Calibrated date: *1σ:* 3790–3640 cal BC
                       2σ: 3950–3530 cal BC

Final comment: see OxA-2434

References: Hedges *et al* 1991b, 287–8

UB–3289 4745 ±88 BP

$\delta^{13}C$: -25.7 ±0.2‰

Sample: BLF 0275 h, submitted on 13 February 1990 by D Garton

Material: charcoal: *Quercus* sp., est. min age 5+ (18.50g) (G Morgan)

Initial comment: this sample could have been building material or represent other activities conducted within the area. The concentration of charred material within this deposit suggests that it originates from a single event, probably the demise of the building. Fast-grown oak of 5+ years only is sampled for radiocarbon.

Objectives: the posthole forms part of building II. The sampled material was from the postpipe below stones and is interpreted as deliberate backfill of the hole after the post had been removed. This sample, together with OxA-2435, dates the construction or demise of the building.

Calibrated date: 1σ: 3640–3370 cal BC
2σ: 3700–3350 cal BC

Final comment: see OxA-2435

UB–3290 5024 ±126 BP

$\delta^{13}C$: -26.4 ±0.2‰

Sample: BLF 0138b, submitted on 13 February 1990 by D Garton

Material: charcoal (9g): *Populus* sp., est. min age 2; *Sorbus* sp., est. min age 6; *Fraxinus* sp., est. min age 10; *Corylus* sp., 20+ fragments, est. min age 5 (G Morgan)

Initial comment: the sample is a mixture of charcoals with minimum age estimates of <20 years. The sample came from the subsidence filling of the posthole; the concentration of charred material suggests that it originates from a single event. The charcoal could represent actual building material or other activities conducted within the confines of the building.

Objectives: the posthole forms part of the western unit of building I. The sampled material was from the subsidence ie the material that had fallen into the void when the post was withdrawn. This sample, together with OxA-2547, dates the construction or demise of this unit of the building (any time gap is probably too small to be determined by radiocarbon).

Calibrated date: 1σ: 3970–3650 cal BC
2σ: 4060–3530 cal BC

Final comment: J B Kenworthy (1992), three of the Belfast results (UB-3290, 3296, and 3297), although derived from reasonably-sized samples of charcoal, have standard errors well in excess of 100 years as a result of sample-independent problems in the laboratory. It is arguable, especially in the case of UB-3296, that they will contribute little to any analysis of site chronology, apart from the observation that the mean radiocarbon 'age' in each case corresponds reasonably well with the range established by the other results.

Laboratory comment: English Heritage (30 January 2012), this result is statistically consistent with two single entity samples of short-lived plant remains from this deposit (SUERC-24131, 4935 ±30 BP; 3780–3640 cal BC at 95% confidence; Reimer *et al* 2004; OxA-20743, 4968 ±33 BP, 3900–3650 cal BC; T'=0.9; T'(5%)=6.0; ν=2; Ward and Wilson 1978).

References: Reimer *et al* 2004
Ward and Wilson 1978

UB–3293 4783 ±78 BP

$\delta^{13}C$: -25.3 ±0.2‰

Sample: BLF 0224 l, submitted on 13 February 1990 by D Garton

Material: charcoal: *Quercus* sp., fragments (11g) (G Morgan)

Initial comment: from fill 1 which was the charcoal-rich layer immediately above the base of the postpipe; it can be interpreted as either material fallen into the hole when the post was removed, or the charred edge of the post which disintegrated on its removal. Since oak fragments only have been identified, it may represent the other part of a charred post.

Objectives: from one of a line of postholes running east-west across the excavation. The subsidence/backfill of posthole 0224 was cut by post-ring 0149. If the radiocarbon date proves to be consistent with that from the sample submitted from posthole 0158 it should date this posthole construction. The only artefact diagnostic of date is from a Group VI axe flake, but this was from the subsidence above one of the postholes, ie it was not in a primary context.

Calibrated date: 1σ: 3650–3380 cal BC
2σ: 3710–3370 cal BC

Final comment: see OxA-2433

UB–3294 7042 ±124 BP

$\delta^{13}C$: -26.4 ±0.2‰

Sample: BLF 0149, submitted on 13 February 1990 by D Garton

Material: charcoal (7.50g): unidentified; *Quercus* sp.; *Corylus* sp. (G Morgan)

Initial comment: the fills of all the individual postholes were floated: the sample is an amalgamation of all the available charcoals ie a bulked sample. There were no concentrations of charcoal-rich material in any of the postholes.

Objectives: the post-rings (2) and ring-slots (7) are of one of two sizes (the larger one is also found as a half-ring) and constructed in segments; they are thought to be contemporaneous structures although their date and function are unknown. Two were dug (a ring-slot and post-ring 0149) through the backfill of postholes on the east-west line and are therefore later than the removal of the posts from this line. No diagnostic artefacts were recovered from them.

Calibrated date: 1σ: 6030–5780 cal BC
2σ: 6210–5670 cal BC

Final comment: J B Kenworthy (1992), this date also had a relatively large error term. The general statistical problem is that presented by the expectation that in a series of 16 results on average five will represent true 'ages' outside the 1σ range: in any given set of results we cannot predict how many will actually do so, or which individual 'dates' are statistically extreme. In addition, if it is judged that a result is aberrant, then it must further be decided whether the result is merely statistically extreme, or whether the sample is unreliable or of an age unrelated to its supposed context.

This result is more reasonably associated with Mesolithic activity known from flint scatters elsewhere on the site. This does not, of course, imply that all the matter dated was of this age, since the sample has been amalgamated, but surely there must be a substantial pre-Neolithic component in it.

Final comment: J Meadows (27 November 2011), this result is clearly earlier than either of the single-entity samples of hazelnut shells from this structure (SUERC-31289, 5455 ±30 BP; 4360–4250 cal BC at 95% confidence; OxA-23368, 6840 ±65 BP, 5880–5620 cal BC; Reimer *et al* 2004). All three samples are apparently residual.

References: Reimer *et al* 2004

UB–3295 4703 ±75 BP

δ¹³C: -27.3 ±0.2‰

Sample: BLF 0266 t, submitted on 13 February 1990 by D Garton

Material: charcoal (20g): *Quercus sp.*, est. min age, 25+, and 30+ (G Morgan)

Initial comment: pit 0266 is the largest of a series of pits all with a charcoal-rich basal layer covered by burnt and unburnt gritstones. All the larger pieces of charcoal bar one were oak (hazel not submitted), as are the floted fragments; the oldest are slow-grown with estimated minimum ages of 25+ and 30+.

Objectives: ten pits had similar fill sequences to pit 0266, though they were smaller. One, a pit dug in 1984 (0014), produced a radiocarbon date of 6230–5890 cal BC (HAR-6500; 7170 ±80 BP). Pit 0266 was dug through a pit containing Plain Bowl pottery sherds and a group VI axe fragment, so must be Neolithic or later; this pit type had a long currency. The bases of the pits were not burnt (magnetic susceptibility values) so the material is disposed within them from another activity. Pit 0266 is one of the few features that cut through a demonstrably Neolithic feature (pit 0270), and could be one of the latest features within the excavated area.

Calibrated date: *1σ:* 3640–3370 cal BC
                      2σ: 3650–3350 cal BC

Final comment: J B Kenworthy (1992), it is clear that UB-3295, although chosen for its stratigraphic position, does not allow chronological separation of pit 0266 from the other pits. If, and only if, the coherence of the results represents an 'event' the pooled mean, 4694 ±47 BP (2σ range: 3640–3360 cal BC; Reimer *et al* 2004), would be an adequate estimate of the date of deposition of material in these pits.

Laboratory comment: English Heritage (30 January 2012), this result is significantly later than a result on a single fragment of hazel charcoal from this deposit (OxA-23585, 4914 ±37 BP; 3780–3640 cal BC at 95% confidence; Reimer *et al* 2004; T'=6.3; T'(5%)=3.8; ν=1; Ward and Wilson 1978).

References: Reimer *et al* 2004
                  Ward and Wilson 1978

UB–3296 4670 ±330 BP

δ¹³C: -26.6 ±0.2‰

Sample: BLF 0316d/e, submitted on 13 February 1990 by D Garton

Material: charcoal (7.50g): *Populus* sp., fragments; *Fraxinus* sp., est. min age 10; *Crataegus* sp., fragments; *Corylus* sp., est. min age 8 (G Morgan)

Initial comment: from a discrete charcoal-rich layer within pit 0316 from which was identified oak, hazel, ash, and hawthorn. The oak is excluded from the sample.

Objectives: from one of the three pits with diagnostic artefacts; the sample layer contained Plain Bowl Neolithic pottery sherds and flakes of struck quartz.

Calibrated date: *1σ:* 3790–2920 cal BC
                      2σ: 4240–2500 cal BC

Final comment: see UB-3290

UB–3297 4567 ±164 BP

δ¹³C: -26.4 ±0.2‰

Sample: BLF 0270a, submitted on 13 February 1990 by D Garton

Material: charcoal (23g): *Quercus sp.*, est. min age 10+ (G Morgan)

Initial comment: from a discrete charcoal-rich layer from which only oak was identified.

Objectives: the sample came from one of the three pits with diagnostic artefacts: the sampled layer also contained Plain Bowl pottery and a group VI axe fragment. This pit was cut by pit 0266.

Calibrated date: *1σ:* 3630–3020 cal BC
                      2σ: 3660–2880 cal BC

Final comment: see UB-3290

Laboratory comment: English Heritage (30 January 2012), this result is significantly later than a result on a single fragment of hazel charcoal from this deposit (SUERC-32293, 4925 ±30 BP; 3780–3640 cal BC at 95% confidence; Reimer *et al* 2004; T'=4.4; T'(5%)=3.8; ν=1; Ward and Wilson 1978).

References: Reimer *et al* 2004
                  Ward and Wilson 1978

UB–3377 4709 ±66 BP

δ¹³C: -26.1 ±0.2‰

Sample: BLF 0021 b/c/d, submitted on 8 January 1991 by D Garton

Material: charcoal (10g) (and hazelnut shell): *Sorbus sp.*, est. min age 12; *Quercus* sp., fast grown, est. min age 15+; *Populus* sp., fragments; *Corylus* sp., est. min age 5 and 15 (G Morgan)

Initial comment: from a floated sample from a charcoal-rich layer in pit.

Objectives: the pit is one of only three from the excavation, which produced any diagnostic artefacts. The charcoal-rich layer sampled overlay a large sherd of Plain Bowl pottery and fragments of 'daub'. The proximity of pit 0021 to building I, and the recovery of similar pottery fragments from the postholes of building I, would suggest that the pit and building were contemporaneous.

Calibrated date: 1σ: 3640–3370 cal BC
                       2σ: 3650–3350 cal BC

Final comment: J B Kenworthy (1992), UB-3377 was one of the four Neolithic dates yielded from the pits. In this case we can not assume that they are dating a single event, but the results are highly coherent (p=0.88), and it is at least worth investigating what this might imply.

Laboratory comment: English Heritage (30 January 2012), this result is statistically significantly different from two results on single nutshells from this deposit (SUERC-32535, 4960 ±40 BP; 3910–3650 cal BC at 95% confidence; OxA-23545, 4900 ±30 BP; 3372–3640 cal BC Reimer *et al* 2004; T'=10.4; T'(5%)=6.0; v=2; Ward and Wilson 1978).

References: Reimer *et al* 2004
                  Ward and Wilson 1978

UB–3378 4770 ±52 BP

$\delta^{13}C$: -27.1 ±0.2‰

Sample: BLF 0311 h (UB-3378 & -3379 combined), submitted on 8 January 1991 by D Garton

Material: charcoal: *Quercus* sp., young oak (G Morgan)

Initial comment: the fill h was the charcoal-rich layer immediately above the base of the postpipe; it may be interpreted as either material fallen into the hole when the post was removed, or the charred edge of the post which disintegrated on its removal. The identification of oak only from the postpipe and lower subsidence layers makes the latter interpretation the most likely.

Objectives: BLF0311 is one of a line of postholes running east-west across the excavated area. If the radiocarbon date proves to be consistent with that from the sample submitted from posthole 0224 (UB-3293) it should date this posthole construction. The only artefact diagnostic of date is from a group VI axe flake, but this was from the subsidence in one of the postholes, ie not in a primary context.

Calibrated date: 1σ: 3640–3510 cal BC
                       2σ: 3660–3370 cal BC

Final comment: see OxA-2433

Lismore Fields, Buxton II, Derbyshire

Location: SK 053733
                     Lat. 53.15.23 N; Long. 01.55.14 W

Project manager: D Garton (Trent and Peak Archaeological
                     Trust), August 1989

Archival body: Trent and Peak Archaeological Trust

Description: in 1984 work prompted by a housing development and funded by Derbyshire County Council, English Heritage, and the Trustees of the Chatsworth Settlement sought to investigate the supposed line of a Roman road at Lismore Fields in Buxton. What emerged, in place of the resoundingly absent Roman road, after some three seasons of excavation, was an earlier Neolithic settlement consisting of a lithic and pottery assemblage associated with a group features including sub-rectangular buildings with preserved floors, postholes and pits (Garton 1991). Analysis of the ground plans has suggested that three similar structures are present. Charred plant remains from the buildings included emmer grains and chaff, flax seeds, hazelnuts, and crab apple fruits and seeds. Taken together with a series of five dates ranging between 3990 and 3105 cal BC, this site arguably challenges previous views of the earlier Neolithic in the Peak and asks us to test our ideas on how settlement of varying levels of permanency or seasonality might be expected to appear. The location of the site, within an upland basin formed by the Wye Valley at 300m OD and surrounded on all sides by hills, challenges the models with which so much has already been achieved. Quite incidentally, the spatially coincident but quite distinct later Mesolithic assemblage and possible features at Lismore Fields also reinforce the emergent picture gained from the surface collection surveys. The dated charcoal from a posthole associated with a ring-slot feature perhaps places the assemblage around the late fifth or early fourth millennium (calibrated) BC. The character of the later Mesolithic to earlier Neolithic transition is perhaps a subject worthy of further research in its own right.

Objectives: the resampling of the site will allow two important steps forward: 1) to study the basal peat to understand the causes of peat initiation, and 2) to date the inceptions of clearances to compare with the radiocarbon dates from the Neolithic occupation.

References: Garton 1987
                  Garton 1991
                  Hedges *et al* 1991b, 287–8

OxA–2300 2495 ±60 BP

$\delta^{13}C$: -29.4‰

Sample: B4/36, submitted in August 1989 by P Wiltshire

Material: peat

Initial comment: the peat core was taken from a very narrow river terrace downslope from the archaeological site and above the present stream bed of the Wye. Builder's spoil had been dumped on the surface approximately six months before sampling but this and some surface peat was removed before peat coring was attempted. The sample contains carbonate and humic acids. The nearness of the water table is not known since the hydrology of the whole site is puzzling. The plateau above the sample site is very wet and the water table appears perched. As the sample was wet peat, presumably the water table is near. The sample was taken approximately 45cm from the original surface (taking into account the removal of some surface peat during sampling).

Objectives: samples OxA-1976–8 from a peat core taken from the site at an earlier date indicated that the basal peat might be of Mesolithic age. Unfortunately, the actual basal sediment was lost so that the chronology could not be verified. Pollen analysis of the original core indicated that peat initiation was Mesolithic. Also, large graminaceous pollen grains (possibly cereals) were found in the basal deposits. These findings imply pre-Neolithic agriculture and are therefore of critical importance. The present core has also yielded large cereal-type pollen, and evidence of woodland clearance at the base. There are indications of a long history of occupation in the immediate vicinity and this is contrary to the evidence revealed by the archaeology. It is considered important, therefore, that an accurate chronology be established for peat initiation and subsequent land-use patterns at the site.

Calibrated date: 1σ: 780–510 cal BC
                       2σ: 800–400 cal BC

Final comment: A Bayliss (30 January 2012), this sediment sequence post-dates the Neolithic activity at Lismore Fields.

OxA–2301 3940 ±60 BP

δ¹³C: -28.1‰

Sample: B4/64, submitted in August 1989 by P Wiltshire

Material: peat

Initial comment: as OxA-2300

Objectives: as OxA-2300

Calibrated date: 1σ: 2560–2340 cal BC
                       2σ: 2580–2210 cal BC

Final comment: see OxA-2300

OxA–2302 4040 ±70 BP

δ¹³C: -28.1‰

Sample: B4/93, submitted in August 1989 by P Wiltshire

Material: peat

Initial comment: as OxA-2300

Objectives: as OxA-2300

Calibrated date: 1σ: 2840–2470 cal BC
                       2σ: 2880–2410 cal BC

Final comment: see OxA-2300

Mancetter, Warwickshire

Location: SP 320965
                     Lat. 52.33.54 N; Long. 01.31.40 W

Project manager: K Scott (Atherstone Archaeological Society), 1990

Archival body: Atherstone Archaeological Society

Description: a major military site of the Roman period *c* 47/57 AD in its first phase. In the 1990 excavations, sealed by the later military activity a pit containing carbonised grain was located, and some 200ml recovered.

Objectives: the dating of this grain is of paramount importance as grain preservation is very rare in the West Midlands, and it is believed that this may be an Iron Age sample, but there is no confirmed datable material.

UtC–2098 2100 ±80 BP

δ¹³C: -22.9‰

Sample: M257F4, submitted in February 1991 by K Scott

Material: grain: *Hordeum vulgare; Triticum dicoccum* (L Moffett 1990)

Initial comment: the site is built on glacial soils, which are extremely variable, consisting mainly of free draining sandy deposits, where the underlying Keuper marl has been found.

Objectives: to date the well-preserved grain.

Calibrated date: 1σ: 350 cal BC–cal AD 1
                       2σ: 380 cal BC–cal AD 70

Final comment: K Scott (2 November 1992), the sample appeared to be in an extremely good state of preservation. It is surprising that the small amount of carbon in the material would only give a date after being sent to Utrecht for analysis by Accelerator Mass Spectrometry. The dates do not pinpoint as well as one would have liked, nevertheless a similar time period is bracketed. Site stratigraphy suggests a date earlier than AD 50 and the analysis more or less confirms a fairly late Iron Age. There now remains the question, why so much emmer in the sample?

Laboratory comment: English Heritage (1 February 2012), the two measurements on this sample are statistically consistent (T'=1.1; T'(5%)=3.8; ν=1; Ward and Wilson 1978). The weighted mean (2038 ±53 BP) calibrates to 200 cal BC–cal AD 80 (95% confidence; Reimer *et al* 2004), or 110 cal BC–cal AD 20 (68% confidence).

References: Reimer *et al* 2004
                     Ward and Wilson 1978

UtC–2099 1990 ±70 BP

δ¹³C: -22.9‰

Sample: M257F4, submitted in February 1991 by K Scott

Material: grain: *Hordeum vulgare; Triticum dicoccum* (L Moffett 1990)

Initial comment: a repliate of UtC-2098.

Objectives: as Utc-2098

Calibrated date: 1σ: 60 cal BC–cal AD 80
                       2σ: 180 cal BC–cal AD 140

Final comment: see Utc-2098

Laboratory comment: see UtC-2098

Market Lavington, Wiltshire

Location: SU 132574
                     Lat. 51.18.54 N; Long. 01.48.38 W

Project manager: M Canti and D Jordan (Ancient Monument Laboratory), 1990

Archival body: Wessex Archaeology

Description: the site mainly comprises a series of negative features sealed by a mid–late Saxon occupation homogeneous deposit. There is limited late Neolithic/early Bronze Age faunal material from linear ditch features, and some Roman material, but most of the features and material are attributable to the Saxon–early medieval period.

Objectives: up to 3m of peat was located at the base of the Upper Greensand ridge. As the adjacent slope had produced flint artefacts of Neolithic and Bronze Age date and there were earthworks and other artefacts dating from Roman, Saxon, and medieval periods it was suspected that the deep stratified peat deposits would contain a long palaeo-vegetational history. Such sequences within Wessex are extremely rare, and its close association with dated archaeology and proximity to the chalk made it of national importance. A number of cores and monoliths were obtained from two locations along the ancient infilled channel immediately adjacent to the archaeological excavations.

References: Hedges *et al* 1992, 147
Williams and Newman 2006

OxA–2996 970 ±70 BP

δ¹³C: -26.0‰ (assumed)

Sample: 9605, submitted in 1991 by M J Allen

Material: peat

Initial comment: from borehole 2, core 1, at a depth of 17–20cm.

Objectives: to provide a chronology for pollen analysis and determine if the peat and its vegetation history relates to the settlement.

Calibrated date: *1σ:* cal AD 1010–1160
2σ: cal AD 900–1220

Final comment: M J Allen (1992), the basal dates from the two cores (OxA-2998 to OxA-3000) indicate peat formation from at least the mid-to-late Iron Age and that the channel continued to fill with peats throughout the Romano-British period to the twelfth/thirteenth centuries AD (OxA-2996). The significance of these dates is twofold: firstly they indicate that the unsampled channel peats pre-date the Iron Age and therefore potentially contain a very significant early prehistoric palynological record in Wessex; and secondly, the sequence obtained is entirely contemporary with the occupation excavated on the adjacent slope (only 50m away), that includes Romano-British structures, Saxon settlement, a cemetery of the sixth/seventh centuries AD, and early medieval occupation. Consequently, the palaeoenvironmental record from the pollen cores will be directly relevant to the adjacent archaeological site, and potentially will make a significant contribution to our understanding of land-use and economy in central Wessex during the later prehistoric and earlier historic periods.

OxA–2997 1500 ±70 BP

δ¹³C: -26.0‰ (assumed)

Sample: 9604, submitted in 1991 by M J Allen

Material: peat

Initial comment: from borehole 2, core 2, at a depth of 79–82cm.

Objectives: as OxA-2996

Calibrated date: *1σ:* cal AD 440–640
2σ: cal AD 410–660

Final comment: see OxA-2996

OxA–2998 2370 ±80 BP

δ¹³C: -26.0‰ (assumed)

Sample: 9603, submitted in 1991 by M J Allen

Material: peat

Initial comment: from borehole 2, core 2, at a depth of 68–72cm.

Objectives: as OxA-2996

Calibrated date: *1σ:* 710–380 cal BC
2σ: 770–210 cal BC

Final comment: see OxA-2996

OxA–2999 2110 ±70 BP

δ¹³C: -26.0‰ (assumed)

Sample: 9601.1, submitted in 1991 by M J Allen

Material: peat (cellulose)

Initial comment: cellulose from peat from the base of borehole 1 where the peat overlies greensand. OxA-3000 dates the humic acid from the same sample.

Objectives: the peat at the base of the valley maybe associated with Neolithic–medieval occupation on the adjacent slope. Dating the peat will provide a chronology in which the pollen analysis can be done and also dates the peat initiation.

Calibrated date: *1σ:* 350–40 cal BC
2σ: 380 cal BC–cal AD 50

Final comment: see OxA-2996

Laboratory comment: English Heritage (1 February 2012), the two measurements from this sample are statistically consistent (T′=0.0; T′(5%)=3.8; ν=1; Ward and Wilson 1978), and their weighted mean (2105 ±50 BP) calibrates to 360 cal BC–cal AD 10 (95% confidence; Reimer *et al* 2004) or 200–50 cal BC (68% confidence).

References: Reimer *et al* 2004
Ward and Wilson 1978

OxA–3000 2100 ±70 BP

δ¹³C: -26.0‰ (assumed)

Sample: 9601.2, submitted in 1991 by M J Allen

Material: peat (humic acids)

Initial comment: humic acid from peat from the base of borehole 1. See OxA-2999.

Objectives: as OxA-2999

Calibrated date: *1σ:* 210–40 cal BC
2σ: 370 cal BC–cal AD 60

Final comment: see OxA-2996

Laboratory comment: see OxA-2999

Market Weighton Bypass, Yorkshire (East Riding)

Location:	SE 870410
	Lat. 53.51.28 N; Long. 00.40.38 W
Project manager:	P Wagner (East Riding Archaeological Research Committee, University of Durham), 1990
Archival body:	Kingston upon Hull Museums

Description: excavation before the construction of the Market Weighton Bypass.

Objectives: to tie down the ring sequence for dendrochronology.

References:	Creighton 1990
	Halkon and Millett 1999

GU–5001 5850 ±50 BP

δ¹³C: -23.5‰

Sample: MW90, submitted on 9 July 1990 by J Hillam

Material: wood (waterlogged): *Quercus* sp. (J Hillam 1990)

Initial comment: the trunk was lying on a possible Neolithic horizon.

Objectives: this tree has 221 annual growth rings, but is so far undatable by dendrochronology. A radiocarbon date may help to date the tree-ring sequence by providing an approximate date.

Calibrated date:	*1σ:* 4790–4680 cal BC
	2σ: 4840–4550 cal BC

Final comment: J Hillam (28 January 1991), the result shows that the horizon is even older than anticipated and the excavator is delighted. I have not been able to date the ring sequence as yet. It is from a period from which we have very little English data.

Maryport: Ewanrigg, Romano-British settlement, Cumbria

Location:	NY 035350
	Lat. 54.42.02 N; Long. 03.29.51 W
Project manager:	R Bewley (Historic Buildings and Monuments Commission), August 1986 and August 1987
Archival body:	Carlisle Museum

Description: a Romano-British curvilinear enclosure at Ewanrigg. Excavation in the 1950s and again the 1980s not only confirmed its fourth-century AD date, but also identified a Bronze Age cremation cemetery in an adjacent field.

Objectives: the aim of the excavation in 1986 and 1987 was to confirm the date of the site, assess the state of its preservation, and to see if there was any prehistoric settlement activity on the site.

Final comment: R H Bewley (28 December 1995), the samples were taken to date the earlier features on the Romano-British settlement site at Ewanigg. The pottery from the site confirmed a fourth-century AD date, but there was possibly an earlier feature (contexts 346 and 349) pre-dating the Romano-British settlement, and perhaps being contemporary with the associated Bronze Age cremation cemetery.

Laboratory comment: English Heritage (17 January 2012), two further dates (HAR-8789–90) were funded in 1986 and published in Bayliss *et al* (2012, 201).

References:	Bayliss *et al* 2012
	Bewley *et al* 1992
	Bewley 1960
	Blake 1960
	Hardiman *et al* 1992, 63–4

HAR–9459 1450 ±80 BP

δ¹³C: -27.9‰

Sample: EWR87346, submitted on 29 February 1988 by R H Bewley

Material: charcoal: unidentified

Initial comment: from an oval feature, the earliest feature on the site, which may be a storage pit.

Objectives: to obtain a date for the earliest context on the settlement.

Calibrated date:	*1σ:* cal AD 540–660
	2σ: cal AD 420–690

Final comment: R H Bewley (28 December 1995), this sample from the oval feature, which is the earliest feature on the settlement site, provided a date which is not too far off the Romano-British pottery dates.

HAR–9460 2970 ±60 BP

δ¹³C: -25.9‰

Sample: EWR87349, submitted on 29 February 1988 by R H Bewley

Material: charcoal (remaining subsample identified): unidentified (0.12g); *Alnus* sp. (0.02g, 100%) (R Gale 1999)

Initial comment: from a burnt layer within context number 346, the earliest feature of the site.

Objectives: as HAR-9459

Calibrated date:	*1σ:* 1310–1110 cal BC
	2σ: 1400–1000 cal BC

Final comment: R H Bewley (28 December 1995), this sample was taken to date the earliest feature on the settlement. There was possibility that it may be contemporary with the Bronze Age cremation cemetery. The date is an indication that there was activity, other than burials at Ewanrigg in the Bronze Age, but it must be treated with caution because of the grains of spelt, which were also found in the pit. If the date is reliable these would be the oldest spelt grains in northern England.

Meole Brace, Shropshire

Location: SJ 492103
                     Lat. 52.41.16 N; Long. 02.45.06 W

Project manager: E G Hughes (Birmingham University
                     Field Archaeology Unit), 1990

Archival body: Shrewsbury Museum and Art Gallery

Description: a ring ditch and group of associated pits on the outskirts of Shrewsbury.

Objectives: the dates will be used as an aid to establishing a site chronology and in support of regional and national Bronze Age chronologies.

Final comment: G Hughes (1996), the three dates all suggest that activity began at the site during the mid-to-late fourth millennium cal BC. This evidence together with the Neolithic pottery from the pit cluster, suggest that the ring ditch is of Neolithic rather than early Bronze Age date. One of the dates (OxA-4205) was for charcoal found in association with later Bronze Age pottery and is likely to be residual.

References: Hedges *et al* 1994, 361
                     Hughes and Woodward 1995

OxA–4204 4535 ±100 BP

$\delta^{13}C$: -25.1‰

Sample: 1/F1 (1020), submitted in January 1993 by
E G Hughes

Material: charcoal: unidentified

Initial comment: this sample is from the primary fill (1020) of ring ditch (F1). The fill consisted of sandy silt and gravel, which had accumulated on the outside edge of the ring ditch, cut on its western side. It seems likely that the charcoal was deposited in the edge of the cut for the ring ditch soon after its construction.

Objectives: the date should allow for an approximation of the date for the construction of the ring ditch and consequently for the establishment of the monument.

Calibrated date: *1σ:* 3490–3030 cal BC
                     2σ: 3630–2910 cal BC

Final comment: E G Hughes (1996), this date seems surprisingly early. The dated material could be residual and this appears to be supported by a fragment of early Bronze Age pottery recovered from overlying fills. However, morphological similarities with other Neolithic ring ditches, and fragments of Mortlake pottery in a group of nearby pits, appear to support an early date for the feature.

References: Mullin 2001

OxA–4205 4715 ±80 BP

$\delta^{13}C$: -24.2‰

Sample: 2/F8 (1024), submitted in January 1993 by
E G Hughes

Material: charcoal: *Salix/Populus sp.*, heartwood (2.28g, 97%); *Quercus sp.*, 11 fragments, stem (R Gale 1990)

Initial comment: this sample is from the fill of a small, shallow circular pit (F8) - 0.6m across and 0.2 deep, containing a few flecks and fragments of cremated bone, and fragments from possibly two pottery vessels.

Objectives: the date will be used as an aid to establishing a site chronology and in support of regional and national Bronze Age chronologies.

Calibrated date: *1σ:* 3640–3370 cal BC
                     2σ: 3660–3350 cal BC

Final comment: E G Hughes (1996), the presence of pottery dated to the late Bronze Age within this feature suggests that the charcoal is residual. However, the date is comparable (although slightly earlier) than those from the ring ditch (OxA-4204) and a nearby pit (OxA-4206).

OxA–4206 4570 ±85 BP

$\delta^{13}C$: -24.3‰

Sample: 3/F10 (1013), submitted in January 1993 by
E G Hughes

Material: charcoal: Rosaceae, sub-family Pomoideae; *Quercus sp.*, 7 fragments, stem; *Corylus sp.*, 6 fragments, stem (R Gale 1990)

Initial comment: sample is from the fill (1013) of a small shallow circular pit (F10) - 0.75m across and 0.16m deep, containing fragments from two pottery vessels (decorated food vessels).

Objectives: as OxA-4205

Calibrated date: *1σ:* 3500–3100 cal BC
                     2σ: 3630–3020 cal BC

Final comment: E G Hughes (1996), the dated charcoal was found in association with fragments of Neolithic Mortlake pottery. The date falls at the earlier end of the date range for Peterborough Ware and is comparable with charcoal from the primary fill of the ring ditch (OxA-4204).

Mildenhall: Swales Fen, MNL-204, Suffolk

Location: TL 65017556
                     Lat. 52.21.10 N; Long. 00.25.23 E

Project manager: E A Martin (Suffolk Archaeological Unit),
                     1986

Archival body: Suffolk Archaeological Unit

Description: a Bronze Age spread of burnt flints with an associated withy-lined trough. Swales Fen is now an island between the old and the canalised courses of the River Lark. Excavations were carried out in connection with the development of Isleham Marina, and brought to light a perforated stone axe-hammer, and a dense concentration of burnt flints and charcoal of the type often described as 'burnt mounds' or 'pot-boiler mounds'.

Objectives: to confirm the date of the site.

References: Martin 1988

HAR–9271 3760 ±60 BP

δ¹³C: -26.7‰

Sample: 2040005, submitted in December 1987 by P Murphy

Material: charcoal: unidentified

Initial comment: from layer 0005 at the base of wood-lined pit 0001, is one of several known 'burnt flint' sites with troughs and pits.

Objectives: to confirm an assumed Bronze Age date.

Calibrated date: 1σ: 2290–2040 cal BC
          2σ: 2410–1980 cal BC

Final comment: E Martin (9 November 1995), the date has come out very close to other dates from similar features in the same area, eg Mildenhall: West Row Fen, MNL-124; HAR-1876 (3720 ±70 BP; 2340–1920 cal BC at 95% confidence) and Mildenhall: West Row Fen; MNL-137, HAR-2690 (3650 ±100 BP; 2300–1740 cal BC at 95% confidence; Jordan *et al* 1994, 110–11; Reimer *et al* 2004).

References: Jordan *et al* 1994, 110–11

Mildenhall: West Row Fen, MNL-165, Suffolk

Location: TL 854769
          Lat. 52.21.30 N; Long. 00.43.22 E

Project manager: E A Martin (Suffolk County Council), 1981–2, and 1985

Archival body: Suffolk County Council

Description: a Bronze Age settlement on the south-eastern edge of the Fenland region, an area of peat fen, part of Mildenhall Common Fen (drained following a Parliamentary Act of AD 1759). The area consists of 'hummock and hollow micro-relief'.

Objectives: to provide a suite of dates for the settlement and to check for any chronological variations that could be linked with the spatial development of this open site.

Final comment: E Martin (9 November 1995), overall, the dates have confirmed the expected Bronze Age date for the settlement. The attempt to date the Neolithic phase of occupation was less successful, with one date coming out too late and the other too early. An episode of woodland clearance appears to have taken place around 2200–1890 BC, followed by activity in the southern part of the site between 2020 and 1740 BC and between 1880 and 1410 BC in the northern part.

Laboratory comment: Ancient Monuments Laboratory (2003), one further sample, HAR-5633 (1659274) was submitted but failed. Seven further dates (HAR-4629 and HAR-5634–9) were published in Bayliss *et al* (2012, 202–4).

References: Bayliss *et al* 2012
          Martin and Murphy 1988

HAR–9268 3510 ±60 BP

δ¹³C: -26.2‰

Sample: 165 4284, submitted in December 1987 by P Murphy

Material: charcoal: unidentified

Initial comment: from pit 4284, used for soaking antler prior to working. The sample consists of charcoal from layers 4284 and 4287.

Objectives: to establish which phase of activity at the site involved antler working.

Calibrated date: 1σ: 1930–1740 cal BC
          2σ: 2020–1680 cal BC

Final comment: E Martin (9 November 1995), the date confirms the Bronze Age date of the pit and indicates that it was broadly contemporary with an adjacent water pit or well (*see* HAR-9272).

HAR–9269 3520 ±60 BP

δ¹³C: -27.1‰

Sample: 165 4379, submitted in December 1987 by P Murphy

Material: charcoal: unidentified

Initial comment: from the top fill of layer 4379 of Neolithic pit 4377, which cut into a sand hummock.

Objectives: the feature produced Neolithic pottery but of a rather undiagnostic plain type. A radiocarbon determination is required to date the Neolithic phase of activity at the site.

Calibrated date: 1σ: 1940–1750 cal BC
          2σ: 2030–1690 cal BC

Final comment: E Martin (9 November 1995), the date has not confirmed the suspected Neolithic date for the plain pottery. The dated material appears to be Bronze Age in date.

HAR–9270 8470 ±80 BP

δ¹³C: -25.7‰

Sample: 165 4405, submitted in December 1987 by P Murphy

Material: charcoal: unidentified

Initial comment: from charcoal layer 4405 within pit/hollow 4403.

Objectives: to confirm the date of Neolithic pottery found in the feature.

Calibrated date: 1σ: 7590–7480 cal BC
          2σ: 7610–7350 cal BC

Final comment: E Martin (9 November 1995), this date has also failed to confirm a suspected Neolithic date. The dated material appears to be significantly older and probably Mesolithic in origin. Mesolithic artefacts are recorded from the site.

HAR–9272 3530 ±80 BP

δ¹³C: -31.0‰

Sample: 165 4249, submitted in December 1987 by P Murphy

Material: wood (waterlogged): wood fragments

Initial comment: from layer 4249 in water pit 4226, a large pit with sandy wet fills.

Objectives: to establish the phase of activity to which this feature belongs. This is one of several similar large Bronze Age pits at the site, none of which has yet been dated by radiocarbon.

Calibrated date: 1σ: 1960–1740 cal BC
                     2σ: 2130–1670 cal BC

Final comment: E Martin (9 November 1995), this was the third water pit dated. The date suggests that it was slightly earlier than the other two and may therefore suggest that the focus of the settlement shifted northwards over time.

Milwich Burnt Mound, Staffordshire

Location: SK 97563153
                     Lat. 52.52.19 N; Long. 00.33.01 W

Project manager: C Welch (Staffordshire County Council), 1991

Archival body: Staffordshire County Council

Description: a burnt mound, exposed by the collapse of a length of the bank of Gayton Brook.

Objectives: no mound in Staffordshire has so far been dated by radiocarbon dating; a Bronze Age date is assumed by analogy with mounds in the south Birmingham area and elsewhere. This remained to be confirmed.

Final comment: C Welch (29 November 1995), the purpose of the dating was to confirm that this burnt mound was in use in the Bronze Age, in common with others in this area and elsewhere in Britain. The difference between the two results (taken from the vertical column 170mm apart) is interesting and supports the idea that, in this case at least, the site was at a favoured location and was visited over a long period of time.

References: Brindley *et al* 1990
                     Welch 1997

GU–5095 3080 ±60 BP

δ¹³C: -26.5‰

Sample: MBM5, submitted on 12 February 1991 by C Welch

Material: charcoal: unidentified

Initial comment: charcoal from the burnt mound was sampled along with stones, sieved and concentrated in the laboratory. The only evident contaminants are a few modern rootlets. This is the upper of two samples from the mound material.

Objectives: the burnt mound is an unusual isolated example and the date of it is sought by dating the charcoal that it contains.

Calibrated date: 1σ: 1430–1260 cal BC
                     2σ: 1500–1130 cal BC

Final comment: C Welch (29 November 1995), confirms initial dating of this burnt mound to the Bronze Age. Taken 170mm above GU-5096 within total deposit thickness of 350mm.

GU–5096 3290 ±100 BP

δ¹³C: -27.5‰

Sample: MBM6, submitted on 12 February 1991 by C Welch

Material: charcoal: unidentified

Initial comment: as GU-5095. This is the lower sample.

Objectives: as GU-5095

Calibrated date: 1σ: 1690–1450 cal BC
                     2σ: 1880–1390 cal BC

Final comment: C Welch (29 November 1995), confirms initial dating of this burnt mound to the Bronze Age. Taken 170mm below GU-5095.

North Cave, Yorkshire (East Riding)

Location: SE 879331
                     Lat. 53.47.12 N; Long. 00.39.56 W

Project manager: J Watt (Humberside Archaeology Unit), 1986

Archival body: Hull and East Riding Museum

Description: an Iron Age settlement on the western escarpment of the Yorkshire Wolds. The samples were from a previously waterlogged pit in an Iron Age Roman settlement at North Cave. One pit had stood open as a shallow well or waterhole in the Iron Age, and contained organic material as well as pottery and animal bone. Wooden steps into the well were made from a reused ox-collar and a possible rake.

Objectives: to provide a date for the well pit.

References: Hardiman *et al* 1992, 52

HAR–10225 2160 ±80 BP

δ¹³C: -27.5‰

Sample: NC86MS, submitted on 6 February 1989 by J Dent

Material: wood (waterlogged): unidentified

Initial comment: a wood chipping preserved in an Iron Age well pit from feature NC86/100.

Objectives: to relate pottery and wooden artefacts to the Iron Age chronology, to anchor the chronology of the environmental evidence, and to compare the dates for the wood and charcoal of HAR-10225 and HAR-10226. The wood could have been re-used, but it's more likely to be newly felled timber.

Calibrated date: 1σ: 370–60 cal BC
                     2σ: 400 cal BC–cal AD 10

Final comment: J Dent (1992), HAR-10226, from the same pit, is some centuries older.

Laboratory comment: AERE Harwell (18 December 1989), this sample was measured in the miniature gas proportional counter (Otlet *et al* 1983).

References: Otlet *et al* 1983

HAR–10226 2410 ±80 BP

δ¹³C: -80.0‰

Sample: NC86NC, submitted on 6 February 1989 by J Dent

Material: charcoal (remaining subsample identified): unidentified (0.13g); *Alnus* sp. (0.76g, 100%) (R Gale 1999)

Initial comment: from an Iron Age well pit from feature NC86/100.

Objectives: to compare with HAR-10225 and to provide a start date for Iron Age/Roman occupation.

Calibrated date: *1σ:* 750–390 cal BC
                       2σ: 790–360 cal BC

Final comment: J Dent (1992), HAR-10225, from the same pit, is some centuries younger.

Laboratory comment: AERE Harwell (2 January 1990), this sample was measured in the miniature gas proportional counter (Otlet *et al* 1983).

References: Otlet *et al* 1983

North Furzton, Buckinghamshire

Location: SP 84763522
                       Lat. 52.00.31 N; Long. 00.45.54 W

Project manager: R J Williams (Milton Keynes Archaeology Unit), 1987

Archival body: Buckinghamshire County Museum

Description: a late Iron Age settlement excavated at North Furzton near Bletchley in 1987, in advance of the then proposed construction of the North Furzton balancing lake and subsequent housing development. The site had been recognised on aerial photographs, and trial trenches were excavated in October 1985. Two areas of occupation were identified: areas A and B. Area A contained a large ditched, rectangular enclosure, thought to be a stockade for animals. Several further smaller enclosures represented by ditches and gullies were also excavated, most of which were interpreted as further stock control areas, although one was possibly the remains of a substantial building. A further substantial pennanular ditch was interpreted as a building and had two large postholes at its entrance. Other features in area A included clay-lined pits and narrow gullies. The few finds recovered from the site included late Iron Age pottery vessels, animal bone, a sharpened wooden stake from one of the enclosure ditches, and two fragments of red deer antler. Area B lay 400 metres to the north east of area A, and comprised a square-ish enclosure with some ephemeral internal features, partially damaged by later medieval ploughing. At the time of excavation it was thought that area B was earlier than the features encountered in area A, and may have been prone to seasonal flooding.

Objectives: radiocarbon dates would be useful supportive evidence for our proposed dating of the site, which is based on rather undiagnostic pottery.

Final comment: R J Williams (13 January 2003), following the closure of the Milton Keynes Archaeological Unit, no further post-excavation analysis has yet been possible. The significance of the radiocarbon dates can only be properly assessed when this work resumes.

UB–3230 2110 ±56 BP

δ¹³C: -26.0 ±0.2‰

Sample: MK158 123, submitted in November 1989 by R J Williams

Material: charcoal: *Acer* sp., several fragments, badly compressed (R Gale 1989)

Initial comment: this sample was found as a pocket of charcoal in the middle fill of a substantial rectangular-shaped enclosure ditch.

Objectives: UB-3230 and UB-3232 should give a date range for the usage of the large enclosure ditch.

Calibrated date: *1σ:* 210–40 cal BC
                       2σ: 360 cal BC–cal AD 10

UB–3231 2520 ±136 BP

δ¹³C: -25.4 ±0.2‰

Sample: MK158 232, submitted in November 1989 by R J Williams

Material: charcoal: *Fraxinus* sp.; *Quercus* sp.; Rosaceae, sub-family Pomoideae, several fragments; *Prunus* sp.; *Acer* sp. (R Gale 1989)

Initial comment: this sample was recovered during flotation of the upper/middle layer of the polygonal-shaped enclosure ditch.

Objectives: the lack of diagnostic pottery from the associated feature has made dating difficult. The date from this sample should confirm the period of usage of the ditch.

Calibrated date: *1σ:* 810–400 cal BC
                       2σ: 970–370 cal BC

UB–3232 2149 ±44 BP

δ¹³C: -28.9 ±0.2‰

Sample: MK158 17, submitted in November 1989 by R J Williams

Material: wood (waterlogged): *Acer* sp. (R Gale 1989)

Initial comment: part of a 1m-long pointed wooden stake, showing approximately 23 annual rings. The stake was found lying along the base of the large enclosure ditch.

Objectives: the stake may be part of the revetting of the internal bank of the enclosure, which fell into the ditch; hence the date of the stake should approximately be the date of construction of the ditch/bank.

Calibrated date: *1σ:* 350–110 cal BC
                       2σ: 370–50 cal BC

Laboratory comment: University of Belfast (20 February 1990), this sample was pretreated using the acid based acid protocol.

North West Wetlands Survey, Cheshire, Cumbria, Greater Manchester, Lancashire, Merseyside, Shropshire, and Staffordshire

Location: *see* individual sites

Project manager: R Middleton (Lancaster University Archaeology Unit), 1990–6

Description: a major programme of archaeological and palaeoecological work on the lowland wetlands of the seven counties, undertaken in partnership with the National Museums and Galleries on Merseyside and the Greater Manchester Archaeological Unit. A pilot study (Howard-Davis *et al* 1988) had identified areas of peat and collated the known archaeological and palaeoecological data for prehistoric activity associated with the lowland wetlands in the northern area of this study, and highlighted the need for detailed field investigation.

Objectives: to assess the archaeological and palaeoenvironmental potential of the lowland wetlands of the north-west.

References: Cowell and Innes 1994
            Hall *et al* 1995
            Hodgkinson *et al* 2000
            Howard-Davis *et al* 1988
            Leah *et al* 1996
            Leah 1997
            Middleton *et al* 1995
            Tooley *et al* forthcoming

North West Wetlands Survey: Bonds Farm, Lancashire

Location: SD 41904688
            Lat. 53.54.53 N; Long. 02.53.05 W

Project manager: B J Edwards (Pilling Historical Society), 1979, 1989–1993

Archival body: Oxford Archaeology North

Description: Bronze Age settlement with metal work at the farm on the northern edge of the moss in the late 1970s.

Objectives: to date the activity at the site.

References: Middleton *et al* 1995

GU–5063 3120 ±60 BP

$\delta^{13}C$: -27.9‰

Sample: BF1, submitted in 1991 by R Middleton

Material: wood (worked wooden stake): unidentified

Initial comment: worked wood stake collected from the former stream bed adjacent to the site.

Objectives: to date the wooden stake which in turn will date the site's activity.

Calibrated date: *1σ:* 1450–1310 cal BC
                        2σ: 1510–1260 cal BC

Final comment: R Middleton, C Wells, and E Huckerby (1995), it appears likely that this provides a date for the occupation of the main site.

Laboratory comment: English Heritage (12 December 2012), the two results on this stake are statistically consistent (T'=0.1; T'(5%)=3.8; ν=1; Ward and Wilson 1978), and their weighted mean (3133 ±46 BP) calibrates to 1500–1300 cal BC (95% confidence; Reimer *et al* 2004), or 1450–1380 cal BC (68% confidence).

References: Reimer *et al* 2004
            Ward and Wilson 1978

GU–5064 3150 ±70 BP

$\delta^{13}C$: -27.5‰

Sample: BF2, submitted in 1991 by R Middleton

Material: wood: unidentified

Initial comment: as GU-5063

Objectives: as GU-5063

Calibrated date: *1σ:* 1500–1320 cal BC
                        2σ: 1610–1260 cal BC

Final comment: see GU-5063

Laboratory comment: see GU-5063

North West Wetlands Survey: Brook Farm, Lancashire

Location: SD 41014481
            Lat. 53.53.46 N; Long. 02.53.52 W

Project manager: C Wells (Lancaster University Archaeology Unit), 1991

Archival body: Oxford Archaeology North

Description: the Brook Farm site is positioned close to an extensive area of mineral ground and so may have been located near to a margin of the expanding mire system in prehistoric times.

Objectives: the date is one in a series dating the chronology and is believed to be on the same level as Kate's Pad.

Final comment: C Wells (1993), the single date from this series fits into the chronological framework provided by the Fenton Cottage series, which is *c* 5000m west of the site. It dates charcoal excavated from the wood peats above the Scheuchzeria flooding horizon. This is thought to be the level of the prehistoric trackway of Kate's Pad previously dated to the Iron Age (1270–670 cal BC at 95% confidence; Reimer *et al* 2004; 2760 ±120 BP; Q-68).

References: Middleton *et al* 1995, 152–9
            Middleton 1991
            Reimer *et al* 2004

GU–5206 3420 ±50 BP

$\delta^{13}C$: -28.7‰

Sample: BF1A, submitted in 1992 by C Wells

Material: charcoal (from peat): unidentified (C Wells 1991)

Initial comment: 75cm in a section 150cm in depth of humified peats.

Objectives: to date a clear band of charcoal in the wood peats above the *Scheuchzeria* layer, which was thought to be the level of Kate's Pad a prehistoric trackway excavated in 1949–50 and dated then to the Iron Age.

Calibrated date: 1σ: 1770–1660 cal BC
                       2σ: 1890–1610 cal BC

Final comment: C Wells (1993), the sample dates the formation of the charcoal from Brook Farm to the Bronze Age.

North West Wetlands Survey: Chat Moss, Greater Manchester

Location: SJ 71169816
                     Lat. 53.28.45 N; Long. 02.26.05 W

Project manager: C Wells (Lancaster University Archaeology Unit), 1992

Archival body: Oxford Archaeology North

Description: Chat Moss, the largest of the mosses in Manchester, lies north of the Mersey and west of central Manchester. The samples were taken from Nook Farm on the northern edge of Chat Moss, approximately 700m south of the Moss Brook.

Objectives: to date the artefactual evidence and provide a date for a possible clearance in this area.

Final comment: E Huckerby (27 July 1994), this series gives results for the initiation of peat development in a north/south transect adjacent to a possible late Mesolithic lithic scatter at Nook Farm on Chat Moss, Greater Manchester. The Neolithic to early Bronze Age dates are consistent with the pollen analytical results which suggest a Neolithic age. The increase in age from GU-5272 to -5271 to -5273 is acceptable as probably the peat gradually spread outwards up the slope of the mineral surface. The date GU-5280 for a birch stump embedded in peat of GU-5273 is in agreement, as is that for the carbonised wood GU-5325.

References: Hall *et al* 1995, 50–62

GU–5271 4590 ±70 BP

$\delta^{13}C$: -26.3‰

Sample: Chat 1 25–40cm, submitted on 6 January 1993 by E Huckerby

Material: peat (wood peat) (C Wells 1992)

Initial comment: basal peats overlying a sand island in a raised mire. Peat has been removed from the site mechanically leaving approximately 50cm.

Objectives: to date the basal peat overlying a sand island on which there is a possible late Mesolithic site. A scatter of lithic material was found on the sand nearby.

Calibrated date: 1σ: 3500–3130 cal BC
                       2σ: 3630–3090 cal BC

Final comment: E Huckerby (27 July 1994), this result gives a Neolithic date for the initiation of peat above the sand island on Chat Moss, Greater Manchester. The sample was taken immediately adjacent to lithic scatter of possible late Mesolithic age. The date is supported by the pollen analytical evidence.

GU–5272 3710 ±60 BP

$\delta^{13}C$: -29.2‰

Sample: Chat 2 South, submitted on 6 January 1993 by E Huckerby

Material: peat (wood peat) (C Wells 1993)

Initial comment: as GU-5271

Objectives: to date the basal peat overlying a sand island on which there is a possible late Mesolithic site.

Calibrated date: 1σ: 2200–2020 cal BC
                       2σ: 2290–1940 cal BC

Final comment: E Huckerby (27 July 1994), this result gives a later date for the initiation of peat growth for the south of the lithic scatter see GU-5271 on Chat Moss, but is consistent with the slope of the underlying mineral substrate.

GU–5273 4670 ±60 BP

$\delta^{13}C$: -29.1‰

Sample: Chat 3 North, submitted on 6 January 1993 by E Huckerby

Material: peat (wood peat) (C Wells 1992)

Initial comment: as GU-5271

Objectives: as GU-5272

Calibrated date: 1σ: 3630–3360 cal BC
                       2σ: 3640–3340 cal BC

Final comment: E Huckerby (27 July 1994), this result gives a similar date to GU-5271 for the development of peat deposits on Chat Moss. It is supported by the pollen analytical evidence.

GU–5280 4570 ±50 BP

$\delta^{13}C$: -25.7‰

Sample: Chat4, submitted on 1 February 1993 by C Wells

Material: wood (waterlogged): *Betula* sp. (C Wells 1992)

Initial comment: the sample is a tree stump embedded in the basal peats above a sand island. The upper layers of peat have been removed mechanically leaving approximately 50cm.

Objectives: this sample is to be dated to see if the tree was contemporary with the peat in which it is embedded.

Calibrated date: *1σ:* 3370–3130 cal BC
                       2σ: 3500–3100 cal BC

Final comment: E Huckerby (1994), the result suggests that the birch tree may have been growing on the developing peat of GU-5273 in the Neolithic period.

GU–5325 3930 ±80 BP

δ¹³C: -27.2‰

Sample: Chat5, submitted in January 1993 by C Wells

Material: wood (carbonised): unidentified (C Wells)

Initial comment: embedded in sand from which the peat has been removed by peat extraction company.

Objectives: this sample should be dated because it was embedded in sand beneath a lithic find of possible late Mesolithic date.

Calibrated date: *1σ:* 2570–2290 cal BC
                       2σ: 2630–2150 cal BC

Final comment: E Huckerby (1994), the date is more recent than the proposed date of the lithic finds but it is in agreement with those from the basal peats of GU-5271 and GU-5272.

North West Wetlands Survey: Ditton Brook, Merseyside

Location: SJ 478853
                     Lat. 53.21.42 N; Long. 02.47.04 W

Project manager: J B Innes (University of Durham), 1992

Archival body: Oxford Archaeology North

Description: the site lies at the confluence of two major glacial channels (the Mersey and the Ditton) and geotechnical borings show that the peat is up to 5m deep in some parts. This could have important implications for vegetation studies in an area for which there is little coverage at the moment.

Objectives: dates may show that Neolithic settlement evidence is present in the area. Within 100–3000m on the opposite valley side there is a late prehistoric bivallate enclosure and reported Roman finds from nineteenth-century construction works.

Final comment: J B Innes (31 March 1994), the three dates were intended to date the change from clay to organic deposition at the three points in the stratigraphy. The series of dates show this point of the diagram to be early Flandrian III, post-elm decline, in age. The age inversion of the lower two dates is unfortunate, but the two dates are close enough to make it important. The dates agree with the pollen data. Data inversions are not expected in valley peats and clays of this type.

References: Cowell and Innes 1994

GU–5207 5070 ±90 BP

δ¹³C: -29.0‰

Sample: DB3-1, submitted in April 1992 by J B Innes

Material: peat (Gyttja - detrital peat from sediment profile)

Initial comment: the site contains a sequence of organic and inorganic deposits, which reflect changes in water level, which may be due to sea-level change. The sample is on peat at 345–350cm, which overlies clay.

Objectives: the sample will date the base of a peat layer, which overlies a grey-blue clay horizon. Pollen suggests this contact will be of late Flandrian II to early Flandrian III age. The clay may be marine in origin but is more likely to be freshwater. It and the other samples will clarify the sequence of water level changes at the site.

Calibrated date: *1σ:* 3970–3710 cal BC
                       2σ: 4050–3650 cal BC

Final comment: J B Innes (31 March 1994), the date agrees with the pollen data in being post-elm decline, although only by a short period. It dates the transition from a period of clay deposition in later Flandrian II, to a period of organic deposition.

GU–5208 5200 ±90 BP

δ¹³C: -28.9‰

Sample: DB3-2, submitted in April 1992 by J B Innes

Material: peat (Gyttja - detrital peat from sediment profile)

Initial comment: the site contains a sequence of organic and inorganic deposits, which reflect changes in water level, which may be due to sea-level change. The sample is on peat at 285–290cm, which overlies clay.

Objectives: the sample will date the base of a peat layer, which overlies a grey-blue clay horizon. Pollen suggests this contact will be of late Flandrian II to early Flandrian III age. The clay may be marine in origin but is more likely to be freshwater. It and the other samples will clarify the sequence of water level changes at the site.

Calibrated date: *1σ:* 4220–3950 cal BC
                       2σ: 4260–3790 cal BC

Final comment: J B Innes (31 March 1994), the date appears to be immediately post-elm decline, which would fit with the pollen data, although a single-level elm peak occurs at the dated horizon. Elm values are low beneath this point. It dates the transition from a short period of clay deposition to a period of organic deposition.

GU–5209 4430 ±70 BP

δ¹³C: -29.3‰

Sample: DB3-3, submitted in April 1992 by J B Innes

Material: peat (Gyttja - detrital peat from sediment profile)

Initial comment: the site contains a sequence of organic and inorganic deposits, which reflect changes in water level, which may be due to sea-level change. The sample is on peat at 243–248cm, which overlies clay.

Objectives: the sample will date the base of a peat layer, which overlies a grey-blue clay horizon. Pollen suggests this contact will be of late Flandrian II to early Flandrian III age. The clay may be marine in origin but is more likely to be freshwater. It and the other samples will clarify the sequence of water level changes at the site.

Calibrated date: *1σ:* 3330–2920 cal BC
                     2σ: 3360–2900 cal BC

Final comment: J B Innes (31 March 1994), the date agrees with the pollen date in being post-elm decline, Flandrian III, in date. It dates the transition from a period of clay deposition to a period of organic deposition.

North West Wetlands Survey: Fenton Cottage, Lancashire

Location: SD 404449
                     Lat. 53.53.48 N; Long. 02.54.26 W

Project manager: C Wells (Lancaster University Archaeology Unit), 1989

Archival body: Oxford Archaeology North

Description: the Over Wyre region of Lancashire was formerly dominated by a complex of ombrotrophic intermediate raised mires, most of which have been severely damaged by agricultural activity during the last 250 years. At Fenton Cottage a relict, non-truncated portion of original mire survives and forms an environmental archive spanning the second half of the Holocene.

Objectives: this series was submitted to determine the general chronology of the stratigraphy of the raised mire.

Final comment: C Wells (7 February 1994), the upper dates confirmed that the site is a rare relic of 'top moss' from the Over Wyre district of Lancashire. It also confirms that the marine clays at the base were from Lytham VI marine transgression (Tooley 1978). Organic deposition occurred from the Neolithic to the present day. The dates have enabled the North West Wetlands Survey to provide a chronological framework for the peat stratigraphy giving the local mire conditions, the pollen diagram, which provide a more regional view of the vegetation, the local archaeology (prehistoric trackway of Kate's Pad), possible climatic shifts, and the find of tephra (Hekla 4) at 358–359cm. A sample at 380–385cm gives a date of 2910–2590 cal BC and one at 345–350cm of 2559–1950 cal BC (Pilcher *et al* 1995), which are in agreement with Hekla 4 dates elsewhere.

References: Middleton *et al* 1995, 141–52
                     Pilcher *et al* 1995
                     Tooley 1978
                     Wells *et al* 1997

GU–5141 390 ±50 BP

δ¹³C: -26.9‰

Sample: 1a 25-30cm, submitted on 27 March 1991 by C Wells

Material: peat (*Sphagnum/Molinia*) (C Wells 1989)

Initial comment: 25–30cms in a 480cm peat core. There is possible contamination of rootlets.

Objectives: the sample is to be dated because it marks the boundary between *Sphagnum* peat and one of predominately *Molinia*. It is one of a series to determine the general chronology of the stratigraphy of the raised mire. It is also hoped to confirm that the site is a relic of top moss in the Over Wyre district of Lancashire.

Calibrated date: *1σ:* cal AD 1440–1620
                     2σ: cal AD 1420–1650

Final comment: C Wells (7 February 1994), the sample dates the boundary between the *Sphagnum* peat and one of *Molinia*. It confirms that the site is a rare relic of 'top moss' in the Over Wyre area of Lancashire.

GU–5142 820 ±50 BP

δ¹³C: -27.2‰

Sample: 1b 45–50cm, submitted on 27 March 1991 by C Wells

Material: peat (*Sphagnum*) (C Wells 1989)

Initial comment: 45–50cm in a peat core of 480cm.

Objectives: to date a minor drier perturbation of the mire surface and the start of very extensive clearance of the woodland. It is one of a series to determine the general chronology of the stratigraphy of the raised mire.

Calibrated date: *1σ:* cal AD 1170–1270
                     2σ: cal AD 1050–1280

Final comment: C Wells (7 February 1994), the sample dates the start of the major clearance of the woodland vegetation, which continues progressively to the present day from the Norman period. It also dates a minor drier perturbation of the mire surface.

GU–5143 1380 ±60 BP

δ¹³C: -27.4‰

Sample: 1c 90–95cm, submitted on 27 March 1991 by C Wells

Material: peat (*Sphagnum*) (C Wells 1989)

Initial comment: 90–95cm in a peat core of 480cm.

Objectives: the sample is to be dated as it marks the return to wetter conditions on the bog surface. It is one of a series to determine chronology of stratigraphy of the raised mire.

Calibrated date: *1σ:* cal AD 610–680
                     2σ: cal AD 560–770

Final comment: C Wells (7 February 1994), the sample dates the return to wetter conditions on the bog surface to the early medieval period. It also dates a period of reforestation in the pollen diagram. The date seems to be consistent with GU-5156 and GU-5144.

GU–5144 1590 ±50 BP

δ¹³C: -27.2‰

Sample: 1d 135–140cm, submitted on 27 March 1991 by C Wells

Material: peat (*Spahgnum*) (C Wells 1989)

Initial comment: 135–140cm in a peat core of 480cm.

Objectives: to date a period of reforestation shown in the pollen diagram and also a period of drier conditions on the mire surface with *Sphagnum sect.* Acutifolia dominant. The sample is one of a series to determine general chronology of stratigraphy of the raised mire.

Calibrated date: *1σ:* cal AD 410–550
                     2σ: cal AD 350–590

Final comment: C Wells (7 February 1994), the sample gave a date for a period of reforestation in the pollen diagram and of the start of a drier phase on the mire surface. It fits into the sequence of GU-5143 and GU-5157.

GU–5145 4370 ±50 BP

δ¹³C: -29.5‰

Sample: 1e 420–431cm, submitted on 27 March 1991 by C Wells

Material: peat (*Phragmites*) (C Wells 1989)

Initial comment: 420–431cm in a peat/clay core of 480cm lying above marine clays.

Objectives: this sample marks the upper boundary of the *Phragmites* deposits prior to the development of fen wood peats. It is one of a series to determine general chronology of stratigraphy of the raised mire.

Calibrated date: *1σ:* 3090–2910 cal BC
                     2σ: 3270–2890 cal BC

Final comment: C Wells (7 February 1994), the sample gives a date for the transition from *Phragmites* peat (reed swamp) to fen wood peat. It fits into the sequence of GU-5146 and GU-5169.

GU–5146 4410 ±80 BP

δ¹³C: -28.4‰

Sample: 1f 431–438cm, submitted on 27 March 1991 by C Wells

Material: peat (*Phragmites*) (C Wells 1989)

Initial comment: 431–438cm of a peat/clay core of 480cm with marine clays at the base.

Objectives: this sample is taken at the boundary of the clay and organic deposit when the salt marsh was colonised by reeds. It is one of a series to determine general chronology of stratigraphy of the raised mire.

Calibrated date: *1σ:* 3330–2910 cal BC
                     2σ: 3360–2880 cal BC

Final comment: C Wells (7 February 1994), the sample gives a date for the development of organic sediments at Fenton Cottage and the transition from a marine to freshwater environment.

GU–5147 4590 ±90 BP

δ¹³C: -27.8‰

Sample: 1g 438–450cm, submitted on 27 March 1991 by C Wells

Material: peat (with clay component: monocote cf *Phragmites*) (C Wells 1989)

Initial comment: 438–450cm of a peat/clay core of 480cm with marine clays at the base.

Objectives: to date the change of a predominately organic clay. The sample is one of a series to determine general chronology of stratigraphy of the raised mire. The conditions at this point have become less brackish.

Calibrated date: *1σ:* 3500–3120 cal BC
                     2σ: 3640–3020 cal BC

Final comment: C Wells (7 February 1994), the sample gives a date for the transition from a minerogenic clay to one with a higher organic content.

GU–5148 4860 ±110 BP

δ¹³C: -27.0‰

Sample: 1h 450–480cm, submitted on 27 March 1991 by C Wells

Material: organic matter (in clay: monocote cf *Phragmites*) (C Wells 1989)

Initial comment: 450–480cm of a peat/clay core of 480cm with marine clays at the base.

Objectives: to date the initialisation of the development of organic deposits. It is one of a series to determine general chronology of stratigraphy of the raised mire.

Calibrated date: *1σ:* 3760–3520 cal BC
                     2σ: 3950–3370 cal BC

Final comment: C Wells (7 February 1994), the sample gives a date which agrees with dates from other areas of north-west England for post Tooley's (1978) Lytham VII marine transgression. It dates the initiation of mire development to the Neolithic, which was suggested by the palynological evidence.

References: Tooley 1978

GU–5156 1200 ±70 BP

δ¹³C: -27.4‰

Sample: 1l 70–75cm, submitted on 27 August 1991 by C Wells

Material: peat (*Sphagnum*) (C Wells 1989)

Initial comment: 70–75cm of a peat core of 480cm.

Objectives: the sample is one of a series to determine general chronology of stratigraphy of the raised mire. It marks the return to wetter conditions after a minor drier perturbation and should therefore be dated. It will also date a brief period of forest clearance in the pollen diagram.

Calibrated date: *1σ:* cal AD 700–940
                     2σ: cal AD 660–990

Final comment: C Wells (7 February 1994), the sample gives an early medieval date for the return to wetter conditions on the mire surface. It dates a brief period of forest clearance in the pollen diagram.

GU–5157 1810 ±90 BP

δ¹³C: -27.3‰

Sample: 1j 160–165cm, submitted on 27 August 1991 by C Wells

Material: peat (*Sphagnum, Eriophorum,* and *Calluna*) (C Wells 1989)

Initial comment: 160–165cm of a peat core of 480cm.

Objectives: the sample is one of a series to determine general chronology of stratigraphy of the raised mire. It marks a brief period of drier conditions on the mire surface and one of extensive forest clearance and should therefore be dated.

Calibrated date: *1σ:* cal AD 80–340
                      2σ: cal AD 1–420

Final comment: C Wells (7 February 1994), the sample gives a Romano-British date for a period of extensive forest clearance and a brief phase shift to drier conditions. It fits into the sequence of other dates from the core.

GU–5158 1940 ±110 BP

δ¹³C: -27.4‰

Sample: 1k 173–178cm, submitted on 27 August 1991 by C Wells

Material: peat (*Sphagnum, Eriophorum,* and *Calluna*) (C Wells 1989)

Initial comment: 173–178cm of a peat core of 480cm.

Objectives: the sample is one of a series to determine general chronology of stratigraphy of the raised mire. It marks a brief period of drier conditions on the mire surface and pollen analytical evidence suggests the rapid deforestation of the area.

Calibrated date: *1σ:* 50 cal BC–cal AD 220
                      2σ: 210 cal BC–cal AD 340

Final comment: C Wells (7 February 1994), the sample gives a date for the rapid deforestation of the area and a brief period of dry conditions on the mire surface.

GU–5159 2080 ±90 BP

δ¹³C: -28.3‰

Sample: 1l 195–200cm, submitted on 27 August 1991 by C Wells

Material: peat (*Sphagnum, Eriophorum,* and *Calluna*) (C Wells 1989)

Initial comment: 195–200cm of a peat core of 480cm.

Objectives: the sample is one of a series to determine general chronology of stratigraphy of the raised mire. It marks a brief period of drier conditions on the mire surface and also the lower boundary of a period of forest clearance, which should be dated.

Calibrated date: *1σ:* 210 cal BC–cal AD 20
                      2σ: 380 cal BC–cal AD 120

Final comment: C Wells (7 February 1994), the sample gives an Iron Age/ Romano-British date for the lower boundary of

a major forest clearance stage in the pollen diagram, with evidence of pastoral and arable farming. It also dates a minor drier perturbation of the mire surface.

GU–5160 2260 ±110 BP

δ¹³C: -28.1‰

Sample: 1m 203–208cm, submitted on 27 August 1991 by C Wells

Material: peat (*Sphagnum, Eriophorum,* and *Calluna*) (C Wells 1989)

Initial comment: 203–208cm of a peat core of 480cm.

Objectives: the sample is one of a series to determine general chronology of stratigraphy of the raised mire. It marks a brief period of drier conditions on the mire surface.

Calibrated date: *1σ:* 410–190 cal BC
                      2σ: 750–40 cal BC

Final comment: C Wells (7 February 1994), this sample dates a minor drier perturbation of the mire surface to the Iron Age.

GU–5161 2570 ±100 BP

δ¹³C: -28.6‰

Sample: 1n 220–230cm, submitted on 27 August 1991 by C Wells

Material: peat (*Sphagnum imbricatum*) (C Wells 1989)

Initial comment: 220–230cm of a peat core of 480cm.

Objectives: the sample is one of a series to determine general chronology of stratigraphy of the raised mire. It marks the point where *Sphagnum imbricatum* becomes the dominant macrofossil, therefore of very wet surface conditions and should be dated.

Calibrated date: *1σ:* 820–540 cal BC
                      2σ: 920–400 cal BC

Final comment: C Wells (7 February 1994), this sample dates a level in the stratigraphy of the raised mire, when *Sphagnum imbricatum* becomes the dominant macrofossil. The date suggests that local conditions at Fenton Cottage were wet during the late Bronze-middle Iron Age.

GU–5162 2530 ±80 BP

δ¹³C: -28.3‰

Sample: 1o 237–242cm, submitted on 27 August 1991 by C Wells

Material: peat (*Sphagnum, Eriophorum,* and *Calluna*) (C Wells 1989)

Initial comment: 237–242cm of a peat core of 480cm.

Objectives: the sample is one of a series to determine general chronology of stratigraphy of the raised mire. It marks the start of the development of wetter mire conditions and should therefore be dated.

Calibrated date: *1σ:* 800–520 cal BC
                      2σ: 830–400 cal BC

Final comment: C Wells (7 February 1994), this sample dates the initiation of *Sphagnum* peat formation at Fenton Cottage to the late Bronze Age-middle Iron Age. It overlaps with GU-5161, which is 12–17cm above it, possibly this is because the samples were small.

GU–5163 2730 ±110 BP

δ¹³C: -28.9‰

Sample: 1p 245–250cm, submitted on 27 August 1991 by C Wells

Material: peat (*Calluna* and *Eriophorum*) (C Wells 1989)

Initial comment: 245–250cm of a peat core of 480cm.

Objectives: the sample is one of a series to determine general chronology of stratigraphy of the raised mire. To date a brief period of stable and relatively dry mire conditions.

Calibrated date: *1σ:* 1010–800 cal BC
                     2σ: 1200–670 cal BC

Final comment: C Wells (7 February 1994), this sample dates a period of stable and relatively dry mire conditions to the Bronze Age. The large standard deviation is probably caused by the small sample size. There is minimal evidence of interference with the vegetation in the pollen diagram at this point.

GU–5164 2940 ±60 BP

δ¹³C: -28.7‰

Sample: 1q 260–265cm, submitted on 27 August 1991 by C Wells

Material: peat (*Calluna, Eriophorum* and *Aulocomnium palustre*) (C Wells 1989)

Initial comment: 260–265cm of a peat core of 480cm.

Objectives: the sample is one of a series to determine general chronology of stratigraphy of the raised mire. It marks the upper boundary of the relatively very dry conditions and needs to be dated.

Calibrated date: *1σ:* 1270–1040 cal BC
                     2σ: 1380–940 cal BC

Final comment: C Wells (7 February 1994), this date of the upper boundary of the relatively very dry conditions on the mire surface places it in the Bronze Age.

GU–5165 3180 ±60 BP

δ¹³C: -27.8‰

Sample: 1r 280–285cm, submitted on 27 August 1991 by C Wells

Material: peat (*Aulocomnium palustre* and *Eriophorum*) (C Wells 1989)

Initial comment: 280–285cm of a peat core of 480cm.

Objectives: the sample is one of a series to determine the general chronology of stratigraphy of the raised mire. It marks a period of relatively very dry conditions. There is some evidence of forest clearance and pastoral agriculture in the pollen diagram, and this therefore needs to be dated.

Calibrated date: *1σ:* 1510–1410 cal BC
                     2σ: 1610–1310 cal BC

Final comment: C Wells (7 February 1994), this sample dates a period of relatively very dry conditions on the mire surface to the Bronze Age. There is some evidence of forest clearance and pastoral agriculture in the pollen diagram.

GU–5166 3370 ±70 BP

δ¹³C: -29.0‰

Sample: 1s 305–310cm, submitted on 27 August 1991 by C Wells

Material: peat (*Aulocomnium* and *Eriophorum*) (C Wells 1989)

Initial comment: 305–310cm of a peat core of 480cm.

Objectives: the sample is one of a series to determine the general chronology of stratigraphy of the raised mire. It marks the upper boundary of the band of *Polytrichum* and should be dated.

Calibrated date: *1σ:* 1750–1530 cal BC
                     2σ: 1880–1490 cal BC

Final comment: C Wells (7 February 1994), this sample dates the upper boundary of a band of *Polytrichum* peat.

GU–5167 3790 ±100 BP

δ¹³C: -27.9‰

Sample: 1t 345–350cm, submitted on 27 August 1991 by C Wells

Material: peat (*Aulocomnium, Polytrichum, Calluna* and *Eriophorum*) (C Wells 1989)

Initial comment: 345–350cm of a peat core of 480cm.

Objectives: the sample is one of a series to determine the general chronology of stratigraphy of the raised mire. It marks a major stratigraphic boundary and also a very marked horizon in the pollen diagram and should be dated.

Calibrated date: *1σ:* 2460–2040 cal BC
                     2σ: 2550–1940 cal BC

Final comment: C Wells (7 February 1994), this sample dates a major stratigraphic boundary in the peat stratigraphy and a very marked horizon in the pollen diagram. It dates the culmination of a flooding horizon and the development of relatively very dry conditions on the mire surface to late Neolithic–early Bronze Age.

GU–5168 4170 ±50 BP

δ¹³C: -29.3‰

Sample: 1u 380–385cm, submitted on 27 August 1991 by C Wells

Material: peat (*Eriophorum* and wood) (C Wells 1989)

Initial comment: 380–385cm of a peat/clay core of 480cm above marine clays.

Objectives: the sample is one of a series to determine the general chronology of stratigraphy of the raised mire. It is to be dated because it is prior to a very marked flooding horizon in the stratigraphy.

Calibrated date: 1σ: 2880–2630 cal BC
                      2σ: 2900–2570 cal BC

Final comment: C Wells (7 February 1994), this sample dates the wood peats underlying a marked flooding horizon (3.50–3.70m) to the late Neolithic.

GU–5169 4220 ±60 BP

δ¹³C: -29.0‰

Sample: 1v 400–405cm, submitted on 27 August 1991 by C Wells

Material: peat (wood peats) (C Wells 1989)

Initial comment: 400–405cm of a peat/clay core of 480cm above marine clays.

Objectives: the sample is one of a series to determine general chronology of stratigraphy of the raised mire. Specifically, it is to date the Fen Carr peats.

Calibrated date: 1σ: 2900–2700 cal BC
                      2σ: 2920–2620 cal BC

Final comment: C Wells (7 February 1994), this sample gives a date for the Fen Carr peats, which formed as conditions became drier in the hydroseral succession. There is a dendrochronological date of 3023 ±9 BC for a bog oak from this stratum 500m south of Fenton Cottage (Q-8013).

North West Wetlands Survey: Ince Blundell, Merseyside

Location: SJ 342031
                     Lat. 52.37.16 N; Long. 02.58.19 W

Project manager: J B Innes (University of Durham), 1992

Archival body: Lancaster University Archaeological Unit

Description: radiocarbon dating of deposits identified during palaeoecological study of the wetlands of Merseyside. The site at Ince Blundell was chosen due to the density of flint sites recovered from the survey of the Alt Valley which made it advisable to sample a site there.

Objectives: to identify and date palaeoenvironments associated with human activity represented by the archaeological evidence around the wetlands. The main technique used was pollen anlaysis of borehole data, through which broad changes in the composition of the regional vegetation can be recorded over time. It also allows identification of human activity associated with woodland clearance and farming, aiding interpretation of the archaeological evidence (Cowell and Innes 1994, 19–20).

Final comment: J Innes (1994), the three dates form a series covering early to mid Flandrian II, all agreeing in age terms with the pollen data. The upper two dates are on the contacts of the thin marine clay at this site and are slightly reversed. The marine episode is likely to have been short-lived and the two dates should best be regarded as one, providing a mean date for the marine event.

References: Cowell and Innes 1994

GU–5210 7130 ±110 BP

δ¹³C: -28.3‰

Sample: IB-1, submitted in October 1992 by J B Innes

Material: peat

Initial comment: peat from borehole, from a depth of 80–82cm.

Objectives: to establish the age of peat initiation at this site in the upper Alt valley.

Calibrated date: 1σ: 6080–5900 cal BC
                      2σ: 6230–5760 cal BC

Final comment: J B Innes (April 1994), the date suggests the start of chronozone Flandrian II, agreeing with other sites in Merseyside. The declining pine and rising alder pollen curves agree very well the radiocarbon date.

References: Cowell and Innes 1994, 76

GU–5211 6040 ±60 BP

δ¹³C: -28.7‰

Sample: IB-2, submitted in October 1992 by J B Innes

Material: peat

Initial comment: peat from borehole.

Objectives: to date the transitions from an organic gyttja/peat deposit to a blue clay, from a depth of 30–32cm.

Calibrated date: 1σ: 5010–4840 cal BC
                      2σ: 5210–4790 cal BC

Final comment: J B Innes (April 1994), this dates the transitions from an organic gyttja/peat deposit to a blue clay, which is shown to be marine by saltmarsh pollen taxa at the transition. This transgression by marine water is a similar date to that recorded lower in the Alt valley and elsewhere in Merseyside, in mid Flandrian II.

References: Cowell and Innes 1994, 77

GU–5212 6080 ±90 BP

δ¹³C: -27.8‰

Sample: IB-3, submitted in October 1992 by J B Innes

Material: peat

Initial comment: peat from borehole, from a depth of 18–20cm.

Objectives: to date the end of clay accumulation and transition to an organic gyttja-peat.

Calibrated date: 1σ: 5210–4840 cal BC
                      2σ: 5290–4780 cal BC

Final comment: J B Innes (April 1994), dates the end of clay accumulation and transition to an organic gyttja-peat. This regressive contract is shown to be caused by the removal of marine conditions by high levels of saltmarsh pollen. The mid Flandrian II date agrees with dates for this event from elsewhere in Merseyside.

References: Cowell and Innes 1994, 77

North West Wetlands Survey: Knowsley Park, Merseyside

Location: SJ 45509610
Lat. 53.27.31 N; Long. 02.49.42 W

Project manager: J B Innes (University of Durham), 1982

Archival body: Lancaster University Archaeological Unit

Description: Knowsley Park Moss, lies within the northern end of the Park. The moss is known to be over 7m deep from stratigraphic survey.

Objectives: it is of regional importance in showing the natural vegetational succession if certain boundaries could be dated.

Final comment: J B Innes (31 March 1994), these dates form an excellent series and date the major pollen zone foundation from the early Flandrian I to the end of Flandrian II. These features can now be compared with similar from other parts of the region and allow Knowsley Park to be used as a standard diagram for Merseyside. Only the date on the rise of *Alnus* pollen at the start of Flandrian II did not give a sensible age and this horizon needs to be redated.

Laboratory comment: English Heritage (12 February 2012), three further radiocarbon dates are available from this pollen sequence: SRR-4515 (9305 ±65 BP; 8750–8320 cal BC; Reimer *et al* 2004) from 676–684cm; Birm-1191 (5290 ±80 BP; 4340–3960 cal BC) from 320–327cm; and Birm-1177 (1680 ±50 BP; cal AD 240–540) from approximately 25cm.

References: Cowell and Innes 1994, 139–51
Reimer *et al* 2004

GU–5237 6190 ±80 BP

δ¹³C: -28.0‰

Sample: KP-1, submitted on 19 April 1992 by J B Innes

Material: peat

Initial comment: this sample is from 441–449cm depth in a raised bog.

Objectives: pollen analysis suggests forest clearance, as well as a rise in *Tilia* pollen and a fall in *Pinus* at this level.

Calibrated date: 1σ: 5300–5020 cal BC
2σ: 5330–4930 cal BC

Final comment: J B Innes (31 March 1994), the mid-Flandrian II date confirmed the pollen date. It dates a major rise in *Quercus* and *Corylus* pollen and falls in *Betula* and *Pinus*.

GU–5238 9030 ±100 BP

δ¹³C: -27.8‰

Sample: KP-2, submitted on 19 April 1992 by J B Innes

Material: peat

Initial comment: this sample is from 636–644cm depth in a raised bog.

Objectives: this sample will date the decline of *Betula* and *Pinus* and a rise in *Quercus* pollen at this level.

Calibrated date: 1σ: 8300–8210 cal BC
2σ: 8470–7950 cal BC

Final comment: J B Innes (31 March 1994), this dates the first appearance of *Quercus* pollen (empirical limit) and the start of consistently high percentages of *Ulmus* pollen (rational limit). The date agrees with other dates from the region for these pollen changes.

GU–5239 5440 ±80 BP

δ¹³C: -27.9‰

Sample: KP-3, submitted on 19 April 1992 by J B Innes

Material: peat

Initial comment: this sample is from 336–344cm depth in a raised bog.

Objectives: this sample will date the decline of *Pinus* and the rise of *Alnus* pollen at this level.

Calibrated date: 1σ: 4360–4230 cal BC
2σ: 4460–4050 cal BC

Final comment: J B Innes (31 March 1994), this dates the late Flandrian II rise in *Tilia* and fall in *Pinus* pollen. A phase of forest clearance occurs with *Plankago lanceslata* and other ruderal weeds. The tree pollen data agree with the late Flandrian II date.

GU–5240 7700 ±80 BP

δ¹³C: -28.0‰

Sample: KP-4, submitted on 19 April 1992 by J B Innes

Material: peat

Initial comment: this sample is from 516–524cm depth in a raised bog.

Objectives: this sample will date the empirical limit (first record) of *Alnus* pollen.

Calibrated date: 1σ: 6640–6460 cal BC
2σ: 6690–6420 cal BC

Final comment: J B Innes (31 March 1994), this dates the first appearance (empirical limit) of *Alnus* in late Flandrian I.

GU–5241 8060 ±80 BP

δ¹³C: -25.8‰

Sample: KP-5, submitted on 19 April 1992 by J B Innes

Material: peat

Initial comment: this sample is from 551–559cm depth in a raised bog.

Objectives: this sample will date the rise of *Pinus* and fall of *Betula* pollen at this level.

Calibrated date: 1σ: 7090–6840 cal BC
2σ: 7300–6690 cal BC

Final comment: J B Innes (31 March 1994), this sample dates a mid Flandrian I fall in *Pinus* pollen and rise in *Betula* and *Corylus*.

GU–5242 8650 ±80 BP

δ¹³C: -27.5‰

Sample: KP-6, submitted on 19 April 1992 by J B Innes

Material: peat

Initial comment: this sample is from 581–589cm depth in a raised bog.

Objectives: this sample will date a rise of *Quercus* pollen.

Calibrated date: 1σ: 7750–7580 cal BC
                        2σ: 7950–7540 cal BC

Final comment: J B Innes (31 March 1994), this dates the mid Flandrian I rational limit of *Quercus* pollen, which is accompanied by a fall in *Betula* and by the end of the *Empetrum* curve.

GU–5243 8880 ±90 BP

δ¹³C: -27.2‰

Sample: KP-7, submitted on 19 April 1992 by J B Innes

Material: peat

Initial comment: this sample is from 616–624cm depth in a raised bog.

Objectives: this sample will date the rise of *Pinus* and fall of *Betula* pollen.

Calibrated date: 1σ: 8240–7820 cal BC
                        2σ: 8290–7680 cal BC

Final comment: J B Innes (31 March 1994), this sample dates the mid Flandrian I rational limit of *Pinus*, which is accompanied by a fall in *Betula* and *Corylus*.

GU–5244 9520 ±80 BP

δ¹³C: -27.1‰

Sample: KP-8, submitted on 19 April 1992 by J B Innes

Material: peat

Initial comment: this sample is from 476–484cm depth in a raised bog.

Objectives: this sample will date rise of *Alnus* pollen at this level.

Calibrated date: 1σ: 9130–8730 cal BC
                        2σ: 9220–8620 cal BC

Final comment: J B Innes (31 March 1994), this sample was on peat from the level of the *Alnus* rise in the pollen diagram and so was expected to be about 7000 BP in age. The early Holocene age of older than 9000 BP is clearly much too old and contamination by older carbon must have occurred during storage or sampling.

Laboratory comment: English Heritage (5 February 2012), the two measurements from this sample are statistically significantly different (T'=701.0; T'(5%)=3.8; ν=1; Ward and Wilson 1978), and neither gives the age expected from the associated pollen flora.

References: Ward and Wilson 1978

GU–5245 9160 ±80 BP

δ¹³C: -27.9‰

Sample: KP-9, submitted on 19 April 1992 by J B Innes

Material: peat

Initial comment: this sample is from 651–659cm depth in a raised bog.

Objectives: this sample will date the rise of *Corylus* pollen.

Calibrated date: 1σ: 8530–8280 cal BC
                        2σ: 8610–8240 cal BC

Final comment: J B Innes (31 March 1994), this sample dates the early Flandrian I rational limit of *Corylus*, and agrees well with other dates from the region for this event. It is accompanied by a phase of clearance with *Melampyrum* and *Artemisia*.

GU–5246 9280 ±80 BP

δ¹³C: -28.0‰

Sample: KP-10, submitted on 19 April 1992 by J B Innes

Material: peat

Initial comment: this sample is from 676–684cm depth in a raised bog.

Objectives: this sample will date the rise of *Corylus* pollen.

Calibrated date: 1σ: 8630–8340 cal BC
                        2σ: 8750–8290 cal BC

Final comment: J B Innes (31 March 1994), this sample dates the empirical limit of *Corylus* and the end of the *Juniperus* curve.

Laboratory comment: English Heritage (12 February 2012), this result is statistically consistent with SRR-4515 (9305 ±80 BP) from the same level (T'=0.0; T'(5%)=3.8; ν=1; Ward and Wilson 1978).

References: Ward and Wilson 1978

GU–5287 6140 ±90 BP

δ¹³C: -28.6‰

Sample: 476–484cm, submitted in 1993 by J B Innes

Material: peat

Initial comment: this sample is from 476–484cm depth in a raised bog (a replicate for GU-5244).

Objectives: this sample will date the rise of *Alnus* pollen.

Calibrated date: 1σ: 5220–4940 cal BC
                        2σ: 5320–4830 cal BC

Final comment: J B Innes (29 August 1995), this sample was on peat from the level of the *Alnus* rise in the pollen diagram and so was expected to be about 7000 BP in age. The date yielded is very young for this pollen feature and causes an inversion in the radiocarbon sequence. Contamination by younger carbon during sampling or storage seem probably.

Laboratory comment: see GU-5244

North West Wetlands Survey: Peel, Lancashire

Location:	SD 350311
	Lat. 53.46.19 N; Long. 02.59.11 W
Project manager:	C Wells (University of Lancaster), 1993
Archival body:	Oxford Archaeology North

Description: a small relict peat site, which represents a scarce remnant of the formerly extensive Lytham Moss.

Objectives: to date the development of freshwater conditions following the marine conditions of Lytham VI.

Final comment: C Wells (1995), the series from Peel gives a date for the development of freshwater conditions following the marine conditions of Lytham VI, which is in accordance with dates from other sites. They date the evidence of clearance episodes in the pollen diagram to the Neolithic and early Bronze Age.

References:	Middleton *et al* 1995, 179–82

GU–5321 3810 ±60 BP

$\delta^{13}C$: -29.0‰

Sample: PEEL 1, submitted in March 1993 by C Wells

Material: wood and peat

Initial comment: this sample is from vestigial truncated peats, at a depth of 55–60cm.

Objectives: the sample is to be dated to give a date for the extensive evidence of clearance (woodland) in the pollen diagram from a peat core adjacent to known archaeological sites.

Calibrated date:	*1σ:* 2350–2140 cal BC
	2σ: 2470–2040 cal BC

Final comment: C Wells (April 1994), the sample gave a Bronze Age date for the upper peats at Peel. It seems likely that there is no hiatus at 0.35cm in the pollen diagram. It shows that there was some clearance of woodland in the Bronze Age.

GU–5322 5000 ±60 BP

$\delta^{13}C$: -28.2‰

Sample: PEEL 2, submitted in March 1993 by C Wells

Material: wood and peat

Initial comment: wood peat from near the base of a core of 1.24m overlying marine clay, from a depth of 114–119cm.

Objectives: the sample is to be dated to determine the age of the basal peats formed above the marine clays. The site is adjacent to known archaeological sites. There is evidence of burning in the peat.

Calibrated date:	*1σ:* 3940–3700 cal BC
	2σ: 3960–3650 cal BC

Final comment: C Wells (April 1994), the date for the peats above the marine transgression (Lytham VI) is in agreement with the dates from the basal peats at Winmarleigh Moss and Fenton Cottage, Over Wyre, Lancaster. It gives a Neolithic date for carbonised material and evidence of change to the vegetation.

North West Wetlands Survey: Queensway, Lancashire

Location:	SD 3328730831
	Lat. 53.46.10 N; Long. 03.00.04 W
Project manager:	C Wells (Lancaster University Archaeology Unit), 1992
Archival body:	Oxford Archaeology North

Description: in south-west Fylde sand dunes appear to have been subjected to periods of instability in the medieval period and this may have hindered settlement farming along the coast during the twelfth and thirteenth centuries (Wells in Middleton *et al* 1995, 198).

Objectives: this work forms part of the attempts to synthesise all the palaeoenvironmental information available within the North West Wetlands Survey of Lancashire and present it as a series of environmental reconstructions against which to view the archaeological record (Wells in Middleton *et al* 1995, 191).

Final comment: C Wells (1995), this radiocarbon determination from an intercalated peat-sand interface, in addition to one of cal AD 1040–1280 (830 ±50 BP; Hv-3846; Reimer *et al* 2004) from Lytham Hall Park (Tooley 1978, table 1), add objective evidence to the historical records from Lytham Priory and the Clifton monuments bemoaning the effects of drifting sand on agricultural land and buildings during the mid to late medieval period.

References:	Middleton *et al* 1995
	Reimer *et al* 2004
	Tooley 1978

GU–5247 800 ±60 BP

$\delta^{13}C$: -28.2‰

Sample: Queensway, submitted in 1992 by C Wells

Material: peat

Initial comment: the sample was taken from peat in a ditch section and was overlain by sand dunes.

Objectives: the sample is to date the period when the moss was overlain by sand dunes.

Calibrated date:	*1σ:* cal AD 1180–1280
	2σ: cal AD 1050–1290

Final comment: C Wells (23 July 1993), this date was similar to that obtained from peat in a similar situation by Tooley (1978). It was thought that it would probably be medieval.

North West Wetlands Survey: Rawcliffe 1, Lancashire

Location: SD 43504355
Lat. 53.53.05 N; Long. 02.51.35 W

Project manager: C Wells (Lancaster University Archaeology Unit), 1991

Archival body: Oxford Archaeology North

Description: Rawcliffe peat possessed a markedly different stratigraphy from the other Over Wyre systems and detailed plant macrofossil analysis from two cores (Rawcliffe 1 and 2) was undertaken to test the observation.

Objectives: to compare the initiation of the peat development on Rawcliffe Moss with that of sites in the north of Over Wyre and to date the major stratigraphic boundaries in the peat core.

Final comment: E Huckerby (2 December 1993), originally it was expected that the basal date would be Neolithic but subsequent pollen analyses are in accordance with the radiocarbon dates. In the future these dates will provide information about the palaeoecological potential of Rawcliffe Moss.

References: Middleton *et al* 1995, 170–9

GU–5198 8840 ±90 BP

$\delta^{13}C$: -26.9‰

Sample: Rawcliffe 1A, submitted on 28 February 1992 by C E Wells

Material: peat (wood and indeterminate monocot) (C Wells 1992)

Initial comment: peat sample at 300–317cm depth overlying marine clays.

Objectives: the sample is being dated so that the start of peat formation can be compared with other sites in the Over Wyre district of Lancashire.

Calibrated date: 1σ: 8220–7750 cal BC
2σ: 8270–7600 cal BC

Final comment: E Huckerby (3 December 1993), the result dates the initiation of peat development at the site. The date was expected to be of a similar age to those from Fenton Cottage (GU-5148; 3950–3370 cal BC; 4860 ±110 BP; Reimer *et al* 2004) and Winmarleigh Moss (GU-5036; 3790–3020 cal BC; 4700 ±150 BP; Reimer *et al* 2004) but was found to be consistently older. Subsequent pollen analysis is consistent with this date.

References: Reimer *et al* 2004

GU–5199 8250 ±100 BP

$\delta^{13}C$: -26.5‰

Sample: Rawcliffe 1B, submitted on 28 February 1992 by C E Wells

Material: peat (*Eriophorum* and *Calluna*) (C Wells 1992)

Initial comment: peat sample at 208–220cm and about 100cm above the marine clays at the base of the organic deposits.

Objectives: the sample is being dated as it marks the development of a predominately *Eriophorum/Calluna* community.

Calibrated date: 1σ: 7480–7080 cal BC
2σ: 7540–7050 cal BC

Final comment: E Huckerby (3 December 1993), the date is consistent with GU-5198 and GU-5200 giving an accumulation rate of approximately 1cm per 6 years. It dates the development of a drier *Calluna/Eriophorum* community on the mire surface.

GU–5200 6800 ±80 BP

$\delta^{13}C$: -26.7‰

Sample: Rawcliffe 1C, submitted on 28 February 1992 by C E Wells

Material: peat (*Eriophorum* and *Calluna*) (C Wells 1992)

Initial comment: sample at 130–150cm in a core 300cm of peat depth overlying marine clays.

Objectives: the sample is being dated because it is a stratigraphic boundary between the older drier conditions and the younger wetter ones. It is also contemporary with a peak of carbonised material.

Calibrated date: 1σ: 5740–5630 cal BC
2σ: 5850–5560 cal BC

Final comment: E Huckerby (3 December 1993), the date is consistent with GU-5199 and GU-5201. The accumulation rate of the peat is approximately 1cm per 14 years. It gives a Mesolithic date for the carbonised material in the samples. The drier conditions were replaced at this date by wetter ones on the mire surface.

GU–5201 5750 ±100 BP

$\delta^{13}C$: -25.6‰

Sample: Rawcliffe 1D, submitted on 28 February 1992 by C E Wells

Material: peat (*Eriophorum angustifolium* and *Sphagnum* sect *cuspidata*) (C Wells 1992)

Initial comment: sample at 63–77cm in a core 300cm of peat depth overlying marine clays.

Objectives: to date the completion of a wetter phase in the mire development and a return to drier conditions.

Calibrated date: 1σ: 4720–4460 cal BC
2σ: 4840–4360 cal BC

Final comment: E Huckerby (3 December 1993), the date is consistent with GU-5200. The accumulation rate of the peat is approximately 1cm per 15 years. It dates the stratigraphic boundary of wetter to drier conditions in the mire development.

North West Wetlands Survey: Rawcliffe 2, Lancashire

Location: SD 43554340
Lat. 53.53.01 N; Long. 02.51.32 W

Project manager: C E Wells (Lancaster University Archaeology Unit), 1991

Archival body: Oxford Archaeology North

Description: Rawcliffe peat possessed a markedly different stratigraphy from the other Over Wyre systems and detailed plant macrofossil analysis from two cores (Rawcliffe 1 and 2) was undertaken to test the observation.

Objectives: to compare the initiation of the peat development on Rawcliffe Moss with that of sites in the north of Over Wyre, to date the deeper peats from a more central site on the mire, and to date the major stratigraphic boundaries in the peat core.

Final comment: E Huckerby (3 December 1993), originally it was expected that the basal dates would be Neolithic but subsequent pollen analyses are in accordance with the radiocarbon dates. These dates in the future will provide information about the palaeoecological potential of Rawcliffe Moss.

References: Middleton *et al* 1995, 170-9

GU–5202 9980 ±180 BP

δ¹³C: -27.5‰

Sample: Rawcliffe 2A, submitted on 28 February 1992 by C E Wells

Material: peat (monocot) (C Wells 1992)

Initial comment: peat sample at 402–418 depth overlying mineral substrate.

Objectives: this sample should be dated to give the age of the initiation of peat from a more central part of the mire.

Calibrated date: 1σ: 10000–9270 cal BC
                        2σ: 10190–8950 cal BC

Final comment: E Huckerby (3 December 1993), the date was expected to be Neolithic but was found to be considerably older. Subsequent pollen analysis is consistent with this date.

GU–5203 8560 ±120 BP

δ¹³C: -25.0‰

Sample: Rawcliffe 2B, submitted on 28 February 1992 by C E Wells

Material: peat (*Eriophorum vaginatum*, *Sphagnum*, and *Calluna*) (C Wells 1992)

Initial comment: peat sample at 315–325cm of a 418cm core.

Objectives: to date the transition from a *Polytrichum* and *Sphagnum* peat to drier one of *Calluna* and *Eriophorum,* and also a peak in carbonised material.

Calibrated date: 1σ: 7650–7520 cal BC
                        2σ: 7940–7360 cal BC

Final comment: E Huckerby (3 December 1993), the result dates to the Mesolithic, which is in accordance with the dates of Rawcliffe 2A and 2C suggesting an accumulation rate of approximately 1cm per 16 years between 410cm and 320cm.

GU–5204 7680 ±100 BP

δ¹³C: -27.1‰

Sample: Rawcliffe 2C, submitted on 28 February 1992 by C Wells

Material: peat (*Eriophorum*, *Sphagnum*, and *Calluna*) (C Wells 1992)

Initial comment: sample at 270–285cm of a 418cm peat core.

Objectives: to date the stratigraphic boundary in the *Calluna/Eriophorum* with a peak in macrofossils of *Sphagnum* sect *acutifolia* cf *subnitens* and carbonised material.

Calibrated date: 1σ: 6640–6440 cal BC
                        2σ: 6700–6380 cal BC

Final comment: E Huckerby (3 December 1993), this result is in accordance with Rawcliffe 2B and 2D, suggesting an accumulation rate of 1cm per 18 years approximately between 320cm and 277cm.

GU–5205 4960 ±70 BP

δ¹³C: -27.4‰

Sample: Rawcliffe 2D, submitted on 28 February 1992 by C E Wells

Material: peat (*Eriophorum* and *Calluna*) (C Wells 1992)

Initial comment: sample at 110–115cm in a 418cm core.

Objectives: to date a stratigraphic boundary in the peat when *Eriophorum angustifolium* is replaced by *Eriophorum vaginatum.*

Calibrated date: 1σ: 3900–3650 cal BC
                        2σ: 3960–3630 cal BC

Final comment: E Huckerby (3 December 1993), this result is in agreement with Rawcliffe 2C and suggests an accumulation rate of approximately 1cm per 16 years between 277 and 107cm.

North West Wetlands Survey: Solway Cow, Cumbria

Location: NY 34507030
Lat. 55.01.22 N; Long. 03.01.29 W

Project manager: R Middleton (Lancaster University Archaeology Unit), 1991

Archival body: Oxford Archaeology North

Description: the discovery and excavation of the remain of the Solway cow (SMR 16788) took place in July 1991, during routine commercial peat extraction.

Objectives: to test the consistency of radiocarbon dates taken on different tissues of a single individual and to ascertain whether or not the expected date of Iron Age/Roman period is correct.

Laboratory comment: English Heritage (5 February 2012), the three results from the cow are statistically consistent (T'=0.1; T'(5%)=6.0; ν=2; Ward and Wilson 1978). The weighted mean (1204 ±44 BP) calibrates to cal AD 680–970 (95% confidence; Reimer *et al* 2004), or cal AD 720–890 (68% confidence).

References: Hedges *et al* 1993, 163
                  Hodgkinson *et al* 2000, 123–30

OxA–3640 1185 ±70 BP

δ¹³C: -22.9‰

Sample: SM91 S16, submitted on 13 March 1992 by R Middleton

Material: organic matter (*Bos* sp. (hoof)) (S Stallibrass 1991)

Initial comment: the sample was first found near the peat surface by a peat cutting machine. It came from an acid raised bog and presumably is heavily contaminated by peat organic matter.

Objectives: firstly this is a possible ritual deposit. Is this type of activity an Iron Age phenomenon or does it continue through/beyond the Roman occupation of the area? There are no other means of dating. Secondly, this is useful material to test the methodology of radiocarbon dating of mammalian remains from peat bogs (relevant to human bog bodies etc).

Calibrated date: 1σ: cal AD 720–970
                       2σ: cal AD 660–1020

Final comment: R Middleton (1993), the finds represent the remains of two partial skeletons with associated soft tissues. Examination has established that they comprise the skull and foreleg remains only which probably derive from a large pool on the mire surface. Parallels from other contexts suggest that this may have been a structural deposit of feasting remains at a special place within the wetland landscape. It was anticipated that their date would lie in the Iron Age on the basis of the surrounding peat stratigraphy and an approximate analogy with similar examples reported from Scandinavia. The mire is, however, largely unstudied and no previous absolute dates are known. The later date is not, therefore, a surprise and reinforces the lack of parallels and contemporary settlement evidence in the area of the find. Further work on the moss will be aimed at the reconstruction of the contemporary environment, and on the analysis and dating of sheep remains from a similar context to the finds reported here.

OxA–3641 1210 ±80 BP

δ¹³C: -22.4‰

Sample: SM91 S10, submitted on 13 March 1992 by R Middleton

Material: animal bone: *Bos* sp., proximal phalange (fused) (S Stallibrass 1991)

Initial comment: as OxA-3640

Objectives: as OxA-3640

Calibrated date: 1σ: cal AD 680–940
                       2σ: cal AD 650–1000

Final comment: see OxA-3640

OxA–3642 1220 ±75 BP

δ¹³C: -21.2‰

Sample: SM91 S1, submitted on 13 March 1992 by R Middleton

Material: organic matter: *Bos* sp., probably skin, attached to the skull, S1 (S Stallibrass 1991)

Initial comment: as OxA-3640

Objectives: as OxA-3640

Calibrated date: 1σ: cal AD 680–900
                       2σ: cal AD 650–990

Final comment: see OxA-3640

North West Wetlands Survey: Solway Moss, Cumbria

Location: NY 345695
                     Lat. 55.00.56 N; Long. 03.01.28 W
Project manager: E Huckerby (Lancaster University Archaeology Unit), 1992
Archival body: Oxford Archaeology North

Description: located 2.5km from the north coast of the Solway Farm, and 1.5km from Gretna Green, on a interfluve between the Rivers Esk and Sark.

Objectives: a series of dates is required to enable independent chronology for these events and to provide a control against which to compare radiocarbon dating of the sheep body.

Final comment: C Wells (1993), the peat core was taken from the site of ancient sheep body at Solway Moss, Cumbria. Pollen and plant macrofossil analysis indicated stratigraphical and palynological significance (ie clearance episodes, charcoal peaks). These results confirmed Mesolithic and Neolithic ages for disturbance indicators, and also helped elucidate the relationship between the sheep and peat (ie the sheep was much more recent than the peat surrounding it).

References: Hodgkinson *et al* 2000

GU–5274 4520 ±50 BP

δ¹³C: -28.3‰

Sample: SOLWAY 1A 0–5cm, submitted in January 1993 by C Wells

Material: peat (*Sphagnum cuspidatum*) (C Wells 1992)

Initial comment: 0–5cm of a peat monolith from which an unknown depth of peat has been removed by a peat extraction company.

Objectives: the sample should be dated because it was immediately below the level of the remains of a sheep of unknown age. From pollen analytical evidence the peat was of Neolithic age.

Calibrated date: 1σ: 3360–3100 cal BC
                       2σ: 3370–3020 cal BC

Final comment: C Wells (1993), this sample was dated because the remains of a sheep were situated at this level. The date is in agreement with the pollen analytical evidence.

GU–5275 5110 ±60 BP

$\delta^{13}C$: -28.4‰

Sample: SOLWAY 1B 45–50cm, submitted in January 1993 by C Wells

Material: peat (*Eriophorum*, *Calluna*, and *Sphagnum*) (C Wells 1992)

Initial comment: 45–50cm of a peat monolith from which an unknown depth of peat has been removed by a peat extraction company.

Objectives: the sample should be dated because it was below the level of the remains of a sheep of unknown age. From pollen analytical evidence the peat was of Neolithic age.

Calibrated date: *1σ:* 3980–3800 cal BC
                      2σ: 4040–3770 cal BC

Final comment: C Wells (1993), this date supports the pollen analytical evidence, which suggested a Neolithic date for the peat.

GU–5276 5470 ±60 BP

$\delta^{13}C$: -28.8‰

Sample: SOLWAY 1C 87–93, submitted in January 1993 by C Wells

Material: peat (*Eriophorum*, *Calluna*, and *Sphagnum* sect. *Acutifolia*) (C Wells 1992)

Initial comment: 87–93cm of a core of 170cm, with the upper layer of peat removed mechanically.

Objectives: to date the boundary where *Sphagnum* sect. *Acutifolia* becomes a prominent component of the *Eriophorum* dominated community.

Calibrated date: *1σ:* 4360–4260 cal BC
                      2σ: 4450–4230 cal BC

Final comment: C Wells (1993), this date supports the evidence from the pollen analysis, which is of a pre-elm decline deposit.

GU–5277 7080 ±50 BP

$\delta^{13}C$: -28.8‰

Sample: SOLWAY 1D 160–170cm, submitted in January 1993 by C Wells

Material: peat (wood) (C Wells 1992)

Initial comment: 160–170cm, basal sample of a peat core. The peat above 0cm has been removed by the peat extraction company.

Objectives: the sample should be dated to date the development of the basal wood peat in which there is extensive evidence of burning.

Calibrated date: *1σ:* 6010–5910 cal BC
                      2σ: 6060–5840 cal BC

Final comment: C Wells (1993), this sample dates the development of the basal peat and expansion of alder pollen is in accordance with dates for the Boreal/Atlantic transition in the British Isles. It gives a Mesolithic date for the extensive evidence of burning on Solway Moss at the site of the core.

GU–5312 4420 ±90 BP

$\delta^{13}C$: -26.3‰

Sample: SOLWAY 1E 0–15cm, submitted in March 1993 by C Wells

Material: peat (*Sphagnum imbricatum*) (C Wells 1992)

Initial comment: top of the peat core of 170cm; the upper layers of peat have been removed by the peat extraction company.

Objectives: to date the development of the *Sphagnum imbricatum* peat.

Calibrated date: *1σ:* 3340–2910 cal BC
                      2σ: 3370–2880 cal BC

Final comment: C Wells (1993), this sample was submitted to tie in top of peat core taken adjacent to the ancient sheep body. Dating confirmed the prehistoric nature of the peat enclosing the sheep body, and also facilitated matching of the core stratigraphy to the sheep context.

GU–5313 4400 ±80 BP

$\delta^{13}C$: -26.1‰

Sample: SOLWAY 1F 20–25cm, submitted in March 1993 by C Wells

Material: peat (*Sphagnum* sect. *Acutifolia*) (C Wells 1992)

Initial comment: 20–25cm of a core 170cm deep. The upper layers of peat have been removed by the peat extraction company.

Objectives: to date the replacement of *Sphagnum* sect. *Cuspidata* peat by *Sphagnum* sect. *Acutifolia* suggesting that the surface was no longer a pool.

Calibrated date: *1σ:* 3310–2910 cal BC
                      2σ: 3360–2880 cal BC

Final comment: C Wells (1993), this sample was submitted to date the peat immediately above the *Sphagnum cuspidatum* pool peats thought to be contemporary with the ancient sheep body in Solway Moss. The result indicates a Neolithic age for the pool peats.

GU–5314 4370 ±90 BP

$\delta^{13}C$: -29.1‰

Sample: SOLWAY 1G 25–30cm, submitted in March 1993 by C Wells

Material: peat (*Sphagnum* sect. *Cuspidata*) (C Wells 1992)

Initial comment: 25–30cm of a core 170cm deep. The upper layers of peat have been removed by the peat extraction company.

Objectives: to date the *Sphagnum* sect. *Cuspidata* peat in which the remains of a sheep were found.

Calibrated date: *1σ:* 3270–2890 cal BC
                      2σ: 3360–2870 cal BC

Final comment: C Wells (1993), this sample was submitted to determine age of *Sphagnum cuspidatum* pool peats enclosing the ancient sheep body from Solway Moss. The result indicates a Neolithic age for the pool peats.

GU–5315 6180 ±60 BP

δ¹³C: -28.9‰

Sample: SOLWAY 1H 142–150cm, submitted in March 1993 by C Wells

Material: peat (wood peat and charcoal) (C Wells 1992)

Initial comment: 145–150cm of a core of 170cm. The upper layers of peat have been removed by the peat extraction company.

Objectives: to date the peak in the curve of macroscopic charcoal prior to the development of an *Eriophorum/Calluna* dominated community.

Calibrated date: 1σ: 5220–5040 cal BC
                      2σ: 5310–4950 cal BC

Final comment: C Wells (1993), this sample was submitted to date the peak of carbonised material identified from macrofossil analysis of peats from Solway Moss. The result indicates a Mesolithic age for the charcoal peak.

North West Wetlands Survey: Solway Sheep, Cumbria

Location: NY 345695
                   Lat. 55.00.56 N; Long. 03.01.28 W

Project manager: R Middleton (Lancaster University Archaeology Unit), 1992

Archival body: Oxford Archaeology North

Description: the discovery and excavation of the remains of the 'solway sheep' (SMR 16789) took place in June 1992 during routine commercial peat extraction at the southern end of the moss.

Objectives: to date the peat around the sheep as well as the sheep itself to see whether it is contemporary.

Final comment: S Stallibrass (20 August 1993), the fleece and bone samples from a juvenile sheep give synchronous dates (mid-seventeenth century AD) and differ very significantly from the two samples on adjacent peat (Neolithic). The peat samples differ by a millennium but are not strictly comparable stratigraphically due to complex vegetative formations in the peat. Conventional radiocarbon dates on an adjacent pollen core (*see* Solway Moss) are also Neolithic. The sheep appears to have been buried within a pool in the bog. The dates suggest that such pools may take millennia to infill, with serious implications for stratigraphic interpretations.

References: Hedges *et al* 1995, 422–3
                   Hodgkinson *et al* 2000, 130–4
                   Middleton 1992

OxA–4213 3840 ±85 BP

δ¹³C: -24.9‰

Sample: SOL Sheep 1, submitted on 11 March 1993 by S Stallibrass

Material: peat (E Huckerby 1992)

Initial comment: a peat sample surrounding the remains of a dead sheep; the precise location may have been a pool within the bog when the sheep became deposited.

Objectives: to compare dates on different materials, ie peat, fleece, and bone; to compare dates of a body with those of the encasing peat; and to compare with the conventional radiocarbon date on the pollen core (different peat samples).

Calibrated date: 1σ: 2470–2140 cal BC
                      2σ: 2570–2030 cal BC

Final comment: S Stallibrass (20 August 1993), the Neolithic peat date compares well with conventional dates analysed elsewhere on a nearby pollen core. The peat date is different to the dates on the sheep remains (fleece and bone - which were dated to the post-medieval period) found within the peat. The peat date also differs by a millennium from a second peat sample also taken adjacent to the sheep.

OxA–4214 4595 ±90 BP

Sample: SOL Sheep 2, submitted on 11 March 1993 by S Stallibrass

Material: peat (E Huckerby 1992)

Initial comment: as OxA-4213

Objectives: as OxA-4213

Calibrated date: 1σ: 3510–3120 cal BC
                      2σ: 3640–3020 cal BC

Final comment: see OxA-4213

OxA–4215 265 ±95 BP

δ¹³C: -24.7‰

Sample: SOL Sheep 3, submitted on 11 March 1993 by S Stallibrass

Material: organic matter (*Ovis* sp. (fleece)) (S Stallibrass 1992)

Initial comment: the fleece was completely encased in peat, probably 1m below the surface. The peat may have had a localised pool in the bog.

Objectives: fleece remains very rare - there is a need for a date to investigate the evolution of fleece type, fibre, and pigmentation; to compare radiocarbon dates on different materials, ie fleece, bone, and peat; and to investigate the stratigraphic relationship of the bog body with the encasing peat.

Calibrated date: 1σ: cal AD 1480–1955*
                      2σ: cal AD 1440–1955*

Final comment: S Stallibrass (20 August 1993), the absolute date is useful for studies of fleece types of domestic sheep. The seventeenth-century AD date is very different to that of enclosing peat (Neolithic). The date of the fleece is very similar to the date on bone (OxA-4216) from the same individual.

Laboratory comment: English Heritage (5 February 2012), the two results on this sheep are statistically consistent (T'=0.1; T'(5%)=3.8; ν=1; Ward and Wilson 1978). The weighted mean (248 ±54 BP) calibrates to cal AD 1490–1955* (95% confidence; Reimer *et al* 2004), or cal AD 1630–1950 (68% confidence).

References: Reimer *et al* 2004
                   Ward and Wilson 1978

OxA–4216 230 ±75 BP

δ¹³C: -22.7‰

Sample: SOL Sheep 4, submitted on 11 March 1993 by S Stallibrass

Material: animal bone: *Ovis* sp. (S Stallibrass 1992)

Initial comment: the commercial peat extraction machine scraped peat off and stopped at a large exposure of fleece. The bone was found in the spoil from the scraping.

Objectives: to date the bog body and relate it to the skeletal type and associated fleece type; to compare radiocarbon dates on different materials, ie fleece, bone, and peat; and to compare the dates of the body with the associated peat.

Calibrated date: 1σ: cal AD 1530–1955*
2σ: cal AD 1460–1955*

Final comment: S Stallibrass (20 August 1993), the absolute date is useful for studies of the evolution of skeletal morphology of domestic sheep. The seventeenth-century AD date is very different to that of enclosing peat (Neolithic). The date of the bone is very similar to the date on the fleece (OxA-4215) from the same individual.

Laboratory comment: see OxA-4215

North West Wetlands Survey: Stafford's Dyke, Lancashire

Location: SD 39934455
Lat. 53.53.36 N; Long. 02.54.51 W

Project manager: C Wells (Lancaster University Archaeology Unit), 1991

Archival body: Oxford Archaeology North

Description: the site is situated 500m to the south west of Fenton Cottage.

Objectives: to determine whether the flooding horizon was contemporary throughout the Over Wyre area.

References: Middleton *et al* 1995

GU–5182 3780 ±60 BP

δ¹³C: -28.1‰

Sample: SD1, submitted in 1991 by C Wells

Material: peat (*Scheuchzeria*) (C Wells 1991)

Initial comment: the sample was taken from a cleaned ditch-side.

Objectives: the sample should be dated to try and elucidate whether the flooding horizon was contemporary throughout the Over Wyre area.

Calibrated date: 1σ: 2300–2130 cal BC
2σ: 2460–2030 cal BC

Final comment: C Wells (1993), it dated the layer of *Scheuchzeria* peat, which is indicative of a flooding horizon episode. The date was similar to the one from Fenton Cottage, Over Wyre (GU-5167; 3790 ±100 BP; 2550–1940 cal BC at 95% confidence; Reimer *et al* 2004) for *Scheuchzeria* peat.

References: Reimer *et al* 2004

North West Wetlands Survey: Winmarleigh Moss, Lancashire

Location: SD 438476
Lat. 53.55.17 N; Long. 02.51.21 W

Project manager: C Wells (Lancaster University Archaeology Unit), 1989

Archival body: Oxford Archaeology North

Description: Winmarleigh Moss is located to north-east of Pilling Water. To the south and east the moss is bounded by a ridge of boulder clay. The peat soils merge into the underlying complex of marine silts and clays and the alluvium around the river Cocker.

Objectives: this series of dates from a peat core was carried out to date the ontogeny of the deposits from Winmarleigh Moss.

Final comment: E Huckerby (1993), it provided dates for the major changes in the macrofossil, pollen, and charcoal diagrams. It aided interpretation of the diagrams suggesting during which periods there may have been human impact on the landscape. The inception of acid mire conditions is shown to have taken place at an earlier date than at Fenton Cottage, Over Wyre, Lancashire, suggesting a separate mire mesotope. The dates GU-5025 and GU-5026 are chronologically in reverse order as are those of GU-5034 and GU-5035. This may be a result of sampling errors, inversion of the peat, or some factor in the peat composition.

Laboratory comment: SURRC Radiocarbon Dating Laboratory (25 February 1991), one further sample was submitted for dating but failed to produce a result as there was insufficient organic material. GU-5037 (Sample 16 (260–270cm).

References: Middleton *et al* 1995, 161–70

GU–5022 1680 ±80 BP

δ¹³C: -27.6‰

Sample: 1 (40–45cm), submitted in 1990 by C Wells

Material: peat (*Sphagnum* (humic acid fraction)) (C Wells 1989)

Initial comment: this sample was from a peat core 270cm deep. The sample was 40-45cm from the present surface, which had a semi-natural vegetation of largely *Molinietum*. There was possible contamination from modern roots.

Objectives: to date a stratigraphic boundary from a *Calluna*, *Eriophorum*, and *Sphagnum* peat to a predominant *Sphagnum imbricatum* one.

Calibrated date: 1σ: cal AD 250–430
2σ: cal AD 130–560

Final comment: E Huckerby (1993), thin sample gave a date in the Romano-British period for the development of a predominantly *Sphagnum imbricatum* peat. It confirmed the original interpretation of the pollen diagram in conjunction with Oldfield and Statham (1965). But the date at 45–50cm (GU-5023; 2460 ±70 BP; 800–390 cal BC; Reimer *et al* 2004) suggests the possibility that it is younger than would be expected. This could be the result of contamination from modern *Molinia* roots or a hiatus in the core as the result of peat cutting.

References: Oldfield and Statham 1965
Reimer *et al* 2004

GU–5023 2460 ±70 BP

δ¹³C: -28.6‰

Sample: 2 45–50cm, submitted in 1990 by C Wells

Material: peat (*Sphagnum, Eriophorum,* and *Calluna* (humic acid fraction)) (C Wells 1989)

Initial comment: the sample was from a peat core 270cm deep. The sample was 45–50cm from the present surface, which had a semi-natural vegetation of largely *Molinietum.*

Objectives: to date a transition from *Sphagnum imbricatum* peat to one of *Eriophorum* and *Calluna.*

Calibrated date: *1σ:* 770–400 cal BC
                       2σ: 800–390 cal BC

Final comment: E Huckerby (1993), this sample gave the date for the upper boundary of the *Eriophorum* peat.

GU–5024 2500 ±90 BP

δ¹³C: -27.5‰

Sample: 3 (65–68.5cm), submitted in 1990 by C Wells

Material: peat (*Sphagnum, Eriophorum,* and *Calluna* (humic acid fraction)) (C Wells 1989)

Initial comment: the sample was from a peat core 270cm deep. The sample was 65–68.5cm from the present surface.

Objectives: to date a transition from *Sphagnum imbricatum* peat to one of *Eriophorum.*

Calibrated date: *1σ:* 800–410 cal BC
                       2σ: 830–390 cal BC

Final comment: E Huckerby (1993), this sample dates the transition from a *Sphagnum imbricatum* peat (indicating wetter conditions) to one of *Eriophorum vaginatum* and *Calluna.*

GU–5025 3310 ±130 BP

δ¹³C: -27.8‰

Sample: 4 (85–90cm), submitted in 1990 by C Wells

Material: peat (*Sphagnum, Eriophorum,* and *Calluna* (humic acid fraction)) (C Wells 1989)

Initial comment: this sample was from a peat core 270cm deep. The sample was 85–90cm from the present surface.

Objectives: to date a stratigraphic boundary from *Sphagnum imbricatum* to *Eriophorum* and *Calluna* peat.

Calibrated date: *1σ:* 1750–1440 cal BC
                       2σ: 1930–1310 cal BC

Final comment: E Huckerby (1993), the date for this sample seems unlikely if that of GU-5026 is correct. It suggests that either the core has been wrongly sampled, the peat for some reason has inverted, or that the peat type (*Eriophorum, Calluna,* and *Sphagnum*) gave an anomalous result. Normally it is assumed that the peat develops in a succession of layers.

GU–5026 2700 ±120 BP

δ¹³C: -28.1‰

Sample: 5 (90-95cm), submitted in 1990 by C Wells

Material: peat (*Sphagnum imbricatum* (humic acid fraction)) (C Wells 1989)

Initial comment: this sample was from a peat core 270cm deep. The sample was 90–95cm from the present surface.

Objectives: to date the upper boundary of a period of wetter conditions when *Sphagnum imbricatum* was the major peat component.

Calibrated date: *1σ:* 980–790 cal BC
                       2σ: 1190–540 cal BC

Final comment: E Huckerby (1993), the date for this sample seems unlikely if that of GU-5025 is correct. It suggests that either the core has been wrongly sampled, the peat for some reason has inverted, or that the peat type (*Sphagnum imbricatum*) gave an anomalous result. Normally it is assumed that the peat develops in a succession of layers.

GU–5027 3500 ±80 BP

δ¹³C: -28.6‰

Sample: 6 (115-120cm), submitted in 1990 by C Wells

Material: peat (*Eriophorum, Calluna,* and *Sphagnum* (humic acid fraction)) (C Wells 1989)

Initial comment: this sample was from a peat core 270cm deep. The sample was 115–120cm from the present surface.

Objectives: to date the transition from *Eriophorum, Calluna* and *Sphagnum* peat to one of *Sphagnum imbricatum.*

Calibrated date: *1σ:* 1940–1690 cal BC
                       2σ: 2040–1620 cal BC

Final comment: E Huckerby (1993), this sample gave a date for the transition from *Eriophorum/Calluna* peat to one of *Sphagnum imbrication.* It seems to be in accordance with that of GU-5028.

GU–5028 3680 ±230 BP

δ¹³C: -28.4‰

Sample: 7 (128-133cm), submitted in 1990 by C Wells

Material: peat (*Eriophorum vaginatum* (humic acid fraction)) (C Wells 1989)

Initial comment: this sample was from a peat core 270cm deep. The sample was 128–133cm from the present surface.

Objectives: to date the fairly long period when the mire was dominated by *Eriophorum vaginatum* from 1.42m–1.16m.

Calibrated date: *1σ:* 2470–1740 cal BC
                       2σ: 2860–1500 cal BC

Final comment: E Huckerby (1993), this sample gave a date for a period of fairly stable conditions on the mire surface with a community of *Eriophorum vaginatum.* The large standard deviation is possibly the result of a small sample.

GU–5029 3630 ±100 BP

δ¹³C: -28.6‰

Sample: 8 (138–143cm), submitted in 1990 by C Wells

Material: peat (*Eriophorum vaginatum* (humic acid fraction)) (C Wells 1989)

Initial comment: this sample was from a peat core 270cm deep. The sample was 138–143cm from the present surface.

Objectives: to date the initiation of the *Eriophorum vaginatum* peat.

Calibrated date: 1σ: 2140–1880 cal BC
2σ: 2290–1740 cal BC

Final comment: E Huckerby (1993), this sample gave a date for the initiation of a prolonged period of *Eriophorum vaginatum* peat formation. The date seems to be in accordance with those above and below.

GU–5030 3810 ±100 BP

δ¹³C: -28.5‰

Sample: 9 (145–150cm), submitted in 1990 by C Wells

Material: peat (*Aulocomnium palustre* and *Eriophorum vaginatum* (Humic acid fractions)) (C Wells 1989)

Initial comment: sample from a peat core 270cm. Sample was 145–150cm from the present surface.

Objectives: to date the upper boundary of the *Aulocomnium/Eriophorum* peat.

Calibrated date: 1σ: 2470–2060 cal BC
2σ: 2570–1950 cal BC

Final comment: E Huckerby (1993), this sample gave a date for the upper boundary of the *Aulocomnium palustre/Eriophorum vaginatum* peat. It seems to be in accordance with the adjacent dates.

GU–5031 3970 ±140 BP

δ¹³C: -27.4‰

Sample: 10 (160–165cm), submitted in 1990 by C Wells

Material: peat (*Aulocomnium palustre* (humic acid fraction)) (C Wells 1989)

Initial comment: this sample was from a peat core 270cm deep. The sample was 160-165cm from the present surface.

Objectives: to date the transition from *Eriophorum/Hylocomium* peat to one of *Eriophorum/Aulocomnium*.

Calibrated date: 1σ: 2840–2280 cal BC
2σ: 2900–2040 cal BC

Final comment: E Huckerby (1993), this sample gave a date for the transition from a *Eriophorum/Hylocomium* peat to one of *Eriophorum/Aulocomnium*. It seems to be in accordance to the adjacent dates.

GU–5032 4090 ±80 BP

δ¹³C: -28.2‰

Sample: 11 (168–173cm), submitted in 1990 by C Wells

Material: peat (*Eriophorum vaginatum/ Hylocomium splendens* (humic acid fraction)) (C Wells 1989)

Initial comment: this sample was from a peat core 270cm deep. The sample was 168–173cm from the present surface.

Objectives: to date the upper levels of the *Eriophorum vaginatum/Hylocomium splendens* peat.

Calibrated date: 1σ: 2870–2490 cal BC
2σ: 2890–2460 cal BC

Final comment: E Huckerby (1993), this sample gave a date for the upper part of the *Eriophorum/Hylocomium* peat. It seems to be in accordance with the adjacent dates.

GU–5033 4410 ±140 BP

δ¹³C: -28.6‰

Sample: 12 (195–200cm), submitted in 1990 by C Wells

Material: peat (*Eriophorum/Calluna/Hylocomium* (humic acid fraction)) (C Wells 1989)

Initial comment: this sample was from a peat core 270cm deep. The sample was 195–200cm from the present surface, which is above a marine clay.

Objectives: to date the initiation of acid mire conditions.

Calibrated date: 1σ: 3350–2890 cal BC
2σ: 3520–2670 cal BC

Final comment: E Huckerby (1993), this sample gave a date for the initiation of ombrotrophic mire conditions. In comparison with other dates in the series it is in agreement. However, on gross stratigraphical evidence it was expected to be comparable to the dates at Fenton Cottage at 345–350cm (GU-5167), which was 3760 ± 100 BP (2550–1940 cal BC; Reimer *et al* 2004).

References: Reimer *et al* 2004

GU–5034 4570 ±90 BP

δ¹³C: -28.8‰

Sample: 13 (215–220cm), submitted in 1990 by C Wells

Material: peat (wood peat including *Betula* sp. remains (humic acid fraction)) (C Wells 1989)

Initial comment: this sample was from a peat core 270cm deep. The sample was 215–220cm from the present surface, which is above a marine clay.

Objectives: to date the wood peats, which developed after the Fen.

Calibrated date: 1σ: 3500–3100 cal BC
2σ: 3630–3010 cal BC

Final comment: E Huckerby (1993), this sample gave a date for the formation of the wood peats as the site became drier. The date seems to fall within the sequence of the upper dates but not of the lower one GU-5035. Normally the lower date would be earlier if deposits form in a succession. This could be caused as the result of a sampling error or as the result of some natural cause.

GU–5035 4470 ±90 BP

δ¹³C: -29.1‰

Sample: 14 (230–235cm), submitted in 1990 by C Wells

Material: peat (including *Betula* sp.) (C Wells 1989)

Initial comment: this sample was from a peat core 270cm deep. The sample was 230–235cm from the present surface, which is above a marine clay.

Objectives: to date the start of development of drier conditions shown by the formation of wood peats.

Calibrated date: *1σ:* 3360–2940 cal BC
 2σ: 3500–2900 cal BC

Final comment: E Huckerby (1993), this sample gave a date for the wood peat, it is more recent than GU-5034 at 215–220cm. It is assumed that deposits form in a succession therefore the dates would be expected to be in reverse order. This could be caused as the result of a sampling error or as the result of some natural cause.

GU–5036 4700 ±150 BP

δ¹³C: -28.5‰

Sample: 15 (240–250cm), submitted in 1990 by C Wells

Material: peat (*Phragmites, Triglochin maritima,* and *foraminifera* (humic acid fraction)) (C Wells 1989)

Initial comment: this sample was from a peat core 270cm deep. The sample was 240–250cm from the present surface, which is above a marine clay.

Objectives: to date the formation of a *Phragmites* swamp.

Calibrated date: *1σ:* 3650–3350 cal BC
 2σ: 3790–3020 cal BC

Final comment: E Huckerby (1993), this sample gave a date for the formation of the *Phragmites* swamp. It is in agreement with the pollen analytical evidence of a post-elm decline age for the development of the organic deposits. It also supports the work of Barnes (1975) and Tooley (1978).

References: Barnes 1975
   Tooley 1978

GU–5038 900 ±90 BP

δ¹³C: -27.9‰

Sample: 17 (22–27cm), submitted in 1990 by C Wells

Material: peat (*Sphagnum imbricatum*) (C Wells 1989)

Initial comment: this sample was from a peat core 270cm deep. The sample was 22-27cm from the present surface, which is above a marine clay. It is probably contaminated by modern *Molinia* roots.

Objectives: to date a significant period of clearance shown in the pollen diagram with records of cereal-type pollen.

Calibrated date: *1σ:* cal AD 1020–1230
 2σ: cal AD 980–1280

Final comment: E Huckerby (1993), this sample gave a date for the upper deposits at Winmarleigh and dates a significant period of clearance shown in the pollen diagram.

Laboratory comment: SURRC Radiocarbon Dating Laboratory (25 February 1991), all the material was wet oxidised after an acid wash.

Norwich: southern bypass, Norfolk

Location: TG 2400500
   Lat. 52.35.00 N; Long. 01.18.00 E

Project manager: T Ashwin (Norfolk Archaeological Unit), 1990

Archival body: Norwich Castle Museum

Description: eight Bronze Age barrows have been examined in the excavation which was following the line of the southern bypass.

Objectives: to establish the date-range of round barrow construction and use, and to date possible occupation features pre-dating the barrow construction, episodes of later prehistoric occupation, and a peat deposit in the Yare valley disturbed by engineering work.

Final comment: T Ashwin (27 September 1993), the samples from the Bronze Age barrows have been considered as a group and compared where possible with dates which can be suggested for associated ceramics on typological grounds. They often accord well with each other but are consistently somewhat earlier than was expected by both excavator and ceramic specialists: this is especially true of GU-5187. A useful date was obtained for a possible later Bronze Age pottery production site, but an undisturbed Iron Age deposit produced an anomalous result (GU-5190).

References: Ashwin and Bates 2000

GU–5184 4090 ±50 BP

δ¹³C: -24.1‰

Sample: 9585 033, submitted on 17 October 1991 by P Murphy

Material: charcoal: *Quercus* sp. (P Murphy 1991)

Initial comment: this sample is of charcoal from an undisturbed un-urned cremation, accompanied by a small accessory Collared Urn, contained by a small pit and cut into the barrow mound.

Objectives: this sample forms part of a series collected from cremated and inhumed burials from the two barrow groups excavated on the line of the Norwich southern bypass. Dating will assist in identifying changes in burial-rite and in studying the spatial development of the barrow cemetery.

Calibrated date: *1σ:* 2860–2500 cal BC
 2σ: 2880–2480 cal BC

Final comment: T Ashwin (27 September 1993), this date is one of a series of five determinations from Bronze Age barrow burials. It is from un-urned cremation accompanied by a small accessory Collared Urn. The result accords well with GU-5185 from a cremation in the adjacent barrow.

GU–5185 4020 ±70 BP

δ¹³C: -24.5‰

Sample: 6099 251, submitted on 17 October 1991 by P Murphy

Material: charcoal: *Quercus* sp., >6mm (P Murphy 1991)

Initial comment: charcoal from a substantial un-urned cremation deposit. The deposit was in a small round pit (300), one of a series of putative graves and cremations in the central area of a large round barrow. A small copper-alloy pin was associated with this cremation.

Objectives: this sample is intended as part of a comparative series of dates taken from cremated and inhumed burials from the two barrow groups excavated on the Norwich southern bypass. The dates should assist in identifying changes in burial-rite and studying the spatial development of the barrow cemetery.

Calibrated date: 1σ: 2630–2470 cal BC
2σ: 2870–2340 cal BC

Final comment: T Ashwin (27 September 1993), this result indicates that this deposit pre-dated the enlargement/reconstruction of the barrow. A *terminus post quem* for this event is provided by determination GU–5188. This result accords well with GU–5184, from a cremation in an adjacent barrow.

GU–5186 8990 ±100 BP

δ¹³C: -24.2‰

Sample: 9585 1106, submitted on 17 October 1991 by P Murphy

Material: charcoal: *Pinus* sp., >6mm (P Murphy 1991)

Initial comment: this sample was taken from the fill of a pit (1122), one of a localised group within the area enclosed by a circular barrow ditch.

Objectives: the character of this feature is entirely different from the cremation pits and putative graves. The date could indicate the period of the possible pre-barrow activity which these features may represent. The sample is potentially of considerable palaeoecological interest as it could indicate very late persistence of pine woodland on marginal sandy soils in this area.

Calibrated date: 1σ: 8290–7990 cal BC
2σ: 8420–7820 cal BC

Final comment: T Ashwin (27 September 1993), the sample was collected from a pit sealed by the Bronze Age barrow, and was intended to date an episode of pre-barrow activity. The result confirms that this group of 'occupation' features were actually natural depressions of immediate post-glacial date.

GU–5187 3740 ±80 BP

δ¹³C: -24.5‰

Sample: 9585 1215, submitted on 17 October 1991 by P Murphy

Material: charcoal: *Quercus* sp., >6mm (P Murphy 1991)

Initial comment: charcoal from a large cremation deposit contained by a Collared Urn; this formed the central deposit within the barrow ring ditch.

Objectives: the sample was taken as part of a series collected from cremated and inhumed burials from the two barrow groups excavated on the line of the Norwich southern bypass. Dating will assist in identifying changes in burial-rite and in studying the spatial development of the barrow cemetery.

Calibrated date: 1σ: 2290–2030 cal BC
2σ: 2460–1920 cal BC

Final comment: T Ashwin (27 September 1993), this determination is substantially earlier than predicted date of the deposit on grounds of ceramic typology (c 1750–1450 cal BC).

GU–5188 3860 ±60 BP

δ¹³C: -24.3‰

Sample: 6099 312, submitted on 17 October 1991 by P Murphy

Material: charcoal: *Quercus* sp., >6mm (P Murphy 1991)

Initial comment: this sample was taken from a substantial deposit contained by a shallow ring ditch representing one phase in the development of a major barrow monument. The sample's position was shallow, but appeared undisturbed and would until recently have been completely sealed by a barrow mound. The sample appeared to be an undisturbed small branch/twig.

Objectives: this result will indicate the date at which the secondary ring ditch of this barrow became silted up. This deposit would have been sealed by the large mound associated with the barrow's tertiary phase, and thus the sample could provide a *terminus post quem* for its construction.

Calibrated date: 1σ: 2470–2200 cal BC
2σ: 2480–2140 cal BC

Final comment: T Ashwin (27 September 1993), this result provides a valuable *terminus post quem* for the major remodelling and enlargement of the monument.

GU–5189 4060 ±200 BP

δ¹³C: -25.5‰

Sample: 9794 1672, submitted on 17 October 1991 by P Murphy

Material: charcoal: *Quercus* sp. (P Murphy 1991)

Initial comment: this sample comprises charcoal from a monoxylous oak coffin, deposited deeply in the central grave contained by a barrow ring ditch.

Objectives: dating will assist in identifying changes in burial-rite and in studying the spatial development of the barrow cemetery.

Calibrated date: 1σ: 2900–2300 cal BC
2σ: 3270–2030 cal BC

Final comment: T Ashwin (27 September 1993), this sample is from a grave containing a tree-trunk coffin, and is potentially important in establishing the relatively earlier date of this deposit compared with sample GU-5191 from a burial in an adjacent barrow. The wide calibration age ranges, however, demand caution.

GU–5190 3460 ±60 BP

δ¹³C: -24.7‰

Sample: 9794 5127, submitted on 17 October 1991 by P Murphy

Material: charcoal: unidentified (P Murphy 1991)

Initial comment: the charcoal collected from the fill of an ovate pit adjacent to, and apparently contemporary with, a circular posthole structure. The deposit contained abundant Iron Age coarse pottery and loom weights.

Objectives: to provide an indication of the date of Iron Age activity represented by a dispersed scatter of distinctive pits across the Harford Farm site. It will also be invaluable in dating the ceramic types with which it was stratified.

Calibrated date: *1σ:* 1890–1690 cal BC
               2σ: 1940–1620 cal BC

Final comment: T Ashwin (27 September 1993), the excavator had expected a date centering on the mid-first century BC due to the presence of abundant Iron Age coarse pottery.

GU–5191 3840 ±70 BP

δ¹³C: -25.5‰

Sample: 9794 148, submitted on 17 October 1991 by P Murphy

Material: charcoal: unidentified (P Murphy 1991)

Initial comment: charcoal from a coffin containing an inhumation burial and Food Vessel. It was the central burial deposit in the barrow ring ditch.

Objectives: dating will assist in identifying changes in burial-rite and in studying the spatial development of the barrow cemetery.

Calibrated date: *1σ:* 2470–2150 cal BC
               2σ: 2480–2040 cal BC

Final comment: T Ashwin (27 September 1993), this result is one of a series of five samples from Bronze Age barrow burials. It is from an inhumation grave containing a complete bipartite Food Vessel.

GU–5192 860 ±60 BP

δ¹³C: -27.0‰

Sample: TV 135, submitted on 17 October 1991 by P Murphy

Material: wood (waterlogged; twigs and wood fragments): *Quercus* sp.; *Salix* sp. (P Murphy 1991)

Initial comment: this sample taken from a depth of 135cm below the surface, came from a contractors' excavation through sediments of the Yare valley at the new Trowse Viaduct. Waterlogged mineral sediment with abundant weed seeds, charcoal, and carbonised cereals, indicated a phase of intensive agriculture nearby.

Objectives: it will provide information on the land use complementary to that from the excavated sites on the Norwich southern bypass.

Calibrated date: *1σ:* cal AD 1050–1260
               2σ: cal AD 1020–1280

Final comment: T Ashwin (27 September 1993), this result suggests (an unexpected) post-Roman date for the agricultural episode this sediment represents.

GU–5290 3110 ±60 BP

δ¹³C: -25.7‰

Sample: 29057 context 301, sample 1, submitted in December 1992 by P Murphy

Material: charcoal: *Quercus* sp. (P Murphy 1992)

Initial comment: this charcoal was collected from a fill of a small round pit, one of several dug under salvage conditions on the Norwich southern bypass watching brief, at the intersection of the Norwich southern bypass and the B1108 Watton Road.

Objectives: the charcoal was found in association with a *c* 7kg 'Bucket Urn' and other later Bronze Age pottery in a rubbish deposit. This material is scarce in Norfolk and a date for this deposit would be of regional importance (Lawson 1980).

Calibrated date: *1σ:* 1440–1310 cal BC
               2σ: 1500–1210 cal BC

Final comment: T Ashwin (27 September 1993), this result suggests a date for the possible manufacture of pottery at this site.

References: Lawson 1980

Norwich: St Martin-at-Palace, Norfolk

Location: TG 2346509103
             Lat. 52.37.59 N; Long. 01.18.07 E

Project manager: O Beazley (Norfolk Archaeological Unit), 1987

Archival body: English Heritage and Norfolk Museums Service

Description: two timber structures were excavated; one dated to the tenth/eleventh centuries and the other to eleventh century, both of which are interpreted as churches. Subsequently, chalk and flint foundations for a bicellular structure were built, contemporary with the extant east wall of the church. The building erected on these footings has been dated, on stylistic grounds only, to the eleventh century.

Objectives: the interpretation of the burial is most important in the history of occupation of St Martin-at-Palace Plain.

References: Beazley 2001
Hedges *et al* 1991b, 289–90

OxA–2320 1460 ±90 BP

δ¹³C: -23.0‰

Sample: 584N746, submitted on 20 January 1989 by P Murphy

Material: human bone (O Beazley 1988)

Initial comment: skeleton 746 was in a grave cut into the gravel subsoil. The grave was truncated to the west by stone church foundations dating from the early eleventh century, and by a later grave to the east. Only the lower part of the skeleton therefore survived. It had been buried beneath successive church floors, inside a standing roofed building.

Objectives: skeleton 746 was associated with one of two timber buildings, pre-dating the stone church and provisionally interpreted as earlier ecclesiastical buildings. In the absence of any artefactual dating, the sample provides the only possible dating evidence, by association, for these buildings. To be of any use a high-precision date is needed.

Calibrated date: *1σ:* cal AD 530–660
2σ: cal AD 410–770

Final comment: B Ayers (1991), the calibrated (2 sigma) result is of considerable interest and importance as we would be most surprised to find any burial on the site pre-dating the eighth century AD. The possibility implied by the result, that we could have a burial as early as the eighth century AD in this part of Norwich has considerable implications for our understanding of the development of the city. It certainly provides food for thought.

Oakham, Leicestershire

Location: SK 867095
Lat. 52.40.33 N; Long. 00.43.03 W

Project manager: P Clay (Leicestershire Archaeological Field Unit), 1986

Archival body: Leicestershire Museums Arts and Records Service

Description: the site is situated on a ridge of middle Liassic marlstone bedrock and although suffering considerable erosion from ploughing and subsoiling, several periods of activity could be identified.

Objectives: dating will help in the understanding of the association between the burial and pit circles of the site.

Final comment: P Clay (1994), overall the dates were variable, two being later than predicted (OxA-2419 and -2420), perhaps due to intrusive material. The other two were consistent with the late Neolithic and early Bronze Age material from the site, although perhaps a little later than expected.

References: Clay 1998
Frere *et al* 1988
Hedges *et al* 1992, 147–8
Liddle 1987

OxA–2419 1020 ±65 BP

δ¹³C: -23.7‰

Sample: A64.1986.1417-24, submitted on 5 December 1989 by P Clay

Material: human bone (A Stirland 1986)

Initial comment: from the base of the grave, beneath stones. Some erosion of the upper grave levels was apparent due to ploughing. The grave was on the interface of calcareous marlstone and liassic clay bedrock.

Objectives: the human bone was associated with late Neolithic flint knives and an unabraded sherd of late Neolithic Peterborough ware. The association between the burial and pit circles (other samples) is important in our understanding of the site.

Calibrated date: *1σ:* cal AD 970–1040
2σ: cal AD 880–1170

Final comment: P Clay (23 September 1994), this date was very much later than predicted due to incorrect selection of material from the sample provided. It was re-run by the laboratory using more appropriate skeletal material (OxA-2578).

OxA–2420 2450 ±80 BP

δ¹³C: -25.1‰

Sample: A64.1986.8, submitted on 5 December 1989 by P Clay

Material: charcoal: *Fraxinus* sp.; *Corylus* sp. (G C Morgan 1986)

Initial comment: charcoal from the base of a pit in the phase 2 pit circle.

Objectives: to provide a date for later Neolithic activity associated with Peterborough ware, the relationship with the burial may also be significant. Peterborough ware joins with the sherds from the burial and two other features.

Calibrated date: *1σ:* 770–400 cal BC
2σ: 800–380 cal BC

Final comment: P Clay (23 September 1994), this date was later than expected and maybe due to intrusive charcoal material. A late Neolithic–early Bronze Age date would be more consistent with the monument.

OxA–2421 3565 ±80 BP

δ¹³C: -27.1‰

Sample: A64.1986.104, submitted on 5 December 1989 by P Clay

Material: charcoal: *Corylus* sp. (G C Morgan 1986)

Initial comment: charcoal from a pit in the phase 1 pit circle. The upper surface of the pit was plough-eroded. The sample came from 160mm from the top of the feature.

Objectives: this sample will date the earliest phase of the pit group associated with a blade industry flint. The date may provide evidence of the earliest activity on the site.

Calibrated date: *1σ:* 2030–1770 cal BC
2σ: 2140–1690 cal BC

Final comment: P Clay (23 September 1994), this date is acceptable for the first phase of the pit circle although an earlier date was predicted.

OxA–2578 3390 ±70 BP

δ¹³C: -22.1‰

Sample: A64.1986.1417-24, submitted in 1990 by P Clay

Material: human bone (mandible) (A Stirland 1986)

Initial comment: as OxA-2419

Objectives: as OxA-2419

Calibrated date: *1σ:* 1760–1610 cal BC
                 2σ: 1890–1510 cal BC

Final comment: P Clay (23 September 1994), this date is acceptable for the crouched burial and associated artefacts.

Laboratory comment: Oxford Radiocarbon Accelerator Unit (24 October 1990), this is a second dating of the human burial from Oakham. The first dating result was on a fragment of bone from high in the grave. OxA-2578 is on the mandible and gives a Bronze Age determination.

Orton Longueville, Cambridgeshire

Location: TL 165963
               Lat. 52.33.06 N; Long. 00.16.54 W

Project manager: F O'Neill (Nene Valley Research Committee), 1979

Archival body: Peterborough City Museum and Art Gallery

Description: the site consists of two barrows, which by their contents, appear to be related. OLB 1 represents a phase missing in OLB 2, and the two monuments were a matter of only 170m apart.

Objectives: the dating evidence from within the mound and associated with the burials is not enough in itself to fix an overall date-range to either, or to date the change in structure in OLB 2.

Final comment: D F Mackreth (16 February 1992), all six samples have proved to be highly satisfactory. The two from the barrow define the creation of that as being of the Beaker period (UB-3243 and -3244). The remaining four belong to a Neolithic to early Bronze Age monument, and demonstrate that the perceived development is sound, not only that but UB-3247 helps to show that the Beaker burials were quite deliberately placed on a fresh site only a few score metres away, and that burials reverted to the monument after the change in culture.

Laboratory comment: Ancient Monuments Laboratory (1 February 1990), two further samples OLB1F22 and OLB2F48 (UB-3242 and UB-3245) failed to produce a result because they contained too little carbon.

UB–3243 3396 ±52 BP

δ¹³C: -21.2 ±0.2‰

Sample: OLB1F19, submitted on 1 December 1989 by D F Mackreth

Material: human bone (male, aged about 25) (F O'Neill 1979)

Initial comment: barrow 1; burial 2, a crouched burial laid on topsoil and sealed by the turf stack of the barrow. There was no grave pit. The body was placed immediately before the building of the barrow, possibly in the Beaker period.

Objectives: to date the construction of the barrow.

Calibrated date: *1σ:* 1750–1620 cal BC
                 2σ: 1880–1530 cal BC

Final comment: D F Mackreth (16 July 1992), the burial was sealed under the barrow and was either contemporary with the other burial or is later and dates the construction of the barrow. The date is earlier than UB-3244 cutting the mound, but the two dates are reconcilable. The barrow is of the Beaker period.

UB–3244 3468 ±38 BP

δ¹³C: -23.9 ±0.2‰

Sample: OLB1F4, submitted on 1 December 1989 by D F Mackreth

Material: human bone (male, 30–40 yrs) (F O'Neill 1979)

Initial comment: barrow 1; burial 6, a crouched inhumation inserted into the top of the barrow. There were no grave goods.

Objectives: to determine whether the body is of prehistoric or early Saxon date.

Calibrated date: *1σ:* 1880–1740 cal BC
                 2σ: 1900–1680 cal BC

Final comment: D F Mackreth (16 February 1992), one of a group of six burials. Two had beakers, unfortunately one cutting the other. Two other burials were similarly associated and the sample came from the upper one. It is of the Beaker period and the other may be assumed to be also, as UB-3243 came from under the mound. A beaker sunk into the surface of the barrow probably dates the remaining two, indeed the whole group.

UB–3246 4741 ±43 BP

δ¹³C: -20.7 ±0.2‰

Sample: OLB2F58, submitted on 1 December 1989 by D F Mackreth

Material: human bone (male, 35–45 yrs) (F O'Neill 1988)

Initial comment: barrow 2; burial 6, a crouched inhumation on a stone bed in the base of a large pit. This cuts the presumed facade of the period 1 long barrow and is sited in the 'apron' extension to the platform formed by the flattening of the long barrow.

Objectives: period 2 is a theoretical construct, if the real body is Neolithic, it could be as late as the early Bronze Age and be late in period 3.

Calibrated date: 1σ: 3640–3380 cal BC
2σ: 3640–3370 cal BC

Final comment: D F Mackreth (16 February 1992), burial F 53 was assigned to period 2 on the grounds of probability as period 1 and 3 were Neolithic. The date of F53 has to conform to demonstrate that the chief act defining period 2 was properly placed. The date is highly satisfactory.

UB–3247 3665 ±42 BP

δ¹³C: -22.1 ±0.2‰

Sample: OLB2F60, submitted on 1 December 1989 by D F Mackreth

Material: human bone (F O'Neill 1979)

Initial comment: barrow 2; burial 13, period 3. A crouched burial in a container at the base of a large and deep grave, assumed to be of early Bronze Age date. There were no grave goods. This grave was also assumed to be the first of the second series of burials of period 3.

Objectives: to establish whether or not this burial was of early Bronze Age date and to mark the end of the chronological gap estimated to have existed in the middle of period 3.

Calibrated date: 1σ: 2140–1970 cal BC
2σ: 2200–1920 cal BC

Final comment: D F Mackreth (16 February 1992), this burial was one of three marking a change of burial practice and was sealed under the period 4 platform. Only one of the three graves had goods - a Collared Urn, and lay away from the other two. F60 has been taken to be the last of the three. The date redefines the order and helps to highlight the perceived absence of Beaker burials on this site.

UB–3248 4713 ±84 BP

δ¹³C: -22.2 ±0.2‰

Sample: OLB2F35, submitted on 1 December 1989 by D F Mackreth

Material: human bone (F O'Neill 1979)

Initial comment: barrow 2; burial 11, period 3. A crouched burial (Neolithic) placed between the stele and the stone facade and sealed under a stone bed. It is assumed to be the latest burial in the secondary linear burial zone.

Objectives: to date the end of the Neolithic period and the beginning of the chronological gap assumed to exist between this phase and the later early Bronze Age burials of period 3.

Calibrated date: 1σ: 3640–3370 cal BC
2σ: 3660–3340 cal BC

Final comment: D F Mackreth (16 February 1992), one of the earlier burials of period 3 and associated with a burial trench very similar to period 3; culturally, the burial had to be Neolithic. The date is very satisfactory.

UB–3249 3333 ±84 BP

δ¹³C: -25.3 ±0.2‰

Sample: OLB2F48, submitted on 1 December 1989 by D F Mackreth

Material: human bone (possibly female, aged 15–17 years) (F O'Neill 1979)

Initial comment: barrow 2; burial 17, period 4. The body was crouched in a tight, lined, gravel pit. The burial is assumed to be the last on the site and to be of early Bronze Age date, the actual date is unknown. There were no grave goods.

Objectives: if this was the last burial, it would provide a closing date for the burial phase for the monument. No other dating is available except for a few Roman sherds associated with sealing deposit.

Calibrated date: 1σ: 1740–1510 cal BC
2σ: 1880–1430 cal BC

Final comment: D F Mackreth (16 February 1992), F78 of period 4 is argued to be the earliest of three burials next to a stele but need not be. There were three early Bronze Age pots, not associated with the bodies, dating on archaeological grounds to 2150–1650 BC. The calibrated date is basically satisfactory.

Peterborough: Cathedral Cloisters, Cambridgeshire

Location: TL 194986
Lat. 52.34.17 N; Long. 00.14.18 W

Project manager: C J S Rollo (Nene Valley Research Committee), 1982

Archival body: Peterborough City Museum and Art Gallery

Description: the excavations made in AD 1894 were reopened in the north-east corner of the cloisters. The walls previously recorded by J T Irvine were uncovered and, because of their alignment with the walls of the monastic church burnt in AD 1116 and found when the central tower of the present Cathedral was rebuilt, were clearly part of the central elements of the same church. Outside the building a mixed cemetery had developed against what should be the first church on the site; for there were no burials within it, and had it been an extension to a yet earlier building, then it should have sealed burials associated with that. The cemetery was of more than one generation before a foundation trench was cut into it for a wall running south from the primary building.

Objectives: middle Saxon cemeteries are rare, and the only dating evidence available for the cemetery consists of the application of one historic 'date' - the third quarter of the seventh century, and the assessed date of the addition to the primary church, c AD 800 plus, but before AD 900; and the two bones provide the only archaeological dating, there being no pottery or small finds at all.

Laboratory comment: English Heritage (12 February 2012), very little documentation relating to these samples can be traced.

References: Mackreth 1983a
Mackreth 1983b
Mackreth 1984

HAR–8580 1020 ±80 BP

δ¹³C: -22.1‰

Sample: 3440PCC, submitted on 20 January 1987 by
D F Mackreth

Material: human bone

Initial comment: probably from the cemetery outside the
first church.

Calibrated date: *1σ:* cal AD 900–1150
                2σ: cal AD 870–1210

HAR–8581 1180 ±70 BP

δ¹³C: -19.7‰

Sample: 3399PCC, submitted on 20 January 1987 by
D F Mackreth

Material: human bone (right femur)

Initial comment: as HAR-8581

Calibrated date: *1σ:* cal AD 720–970
                2σ: cal AD 670–1020

Radley: Barrow Hills, Oxfordshire

Location: SU 51359815
            Lat. 51.40.45 N; Long. 01.15.26 W

Project manager: C Halpin (Central Excavation Unit),
            1983–5

Archival body: Ashmolean Museum, Natural History
            Museum

Description: the excavations conducted in advance of housing construction over the west end of the early Bronze Age barrow cemetery at Barrow Hills, close to the Abingdon causewayed enclosure, yielded evidence for ceremonial and funerary use of the complex from the earlier Neolithic to at least the middle Bronze Age. The site consists of 17 barrows in two rows forming an 'avenue' which appeared to be aligned upon an earlier causewayed enclosure to the west. Eleven of the barrows had been excavated in the past to varying degrees. Current excavations involved barrows 1, 12, and 13 sited at the south-west end of the cemetery.

Objectives: to determine the use and chronological sequence of the Barrow Hills complex, incorporating evidence from the 1983–5 and earlier excavations.

Final comment: F Healy (17 October 1995), the Oxford AMS dates for Barrow Hills, combined with a series of 25 British Museum dates for the site, some of them published by Bradley (1992), and the British Museum dates for the Abingdon causewayed enclosure (Avery 1982), provide a suite of over 50 dates for the monument as a whole. All are listed in full and individually evaluated and discussed in detail by Ambers *et al* (1999). Collectively they document ritual and funerary use of the site over more than two thousand years, from the mid-fourth to the late second millennium cal BC, with a probable lull in monument building in the early third millennium. The large number of high-quality dates has made it possible to define the development of the complex and its spatial organisation at

different periods. Individually, some dates elucidate the chronology of generally poorly-dated feature, monument or artefact types, such as non-monumental early and middle Neolithic burials (OxA-1881-2, OxA-4359; 4700 ±100 BP; 3690–3120 cal BC at 95% confidence (Reimer *et al* 2004), BM-2709; 4270 ±100 BP; 3270–2570 cal BC at 95% confidence (Reimer *et al* 2004), BM-2710; 4530 ±50 BP; 3490–3020 cal BC at 95% confidence (Reimer *et al* 2004), BM-2714; 4470 ±70 BP; 3370–2910 cal BC at 95% confidence (Reimer *et al* 2004), and BM-2716; 4600 ±70 BP; 3630–3090 cal BC at 95% confidence (Reimer *et al* 2004)), pond barrows (OxA-1879-80, OxA-1903, BM-2697; 3320 ±50 BP; 1740–1490 cal BC at 95% confidence (Reimer *et al* 2004), and BM-2698; 3500 ±50 BP; 1960–1680 cal BC at 95% confidence (Reimer *et al* 2004)), early metalwork (OxA-1874-5 and OxA-4356; 3880 ±90 BP; 2580–2040 cal BC at 95% confidence (Reimer *et al* 2004)), and a 'Wessex' grave group (OxA-1886).

References: Ambers *et al* 1999
            Avery 1982
            Barclay and Halpin 1999
            Bradley 1992
            Hedges *et al* 1990, 218–21
            Reimer et al 2004

OxA–1872 3450 ±80 BP

δ¹³C: -21.0‰ (assumed)

Sample: 601B3, submitted in March 1987 by C Halpin

Material: human bone (cremated unidentifiable fragments)

Initial comment: an infant cremation from one of two miniature Biconical vessels (?Biconical Urn) placed side-by-side on the surface of the stabilised secondary fill of the outer (phase 2) ditch of barrow 12 on the north-east side of the barrow.

Objectives: to date the charred bone, which will provide a *terminus post quem* for later silt accumulation/soil development in the barrow ditch.

Calibrated date: *1σ:* 1890–1670 cal BC
                2σ: 1960–1530 cal BC

Final comment: F Healy (17 October 1995), an important result since it dates the miniature vessels. The date is compatible with the context and the pottery, and forms a conformable sequence with dates for other contexts in the same barrow (OxA-1884, -1887; BM-2699; 3720 ±60 BP; 2300–1940 cal BC at 95% confidence; Reimer *et al* 2004). Doubts about the general accuracy of radiocarbon determinations on charred bone samples, however, reduce the confidence which can be put in it.

OxA–1873 3510 ±80 BP

δ¹³C: -21.0‰ (assumed)

Sample: 611D2, submitted in March 1987 by C Halpin

Material: human bone (cremated unidentifiable fragments)

Initial comment: cremated bone associated with a fragmentary Bronze Age vessel (not diagnostic). Found at the centre of a pond barrow, which overlay a Neolithic ring ditch. The pond barrow was out by the outer ditch of barrow 12.

Objectives: this burial was found at the centre of pond barrow (F611). It is the only evidence available to date this uncommon monument.

Calibrated date: *1σ:* 1950–1740 cal BC
                       2σ: 2040–1630 cal BC

Final comment: F Healy (17 October 1995), OxA-1873 dates the cremated bones of the 2–3 year old found beneath a fragmentary, inverted indeterminate urn of early Bronze Age fabric at the centre of a partially silted late Neolithic hengiform ring ditch (611). It is compatible with the context and the pottery and forms a conformable sequence with the dates for other contexts in 611 (OxA-1889; BM-2712 (3860 ±80 BP; 2570–2050 cal BC at 95% confidence; Reimer *et al* 2004; BM-2713 (3950 ±80 BP; 2840–2200 cal BC at 95% confidence), and BM-2896; 2820 ±40 BP; 1120–850 cal BC at 95% confidence (Reimer *et al* 2004), and it rightly pre-dates OxA-1872.

References: Reimer et al 2004

OxA–1874 3930 ±80 BP

δ¹³C: -21.0‰ (assumed)

Sample: 919, submitted in March 1987 by C Halpin

Material: human bone (child skull fragments and radius)

Initial comment: from an unmarked beaker burial *c* 55m west of barrow 12, close to beaker burial F950. It was a shallow grave pit (*c* 20cm) with the burial disturbed by animal burrowing. The grave contained a child inhumation and 'barbed-wire' Beaker, Wessex/Middle Rhine beaker, bone disc, and three copper rings. The bones of a newborn baby were found in the Middle Rhine beaker (F919 SF597).

Objectives: to date the human burial and grave context and provide a *terminus post quem* for the grave backfill.

Calibrated date: *1σ:* 2570–2290 cal BC
                       2σ: 2630–2150 cal BC

Final comment: C Halpin (1990), the date is satisfactory for the step 3 Beakers. It indicates the age of an important grave group, in particular the three copper rings, which previously had been unrecorded from graves in this country. A second burial (dated by OxA-1875) seems to have been inserted into the grave. This and OxA-1875 are among the earliest dates for metalwork and for Beaker pottery in mainland Britain.

OxA–1875 3990 ±80 BP

δ¹³C: -21.0‰ (assumed)

Sample: 919 sf 597, submitted in March 1987 by C Halpin

Material: human bone (new born right humerus and ribs)

Initial comment: bones of a new born found with a small quantity of cremated bone from a 2 to 3 year-old deposited in a Wessex/Middle Rhine Beaker, apparently inserted into the grave (919) which already contained the child dated by OxA-1874.

Objectives: as OxA-1874

Calibrated date: *1σ:* 2580–2460 cal BC
                       2σ: 2860–2280 cal BC

Final comment: F Healy (17 October 1995), this and OxA-1874 are among the earliest dates for metalwork and for Beaker pottery in mainland Britain.

OxA–1876 2740 ±70 BP

δ¹³C: -21.0‰ (assumed)

Sample: 4245I, submitted in March 1987 by C Halpin

Material: human bone (cremated unidentifiable fragments)

Initial comment: two associated Collared Urn cremations from a pit *c* 10m north of barrow 13, one upright, one inverted - a sample was taken from one of these urns.

Objectives: to date the burial and this phase of the Barrow Hills cemetery, ie the deposition of urned cremations outside the monuments.

Calibrated date: *1σ:* 980–810 cal BC
                       2σ: 1050–790 cal BC

Final comment: F Healy (17 October 1995), the date is late for the pottery style and doubts about the general accuracy of radiocarbon determinations on charred bone samples reduce the confidence which can be put in it.

Laboratory comment: Oxford Radiocarbon Accelerator Unit (1990), chemically the anomalous charred bones were no different from the other charred bones, which have produced acceptable dates. Environmental contamination is possible, although it would be unusual for the same process to make dates both too old and too young.

OxA–1877 2770 ±70 BP

δ¹³C: -21.0‰ (assumed)

Sample: 4321, submitted in March 1987 by C Halpin

Material: human bone (cremated unidentifiable fragments)

Initial comment: from an urned cremation at the west end of the barrow cemetery, *c* 20m north of barrow 12. It was contained within a tripartite Collared Urn decorated with twisted cord impressions.

Objectives: as OxA-1876

Calibrated date: *1σ:* 1010–830 cal BC
                       2σ: 1120–800 cal BC

Final comment: see OxA-1876

Laboratory comment: see OxA-1876

OxA–1878 4150 ±70 BP

δ¹³C: -21.0‰ (assumed)

Sample: 4700, submitted in March 1987 by C Halpin

Material: human bone (cremated unidentifiable fragments)

Initial comment: from an urned cremation contained within a tripartite Collared Urn decorated with whipped cord impressions. It was located in a pit at the west end of the barrow cemetery.

Objectives: as OxA-1876

Calibrated date: *1σ:* 2880–2580 cal BC
                       2σ: 2910–2490 cal BC

Final comment: see OxA-1876

OxA–1879 3720 ±80 BP

δ¹³C: -21.0‰ (assumed)

Sample: 4866A5I, submitted in March 1987 by C Halpin

Material: human bone (cremated unidentifiable fragments)

Initial comment: one of two unaccompanied cremations found in shallow scoops cut into the base of a pond barrow. On the south-east side of the barrow, an arc of six inhumations associated with Food Vessels was excavated. An isolated inhumation (sample 5274) was found 4m north-east of the barrow.

Objectives: the pond barrow showed three phases of deposition: two unaccompanied cremations, an arc of burials, and an isolated inhumation. It is a rare monument, being one of only two excavated in the last 40 years. Dates for each phase of deposition would indicate the period over which the barrow served as a focus for burial.

Calibrated date: 1σ: 2280–1980 cal BC
                     2σ: 2410–1890 cal BC

Final comment: F Healy (17 October 1995), the date is compatible with the context and with the dates for burials in the graves surrounding the pond barrow (OxA-1880, OxA-1903, BM-2697 (3320 ±50 BP; 1740–1490 cal BC at 95% confidence; Reimer *et al* 2004), and BM-2698 (3500 ±50 BP; 1960–1680 cal BC at 95% confidence; Reimer *et al* 2004). If reliable, OxA-1879 should approximate to the construction date of the monument. Doubts about the general accuracy of radiocarbon determinations on charred bone samples, however, reduce the confidence which can be put in it.

References: Reimer et al 2004

OxA–1880 3490 ±80 BP

δ¹³C: -21.0‰ (assumed)

Sample: 4969/1, submitted in April 1987 by C Halpin

Material: antler: *Cervus elaphus*

Initial comment: one of an arc of six inhumations (three of which were associated with Food Vessels) located on the south-east side of the pond barrow. Two unaccompanied cremations were found at the base of the barrow (samples 4855 D5I, 4866 DSII). An isolated inhumation was found 4m north-east of the pond barrow (sample 5274). 4969/1 was a child inhumation accompanied by a flint borer and laid in a tree-trunk coffin. A large number of antlers were found in the backfill of the grave.

Objectives: the pond barrow showed three phases of deposition. Such monuments have rarely been excavated, and dates for each phase of deposition would indicate the period during which the barrow served as a focus for burial. In addition F4969 produced an uncommon collection of antler, these together with antlers from three Neolithic monuments at Barrow Hills, comprise a collection of national importance.

Calibrated date: 1σ: 1920–1690 cal BC
                     2σ: 2030–1610 cal BC

Final comment: F Healy (17 October 1995), the date is one of six red deer antlers placed, together with a cattle skull and a pig calcaneum, around the sides of a grave (4969), above

the level of the top of a wooden coffin containing a subadult inhumation accompanied by a flint piercer. This was one of eight early Bronze Age burials around pond barrow 4866. The measurement is likely to date the burial and is compatible with other dates relating to the pond barrow (OxA-1879, OxA-1903, BM-2697 (3320 ±50 BP; 1740–1490 cal BC at 95% confidence; Reimer *et al* 2004), and BM-2698 (3500 ±50 BP; 1960–1680 cal BC at 95% confidence; Reimer *et al* 2004).

References: Reimer et al 2004

OxA–1881 5140 ±100 BP

δ¹³C: -21.0‰ (assumed)

Sample: 5352/13, submitted in April 1987 by C Halpin

Material: antler: *Cervus elaphus*

Initial comment: the sample was from the primary fill of a large pit located outside the linear barrow cemetery, c 15m north-west of barrow 2. The pit was overlain by an elongated grave within which were found three inhumations (1 articulated, 2 disarticulated; Neolithic?).

Objectives: the pit was apparently related to the overlying grave. A date for each feature would contribute to their interpretation. In addition four monuments at Barrow Hills produced antlers and together these comprise a collection of national importance.

Calibrated date: 1σ: 4050–3800 cal BC
                     2σ: 4240–3700 cal BC

Final comment: F Healy (17 October 1995), the date provides a *terminus post quem* for the silting of the pit and the creation of the overlying mortuary structure. It is exceptionally early but compares with at least two dates from within the inner ditch of the nearby causewayed enclosure (BM-351; 5060 ±130 BP, 4230–3630 cal BC at 95% confidence; BM-352; 4970 ±130 BP, 4040–3380 cal BC at 95% confidence; Reimer *et al* 2004).

References: Reimer *et al* 2004

OxA–1882 4650 ±80 BP

δ¹³C: -21.0‰ (assumed)

Sample: 5354, submitted in March 1987 by C Halpin

Material: human bone (right ulna and radius)

Initial comment: an unmarked articulated child inhumation. Adjacent to inhumations F5355 and F5356, it was found in a large deep (0.80m) grave pit, and was undisturbed. The burial lies outside the line of the Bronze Age barrow and may have been related to the Neolithic causewayed camp.

Objectives: lying as it does outside the avenue of the Bronze Age barrows it is suspected that this burial may have been related to the Neolithic causewayed enclosure. A date is required to substantiate this opinion.

Calibrated date: 1σ: 3630–3350 cal BC
                     2σ: 3640–3110 cal BC

Final comment: F Healy (17 October 1995), OxA-1882 dates the skeleton of a 10–12 year old buried in one (5354) of a group of three single graves. The date and those on the skeletons from the two other graves (OxA-4359; BM-2710;

4530 ±50 BP; 3490–3030 cal BC at 95% confidence; Reimer *et al* 2004) place them in the fourth millennium cal BC. The grouping of three burials seems so far unique among early or middle Neolithic flat graves, most of which appear to have been isolated. The burial pre-dates the earliest phase of the oval barrow (BM-2392; 4500 ±60 BP; 3370–2930 cal BC at 95% confidence; Reimer *et al* 2004).

References: Reimer et al 2004

OxA–1883 8100 ±120 BP

δ¹³C: -26.0‰ (assumed)

Sample: 5353/4, submitted in April 1987 by C Halpin

Material: charcoal: *Quercus* sp.

Initial comment: a sample from a charcoal lens in a naturally treethrow hole (5353) originally thought to be a pit, which also contained an ?auroch tibia fragment and woodland molluscan fauna. From a large pit, which lay north of the linear barrow cemetery.

Objectives: the importance of this feature lies in the fact that it may be the only feature associated with a settlement as opposed to funerary monuments.

Calibrated date: 1σ: 7300–6840 cal BC
2σ: 7460–6680 cal BC

Final comment: F Healy (17 October 1995), it is believed to be important to date this feature as it was possibly the only discrete feature to be excavated. Small quantities of Mesolithic artefacts were found elsewhere in the excavated area; the charcoal could conceivably have resulted from contemporary woodland clearance.

OxA–1884 3670 ±80 BP

δ¹³C: -21.0‰ (assumed)

Sample: 605I, submitted in March 1987 by C Halpin

Material: human bone (left humerus and skull fragment)

Initial comment: an infant inhumation, with the pelvis and leg bones absent. A Food Vessel was deposited with burial, an it was within the central grave pit of the double-ditched barrow, barrow 12. It was deposited in a pit which cut through the backfill of the primary burial (F607). In the same pit, immediately beneath this burial, an unaccompanied cremation was found.

Objectives: barrow 12 was a double-ditched barrow representing two main structural phases. The primary grave was re-opened and F605 deposited. A date for this feature would demonstrate if there was a significant hiatus between phases I and II, and over what period the barrow was in use.

Calibrated date: 1σ: 2200–1940 cal BC
2σ: 2290–1820 cal BC

Final comment: F Healy (17 October 1995), OxA-1884 dates the skeleton of an infant aged approximately one year, accompanied by a Food Vessel, which formed the upper of two deposits in the central grave (605) of phase 2 of barrow 12, the underlying deposit being the cremation dated by OxA-1887. This date forms a conformable sequence with the others from barrow 12: BM-2699 (3720 ±60 BP;

2300–1940 cal BC at 95% confidence; Reimer *et al* 2004), OxA-1872, and OxA-1887). It is also one of surprisingly few reliable dates directly associated with Food Vessel pottery.

References: Reimer et al 2004

OxA–1885 1710 ±70 BP

δ¹³C: -26.0‰ (assumed)

Sample: 411/1, submitted in April 1987 by C Halpin

Material: carbonised plant macrofossil (wheat grains)

Initial comment: charred wheat grains from the upper fill of a small (originally thought to be prehistoric) pit, close to barrows 12 and 13 which contained charcoal and charred grain, including free-threshing wheat, but no artefacts.

Objectives: this sample was recommended by the environmentalist (Dr Mark Robinson) to be submitted for radiocarbon dating because the material is uncommon.

Calibrated date: 1σ: cal AD 240–420
2σ: cal AD 130–540

Final comment: F Healy (17 October 1995), it was important to know if this deposit dated to the prehistoric period. The date relates to the Roman cemetery or, less probably, the Saxon settlement, both of which lay within the excavated area.

OxA–1886 3520 ±70 BP

δ¹³C: -26.0‰ (assumed)

Sample: 11/4, submitted in April 1987 by C Halpin

Material: charcoal: *Quercus* sp., and leguminosae seeds

Initial comment: charcoal from remains of a funeral pyre deposited with central cremation of barrow 1. Associated finds included a copper/bronze knife, bone tweezers, and a bone ring-headed pin. The grave goods may have been inside a container of so far unidentified organic material.

Objectives: to provide an age for the cremation and grave goods.

Calibrated date: 1σ: 1950–1740 cal BC
2σ: 2040–1680 cal BC

Final comment: F Healy (17 October 1995), the date confirms the final early Bronze Age, ie Wessex II, age indicated by the associated grave goods. It is one of relatively few reliable dates for 'Wessex' grave assemblages.

OxA–1887 3830 ±70 BP

δ¹³C: -26.0‰ (assumed)

Sample: 605/1, submitted in April 1987 by C Halpin

Material: charcoal: *Quercus* sp.

Initial comment: a charred oak bier or tray on which lay the unaccompanied cremated remains of a 17–23 year old. This was the lower of two deposits in the central grave (605) of phase 2 of barrow 12, the overlying deposit being the inhumation dated by OxA-1884. This grave cut the phase 1 grave (607), the primary burial in which is dated by BM-2699.

Objectives: to date the wooden object, associated with the cremation, and provide a *terminus post quem* for the grave backfill.

Calibrated date: *1σ:* 2460–2140 cal BC
                     2σ: 2480–2040 cal BC

Final comment: F Healy (17 October 1995), the earlier result for OxA-1887 may be explained by the use of long lived oak wood. The date forms a conformable sequence with the others from barrow 12 (OxA-1872, -1884; BM-2699; 3720 ±60 BP, 2300–1940 cal BC at 95% confidence; Reimer *et al* 2004), although the oak, which comprised the sample, could have had a considerable age-at-death offset.

References: Reimer *et al* 2004

OxA–1888 3450 ±70 BP

δ¹³C: -26.0‰ (assumed)

Sample: 802/1, submitted in April 1987 by C Halpin

Material: charcoal (onion couch tubers): *Quercus* sp.; *Crataegus* sp.

Initial comment: charcoal flecks from the fill of cremation pit 802 at the centre of ring ditch 801. The centre of the pit contained a cremation deposit surrounded by a rim of charcoal (mainly hawthorn-type) and including tubers and grasses. Grave goods were a bronze awl and a fired clay bead.

Objectives: to establish the date of the ring ditch which has not been dated.

Calibrated date: *1σ:* 1890–1680 cal BC
                     2σ: 1950–1600 cal BC

Final comment: C Halpin (1990), this result dates an otherwise undated ring ditch but it may date the cremation event. However, given the anomalies of OxA-1876, -1877, and -1878 it should be treated with caution.

Laboratory comment: Oxford Radiocarbon Accelerator Unit (1990), a possible explanation for the anomalous charred bone dates is described in OxA-1876, -1877, and -1878. It is hard to see how OxA-1888 could have been affected by the same problem though, given the fact that different material was dated.

OxA–1889 3600 ±70 BP

δ¹³C: -26.0‰ (assumed)

Sample: 611/C/2, submitted in April 1987 by C Halpin

Material: charcoal: *Prunus spinosa*; *Quercus* sp.

Initial comment: charcoal from layer 2 of ring ditch 611, the same layer in the upper silts as the urned cremation dated by OxA-1873.

Objectives: to provide a date for the pond barrow.

Calibrated date: *1σ:* 2040–1880 cal BC
                     2σ: 2200–1750 cal BC

Final comment: F Healy (17 October 1995), the similarity between this date and that of OxA-1873 suggests that the charcoal sample was pyre debris from the cremation, although this is not demonstrable. Both for a conformable

sequence with dates for other contexts in 611 (BM-2712; 3860 ±80 BP; 2570–2040 cal BC at 95% confidence, BM-2713; 3950 ±80 BP; 2840–2200 cal BC at 95% confidence, and BM-2896; 2820 ±40 BP; 1120–850 cal BC at 95% confidence (Reimer *et al* 2004).

References: Reimer *et al* 2004

OxA–1903 3480 ±80 BP

δ¹³C: -21.0‰ (assumed)

Sample: 5274, submitted in March 1987 by C Halpin

Material: human bone (skull and long bone shaft fragments)

Initial comment: an isolated inhumation found 4m north-east of a pond barrow (F4866). On the south-east side of the barrow an arc of six burials (inhumations associated with Food Vessels) was excavated. Two unaccompanied cremations were found at the base of the barrow. This burial was an articulated infant inhumation with six struck flints (including a transverse arrowhead) laid by the hands. The grave pit was 0.25m deep and apparently undisturbed.

Objectives: the pond barrow is a rare monument, there being only two excavated in the last 40 years. Dates for each phase of deposition would indicate the period over which the barrow served as a focus for burial.

Calibrated date: *1σ:* 1910–1690 cal BC
                     2σ: 2030–1610 cal BC

Final comment: F Healy (17 October 1995), the date is likely to age the burial and is compatible with other dates relating to the pond barrow (BM-2697; 3320 ±50 BP; 1740–1490 cal BC, at 95% confidence, BM-2698; 3500 ±50 BP; 1960–1680 cal BC, at 95% confidence (Reimer *et al* 2004), OxA-1879, and OxA-1880).

References: Reimer *et al* 2004

Raunds prehistoric, Northamptonshire

Location: SP 976925
                  Lat. 52.20.29 N; Long. 00.34.02 W

Project manager: A Chapman and D Windell
                  (Northampton County Council), 1985–92

Description: since 1985 large-scale excavation and survey has been carried out around Raunds, Northamptonshire, in the midlands of England. This has led to the discovery of a monumental prehistoric landscape, which lasted more than 2000 years. The complex comprises an early Neolithic long barrow, turf mound, and long mound, a later Neolithic long enclosure and causewayed ring ditch, and at least 14 Bronze Age barrows. There are also a number of undated enclosures and ring ditches. The northern part of this complex lies under a deserted medieval hamlet at West Cotton.

Objectives: to help construct a chronological framework for the site.

Final comment: J Harding and F Healy (2008), the Raunds Area Project investigated more than 20 Neolithic and Bronze Age monuments in the Nene Valley. From *c* 5000 BC to the early first millennium cal BC a succession of ritual mounds and burial mounds were built as settlement along the valley sides increased and woodland was cleared. Starting as a regular stopping-place for flint knapping and domestic tasks, first the Long Mound, and then Long Barrow, the north part of the Turf Mound and the Avenue were built in the fifth millennium BC. With the addition of the Long Enclosure, the Causewayed Ring Ditch, and the Southern Enclosure, there was a chain of five or six diverse monuments stretched along the river bank by *c* 3000 cal BC. Later, a timber platform, the Riverside Structure, was built and the focus of ceremonial activity shifted to the Cotton 'Henge', two concentric ditches on the occupied valley side. From *c* 2200 cal BC monument building accelerated and included the Segmented Ditch Circle and at least 20 round barrows, almost all containing burials, at first inhumations, then cremations down to *c* 1000 cal BC, by which time two overlapping systems of paddocks and droveways had been laid out. Finally, the terrace began to be settled when these had gone out of use, in the early 1st millennium cal BC.

References: Harding and Healy 2007
               Harding and Healy 2011
               Parry 2006
               Windell *et al* 1990

Raunds prehistoric: Irthlingborough, Northamptonshire

Location: SP 965715
               Lat. 51.56.25 N; Long. 01.16.40 W

Project manager: C Halpin (Central Excavation Unit), 1987

Archival body: English Heritage

Description: a ceremonial and mortuary monument complex excavated in advance of gravel extraction and road building in the Nene valley at Irlingborough, Stanwick, and West Cotton.

Objectives: to date the features and phases of the complex.

References: Dix 1987, 3–30
               Harding and Healy 2007
               Kinnes 1979
               Macphail and Goldberg 1990, 425–9

OxA–3051 3590 ±70 BP

$\delta^{13}C$: -22.9‰

Sample: 291-33027, submitted on 13 February 1991 by J Humble

Material: charcoal: *Quercus* sp. (G Campbell 1991)

Initial comment: from the fill of a posthole which appeared to have been cut during the deposition of the fill of the central ?burial pit within the mound of barrow 3.

Objectives: a radiocarbon date will provide a *terminus ante quem* for the cutting of the central ?burial pit and the concentric postcircles below the mound.

Calibrated date: *1σ:* 2040–1880 cal BC
                  2σ: 2140–1740 cal BC

Final comment: J Humble (2 June 1993), due to a dearth of suitable sample material, OxA-3051 is the only determination from barrow 3: it provides a date for the central post-built structure which, in conjunction with a series of post-circles and post-arcs, preceded the raising of the mound.

References: Hedges *et al* 1993, 158

OxA–3052 3450 ±70 BP

$\delta^{13}C$: -22.5‰

Sample: 291-33467, submitted on 13 February 1991 by J Humble

Material: plant macrofossils (charred tubers) (G Campbell 1991)

Initial comment: the sample was taken from a cremation located in mound material within the western quadrant of barrow 4. The tubers are associated with cremation 291-6460.

Objectives: to provide a date for the secondary burial activity on the mound and also a *terminus ante quem* for the construction of the mound.

Calibrated date: *1σ:* 1890–1680 cal BC
                  2σ: 1950–1600 cal BC

Final comment: J Harding and F Healy (2007), if the cremation deposit was indeed cut into the mound, rather than inserted during construction, the mound must have been built between the dates of the two samples (OxA-3053 and OxA-3052), and so, despite the lack of material directly dating this event, the date of construction can be estimated as *2020–1600 cal BC at 95% probability*. If the cremation deposit was inserted during construction, its age provides a second *terminus post quem* for the construction of the mound, the date of which can be estimated as *1880–1520 cal BC at 95% probability* (Harding and Healy 2007, 165).

References: Hedges *et al* 1993, 158–9

OxA–3053 3530 ±70 BP

$\delta^{13}C$: -25.1‰

Sample: 291-33478, submitted on 13 February 1991 by J Humble

Material: charcoal (charred timber): *Quercus* sp., poorly preserved charcoal, most of which appears to be heartwood. 1 piece possibly sapwood (R Gale 1998)

Initial comment: from carbonised wood remains located within mound material near the centre of the barrow mound of barrow 4.

Objectives: there is a strong likelihood that the deposition of the wood is contemporary with the construction of the mound. The sample is expected to be late Neolithic/early Bronze Age.

Calibrated date: *1σ:* 1950–1750 cal BC
                  2σ: 2040–1680 cal BC

Final comment: J Harding and F Healy (2007), the planks heaped in the mound did not appear to be of heartwood, although the outside of the trees could not be identified.

A date for this sample is therefore a *terminus post quem* for the construction of the mound (Harding and Healy 2007, 165). *See* also OxA-3052.

References:　　　　Hedges *et al* 1993, 158

OxA–3054 4460 ±70 BP

δ¹³C: -24.6‰

Sample: 291-33308, submitted on 13 February 1991 by J Humble

Material: charcoal (highly burnt twigs): unidentified (G Cambell 1991)

Initial comment: from the fill of a small pit containing the cremation. The pit was located between the inner and outer ditches of the mound for barrow 5 and the fill was sealed below buried soil of post-early Bronze Age, yet pre-Romano-British or Romano-British date.

Objectives: to provide a date for secondary burial activity in the barrow. It may also indicate a likely *terminus post quem* for the digging of the outer ditch although it is acknowledged that there is no stratigraphic evidence that it does pre-date the outer ditch.

Calibrated date:　　1σ: 3340–3010 cal BC
　　　　　　　　　2σ: 3370–2910 cal BC

Final comment: J Humble (2 June 1993), this is the earliest date for a cremation burial within the complex to date. In the absence of supporting evidence, however, the date can be regarded as spuriously early, or as evidence for a flat burial incorporated within the platform of the much later round barrow.

References:　　　　Hedges *et al* 1993, 158–9
　　　　　　　　　Parry 2006, 45

OxA–3055 4480 ±70 BP

δ¹³C: -23.4‰

Sample: 291-33421, submitted on 13 February 1991 by J Humble

Material: charcoal: *?Quercus sp* (G Campbell 1991)

Initial comment: from the primary silts in the northern ditch terminus of the monument in trench B118. The deposit containing the charcoal was sealed by overlying ditch fills and there is no record of disturbance or contamination.

Objectives: to provide a *terminus ante quem* for the digging of the ring ditch and a *terminus post quem* for the recutting of this ditch.

Calibrated date:　　1σ: 3350–3020 cal BC
　　　　　　　　　2σ: 3370–2910 cal BC

Final comment: J Humble (2 June 1993), two dates for a causewayed ring ditch (*c* 22m diameter) supplement the growing body of evidence for the construction of circular enclosures during the middle Neolithic (Kinnes 1979); OxA-3055 is from material contained within the fills of the first ditch; and OxA-3121 is from a deposit of *Cervus elaphus* antler placed in one of the terminals of the ditch after it had been partly infilled and then redefined.

References:　　　　Hedges *et al* 1993, 158
　　　　　　　　　Kinnes 1979

OxA–3056 4210 ±70 BP

δ¹³C: -24.3‰

Sample: 291-33382, submitted on 13 February 1991 by J Humble

Material: plant macrofossils (hazelnut shells) (G Cambell 1991)

Initial comment: from the fill of a small circular pit on the west side of trench B1 0.

Objectives: the fill of the pit contained Grooved Ware sherds, worked flint, grain, and hazelnut shells. A date on material directly associated with grooved ware would provide a date for the local and regional Grooved Ware horizon. For example the only diagnostic artefact in terms of date from the ditched enclosure at West Cotton (cut by the outer ditch of barrow 1) is a Grooved Ware rim sherd.

Calibrated date:　　1σ: 2900–2680 cal BC
　　　　　　　　　2σ: 2930–2580 cal BC

Final comment: J Humble (2 June 1993), OxA-3056 was obtained from hazelnut shells associated with charred cereal grain, apple and sloe fragments, and Grooved Ware (sherds too small to be attributed to substyle) contained in a pit, and is compatible with the span of radiocarbon dates for samples with Grooved Ware from elsewhere in the East Midlands and East Anglia (eg OxA-2310; 4005 ±90 BP; 2880–2230 at 95% confidence, and OxA-2311; 4170 ±90 BP; 2930–2480 cal BC at 95% confidence; Reimer *et al* 2004).

References:　　　　Hedges *et al* 1993, 158
　　　　　　　　　Parry 2006, 33
　　　　　　　　　Reimer *et al* 2004

OxA–3057 5370 ±80 BP

δ¹³C: -26.6‰

Sample: 291-33047, submitted on 13 February 1991 by J Humble

Material: charcoal (short-lived species): unidentified (G Campbell 1991)

Initial comment: the soil sample from which the charcoal was recovered was taken from the bottom fill of cut 63123, a treehole located in trench B140.

Objectives: the sample forms part of a series of three samples from different treeholes within the same trench. They are being dated to establish whether the burning in them represents a single event and is associated with a clearance episode, to establish a framework for soil micromorphology work on treeholes 62113 and 63123, and to date flintwork found in treehole 63123.

Calibrated date:　　1σ: 4340–4050 cal BC
　　　　　　　　　2σ: 4360–3990 cal BC

Final comment: J Humble (2 June 1993), the results indicate that tree clearance commenced in the period conventionally encompassing the transition from Mesolithic to Neolithic and continued, perhaps especially, into the middle Neolithic. It is not possible to establish if the trees were felled by natural or human agencies (eg by ring-barking), but the fallen trees had been burnt out *in situ* (Macphail and Goldberg 1990). Environmental evidence from the earlier

Neolithic monuments in the complex confirms that they were built in a landscape which had been cleared, at least locally, of its tree cover.

References: Hedges *et al* 1993, 158
Macphail and Goldberg 1990

OxA–3058 4700 ±80 BP

δ¹³C: -25.7‰

Sample: 291-33044, submitted on 13 February 1991 by J Humble

Material: charcoal: *?Quercus sp* (G Campbell 1991)

Initial comment: from the upper fill of cut 62113, a treehole located in trench B140.

Objectives: as OxA-3057

Calibrated date: 1σ: 3640–3360 cal BC
2σ: 3650–3340 cal BC

Final comment: see OxA-3057

References: Hedges *et al* 1993, 158
Parry 2006, 32

OxA–3059 6130 ±80 BP

δ¹³C: -26.6‰

Sample: 291-33037, submitted on 13 February 1991 by J Humble

Material: charcoal (short-lived species): unidentified (G Campbell 1991)

Initial comment: the sample was taken as a soil sample from the upper fill of cut 62126, a tree hole located in trench B140.

Objectives: as OxA-3057

Calibrated date: 1σ: 5220–4940 cal BC
2σ: 5310–4840 cal BC

Final comment: see OxA-3057

References: Hedges *et al* 1993, 158

OxA–3089 2950 ±80 BP

δ¹³C: -26.0‰ (assumed)

Sample: 291-11076, submitted on 13 February 1991 by J Humble

Material: carbonised plant macrofossil (*Arrhenatherum elatius* plant tubers) (G Campbell 1991)

Initial comment: from a pit containing a cremation. The pit was located on the berm between the middle and outer quarry ditches of the mound for barrow 1. The upper fill of the pit was sealed by mound material.

Objectives: to provide a *terminus post quem* for the outer phase 3 ditch of the barrow and tentatively a *terminus ante quem* for the middle ditch. A result will also provide a date for secondary burial activity in the barrow.

Calibrated date: 1σ: 1310–1020 cal BC
2σ: 1410–920 cal BC

Final comment: J Humble (2 June 1993), the pit was not cut through the overlying barrow mound, and as the outer ditch was dug prior to the deposition of the cremation, it appears that the mound has slumped outwards, sealing the pit. This is the latest date obtained from a Bronze Age cremation burial within the monument complex.

References: Hedges *et al* 1993, 158–9
Parry 2006, 33 and 46

OxA–3120 3680 ±100 BP

δ¹³C: -22.9‰

Sample: AOR 55243, submitted on 13 February 1991 by J Humble

Material: animal bone (large artiodactyl, tibia) (S Davis 1991)

Initial comment: the bone was recovered from the basal fill of a pit at the centre of the mound for barrow 5. The upper fill of the pit was sealed by remnant mound material. The pit cut another pit at the centre of the barrow, which contained five arrowheads and a Beaker, but no human remains.

Objectives: to provide a *terminus ante quem* for the pit containing the grave goods and a *terminus post quem* for the construction of the mound. The sample is one of two (OxA-3120 and OxA-3121) to be dated from barrow 5.

Calibrated date: 1σ: 2210–1920 cal BC
2σ: 2430–1770 cal BC

Final comment: J Humble (2 June 1993), barrow 5 contained a Wessex/middle Rhine Beaker and five Sutton B type barbed and tanged arrowheads, but no skeletal remains were present. The date of the animal bone provides a *terminus ante quem* for the deposition of the grave goods.

References: Hedges *et al* 1993, 158–9

OxA–3121 4450 ±90 BP

δ¹³C: -23.0‰

Sample: AOR 55372, submitted on 13 February 1991 by J Humble

Material: antler: *Cervus elaphus*, tine (S Davis 1991)

Initial comment: the antler appeared to be a placed deposit within the secondary fill of a ditch recut within the southern terminus of the causewayed ring ditch in trench B118.

Objectives: to provide a *terminus ante quem* for the digging of the ditch recut. The sample is one of two to be dated from this ring ditch (*see* OxA-3055).

Calibrated date: 1σ: 3350–2920 cal BC
2σ: 3490–2890 cal BC

Final comment: J Humble (2 June 1993), the date overlaps at 68% confidence with the determination for OxA-3055 obtained on hazel/alder charcoal in the primary ditch fills, and confirms the middle Neolithic construction of the monument.

References: Hedges *et al* 1993, 158

OxA–4067 4100 ±80 BP

δ¹³C: -22.4‰

Sample: 291-35126, submitted on 13 February 1991 by J Humble

Material: animal bone (boar tusk): *Sus* sp. (A Foxon 1991)

Initial comment: this sample is one of 27 items deposited as grave goods with primary inhumation 6410 in barrow 1. The grave goods were tightly grouped by the feet of the partly disarticulated skeleton. The burial was in a pit at the centre of the barrow and had been 'roofed' with some form of timber structure and overlain with a cairn comprised of limestone and over 200 cattle skulls. Collapse of the timber structure resulted in the cairn subsiding into the burial pit, causing movement but no contamination.

Objectives: to refine a date for the deposition of the primary inhumation and associated grave goods.

Calibrated date: *1σ:* 2880–2490 cal BC
             2σ: 2900–2460 cal BC

Final comment: J Humble (2 June 1993), the date is the earliest in the series and does not overlap with the calibrated determination on the human burial UB-3148 at 95% confidence. It appears that upon deposition, the tusk was of considerable antiquity, and thus of no value in refining the chronology for the other grave goods.

UB–3147 3504 ±38 BP

δ¹³C: -22.1 ±0.2‰

Sample: 291-6409, submitted in 1989 by N Balaam

Material: human bone (adult male) (J Henderson 1989)

Initial comment: this sample is an adult skeleton, which was recovered from a deep steep-sided grave, pit located 4.5m north-north-east of the centre of barrow 1. A bone pin (no. 38143) was found close by the hands.

Objectives: to attempt to identify a chronology for the burials and to test contemporarily with the cairn of cattle skulls.

Calibrated date: *1σ:* 1890–1750 cal BC
             2σ: 1940–1690 cal BC

Final comment: J Harding and F Healy (2007), the date confirms this was a secondary burial.

UB–3148 3681 ±47 BP

δ¹³C: -21.0 ±0.2‰

Sample: 291-6410, submitted in 1989 by N Balaam

Material: human bone (J Henderson 1989)

Initial comment: primary inhumation from barrow 1. Burial and grave goods, including a Beaker vessel, were found on the floor of a large central grave pit. A timber structure was constructed over the pit, *see* OxA-4067. The skeleton was partially disarticulated and the mandible was missing. It is unclear whether the burial was disarticulated when deposited or subsequently disturbed if the coffin was left open for a period.

Objectives: to compare with animal bones from overlying cairn. The bone fragments are too small for conventional radiocarbon dating so are to be dated separately by AMS.

Calibrated date: *1σ:* 2140–1980 cal BC
             2σ: 2210–1930 cal BC

Final comment: Harding and Healy (2007), this provides a date for the primary burial. The measurements on the skeleton and on the sapwood from the chamber are statistically consistent, and the date of the construction of the mound is estimated as *2140-1800 cal BC at 95% probability* (Harding and Healy 2007, 163).

References: Harding and Healy 2007, 163

Raunds prehistoric: Irthlingborough skulls, Northamptonshire

Location: SP 96247127
                 Lat. 52.19.50 N; Long. 00.35.15 W

Project manager: C Halpin (Central Excavation Unit), 1986

Archival body: English Heritage

Description: barrow 1 at Irthlingborough was one of a group of barrows and other monuments on the floodplain of the Nene. A bone deposit found in a round barrow overlying a rich Beaker-period burial contained at least 184 domestic cattle skulls and one aurochs skull, but very few other cattle bones or bones of other animals. Most of the cattle were young adults. The relative scarcity of premolars suggests that they were deposited on the cairn some time after death.

Objectives: to provide a date for the skulls, discover if they are contemporaneous, and compare the dates with that of the Beaker burial.

References: Davis 1993
                 Hedges *et al* 1990, 222
                 Parry 2006, 34

OxA–2084 3610 ±110 BP

δ¹³C: -21.0‰ (assumed)

Sample: AOR 34628R, submitted in 1989 by S Davis

Material: animal bone: *Bos* sp., cattle tooth

Initial comment: the bone deposit was up to 0.8m thick and covered an area of 10–15² metres, and contained abundant cattle teeth and bone fragments. Loss from ploughing and the construction of an anthrax pit means that the original deposit may have been somewhat larger. Most of the teeth are from maxillae (upper jaws). They and the other bones were scattered at random, but their distributions form a single cluster over and around the grave.

Objectives: to establish a date for the sample and to try and establish whether samples OxA-2084–7 are contemporary.

Calibrated date: *1σ:* 2140–1780 cal BC
             2σ: 2290–1680 cal BC

Final comment: S Davis (1990), the spread of dates for OxA-2084–7 is slightly wider than might be expected for a single event. In general terms though these dates confirm the Beaker period age of the burial, the cattle, and the aurochs bones.

Laboratory comment: English Heritage (12 February 2012), the four measurements on cattle skulls from this barrow are not statistically consistent at 95% confidence (T'=10.9; T'(5%)=7.8; ν=3; Ward and Wilson 1978).

References: Ward and Wilson 1978

OxA–2085 4040 ±80 BP

$\delta^{13}C$: -21.0‰ (assumed)

Sample: AOR 34873R, submitted in 1989 by S Davis

Material: animal bone: *Bos taurus*, tooth

Initial comment: as OxA-2084

Objectives: as OxA-2084

Calibrated date: 1σ: 2840–2470 cal BC
2σ: 2880–2340 cal BC

Final comment: see OxA-2084

OxA–2086 3810 ±80 BP

$\delta^{13}C$: -21.0‰ (assumed)

Sample: AOR 34873L, submitted in 1989 by S Davis

Material: animal bone: *Bos taurus*, tooth

Initial comment: as OxA-2084

Objectives: as OxA-2084

Calibrated date: 1σ: 2460–2130 cal BC
2σ: 2480–2020 cal BC

Final comment: see OxA-2084

OxA–2087 3810 ±80 BP

$\delta^{13}C$: -21.0‰ (assumed)

Sample: AOR 35082R, submitted in 1989 by S Davis

Material: animal bone: *Bos* sp., tooth

Initial comment: as OxA-2084

Objectives: as OxA-2084

Calibrated date: 1σ: 2460–2130 cal BC
2σ: 2480–2020 cal BC

Final comment: see OxA-2084

Raunds prehistoric: peat profile, Northamptonshire

Location: SP 975728, SP 973724, and SP 969723
Lat. 52.20.38 N; Long. 00.34.08 W,
Lat. 52.20.25 N; Long. 00.34.19 W,
Lat. 52.20.22 N; Long 00.34.40 W

Project manager: A G Brown (Leicester University), 1987

Archival body: Northampton Museum

Description: the floodplain of the River Nene within the Raunds Project area comprises a block of the valley floor up to 1km wide, running for about 3.5km along the eastern bank of the present channel of the river (Harding and Healy 2007, 19). This series of radiocarbon dates on monolith cores from palaeochannels was taken to reconstruct local environmental sequences. The samples derive from the base of pollen columns from three palaeochannel fragments in the floodplain.

Objectives: preliminary study has shown a good pollen sequence probably beginning in the late prehistoric period and running continuously to the present. Radiocarbon dates will help to place the samples within a firm chronology, help to date the channel abandonment, and provide a basal date for a pollen profile and macrofossil column.

Laboratory comment: Ancient Monuments Laboratory (9 October 2003), one further sample RAPWCTI (HAR-9240) was submitted for dating but failed to produce a result.

References: Hardiman *et al* 1992, 68–9
Harding and Healy 2007

HAR–9241 4300 ±150 BP

$\delta^{13}C$: -31.6‰

Sample: RAPCI, submitted on 9 June 1988 by A G Brown

Material: sediment (organic mud with wood) (A G Brown 1987)

Initial comment: from a palaeochannel sampled from the floodplain in the Raunds Survey area. The channel pre-dates forest clearance, with high alder, relatively high hazel (Coryloid pollen which can be assumed to be hazel in this environment), low herbs, and no introduced species (Brown in Parry 2006, 28). Basal 5cm from a monolith from a small exposed section through the palaeochannel.

Objectives: to date palaeochannel abandonment and to provide a basal age for the pollen profile.

Calibrated date: 1σ: 3100–2700 cal BC
2σ: 3370–2490 cal BC

Final comment: J Harding and F Healy (2007), this sample dates the palaeochannel abandonment to the late Neolithic and provides a basal age for the pollen profile which suggests a very different picture downstream from the West Cotton monuments (Harding and Healy 2007, 23).

References: Harding and Healy 2007, 23
Parry 2006, 28 and 32

HAR–9242 1970 ±80 BP

$\delta^{13}C$: -29.9‰

Sample: RAPDI, submitted on 9 June 1988 by A G Brown

Material: sediment (organic mud with fragile shells) (A G Brown 1987)

Initial comment: from basal 5cm from a monolith taken from an excavation trench (no. B139) cut across a palaeochannel on the Nene floodplain. The depth below the trench step is 167–172cm, monoliths were taken in the middle of the palaeochannel and the trench was cut into terrace gravels.

Objectives: to date palaeochannel abandonment and provide a basal date for the pollen profile. This should provide a reliable *terminus post quem* date.

Calibrated date: *1σ:* 50 cal BC–cal AD 130
                      2σ: 180 cal BC–cal AD 240

Final comment: A G Brown (1996), the result should provide a reliable *post terminum* date of palaeochannel abandonment.

HAR–9243 9370 ±170 BP

δ¹³C: -31.6‰

Sample: RAPEI, submitted on 9 June 1988 by A G Brown

Material: sediment (organic mud and peat with wood) (A G Brown 1987)

Initial comment: basal 5cm from a monolith collected from a trench (no. B141) cut across a palaeochannel on the Nene floodplain. The trench was within 100m of the Neolithic/Bronze Age land surface in the alluvium. The sample was from 26–21m from the base of the trench, 2.47m below the floodplain surface.

Objectives: to date the abandonment of the palaeochannel and to provide a basal age for the pollen profile.

Calibrated date: *1σ:* 8830–8340 cal BC
                      2σ: 9240–8270 cal BC

Final comment: J Harding and F Healy (2007), gravel aggradation had ceased and an anastomosing (multiple cross-linked) system of relatively stable channels had become established just before the start of the Flandrian (ie shortly before 10,100 BP, *c* 9700 cal BC). Channel E (in trench B141), which was only traced for a short length, was abandoned in the early Flandrian according to this radiocarbon date from the organic sediments from the bottom (Harding and Healy 2007, 19).

References: Harding and Healy 2007, 19
                Parry 2006, 31

Raunds prehistoric: South Stanwick, Northamptonshire

Location: SP 972716
               Lat. 52.20.01 N; Long. 00.34.24 W

Project manager: F Blore (Central Archaeological Service), 1992

Archival body: Northampton Museum

Description: excavation of the Iron Age and Roman settlement at Stanwick as part of the Raunds Area Project led to the discovery of Neolithic and Bronze Age features. Most notably a Neolithic causewayed ring ditch and an early Bronze Age barrow. An extensive system of ditched enclosures and droveways with associated post-built structures was also uncovered. Trial trenching undertaken in order to recover dating evidence revealed further settlement activity, and subsequent stripping of the area uncovered the previously undiscovered avenue and segmented-ditch circle monuments.

Objectives: to date the unique monuments uncovered during the course of the project, and to add to the sparse dating evidence available for this period from this area.

References: Harding and Healy 2007

GU–5316 3570 ±70 BP

δ¹³C: -22.6‰

Sample: 291-91805, submitted on 11 March 1993 by F Blore

Material: antler: *Cervus elaphus* (S Davis 1992)

Initial comment: the antler was recovered from the very base of the pit-ring cut. The pit-ring was constructed from a series of sub-oval pits forming an unbroken circular ditch. The original pits appeared to have been excavated all at the same time. The antlers were the only artefacts found from the base. The whole feature appeared to have been backfilled with burnt material shortly after it had been constructed.

Objectives: both the pit-ring and associated avenue are unique features to this area. Comparable sites elsewhere appear to be Neolithic in date. Little dating evidence was found so any information regarding date would be invaluable.

Calibrated date: *1σ:* 2030–1780 cal BC
                      2σ: 2140–1740 cal BC

Final comment: J Harding and F Healy (2007), the two antler picks, from within and on the surface of the primary silt, provide two statistically consistent measurements (GU-5316 and -5317), which give an estimated date for the construction of the circle of *2020–1680 cal BC at 95% probability* (Harding and Healy 2007, 147).

Final comment: J Humble (17 December 1993), GU-5316 and GU-5317 were obtained from *Cervus elaphus* antler in the fill of the pits making up the pit ring. If these two very close determinations date the main period of monument use, they are somewhat later than anticipated. The best parallel for this monument is the classic group of segmented ditch circles at Dorchester, Oxfordshire; although many of the other Dorchester monuments have radiocarbon dates, the segmented ditch circles do not. These dates are exciting because the pit-ring appears to represent a non-round barrow early Bronze Age tradition of monument building and the only substantiated example from Raunds. If the dates on the avenue are correct, there is a very long time gap between the avenue and the pit-ring indicating continuity of 'presence' for the avenue, perhaps supporting the notion that the avenue was of episodic construction. As the pit-ring is bisected by the long barrow-Cotton Henge alignment, the argument for continuity in the significance of the alignment is also supported. In this context it is relevant to note the round barrow on the alignment to the south-west of the long barrow.

References: Harding and Healy 2007, 147

GU–5317 3560 ±70 BP

δ¹³C: -22.9‰

Sample: 291-91806, submitted on 11 March 1993 by
F Blore

Material: antler: *Cervus elaphus* (S Davis 1992)

Initial comment: as GU-5316. This antler was found to the
eastern edge of the pit-ring at the very base of the cut. Again
in this area it was very apparent that the ditch had been
backfilled very shortly after it had been constructed.

Objectives: as GU-5316

Calibrated date: *1σ:* 2020–1770 cal BC
                     2σ: 2140–1690 cal BC

Final comment: see GU-5317

GU–5318 5090 ±60 BP

δ¹³C: -23.7‰

Sample: 291-99228, submitted on 11 March 1993 by
F Blore

Material: charcoal: *Quercus* sp. (G Campbell 1992)

Initial comment: the sample was taken from a section face of
the segment cut through the avenue ditch. This avenue
consisted of two parallel lines of segmented ditch lengths
plus various sized treeholes. The avenue leads up to and is
cut by a circular pit-ring. No finds were recovered from
the ditch lengths or treeholes, but fills of the ditch were
full of burnt material, some of which may well have been
burnt *in situ*.

Objectives: both the avenue and associated circular pit-ring
are unique features to this area's excavation. No finds were
recovered but comparable sites elsewhere appear to be
Neolithic in date. Any information regarding the date of
this activity is vital to our understanding of the prehistory
in this area.

Calibrated date: *1σ:* 3970–3790 cal BC
                     2σ: 4040–3710 cal BC

Final comment: J Humble (17 December 1993), GU-5318
and GU-5319 are two early Neolithic dates from the avenue,
and much earlier than anticipated. These are interesting
because they are the earliest dates from deposits integral to
any of the Raunds monuments, albeit they are close to the
turf mound and the long barrow dates. The avenue
represents the only non-mounded early Neolithic
monument. In view of the long barrow-avenue-Cotton
Henge alignment, they add support to the notion that
Cotton Henge, or a precursor to Cotton Henge, existed at a
very early date. This was already suggested, of course, by the
orientation of the long mound.

GU–5319 4990 ±110 BP

δ¹³C: -24.6‰

Sample: 291-99251, submitted on 11 March 1993 by
F Blore

Material: charcoal: *Quercus* sp. (G Campbell 1992)

Initial comment: as GU-5318. Many rootlets were evident
within the charcoal. Some attempt has been made to
remove these.

Objectives: as GU-5318

Calibrated date: *1σ:* 3960–3650 cal BC
                     2σ: 4040–3530 cal BC

Final comment: see GU-5319

GU–5320 2990 ±50 BP

δ¹³C: -24.6‰

Sample: 291-80523, submitted on 11 March 1993 by
F Blore

Material: charcoal: *Fraxinus* sp. (G Campbell 1990)

Initial comment: the charcoal sample comes from a burnt
stake found *in situ* within a shallow (30cm depth) circular
posthole. This posthole was part of a possible fence line
associated with a circle of postholes, which has been
interpreted as a hut circle.

Objectives: only a few sherds of pottery were recovered from
all the postholes in this area. The pot has been identified as
Bronze Age in character. Generally there is a dearth of
datable artefacts from possible prehistoric features in this
area. A date from this posthole will give us a clearer
impression of the date of this activity in this area.

Calibrated date: *1σ:* 1320–1120 cal BC
                     2σ: 1400–1050 cal BC

Final comment: J Humble (17 December 1993), a good middle
Bronze Age date. The sample was taken from a posthole
forming part of the fence line, seemingly associated with the
hut, which appeared to be contemporary with the field system.
The association maybe slightly tenuous, but barring some flints
and a couple of pieces of pot, it provides the only dating for
what appears to represent a fundamental change in the land
use. The determination is entirely in keeping with those
obtained from the comparable field system and huts at Fengate.

Raunds prehistoric: Stanwick, Redlands Farm, Northamptonshire

Location: SP 965710
                  Lat. 52.19.42 N; Long. 00.35.02 W

Project manager: M Robinson (University Museum,
                  Oxford), 1989

Archival body: Northampton Museum

Description: a long barrow.

Objectives: to date the construction of the long barrow; to
establish whether its construction fell within the date range
of the other earlier Neolithic monuments on the valley
bottom of the River Nene which comprise the ritual complex
in the Raunds area; to show whether the organic sediments
in the southern barrow ditch belonged to the early life of the
barrow; to date the secondary use of the monument as a
focus for cremation burial; and finally to establish whether
this secondary use fell within the date range of the Bronze
Age round barrow cemetery in the valley bottom.

Final comment: M Robinson (1993), all the objectives are satisfactorily achieved by these results.

References: Harding and Healy 2007
Hedges *et al* 1993, 157–8
Whittle *et al* 2011, 300-14

OxA–2989 3320 ±80 BP

δ¹³C: -27.2‰

Sample: ST 126, submitted on 25 January 1991 by M Robinson

Material: charcoal: *Quercus* sp. (M Robinson 1991)

Initial comment: the sample was comprised charcoal from a cremation, which had been inserted into the top of the barrow.

Objectives: to show whether the reuse of the monument corresponded to the Bronze Age construction of the barrow cemetery at Irthlingborough and West Cotton.

Calibrated date: 1σ: 1730–1500 cal BC
2σ: 1870–1430 cal BC

Final comment: M Robinson (1993), OxA-2989 comes from a cremation of the north-east of the long barrow. It provides a middle Bronze Age date for the cremations and indeed falls within the range of dates for the use of the round barrows eg Raunds: Irthlingborough, OxA-3052.

OxA–3001 4810 ±80 BP

δ¹³C: -26.0‰ (assumed)

Sample: ST 128, submitted on 25 January 1991 by M Robinson

Material: waterlogged plant macrofossils (seeds; 12 species identified, submerged aquatics excluded) (M Robinson 1991)

Initial comment: waterlogged seeds from the top of the permanently waterlogged organic sediments in the barrow ditch.

Objectives: to provide a date for the top of the column being subjected to full-scale environmental analysis; pollen, seeds, and insects. At present, there is no evidence for the rate of sedimentation.

Calibrated date: 1σ: 3660–3520 cal BC
2σ: 3760–3370 cal BC

Final comment: M Robinson (1993), OxA-3001 and OxA-3002 show the organic sediments of the barrow ditch, which are being subjected to detailed palaeoecological analyses and contain two scarab beetles now extinct in Britain, *Caccobius schreberi* and *Valgus hemipterus*, belong to the earlier Neolithic.

OxA–3002 4560 ±140 BP

δ¹³C: -26.0‰ (assumed)

Sample: ST 131, submitted on 25 January 1991 by M Robinson

Material: waterlogged plant macrofossils (seeds; 13 species all identified, aquatics excluded) (M Robinson 1991)

Initial comment: waterlogged seeds from the earliest, permanently waterlogged sediments in the bottom of the ditch.

Objectives: to provide a date for the bottom of the column being subjected to full-scale environmental analysis; pollen, seeds, and insects.

Calibrated date: 1σ: 3520–3020 cal BC
2σ: 3650–2900 cal BC

Final comment: M Robinson (1993), the result from OxA-3002 is 200 years younger than might have been expected given OxA-3001 and OxA-3003. However, once the dates are calibrated, it is possible to construct the following sequence which all fits within the one sigma range and has plausible sedimentation rates: outermost rings of oak plank laid down in *c* 3525 cal BC, revetment collapses and earliest organic deposits form in *c* 3500 cal BC, and uppermost organic deposits form in *c* 3400–3450 cal BC. *See also* OxA-3001.

OxA–3003 4790 ±90 BP

δ¹³C: -26.0‰ (assumed)

Sample: ST 140, submitted on 25 January 1991 by M Robinson

Material: wood (waterlogged): *Quercus* sp., outer rings of plank (M Robinson 1991)

Initial comment: the sample consisted of numerous oak planks which had collapsed from the barrow revetment into the organic sediments at the bottom of the ditch.

Objectives: to date the structure of the barrow itself and to show whether, as suspected, the earliest organic sediments in the ditch (ST131) were almost contemporaneous with the construction of the monument.

Calibrated date: 1σ: 3660–3380 cal BC
2σ: 3760–3360 cal BC

Final comment: M Robinson (1993), the early Neolithic date of OxA-3003 falls within the range of those obtained from other earlier Neolithic monuments, eg Raunds: West Cotton, (UB-3313 and UB-3317).

References: Parry 2006, 32

Raunds prehistoric: West Cotton, barrow 6, Northamptonshire

Location: SP 97607256
Lat. 52.20.30 N; Long. 00.34.02 W

Project manager: D Windell and A Chapman (Northamptonshire County Council Archaeological Unit), 1987

Archival body: Northampton Museum

Description: barrow 6 was a complex, multi-phase round barrow, with three concentric ditches, each associated with a mound. The first ditch may have been centred on a pre-existing tree, perhaps in conjunction with a large open pit immediately to the north-west. The Beaker grave truncated the tree throw hollow at its eastern end, suggesting that the tree was no longer present. The main burial, of a male crouched on his left side, contained many grave goods. Under the grave there was a small pit containing the disarticulated remains of a male and another individual. There is evidence that the bones had been exhumed from elsewhere after partial decomposition. The initial mound was of turf and topsoil, and appears to have closely followed the Beaker burial. The middle ditch was then cut around the mound, which was extended, incorporating the extracted gravel over the heavily silted inner ditch. A large postpit was dug into the upper fills of this ditch. The final, outer, ditch was *c* 31m in diameter. A further arc on the eastern side formed part of this enclosure, although interrupted by a causeway on either side where the outer ditch intersected with the Ditched Enclosure, suggesting that the latter's internal bank was visible and deliberately respected. Topsoil, probably from the outer ditch and berm, was dumped around the mound perimeter, which was then gravel-capped. Two infant cremations (one beneath a small Collared Urn) were inserted into secondary fills of the outer ditch, and an adult cremation in a Collared Urn was buried in the berm, all in the area shared with the ditched enclosure. Prior to ploughing there was deliberate backfilling of parts of the outer ditch.

Objectives: to date the burial sequence within barrow 6.

Final comment: A Bayliss and F Healy (2011), a bone from one of two incomplete disarticulated skeletons in a grave beneath the primary burial of the barrow was dated by *UB-3310* to *3360–3090 cal BC at 95% probability*. Around a thousand years later, the primary burial was made, an event which would have been almost immediately followed by the construction of the first mound and ditch. The articulated skeleton, which was accompanied by a Beaker and elaborate grave goods, is dated to *2140–2080 cal BC at 14% probability* or *2050–1890 cal BC at 82% probability* (*UB-3311*). Pomoideae charcoal fragments from a stakehole in a cremation pit cut into the silted outer ditch (*OxA-7866*) are later than the construction of the mound, and provide an estimate for the date of the cremation of *2030–1870 cal BC at 89% probability*. The charcoal seems to have formed part of the surrounding cremation and to have fallen into the stakehole together with fragments of cremated bone after the stake had decayed. It is likely to be close in age to the cremation. Material from the second dated cremation from this ditch was mature oak and so provides only a *terminus post quem* of *1750–1490 cal BC at 95% probability* (*UB-3315*) (Bayliss *et al* 2011, fig SS6.11).

References: Bayliss *et al* 2011
                      Harding and Healy 2007
                      Windell *et al* 1990

UB–3310 4500 ±33 BP

$\delta^{13}C$: -21.1 ±0.2‰

Sample: Unit 3390, submitted on 14 February 1990 by D Windell

Material: human bone (S Mays)

Initial comment: disarticulated human bone representing two individuals found in a pit sealed beneath the primary Beaker burial of barrow 6. Presumed reinterment from elsewhere and thus pre-dating the primary burial of barrow 6.

Objectives: one of a series of samples to date the stratified sequence in barrow 6.

Calibrated date: *1σ:* 3350–3090 cal BC
                            2σ: 3360–3030 cal BC

Final comment: S Parry (2006), this result indicates that the two disarticulated burials were a thousand years older than the burial placed above them (UB-3311), and is a possible example of ancestor rites.

References: Parry 2006, 45

UB–3311 3608 ±41 BP

$\delta^{13}C$: -22.3 ±0.2‰

Sample: Unit 3259, submitted on 14 February 1990 by D Windell

Material: human bone (S Mays)

Initial comment: human bone from primary Beaker inhumation of barrow 6. The turf mound of the barrow partly stood *c* 0.3m immediately over the burial. The mound had been mainly removed by Saxon and medieval activity, but this had not disturbed the grave at all.

Objectives: as UB-3310

Calibrated date: *1σ:* 2030–1900 cal BC
                            2σ: 2130–1880 cal BC

Final comment: see UB-3310

UB–3315 3347 ±54 BP

$\delta^{13}C$: -27.0 ±0.2‰

Sample: SAMPLE 47; Unit 3206, submitted on 14 February 1990 by D Windell

Material: charcoal: *Quercus* sp., mainly; no twiggy material (G Campbell)

Initial comment: from a pit cutting the secondary fills and sealed by the final fills of the outer ditch of barrow 6 (F3177). The fill comprised of a grey/black loam with frequent fragments of charcoal and a small amount of cremated bone. The pit lay *c* 0.9m from F3219, the miniature Urn covering the cremated bone, which was stratigraphically contemporary.

Objectives: the sample dates the third phase of barrrow 6 and is also associated stratigraphically with the miniature Urn and cremation.

Calibrated date: *1σ:* 1730–1530 cal BC
                            2σ: 1760–1500 cal BC

Final comment: J Harding and F Healy (2006), material from F3206, the second dated cremation burial from this ditch, was mature oak, and so provides a *terminus post quem*.

References: Harding and Healy 2007, 135

Raunds prehistoric: West Cotton, long enclosure, Northamptonshire

Location: SP 97547245
Lat. 52.20.27 N; Long. 00.34.06 W

Project manager: D Windell (Northamptonshire County Council Archaeology Unit), 1986

Archival body: Northampton Museum

Description: the long enclosure at West Cotton measured 117m long by 17m wide internally, was oriented south-west to north-east, and was defined by a single and probably continuous ditch. The northernmost 26m of the enclosed area lay within the area of total excavation. To the south of this area, the two sides and the southern end of the ditch were located by machine-cut trial trenches. The ditch fills indicated the former presence of internal banks along the sides, and episodes of localised recutting. The only artefacts were a sparse scatter of struck flint, without pottery. A red deer antler rake and two cattle bones were recovered from the primary ditch fills. There were no archaeological features within the excavated part of the enclosed area, although there were two tree-hollows.

Objectives: to date the sequence within the long enclosure.

Final comment: A Bayliss and F Healy (2011), the two measurements (UB-3308 and UB-3312) are statistically consistent (T'=0.6, T'(5%)=3.8, v=1; Ward and Wilson 1978). The samples were respectively 0.1m and 0.15m above the base of the ditch in gravel primary silts. It seems probable that the antler was used to build the enclosure, in which case it is likely to be close in age to its construction. Because of the large error term on UB-3308, which was a very small sample, *UB-3312*, made on the antler rake, is preferred as a more robust estimate for the date of construction. This is *3350–2890 cal BC at 95% probability* (Bayliss *et al* 2011, fig SS6.9).

References: Bayliss *et al* 2011
Harding and Healy 2011
Ward and Wilson 1978

UB–3308 4278 ±156 BP

δ¹³C: -28.4 ±0.2‰

Sample: Sample 32; Unit 2102, submitted on 14 February 1990 by D Windell

Material: animal bone: *Bos* sp., proximal tibia (S Davis)

Initial comment: from the primary fill of the eastern arm of the long enclosure ditch. The ditch cuts through the natural gravel to a depth of 1.10m and the sample was found near the base.

Objectives: although the bone has no functional relationship with the ditch construction, a date should be closely related to the use of the monument and date the earliest siltings of the enclosure ditch.

Calibrated date: 1σ: 3100–2660 cal BC
2σ: 3370–2470 cal BC

Final comment: J Harding and F Healy (2006), because of the very large error term on this measurement, which was a

very small sample, UB-3312 is preferred as a more robust estimate for the date of construction (Harding and Healy 2007, 98).

References: Harding and Healy 2007, 98

UB–3312 4411 ±77 BP

δ¹³C: -23.5 ±0.2‰

Sample: Sample 56; Unit 2102, submitted on 14 February 1990 by D Windell

Material: antler: *Cervus elaphus*, shed (S Davis)

Initial comment: the antler pick or rake was found in the base of the primary fill from the eastern arm of the long enclosure ditch.

Objectives: to date the construction and the use of the long enclosure monument.

Calibrated date: 1σ: 3320–2910 cal BC
2σ: 3360–2890 cal BC

Final comment: see UB-3308

UB–3324 3883 ±58 BP

δ¹³C: -26.1 ±0.2‰

Sample: SAMPLE 20; Unit 990, submitted on 14 February 1990 by D Windell

Material: charcoal: *?Quercus sp*, 20 years growth, rootlet penetration (G Campbell and M Robinson)

Initial comment: as UB-3320

Objectives: as UB-3320

Calibrated date: 1σ: 2470–2230 cal BC
2σ: 2570–2150 cal BC

Final comment: see UB-3320

Raunds prehistoric: West Cotton, long mound, Northamptonshire

Location: SP 97512725
Lat. 51.56.04 N; Long. 00.34.55 W

Project manager: D Windell (Northamptonshire County Council Archaeological Unit), 1987–9

Archival body: Northampton Museum

Description: the long mound was 135m long, and between 13m and 18m wide. It was aligned a few degrees north-east of true east-west. Almost exactly half of the mound was fully excavated. It was built of turf and incorporated struck flint, pottery, and animal bone. A pit beneath the probably pre-dated the construction of the mound by several centuries. It is suggested that initially the structure comprised regular bays defined by transverse and longitudinal stake lines along the northern and southern edges of a mound. At the eastern end there may have been a 'chamber' defined by stake lines and possibly flanked by open bays, with a forecourt and facade. Subsequently, a simple dumped mound with no bay structure was constructed beyond the easternmost stake line, the possible facade, with the 'chamber' area perhaps being covered by a low mound. Following the extension of the mound to its full length, a gully was cut around the top edge of the mound the fills of which contained quantities of burnt debris. At the eastern end stakes were set into the gully fill and may suggest the presence of some form of facade, which was probably refurbished at intervals. The mound was at least partially flanked by broad shallow 'quarry pits', although no material from these was used in the mound make-up, and they may have post-dated its construction.

Objectives: to date all the major phases of the monument.

Final comment: A Bayliss (2012), the dating of the long mound is problematic. It appears that the bulk charcoal samples may have contained differing proportions of intrusive charcoal from the overlying Saxon and medieval deposits. The interpretation of these dates is fully discussed by Bayliss *et al* (2011, 870–7).

Laboratory comment: English Heritage, eight further samples were dated from the long mound but submitted after March 1993 (Bayliss *et al* 2011, table SS6.1).

Laboratory comment: English Heritage (26 July 2012), one further sample (128 from unit 5549) failed to produce a result.

References: Bayliss *et al* 2011
                Harding and Healy 2007
                Harding and Healy 2011
                Windell *et al* 1990

UB–3313 4602 ±72 BP

$\delta^{13}C$: -26.1 ±0.2‰

Sample: Sample 28; Unit 2062, submitted on 14 February 1990 by D Windell

Material: charcoal: *Quercus* sp. (c 15g) (G Campbell)

Initial comment: the sample consists of a portion of carbonised oak plank from the surface on the long mound and relates to the refurbishment or reuse of the monument. The sample lay within 2062 and 2065, which formed either a capping containing gravel or the upper surface to the refurbished long mound.

Objectives: to date the refurbishment of the long mound.

Calibrated date: *1σ:* 3500–3190 cal BC
                      2σ: 3630–3090 cal BC

Final comment: J Harding and F Healy (2006), the measurement calibrates to the fourth millennium BC, unfortunately the oak was of unknown maturity, and so this measurement cannot be used as a *terminus ante quem* for the construction of the mound. As it was a plank, it may also have come from an earlier structure (Harding and Healy 2007, 63)

References: Harding and Healy 2007, 63

UB–3320 4417 ±75 BP

$\delta^{13}C$: -27.2 ±0.2‰

Sample: Sample 24; Unit 990, submitted on 14 February 1990 by D Windell

Material: charcoal: *?Quercus sp*, 10–20 years growth (G Campbell)

Initial comment: from a stake burnt *in situ* in the gully of the secondary facade of the long mound. The sample was located towards the east end of the mound, and was overlaid by Saxon-medieval strata.

Objectives: the stake formed part of the structure of the reformation of the long mound monument. The objective was to date this reformation.

Calibrated date: *1σ:* 3330–2910 cal BC
                      2σ: 3360–2890 cal BC

Final comment: J Harding and F Healy (2006), this result, plus four others measured from the gully, were not statistically consistent, and their calibrated date ranges cover well over a thousand years, thus making an estimation for the *terminus ante quem* for the long barrow mound construction problematic (Harding and Healy 2007, 63).

References: Harding and Healy 2007, 63

UB–3329 5767 ±58 BP

$\delta^{13}C$: -24.8 ±0.2‰

Sample: SAMPLE 139; Unit 5460, submitted on 14 February 1990 by D Windell

Material: charcoal: *Quercus* sp., trunk (G Campbell)

Initial comment: from a small pit sealed by the construction of the long mound. The sample was located towards the western end of the excavated part of the mound and it was sealed under a turf/topsoil construction of mound but cut into the relict soil under the mound.

Objectives: the sample was from a pit, which proceeded, and probably immediately proceeded, the construction of the first phase of the long mound.

Calibrated date: *1σ:* 4710–4540 cal BC
                      2σ: 4770–4460 cal BC

Final comment: J Harding and F Healy (2006), this fifth millennium date provides a *terminus post quem* for the construction of the west and central parts of the mound, in which there was at least one fragment of Neolithic Bowl pottery (Hatrding and Healy 2007, 62).

References: Harding and Healy 2007, 62

UB–3417 4795 ±71 BP

$\delta^{13}C$: -24.6 ±0.2‰

Sample: S.127, submitted on 21 February 1991 by D Windell

Material: charcoal: *Quercus* sp., stake (G Campbell)

Initial comment: from a stake burnt *in situ* in the gully of the long mound. The sample was located at the western end of the monument within recognisable fill of the gully, extracted during excavation of that fill.

Objectives: to date this structural element of the western part of the long mound.

Calibrated date: *1σ:* 3650–3520 cal BC
                      2σ: 3710–3370 cal BC

Final comment: see UB-3320

Raunds prehistoric: West Cotton, palaeochannel and riverine structure, Northamptonshire

Location: SP 97552726
                Lat. 51.56.04 N; Long. 00.34.52 W

Project manager: D Windell (Northamptonshire County
                Council Archaeology Unit), 1987–8

Archival body: Northampton Museum

Description: deposits of brushwood and alder trunks which lay at the southern edge of the earliest of a long sequence of palaeochannels have been interpreted as a constructed platform. The brushwood platform, which extended several metres into the river channel, was formed of smaller wood and some trunk timbers, apparently derived largely from the clearance of the tree cover along the adjacent riverside. Dumps of gravel, clay, and further brushwood were used to retain and consolidate the platform, which was overlain towards its outer edge by larger trunks. No artefacts were recovered from these deposits but direct evidence of human activity was provided by axe marks, split trunks, and the trimmed ends of some trunks. The final form of the platform is unknown. The consolidated platform would have lain below water level and probably provided a shallow water shelf adjacent to the riverside. At the outer edge the larger trunks probably acted as a revetment for the main platform. However, it is possible that these larger trunks had also supported further timbers which may have formed a raised platform standing above water-level. In this form the effect might have been of an 'island' set several metres from the riverside. The excavated area lay at the eastern end of the structure and its extent to the west is unknown. The wood and associated waterlogged deposits have produced a wealth of environmental evidence. Deposits of animal and human bone lay within the gravels and silts forming and overlying the platform. A direct association with the adjacent monuments is suspected, the platform having a ritual function. Most speculatively, it can be suggested that the intention was to create a ritual island, the bone deposits being the results of the dumping of feasting debris.

Objectives: to date the riverine deposits and structures.

Final comment: A Bayliss and F Healy (2011), a stratigraphic sequence is formed by UB-3419 from a lens of clay and sand containing tightly packed wood debris within the underlying natural gravels, and by UB-3321 and UB-3319 from the structure itself. The estimated date for the construction of the riverine structure is *2870–2800 cal BC at 13% probability* or *2760–2470 cal BC at 82% probability* (*Riverside Structure*; Bayliss *et al* 2011, fig SS6.10).

References: Bayliss *et al* 2011
                Harding and Healy 2011

UB–3319 3990 ±54 BP

$\delta^{13}C$: -29.2 ±0.2‰

Sample: SAMPLE 146; 147; Unit 6765, submitted on 14 February 1990 by D Windell

Material: wood (waterlogged): *Corylus/Alnus* sp., ?50+ years (G Campbell)

Initial comment: sample from one of two 7m long trunks laid on top of a brushwood platform and partially sealed by

subsequent deposits of brushwood. The timbers were found *in situ* within the Nene palaeochannel beneath the ancient and modern water tables. The timber was sealed by later water deposited clays and gravels.

Objectives: to date the Neolithic riverine structure.

Calibrated date: 1σ: 2580–2460 cal BC
                  2σ: 2830–2340 cal BC

Final comment: J Harding and F Healy (2007), a stratigraphic sequence is formed by dates on a sample of hazel or alder from the underlying gravels (UB-3419), an ash pole from the base of the structure (UB-3321), and the inner alder trunk (UB-3319).

Laboratory comment: University of Belfast (31 May 1990), this sample was bleached.

References: Harding and Healy 2007, 115
                Parry 2006, 32

UB–3321 4062 ±54 BP

$\delta^{13}C$: -27.7 ±0.2‰

Sample: SAMPLE 163; Unit 7141, submitted on 14 February 1990 by D Windell

Material: wood (waterlogged): *Fraxinus* sp., outer rings available, *c* 10years (G Campbell)

Initial comment: sample from one of several long poles *c* 1m at the base of the brushwood platform of the the the riverside/riverine structure which lay on a gritty water-lain sand deposit which directly overlies the natural gravel of the river bank.

Objectives: to date the probably Neolithic riverine structure.

Calibrated date: 1σ: 2840–2490 cal BC
                  2σ: 2870–2470 cal BC

Final comment: see UB-3319

Laboratory comment: see UB-3319

References: Parry 2006, 28 and 32

UB–3419 4268 ±32 BP

$\delta^{13}C$: -29.0 ±0.2‰

Sample: length of branch, palaeochannel, submitted on 21 February 1991 by D Windell

Material: wood (waterlogged): *Corylus/Alnus* sp. (G Campbell)

Initial comment: the sample was found in a localised lens of clay, which provides the earliest datable context in the riverside sequence. It was sealed by *c* 0.15m of clean calcareous gravel, which in turn was sealed by the brushwood of the late Neolithic timber platform.

Objectives: to provide a date for the earliest organic deposit within the palaeochannel sequence.

Calibrated date: 1σ: 2910–2880 cal BC
                  2σ: 2920–2870 cal BC

Final comment: see UB-3319

Laboratory comment: University of Belfast (14 March 1991), this sample was pretreated using the acid based acid protocol.

Raunds prehistoric: West Cotton, turf mound, Northamptonshire

Location:	SP 97477236
	Lat. 52.20.29 N; Long. 00.34.10 W
Project manager:	A Chapman and D Windell
	(Northamptonshire County Council
	Archaeological Unit), 1987
Archival body:	Northampton Museum

Description: the turf mound was to the immediate north of barrow 2. Roughly circular in plan, of *c* 19m diameter, it stood to a height of 0.5m at the centre. A full understanding of the development of the monument was not possible because much of the evidence was obtained during a watching brief and salvage excavations. Part of the north-eastern end of the mound was fully excavated and the general outline of the monument's plan-form obtained within the quarry area. It consisted of a slightly elongated, unditched mound, onto the southern tail of which a later, ditched, subcircular mound was built. Fences were built, and burnt, in two gullies cut into the original north mound. Both mounds were of turf or turf and topsoil construction. A probable tree-hollow, containing a flint scatter including two leaf arrowheads, pre-dated the construction of the north mound. A pit containing a sherd of Grooved Ware or Beaker and a red deer antler underlay the south mound. There was no evidence that this pit had contained an inhumation burial. A scatter of Beaker sherds on top of the north mound and in a pit cut into it reflect activity perhaps contemporary with the construction of the south mound.

Objectives: to provide further evidence for the chronology and phasing of what was believed to be the earliest monument in the Raunds complex.

Final comment: A Bayliss and F Healy (2011), the gully which contained the samples for OxA-7865 (4975 ±35 BP), OxA-7945 (5035 ±35 BP), UB-3314, and UB-3317 was one of two cut into the northern part of the mound. All four measurements are statistically consistent (T'=6.7, T'(5%)=7.8, ν=3; Ward and Wilson 1978). The intervals between the construction of the mound and the cutting of two successive gullies can only be guessed at. If they were negligible, the mound would have been built in *3750–3620 at 77% probability or 3600–3520 cal BC at 18% probability (Turf Mound 1;* Bayliss *et al* 2011, fig SS6.8). A stake charred *in situ* can scarcely have been derived from an earlier context, and the consistency of all the dates reinforces the argument that a tightly defined concentration of Beaker pottery in the mound was in fact in a pit undetected at the time of excavation.

References:	Bayliss *et al* 2011
	Harding and Healy 2007
	Ward and Wilson 1978
	Windell *et al* 1990

UB–3314 4937 ±56 BP

δ¹³C: -24.1 ±0.2‰

Sample: Sample 99; Unit 6302, submitted on 14 February 1990 by D Windell

Material: charcoal: *Quercus* sp. (G Campbell)

Initial comment: a stake found *in situ* set within the fill of a shallow linear gully cut into the top of the turf mound. The gully fill included scattered charcoal associated with patches of reddened burnt sand. The top of the mound had been disturbed by ploughing, but the sample was sealed under alluvium.

Objectives: the sample represents the use of the gully on the turf mound.

Calibrated date:	*1σ:* 3780–3650 cal BC
	2σ: 3930–3630 cal BC

Final comment: J Harding and F Healy (2007), the stake had occupied a circular stakehole *c* 80mm in diameter, which strongly suggests that the stake was of fairly young wood and thus close in age to its insertion. A stake charred *in situ* can scarcely have derived from an earlier context, and the consistency of this and other measurements from the recut of the eastern gully, strongly suggests that the real age of the second fence in the estern gully is likely to be close to its estimated date of *3750-3620 cal BC at 77% probability or 3600–3520 cal BC at 18% probability* (Harding and Healy 2007, fig 3.68).

References:	Harding and Healy 2007, 72–3

UB–3317 4873 ±56 BP

δ¹³C: -24.8 ±0.2‰

Sample: SAMPLE 98; Unit 6302, submitted on 14 February 1990 by D Windell

Material: charcoal: *Quercus* sp., fragments (c 20g) (G Campbell)

Initial comment: fragments of charcoal from within the fill of the gully cut into the top of the turf mound.

Objectives: the charcoal is almost certainly associated with the filling of the gully and therefore with the cessation of use of the turf mound.

Calibrated date:	*1σ:* 3710–3630 cal BC
	2σ: 3780–3530 cal BC

Final comment: J Harding and F Healy (2007), one of several samples from the recut of the eastern gully. *See also* UB-3314.

Raunds: Burystead, Northamptonshire

Location:	TL 0017315
	Lat. 52.20.48 N; Long. 00.31.55 W
Project manager:	M Audouy (Northamptonshire County
	Council Archaeological Unit), 1987
Archival body:	Northamptonshire County Council
	Archaeology Unit

Description: part of the Raunds Area Project. Saxon and medieval features were excavated adjacent to the parish church, in addition to a small area to the north on the Midland Road frontage, which explored parts of the late medieval to post-medieval tenements (Audouy and Chapman 2009, 6). A large quantity of early–middle Saxon pottery, including imported middle Saxon wares, was recovered during the Burystead excavations, possibly enough to suggest it was more intensively occupied than the western stream bank during the middle Saxon period. Unfortunately, little pattern could be discerned in the features dated to this period, although both the features and the pottery distribution indicate that the centre of activity probably lay to the north-east, in an area largely destroyed by post-medieval stone quarrying (Audouy and Chapman 2009, 27).

Objectives: to provide a *terminus post quem* for the assemblage of middle Saxon pottery found in one of the features, and hence help to build a chronology for the site, and for the Raunds Area Project as a whole.

References: Audouy and Chapman 2009

UB–3420 1308 ±26 BP

δ¹³C: -25.4 ±0.2‰

Sample: BSTD 0376 S606, submitted on 15 February 1991 by D Windell

Material: wood (waterlogged): *Quercus* sp., trunk wood (G Campbell 1991)

Initial comment: the sample derived from the remains of oak planks used to line from the sides of a 1m-deep pit cut in clay. Although sub-circular in plan at the top, the pit tapered down into a rectangular section measuring 1.10m × 0.55m × 0.41m. The rectangular section only was lined with wood. The feature has been interpreted as a water pit. It is thought to be middle Saxon in date on the basis of the pottery assemblage contained in the backfill material. The pit and fill were sealed by the wall of a medieval dovecot with no intervening stratae.

Objectives: it is hoped that the results will provide a *terminus post quem* to the assemblage of middle Saxon Maxey type ware found in the backfill of the feature. This type of pottery, together with Ipswich Ware, are the only types datable to the middle Saxon period. The test will hopefully support their dating and will confirm the occurrence of such ceramics as being of chronological significance.

Calibrated date: 1σ: cal AD 660–770
2σ: cal AD 650–780

Final comment: M Audouy and A Chapman (2009), at Burystead occupation continued through the middle Saxon period, as indicated by the pottery, and confirmed by the radiocarbon date (Audouy and Chapman 2009, 52), which coincides with the first century of the 200 year currency of Maxey ware (Audouy and Chapman 2009, 60).

Laboratory comment: University of Belfast (25 March 1991), this sample was bleached.

References: Audouy and Chapman 2009
Parry 2006, 35

Raunds: West Cotton, medieval activity, Northamptonshire

Location: SP 976725
Lat. 52.20.49 N; Long. 00.34.03 W

Project manager: G Campbell (University Museum, Oxford), 1985–90

Archival body: Northampton Museum

Description: a palaeochannel adjacent to the deserted medieval village at West Cotton, which revealed a series of watermills and associated activity.

Objectives: to date flax retting activity in the palaeochannel and a series of watermills and associated activity.

Final comment: A Chapman (2010), the radiocarbon dates UB-3323 and OxA-4079 have demonstrated that the flax retting activity occurred in the middle Saxon period. It was probably a short-lived phase centred on the mid-eighth century, with the flax seeds and capsules in the silts being the debris from the retting.

References: Chapman 2010
Windell *et al* 1990

OxA–4079 1295 ±70 BP

δ¹³C: -27.8‰

Sample: WC85 BC5, submitted on 25 November 1992 by G Campbell

Material: waterlogged plant macrofossil (Flax seeds and capsules (*Limum usitatissimum* L.)) (G Campbell)

Initial comment: the sample was extracted from waterlogged black silty clay, which formed the bottom-most layer in the centre of a silted-up palaeochannel adjacent to the deserted medieval village of West Cotton. The deposit represents the onset of final infilling of the channel, which during the late Neolithic was much wider, and had a brushwood platform constructed on its southern bank.

Objectives: the sample will date the flax retting activity in the channel and determine whether or not this relates to activity on the adjacent site or is of early Saxon, late Saxon, or medieval date. It will also give a date for the existence of managed hay meadows in the vicinity of the site.

Calibrated date: 1σ: cal AD 650–780
2σ: cal AD 620–890

Final comment: A Chapman (2010), this date demonstrates that the flax retting activity in the channel occurred during the middle Saxon period.

UB–3322 1258 ±69 BP

δ¹³C: -30.3 ±0.2‰

Sample: SAMPLE 164; Unit 7323, submitted on 14 February 1990 by D Windell

Material: wood (waterlogged stake): *Corylus* sp., *c* 15–20 years growth (G Campbell)

Initial comment: from a stake lying at the base of a wheel pit of the earliest of the sequence of three mills. The sample was adjacent to the badly decayed remnants of a stake-and-wattle revetment of the wheel pit. The base of the wheel pit was surfaced with limestone and non-calcareous gravel. The fill of the pit was a dark grey clay-loam.

Objectives: to date the earliest phase of the watermill. By association the sample is also related to the introduction of the late Saxon manorial establishment.

Calibrated date: 1σ: cal AD 660–880
2σ: cal AD 640–950

Final comment: A Chapman (2010), this result suggests the stake was residual, or reused from some earlier activity. The result is statistically consistent with three radiocarbon measurements (UB-3323, -3328, and OxA-4079; T'=0.4; T'(5%)=7.8; ν=3; Ward and Wilson 1978) for stakes and flax retting within the river channel to the immediate north.

Laboratory comment: University of Belfast (26 July 2012), no record survives of whether this sample was pretreated using the acid based alkali protocol or was bleached.

References: Ward and Wilson 1978

UB–3323 1264 ±52 BP

$\delta^{13}C$: -28.1 ±0.2‰

Sample: Sample 165 Unit 7120, submitted on 14 February 1990 by D Windell

Material: wood: *Quercus* sp., *c* 25 years growth (G Campbell)

Initial comment: sample from a peg driven into, but not fully through a prehistoric alder trunk (*see* UB-3319). The top projected above the level of the trunk.

Objectives: to date the possibly Neolithic riverine structure.

Calibrated date: 1σ: cal AD 670–810
2σ: cal AD 650–890

Final comment: A Chapman (2010), this peg is not related to the Neolithic riverine structure, but is part of activity in the palaeochannel during the middle Saxon period, probably related to flax retting.

Laboratory comment: University of Belfast (26 April 1990), this sample was pretreated using the acid based acid protocol.

UB–3325 941 ±53 BP

$\delta^{13}C$: -26.4 ±0.2‰

Sample: SAMPLE 143; Unit 6644, submitted on 14 February 1990 by D Windell

Material: wood (waterlogged): *Quercus* sp., outer rings available; 30 years growth (G Campbell)

Initial comment: from a split trunk with mortice holes at either end found *in situ* at the base of the wheel pit of the third and final mill of the sequence.

Objectives: the sample is a structural timber from the third and final phase of the water mill. The outermost rings should relate closely to the construction date. There were insufficient rings to provide a dendrochronological date for the timber.

Calibrated date: 1σ: cal AD 1020–1170
2σ: cal AD 990–1220

Final comment: A Chapman (2010), the radiocarbon dates UB-3225-7, alongside the pottery evidence, indicate a construction date for the third watermill at around the middle of the eleventh century AD, with abandonment before the middle of the twelfth century AD. This would imply that this was the final, horizontal-wheeled mill that was in use both at the time of the Conquest and the Domesday Survey (Chapman 2010, 136).

Laboratory comment: University of Belfast (31 May 1990), this sample was bleached.

References: Parry 2006, 36

UB–3326 1086 ±29 BP

$\delta^{13}C$: -26.1 ±0.2‰

Sample: Sample 142; Unit 6665, submitted on 14 February 1990 by D Windell

Material: wood (waterlogged): *Quercus* sp., outer rings available; 40 years growth (G Campbell)

Initial comment: from an unworked branch or trunk set on, and slightly behind, a clay and limestone revetment of the latest phase of the watermill leat.

Objectives: the sample is from the third and final phase of the mill-leat revetment and should relate closely to construction of the third leat. There were insufficient rings to provide a dendrochronological date.

Calibrated date: 1σ: cal AD 890–1000
2σ: cal AD 890–1020

Final comment: A Chapman (2010), the unworked oak trunk from within the wheel pit revetment dates to the tenth century AD, and may be regarded as a residual timber (Chapman 2010, 136).

Laboratory comment: see UB-3325

UB–3327 1014 ±51 BP

$\delta^{13}C$: -26.5 ±0.2‰

Sample: SF 9075; unit 6691, submitted on 14 February 1990 by D Windell

Material: wood (waterlogged): *Quercus* sp., less than 10 years old (G Campbell)

Initial comment: from a post found *in situ* set in the gravel at the base of a postpit. Thought to be a minor post forming part of the sluice gate of the mill last in the sequence. The surrounding fills contained limestone rubble and therefore were somewhat calcareous.

Objectives: to date the final phase of the watermill.

Calibrated date: 1σ: cal AD 980–1040
2σ: cal AD 890–1160

Final comment: see UB-3325

Laboratory comment: see UB-3325

References: Parry 2006, 36

UB–3328 1297 ±49 BP

$\delta^{13}C$: -27.0 ±0.2‰

Sample: SF 9236; Unit 6778, submitted on 14 February 1990 by D Windell

Material: wood (waterlogged): *Quercus* sp., *c* 5 years growth (G Campbell)

Initial comment: as UB-3323

Objectives: as UB-3323

Calibrated date: *1σ:* cal AD 660–780
                    2σ: cal AD 640–870

Final comment: A Chapman (2010), this peg probably derived from a timber structure related to middle Saxon flax retting in the channel.

Laboratory comment: see UB-3325

UB–3418 1548 ±33 BP

δ¹³C: -25.5 ±0.2‰

Sample: SS 782; Unit 4952, submitted on 21 February 1991 by D Windell

Material: charcoal: *Corylus* sp. (G Campbell)

Initial comment: from the bottom fill (4952) of an early Saxon *Grubenhaus* and is associated with early Saxon ceramics. The sample is probably contemporary with the use of the Grubenhaus rather than the backfill.

Objectives: the sample is directly associated with the short-lived early Saxon occupation and associated poorly with ceramics dated AD 450–850 cal. A date would also make clear the relationship between the *Grubenhaus* and the riverine activity already dated.

Calibrated date: *1σ:* cal AD 430–560
                    2σ: cal AD 420–600

Final comment: A Chapman (2010), this radiocarbon date is compatible with the artefactual evidence from this structure.

Reawla, Cornwall

Location: SW 605363
                    Lat. 50.10.39 N; Long. 05.21.17 W

Project manager: P O'Hara (Cornwall Archaeology Unit), 1987

Archival body: Royal Cornwall Museum Truro

Description: a Romano-British univallate enclosed settlement or 'round' of the second to early fourth centuries AD. Five samples were submitted, all samples were charcoal, but no species identification was attempted because most samples were comminuted.

Objectives: to establish the date range and to investigate the sequence of the defences.

Final comment: H Quinnell (1992), these dates, together with UB-3250 to UB-3255 from a similar enclosed site at Trethurgy, are the first series to be obtained from Roman period settlements in Cornwall. Both series considered together suggest that the ceramic sequence proposed from Roman Cornwall is reasonably secure in broad outline. Dates such as UB-3181 are as consistent with the ceramic evidence as can be expected. This confirmation is important because the local Cornish ceramic series for the period is *sui generis* and the implications of ceramic material imported from outside the county were uncertain. These remarks apply only to contexts, from both Trethurgy and Reawla, where there are deposits including ceramic material of reasonable size. The relationship between ceramic and radiocarbon dating for Roman Cornwall

is further discussed in Quinnell (2004). The complexity of calibrations involves difficulties in conceptualising and discussing these dates. As a form of shorthand it is suggested that each of the Reawla dates be discussed with reference to the 1σ probability. UB-3180 and UB-3181 provide reasonable confirmation for the broad dating framework for the site based on ceramics; the only proviso must be that these deposits may have been dated rather too early. UB-3182 and UB-3183 cannot be easily reconciled with the ceramic evidence, which indicates, by comparison with Trethurgy (Quinnell 2004), that the site was not occupied far into the fourth century AD. UB-3183 also raises the possibility of sixth century AD occupation but, because the deposit contains intrusive medieval material, is probably best discounted. Both UB-3182 and UB-3183 come from contexts just below recent agricultural levels where some intrusive material might be expected. UB-3184 could be an acceptable date for rampart collapse into the ditch; there is no other dating for this episode. There is no obvious evidence for disturbance or intrusion. If UB-3184 were a correct indication of actual date this would imply activity on the site involving burning and levelling which left no artefactual record. The artefacts most appropriate for this date would be sherds of post-Roman imported pottery. While such sherds occur on a wide range of sites in west Cornwall, they are not usually common, and insufficient is still known about their distribution for their absence to be definitely regarded as significant. If UB-3184 is regarded as acceptable, activities, presumably agricultural, which need not have involved ceramics, may have continued after the domestic abandonment of Reawla and account for UB-3182-3 rather than disturbance and intrusion.

References: Quinnell 1992
                   Quinnell 2004

UB–3180 1744 ±46 BP

δ¹³C: -25.8 ±0.2‰

Sample: R87 340 HB, submitted in April 1989 by N Appleton

Material: charcoal (fragments of large wood): unidentified

Initial comment: from the lowest fill of hearth [324] in house B/300. The charcoal was burnt *in situ* and therefore derived from the last use of the hearth.

Objectives: to provide a date for house B which is stratigraphically isolated from main activity areas.

Calibrated date: *1σ:* cal AD 230–380
                    2σ: cal AD 130–410

Final comment: H Quinnell (5 September 1991), pottery from a midden dump after disuse of the house had been dated to the later third century AD; sparse pottery from occupation contexts, presumed contemporary with the hearth from which UB-3180 was taken, would be consistent with its use during the third century AD. The date confirms that derived from ceramic data.

UB–3181 1708 ±39 BP

δ¹³C: -26.2 ±0.2‰

Sample: R87 307 P1, submitted in April 1989 by N Appleton

Material: charcoal (fragments of large wood): unidentified

Initial comment: from the occupation level of house C/300 which seals pits from the primary occupation.

Objectives: to date the second occupation of house B.

Calibrated date: 1σ: cal AD 250–400
                      2σ: cal AD 230–430

Final comment: H Quinnell (5 September 1991), R87 307 P1 is the midden dump over house C/300, and therefore stratigraphically above the context of UB-3180. Context 307 has been dated to the later third century AD on ceramic evidence. The date is acceptable, but the range indicated by the calibrations suggests that it might be wise to consider extending the date range of the ceramics to the earlier fourth century AD.

UB–3182 1619 ±45 BP

δ¹³C: -26.6 ±0.2‰

Sample: R87 151 P3, submitted in April 1989 by N Appleton

Material: charcoal (fragments of large wood): unidentified

Initial comment: from a midden deposit which represents the last phase of activity before abandonment of the site.

Objectives: to date the end of Roman-British occupation. This is important as the site produced Cordoned Ware, but no south-west decorated (Glastonbury) Ware. Most similar sites in Cornwall have both.

Calibrated date: 1σ: cal AD 390–540
                      2σ: cal AD 330–550

Final comment: H Quinnell (5 September 1991), context R87 151 P3 forms part of a midden, below ploughsoil, which contained much pottery with fresh breaks dating to the earlier fourth century AD. The date as calibrated suggests a date range one or two centuries later. The context is effectively unstratified and disturbance may account for the discrepancy between the ceramic-derived and radiocarbon dating.

UB–3183 1523 ±41 BP

δ¹³C: -29.1 ±0.2‰

Sample: R87 23 P3, submitted in April 1989 by N Appleton

Material: charcoal (small branches): unidentified

Initial comment: from the fill of a depression left by the abandonment of a house, probably directly related to later 'industrial' use of the site. [23] is a possible midden layer. The layer was located directly beneath medieval plough soil, therefore there is a slight possibility of later contamination.

Objectives: to provide an end date for the industrial activity. This date is important with regard to the range of pottery types discovered.

Calibrated date: 1σ: cal AD 460–600
                      2σ: cal AD 420–640

Final comment: H Quinnell (5 September 1991), context R87 23 P3 is a gradual accumulation, within a hollow below ploughsoil, containing ceramics dating from the second to the fourth centuries; there has been some medieval/post-medieval disturbance. UB-3183, as calibrated, cannot be reconciled with the ceramic data, and the difference is almost certainly due to intrusive material.

UB–3184 1496 ±42 BP

δ¹³C: -26.0 ±0.2‰

Sample: R87 35 0D, submitted in April 1989 by N Appleton

Material: charcoal (fragments of large wood): unidentified

Initial comment: from the first backfill layer of the outer defensive ditch. The material derived from the rampart.

Objectives: there was no stratigraphic link between this ditch and the main occupational activity. No datable pottery was recovered. This is the only possibility of fixing the ditch into the history of the site.

Calibrated date: 1σ: cal AD 540–610
                      2σ: cal AD 430–650

Final comment: H Quinnell (5 September 1991), context R87 35 OD represents collapse with some burnt material, or possible deliberate demolition, of rampart material into the defensive ditch around the site; it lies above some depth of silting and possible earlier collapse. There is no independent dating for any of the ditch infill. Ceramic evidence suggests that the site was abandoned during the earlier fourth century AD. Rampart collapse could well have been two or three centuries later.

Richmond: St Giles Hospital, North Yorkshire

Location: SE 209996
                       Lat. 54.23.29 N; Long. 01.40.41 W

Project manager: P Cardwell (North Yorkshire County Council), 1990

Archival body: Yorkshire Museum, York, North Yorkshire County Council

Description: the medieval chapel of St Giles Hospital, situated on the south bank of the river Swale near Richmond. The site has suffered substantial river erosion.

Objectives: to establish dates for pre-hospital features.

Final comment: P Cardwell (25 May 1994), the dates confirm two separate and distinct phases of prehistoric activity on the river terrace. This was initially cleared in the late Neolithic (GU-5236), but was subsequently sealed by a depth of colluvium. The site was occupied for a period in the late Iron Age (OxA-3653), with further colluvium being deposited at a slower rate up until the foundation of the medieval hospital.

References: Cardwell 1990
                       Cardwell 1995
                       Cardwell and Speed 1996
                       Taylor *et al* 2000

GU–5236 3860 ±170 BP

δ¹³C: -26.4‰

Sample: BSG 90 2092 AA, submitted on 19 March 1992 by P Cardwell

Material: charcoal (*Carpinus* (hornbeam); 0.8g (6.9%)): unidentified, <3mm (5.30g, 45.7%); *Quercus* sp. (0.20g, 1.7%); *Ulmus* sp. (0.20g, 1.7%); *Salix* sp. (0.10g, 0.9%);

Prunus spinosa, blackthorn type (0.20g, 1.7%); *Alnus* sp. (4.20g, 36.2%); *Corylus* sp. (0.60g, 5.2%) (C Dickson 1990)

Initial comment: the sample was taken from a charcoal-rich horizon about 30cm below the earliest recognisable medieval feature. This layer was only clearly defined within a 3m × 1.5m box section, and the charcoal was collected by hand. The layer was a silty clay loam up to 5cm thick containing pebbles and had void root channels and some earthworm burrows. The charcoal formed up to 20% of the soil and was randomly distributed.

Objectives: the sample would aim to determine a probable Mesolithic baseline within the stratigraphic sequence of the site and indicate the depth of colluvium built up over this prior to the medieval occupation. The date would also aim to confirm the probable horizon from which residual Mesolithic artefacts were originally derived, although possible Anglo-Saxon occupation of the site is suggested by evidence recovered from other horizons.

Calibrated date: *1σ:* 2570–2040 cal BC
               2σ: 2880–1880 cal BC

Final comment: P Cardwell (25 May 1994), later than the Mesolithic date anticipated suggests initial clearance of the river terrace contemporary with lithic artefacts recovered from elsewhere on the site.

OxA–3653 2130 ±65 BP

δ¹³C: -24.4‰

Sample: BSG 1551AA, submitted on 6 May 1992 by P Cardwell

Material: grain (carbonised cereal grain and grass seeds; heath grass, sedge, hulled barley; (unidentified)) (J Huntley 1990)

Initial comment: the sample was produced from a palaeobotanical sample taken from the fill of a pit measuring 2.0m by 0.6m and up to 0.2m deep. The fill had evidence of being rooted. The sample was processed on site through a flotation tank, through a 200 micron mesh and the flot was collected in a 500 micron mesh.

Objectives: the sample is from a feature associated with occupation prior to the founding of the hospital. Pottery from this phase is mostly late Iron Age in date, but may include Anglo-Saxon material. If an Anglo-Saxon date was obtained from the sample, this would resolve a conflict of evidence, and be crucial to the understanding of the foundation of the hospital.

Calibrated date: *1σ:* 350–50 cal BC
               2σ: 380 cal BC–cal AD 10

Final comment: P Cardwell (25 May 1994), the late Iron Age date for pre-hospital occupation on the site was confirmed, in agreement with most of the pottery related to this occupation. This indicated that the possible Anglian attribution for a small proportion of this pottery was incorrect.

References: Hedges *et al* 1993, 161

Ripon: Ailcy Hill, Yorkshire (North Riding)

Location:	SE 31717114
	Lat. 54.08.06 N; Long. 01.30.53 W
Project manager:	R A Hall (York Archaeological Trust), 1986–7
Archival body:	English Heritage and York Archaeological Trust

Description: twenty-six intact, or fragmentary but articulated, inhumations were retrieved from the cemetery which sat on the summit of a mound of glacially deposited material at Ailcy Hill, Ripon. No closely datable artefacts were recovered from contexts closely associated with any of the skeletons, although parallels with the iron chest fittings accompanying a number of the burials suggest a broad date range in the seventh–tenth centuries AD.

Objectives: to test the validity of the broad date range of the cemetery as seventh–tenth century AD. Also to determine whether the cemetery in its different phases extended over a significantly longer period than that suggested above.

Final comment: R A Hall (29 November 1995), the samples derived from human bones excavated in 1986/7. The cemetery in which they were found was believed to be of the Anglo-Saxon date indicated because of evidence for burial in coffins/chests (hinges, locks, other fittings), and in one instance an iron knife and buckle accompanying a burial. It was hoped that the samples would confirm this broad date span, and possibly allow narrower date ranges to be attributed to the three phases of burial (phases 2, 3, and 4) identified. The pattern of the radiocarbon determinations corresponds extremely well with this phasing, although in no case is there complete separation between successive phases.

References: Anderson 1988
                     Hall 1987
                     Hall and Whyman 1986
                     Hall and Whyman 1996

UB–3149 1143 ±43 BP

δ¹³C: -27.5 ±0.2‰

Sample: 50001044, submitted on 5 December 1988 by R A Hall

Material: human bone

Initial comment: this sample was recovered from a shallow (*c* 0.4m) much disturbed deposit, which over much of the summit area formed the modern ground surface. There was disturbance by further burials in antiquity, modern tree roots, and slippage of material from the summit, as well as modern digging by children and treasure hunters. It was impossible to detect and excavate individual grave cuts due to this disturbance - the soil from which the burials were excavated was thus homogenous. Different phases of burial on the hill seem to be represented by certainly two, and possibly three, alignments which were labelled A, B, and C. This sample has been taken from alignment C. A total of 26 intact or partially intact inhumations were recovered from the summit area, and an uncertain (but at least comparable) number were represented by charnel. This sample is from an intact inhumation.

Objectives: to test the view that the Ailcy Hill cemetery has a date range broadly in the seventh-tenth centuries AD, and whether its earliest use pre- or post-dates the introduction of Christianity to the area (seventh century). Also to determine whether the cemetery was in use over several centuries, or for a relatively brief period.

Calibrated date: *1σ:* cal AD 870–980
                     2σ: cal AD 770–1000

Final comment: R A Hall (29 November 1995), the stratigraphic position and the orientation of the skeleton indicated that it belonged to the latest of the three burial phases. Although overlapping with that from a burial from the preceding phase, the span on this result allows that it possibly could be considerably later. This may account for the fact that this phase 4 burial was cut into a phase 3 inhumation, unusual on the site.

UB–3150 1281 ±35 BP

δ¹³C: -20.9 ±0.2‰

Sample: 50001045, submitted on 5 December 1988 by R A Hall

Material: human bone

Initial comment: as UB-3149, except this sample came from an intact inhumation in alignment B.

Objectives: as UB-3149

Calibrated date: *1σ:* cal AD 670–780
                     2σ: cal AD 660–810

Final comment: R A Hall (29 November 1995), the result from this phase 3 burial overlaps (only) slightly with that from a sample from the succeeding phases, and by the tiniest of margins with that from one which precedes it. The late seventh/early ninth-century AD date accords well with the date span recognised for the iron coffin fittings of the type found in association with this burial.

UB–3151 1427 ±35 BP

δ¹³C: -22.0 ±0.2‰

Sample: 50001064, submitted on 5 December 1988 by R A Hall

Material: human bone

Initial comment: as UB-3149

Objectives: as UB-3149

Calibrated date: *1σ:* cal AD 600–660
                     2σ: cal AD 560–670

Final comment: R A Hall (29 November 1995), the phasing of the cemetery on stratigraphic and (in this case) spatial grounds suggested this as one of the earliest burials encountered. Its accompanying knife and buckle suggested a date in the seventh century AD. The result is consistent with this, and the (only) marginal overlap with the result from a sample from the next phase accords well with conclusions about the cemetery's development drawn from spatial and stratigraphic considerations.

UB–3152 1267 ±36 BP

δ¹³C: -21.1 ±0.2‰

Sample: 50002005, submitted on 5 December 1988 by R A Hall

Material: human bone

Initial comment: as UB-3149, except that the sample is from an intact inhumation from alignment A.

Objectives: as UB-3149

Calibrated date: *1σ:* cal AD 670–780
                     2σ: cal AD 660–870

Final comment: R A Hall (29 November 1995), located in a separate but adjacent excavated area to the previous three burials cited, this inhumation was interpreted as an instance of 'infilling' of the spaces between phase 3 burials. The extensive overlap of the date span with that from UB-3153 is to be expected, as such infilling need not be widely separated in time from the creation of the original rows.

UB–3153 1236 ±35 BP

δ¹³C: -22.0 ±0.2‰

Sample: 50002006, submitted on 5 December 1988 by R A Hall

Material: human bone

Initial comment: as UB-3149, except that the sample is from an intact inhumation from alignment A.

Objectives: as UB-3149

Calibrated date: *1σ:* cal AD 690–860
                     2σ: cal AD 670–890

Final comment: R A Hall (29 November 1995), located in a separate but adjacent excavated area, this burial was associated with the phase 3 burials on the grounds of its alignment. The result accords well with this interpretation.

Roadford Reservoir, Devon

Location: SX 42669165 (transect 46 and soil pit 36), SX 41959130 (transect 1009), and SX 42439256 (soil pit 18)
                    Lat. 50.42.09 N; Long. 01.13.42 W,
                    Lat. 50.42.09 N; Long. 01.13.42 W,
                    Lat. 50.42.37 N; Long. 04.13.53 W

Project manager: T Pearson and S Reed (Exeter Museums Archaeological Field Unit), 1988–9

Archival body: University of Bristol

Description: samples were taken from an area within Lower Great Moor (tithe field 1423), on the flood plain gravels of the river Wolf in the Culm Measures of Devon. Samples were taken from transect 46 across the terrace, and soil pit 36 was excavated through alluvial deposits, 2m from the present bank of the river Wolf. Transect 1009 sampled a peat accumulation in the floodplain of a small valley tributary to the river Wolf. Soil pit 18 was also situated on a tributary below Toft Farm. They were *c* 1km to the north of transect 46 and soil pit 36.

Objectives: the sequences are from natural deposits and buried soils sampled to establish a chronology of vegetation and soil development and change in the Wolf valley and its tributaries. This was part of a landscape archaeology project in a previously unstudied part of lowland west Devon which was shortly to be flooded by Roadford reservoir.

Laboratory comment: Ancient Monuments Laboratory (6 October 2003), two further samples RDFORD24 (HAR-9214) and RDFORD20 (HAR-9213), were submitted for dating but failed to produce results.

References: Straker 1986

HAR–10196 2310 ±70 BP

δ¹³C: -31.7‰

Sample: x 4802530, submitted on 28 October 1988 by V Straker

Material: peat (V Straker 1988)

Initial comment: this sample came from the top of fibrous silty peat (1.58m from surface) at 0.19–0.21m from the base of the peat layer.

Objectives: pollen and sediment analysis of the peat and overlying sediments is in progress and dates are required to place the sequence chronologically as well as to provide a *terminus ante quem* for the build up of sediments above the peat.

Calibrated date: 1σ: 410–260 cal BC
2σ: 710–200 cal BC

Final comment: V Straker (29 February 2012), peat formation continued in the Iron Age before it was inundated by sediment-rich waters depositing silty clays on the floodplain.

HAR–10197 2470 ±110 BP

δ¹³C: -32.2‰

Sample: x 4802531, submitted on 28 October 1988 by V Straker

Material: peat (V Straker 1988)

Initial comment: this sample came from a fibrous silty peat (1.72m from surface, and 0.3m above the base of the peat).

Objectives: as HAR-10196

Calibrated date: 1σ: 800–400 cal BC
2σ: 830–370 cal BC

Final comment: V Straker (29 February 2012), this result and that for HAR-10198 suggest initial peat formation in the final Bronze Age or Iron Age.

HAR–10198 2450 ±70 BP

δ¹³C: -31.3‰

Sample: x 4802532, submitted on 28 October 1988 by V Straker

Material: peat (V Straker 1988)

Initial comment: this sample came from the base of the fibrous silty peat (1.75m from surface).

Objectives: as HAR-10196

Calibrated date: 1σ: 770–400 cal BC
2σ: 800–390 cal BC

Final comment: V Straker (29 February 2012), this result and that for HAR-10197 suggest initial peat formation in the final Bronze Age or Iron Age

HAR–9144 180 ±60 BP

δ¹³C: -30.7‰

Sample: X4802511 (RFORDTP1), submitted in January 1988 by V Straker

Material: peat (V Straker 1988)

Initial comment: the sample came from a red/brown fibrous peat deposit 1.05m deep, at 0.25–0.26m, which overlay organic silty clay and fine gravel. Pollen analysis is currently in progress.

Objectives: to establish a chronology of vegetation and soil development and change. As the area is shortly to be flooded, dates are urgently required to provide feedback on the current investigations and ensure that adequate sampling is carried out before the opportunity is lost.

Calibrated date: 1σ: cal AD 1650–1955★
2σ: cal AD 1630–1955★

Final comment: C Henderson (1989), this result helps with a general survey of the soils, the effects of the agriculture on soil erosion, and the vegetational history of the area, which is shortly to be flooded.

HAR–9145 1560 ±60 BP

δ¹³C: -30.6‰

Sample: X4802512, submitted in January 1988 by V Straker

Material: peat (V Straker 1988)

Initial comment: this sample came from a black greasy humified peat at 0.52–0.53m.

Objectives: as HAR-9144

Calibrated date: 1σ: cal AD 420–570
2σ: cal AD 380–640

Final comment: C Henderson (1989), archaeological excavations and pollen analysis of the Wolf Valley are underway before the area is flooded by the Roadford reservoir.

References: Hardiman *et al* 1992, 69

HAR–9146 3930 ±60 BP

δ¹³C: -30.1‰

Sample: X4802513 (RFORDTP3), submitted in January 1988 by V Straker

Material: peat (V Staker 1988)

Initial comment: this sample came from a brownish-black greasy humified peat grading into pale grey organic silty clay at 0.85–0.86m.

Objectives: as HAR-9144

Calibrated date: *1σ:* 2490–2340 cal BC
                       2σ: 2580–2200 cal BC

Final comment: C Henderson (1989), this result helps with a general survey of the soils, the effects of the agriculture on soil erosion, and the vegetational history of the area, which is shortly to be flooded.

OxA–3038 3850 ±100 BP

δ¹³C: -28.2‰

Sample: x 48025851, submitted on 18 February 1991 by V Straker

Material: wood: *Corylus/Alnus* sp., fragments (V Straker 1991)

Initial comment: a sample from transect 46; from pale grey organic silts from 1.13–1.14m depth. The sample should date to before *c* 2550 BC, as it is stratigraphically below HAR-9146.

Objectives: the series of deposits in transect 46 gives the longest sequence available in the area and therefore the most comprehensive pollen diagram to which the other, shorter diagrams can be related.

Calibrated date: *1σ:* 2470–2140 cal BC
                       2σ: 2580–2020 cal BC

Final comment: V Straker (1993), OxA-3038 and OxA-3039 were required to complete the dating of the pollen sequence. The earliest date that had previously been obtained from the sequence had been HAR-9146, from the base of the peat deposit. The base date (OxA-3039) is within expected limits, and although the upper date (OxA-3038) is marginally younger than the stratigraphically higher conventional measurement of 3930 ±60 BP (HAR-9146), the age difference is not significant.

References: Hedges *et al* 1994, 359

OxA–3039 5420 ±90 BP

δ¹³C: -26.2‰

Sample: x 48025852, submitted on 18 February 1991 by V Straker

Material: wood: *Corylus avellana*, fragments (V Straker 1991)

Initial comment: this sample came from a silty clay at 1.33–1.34m depth. It should date to before *c* 2550 BC, the earliest radiocarbon date obtained from peat which is 0.47m above this sample (HAR-9146).

Objectives: as OxA-3038

Calibrated date: *1σ:* 4350–4170 cal BC
                       2σ: 4460–4000 cal BC

Final comment: see OxA-3038

References: Hedges *et al* 1994, 359

UB–3207 1889 ±72 BP

δ¹³C: -27.3 ±0.2‰

Sample: Soil pit 36; x4802533/4, submitted on 5 July 1989 by T Pearson

Material: charcoal: unidentified (V Straker 1989)

Initial comment: this sample was taken from 1.35–1.40m below the surface. No charcoal fragments were found immediately above this depth. The occurrence of charcoal and the deposition of alluvial sediments may be associated with earlier phases of land use in the valley.

Objectives: to provide a framework for the interpretation of these deposits.

Calibrated date: *1σ:* cal AD 30–230
                       2σ: 50 cal BC–cal AD 330

Final comment: V Straker (29 February 2012), the Roman date for the charcoal is consistent with the earlier (Iron Age) peat below the alluvial silty clays. Pollen analysis will help understanding of whether the burning was related to large-scale clearance or a local activity.

UB–3208 3521 ±54 BP

δ¹³C: -27.3 ±0.2‰

Sample: Soil pit 18; 480 2535, submitted on 5 July 1989 by T Pearson

Material: charcoal: unidentified (V Straker 1989)

Initial comment: this sample came from soil pit 18, 0.85–86m below the ground surface on the floodplain of a tributary of the river Wolf, below Toft Farm. The occurrence of charcoal and the deposition of alluvial sediments may be associated with early phases of land use in the valley.

Objectives: to provide a time framework for the interpretation of these deposits. The occurrence of charcoal and the rate of alluvial sedimentation may be associated with earlier phases of land-use in the valley. It is hoped that radiocarbon dating along with analysis of these deposits will provide a link between the deposits and the settlement sites in the valley.

Calibrated date: *1σ:* 1930–1750 cal BC
                       2σ: 2020–1690 cal BC

Final comment: V Straker (29 February 2012), both episodes of burning, falling within the early to middle Bronze Age, are substantially earlier than those noted in soil pit 36.

UB–3209 3340 ±51 BP

δ¹³C: -27.0 ±0.2‰

Sample: Soil pit 18; 480 2536, submitted on 5 July 1989 by T Pearson

Material: charcoal: unidentified (V Straker 1989)

Initial comment: as UB-3208

Objectives: as UB-3208

Calibrated date: *1σ:* 1690–1530 cal BC
                       2σ: 1750–1500 cal BC

Final comment: see UB-3208

UB–3225 1828 ±50 BP

δ¹³C: -29.2 ±0.2‰

Sample: x 48025837, submitted on 7 December 1989
by S Reed

Material: peat

Initial comment: from a transect across a small valley
containing a small stream tributary of the river Wolf. The
peat was probably waterlogged all through the year since the
valley floor is very marshy. Depth of sample below ground
level is 0.63–0.64m. Possibly medieval in date.

Objectives: the dates are required to place the sequence
chronologically and to provide a *terminus ante quem* for the
build up of sediments above the peat. Pollen analysis to follow.

Calibrated date: *1σ:* cal AD 120–250
               2σ: cal AD 70–340

Final comment: V Straker (29 February 2012), UB-3225,
UB-3226, and UB-3227 demonstrate that this local peat in a
tributary of the river Wolf started to accumulate in the late
Bronze Age and ended in the Roman period. Approximately
0.6m of waterlain silty clays were deposited above the peat
suggesting a change in hydrology and possibly land-use,
sometime in the first four centuries AD.

UB–3226 2821 ±46 BP

δ¹³C: -29.6 ±0.2‰

Sample: x 48025838, submitted on 7 December 1989
by S Reed

Material: peat

Initial comment: as UB-3225. From base of black peat build
up, 1.02–1.04m depth from surface. It is possibly of
prehistoric date.

Objectives: as UB-3225

Calibrated date: *1σ:* 1030–910 cal BC
               2σ: 1130–840 cal BC

Final comment: see UB-3225

UB–3227 3124 ±42 BP

δ¹³C: -30.0 ±0.2‰

Sample: x 48025839, submitted on 7 December 1989
by S Reed

Material: peat

Initial comment: as UB-3225. This sample came from the
base of the earliest peat deposit on top of river gravels. The
sample was taken 1.27-1.28m below the surface. It is
possibly of prehistoric date.

Objectives: this sample will give a date for the initial build up
of peat over river gravels which may represent a change in
the processes of drainage and alluvial build up in the valley.

Calibrated date: *1σ:* 1440–1320 cal BC
               2σ: 1500–1300 cal BC

Final comment: see UB-3225

Romsey Abbey, Hampshire

Location: SU 35062127
           Lat. 50.59.21 N; Long. 01.30.02 W

Project manager: F J Green (Test Valley Archaeological
           Trust), 1988

Archival body: Test Valley Archaeological Trust,
           Hampshire County Museum Service

Description: excavation of a soakaway 5m north of Romsey
Abbey revealed at least three phases of activity, almost
certainly preceding the construction of the extant Norman
Abbey.

Objectives: to enable us to tie down the stratigraphic
sequence, which is presently undated. More specifically it is
wished to confirm the probable middle Saxon date for the
soil horizon (30), to date the later floor (29) and see how
much earlier than the Norman Abbey it is, and to date the
floor (25), which is near the top of the stratigraphic
sequence, to enable us to date the latter part of the
stratigraphic sequence.

References: Hedges *et al* 1991b, 286

OxA–2318 330 ±70 BP

δ¹³C: -23.3‰

Sample: A.1988.7 (25), submitted on 16 August 1989
by F J Green

Material: animal bone: *Bos* sp., proximal metatarsus,
fragment of radius, ulna, and femur (J Bourdillon 1988)

Initial comment: gravel floor deposit A.1988.7 (25), later than
A.1988 (30) and (29); site phase 2.

Objectives: to know whether this phase is pre-Norman Abbey.

Calibrated date: *1σ:* cal AD 1450–1650
               2σ: cal AD 1430–1950

Final comment: F J Green (1991), this sample came from the
third of a series of four gravel surfaces on the north side of
the Abbey. The earliest surface sealed a charcoal layer and a
pre-Conquest clay floor (context 29), and was probably laid
down after the start of the construction of the present
Norman Abbey in the early twelfth century AD.
Stratigraphically a late medieval to post-medieval date for
the third surface is quite acceptable.

OxA–2319 1125 ±80 BP

δ¹³C: -23.1‰

Sample: A.1988.7 (30), submitted on 16 August 1989
by F J Green

Material: animal bone: *Bos* sp., rib, lumbar and thoracic
vertebrae (J Bourdillon 1988)

Initial comment: post-Roman soil horizon, between phases of
occupation (A.1988 (30)). Site phase 1B and immediately
below clay floor (site phase 1C) A.1988.7 (29).

Objectives: to provide a date for the animal bone contained
within the soil horizon (30).

Calibrated date: 1σ: cal AD 780–1020
2σ: cal AD 680–1040

Final comment: F J Green (1991), this date came from a soil horizon which was sealed beneath the pre-Conquest clay floor (context 29). Context 30 contained no ceramics, but a sizeable group of animal bone, which would not be out of place in a middle to late Saxon context. The horizon had been provisionally dated to the same periods on stratigraphic grounds. This dating matches with the result of the radiocarbon assay.

Samson: East Porth, Isle of Scilly

Location: SV 87941263
Lat. 49.55.53 N; Long. 06.20.56 W

Project manager: J Ratcliffe (Cornwall Archaeology Unit), 1990

Archival body: Isles of Scilly Museum

Description: on the south side of East Porth, on the north-east side of Samson South Hill, the dune has eroded back to expose a narrow, 3m-wide shelf of old land surface overlying the natural *ram*. Visible in cross-section in the dune face are a series of walls assumed to be part of the prehistoric field system which covers most of South Hill, and to also relate to field wall remains recorded in the intertidal zone to the east and north.

Objectives: to date the grain which would place the buried land surface and fieldwalls in archaeological sequence for the Isles of Scilly, as well as providing a date for the use of naked barley on the Islands.

References: Hedges *et al* 1994, 363
Ratcliffe 1991
Ratcliffe and Straker 1996

OxA–3649 3620 ±70 BP

δ¹³C: -23.3‰

Sample: SAMEP1, submitted in March 1992 by V Straker

Material: grain (charred; *Hordeum sativum var. nudum* (naked barley)) (V Straker 1992)

Initial comment: the grain is from a small 'cache' that was found in a burnt area of old land surface associated with prehistoric field walls. Two pieces of pottery that appear to be prehistoric were also found. Naked barley is rarely found on archaeological sites.

Objectives: a date for the grain would enable the buried land surface and fieldwalls to be placed in archaeological sequence for the Isles of Scilly, as well as providing a date for the use of naked barley on the Islands. At present it is not known if it is contemporary with that at West Porth or not. The grain from West and East Porth are the best assemblages to be studied from the Islands.

Calibrated date: 1σ: 2130–1890 cal BC
2σ: 2200–1770 cal BC

Final comment: J Ratcliffe (1994), this is a wonderfully early date and, since it was obtained for an old land surface apparently associated with a field system which stretches both inland and out onto the intertidal sand flats, it allows an early Bronze Age date to be suggested for this field system. The radiocarbon determination also provides an early date for the use of naked barley in Scilly.

Samson: West Porth, Isle of Scilly

Location: SV 87601304
Lat. 49.56.05 N; Long. 06.21.14 W

Project manager: J Ratcliffe (Cornwall Archaeology Unit), 1990

Archival body: Isles of Scilly Museum

Description: the West Porth remains were visible in plan on the cliff top and in section in the adjacent cliff face. The remains of a late Bronze Age to early Iron Age hut circle lay on the seaward side of this area, most of it having already been removed by the sea.

Objectives: to date the occupation horizon for one of the huts as well as providing a date for the use of naked barley on the Islands.

References: Hedges *et al* 1994, 363
Ratcliffe 1991
Ratcliffe and Straker 1996

OxA–3650 2545 ±65 BP

δ¹³C: -22.7‰

Sample: SAMWPH1, submitted in March 1992 by V Straker

Material: grain (*Horseum sativum var. nudum* (naked barley)) (V Straker 1992)

Initial comment: the charred grain came from an occupation layer within the remains of a Bronze Age house. The samples were collected (from context 8) when the remains of the house were excavated by J Ratcliffe for the Cornwall Archaeological Unit. The occupation layer (8) was sealed by a post-occupation deposit.

Objectives: the grain comes from a sealed occupation horizon within a house that contained pottery that can only be dated as 'prehistoric'. The identification of naked barley is comparatively rare, and a radiocarbon date for this would enable it to be placed more accurately within the archaeological record for the crop, as well as dating the structure in which it was found.

Calibrated date: 1σ: 800–550 cal BC
2σ: 820–410 cal BC

Final comment: J Ratcliffe (1994), both SAMWPH1 and SAMWPH2 are from the same context (a thin occupation layer within eroding hut circle), so it is not surprising that they are so similar. These determinations provide a secure date for the final occupation phase of the hut (assuming earlier occupation material may have been removed during floor cleaning), as well providing further dating evidence for Scilly's prehistoric pottery sequence.

OxA-3651 2570 ±65 BP

$\delta^{13}C$: -23.1‰

Sample: SAMWPH2, submitted in March 1992 by V Straker

Material: charcoal: *Ulex* sp. (R Gale 1990)

Initial comment: as OxA-3651

Objectives: as OxA-3651; it would also be useful to date charcoal and grain from the same context.

Calibrated date: 1σ: 810–600 cal BC
           2σ: 840–510 cal BC

Final comment: see OxA-3651

Shepton Mallet: Fosse Lane, Somerset

Location:	ST 630424
	Lat. 51.10.45 N; Long. 02.31.46 W
Project manager:	P Leach (Birmingham University Field Archaeology Unit), 1990
Archival body:	Somerset County Museum

Description: an extensive roadside Romano-British settlement along the Fosse Way, which has revealed a number of late Roman features and human burials. No occupation of the site can be demonstrated after the fifth century AD, although it is perhaps significant that Shepton Mallet's medieval parish boundary crosses the Fosse Way at this point to enclose the site and immediate environs of the former Roman town.

Objectives: to date the burials and form a chronology for the graves in the different cemeteries.

Final comment: J Evans (1994), the samples submitted were from three small separate cemeteries within late Roman roadside settlement areas. Two with late Roman Pagan characteristics (GU-5293 and GU-5294), one possibly Christian (GU-5295 and GU-5296), and one separate burial (GU-5297). All were originally interpreted archaeologically as late Roman burials, which is broadly confirmed by the radiocarbon determinations. Only GU-5297 appears significantly anomalous (too young), although GU-5296 seems slightly too old.

References: Leach 1991
         Leach and Evans 2001

GU-5293 1450 ±70 BP

$\delta^{13}C$: -24.5‰

Sample: SM90 HB9, submitted in February 1993 by J Evans

Material: human bone (right femur) (S Pinter-Bellows 1990)

Initial comment: from an extended, north-south aligned, adult inhumation within a shallow (*c* 0.30m deep) rock-cut grave. The fill was a stony, clay soil with minor root penetration within a rectangular cut into lias limestone. Some iron nails were present, although there were no other grave goods. The burial lay within 0.50m of the modern surface, one from a small scattered cemetery in a ditched enclosure.

Objectives: this burial is a representative from one of three small cemeteries at Shepton Mallet. These appear to be the latest in a sequence of events relating to the Roman roadside settlement. Are these of post-Roman date? Were they all approximately contemporary, or do they fit within a chronological sequence?

Calibrated date: 1σ: cal AD 540–660
           2σ: cal AD 430–680

Final comment: J Evans (1994), this date range supports the hypothesis of an early post-Roman burial in a small cemetery (IV) of variably orientated burials with pagan attributes cut through late-fourth century deposits. A late fourth- or fifth-century date was anticipated.

GU-5294 1440 ±90 BP

$\delta^{13}C$: -23.1‰

Sample: SM90 HB12, submitted in February 1993 by J Evans

Material: human bone (right femur) (S Pinter-Bellows 1990)

Initial comment: from an extended, north-south aligned, adult inhumation within a lead coffin, set into a *c* 0.40m deep rock-cut grave. The fill was a loamy, worm-sorted soil, with few stones, and slight root penetration. The grave cut into the natural clay and bedded lias limestone in a cemetery of similarly aligned graves.

Objectives: as GU-5293

Calibrated date: 1σ: cal AD 540–670
           2σ: cal AD 420–770

Final comment: J Evans (February 1993), this date range supports a late fourth–fifth-century AD date suggested for a small cemetery (II) adjacent to a contemporary building. This burial, within a lead coffin, was prominent within the cemetery.

GU-5295 1610 ±60 BP

$\delta^{13}C$: -24.2‰

Sample: SM90 HB21, submitted in February 1993 by J Evans

Material: human bone (left femur) (S Pinter-Bellows 1990)

Initial comment: from an extended, east-west aligned, adult inhumation within a shallow rock-cut grave (*c* 0.30m deep). The fill was a stony clay soil. The burial was resting on the limestone bedrock *c* 0.50m below the modern ploughsoil. There were no grave goods, and it was one of a closely set group of five similar burials within a larger cemetery of *c* 20 burials.

Objectives: as GU-5293

Calibrated date: 1σ: cal AD 390–540
           2σ: cal AD 260–580

Final comment: J Evans (1994), this date range supports a late fourth–fifth-century date suggested for a small cemetery (III) of east-west graves. One (HB22) contained a possible fifth-century AD Christian artefact and suggests that this was a late/post-Roman Christian cemetery.

GU–5296 1790 ±70 BP

δ¹³C: -23.2‰

Sample: SM90 HB22, submitted in February 1993 by J Evans

Material: human bone (right femur) (S Pinter-Bellows 1990)

Initial comment: from an extended, east-west aligned adult inhumation within a shallow rock-cut grave (*c* 0.30m deep). The fill was a stony clay soil with minor root penetration within a rectangular cut in the bedded lias limestone. Some iron coffin nails and a silver amulet cross accompanied the burial. The grave lay below *c* 0.20m of stony ploughsoil. It was one of a small (<20 individuals) cemetery of east-west, possibly Christian graves within a ditched enclosure.

Objectives: as GU-5293

Calibrated date: *1σ:* cal AD 130–340
                              2σ: cal AD 70–410

Final comment: J Evans (1994), this date was obtained from a burial containing a probable fifth-century Christian silver amulet, within the same cemetery (III) as HB21. The radiocarbon age appears to be too old for this and the other burials in the cemetery, believed to be of fourth- or fifth-century AD date (*see* GU-5295).

GU–5297 1160 ±50 BP

δ¹³C: -25.6‰

Sample: SM90 HB33, submitted in February 1993 by J Evans

Material: human bone (right femur) (S Pinter-Bellows 1990)

Initial comment: from an extended, east-west aligned adult inhumation within a shallow rock-cut grave (*c* 0.10m deep). The fill was a stony, brown clay soil. The grave was badly disturbed, probably by ploughing, and the top half was missing. It was cut into the bedded lias limestone, and lay *c* 0.30m below the modern surface and within an earlier demolished Roman building. There were no grave goods, and there was similar burial adjacent.

Objectives: as GU-5293. This burial may belong to the east-west Christian cemetery. It was cut into the remains of a fourth-century AD building with a later timber-framed structure above it. Was it contemporary or later than the secondary building?

Calibrated date: *1σ:* cal AD 770–970
                              2σ: cal AD 710–990

Final comment: J Evans (1994), this date range appears to be too young. Although this was an isolated burial (with HB32) cut into an early fifth-century AD structure. There is no other evidence for any later Anglo-Saxon activity on the site. Being a shallow and disturbed burial could this date have been affected by contamination?

Slough House Farm, Essex

Location: TL 873091
                        Lat. 51.44.55 N; Long. 00.42.49 E

Project manager: O Bedwin (Essex County Council),
                        1988–9

Archival body: Essex County Council Archaeology
                        Section, Colchester and Essex Museum

Description: a multi-period settlement with evidence of activity from the Neolithic to the early Middle Ages. The site was known to have a large complex of cropmarks and excavation took place in advance of gravel extraction.

Objectives: to help provide a chronology for the site.

References: Hedges *et al* 1992, 148
                        Wallis 1989
                        Wallis and Waughman 1998

OxA–2932 1620 ±70 BP

δ¹³C: -24.8‰

Sample: SHF 204, submitted in August 1990 by P Murphy

Material: charcoal (very large quantity, but mostly too comminuted to identify; 25% subsample mostly oak): unidentified (363g); Pomoideae, hawthorn, apple, pear, rowan, service tree, whitebeam (0.02g, 0.4%); Salicaceae, willow or poplar (0.03g, 0.5%); *Quercus* sp., heartwood (5.39g, 98.4%); *Corylus* sp., hazel (0.04g, 0.7%) (R Gale 1998)

Initial comment: from the middle fill of an isolated pit. The lower fill was largely silting and slumping, and the upper fill capping or similar. This middle fill contained quantities of debris, pottery of probably sixth-century AD in date, and a high charcoal content.

Objectives: dating of the metal-working activity depends at present on ceramic styles. An independent source of dating evidence is desirable.

Calibrated date: *1σ:* cal AD 350–540
                              2σ: cal AD 250–600

Final comment: O Bedwin (1994), this result gives general confirmation of an early Saxon date from a pit containing much debris from iron-working.

OxA–3036 1570 ±100 BP

δ¹³C: -22.8‰

Sample: SHF 233/330, submitted in August 1990 by P Murphy

Material: grain: *Triticum dicoccum, Triticum aestivum* (P Murphy 1990)

Initial comment: from the silty lower fills of two of the ditches that made up the enclosure. Other dating evidence was limited and included part of a Beaker vessel in the upper fill of the west ditch, flint flakes spot-dated to the late Neolithic/early Bronze Age in the east ditch, and an early Neolithic sherd in the pits just north of the enclosure. The feature was shallow and its fill included some rootlets.

Objectives: to provide further evidence for the chronology of Neolithic activity in Essex, and help to relate this enclosure to the nearby settlement site of the Stumble from which dates are available. It will in addition provide another date for Neolithic agriculture in the area.

Calibrated date: *1σ:* cal AD 390–600
                              2σ: cal AD 240–660

Final comment: O Bedwin (1994), this result gives general confirmation of a likely early Saxon date for a ditch containing very little dating material.

OxA–3037 530 ±90 BP

δ¹³C: -23.3‰

Sample: SHF 470, submitted in August 1990 by P Murphy

Material: grain: Cereal indet; *Avenena* sp. (P Murphy 1990)

Initial comment: from the only fill of enclosure B, which appears to be the first major element of the Iron Age settlement. Pottery from the fill has been spot-dated to the early Iron Age. The ditch was shallow and included rootlets.

Objectives: this is one of very few Iron Age enclosures excavated in Essex. More data on the chronology of settlement activity and ceramic styles are required.

Calibrated date: *1σ:* cal AD 1310–1450
                   2σ: cal AD 1280–1620

Final comment: O Bedwin (1994), a very recent date and not compatible with the ceramic evidence. The sample was probably contaminated with modern charred grain.

Snail Down, Wiltshire

Location: *see* individual sites

Project manager: N Thomas (Devizes Museum for the Ministry of Works), 1953–7

Description: Snail Down is an early Bronze Age barrow cemetery on Salisbury Plain, located eight miles north-east of Stonehenge. Thirty-three mounds include examples of almost every type of Wessex barrow, several of which were fully excavated between 1953 and 1957 (Thomas 2005, xiii). In total eleven radiocarbon dates were obtained from charcoal fragments and human bones from seven of the barrows (Ashbee in Thomas 2005, 253).

Objectives: to provide a chronological framework for the barrow cemetery.

Final comment: N Thomas (2005), radiocarbon determinations from charcoal and bone associated with some of the burials suggest that the early Bronze Age cemetery could have begun between 2140 and 1810 cal BC, and ended between 1750 and 1440 cal BC, the use spanning between 150 and 600 years (Thomas 2005, xiii).

References: Thomas 2005

Snail Down: Site II, Wiltshire

Location: SU 21555194
               Lat. 51.15.56 N; Long. 01.41.28 W

Project manager: N Thomas (Devizes Museum), 1953

Archival body: Wiltshire Heritage Museum

Description: a saucer barrow.

Objectives: to date the barrow.

References: Thomas 2005

GU–5301 5690 ±90 BP

δ¹³C: -24.7‰

Sample: SDII 1953 95, submitted in 1 by N Thomas

Material: charcoal: Pomoideae (2.80g); *Quercus* sp. (7.20g); *Corylus* sp. (1.10g) (C Dickson 1993)

Initial comment: the sample was mixed with cremation material in a burial pit associated with the cremation of a youthful person. It is also associated with ?domestic rubbish and food vessel sherds. The whole deposit was 'dirty' with charcoal dust. No contamination was seen.

Objectives: to provide primary dating evidence for the only saucer barrow at Snail Down. It has links with a pond barrow and with a foetus from site II by implication. Foetuses are a rare find in the early Bronze Age.

Calibrated date: *1σ:* 4690–4450 cal BC
                  2σ: 4730–4340 cal BC

Final comment: N Thomas (8 September 1993), the dating could be associated with the central, and also the primary burial, disturbed in AD 1805. GU-5301 is much too early and is thus archaeologically not acceptable.

Snail Down: Site III, Wiltshire

Location: SU 21685205
               Lat. 51.15.58 N; Long. 01.41.21 W

Project manager: N Thomas (Devizes Museum), 1955

Archival body: Wiltshire Heritage Museum

Description: a bell barrow with a funeral pyre beneath containing two secondary cremations in urns.

Objectives: to date and provide phasing for the bell barrow.

Laboratory comment: English Heritage (17 January 2012), two further dates, HAR-61(S) and HAR-130(S), were published in Bayliss *et al* 2012 (252).

References: Bayliss *et al* 2012
              Thomas 2005

GU–5302 3440 ±90 BP

δ¹³C: -26.7‰

Sample: SD III 1955 142, submitted on 16 February 1993 by N Thomas

Material: charcoal (*Prunus avium/Padus* type (0.1g)): unidentified (4.40g); *Quercus* sp. (1.50g); Pomoideae (0.10g) (C Dickson 1993)

Initial comment: from the secondary cremation in a Collared Urn whose grave goods of beads included segmented faience. The sample was mixed with cremation material in a burial pit sealed by a flint cairn on the berm of the bell barrow. It is associated with the cremation of an adult female.

Objectives: to date the faience beads and help with the phasing of the barrow.

Calibrated date: *1σ:* 1890–1630 cal BC
                  2σ: 2020–1520 cal BC

Final comment: N Thomas (8 September 1993), a date for such faience is useful, as well as for the interment and comparison with dates from primary burial (HAR-61(S); 3540 ±140 BP; 2290–1520 cal BC at 95% confidence; HAR-130(S); 3500 ±110 BP; 2140–1530 cal BC at 95% confidence; and NPL-141; 3490 ±90 BP; 2040–1600 cal BC at 95% confidence; Reimer *et al* 2004). The result is satisfactory and interesting and suggests no great time lag between burials.

References: Reimer *et al* 2004

Snail Down: Site XIV, Wiltshire

Location: SU 21685209
Lat. 51.16.01 N; Long. 01.41.21 W

Project manager: N Thomas (Devizes Museum), 1957

Archival body: Wiltshire Heritage Museum

Description: a barrow with four contiguous mounds, occupying a crucial position in Snail Down cemetery. This site is close to site III (NPL-141; 3490 ±90 BP; 2040–1600 cal BC at 95% confidence; Reimer *et al* 2004) and site XVII (OxA-4179 and OxA-4211; *see* below).

Objectives: to date the barrow but, also, thereby dating an associated group of barrows. Sites X to XIV occupy a special place within the cemetery and phasing of important sections of the cemetery depend upon dating these barrows.

References: Hedges *et al* 1995, 421
Reimer *et al* 2004
Thomas 2005

OxA–4178 3555 ±75 BP

$\delta^{13}C$: -23.7‰

Sample: SD IV 1957 352, submitted on 8 February 1993 by N Thomas

Material: charcoal: *Quercus* sp. (0.10g); *Fraxinus* sp., *c* 0.02g sent for dating (young wood) (1.90g) (C Dickson 1993)

Initial comment: from the primary cremation pit associated with the cremation of a young adult. The pit was intact and sealed by a barrow mound.

Objectives: to help decide the phasing of the main alignment of barrows.

Calibrated date: 1σ: 2020–1770 cal BC
2σ: 2140–1690 cal BC

Final comment: N Thomas (8 September 1993), the result suggests, satisfactorily, that this and its four contiguous scraped-up mounds may just be earlier than the main alignment represented by HAR-61(S) (3540 ±140 BP; 2290–1520 cal BC at 95% confidence), HAR-130(S) (3500 ±110 BP; 2140–1530 cal BC at 95% confidence), NPL-141 (3490 ±90 BP; 2040–1600 cal BC at 95% confidence; Reimer *et al* 2004), and also GU-5302 (Snail Down, Site III).

References: Reimer *et al* 2004

Snail Down: Site XIX, Wiltshire

Location: SU 22055202
Lat. 51.15.59 N; Long. 01.41.02 W

Project manager: N Thomas (Devizes Museum), 1957

Archival body: Wiltshire Heritage Museum

Description: a double bell barrow, the largest at Snail Down, which yielded a very important Bronze Age ogival dagger and bronze pin in AD 1805.

Objectives: to date the ogival dagger as these samples were sealed near the base of a very large mound.

References: Thomas 2005

GU–5304 3330 ±80 BP

$\delta^{13}C$: -23.5‰

Sample: SD XIX 1957 305, submitted on 16 February 1993 by N Thomas

Material: charcoal: *Quercus* sp. (9.20g) (C Dickson 1993)

Initial comment: at a depth of *c* 1.2m in the larger of two mounds constituting a double bell barrow. The mound was originally sealed by a chalky crust. The sample came from a core composed of turf and topsoil from the site of the barrow's surrounding ditch.

Objectives: to date the grave goods associated with the site which were removed in AD 1805. The grave goods consist of a wooden box containing an important ogival bronze dagger and bronze ring-headed pin, wrapped in cloth, and a coffin for the cremation, made out of a tree-trunk.

Calibrated date: 1σ: 1740–1510 cal BC
2σ: 1880–1430 cal BC

Final comment: N Thomas (8 September 1993), the date suggests this site may be younger than neighbouring site Snail Down, Site XXII (dated by OxA-4211). This is archaeologically surprising but quite acceptable.

Snail Down: Site XV, Wiltshire

Location: SU 22025208
Lat. 51.16.01 N; Long. 01.41.04 W

Project manager: N Thomas (Devizes Museum), 1955

Archival body: Wiltshire Heritage Museum

Description: a barrow with a Romano-British pottery concentration. The only barrow at Snail Down to yield a series of crouched inhumations under cairns.

Objectives: to add to the overall dating history of the cemetery.

References: Thomas 2005

GU–5305 2920 ±70 BP

$\delta^{13}C$: -21.8‰

Sample: SD XV 1955 58, 60, 62, submitted on 16 February 1993 by N Thomas

Material: human bone (mature female) (I Cornwall)

Initial comment: from a skeleton beneath the modern turf/topsoil and beneath the earlier top of the barrow sealed by rabbit throw out. The burial was roughly covered by the remains of a flint cairn. The skeleton was mostly articulated but was broken or damaged *in situ*. The skull and several other bones were absent. The burial had been disturbed by rabbits and there was some possible intrusion by rootlets.

Objectives: to date the inhumation and associated Romano-British sherds which date to the first and second centuries AD.

Calibrated date: *1σ:* 1260–1000 cal BC
                     2σ: 1380–910 cal BC

Final comment: P Ashbee (2001), this single date obtained from human bone taken from an inhumation burial beneath the crown of barrow XV, stands apart as it was believed that this burials was Romano-British. This date, however, albeit a single one, and thus statistically uncertain, could be thought of as calling into question the nature and age of some of these subsequent burials in barrows.

Snail Down: Site XVII, Wiltshire

Location: SU 21675210
                     Lat. 51.16.02 N; Long. 01.41.22 W

Project manager: N Thomas (Devizes Museum), 1957

Archival body: Wiltshire Heritage Museum

Description: a bowl barrow, an outrider to the main barrow alignment. It was not disturbed when almost all other barrows were trenched by Hoare-Cunnington in AD 1805.

Objectives: to date the barrow and the sequence of phasing in the barrow.

References: Thomas 2005

GU–5303 5310 ±70 BP

δ¹³C: -25.4‰

Sample: SD XVII 1957 359, submitted on 16 February 1993 by N Thomas

Material: charcoal (*Prunus avium/Padus* type (1.5g)): Pomoideae (2.30g); *Corylus* sp. (7.70g) (C Dickson 1993)

Initial comment: from the central burial pit which was undisturbed and sealed by the mound. The burial is associated with a large cremation of a well-built young man. This sample comes from the only barrow in the cemetery not previously dug into.

Objectives: the burial has an important location within the cemetery and its date, therefore, is important for phasing the whole cemetery. The measurement would also date the rare discovery here of a ritually smashed large urn.

Calibrated date: *1σ:* 4260–4000 cal BC
                     2σ: 4340–3970 cal BC

Final comment: N Thomas (8 September 1993), this result is far too early and is archaeologically unacceptable.

OxA–4179 3480 ±70 BP

δ¹³C: -25.5‰

Sample: SD XVII 1957 52, 120, submitted on 8 February 1993 by N Thomas

Material: charcoal (initial sample included *Corylus* (0.1g); unidentified (1.2g)): Pomoideae, *c* 0.07g sent for dating (2.20g) (C Dickson 1993)

Initial comment: from pit 1, one of three possible ritual pits associated with sherds of an incomplete bipartite Collared Urn and human burnt bone. It is secondary to the central grave (dated by GU-5303). The pit cut into the edge of the mound which was full of charcoal and burnt earth and carefully packed sherds of incomplete bipartite Collared Urn.

Objectives: to date the pit. The pit is allied to the central grave (see GU-5303) by broken sherds and a smashed central urn. It gives an example of continuity of practice, seen elsewhere at Snail Down. This sample, together with GU-5303 will give a useful indicator of the length of rituals at Site XVII.

Calibrated date: *1σ:* 1900–1690 cal BC
                     2σ: 2020–1620 cal BC

Final comment: N Thomas (8 September 1993), the result is acceptable; on archaeological grounds these ?ritual pits are not likely to be much later than the primary burial (GU-5303, the date for which is unacceptable). This result is a hint at the barrow's age, as correction to GU-5303.

References: Hedges *et al* 1995, 421

Snail Down: Site XXII, Wiltshire

Location: SU 22065196
                     Lat. 51.15.57 N; Long. 01.41.02 W

Project manager: N Thomas (Devizes Museum), 1957

Archival body: Wiltshire Heritage Museum

Description: a small mound added to the berm of a large bell barrow.

Objectives: this burial is special because, apart from the foetus from Site II, all the burials from Snail Down have been cremations. The result would also help date the bell barrow, one of the largest at Snail Down and in a key position. It is necessary to establish how the burial fits into the overall history of the cemetery.

References: Hedges *et al* 1995, 421
                     Thomas 2005

OxA–4211 3485 ±110 BP

δ¹³C: -21.3‰

Sample: SD XXII 1957, submitted on 16 February 1993 by N THomas

Material: human bone (juvenile) (I Cornwall)

Initial comment: from a crouched complete skeleton of a youth suffering from a tumour. The section showed that the skeleton had been inserted into the mound. It was associated with amber beads and a perforated cockle shell.

Objectives: to provide a date for the burial in order to compare it with the neighbouring double bell barrow (GU-5304). The tumour is possibly the first on record and also therefore a date would have medical interest.

Calibrated date: 1σ: 1950–1680 cal BC
2σ: 2140–1520 cal BC

Final comment: N Thomas (8 September 1993), the result is acceptable, although I expected it to be somewhat later. It makes the overall phasing interesting!

Snape, Suffolk

Location: TM 402593
Lat. 52.10.45 N; Long. 01.30.49 E

Project manager: T Pestell (Suffolk Archaeological Unit), 1991

Archival body: Suffolk County Council

Description: on account of the boat burials excavated in AD 1862 and AD 1998, the Snape cemetery is a site of crucial importance to the understanding of East Anglian pagan Anglo-Saxon cemeteries in general and Sutton Hoo in particular.

Objectives: to date the horse's head burial and the burnt stone features.

References: Filmer-Sankey *et al* 1991
Filmer-Sankey and Pestell 2001

GU–5233 1460 ±70 BP

δ¹³C: -20.9‰

Sample: 1787/1789/1783, submitted on 15 April 1992 by S A Carnegie

Material: animal bone: *Equus* sp., head; bone and teeth (T Pestell 1991)

Initial comment: found directly beneath the ploughsoil, in area of arable; therefore possible contaminates include rootlets, animal disturbance, and regular liming. The top of the head was truncated by ploughing, scattering bone fragments.

Objectives: found adjacent to an Anglo-Saxon boat burial so this association needs to be confirmed. If it is Anglo-Saxon, it is a rare find which will give a more precise date to the boat contents.

Calibrated date: 1σ: cal AD 540–660
2σ: cal AD 420–680

Final comment: T Pestell (6 May 1994), bone from a horse skull was submitted as there was no stratigraphic evidence to date it, and the few associated pieces of tack were stylistically unremarkable. Now confirmed as Anglo-Saxon, the skull is an extremely rare find and must relate to an adjacent inhumation burial of high status.

GU–5234 1580 ±50 BP

δ¹³C: -25.3‰

Sample: 1799, submitted on 15 April 1992 by S A Carnegie

Material: charcoal: unidentified, including small sand grains (11.30g); *Ulex* sp. (5.40g); *Quercus* sp. (0.20g); *Corylus* sp. (0.30g) (C Dickson 1992)

Initial comment: the feature was within an arable area, directly beneath the ploughsoil, and possible contamination include rootlets, animal, and plough disturbances. The field is also continually limed. The feature is one of two found amongst inhumation graves and consisted of a large oval/oblong possible pit, packed with burnt flints, surrounded entirely by an edging of carbonised wood.

Objectives: Anglo-Saxon dating will confirm the use of the feature during the active life of the cemetery. The presence of a Bronze Age urn on the site gives a possibility of earlier dating and use. The feature maybe a cremation pyre/feasting hearth never seen before in Anglo-Saxon cemetery, therefore it is highly important to know the correct date. If it is Anglo-Saxon, it will assist in dating other aspects of the cemetery more closely within the period.

Calibrated date: 1σ: cal AD 410–550
2σ: cal AD 380–600

Final comment: T Pestell (6 May 1994), charcoal from a shallow pit filled with burnt flint was submitted. It was unknown if the pit was of antiquity, lacking both stratigraphic data and finds. The Anglo-Saxon dates agrees with that of sample GU-5235 and suggests that the seven such pits found are contemporary with the cemetery.

GU–5235 1680 ±50 BP

δ¹³C: -25.6‰

Sample: 1897, submitted on 15 April 1992 by S A Carnegie

Material: charcoal: unidentified, includes small sand grains (6.10g); *Ulex* sp. (<0.40g); *Quercus* sp. (0.50g) (C Dickson 1992)

Initial comment: as GU-5234

Objectives: as GU-5234

Calibrated date: 1σ: cal AD 260–420
2σ: cal AD 240–540

Final comment: T Pestell (6 May 1994), charcoal from a second burnt-flint filled pit, also lacking any other dating evidence was submitted. Despite the relatively early date, it broadly agrees with sample GU-5234. This suggests that the pits, including others encountered, were used during the life of the pagan Anglo-Saxon cemetery.

Somerset Levels, Somerset

Location: ST 3542 to ST 4539 approx
Lat. 51.10.23 N; Long. 02.55.48 W to
Lat. 51.08.51 N; Long. 02.47.11W

Project manager: J Coles (Department of the Environment)

Description: a series of prehistoric wooden trackways crossing the wetlands in the area of Glastonbury. They were gradually engulfed, and thereby preserved, through the build up of peat in the Levels.

References: Coles and Dobson 1989
Coles and Orme 1976
Coles and Orme 1979
Coles and Orme 1981
Coles and Orme 1984
Orme 1982

Somerset Levels: Claylands, Binham Moor, Somerset

Location:	ST 382493 Lat. 51.14.20 N; Long. 02.53.07 W
Project manager:	R McDonnell (Somerset County Council), 1986
Archival body:	Somerset County Museum
References:	McDonnell 1985 McDonnell 1986

HAR–9190 2900 ±60 BP

δ¹³C: -28.4‰

Sample: BM01, submitted on 5 January 1988 by R McDonnell

Material: peat

Initial comment: sample taken from junction of clay (above) with peat (beneath) at a depth of 1.7m OD.

Objectives: this sample should provide a date for the end of peat formation and the onset of marine flooding in this part of the Somerset levels.

Calibrated date:	*1σ:* 1210–1000 cal BC
	2σ: 1300–910 cal BC

Somerset Levels: Claylands, Cripps River, Somerset

Location:	ST 369439 Lat. 51.11.25 N; Long. 02.54.11 W
Project manager:	R McDonnell (Somerset County Council), 1986
Archival body:	Somerset County Museum
References:	McDonnell 1985 McDonnell 1986

HAR–9188 2900 ±90 BP

δ¹³C: -28.2‰

Sample: CR01, submitted in September 1987 by R McDonnell

Material: peat

Initial comment: duplicate of CR02, briquetage mound. Sample taken from bottom of peat above clay, feature 13, containing briquetage (trench A).

Objectives: it is anticipated that the date provided by this sample, and sample CR02 (HAR-9189), will provide a date for salt production activity within an area of peat deposition.

Calibrated date:	*1σ:* 1260–930 cal BC
	2σ: 1390–840 cal BC

References:	Hardiman *et al* 1992, 69

HAR–9189 3560 ±60 BP

δ¹³C: -28.1‰

Sample: CR02, submitted in September 1987 by R McDonnell

Material: peat

Initial comment: as HAR-9188

Objectives: as HAR-9188

Calibrated date:	*1σ:* 2010–1780 cal BC
	2σ: 2120–1740 cal BC

Laboratory comment: English Heritage (26 February 2012), the two measurements on this sample are statistically significantly different (T′=36.0; T′(5%)=3.8; ν=1; Ward and Wilson 1978).

References:	Ward and Wilson 1978

South Acre, Norfolk

Location:	TF 80321472 Lat. 52.41.59 N; Long. 00.40.08 E
Project manager:	J Wymer (Centre of East Anglian Studies, University of East Anglia), 1988
Archival body:	Norwich Castle Museum

Description: a group of ring ditches on a wide gravel terrace of the River Nar. The sequence of events on the site can be divided into three phases. The earliest phase, prior to the construction of the ring ditch, is based on the assumption that flint artefacts of Mesolithic type would have been made and used long before such earthworks existed. The second phase is the construction of the ring ditch, the accumulation of the silt by natural processes within it, and the formation of a podzol soil horizon in the fill. The third phase is that represented by the numerous intrusive burials within and external to the ring ditch.

Objectives: to excavate and date the site before being destroyed by gravel quarrying.

References:	Hardiman *et al* 1992, 57
	Wymer 1996

HAR–10238 1150 ±70 BP

δ¹³C: -21.9‰

Sample: SAC14449, submitted in December 1988 by P Murphy

Material: human bone

Initial comment: from skeleton 33, a grave dug immediately outside the ring ditch.

Objectives: no grave goods were recovered with the skeletons. Dating is required to establish the association with similar burials within the ditch fills of the ring ditch.

Calibrated date:	*1σ:* cal AD 770–990
	2σ: cal AD 680–1030

Final comment: J Wymer (1996), the human burials from this excavation constitute the most informative and significant aspect of the site and are of late Saxon date.

HAR–10239 1710 ±90 BP

δ¹³C: -21.8‰

Sample: SAC1305, submitted in December 1988 by P Murphy

Material: human bone

Initial comment: from skeleton 75, a grave dug into the ditch fill of the ring ditch, which is more recent than the formation of a podzol subsoil feature within the ditch filling.

Objectives: no grave goods were recovered with the skeletons but casual finds within the ditch and grave fills included a few sherds of pagan Saxon ware. Dating is required to confirm the association, or otherwise, with the burials.

Calibrated date: *1σ:* cal AD 230–430
                      2σ: cal AD 80–550

Final comment: see HAR-10238

South West Fen Dyke Survey, Cambridgeshire

Location: TF 19200740 to TL 23509950
                Lat. 52.39.03 N; Long. 00.14.16 W, to
                Lat. 52.34.44 N; Long. 00.10.38 W

Project manager: C French (Fenland Archaeological Trust), 1982 and 1985

Description: a series of prehistoric to Roman sites were discovered in the Fenland region to the north-east of Peterborough by the systematic survey and recording of the cleared dyke sections (by the drainage authorities) over a period of three years. Identified sites were dated, delimited, and set in their environment and drift geological contexts.

Objectives: to augment the work of the Fenland Survey Project by systematically looking for buried prehistoric sites buried by the Fenland drift sequence; to investigate and put into practice new methodological approaches to extensive buried archaeology; and to identify well-preserved and waterlogged sites in the Fenland region to the north-east of Peterborough.

References: French 1988
               French and Pryor 1993

South West Fen Dyke Survey: Borough Fen, site 7, Cambridgeshire

Location: TF 19200740
                Lat. 53.29.02 N; Long. 00.14.17 W

Project manager: C French (Fenland Archaeological Trust), 1982–6

Description: the main rampart and ditch covers an approximately circular area of *c* 3.8ha, with a diameter of *c* 220m. There are slight indications of an outer ditch and bank with a diameter of *c* 280m. The eastern third is cultivated and being progressively plough damaged; the western two-thirds is under grass. The interior in its eastern third contains a thick occupation horizon and intact ploughsoil/soil sequence, beneath which define settlement features.

Objectives: to identify the date, preservation, and nature of the monument; to investigate the presence/absence of interior features, and the monument's function.

HAR–8512 2090 ±80 BP

δ¹³C: -26.7‰

Sample: SWFC3, submitted in March 1987 by C French

Material: charcoal (0.03g,100) (remaining sparse subsample identified): unidentified (0.05g); *Alnus* sp. (0.30g, 100%) (R Gale 2000)

Initial comment: the charcoal was obtained by wet-sieving occupation deposits from dyke 5.

Objectives: to provide corroborative evidence for the period of occupation of the only known fort in a Fenland context, and to provide a *terminus ante quem* for the onset of alluviation and upper peat formation.

Calibrated date: *1σ:* 210 cal BC–cal AD 10
                      2σ: 380 cal BC–cal AD 80

Final comment: C French (26 March 1996), this date reflects the opinion of the date range obtained from pottery within the interior feature, and indicates the latest possible use of this high, landward part of Borough Fen, for settlement.

Laboratory comment: AERE Harwell (28 February 1989), this sample was measured in the miniature gas proportional counter (Otlet *et al* 1983).

References: French 1988
               French and Pryor 1993
              Otlet *et al* 1983

South West Fen Dyke Survey: Crowtree Farm, Cambridgeshire

Location: TF 29800101
                Lat. 52.35.28 N; Long. 00.05.01 W

Project manager: C French (Fenland Archaeological Trust), 1985

Archival body: Fenland Archaeological Trust and Peterborough Museum

Description: a later Mesolithic to Neolithic lithic scatter campsite on the extreme landward edge of the fens in the third millennium BC.

Objectives: to define the extent, date, and nature of the site, as well as to elucidate the onset of marine and freshwater influences in this part of the fen.

References: French and Pryor 1993
              Hardiman *et al* 1992, 66–7

HAR–8510 3740 ±100 BP

δ¹³C: -28.1‰

Sample: SWFC1, submitted in April 1987 by C French

Material: peat

Initial comment: sample taken from dyke 14, from the upper 5cm of a buried soil which contained later Mesolithic/earlier Neolithic flint artefacts. The flot came from *c* 1kg of wet-sieved material, plus *c* 0.5kg of unsieved material.

Objectives: to provide firmer evidence of the time period of human settlement, and to provide a *terminus ante quem* for the onset of the lower peat formation. By implication a date will also provide approximate dating of two other nearby sites with a similar stratigraphic location.

Calibrated date: *1σ:* 2300–1980 cal BC
                       2σ: 2470–1880 cal BC

Final comment: C French (26 March 1996), the final use of the fen-edge occurred in the later third/early second millennium BC, thus according with artefactual and sedimentary evidence. This part of the fen-edge was frequented for the last half of the millennia, occasionally and perhaps on a seasonal basis, before the onset of peat growth in the Bronze Age. The dates have also enabled the pollen sequence to be tied down to a similar period, and in particular to record the change from deciduous woodland dominated by lime and oak to brackish and freshwater fen conditions with a rich aquatic flora change.

HAR–8513 3660 ±60 BP

δ¹³C: -27.6‰

Sample: SWFC4, submitted in April 1987 by C French

Material: peat

Initial comment: taken from dyke 14, from the lower 5cm of the lower peat overlying the buried soil. The flot came from *c* 1kg of wet-sieved material plus *c* 0.5kg of unsieved peat.

Objectives: to provide an approximate date for the inception of the lower peat growth on the island.

Calibrated date: *1σ:* 2140–1940 cal BC
                       2σ: 2210–1880 cal BC

Final comment: see HAR-8510

HAR–8913 3190 ±90 BP

δ¹³C: -28.1‰

Sample: SWFC4A, submitted in April 1987 by C French

Material: charcoal: unidentified

Initial comment: from the base of the lower peat in trench 2.

Objectives: for comparative reasons to samples SWFC1 and SWFC4.

Calibrated date: *1σ:* 1530–1390 cal BC
                       2σ: 1690–1260 cal BC

Final comment: see HAR-8510

Laboratory comment: AERE Harwell (5 September 1989), this sample was measured in the miniature gas proportional counter (Otlet *et al* 1983).

References: Otlet *et al* 1983

Staines Road Farm, Surrey

Location: TQ 07686832
                      Lat. 51.24.11 N; Long. 00.27.06 W

Project manager: P Jones (Surrey County Archaeological Unit), 1989

Archival body: Surrey County Archaeology Unit

Description: during the autumn of 1989 a ditched ringwork identified on an aerial photograph was found to be of Neolithic date and totally excavated in advance of gravel extraction. The work was undertaken by archaeological staff of Surrey County Council Planning Department, who were also able to sample an adjacent occupation layer that had been sealed below a 'burnt mound' layer with an associated 'boiling pit', a 'waterhole', some peripheral late Bronze Age pits, a nearby long avenue of pit rows, and some field ditches. Except for the obviously later pits, it was thought that some of these features could have been partly contemporaneous with the use of the ringwork.

Objectives: ten samples were selected to provide dating for the primary and tertiary infillings of the ring ditch, two humans represented by skeletal material in the ditch, the possible 'burnt mound', and an earlier occupation layer that lay outside the ring ditch, an adjacent 'water hole', and a nearby avenue of pit rows.

Final comment: P Jones (4 June 1996), the successful dating of seven of the ten samples dispelled an earlier notion of a possible sequence of later Neolithic features, confirms an earlier Neolithic presence as well as a later one, and extends the period of use of the immediate area around the ring ditch through most, if not all, of the Bronze Age. The early date range of one sample from the second fill of the ring ditch (OxA-4060) could imply that it had been redeposited from an earlier Neolithic occupation that pre-dated its construction, or else belonged to its use before its first infilling. A period of earlier Neolithic activity has been suspected from both the flintwork and the pottery, and this sample confirms it. This means, however, that there can be no certainty that the other three animal bone samples from the ring ditch were not also residual, although their range of dating conforms to what was expected, ie a first deliberate infill in the middle of the fourth millennium cal BC, and a second infill sometime during the second half of the millennium. The only certain primary sample was the human burial, and the date range for this falls between those of the other three. Instead of the ringwork having been contemporary with some of the external features, the dating of samples suggests that the 'burnt mound' layer had been deposited up to half a millennium after the ring ditch was sealed, and that the waterhole was even later and cannot have been open even whilst the burnt layer was being formed. The lack of success in dating the human torso is unfortunate, but the failure of samples from the occupation soil below the burnt layer, and from one of the pits of the avenue, seriously detracts from our understanding of this long-lived complex of buried field monuments.

Laboratory comment: Oxford Radiocarbon Accelerator Unit (11 May 1993), two further samples (sample S (G8) and sample 7 (H7)) failed to provide enough collagen to date. Despite taking quite large amounts of bone, the sample yielded less than 0.2mg of carbon and was therefore too small to be dated.

References: Jones 1990a
                 Jones 1990b
                 Jones 2008

GU–5278 3630 ±90 BP

δ¹³C: -27.1‰

Sample: 9 (H3), submitted on 11 August 1992 by P Jones

Material: wood (waterlogged): *Quercus* sp., 74 rings, no sapwood (J Hillam)

Initial comment: from an oak pile lying on the base of a large pit that had been dug through the contemporaneous watertable and which is interpreted as having been a waterhole, feature H3. The sample was sealed by primary sand and silt infillings with Neolithic material, and a formation of reed peat, and was recovered from below the modern watertable.

Objectives: this sample will assist in the dating of the original digging of the waterhole. Since it may have been dug to supply water for the boiling pit (H4) and other possibly associated features (burnt layer H2, GU-5279, and hearth H5), its dating will clarify the chronological relationship of these contexts. The pile retains 74 growth rings and a sample already taken is to be dated dendrochronologically. A radiocarbon determination will both assist in that procedure and also serve as a check on the dendrochronology.

Calibrated date: *1σ:* 2140–1880 cal BC
                 2σ: 2280–1740 cal BC

Final comment: P Jones (4 June 1996), the 'waterhole' could have been dug a thousand years or more after the infilling of the ring ditch, and certainly after, perhaps by as much as half a millennium, the deposition of the 'burnt mound' layer H2, GU-5279. The feature can be no longer regarded simply as a source of water for the boiling pit H4, and the dating suggests that it had been dug towards the end of the early Bronze Age. This is supported by the evidence of pottery sherds from its later infills above the peat layer, which are of Deverel-Rimbury types. The pile has not been dated dendrochronologically.

GU–5279 3930 ±50 BP

δ¹³C: -26.0‰

Sample: 8 (H2), submitted on 11 August 1992 by P Jones

Material: charcoal: Pomoideae (M Robinson)

Initial comment: from a layer of comminuted charcoal, wood ash, and calcined flints (perhaps a levelled burnt mound) which lay outside of, and was stratigraphically unconnected with, the ring ditch. It is from the second of three layers (above that which yielded 7 (H7)) which survived plough truncation because they had slumped within an earlier linear hollow. The layer is contiguous with the fill of a rectangular pit (H4) which lay within the spread of burnt material, and covered a hearth (H5) next to the pit.

Objectives: the layer is either contemporary with at least one of the ring ditch phases, or else later. It is associated with a rectangular, flat-based pit, which may have been a for boiling water, and a hearth where flints may have been heated before immersion in the water in the pit. The water could have come from the close-by, deep pit, H3. Radiocarbon dates for the burnt layer (GU-5279), its underlying soil (sample 7 (H7)), the waterhole (GU-5278), and the ring ditch samples (OxA-4057 to OxA-4061) should clarify the chronological sequence.

Calibrated date: *1σ:* 2480–2340 cal BC
                 2σ: 2570–2280 cal BC

Final comment: P Jones (4 June 1996), layer H2 of sample 8 had been deposited in the early Bronze age, much later than the final infilling of the ring ditch, but earlier than the digging of the waterhole nearby. Although the associated rectangular pit (H4) could still have been for boiling water, this had not been obtained for the waterhole (H3). As sample 7 from the underlying occupation soil layer H7 could not be dated, it remains uncertain whether this had been of Bronze Age, or earlier or later Neolithic date.

OxA–4057 4670 ±85 BP

δ¹³C: -21.0‰ (assumed)

Sample: 1 (G1 E/F), submitted on 11 August 1992 by P Jones

Material: animal bone: *Bos* sp., humerus (D Sergeantson)

Initial comment: from the primary fill of the ring ditch, found intermittently along the base and sides of the original profile after most had been dug out later in the Neolithic period during a re-cutting of the ring ditch. It was stratified below the second fill (represented by OxA-4059 and OxA-4060) in a cream/buff calcareous clayey silt. Both OxA-4057 and OxA-4058 came from the same context but from different parts of the ring ditch.

Objectives: both OxA-4057 and OxA-4058 were samples used to date the first deliberate backfilling of the ring ditch after its earliest use.

Calibrated date: *1σ:* 3630–3360 cal BC
                 2σ: 3650–3120 cal BC

Final comment: P Jones (4 June 1996), this is a little earlier than expected as the deposit also includes two sherds of impressed ware more typical of the later Neolithic, but *see* OxA-4060.

References: Bronk Ramsey *et al* 2000b, 250

OxA–4058 4740 ±85 BP

δ¹³C: -21.0‰ (assumed)

Sample: 2 (G9 E/F), submitted on 11 August 1992 by P Jones

Material: animal bone: *Bos* sp., metacarpal (D Sergeantson)

Initial comment: as OxA-4057

Objectives: as OxA-4057

Calibrated date: *1σ:* 3640–3370 cal BC
                 2σ: 3700–3350 cal BC

Final comment: P Jones (4 June 1996), this is earlier than OxA-4057 and is unexpected for the same reason, but *see* also OxA-4060.

References: Bronk Ramsey *et al* 2000b, 250

OxA–4059 4595 ±85 BP

δ¹³C: -21.0‰ (assumed)

Sample: 3 (G15 D1), submitted on 11 August 1992 by P Jones

Material: animal bone: *Bos* sp., metatarsal (D Sergeantson)

Initial comment: from the second fill of the ring ditch, found in clayey loam. Most of the first fill represented by OxA-4057 and OxA-4058 was dug out some time in the middle/late Neolithic, respecting much the same alignment as had earlier prevailed. The second fill was either a deliberate backfilling or a gradual accumulation. Both OxA-4059 and OxA-4060 come from the same context but different parts of the ring ditch.

Objectives: OxA-4059 and OxA-4060 should be later than OxA-4057 and OxA-4058, when the ring ditch was first backfilled, but later than when it was backfilled for the second time. They should therefore be partly contemporaneous with the second phase of use of the monument.

Calibrated date: 1σ: 3500–3120 cal BC
2σ: 3640–3020 cal BC

Final comment: P Jones (4 June 1996), the sample is later than OxA-4057 and OxA-4058 of the earlier fill, and its date is in accordance with some of the ceramics in association, such as Ebbsfleet and Mortlake styles of the later Neolithic impressed ware series; but *see* also OxA-4060.

References: Bronk Ramsey *et al* 2000b, 250

OxA–4060 4860 ±85 BP

δ¹³C: -21.0‰ (assumed)

Sample: 4 (G13 D2/3), submitted on 11 August 1992 by P Jones

Material: animal bone: *Bos* sp., tibia (D Sergeantson)

Initial comment: as OxA-4059

Objectives: as OxA-4059

Calibrated date: 1σ: 3710–3530 cal BC
2σ: 3900–3380 cal BC

Final comment: P Jones (4 June 1996), this is much earlier than expected, and even earlier than samples OxA-4057 and OxA-4058 of the earlier fill. The later fill may therefore be contaminated with material from an occupation that pre-dated, or belonged to, the earliest use of the ring ditch before its first infilling. If so, there can be no certainty of knowing whether samples OxA-4057, OxA-4058, or OxA-4059 belonged to either the period immediately before the first infilling, or before the second infilling, or before the ring ditch had been dug.

References: Bronk Ramsey *et al* 2000b, 250

OxA–4061 4645 ±85 BP

δ¹³C: -21.0‰ (assumed)

Sample: 6 (G10), submitted on 11 August 1992 by P Jones

Material: human bone (S Mays)

Initial comment: the crouched inhumation burial lay at the base of a grave pit cut through the first phase ring ditch fill (as of OxA-4057 and OxA-4058), but it is uncertain whether it had lain below the bulk of the second phase fill (as of OxA-4059 and OxA-4060) or been cut through it. It was, therefore, the earliest or the latest context associated with the second phase of infilling, but was filled with brown clayey loam that is very similar to that of the second phase of infilling. The burial lay immediately adjacent to the single causewayed entrance.

Objectives: the burial is of either an early or a late date within the second phase of use of the ring ditch. It is uncertain how the date of the burial relates to the features and layers outside the ring ditch, or to a human torso, sample 5 (G8), which was found elsewhere along the base of the ring ditch.

Calibrated date: 1σ: 3630–3350 cal BC
2σ: 3640–3100 cal BC

Final comment: P Jones (4 June 1996), the date range of sample 6 is little different to those of OxA-4059 and OxA-4057, the second and primary phases of the ring ditch infilling, but note the uncertainties about such dating in the comments on OxA-4060. OxA-4061, therefore, is the only dated sample from the ring ditch that had been, without question, primarily deposited there. It still remains uncertain, however, whether the grave had lain below the second fill, or had been cut through it. Without a date for the human torso of sample 5 it cannot be known whether this was earlier or later than the more formal burial represented by sample 6.

References: Bronk Ramsey *et al* 2000b, 250

Stannon: Bodmin Moor, Cornwall

Location: SX 126797
Lat. 50.35.11 N; Long. 04.38.51 W

Project manager: V Straker (University of Bristol), May 1991

Archival body: Cornwall County Council

Description: a pipeline trench for South West Water was routed over 3km of open moorland between De Lank and Stannon (near the Stannon stone circle) on Bodmin Moor. It cut through several boundaries including part of an 'early' curvilinear field system. One boundary was found to have been proceeded by a wooden fence-line of near-continuous posts.

Objectives: two of the boundary banks ran into a bog giving the opportunity to relate the field systems to a dated sequence of vegetation change derived from pollen analysis and radiocarbon dating. Trench 8 across one boundary provided five samples (GU-5153, GU-5178, GU-5173, and GU-5174) comprising a wooden stake in peat beneath the boundary and three peat samples. Three samples of peat (GU-5170, GU-5180, and GU-5171) were submitted from trench 9 which cut a section across the other boundary.

References: Rose 1992a
Rose 1992b

GU–5153 5340 ±60 BP

δ¹³C: -27.8‰

Sample: STAN 91/01, submitted in June 1991 by V Straker

Material: wood: *Alnus glutinosa* (V Straker 1991)

Initial comment: the wood is from a post recovered from a 2 × 2m trench (trench 8, section A-B) in a peat bog excavated to show the relationship between a stone boundary-bank and the bog into which it runs. The post is one of two pushed into the peat along the line of the boundary. The base of the post rested on natural granite and the post was embedded in peat. A 0.16m thick layer of red/black peat covered the surviving top of the post, separating it from the base of the stone bank.

Objectives: a date for the post coupled with a date on the peat immediately below the stone boundary will determine whether the line of posts is part of the construction of the stone boundary, or part of an earlier boundary. This is the first occasion on which it has been possible to excavate a boundary on Bodmin Moor, which exists on dry-land and also extends into a peat bog. A date for this feature will be important as it is part of a landscape which has been extensively surveyed, but is only possible to date in relative terms.

Calibrated date: *1σ:* 4320–4050 cal BC
                      2σ: 4340–3990 cal BC

Final comment: V Straker (1 March 2012), the early fifth millennium BC date demonstrates that the post is substantially earlier than the stone boundary wall above it which ran on a similar alignment. The date for the top of the peat beneath the wall (GU-5172) is early Bronze Age (mid-late second millennium cal BC).

GU–5170 3310 ±50 BP

δ¹³C: -28.3‰

Sample: STAN91/02, submitted on 1 August 1991 by D Jordan

Material: peat (humic acid fraction)

Initial comment: from a vertical section in a 2m × 2m trench cut into a peat bog immediately beneath a boundary wall (trench 9). The peat may be contaminated by stray roots from above and from any turves laid over it during construction of the wall.

Objectives: to date the wall (*terminus ante quem*) and the top of the pollen sequence.

Calibrated date: *1σ:* 1670–1520 cal BC
                      2σ: 1740–1460 cal BC

Final comment: V Straker (1 March 2012), this date is broadly comparable with GU-5172 which dated the peat immediately beneath the boundary sectioned in trench 8.

GU–5171 6050 ±70 BP

δ¹³C: -28.4‰

Sample: STAN91/04, submitted on 1 August 1991 by D Jordan

Material: peat (humic acid fraction)

Initial comment: from beneath the field wall, at a depth of 17–20 cm, (below GU-5180). May contain old roots not contemporary with its original deposition.

Objectives: to date the wall (*terminus ante quem*) and the pollen sequence.

Calibrated date: *1σ:* 5050–4840 cal BC
                      2σ: 5210–4780 cal BC

Final comment: V Straker (1 March 2012), the peat in trench 9 provides a chronology for the environment and vegetation from the onset of peat growth in the late Mesolithic to the mid-to-late first millennium cal BC.

GU–5172 3380 ±50 BP

δ¹³C: -28.9‰

Sample: STAN91/05, submitted on 1 August 1991 by D Jordan

Material: peat (humic acid fraction)

Initial comment: from a section immediately beneath a field wall (trench 8, section A-B). May be contaminated by roots from above.

Objectives: to date the wall and the pollen sequence beneath it.

Calibrated date: *1σ:* 1750–1610 cal BC
                      2σ: 1870–1520 cal BC

Final comment: V Straker (1 March 2012), this early Bronze Age date for the peat beneath the wall provides a *terminus ante quem* for its construction and dates the top of the pollen sequence beneath it.

GU–5173 5060 ±70 BP

δ¹³C: -29.5‰

Sample: STAN91/07, submitted on 1 August 1991 by D Jordan

Material: peat (humic acid fraction)

Initial comment: from 45–50 cm deep in a section beside a field wall. This sample came from directly below GU-5178 (trench 8, section B–D).

Objectives: to provide a date for the pollen sequence.

Calibrated date: *1σ:* 3960–3770 cal BC
                      2σ: 3990–3690 cal BC

Final comment: V Straker (1 March 2012), the peat in trench 8 provides a chronology for the environment and vegetation from the onset of peat growth in the Mesolithic (early–mid eighth millennium cal BC) to the mid-to-late first millennium cal BC.

GU–5174 8380 ±70 BP

δ¹³C: -29.5‰

Sample: STAN91/08, submitted on 1 August 1991 by D Jordan

Material: peat (humic acid fraction)

Initial comment: from 77–82cm depth in the section beside a field wall, directly beneath GU-5173 (trench 8, section B–D).

Objectives: to provide a date for the pollen sequence.

Calibrated date: *1σ:* 7540–7350 cal BC
                      2σ: 7580–7200 cal BC

Final comment: see GU-5173

GU–5178 2580 ±50 BP

δ¹³C: -28.8‰

Sample: STAN91/06, submitted on 1 August 1991 by D Jordan

Material: peat (humic acid fraction)

Initial comment: from a depth of 18–23cm in a section beside, and stratigraphically immediately below, a field wall (trench 8, section B–D).

Objectives: to date the collapse of the wall, to provide a date for the pollen sequence, and also to compare with GU-5172.

Calibrated date: *1σ:* 810–760 cal BC
                      2σ: 830–540 cal BC

Final comment: V Straker (1 March 2012), the peat dated was under wall collapse. It is younger than GU-5172. One interpretation is that peat continued to grow around the wall for several centuries after it was built, before the wall started to collapse and spread.

GU–5180 4500 ±60 BP

δ¹³C: -28.3‰

Sample: STAN91/03, submitted on 1 August 1991 by D Jordan

Material: peat (humic acid fraction)

Initial comment: from a vertical section in a 2m × 2m trench cut into a peat bog immediately beneath a boundary wall, taken from 11–14cm beneath the wall (trench 9, below GU-5170).

Objectives: to date the wall and also provide a date for the pollen sequence.

Calibrated date: *1σ:* 3360–3090 cal BC
                      2σ: 3370–2930 cal BC

Final comment: see GU-5171

Stansted: British Rail Section, Essex

Location: TL 523250
                    Lat. 51.54.08 N; Long. 00.12.50 E

Project manager: W Wall (Essex County Council Archaeology Section), May 1988

Archival body: Essex County Council

Description: an area of organic deposits visible within the railway cutting for the proposed railway link. No excavation took place but detailed samples were recorded.

Objectives: to obtain a date for the organic layers within the column samples taken.

Final comment: R Havis (24 September 1997), the dating has provided information on the surviving organic deposits and clearly associated them to a particular period in the prehistoric and historic period. This has allowed detailed palynological assessments of the deposits.

References: Brooks 1989
                    Brooks and Bedwin 1989
                    Havis and Brooks 2004

HAR–9238 1430 ±60 BP

δ¹³C: -30.2‰

Sample: BRS117, submitted in June 1988 by P Murphy

Material: sediment (organic mud)

Initial comment: from a layer of organic mud underlying mineral alluvium at a depth of 117–121cm in contractor's excavations.

Objectives: these sediments in the valley of the Stansted Brook will provide information on phases of soil erosion/alluviation and on vegetational history from pollen and macrofossils within the survey area. Radiocarbon dates are necessary in the absence of any artefactual dating evidence.

Calibrated date: *1σ:* cal AD 570–660
                      2σ: cal AD 530–680

Final comment: R Havis (24 September 1997), this result provided initial dating evidence for a layer of organic deposits. This provided the most interesting information on the Saxon period for the whole project, and allowed a view into the landscape of this period.

HAR–9239 3810 ±80 BP

δ¹³C: -30.0‰

Sample: BRS228, submitted in June 1988 by P Murphy

Material: sediment (organic mud with wood)

Initial comment: from the base of a section exposed in contractor's excavations through the valley floor alluvial sediments at a depth of 228–238cm.

Objectives: as HAR-9238

Calibrated date: *1σ:* 2460–2130 cal BC
                      2σ: 2480–2020 cal BC

Final comment: R Havis (24 September 1997), this result provided dating evidence where no artefactual evidence was found. This allowed detailed analysis on the deposits, and has added to the knowledge of the area during the Bronze Age.

References: Hardiman *et al* 1992, 56

Stansted: Social Club, Essex

Location: TL 523224
                    Lat. 51.52.44 N; Long. 00.12.46 E

Project manager: W Wall (Essex County Council Archaeology Section), February 1988

Archival body: Essex County Council

Description: two Bronze Age structures, with associated pits and rubbish pits. In the middle Iron Age a trackway/droveway was constructed running through the site to an area of open fields. Rubbish pits of a similar date were identified. During the late Iron Age and early Roman period two groups of cremations were identified. A Roman ditch, probably a field boundary was also identified.

Objectives: to establish the date of one of the trackway ditches and a large pit containing significant quantities of rubbish.

Final comment: R Havis (24 September 1997), the dating from the radiocarbon results added little to the final dating of the site, as the large pottery assemblage allowed relatively accurate dating. It did help confirm the age of the features.

References: Brooks 1989
Brooks and Bedwin 1989
Havis and Brooks 2004

HAR–9236 2490 ±70 BP

δ¹³C: -25.5‰

Sample: SCS2246, submitted in June 1988 by P Murphy

Material: charcoal (charcoal, remaining subsample consisted of 'cokey' material and charcoal was sparse): unidentified (12.46g); Rosaceae, sub-family Pomoideae (0.17g, 52%); *Corylus* sp. (0.16g, 48%) (R Gale 1997)

Initial comment: from a charcoal rich layer in fill of a pit, which cuts a ditch, outlining a late Bronze Age/early Iron Age trackway.

Objectives: the pit from which the sample derives cuts the ditch of a Bronze Age trackway, the earliest feature on the site, and from the whole of the Stansted project. Further samples have been taken from a pit cut by the trackway ditch (*see* HAR-9237). It is hoped that radiocarbon dates from these features will give good dating evidence for the construction and abandonment of the trackway.

Calibrated date: *1σ:* 790–410 cal BC
2σ: 810–400 cal BC

Final comment: R Havis (24 September 1997), HAR-9236, together with HAR-9237, provided a window for the abandonment of the trackway. They support the pottery dating as being of middle Iron Age date.

HAR–9237 2780 ±70 BP

δ¹³C: -28.0‰

Sample: SCS2260, submitted in June 1988 by P Murphy

Material: charcoal: unidentified

Initial comment: from a layer of charcoal in the fill of a another pit cut by the ditch of the trackway.

Objectives: as HAR-9236

Calibrated date: *1σ:* 1010–830 cal BC
2σ: 1130–800 cal BC

Final comment: see HAR-9236

UB–3179 2353 ±38 BP

δ¹³C: -25.0 ±0.2‰

Sample: SCS2380, submitted in August 1989 by P Murphy

Material: charcoal: unidentified

Initial comment: from a block of charcoal identified within a large pit thought to be of Bronze Age date.

Objectives: to establish a date for the infilling of the pit, which was thought to be a late Bronze Age rubbish pit.

Calibrated date: *1σ:* 410–390 cal BC
2σ: 520–380 cal BC

Final comment: R Havis (24 September 1997), this date provided corroborative dating for the pottery from the large rubbish pits on the site.

Stonea Camp, Cambridgeshire

Location: TL 448931
Lat. 52.30.58 N; Long. 00.08.03 E

Project manager: T Malim (Cambridgeshire County Council Archaeological Field Unit), 1992

Archival body: English Heritage

Description: a multi-vallate Iron Age Fort whose outermost defences enclose 24 acres. It is situated on the very edge of a fen island, at 2.0m OD. In concept and scale Stonea Camp is similar to the hillforts of southern and western England, whilst unparalleled in Cambridgeshire and largely unlike any forts in the surrounding region. However, there is little evidence to suggest much occupation of the site, and instead when viewed in the light of the greater landscape Stonea Camp should be seen as a focal point for the surrounding Iron Age communities, evidence of whose settlement can be found elsewhere in the locality.

Objectives: a programme of work carried out at the camp during 1990–92 has added substantially to our understanding and phasing of this important site. A series of dates if being sought from various parts of the site to get an overall picture of its length of occupation and to try to verify the postulated phasing.

Final comment: T Malim (March 1994), this series of dates was designed to give a chronological frame work for Stonea Camp, independent of dating from classification and morphological means. The series confirms an Iron Age date, and concentrates the construction and use of the Fort to within at least a 100-year range set approximately within the first two centuries BC. The full range of calibrated dates could take early phases back as far as the fourth century BC, with a range for the latest date into the first century AD, but taking the dates as a group it seems that the second–first centuries BC would accommodate all dates. Sequentially the dates conform with stratigraphic evidence, with a definite separation between primary deposits (leaves and twigs) and later human skeletal material. The samples were obtained from three different locations around the outer defensive ditch.

References: Malim 2005

GU–5331 2210 ±90 BP

δ¹³C: -26.2‰

Sample: WIMSC91 9.6, submitted on 30 March 1993 by T Malim

Material: organic matter (leaves and twigs; *Quercus* sp. mainly) (P Murphy 1993)

Initial comment: from an organic-rich deposit, which was a basal fill of an Iron Age defensive ditch. Immediately above this deposit were human remains, some of which were also dated in 1992 (OxA-3620).

Objectives: to establish an accurate date for initial natural infill and to confirm and refine the date OxA-3620 from human bone.

Calibrated date: 1σ: 400–160 cal BC
2σ: 410–40 cal BC

Final comment: T Malim (22 March 1994), this date confirms that of OxA-3620 from the human bone and suggests that the primary fills may be second century (or even earlier) BC. This sample constitutes the earliest of the four dates obtained from Stonea to date.

GU–5332 2110 ±50 BP

δ¹³C: -26.0‰

Sample: WIMSC92 2.5/34, submitted on 30 March 1993 by T Malim

Material: organic matter (wood and leaves, *Quercus* sp. mainly) (P Murphy 1993)

Initial comment: from the dessicated basal fill of the ditch terminal, organic-rich layer. Wood from this layer has been submitted to Cathy Groves at Sheffield for dendrochronological analysis.

Objectives: this particular sample will help give a *terminus ante quem* for the only known entrance way, and will be complemented by a dendrochronological sample.

Calibrated date: 1σ: 200–50 cal BC
2σ: 360 cal BC–cal AD 10

Final comment: T Malim (23 March 1994), the date suggests a second century BC deposition within basal fills of the outer ditch of the fort, presumably indicating the period of construction of the outer defences, and according to the excavator, the initial phase of the fort. This date corresponds well to the other three dates recovered from Stonea and confirms construction to be mid-late Iron Age.

OxA–3620 2070 ±65 BP

δ¹³C: -19.5‰

Sample: WIMSC 91 SK2 (skeleton 2), submitted in November 1991 by T Malim

Material: human bone

Initial comment: from ditch 5, which was about 1.63m deep. Beneath the ploughsoil were layers of peaty loam (5.1) and sandy clay (5.2). Several layers of clay (5.3 and 5.4) lay beneath these, and about 20cm of organic layers lined the bottom of the ditch in damp slightly waterlogged conditions. The burials were found within these organic layers.

Objectives: only limited excavation has taken place at Stonea Camp and previously no secure dating material had been recovered. The skeletal material now submitted was recovered from the earliest fills of one of the ditches and hopefully will help to examine the phasing of the multiple ditches of the camp and further relate the camp to the nearby archaeological remains, particularly the Roman site at Stonea Grange.

Calibrated date: 1σ: 180 cal BC–cal AD 10
2σ: 360 cal BC–cal AD 70

Final comment: T Malim (July 1993), Stonea Camp is presumed to be an Iron Age Fort, possibly the scene of a battle between Romans and Iceni referred to by Tacitus in his annals. The present sample comes from human bone in basal ditch deposits associated with a child's skull displaying sword-cuts. The date confirms an Iron Age date, but indicating one phase of the camp was somewhat earlier than the latest Iron Age, or Conquest times.

References: Hedges *et al* 1993, 161–2

OxA–4064 1985 ±55 BP

δ¹³C: -19.2‰

Sample: WIMSC92 Human Bone <1>, submitted on 29 January 1993 by T Malim

Material: human bone (tibia; 25–35 year old male, 1.78m tall) (C Duhig 1993)

Initial comment: from trench XV, ditch 4; an almost complete human skeleton was found within a layer of waterborne silts. These silts are infilling a ditch and are probably derived from a nearby (now extinct) watercourse. No grave cut was distinguishable, and it is assumed that the body was lowered into wet deposits and sank gently into the silts. Further flooding may have completed sealing the body in silts.

Objectives: this sample is from the same silts as OxA-3620, but from the top of the deposition period. It will provide invaluable evidence not only for the duration of the flooding episode, but also of the period of use of the camp. It will also corroborate the dates obtained from OxA-3620 thus showing many events very condensed in time at Stonea. This is important information for phasing and interpreting the fort.

Calibrated date: 1σ: 50 cal BC–cal AD 80
2σ: 160 cal BC–cal AD 130

Final comment: T Malim (July 1993), this sample from the top of ancient infill tends towards a Conquest date. It therefore confirms the Iron Age date and indicates the complexity of phasing and longevity of use of Stonea Camp.

References: Hedges *et al* 1994, 364

Stonehenge, 20th Century, Wiltshire

Location: *see* individual sites

Project manager: *see* individual sites, 1910, 1919–26, 1950–64, and 1988

Description: a programme of post-excavation analysis of all the unpublished twentieth-century excavations at Stonehenge.

Objectives: the dating programme for this project was designed to address a series of specific aims:- the provision of a series of reliable absolute dates and the construction of a reliable chronology for each major phase of the monument- the elucidation of the chronology and sequence of major events or sub-phases within phase 3- the assigning of specific features to a phase where other evidence was sparse- the dating of specific cultural artefacts with intrinsic significance.

Final comment: M J Allen, this project has produced or identified 52 radiocarbon determinations which are considered reliable.

References: Cleal *et al* 1995

Stonehenge, 20th century: car park 1988, Wiltshire

Location: SU 113424
                  Lat. 51.10.47 N; Long. 01.50.18 W

Project manager: R Trott (Wessex Archaeology), 1988

Archival body: Salisbury and South Wiltshire Museum

Description: the 1966 exacvations revealed three substantial pits. In 1988 a similar pit, further east, was discovered.

Objectives: to establish the Mesolithic date of both the feature and the pine charcoal.

Final comment: M J Allen (25 January 1991), all of these determinations from the postpit features in the car park fall into the eighth or late ninth millennium BC (OxA-4919; 8520 ±80 BP; 7660–7470 cal BC at 95% confidence; OxA-4920; 8400 ±100 BP; 7600–7180 cal BC at 95% confidence; GU-5109 (*see* below); HAR-455; 9130 ±180 BP; 8800–7790 cal BC at 95% confidence; and HAR-456; 8090 ±140 BP; 7490–6640 cal BC at 95% confidence; Reimer *et al* 2004). They cover a period of about one millennium and so it cannot be established whether these features, containing upright pine posts, were exactly contemporary and ever all stood together, but they are certainly Mesolithic and not related to the main Monument.

References: Allen 1995
                  Allen and Bayliss 1995
                  Reimer *et al* 2004

GU–5109 8880 ±120 BP

δ¹³C: -24.5‰

Sample: W243/008, submitted on 25 January 1991 by M J Allen

Material: charcoal: *Pinus* sp. (R Gale)

Initial comment: from the base of the secondary fill of postpit 9580, at *c* 0.7m depth (context 9582). The pit was cut into the chalk, with chalk rubble fill.

Objectives: a date would enable the environmental sequence and pit to be placed within the broader sequence of the Stonehenge environs.

Calibrated date: *1σ:* 8250–7750 cal BC
                    2σ: 8300–7600 cal BC

Final comment: M Allen (25 January 1991), this result confirms that the feature is Mesolithic and can be included as a group with the three postholes excavated in 1966.

Strawberry Hill, Wiltshire

Location: SU 000525
                  Lat. 51.16.16 N; Long. 01.60.00 W

Project manager: M J Allen (Wessex Archaeology),
                  July 1987

Archival body: Wessex Archaeology

Description: the site is situated on the north face of Salisbury Plain. Excavations revealed over 2.5m of hillwash which sealed an undated ditch terminal. The colluvial sequence contained two well-formed buried soils. Both displayed pronounced earthworm-worked stone-free horizons and stony horizons, the upper of which contained sherds of a tripartite Bowl (late Bronze Age) and typical of the Potterne material. Potterne lies approximately 1–2km to the north-east of the site.

Objectives: the dating of the ditch is significant especially in that an excellent palaeoenvironmental sequence has been recovered. Furthermore, the opportunity to date both charcoal and land snails will provide an opportunity to examine the dates from both and compare with the work of Yates (1986).

Final comment: M J Allen (1992), these dates provide important evidence for a late Mesolithic site on the northern scarp of Salisbury Plain. Of particular importance, however, is the potential significant residuality of charcoal within the eroded soil sequences. Such information has implications beyond the interpretation of the land-use history of this site.

References: Allen 1988
                  Hedges *et al* 1992, 145
                  Yates 1986

OxA–3040 9350 ±120 BP

δ¹³C: -22.1‰

Sample: W194/14.1, submitted in March 1991 by M J Allen

Material: charcoal: *Pinus* sp.

Initial comment: from a ditch on a dry chalkland slope beneath 2.5m+ of hillwash. The sample was sealed by weakly calcareous buried soils and highly calcareous hill wash.

Objectives: dating will provide a chronological framework for a molluscan sequence, the ditch and the clearance episode, and also provide comparison with land snails submitted for radiocarbon dating (*see* OxA-3041).

Calibrated date: *1σ:* 8770–8460 cal BC
                    2σ: 9130–8290 cal BC

Final comment: M J Allen (1992), although the two samples (OxA-3040 and OxA-3041) were sieved and extracted from a single bulk sample of the same feature, the two significantly different dates are not inconsistent with the archaeological and palaeoenvironmental record. The pine charcoal date (OxA-3040) corresponds with the Boreal pine maximum in southern England. This provides further confirmation of the existence of pine stands on the chalk (Allen 1988). Whether the charcoal indicates localised anthropogenic clearance or natural fires has not been determined. The shell date (OxA-3041) from the ditch is, however, more likely to be contemporary with the construction/infilling of the ditch and the typical Atlantic mollusc assemblages. This indicates a late Mesolithic date for the site and may be contemporary with a tranchet axe found nearby and recorded in the SMR. The site was subsequently buried by hillwash, later Bronze activity, and associated hillwash, culminating in large scale erosion during Roman tillage of the area.

OxA–3041 6820 ±120 BP

$\delta^{13}C$: -8.6‰

Sample: W194/14.2, submitted on 8 March 1991 by M J Allen

Material: shell (land snails; *Cepaea* sp. *nemoralis/hortensis*) (M J Allen 1991)

Initial comment: from a ditch on a dry chalkland slope 2.5m–3m below the surface, beneath hillwash. The sample was found in weakly calcareous ditch fill and sealed by weakly calcareous buried soils and highly calcareous hillwash.

Objectives: to establish a date for good woodland mollusc fauna; woodland clearance and a date for the ditch. It will also provide a comparative date for OxA-3040.

Calibrated date: 1σ: 5840–5620 cal BC
                    2σ: 5990–5520 cal BC

Final comment: see OxA-3040

Laboratory comment: English Heritage (25 February 2012), since the charcoal appears to be residual in the layer, no assessment is possible of the possible hard-water error inherent in the age on these terrestrial molluscs (Bowman 1990, 26).

References: Bowman 1990

Sulhamstead: Shortheath Lane, Berkshire

Location: SU 643676
               Lat. 51.24.12 N; Long. 01.04.32 W

Project manager: S Lobb (Wessex Archaeology), 1985

Archival body: Reading Museum

Description: the site lies on the plateau gravels overlooking the Kennet Valley about 4km south of the Burghfield area where the Field Farm site is located and where Bronze Age activity is well attested (Knights Farm, Bradley *et al* 1980).

Objectives: a group of eight urns was examined at this site. Urn SF50 is probably of similar date to sample R625 from an urn at Field Farm, and two other urn cemeteries of the same period have been located in the area, although no dates have been recorded. These cremation burials are important in consideration of the social organisation of the middle Bronze Age occupation at these sites and a date from this urn will be useful in comparison with the other urns found at Field Farm.

References: Bradley *et al* 1980
                  Lobb 1992

HAR–9141 3340 ±60 BP

$\delta^{13}C$: -27.6‰

Sample: W104 SF50, submitted in February 1988 by S Lobb

Material: charcoal: unidentified

Initial comment: from the fill of a cremation urn. One of several urns in a small cemetery 4km to the south of the Field Farm site. The urn was incomplete and had been disturbed by animal burrowing. It was probably originally inverted.

Objectives: to date the site and the ceramic type to establish chronological relationship with other cremations in the area.

Calibrated date: 1σ: 1730–1520 cal BC
                    2σ: 1760–1490 cal BC

Final comment: S Lobb (11 June 1996), the date from the Shortheath urn serves to establish a date for this small group of Deverell-Rimbury urns, and is a useful comparison with dates obtained from nearby urn cemeteries at Field Farm and Knights Farm (HAR-9140; 3690 ±120 BP; 2470–1740 at 95% confidence; Butterworth and Lobb 1992, 46; and BM-1594; 3195 ±95 BP; 1690–1260 cal BC at 95% confidence; Reimer *et al* 2004; Bradley *et al* 1980, 268).

References: Bradley *et al* 1980
                  Butterworth and Lobb 1992
                  Reimer *et al* 2004

Swallowfield: Riseley Farm, Berkshire

Location: SU 735637
               Lat. 51.22.02 N; Long. 00.56.39 W

Project manager: R Taylor (Trust for Wessex Archaeology), 1982

Archival body: Reading Museum and Art Gallery

Description: three areas were excavated: part of a double-ditched rectangular enclosure, part of a curvilinear ditch defining a possible enclosure, and a small ring ditch. The ring ditch proved to be early-middle Bronze Age in date, and probably funerary in function. The putative enclosure is of middle Iron Age date, probably not domestic in function, and the double-ditched enclosure dated to the first century AD and may have been occupied, although its primary function may have been iron-working.

Objectives: to evaluate 50ha at Riseley Farm in advance of obtaining planning permission for gravel extraction due to potential importance of this archaeological landscape revealed by aerial photographs taken by the RCHM in 1975. Complex settlement features had been discovered at this location adjacent to the Roman road from Silchester (*Calleva*) to London.

References: Lobb and Morris 1994

HAR–9157 2250 ±60 BP

$\delta^{13}C$: -27.5‰

Sample: W33B363, submitted in July 1987 by S Lobb

Material: charcoal: *Quercus* sp. (R Gale)

Initial comment: primary deposit of charcoal and burnt flint from the bottom of a T-shaped hearth containing 1.11kg of possible Iron Age or Saxon pottery.

Objectives: a date is needed from this unusual T-shaped hearth-like feature, which at present is unique in form and unknown in function. The associated pottery is handmade and so simple in form that it may be Iron Age or Saxon in type. One vessel was recovered in a burnt clay deposit from context 363 suggesting that the feature had been a rudimentary kiln.

Calibrated date: *1σ:* 400–200 cal BC
                       2σ: 410–170 cal BC

Final comment: E Morris (27 June 1996), it was an enormous relief to the pottery analyst that the date of this feature was clearly middle Iron Age. The original doubt was due to the presence of a moderate amount of organic temper in one of the fabric types, and in Berkshire, as in so many other areas, this is often assumed to be a Saxon tradition. This radiocarbon date has now confirmed that 'organic' does not always mean Saxon, and we must be more careful in future of quick spot-dating particularly of field-walking pottery. Dating this unusual T-shaped hearth feature to the middle Iron Age now begs many questions about possible pottery production experimentation occurring prior to the late Iron Age.

Tennyson Down, Isle of Wight

Location: SZ 33648558
                     Lat. 50.40.06 N; Long. 01.31.26 W

Project manager: F Basford (Isle of Wight County
                     Archaeological Centre), 1989

Archival body: Isle of Wight Museum Service

Description: a possible Neolithic earthwork believed to be an embanked enclosure reminiscent of some long mortuary enclosures. The sample was taken from a section revealed by a presumed Second World War trench bisecting the monument.

Objectives: to date the supposed Neolithic earthwork.

References: Grinsell and Sherwin 1941
                     Hedges *et al* 1992, 145
                     RCHME 1979

OxA–3076 3980 ±70 BP

δ¹³C: -26.0‰ (assumed)

Sample: IWCAC 56.5.2, submitted in July 1989 by D L Motkin

Material: charcoal: unidentified

Initial comment: the charcoal was sieved from two 1kg samples of primary gellifracted chalk infill of the shallow chalk-cut side ditch of the monument. This fill (context 5) lies no more than 1m below the present surface and is subject to rootlet interference. Some military disturbance is evident in the ditch (contexts 9–11) but does not affect the sample. Two samples (now combined) were taken 10cm above the floor of the ditch and 10–15cm below the overlying context 4. Context 4 represents the later weathering and denudation of the monument.

Objectives: the date refers to small charcoal fragments sieved from a 2kg sample of primary chalk infill obtained from a single section cut through the flanking ditch of the mortuary enclosure. The section failed to locate any characteristic Neolithic artefacts other than flint debitage. The charcoal offers the only precise means of dating this site other than by means of monument typology.

Calibrated date: *1σ:* 2580–2460 cal BC
                       2σ: 2840–2290 cal BC

Final comment: D L Motkin (1994), this result provides confirmatory dating evidence for the supposed Neolithic earthwork first noted by L V Grinsell who considered it to be a doubtful long barrow (Grinsell and Sherwin 1941, 195). The monument was listed as a discredited long barrow by RCHME (1979, xxxv) and was reclassified as an embanked enclosure reminiscent of some long mortuary enclosures.

References: Grinsell and Sherwin 1941, 195
                     RCHME 1979

Thorn Crag, Cumbria

Location: NY 2809606870
                     Lat. 24.27.07 N; Long. 03.06.33 W

Project manager: P Tostevin (Lancaster University
                     Archaeology Unit), 1989–90

Description: this Neolithic axe factory (site 187) is a small, *in situ* flake deposit, on a glacial bench below the summit of Thorn Crag and about 100m below the band of outcropping fine grained volcanic tuff (group VI). As such it belongs to a characteristic group of relatively small sites (type C), and is distinct in association and form from the considerably larger working sites which exploit rock directly from the outcrop (types A and B).

Objectives: to understand how the sites fit in within a national context it is necessary to have as many dates as possible from as many different types of site as possible.

References: Hedges *et al* 1994, 360–1

OxA–4212 5080 ±90 BP

δ¹³C: -25.6‰

Sample: TC91 T2 5, submitted on 20 May 1992 by J Quartermaine

Material: charcoal: unidentified

Initial comment: the charcoal was sealed by a 0.3m deep loam deposit, containing large quantities of Neolithic waste and there was no evidence of any disturbance through the deposit. Waste flakes were found directly on top of the sample and there is a safe association with the earliest phase of axe production at the site.

Objectives: to establish if the overall axe manufacturing episode was of short or long duration, or whether the more simplistic production methodologies reflect earlier working. Also it is essential in establishing a chronological relationship with the Harrison Path production group on the opposite side of a large beck.

Calibrated date: *1σ:* 3980–3770 cal BC
                       2σ: 4050–3650 cal BC

Final comment: J Quartermaine (1994), the date is earlier than any other radiocarbon date from Great Langdale, the closest date is from a similar type of axe factory site, on the same glacial bench (Harrison Stickle 3760–3530 cal BC at 95% confidence; BM-2625; 4870 ±50 BP; Reimer *et al* 2004; Bradley and Edmonds 1993). It corresponds, however, with the beginning of forestry clearance in this area identified from a pollen section at the nearby Blea Tarn (Pennington 1975). As the charcoal sample was at the interface between the axe waste deposits and natural there is a possibility that it relates to forestry clearance activity rather than the axe production, and as such provides only a *terminus post quem* for the axe factory site. It does, however, confirm that the earliest human activity in this area was from *c* 3800 cal BC.

References: Bradley and Edmonds 1993
            Pennington 1975
            Reimer *et al* 2004

Thwing: Paddock Hill 83, Yorkshire (East Riding)

Location: TA 03057070
            Lat. 54.07.18 N; Long. 00.25.23 W

Project manager: T G Manby (Yorkshire Archaeological Society), 1983–90

Archival body: Hull and East Riding Museums Service

Description: a small Bronze Age hillfort with a box rampart constructed over earlier occupation within the Paddock Hill monument.

Objectives: to date the Bronze Age features within the monument.

OxA–2542 2920 ±100 BP

$\delta^{13}C$: -24.4‰

Sample: T83/J10/F2 layer 2, submitted in 1989 by T G Manby

Material: charcoal: unidentified

Initial comment: the sample came from the lower filling layer of a large rectangular hollow. The fill contained charcoal, burnt stone, animal bone, and pottery.

Objectives: the date should provide a comparative check on sample OxA-2687, which comes from the lower layer of the same feature. However, there is unlikely to be a long interval between the formation of the layers.

Calibrated date: 1σ: 1300–940 cal BC
            2σ: 1420–840 cal BC

Final comment: T G Manby (1991), these dates (OxA-2542 and OxA-2687) are compatible with the later Bronze Age pottery in the trough.

References: Hedges *et al* 1991b, 289

OxA–2543 1230 ±90 BP

$\delta^{13}C$: -26.7‰

Sample: T83/J12/F6, submitted in 1989 by T G Manby

Material: charcoal: unidentified

Initial comment: the sample came from the clay floor of a chalk-cut hollow, concentrated in a deeper section of the floor, and overlaid by burnt clay debris from the furnace or oven.

Objectives: the feature pre-dates the construction of the rampart and is likely to be the source of the spread of charcoal on the adjoining pre-rampart surface.

Calibrated date: 1σ: cal AD 670–900
            2σ: cal AD 640–1000

Final comment: T G Manby (1993), this date and those for OxA-2580 and -2686 are supported by the coinage with a date range from the early-eighth to the mid-ninth centuries AD. There is no ceramic evidence extending over the same period and into the tenth century AD for occupation accompanying successive phases and building and palisade construction.

References: Hedges *et al* 1993, 161

OxA–2579 2510 ±70 BP

$\delta^{13}C$: -27.1‰

Sample: T83/J8/F14 find 120, submitted in 1989 by T G Manby

Material: charcoal: unidentified

Initial comment: the sample came from within the packing material of a posthole, which cut into layer 2 of the central hollow and was sealed by layer 1, the upper layer. Layers 1, 2, and the posthole were cut by a Bronze Age burial pit inserted through the central hollow.

Objectives: the sample relates to the stratigraphical sequence of the central building. The dating will confirm the deposits of the central hollow pre-date the central building represented by sample OxA-2685. This sample comes from a feature post-dating the earliest infilling of the central hollow, layer 2 (OxA-2582 and OxA-2583), and pre-dates the later infilling.

Calibrated date: 1σ: 800–510 cal BC
            2σ: 810–400 cal BC

Final comment: T G Manby (1991), the dates are consistent with the stratigraphical relationship of the lower filling (OxA-2582 and OxA-2583) and the intrusive pit (OxA-2579).

References: Hedges *et al* 1991b, 289

OxA–2580 1190 ±70 BP

$\delta^{13}C$: -22.1‰

Sample: T83/08/450, submitted in 1989 by T G Manby

Material: antler: *Cervus elaphus* (G Mourteney)

Initial comment: the sample was extracted from the chalk rubble core of the rampart.

Objectives: the sample should relate to the construction of the rampart bank, its origin in all probability is a piece of broken antler pick or rake used to quarry the chalk rubble. It should then provide a date relating to the structural phase of the site and be compared with sample 6 for pre-rampart occupation.

Calibrated date: 1σ: cal AD 710–950
2σ: cal AD 660–1000

Final comment: see OxA-2543

Laboratory comment: Ancient Monuments Laboratory (2001), sample 6 was unsuitable for dating.

References: Hedges *et al* 1993, 161

OxA–2581 2590 ±90 BP

δ¹³C: -23.1‰

Sample: T83/08/412, submitted in 1989 by T G Manby

Material: antler: *Cervus elaphus* (J Mourtery)

Initial comment: as OxA-2580

Objectives: as OxA-2580

Calibrated date: 1σ: 830–590 cal BC
2σ: 920–410 cal BC

Final comment: T G Manby (1993), the sample could either have been incorporated in the rampart at the time of its construction or at the time of its collapse following a period of decay.

References: Hedges *et al* 1993, 160–1

OxA–2582 2830 ±80 BP

δ¹³C: -26.9‰

Sample: T83/J8 (343) layer 2, submitted in 1989 by T G Manby

Material: charcoal: unidentified

Initial comment: the sample comes from the lower filling of layer 2 of the central hollow. The layer provided no pottery evidence for dating and should immediately post-date the digging of the hollow whose major feature was a block or 'plinth' of over excavated chalk. This layer covered the floor of the hollow and postholes and pits. The latter digging into it and making feature 14, which provided OxA-2579.

Objectives: the sample should date the first filling inserted into the central hollow following its digging. This is an early feature on the site with probable votive usage centred on the 'plinth'. The overlying surface had pits and a second phase of votive activity before the upper filling buried the surface. An enlarged Food Vessel lay on the surface and the upper layer fill had pottery of Deverel character.

Calibrated date: 1σ: 1120–900 cal BC
2σ: 1260–810 cal BC

Final comment: T G Manby (1991), the dates are consistent with the stratigraphical relationship of the lower filling (OxA-2582 and OxA-2583) and the intrusive pit (OxA-2579).

References: Hedges *et al* 1991b, 289

OxA–2583 2800 ±80 BP

δ¹³C: -27.3‰

Sample: T83/J8 (373) layer 2, submitted in 1989 by T G Manby

Material: charcoal: unidentified

Initial comment: as OxA-2582

Objectives: as OxA-2582; the sample was submitted as a check on Oxa-2582 as there is no other dating evidence for this layer other than its stratigraphy.

Calibrated date: 1σ: 1050–840 cal BC
2σ: 1210–800 cal BC

Final comment: see OxA-2582

References: Hedges *et al* 1991b, 289

OxA–2685 1950 ±70 BP

δ¹³C: -22.2‰

Sample: T83/J7/F14, submitted in 1989 by T G Manby

Material: antler

Initial comment: the sample was recovered from the packing material around a posthole of the inner ring of the central building, which was dug into solid rock.

Objectives: the sample should relate to the construction of the central building, a building of unique Bronze Age design, contemporary to the central hollow. On stratigraphy alone it can not be established whether the central building pre-dated the rampart or if it was contemporary with it. The dating of this sample may indicate an earlier or later period of construction in relation to samples OxA-2580 and OxA-2581.

Calibrated date: 1σ: 40 cal BC–cal AD 130
2σ: 110 cal BC–cal AD 240

Final comment: T G Manby (1991), a late Bronze Age date was expected, the date obtained was too young for the pottery content of the post-packing and postpipe infill.

References: Hedges *et al* 1991b, 289

OxA–2686 1310 ±70 BP

δ¹³C: -22.2‰

Sample: T83/L8/F, submitted in 1989 by T G Manby

Material: antler

Initial comment: the sample was recovered from beneath a bank of chalk rubble floor and some brown soil.

Objectives: the sample should relate to one of the major structural phases of the henge monument and its bank.

Calibrated date: 1σ: cal AD 650–780
2σ: cal AD 600–890

Final comment: see OxA-2543

References: Hedges *et al* 1993, 161

OxA–2687 2770 ±70 BP

$\delta^{13}C$: -27.1‰

Sample: T83/J10/F2 (452), submitted in 1989 by T G Manby

Material: charcoal: unidentified

Initial comment: the sample was recovered from the fill of a rectangular hollow consisting of charcoal burnt stones, animal bones, and pottery, interpreted as a cooking area. It is located *c* 10m east of the central building and should relate to the major occupation phase of the hillfort phase.

Objectives: the sample should date the activity of this feature, a trough like feature with a posthole at each corner.

Calibrated date: 1σ: 1010–830 cal BC
                2σ: 1120–800 cal BC

Final comment: see OxA-2542

References: Hedges *et al* 1991b, 289

Thwing: Paddock Hill 90, Yorkshire (East Riding)

Location: TA 03057070
                Lat. 54.07.18 N; Long. 00.25.23 W

Project manager: T G Manby (Doncaster Museum and Art Gallery), 1990

Archival body: Hull and East Riding Museums Service

Description: these are a stratified series of samples. Collected from successive infillings of the ditch belonging to the 'inner monument' with associated pottery, faunal remains, and burnt stone.

Objectives: this series of samples was submitted to provide clarification on previously dated samples.

Final comment: T G Manby (1993), these dates provide a consistent series which supports the ceramic evidence for occupation late in the second millennium BC. They are compatible with the chronological sequence of the site where the inner monument precedes the central structures that are associated with the previous published dates in Hedges *et al* (1991b, 289).

Laboratory comment: English Heritage (28 March 2012), five further samples from Thwing: Paddock Hill (HAR-1398, HAR-4282–4, and HAR-4285+HAR-4530) were dated before 1981 and are published in Jordan *et al* (1994, 197).

References: Hedges *et al* 1991b, 289
                Hedges *et al* 1993, 160–1
                Jordan *et al* 1994, 197

OxA–2990 2860 ±80 BP

$\delta^{13}C$: -24.6‰

Sample: T90 I11 4 GAM, submitted on 5 February 1991 by T G Manby

Material: charcoal: unidentified

Initial comment: the sample was incorporated with occupational debris in layer 4 of the inner ditch. The upper fill layer, filling the recut of the ditch was inserted and was not deposited as natural silting.

Objectives: samples from this debris layer were previously dated (HAR-4283; 3110 ±80 BP; 1530–1130 cal BC at 95% confidence; HAR-4284; 3010 ±100 BP; 1500–930 cal BC at 95% confidence; and HAR-4285+ HAR-4530; 3400 ±130 BP; 2040–1410 cal BC at 95% confidence; Reimer *et al* 2004; Jordan *et al* 1994, 197). The new dates should provides clarification on the old dates.

Calibrated date: 1σ: 1190–910 cal BC
                2σ: 1300–830 cal BC

Final comment: see series comments

References: Jordan *et al* 1994, 197

OxA–3116 3080 ±80 BP

$\delta^{13}C$: -19.9‰

Sample: T90 J11 2 GAB, submitted on 5 February 1991 by T G Manby

Material: antler: *Cervus elaphus*

Initial comment: from upper fill (B2) of the inner ditch.

Objectives: to date the stratigraphic sequence with the ditch of the 'inner monument'.

Calibrated date: 1σ: 1440–1260 cal BC
                2σ: 1510–1120 cal BC

Final comment: see OxA-2990

OxA–3117 2890 ±70 BP

$\delta^{13}C$: -22.3‰

Sample: T90 I11 GAM42, submitted on 5 February 1991 by T G Manby

Material: antler: *Cervus elaphus* (T G Manby 1990)

Initial comment: as OxA-2990

Objectives: as OxA-2990

Calibrated date: 1σ: 1210–940 cal BC
                2σ: 1310–900 cal BC

Final comment: see series comments

OxA–3118 2880 ±70 BP

$\delta^{13}C$: -22.6‰

Sample: T90 I11 GAP41, submitted on 5 February 1991 by T G Manby

Material: antler: *Cervus elaphus* (T G Manby 1990)

Initial comment: the sample is incorporated into the secondary silting layer (layer 6) of the inner ditch.

Objectives: the sample should establish the activity relationship with the use of the ditch.

Calibrated date: 1σ: 1200–930 cal BC
                2σ: 1300–890 cal BC

Final comment: see series comments

OxA–3119 2880 ±100 BP

$\delta^{13}C$: -22.8‰

Sample: T90 I11 7 GBG55, submitted on 5 February 1991 by T G Manby

Material: antler: *Cervus elaphus* (T G Manby 1990)

Initial comment: the sample was recovered on a ledge of the ditch wall, within the primary features of the ditch fill.

Objectives: the sample should relate to the primary age of the inner ditch of the henge-type monument. Very little cultural material from the primary silting of the inner ditch has been recovered. The only ceramic was an S-Beaker sherd.

Calibrated date: 1σ: 1260–910 cal BC
                   2σ: 1390–820 cal BC

Final comment: see series comments

Thwing: Paddock Hill, cemetery, Yorkshire (East Riding)

Location: TA 03057070
                     Lat. 54.07.18 N; Long. 00.25.23 W

Project manager: T G Manby (Yorkshire Archaeological Society), 1973–1990

Archival body: Hull and East Riding Museums Service

Description: a multi-period site with a henge, hillfort, and a late Bronze Age enclosure that was remodelled in the Anglo-Saxon period. Several Anglo-Saxon features were excavated, and east of the centre of the enclosure was an inhumation cemetery from which 130 burials were recovered. Some of the burials were in coffins.

Objectives: the samples are to provide a time span of the use of the cemetery and its dates in relation to the occupation of the monument. It will also provide dates for the change in alignment of the graves.

Final comment: T Manby (2002), the graves were aligned either true east-west or east-north-east to west-south-west, closely spaced, and frequently intercut. The cemetery was limited to the west by two massive postholes, probably for free-standing crosses, and a rectangular wooden building, which may have been a mortuary chapel. Refinement in the chronology provided by the radicaorbon dates was limited by the low collagen yield of some samples. The full series of dates, however, supports the use of the cemetery during the entire period of Northumbrian Christianity from *c* AD 620 down to AD 879. Such a date range would extend that provided by the coinage for activity on the site (from the early eighth century to AD 841–4).

GU–5087 1140 ±90 BP

$\delta^{13}C$: -23.0‰

Sample: GRAVE 2B T77 J9/F50, submitted on 5 February 1991 by T G Manby

Material: human bone (right femur)

Initial comment: the sample was recovered from a burial from a small cemetery on an east-north-east alignment cutting an east-west aligned grave (GU-5088). The position and alignment of this grave is considered to be late in the life of the cemetery.

Objectives: the small cemetery without grave goods is attributed to the period of AD 700–900 suggested by the coffin fitting evidence. The series of samples has been selected to establish the date of the cemetery usage in relation to the occupation of the monument that extends into the tenth century. A chronological progression in the cemetery is indicated by change of grave alignments from east-west to east-north-east/west-south-west.

Calibrated date: 1σ: cal AD 770–1000
                   2σ: cal AD 670–1040

Final comment: T Manby and A Bayliss (2002), this date is compatible with that for grave 1b (GU-5088), which is stratigraphically earlier.

GU–5088 1340 ±70 BP

$\delta^{13}C$: -23.0‰

Sample: GRAVE 1B T77 J9/F51, submitted on 5 February 1991 by T G Manby

Material: human bone (right femur)

Initial comment: the sample was recovered from a burial in a grave cutting grave 1a and cut by later grave 2.

Objectives: part of the series to establish the date range of the cemetery. *See* GU-5087.

Calibrated date: 1σ: cal AD 640–770
                   2σ: cal AD 590–860

Final comment: T Manby and A Bayliss (2002), this date is compatible with that for grave 2 (GU-5087), which is stratigraphically later.

GU–5089 1260 ±60 BP

$\delta^{13}C$: -20.9‰

Sample: GRAVE 21A T83 J9/F15, submitted on 5 February 1991 by T G Manby

Material: human bone (right femur)

Initial comment: the sample was recovered from the earliest burial of a multi-phase grave alignment east/west.

Objectives: as GU-5088

Calibrated date: 1σ: cal AD 670–860
                   2σ: cal AD 650–900

Final comment: T Manby and A Bayliss (2002), this burial is probably late seventh- or eighth-century AD in date.

GU–5090 1290 ±100 BP

$\delta^{13}C$: -23.1‰

Sample: GRAVE 12C T83 J9/F14, submitted on 5 February 1991 by T G Manby

Material: human bone (right femur)

Initial comment: the sample was recovered from an early burial in a grave east/west alignment and cut by the inserted grave 7.

Objectives: as GU–5088

Calibrated date: *1σ:* cal AD 650–880
                     2σ: cal AD 570–980

Final comment: see GU–5089

GU–5091 1180 ±80 BP

δ¹³C: -24.2‰

Sample: GRAVE 4 T85 J10/F3, submitted on 5 February 1991 by T G Manby

Material: human bone (right femur)

Initial comment: the sample was recovered from a burial in a grave at the extreme southeastern corner of the cemetery, aligned east/west.

Objectives: as GU–5088

Calibrated date: *1σ:* cal AD 710–970
                     2σ: cal AD 660–1020

Final comment: T Manby and A Bayliss (2002), this burial is probably eighth- or early ninth-century AD in date.

GU–5092 1130 ±80 BP

δ¹³C: -23.0‰

Sample: GRAVE 8 T85 J9/F22, submitted on 5 February 1991 by T G Manby

Material: human bone (right femur)

Initial comment: the sample was recovered from a within a coffin which also contained beads. The burial was in the southwest corner of the cemetery, west of the regular graves.

Objectives: as GU–5088

Calibrated date: *1σ:* cal AD 770–1000
                     2σ: cal AD 680–1030

Final comment: see GU–5091

GU–5093 1500 ±90 BP

δ¹³C: -23.7‰

Sample: GRAVE 55D T85 K9/F3, submitted on 5 February 1991 by T G Manby

Material: human bone (right femur)

Initial comment: the sample was recovered from the earliest burial in an east/west grave in the northern part of the cemetery.

Objectives: as GU–5088

Calibrated date: *1σ:* cal AD 430–650
                     2σ: cal AD 380–680

Final comment: T Manby and A Bayliss (2002), this burial has a radiocarbon date range that, at 68% confidence, extends from the pagan period across to the conversion of Northumbria to Christianity during the middle decades of the seventh century AD.

GU–5094 1490 ±150 BP

δ¹³C: -24.0‰

Sample: GRAVE 65 T85 K9/F23, submitted on 5 February 1991 by T G Manby

Material: human bone (right femur)

Initial comment: the sample was recovered from a burial stratigraphically later than the east/west ones. It belongs to a late phase of the cemetery.

Objectives: as GU–5088

Calibrated date: *1σ:* cal AD 410–670
                     2σ: cal AD 230–870

Final comment: T Manby and A Bayliss (2002), this burial is stratigraphically later than the east-west palisade, which is dated by coinage of Eanred to AD 810–840. It must therefore date to the later part of the date range provided by the radiocarbon dating.

Trethellan Farm, Cornwall

Location: SW 80156127
                     Lat. 50.24.34 N; Long. 05.05.40 W

Project manager: J A Nowakowski (Cornwall Archaeology
                     Unit), 1987

Archival body: Cornwall County Archaeology Unit,
                     Royal Institution of Cornwall

Description: open area excavations on either side of the newly constructed estate road revealed the remains of a large open settlement, comprising six to seven round houses, together with the edges of a contemporary field system. The settlement lay on a linear plateau (35m OD) between two major scarps on a south-facing slope, and the houses were regularly spaced along this level area. Immediately to the south of the occupation area two stone-clearance boundaries, representing the elements of a field system, which overlay buried prehistoric soils.

Objectives: to reveal the character and extent of the settlement, as well as to secure the chronological sequence of events on site and to retrieve as much dating and environmental data as possible.

Final comment: J A Nowakowski (28 July 1994), all the samples in this series from Trethellan Farm were taken from well-sealed deposits, and the selection was made on the suitability of the material to address the following issues: to confirm the perceived contemporaneity of major settlement features and to document the life-histories of the four structures so that an outline of the structural development of the settlement could be achieved. Another important consideration was to provide a series of useful radiocarbon determinations on the associated ceramic assemblage, as material of this period has not been adequately dated by these means in the South West. As such this is an extremely important series of dates. The results confirm middle Bronze

Age occupation across the settlement and at least 75% imply a tight span of occupation. The dates did not generally allow us to correlate and cross-link different occupation phases within build-ups and perhaps we were hoping too much for fine-tuning from them and underestimated the degree of potential contamination through intermixing of layers when the site was abandoned in antiquity.

Laboratory comment: University of Belfast (21 June 1989), some of the samples were very small and consequently the precisions were poor, in one case (UB-3108) up to ±335 BP for a single standard deviation. In this case only 0.3g of carbon remained after pretreatment.

References: Nowakowski 1991

UB–3107 3666 ±120 BP

δ¹³C: -25.5 ±0.2‰

Sample: TF87 638, submitted in December 1988 by J A Nowakowski

Material: charcoal with soil

Initial comment: dark reddish-brown soil and charcoal layer from Bronze Age hut (648). Activity layer from the interior of the hut representing one of the earliest occupational phases of activity within this Bronze Age hut.

Objectives: to provide a date for the earliest occupational phase of activity within Bronze Age hut (648) and enable an assessment of the hut's chronological position within the Bronze Age settlement as a whole. This sample forms part of a series from the site of six similar samples submitted for the same reason.

Calibrated date: 1σ: 2210–1890 cal BC
                        2σ: 2470–1740 cal BC

Final comment: J A Nowakowski (28 July 1994), a very poor result from the only sample submitted from hut 648. The precision was unreliable perhaps because only a small charcoal sample was available and contamination (the intermixing of material in antiquity) is highly likely. It does not allow us to pinpoint the date of the abandonment activity, and it is outside the date range for middle Bronze Age pottery.

UB–3108 3855 ±335 BP

δ¹³C: -26.5 ±0.2‰

Sample: TF87 2531, submitted in December 1988 by J A Nowakowski

Material: charcoal with soil

Initial comment: soil layer within ritual structure (2192) represents an activity phase of this Bronze Age structure prior to its final abandonment when it became deliberately backfilled.

Objectives: to provide a date for the use-life of ritual structure (2192) and aid in assessing its chronological position within the larger context of the site during Bronze Age occupation. This sample will also aid in shedding some light on the relationship between 'ritual' and 'domestic' activities on Trethellan Farm.

Calibrated date: 1σ: 2880–1880 cal BC
                        2σ: 3360–1460 cal BC

Final comment: J A Nowakowski (28 July 1994), this is an unreliable date with very poor precision. It may have been contaminated as only a small amount of charcoal was available for dating. It was taken from a layer in ritual structure 2192, and does not help date the use of the building or even confirm its suspected middle Bronze Age credentials.

UB–3109 3088 ±40 BP

δ¹³C: -26.1 ±0.2‰

Sample: TF87 2532, submitted in December 1988 by J A Nowakowski

Material: charcoal with soil

Initial comment: an activity layer from within the base of pit (2503) which lies to the west of ritual structure (2192). This represents secondary burning activities of Bronze Age date on the main scarp (3006) which runs to the north of the settlement area. The exact nature of this activity has not been fully explained but it is considered to be Bronze Age in date.

Objectives: to provide a date for an episode of burning on the scarp (3006) and to assess its chronological position within the larger context of Bronze Age occupation on site. The sample will also provide a *terminus post quem* for the construction of ritual features on the site in relation to the domestic huts of Bronze Age date.

Calibrated date: 1σ: 1420–1310 cal BC
                        2σ: 1440–1260 cal BC

Final comment: J A Nowakowski (28 July 1994), an extremely reliable date, which confirms the general cultural phase of occupation within the settlement. It came, however, from a pre-construction deposit in ritual structure 2192 and can therefore only provide a *terminus post quem*. It hints at earlier activities in this part of the settlement (pre-structure 2912) for which little traces survived.

UB–3110 3070 ±40 BP

δ¹³C: -25.7 ±0.2‰

Sample: TF87 2095, submitted in December 1988 by J A Nowakowski

Material: charcoal with soil

Initial comment: burnt soil layer *in situ* at the base of ritual area (2021). It represents the earliest phase of 'ritual' burning activity within this Bronze Age feature.

Objectives: to provide a date for the earliest episode of fire within Bronze Age ritual feature (2021). This will aid in the examination of the relationship between Bronze Age 'domestic' activity on the site and activities centred around two major features which have been interpreted as 'ritual' or 'non-domestic' in nature. As such this sample forms part of a series of two submitted from the site to resolve the chronological position of ritual features in relation to the Bronze Age domestic huts.

Calibrated date: 1σ: 1410–1290 cal BC
                        2σ: 1430–1210 cal BC

Final comment: J A Nowakowski (28 July 1994), this provides a good reliable date, taken from the base of 'ritual hollow' 136/2021 - one of the earliest burnt spreads in this feature. It places activities centred in this feature comfortably within the main occupation horizon for the settlement and confirms contemporaneity with the houses as well as its neighbouring 'ritual hollow' 2765.

UB–3111 3034 ±20 BP

δ¹³C: -24.9 ±0.2‰

Sample: TF87 2166, submitted in December 1988 by J A Nowakowski

Material: charcoal: unidentified

Initial comment: from a burnt charcoal layer a the base of ritual hollow (2765). It represents the earliest episode of fire within this major Bronze Age feature which has been interpreted as a 'ritual' activity area.

Objectives: to provide a date for the earliest episode of fire within Bronze Age ritual hollow (2765). This will aid in the examination of the relationship between Bronze Age 'domestic' activity on the site and activities centred around two major features which have been interpreted as 'ritual' or 'non-domestic' in nature. As such this sample forms part of a series of two submitted from the site to resolve the chronological position of ritual features in relation to the Bronze Age domestic huts.

Calibrated date: *1σ:* 1375–1265 cal BC
            2σ: 1390–1215 cal BC

Final comment: J A Nowakowski (28 July 1994), an extremely reliable high precision date taken from basal deposit in 'ritual hollow' 2765. It implies the use of this feature is contemporary with that of neighbouring 'ritual hollow' 136/2021 and buildings on the east side of the settlement. It maybe taken as a key date for middle Bronze Age occupation at Trethellan Farm.

Laboratory comment: University of Belfast (21 June 1989), this sample was measured on the high-precision system.

UB–3112 3216 ±60 BP

δ¹³C: -25.3 ±0.2‰

Sample: TF87 1070, submitted in December 1988 by J A Nowakowski

Material: charcoal with soil

Initial comment: from the earliest stratified context within Bronze Age hut (1034). It represents the first phase of activity within the hut and derives from a well-sealed and stratified context.

Objectives: to provide a date, if possible, of the earliest stratified contexts within Bronze Age hut (1034) to enable assessment of the hut's chronological position within the Bronze Age settlement as a whole. This sample forms part of a series of six similar samples submitted for the same reason from Trethellan Farm.

Calibrated date: *1σ:* 1530–1420 cal BC
            2σ: 1630–1390 cal BC

Final comment: J A Nowakowski (28 July 1994), a good result, which falls comfortably into middle Bronze Age occupation from the site. Taken from earliest occupation deposit within house 141/1034 it provides a useful date as a marker (at 95% confidence level) for the probable earliest phase of activity at Trethellan Farm.

UB–3113 3023 ±100 BP

δ¹³C: -26.5 ±0.2‰

Sample: TF87 1067, submitted in December 1988 by J A Nowakowski

Material: charcoal: unidentified

Initial comment: from a reddish burnt spread within Bronze Age hut (1034). This is the best collected context representing the last phases of occupational activity within hut (1034) prior to final abandonment.

Objectives: to provide a date for the last phase of occupation within Bronze Age hut (1034) prior to final abandonment. It will be used to assess the use-life of the hut within the larger context of the Bronze Age settlement, and aid in providing an assessment of the longevity of 'domestic' Bronze age occupation on the site. As such this sample forms part of a series of four similar samples from the site which are being submitted to help resolve his problem.

Calibrated date: *1σ:* 1420–1120 cal BC
            2σ: 1500–970 cal BC

Final comment: J A Nowakowski (28 July 1994), a reliable date taken from the later phase of the activity within house 141/1034. It accords well with its partner (UB-3112) - though has a larger standard deviation and therefore does not allow us to clearly pinpoint the date of the final phase of activity within this feature. It lies within the range of the middle Bronze Age pottery though.

UB–3114 3091 ±20 BP

δ¹³C: -26.2 ±0.2‰

Sample: TF 87 2654, submitted in December 1988 by J A Nowakowski

Material: charcoal with soil

Initial comment: from the fill of large pit cut into the floor of Bronze Age hut (2222). It is from a well-sealed and securely stratified context. Bronze Age hut (2222) is considered to be the earliest hut within the Bronze Age settlement at Trethellan; this observation derives from the fact that, after its abandonment, it was completely buried by a massive midden deposit which altered the Bronze Age ground surface so that it lay at a deeper level than the two neighbouring huts. Hence, this is potentially one of the earliest Bronze Age deposits from the site that comes from a 'domestic' context.

Objectives: to provide a date for the earliest phase of occupation of hut (2222) and enable an assessment of the hut's chronological position within the Bronze Age settlement as a whole. This sample forms part of a series of six similar samples submitted for the same reason from Trethellan Farm.

Calibrated date: 1σ: 1410–1320 cal BC
2σ: 1425–1310 cal BC

Final comment: J A Nowakowski (28 July 1994), this provides an extremely reliable high-precision date. It was taken from a well-sealed deposit in hut 2222, and falls well within a middle Bronze Age occupation horizon as confirmed by the associated material culture. It provides another key date for this site and helps to confirm the co-existence of this hut with other features on the eastern part of the settlement.

Laboratory comment: University of Belfast (21 June 1989), this sample was measured on the high-precision system.

UB–3115 3110 ±40 BP

δ¹³C: -25.4 ±0.2‰

Sample: TF87 3046, submitted in December 1988 by J A Nowakowski

Material: charcoal with soil

Initial comment: from the fill of pit (3047) within Bronze Age hut (3022). It derives from a well-sealed stratified context that represents the last stage of activity within the hut prior to its final abandonment.

Objectives: to provide a date for the final abandonment of Bronze Age hut (3022). It will be used to assess the use-life of this hut within the larger context of the Bronze Age settlement, and aid in providing an assessment of the longevity of 'domestic' Bronze Age occupation on the site. This sample forms part of a series of four similar samples from the site which are being submitted to resolve this problem.

Calibrated date: 1σ: 1430–1320 cal BC
2σ: 1460–1290 cal BC

Final comment: J A Nowakowski (28 July 1994), this provides a good reliable date. One of two samples taken from hut 142/3022, it accords well with its partner (UB-3116) taken from an earlier phase and falls comfortably within the major the middle Bronze Age occupation horizon.

UB–3116 3211 ±70 BP

δ¹³C: -25.8 ±0.2‰

Sample: TF87 3135, submitted in December 1988 by J A Nowakowski

Material: charcoal with soil

Initial comment: from the dark brown loam and charcoal fill of posthole (3136) within Bronze Age hut (3022). It is from a well-sealed and stratified deposit from the first phase of activity within this hut on the Bronze Age settlement of Trehellan Farm.

Objectives: to provide a date, if possible, of one of the earliest stratified contexts within Bronze Age hut (3022), to enable an assessment of the hut's chronological position within the Bronze Age settlement as a whole. This sample forms part of a series of six similar samples submitted for the same reason from Trehellan Farm.

Calibrated date: 1σ: 1530–1410 cal BC
2σ: 1640–1320 cal BC

Final comment: J A Nowakowski (28 July 1994), this provides a reliable date, taken from earliest occupation levels in hut 142/3022 and accords well with its partner UB-3115. It falls comfortably into the major middle Bronze Age occupation horizon.

UB–3117 3460 ±190 BP

δ¹³C: -25.9 ±0.2‰

Sample: TF 87 2313, submitted in December 1988 by J A Nowakowski

Material: charcoal with soil

Initial comment: from a mid-brown sealing layer within the north-east quadrant of Bronze Age hut (2010). It is from a levelling layer marking the final abandonment of occupational activity within this hut.

Objectives: to provide a date for the final abandonment of Bronze Age hut (2010). It will be used to assess the use-life of this hut within the larger context of the Bronze Age settlement and aid in providing an assessment of the longevity of 'domestic' Bronze Age occupation on the site. This sample forms part of a series of four similar samples from the site which as being submitted to help resolve this problem.

Calibrated date: 1σ: 2030–1520 cal BC
2σ: 2300–1390 cal BC

Final comment: J A Nowakowski (28 July 1994), this result has very poor precision, taken from sealing layer in hut 2010. It must be an anomaly since this is one of a few from this feature and it produced a much older date than expected. It may have been contaminated during the abandonment process.

UB–3118 2981 ±40 BP

δ¹³C: -26.2 ±0.2‰

Sample: TF87 2714, submitted in December 1988 by J A Nowakowski

Material: charcoal: unidentified

Initial comment: from the fill of ash pit (2715) within Bronze Age hut (2010) and below central hearth (2371). It derives from a well-sealed and stratified deposit within this Bronze Age hut, and represents the earliest phase of occupational activity within the hut.

Objectives: to provide a date, if possible for the earliest phase of occupation of Bronze Age hut (2010) and to enable an assessment of the hut's chronological position within the Bronze Age settlement as a whole. This sample forms part of a series of six similar samples submitted for the same reason from Trethellan Farm.

Calibrated date: 1σ: 1300–1120 cal BC
2σ: 1380–1050 cal BC

Final comment: J A Nowakowski (28 July 1994), the precision seems fine but this sample produced a much younger date than expected - this is one of a few taken from hut 2010. Therefore an anomaly as far as the use life of hut 2010 is concerned, but it would still fall comfortably within the date range of middle Bronze Age occupation.

UB–3119 3014 ±75 BP

δ¹³C: -25.2 ±0.2‰

Sample: TF87 2354, submitted in December 1988 by J A Nowakowski

Material: charcoal: unidentified

Initial comment: from a dark brown soil layer within the north-east quadrant of Bronze Age hut (2001), representing the final occupational phase of activity prior to abandonment of the hut.

Objectives: to provide a date for the final phase of occupation of Bronze Age hut (2001) prior to its final abandonment. It will be used to assess the use-life of this hut within the larger context of Bronze Age settlement, and aid in providing an assessment of the longevity of 'domestic' Bronze Age on the site. This sample forms part of a series of four similar samples from the site which are being submitted to help resolve this problem.

Calibrated date: 1σ: 1400–1120 cal BC
2σ: 1440–1010 cal BC

Final comment: J A Nowakowski (28 July 1994), this result has good precision and provides a reliable date. This is one of three samples taken from house 2001, and comes from the third phase of occupation. The result accords well with UB-3210 and can provide a marker of phased occupation within the structure which, at 94.5% confidence level, may represent a period of at least 80 years.

UB–3120 3093 ±50 BP

δ¹³C: -25.4 ±0.2‰

Sample: TF87 2459, submitted in December 1988 by J A Nowakowski

Material: charcoal with soil

Initial comment: from an occupational activity layer of burnt material within Bronze Age hut (2001). The sample derives from a well-sealed and stratified context within the hut's interior. This sample is submitted from what has been recognised as the most 'active' occupational phase within the use-life of hut (2001), which stands out from all the other 'domestic' huts on the site as being more complex having witnessed substantial modification throughout its history of use.

Objectives: to provide a date for the most 'active' phase of occupation within Bronze Age hut (2001) which will help in the assessment of its use-life and its role within the larger context of the settlement. This is a good context for dating the pottery sequence from the hut.

Calibrated date: 1σ: 1430–1310 cal BC
2σ: 1490–1220 cal BC

Final comment: J A Nowakowski (28 July 1994), this is a reliable date with good precision taken from the second phase of occupation in hut 2001. It agrees with the stratigraphic phasing and so accords well with UB-3119. It is a useful date for the middle Bronze Age occupation generally at Trethellan Farm.

UB–3156 3184 ±100 BP

δ¹³C: -27.3 ±0.2‰

Sample: TF87 2084, submitted in December 1988 by J A Nowakowski

Material: charcoal with soil

Initial comment: from a mid-brown activity layer within hut (2001) from one of the earliest phases of occupation of this Bronze Age hut. It derives from a well-sealed and stratified deposit. This sample replaced UB-3121 (TF87 2385) which was too small.

Objectives: to provide a date for the earliest occupational phase of activity within Bronze Age hut (2001), and enable an assessment of the hut's chronological position within the Bronze Age settlement as a whole. This sample forms part of a series of six similar samples submitted for the same reason from Trethellan Farm. It is a good context for dating pottery from the site.

Calibrated date: 1σ: 1490–1435 cal BC
2σ: 1495–1425 cal BC

Final comment: J A Nowakowski (28 July 1994), this result has very poor precision. The sample was taken from an abandon-ment layer in hut 2001. A very small amount of charcoal was available and intermixing in antiquity makes contamination highly likely. This result would not have been useful if this had been the only sample dated from this feature at Trethellan Farm.

Trethurgy, Cornwall

Location: SX 03475563
Lat. 50.22.01 N; Long. 04.45.50 W

Project manager: H Quinnell (Field Archaeology Unit, Institute of Archaeology), 1973

Archival body: English Heritage, Royal Institution of Cornwall

Description: a small univallate enclosure located on the edge of the Hensbarrow (St Austell) granite. 'Round' is the term used for later prehistoric and Roman period enclosed settlements in Cornwall: their continuance into the post-Roman period was not recognised in the early 1970s. All samples came from an acid soil formed over a granite head. The water-table was well below the level of the site.

Objectives: to ascertain when oval houses, the main structural domestic form in Roman Cornwall, were first built, when they went out of use, and the date of the end of the formal use of the round.

Final comment: H Quinnell (1992), these dates, together with those from a similar enclosed site at Reawla (UB-3180 to UB-3184), are the first series to be obtained from Roman period settlements in Cornwall. Both series considered together suggest that the ceramic sequence proposed from Roman Cornwall is reasonably secure in broad outline. This confirmation is important because the local Cornish ceramic series for the period is *sui generis* and the implications of ceramic material imported from outside the county were uncertain. These remarks apply only to contexts, from both Trethurgy and Reawla, where there are deposits including ceramic material of reasonable size. The relationship between ceramic and radiocarbon dating for Roman Cornwall is further discussed in Quinnell (2004).

References: Quinnell 2004

UB–3250 1683 ±45 BP

$\delta^{13}C$: -25.8 ±0.2‰

Sample: TGY 932, submitted on 25 October 1989 by
H Quinnell

Material: charcoal: *Calluna* sp., small twigs and branches;
Ulex sp. (C Cartwright 1988)

Initial comment: this sample represents the base of a midden
left to accumulate in deserted structure U. This midden was
of very humic black soil and contained large quantities of
pottery as well as a rare tin ingot. The charcoal was collected
close to the findspot of the ingot. This sample would relate
to the ingot, to a wide range of local pottery, and to an
episode which can be fitted in well to the stratigraphic
sequence on the site. If the interpretation as an undisturbed
midden is correct, it is unlikely that the charcoal is residual.

Objectives: this sample was chosen to represent the use of the
site after a disuse phase. Period 6 is really the latest period
from which we have good samples.

Calibrated date: 1σ: cal AD 260–420
              2σ: cal AD 240–440

Final comment: H Quinnell (5 September 1991), the
determination is consistent with the later fourth-century date
for the midden indicated by ceramic evidence.

UB–3251 1641 ±60 BP

$\delta^{13}C$: -26.2 ±0.2‰

Sample: TGY 849, submitted on 25 October 1989 by
H Quinnell

Material: charcoal: *Fraxinus* sp., ?mature timber; *Corylus* sp.,
twigs and small branches (C Cartwright 1988)

Initial comment: from house Z, phase 2: from the contents of
a 'hearth pit'. The sample is unlikely to be residual or
disturbed. The context relates to a later phase of house Z
and is definitely after the major rebuilding of period 6.

Objectives: this sample, together with TGY 932 (UB-3250)
were chosen to represent later phases of the site. After TGY
932 (UB-3250), this sample is probably the best contexted
sample for periods after the disuse of the site (after period 4).

Calibrated date: 1σ: cal AD 340–530
              2σ: cal AD 250–560

Final comment: H Quinnell (25 September 1991), there was
no direct artefactual dating for the feature, but
stratigraphically it was later than the context for UB-3250.
The finds in associated contexts suggested a date anywhere
from the late fourth century to the sixth century AD would
be possible. The determination is entirely acceptable.

UB–3252 1806 ±52 BP

$\delta^{13}C$: -25.3 ±0.2‰

Sample: TGY 427, submitted on 25 October 1989 by
H Quinnell

Material: charcoal: *Ulex* sp., twigs and small branches;
Fraxinus sp., ?mature timber (C Cartwright 1988)

Initial comment: from the floor of phase 3 of house T,
assigned on reasonable stratigraphic grounds to period 4.
The material was most likely to have been trodden in during
use; disturbance is unlikely.

Objectives: this sample was chosen with TGY 923 (UB-3253)
to establish dates for period 4, a definite building phase
across the site. UB-3252 would provide useful confirmation
of a mid-way point in the round's occupation, and provide a
terminus post quem for the possible disuse after period 4.

Calibrated date: 1σ: cal AD 130–320
              2σ: cal AD 70–380

Final comment: H Quinnell (5 September 1991), period 4
was dated on rather sparse ceramic data to *c* AD 300. The
determination is acceptable as UB-3253 also suggests that
the initial period 4 dating may be up to a century too late.

UB–3253 1842 ±46 BP

$\delta^{13}C$: -25.3 ±0.2‰

Sample: TGY 923, submitted on 25 October 1989 by
H Quinnell

Material: charcoal: *Calluna* sp., twigs and small branches;
Ulex sp. (C Cartwright 1988)

Initial comment: identified during excavation as 'ash-like'
material, this formed part of a dump covered by layer 905.
The material is unlikely to be residual or disturbed. The
context fits in closely with the stratigraphic sequence in the
area of house Z.

Objectives: this sample was chosen with TGY 427 (UB-3252)
to establish dates for period 4, a definite building phase
across the site. UB-3253 represents a good stratigraphic
horizon before temporary disuse of the site. The dating is
principally wanted for its relationship to the sequence. It
would also be helpful for the dating of layer 905 above,
which provided the earliest context on the site for a flanged
bowl in local fabric. These bowls are supposed to provide a
terminus post quem dating of AD 275 but I find the
arguments for this very feeble; even so the introduction of
flanged bowls in gabbroic fabric provides one of the few
ceramic horizons so far discernible in Roman Cornwall.

Calibrated date: 1σ: cal AD 90–240
              2σ: cal AD 60–320

Final comment: see UB-3252

UB–3254 2123 ±47 BP

$\delta^{13}C$: -25.7 ±0.2‰

Sample: TGY 207, submitted on 25 October 1989 by
H Quinnell

Material: charcoal: *Ulex* sp., twigs and small branches;
Fraxinus sp., ?mature timber (C Cartwright 1988)

Initial comment: from a pit sealed by the old land surface
beneath a round bank.

Objectives: this sample has been chosen together with TGY
884 (UB-3255) to bracket an early phase of the site. It
provides a good *terminus post quem* for the site's construction.
The contents of the pit provide a *post quem* for the

construction of the round. It lies immediately beneath the old land surface beneath the main rampart. Admittedly there is no way of knowing how much earlier the pit is than the rampart. The main importance lies in narrowing dates for construction of the main rampart and the start of the use of the round, oval houses etc.

Calibrated date: *1σ:* 210–50 cal BC
                                   2σ: 360–40 cal BC

Final comment: H Quinnell (5 September 1991), the date may be acceptable because it lies within the time span of some sparse residual later Iron Age sherds, and may assist in devising a chronological framework for a sequence of pre-round episodes.

UB–3255 1768 ±47 BP

δ¹³C: -25.8 ±0.2‰

Sample: TGY 884, submitted on 25 October 1989 by H Quinnell

Material: charcoal (all twigs): *Ulex* sp.; *Calluna* sp.; *Corylus* sp. (C Cartwright 1988)

Initial comment: from a posthole covered by a thin soil layer and then by a stone construction of a later house phase. The top of the hole was 1m below the present surface. The material could be residual, but is unlikely to be disturbed.

Objectives: to date the earliest phase of house Z, which relates to the early use of the round. This sample was chosen with TGY 207 (UB-3254) to bracket the foundation of the round.

Calibrated date: *1σ:* cal AD 220–340
                                   2σ: cal AD 130–400

Final comment: H Quinnell (5 September 1991), weak ceramic evidence had suggested a date around AD 200, very much at the earliest end of possible calibrations. The calibrated range for this date is a little later than that of UB-3252 and UB-3253 from period 4, but this amount of discrepancy from a single date may be accepted.

Unstone, Derbyshire

Location: SK 373769
                            Lat. 53.17.15 N; Long. 01.26.26 W

Project manager: T Courtney (North Derbyshire Archaeological Trust), 1977

Archival body: North Derbyshire Archaeological Trust

Description: a hearth in close proximity to a Mesolithic posthole and stakehole structures, from which carbonised grain was recovered.

Objectives: to establish whether the charcoal is Mesolithic or intrusive, and to assess the importance of the site.

Laboratory comment: English Heritage (12 January 2010), one further date was published in Jordan *et al* (HAR-2589; 1994, 198–9). A further sample, U77C2F48 (HAR-2657), was abandoned.

References: Jordan *et al* 1994, 198–9
                            Walker *et al* 1991a, 88

HAR–3339 1980 ±150 BP

δ¹³C: -26.6‰

Sample: U77C2F48, submitted in March 1978 by T Courtney

Material: charcoal: unidentified

Initial comment: from the upper sand fill of a hearth. The sample was sealed by disturbed rubble and ploughsoil.

Objectives: to provide a date for the hearth which is thought to be Mesolithic.

Calibrated date: *1σ:* 180 cal BC–cal AD 220
                                   2σ: 390 cal BC–cal AD 390

Final comment: T Courtney (24 July 1996), the stratigraphic context (F.48) of this sample was that of a hearth close to Mesolithic posthole and stakehole structures, although located outside the most dense concentration of Mesolithic ploughsoil flints. The hearth was not linked stratigraphically with other features. Its lower burnt soil (F.49) had provided a charcoal sample HAR-2589 (2740 ±170 BP; 1340–410 cal BC at 95% confidence; Reimer *et al* 2004; Jordan *et al* 1994, 198–9), indicating either an intrusive origin for the sample or a late phasing for the use of the hearth. This present second sample HAR-3339 suggests the same, and sheds no light on the Mesolithic occupation, and the date of the hearth remains in question.

Laboratory comment: AERE Harwell (1989), this sample was measured in the miniature gas proportional counter (Otlet *et al* 1983).

Laboratory comment: English Heritage (27 February 2012), the two results from this feature are statistically significantly different (T'=11.3; T'(5%)=3.8; ν=1; Ward and Wilson 1978).

References: Jordan *et al* 1994, 198–9
                            Otlet *et al* 1983
                            Reimer *et al* 2004
                            Ward and Wilson 1978

Upwich, Worcestershire

Location: SO 9010063503
                            Lat. 52.16.09 N; Long. 02.08.42 W

Project manager: J Price (Archaeology Section, Hereford & Worcester County Council), 1984

Archival body: Worcestershire County Museum

Description: a multi-period salt production site dating from the Iron Age onwards.

Objectives: HAR-9118 to HAR-9125 form four pairs of samples which were taken during the excavation as part of an overall strategy to analyse discrete and well preserved environmental remains, in this instance, from Saxon occupation levels. The *in situ* furnaces were located at similar stratigraphic horizons, and it is hoped that soil analysis will assist in providing a phase sequence for the intensive pre-medieval activity.

Final comment: J D Hurst (5 July 1996), radiocarbon dating provided a very useful series of dates. These determine the presence of a middle Saxon phase, as well as refining the ceramic dating of an earlier sub-Roman/Anglo-Saxon phase.

Laboratory comment: English Heritage (17 January 2012), eight further dates from this site were published in Bayliss *et al* (2012, 290–1; HAR-9118–25).

References: Bayliss *et al* 2012
              Hurst 1991
              Hurst 1997

UB–3194 1242 ±36 BP

δ¹³C: -25.4 ±0.2‰

Sample: 4575-2189, submitted in June 1989 by J D Hurst

Material: charcoal: unidentified

Initial comment: from part of the lowest infilling of a major east-west watercourse which is cut through the pale grey alluviation deposits.

Objectives: to provide a *terminus post quem* for the construction of the watercourse. A section through the watercourse suggests that infilling along the north bank was deliberate, and ensued soon after the construction as there was no evidence for silting.

Calibrated date: *1σ:* cal AD 690–810
                    2σ: cal AD 670–890

Final comment: J D Hurst (5 July 1996), the radiocarbon date was broadly similar to UB-3195 suggesting that the construction of the watercourse revetment and timber trackway were of similar date, both belonging to the middle Saxon period.

UB–3195 1250 ±36 BP

δ¹³C: -27.8 ±0.2‰

Sample: 4575-3635, submitted in June 1989 by J D Hurst

Material: wood (waterlogged): unidentified

Initial comment: withies/rods from matted twiggy material along the north bank of a water course which postdates the pale grey alluviation deposits. This was 23m long and was interpreted as a trackway.

Objectives: this sample caps the top of the pale grey alluviation episode, and will therefore provide a useful *terminus ante quem* for the termination of alluvial deposition across the site.

Calibrated date: *1σ:* cal AD 680–810
                    2σ: cal AD 660–890

Final comment: J D Hurst (5 July 1996), this radiocarbon date provided a useful indication of the date of the end of alluviation.

Laboratory comment: University of Belfast (26 July 2012), no record survives of whether this sample was pretreated using the acid based alkali protocol or was bleached.

UB–3196 1494 ±37 BP

δ¹³C: -26.0 ±0.2‰

Sample: 4575-3747, submitted in June 1989 by J D Hurst

Material: charcoal: unidentified

Initial comment: from a charcoal layer in the middle of a metre-thick pale grey clay deposition, which probably represents alluviation of the river flood plain.

Objectives: the previous series of radiocarbon dates, HAR-9118 to HAR-9125, has dated an underlying area of saltmaking activity to *c* cal AD 600. At present the alluvial clay deposits overlying this saltmaking horizon can only be dated in broad terms to post- AD 600 and pre- *c* AD 1250, the construction of Upwich Brine Pit. Further samples, UB-3196 and UB-3197, should clarify the chronology associated with alluviation.

Calibrated date: *1σ:* cal AD 540–610
                    2σ: cal AD 430–650

Final comment: JD Hurst (5 July 1996), the radiocarbon date confirmed the general dating based on stratigraphic grounds, and, when combined with UB-3194–5, suggested that the deposition of alluvium occurred in the later seventh and/or eighth century AD.

UB–3197 1527 ±50 BP

δ¹³C: -26.0 ±0.2‰

Sample: 4575-3748, submitted in June 1989 by J D Hurst

Material: charcoal: unidentified

Initial comment: from a charcoal layer positioned between 3747 and the base of the clay alluviation deposits. The latter is varied suggesting many inundation episodes.

Objectives: comparison between this sample and UB-3196 should allow the timespan of the total alluviation episode to be assessed.

Calibrated date: *1σ:* cal AD 430–600
                    2σ: cal AD 410–650

Final comment: see UB-3197

Wallingford Bypass: Whitecross Farm, Oxfordshire

Location: SU 601882
                 Lat. 51.35.20 N; Long. 01.07.57 W

Project manager: G Lambrick (Oxford Archaeological
                 Unit), 1985–6

Archival body: Oxford Archaeology

Description: a late Bronze Age settlement site. The site at Whitecross Farm, included timber structures located on the edge of the eyot, and a substantial midden and occupation deposit. The artefact assemblages are suggestive of a high-status site, with a range of domestic and ritual activities represented.

Objectives: to date the deposit of worked wood, to date and provide a relative sequence for the two structures (A and B), and then provide a date for the first phase of activity (pre-midden).

References: Cromarty *et al* 2006

UB–3138 2776 ±40 BP

δ¹³C: -27.7 ±0.2‰

Sample: WBP1, submitted on 7 October 1988 by
G Lambrick

Material: wood (charred and waterlogged): *Corylus* sp., rod,
9 rings (R Gale 1988)

Initial comment: from a river channel adjacent to the late
Bronze Age settlement site containing late Bronze Age
pottery, flints, copper alloy pin, charred and waterlogged
plant and insect remains, molluscs etc. This sample is one of
many pieces of rod associated with the charred remains of a
wooden structure of beams (*Quercus* sp.) and rods (*Corylus*
sp.) which burnt down.

Objectives: to provide general dating for channel deposits and
the associated late Bronze Age settlement activity; to date the
late Bronze Age wooden structure; and to provide a
comparative date for the base of the magnetic dating column
of silts.

Calibrated date: *1σ:* 980–850 cal BC
                      2σ: 1020–820 cal BC

Final comment: A Bayliss, A Barclay, A M Cromarty &
G Lambrick (7 October 1988), the four results are not
statistically significantly different at 95% confidence (T'=1.4;
T' (5%)=7.8; ν=3; Ward and Wilson 1978). This means that
the period of activity represented by the wooden structures
and the wood deposit was probably fairly short. UB-3141,
from structure A, is not significantly different in date from
UB-3140, from structure B, and so their relative chronology
cannot be determined by radiocarbon analysis. The wooden
deposits are securely late Bronze Age in date and provide a
terminus post quem of *c* 1000 to 800 cal BC for the midden
deposits. If this midden is contemporary with the occupation
layer found widely across the eyot which is associated with a
Decorated Ware assemblage and metal work, then this
independent *terminus post quem* for these deposits fits well
with the current accepted chronologies for the late Bronze
Age (Needham 1996).

Laboratory comment: University of Belfast (26 July 2012), no
record survives of whether this sample was pretreated using
the acid based alkali protocol or was bleached.

References: Needham 1996
                     Ward and Wilson 1978

UB–3139 2713 ±35 BP

δ¹³C: -28.1 ±0.2‰

Sample: WBP2, submitted on 7 October 1988 by
G Lambrick

Material: wood (charred and waterlogged): *Quercus* sp.,
plank, outer rings (R Gale 1988)

Initial comment: as UB-3138

Objectives: as UB-3138

Calibrated date: *1σ:* 910–810 cal BC
                      2σ: 930–800 cal BC

Final comment: see UB-3138

Laboratory comment: University of Belfast (27 April 1989), this
sample was pretreated using the acid based acid protocol.

UB–3140 2739 ±40 BP

δ¹³C: -27.7 ±0.2‰

Sample: WBP3, submitted on 7 October 1988 by
G Lambrick

Material: wood (waterlogged): *Quercus* sp., sapwood of *c* 35
year old pole (R Gale 1988)

Initial comment: from an *in situ* pile of *Quercus* sp. from the
river bed adjacent to the settlement. The sample is part of
either a single structure with other piles, or belongs to
one of two structures, possibly bridges or jetties, one
replacing the other.

Objectives: to date the presumed late Bronze Age *in situ*
waterside/waterfront structures and to provide a general date
for the settlement.

Calibrated date: *1σ:* 920–830 cal BC
                      2σ: 1000–800 cal BC

Final comment: see UB-3138

Laboratory comment: see UB-3138

UB–3141 2736 ±45 BP

δ¹³C: -26.6 ±0.2‰

Sample: WBP4, submitted on 7 October 1988 by
G Lambrick

Material: wood (waterlogged): *Quercus* sp., sapwood rings
from *c* 35 year old pole (R Gale 1988)

Initial comment: from an *in situ* pile of *Quercus* sp. from the
river channel adjacent to the settlement and containing late
Bronze Age settlement debris and biological remains. This
sample is part of either a single structure (with UB-3140) or
belongs to one of two structures, bridges of jetties, of
different phases.

Objectives: as UB-3140

Calibrated date: *1σ:* 930–820 cal BC
                      2σ: 1000–800 cal BC

Final comment: see UB-3138

Laboratory comment: see UB-3138

Watton Carrs, Humberside

Location: TA 06414764
                     Lat. 53.54.50 N; Long. 00.22.47 W

Project manager: J Dent (Borders Regional Council), 1989

Description: a group of bog oaks were taken from the same
large field, which lies at the angle of Watton Beck and the
River Hull. All but one now lie at the side of the field
adjoining the Starberry Drain, the other lies at the north-
west corner of the field with three large, unworked trees.
This second position is very close to the line of a double-
ditched feature, probably a trackway, which appears on aerial
photographs taken in March 1989.

Objectives: these timbers were not prime building timbers
because of the heart-rot, but were deliberately felled and
split. It seems likely that they represent two or more

trackways across the wetlands, of the kind, which is well known in the Somerset Levels. Seven timbers were sampled. Some have sufficient rings for dendrochronological examination to be worthwhile. Radiocarbon dates would give a clear idea of whether one period of activity is represented, presumably within the prehistoric period, or whether a whole series of successive trackways awaits discovery.

Final comment: A Bayliss (27 February 2012), the four radiocarbon results on these timbers are statistically significantly different (T'=44.4; T'(5%)=7.8; ν=3; Ward and Wilson 1978). This need not mean, however, that more than one trackway exists at watton Carrs, since this difference could arise from the different rings sampled for radiocarbon dating. All the samples probably date to the middle centuries of the second millenium cal BC.

References: Ward and Wilson 1978

UB–3267 3414 ±49 BP

δ¹³C: -27.7 ±0.2‰

Sample: WC1AC, submitted on 27 November 1989 by J Dent

Material: wood (waterlogged; split roundwood): *Quercus* sp. (J Hillam 1989)

Initial comment: from a large timber, which had been lying at the side of an arable field for 2–3 years. It had previously been dragged from peat in an adjacent and low-lying part of the field.

Objectives: UB-3267, together with UB-3268, UB-3269 and UB-3270, are from four timbers which probably represent one or more trackways across boggy land in the prehistoric period. Dendrochronological examination shows no overlap, and a complex history may be clarified through radiocarbon dating. Not all phases need be prehistoric.

Calibrated date: 1σ: 1760–1640 cal BC
2σ: 1890–1610 cal BC

Final comment: C Tyers (24 June 2009), a dendrochronological sample of this timber contained 150 rings, but no sapwood or heartwood/sapwood boundary, and dated to 1804–1655 BC. It is not known which rings were included in the radiocarbon sample.

Laboratory comment: University of Belfast (20 March 1990), this sample was pretreated using the acid based acid protocol.

UB–3268 3451 ±35 BP

δ¹³C: -26.2 ±0.2‰

Sample: WC4AJ, submitted on 27 November 1989 by J Dent

Material: wood (waterlogged; split roundwood): *Quercus* sp. (J Hillam 1989)

Initial comment: as UB-3267

Objectives: as UB-3267

Calibrated date: 1σ: 1880–1690 cal BC
2σ: 1890–1680 cal BC

Final comment: C Tyers (24 June 2009), this sample contained 28 heartwood rings and was not measured for tree-ring analysis. There was no sapwood/heartwood boundary.

Laboratory comment: see UB-3267

UB–3269 3140 ±35 BP

δ¹³C: -27.0 ±0.2‰

Sample: WC5AM, submitted on 27 November 1989 by J Dent

Material: wood (waterlogged; split roundwood): *Quercus* sp. (J Hillam 1989)

Initial comment: as UB-3267

Objectives: as UB-3267

Calibrated date: 1σ: 1440–1400 cal BC
2σ: 1500–1320 cal BC

Final comment: C Tyers (24 June 2009), this sample contained 182 heartwood rings, but could not be dated dendrochronologically. There was no sapwood or heartwood/sapwood boundary, and it is not known which rings were included in the radiocarbon sample.

Laboratory comment: see UB-3267

UB–3270 3355 ±36 BP

δ¹³C: -24.8 ±0.2‰

Sample: WC6AQ, submitted on 27 November 1989 by J Dent

Material: wood (waterlogged; split roundwood): *Quercus* sp. (J Hillam 1989)

Initial comment: as UB-3267

Objectives: as UB-3267

Calibrated date: 1σ: 1690–1610 cal BC
2σ: 1750–1520 cal BC

Final comment: C Tyers (24 June 2009), this sample contained 31 heartwood rings and was not measured for tree-ring analysis. There was no sapwood or heartwood/sapwood boundary surviving on the timber.

Laboratory comment: see UB-3267

Wells Cathedral: The Camery, Somerset

Location: ST 552458
Lat. 51.12.33 N; Long. 02.38.29 W

Project manager: W Rodwell (Western Archaeological Trust), 1978–9

Archival body: Wells Cathedral

Description: excavations in the angle between the south transept and the east cloister revealed evidence for prehistoric and unsuspected Roman occupation, a Saxon cemetery, and the medieval lady chapel by the cloister.

Objectives: the dating of the complex Anglo-Saxon phases at Wells can only be achieved through radiocarbon testing, since intrinsically datable artefacts are entirely absent from the pre-Conquest levels. The importance of the mausoleum and the mortuary chapel in terms of the history of the pre-cathedral structures is such that two samples from each are also being tested.

Final comment: W Rodwell (7 March 1995), this series provides the principal dating evidence for the Anglo-Saxon burials and earliest structures on the cathedral site. HAR-3374 and GU-5017 provide dates for the pre-cemetery features, north and south of the minster, respectively. GU-5018, 5019, 5154, and 5155 establish the wide date-range of early tombs that were disinterred in the mid-tenth century, and their contents repacked in the disused Roman mausoleum. HAR-3397, GU-5014, -5015, and -5016 confirm the mid-Saxon origins of the satellite burials around the early mortuary chapel, the focus of the original Minster site. The other samples date the beginnings of early medieval burial sequences around the Saxo-Norman cathedral church.

Laboratory comment: English Heritage (24 June 2009), five samples (HAR-3374–6, and HAR-3397–8) from this site were radiocarbon dated in 1979 and are published in Jordan *et al* 1994, 202–3). One further sample (GU-5013; WC80/01) was submitted but produced insufficient collagen for dating.

References: Jordan *et al* 1994, 202–3
                      Rodwell 1982
                      Rodwell 1987
                      Rodwell 2001

GU–5014 1260 ±50 BP

$\delta^{13}C$: -21.0‰

Sample: WC80/02, submitted in August 1990 by W J Rodwell

Material: human bone (J Rogers 1980)

Initial comment: sealed burial (skeleton 294) within the mid-Saxon mortuary chapel beneath the eastern termination of the Anglo-Saxon cathedral.

Objectives: it is associated with the use of the Saxon mortuary chapel, which is the earliest structural element in the history of the Wells Cathedral. It is important for establishing the beginning date for the whole stratigraphic sequence.

Calibrated date: *1σ:* cal AD 670–810
                      2σ: cal AD 650–890

Final comment: W J Rodwell (7 March 1995), this burial was third in the sequence of graves inside the Saxon mortuary chapel. The date obtained helps to establish that the chapel and its burial formed the earliest Anglo-Saxon focus on the site, which was suspected on stratigraphic grounds.

GU–5015 1080 ±110 BP

$\delta^{13}C$: -20.8‰

Sample: WC80/03, submitted in August 1990 by W J Rodwell

Material: human bone (J Rogers 1980)

Initial comment: skeleton 277 form a small cemetery to the east of the mortuary chapel (as GU 5014).

Objectives: the cemetery was associated with the mortuary chapel and thus with the primary focus of structures and distinguished graves beneath the later Saxon eastern arm of the cathedral.

Calibrated date: *1σ:* cal AD 820–1030
                      2σ: cal AD 680–1210

Final comment: W J Rodwell (7 March 1995), this sample is from one of the small group of burials just east of the Anglo-Saxon mortuary chapel, and confirms a mid-to-late Saxon date for the group. It establishes the suspected chronological association between the chapel and the group of graves.

GU–5016 1360 ±80 BP

$\delta^{13}C$: -21.1‰

Sample: WC80/04, submitted in August 1990 by W J Rodwell

Material: human bone (J Rogers 1980)

Initial comment: skeleton 257 from the main Anglo-Saxon cemetery adjacent to the north side of the eastern arm of the cathedral. One of the earliest graves, well-sealed.

Objectives: this sample is important for establishing a date for the beginnings of the Saxon cemetery adjacent to the cathedral, on the north side of the lady chapel.

Calibrated date: *1σ:* cal AD 610–770
                      2σ: cal AD 540–860

Final comment: W Rodwell (7 March 1995), a sample from one of the earliest burials in the densely used Anglo-Saxon cemetery north of the mortuary chapel. Appropriately, this has returned the earliest date for a grave *in situ*. It has also usefully provided a date indication for timber-lined graves which, at Wells, seem to precede the appearance of carpentered coffins.

GU–5017 1340 ±70 BP

$\delta^{13}C$: -24.9‰

Sample: WC80/05, submitted in August 1990 by W J Rodwell

Material: charcoal: unidentified

Initial comment: from a small pit containing a concentrated quantity of charcoal, which was associated with Anglo-Saxon domestic occupation pre-dating the northern cemetery.

Objectives: there was mid-late Saxon 'domestic' occupation (aceramic) both north and south of the earliest cathedral. The pit that yielded the charcoal underlay the earliest stratum of burials in the Saxon north cemetery, and is thus important for dating the earliest activity here.

Calibrated date: *1σ:* cal AD 640–770
                      2σ: cal AD 590–860

Final comment: W J Rodwell (7 March 1995), underlying the northern cemetery of the Anglo-Saxon minster were features of potentially 'domestic' origin. This sample, taken from a small pit full of charcoal, provides both a date for the feature and a *terminus post quem* for the series of burials and cemetery structures that overlay it, confirming their suspected origin in the middle Saxon period.

GU–5018 1210 ±100 BP

δ¹³C: -16.7‰

Sample: WC80/06, submitted in August 1990 by W J Rodwell

Material: human bone (J Rogers 1980)

Initial comment: part of a carefully stacked mortuary collection, comprising c 30 skeletons, inside a stone-built mausoleum.

Objectives: the mausoleum is sub-Roman, but the disarticulated skeletons may belong to a mid-Saxon reuse. Skeletons were evidently removed from coffins and packed into the sub-structure of the mausoleum in the tenth century, when the whole site was sealed by the eastward expansion of the cathedral.

Calibrated date: 1σ: cal AD 670–970
2σ: cal AD 640–1030

Final comment: W J Rodwell (7 March 1995), an individual result for one of the c 30 disarticulated skeletons packed inside the disused Roman mausoleum. The result suggests a mid-to-late Saxon interment, redeposited during structural alterations in the mid-tenth century AD.

GU–5019 1450 ±60 BP

δ¹³C: -17.6‰

Sample: WC80/07, submitted in August 1990 by W J Rodwell

Material: human bone (J Rogers 1980)

Initial comment: as GU-5018, although the sample is from a different skeleton.

Objectives: as GU-5018. The importance of the mausoleum and its contents warrants two samples being dated, from separate skeletons.

Calibrated date: 1σ: cal AD 550–660
2σ: cal AD 430–670

Final comment: W Rodwell (7 March 1995), an individual result for a second disarticulated and redeposited burial in the disused mausoleum. This suggests the original burial was substantially earlier than GU-5018. Because of this clearcut difference in dates, two further sample were tested, with a view to discovering whether one was aberrant, whether there was genuinely a wide date range represented in the deposit.

GU–5154 1230 ±60 BP

δ¹³C: -20.6‰

Sample: WC80/09, submitted in August 1991 by W J Rodwell

Material: human bone (J Rogers 1980)

Initial comment: as GU-5018. Sample from a different skeleton.

Objectives: as GU-5018. Additional samples are to be dated because of the divergent results obtained from GU-5018 and GU-5019, which are all part of the same contemporary mortuary deposit.

Calibrated date: 1σ: cal AD 680–890
2σ: cal AD 660–970

Final comment: W J Rodwell (7 March 1995), an individual result for a third disarticulated and redeposited burial in the disused mausoleum. This result is comparable with GU-5018.

GU–5155 1070 ±80 BP

δ¹³C: -21.3‰

Sample: WC80/08, submitted in August 1991 by W J Rodwell

Material: human bone (J Rogers 1980)

Initial comment: as GU-5018, although this sample is from a different skeleton.

Objectives: as GU-5018. Additional samples are to be dated because of the divergent results obtained from GU-5018 and GU-5019, which are all part of the same contemporary mortuary deposit.

Calibrated date: 1σ: cal AD 890–1030
2σ: cal AD 770–1160

Final comment: W J Rodwell (7 March 1995), an individual result for a fourth disarticulated and redeposited burial in the disused mausoleum. The result suggests a somewhat later date than the previous three, potentially suggesting that this burial was not very old when it was disinterred and redeposited in the mid-tenth century AD.

Wembdon Hill, Somerset

Location: ST 279278
Lat. 51.02.54 N; Long. 03.01.43 W

Project manager: R A Crofts and H Woods (Somerset County Council), 1984 and 1987

Archival body: Somerset County Museum

Description: an early Christian cemetery with three rows of burials excavated at the top of the hill. The grave cuts were sealed by a layer of hillwash 0.3m thick.

Objectives: due to a lack of other datable artefacts within the graves, radiocarbon dating is the only way to establish a date for the burials.

Final comment: A Bayliss (27 February 2012), the three radiocarbon results from this cemetery are statistically consistent (T'=3.9; T'(5%)=6.0; ν=2; Ward and Wilson 1978), which suggests that this burial ground may have been in use for a restricted period, probably in the eighth or ninth century cal AD.

References: Ward and Wilson 1978

GU–5149 1300 ±90 BP

δ¹³C: -21.3‰

Sample: Burial 4, Skeleton 4, submitted in 1 by R A Croft

Material: human bone (adult male) (J Rogers 1984)

Initial comment: burial 4 was sealed by red earth, an antique hillwash deposit, and cut into natural bedrock. It was cut in the pelvis area by a water pipe.

Objectives: the sample is probably from the same row as burial 8 (GU-5150) and burial 12 (GU-5151), and it may be possible to use the three samples to obtain replicate determinations. There are no other means of dating the cemetery from which these burials came.

Calibrated date: 1σ: cal AD 650–810
                      2σ: cal AD 580–950

Final comment: see series comments

GU–5150 1240 ±70 BP

δ¹³C: -20.1‰

Sample: Burial 8, submitted on 2 May 1991 by R A Croft

Material: human bone (adult male) (J Rogers 1987)

Initial comment: burial 8 was sealed by layer 3, an antique hillwash deposit, and cut into natural sand. It was securely sealed.

Objectives: this sample is one of two from the same row of burials. It is envisaged that GU-5150 and GU-5151 may be nearly contemporary, but there is no other means of dating the cemetery from which the burials come from.

Calibrated date: 1σ: cal AD 670–890
                      2σ: cal AD 650–980

Final comment: see series comments

GU–5151 1060 ±90 BP

δ¹³C: -22.9‰

Sample: Burial 12, submitted on 2 May 1991 by R A Croft

Material: human bone (adult male) (J Rogers 1987)

Initial comment: burial 12 was sealed by layer 3, an antique hillwash deposit, and cut into natural sand. It was securely sealed.

Objectives: as GU-5150

Calibrated date: 1σ: cal AD 890–1030
                      2σ: cal AD 770–1170

Final comment: see series comments

Wessex Linear Ditches, Wiltshire

Location: *see* individual sites

Project manager: R Entwistle (Reading University), 1989 and 1990

Description: an extensive system of prehistoric boundary ditches on the Wiltshire chalk.

Objectives: to provide a chronological framework in order to understand the evolution of the linear ditch system. Not only will this enable the different ditch elements to be related to each other, it will also provide a more precise basis for dating the ceramic evidence. Late Bronze Age Plain Ware is not well-dated in Wiltshire, and the provision of a comprehensive radiocarbon chronology has somewhat wider implications. Locally, it will enable us to relate the construction of the

ditch system to the settlement pattern, but in addition there is the potential for achieving a better definition of the late Bronze Age horizon in this part of Wessex.

Final comment: R Entwistle (1995), the problem of residuality in primary ditch contexts made the selection of appropriate material difficult. This is illustrated by OxA-3130 which, when calibrated, gave a date range of *c* 1260–800 cal BC (at 95% confidence; Reimer *et al* 2004). The structural relationship of this ditch to other elements in the layout and its morphology suggested that it belonged to a middle Iron Age phase. Clearly, this was not confirmed by the radiocarbon assay. Considering all the other evidence, the most likely explanation for the discrepancy is that the sample was indeed residual, and therefore has no direct bearing on the date of the ditch. The other site that must be questioned is OxA-3045. This was given by a sample recovered from a burial soil beneath the bank of linear ditch. When calibrated it gives a date range of *c* 3700–3360 cal BC (at 95% confidence; Reimer *et al* 2004). Although this is far too early to date the associated earthwork, it is of more general value in that it can be related to the environmental sequence from the buried soil. Each of the remaining samples produced a date range consistent with the pottery recovered from the ditch sections and associated sites. As a group, they confirm the long history of remodelling which seems to typify the linear ditch system in the study area. In particular, they highlight major phases in the re-organisation of the landscape which took place during the late Bronze Age to early Iron Age, and again from the middle Iron Age onwards. Characteristic of this latter period is the placing of human and animal skulls in boundary ditches. Sample OxA-3043, -3046, and -3047 are examples of this practice. They produced statistically indistinguishable radiocarbon dates (T'=0.7; T'(5%)=6.0; v=2; Ward and Wilson 1978). Together with the results of more recent work, these point to a tradition of special deposits reflecting the significance of boundary earthworks during a period that witnessed arable production on an increasing scale (Chambers Jones 1984).

References: Bradley *et al* 1994
                      Chambers and Jones 1984
                      Hedges *et al* 1993, 159–60
                      Reimer *et al* 2004
                      Ward and Wilson 1978

Wessex Linear Ditches: Brigmerston Down linear ditch, Tidworth, Wiltshire

Location: SU 20474737
                      Lat. 51.13.29 N; Long. 01.42.25 W

Project manager: R Entwistle (Reading University), August 1989

Archival body: Devizes Museum

Description: a double-banked linear ditch forming the western boundary of the northern core territory. The ditch was flat-bottomed, approximately 3m wide, and 1.4m deep.

Objectives: to date the initial construction and subsequent reuse of a well-preserved and coherent layout of liner ditches on Salisbury Plain.

OxA–3045 4770 ±75 BP

δ¹³C: -20.6‰

Sample: 092 buried soil, Sample 12, submitted on 8 August 1990 by R Entwistle

Material: bone (unidentified)

Initial comment: from a subsoil hollow at base of palaeo-cultivation soil, context 3A. This is buried beneath the bank of the linear ditch. The hollow has been interpreted as a fossil tree-cast and is associated with a land-snail sequence suggesting clearance.

Objectives: to provide a *terminus ante quem* for the phase of clearance and cultivation which appears to precede, by a short interval, the construction of the ditch and bank.

Calibrated date: 1σ: 3650–3380 cal BC
                       2σ: 3700–3360 cal BC

Final comment: R Entwistle (1994), this early Neolithic date is of interest, since it can be tentatively linked to the environmental sequence preserved in the pre-bank soil, perhaps belonging with the woodland conditions preceeding the clearance phase seen in the molluscan sequence (Entwistle in Bradley *et al* 1994, 67).

References: Bradley *et al* 1994, 67

Wessex Linear Ditches: Dunch Hill, Bulford, Wiltshire

Location: SU 24575113
                       Lat. 51.14.13 N; Long. 01.42.25 W

Project manager: R Entwistle (Reading University), December 1989

Archival body: Devizes Museum

Description: this was the only site excavated during the linear ditches project that produced structural features, relating to a late Bronze Age settlement. The earliest feature on the site was a shallow ditch 1m wide and 0.6m deep. This was paralleled by a holloway, with clearly defined wheel ruts containing pulverised flint and compacted silt. At a later date, a midden deposit had accumulated in the holloway and had spread over the silted-up ditch.

Objectives: to date the initial construction and subsequent re-use of a well preserved and coherent layout of liner ditches on Salisbury Plain.

OxA–3048 2420 ±70 BP

δ¹³C: -21.1‰

Sample: 081A, Sample 19, submitted on 8 August 1990 by R Entwistle

Material: animal bone (unidentified; femur) (W Bonner 1990)

Initial comment: this sample was recovered during the excavation of context 3, a midden deposit overlying a holloway (CUT 2). The lower part of context 3 showed signs

of having been penetrated by scrub or small tree roots. However, this sample was chosen because it was from an undisturbed location.

Objectives: dating is important from the point of view of the ceramic evidence recovered from the linear ditches. Although sherds from these sites can be matched to the material from this site, and broadly speaking this can be assigned to the late Bronze Age, there is no reliable absolute date for this cultural horizon in Wessex. Therefore, in order to set the inception and development of the linear ditch system in a broader chronological framework we need a date range for this ceramic transition.

Calibrated date: 1σ: 750–400 cal BC
                       2σ: 790–380 cal BC

Final comment: R Entwistle (1994), the absence of any developed All Cannings Cross or Iron Age pottery in the assemblage from the midden would seem to indicate that a date in the early part of this range is closest to the true time of abandonment of the settlement. Taken together, these dates suggest that the system of territorial boundaries, which was established some time after 1200 BC, was undergoing considerable change by the eighth century BC, and that this involved the abandonment of the Dunch Hill and Brigmerston settlements (Entwistle in Bradley *et al* 1994, 123).

References: Bradley *et al* 1994, 123

Wessex Linear Ditches: Haxton Down pit alignment, Tidworth, Wiltshire

Location: SU 20505085
                       Lat. 51.15.21 N; Long. 01.42.22 W

Project manager: R Entwistle (Reading University), May 1990

Archival body: Devizes Museum

Description: a site excavated along the course of the Old Marlborough Coach Road, which involved a linear feature thought to be a ditch. On the other side of the Coach Road was a series of closely spaced pits.

Objectives: to investigate the relationship between the pit alignment and the Sidbury West linear ditch.

OxA–3042 2310 ±70 BP

δ¹³C: -21.3‰

Sample: Site 099, Sample 3, submitted on 8 August 1990 by R Entwistle

Material: animal bone (unidentified) (W Bonner 1990)

Initial comment: from calcareous primary silts (14) of a pit which is part of a pit alignment, cut through a partly silted-up linear ditch. The sample does not appear to be a deliberately placed deposit and may therefore have been incorporated during erosion of the pit sides.

Objectives: the sample comes from a pit which forms part of an alignment which is cut into a silted-up and rather shallow linear ditch. This arrangement is unique in the study area and has no pottery associated with it. A radiocarbon date is therefore essential to our understanding of how this unusual site fits into the generally more uniform picture of linear ditch morphology.

Calibrated date: 1σ: 410–260 cal BC
                       2σ: 710–200 cal BC

Final comment: R Entwistle (1994), this date provides a *terminus ante quem* for the ditch (Entwistle in Bradley *et al* 1994, 133).

References: Bradley *et al* 1994, 133

Wessex Linear Ditches: Pearl Wood linear ditch, Tidworth, Wiltshire

Location: SU 21564491
                       Lat. 51.12.09 N; Long. 01.41.29 W

Project manager: R Entwistle (Reading University), July 1989

Archival body: Devizes Museum

Description: the ditch excavated was 3.7m wide and 1.3m deep. Originally it was flat-bottomed, but it had been substantially recut to create a V-shaped profile. A full articulated cattle skull, but lacking the lower jaw, was lying just above the base of the recut.

Objectives: to date the initial construction and subsequent reuse of a well-preserved and coherent layout of liner ditches on Salisbury Plain.

OxA–3046 2170 ±70 BP

$\delta^{13}C$: -19.8‰

Sample: 090, Sample 17, submitted on 8 August 1990 by R Entwistle

Material: animal bone: *Bos* sp., cranium (W Bonner 1989)

Initial comment: recovered from the centre of context 5. This layer represents the primary fill of a massive ditch recut which has removed almost all of the original ditch fill. The only trace of original fill was context 6.

Objectives: this sample is from a massively recut ditch which on morphological grounds is thought to be part of a late development in the use of the ditch system. As with the material from the Old Coach Road Section (OxA-3130), the dating of this sample will enable us to determine how much later this apparent selective reuse of ditch elements takes place.

Calibrated date: 1σ: 370–110 cal BC
                       2σ: 400–40 cal BC

Final comment: R Entwistle (1994), this dates the refurbishment of parts of the boundary system (Entwistle in Bradley *et al* 1994, 68)

References: Bradley *et al* 1994, 68

Wessex Linear Ditches: Sidbury double linear ditch, Tidworth, Wiltshire

Location: SU 21505079
                       Lat. 51.15.19 N; Long. 01.41.31 W

Project manager: R Entwistle (Reading University), April 1990

Archival body: Devizes Museum

Description: excavations in five areas (LDP 020, LDP 026, LDP 027, LDP 100, and LDP 101) were undertaken to explore the the earthworks which survived as a series of extant banks and ditches in the environs of Sidbury Hill hillfort.

Objectives: to date the initial construction and subsequent re-use of a well preserved and coherent layout of linear ditches on Salisbury Plain.

OxA–2987 2480 ±80 BP

$\delta^{13}C$: -26.1‰

Sample: East Terminal 100, Sample 5, submitted on 8 August 1990 by R Entwistle

Material: charcoal: *Fraxinus* sp. (R Gale 1990)

Initial comment: from a charcoal lens in context 10 which consisted of a primary chalk rubble mixed with clay and gravel. These latter are derived from a tertiary deposit, which overlies the solid chalk in the vicinity of the ditch, however the matrix of the context was highly calcareous.

Objectives: the presence of charcoal in the basal stratigraphy of the east terminal offers the potential for dating the construction of this ditch, which is one of a pair of parallel ditches whose relative chronology is unknown at present. In addition the charcoal relates to a major clearance horizon in a complicated and detailed environmental sequence. The phasing of this sequence, in relation to the evidence from other ditches, is crucial from the point of view of reconstructing the land-use history for the ditch system as a whole.

Calibrated date: 1σ: 790–410 cal BC
                       2σ: 810–390 cal BC

Final comment: R Entwistle (1994), sometime between the eight and fifth centuries BC, certain changes to the boundary system, and the abandonment of open settlements following the appearance of early All Cannings Cross ceramics, indicate a radical restructuring of the previous territorial arrangements. The dating of this stage relies on the radiocarbon chronology for the remodelling of the Sidbury Hill to Snail Down linear ditch in order to create a monumental double earthwork; *c* 795–410 cal BC (OxA-2987 and -2988) (R Entwistle in Bradley *et al* 1994, 122).

References: Bradley *et al* 1994, 122

OxA–2988 2490 ±80 BP

$\delta^{13}C$: -25.6‰

Sample: West Terminal 101, Sample 9, submitted on 8 August 1990 by R Entwistle

Material: charcoal: *Sambucus* sp.; *Quercus* sp.; *Corylus* sp. (R Gale 1990)

Initial comment: from a concentration of charcoal in the ditch primary silts, which generally contained frequent charcoal fragments. The primary silts, context 27, are probably equivalent to context 10 in the adjacent ditch terminal 100, but the lenses of clay and gravel are absent. As with context 10, the matrix of the context is highly calcareous.

Objectives: OxA-2988 is equivalent to OxA-2987, but in the western ditch of the double linear. The stratigraphic and taphonomic comments of OxA-2987 apply.

Calibrated date: *1σ:* 790–410 cal BC
                     2σ: 810–390 cal BC

Final comment: see OxA-2987

OxA–3043 2090 ±75 BP

δ¹³C: -20.4‰

Sample: East Terminal, Sample 6, submitted on 8 August 1990 by R Entwistle

Material: human bone (mainly cranial fragments) (W Bonner 1990)

Initial comment: the stratigraphic position of this sample resembles that of OxA-3044 and may be contemporary with it. From a shallow pit which cuts context 9 which, like 27 in 101, contains mixed clay and gravel. The pit infill is highly calcareous.

Objectives: from an early feature in the ditch stratigraphy, and possibly very little time elapsed between the incorporation of OxA-2987 and the deposition of the human remains. However, the fragmentary and generally poor condition of this sample suggests that the material might be significantly older than the date of burial. This raises an interesting question about the origin of these remains: were they, for example, selected from a previous internment elsewhere, in order to be placed as a special deposit in a boundary ditch? This is a chronologically significant issue in its own right, since similar deposits are present in other ditches.

Calibrated date: *1σ:* 210 cal BC–cal AD 1
                     2σ: 370 cal BC–cal AD 70

Final comment: R Entwistle (1994), that the significance of this part of the double earthwork was not lost in later times is implied by this date on the human remains, suggesting a continued respect for the site during the hillfort phase (Entwistle in Bradley *et al* 1994, 134).

References: Bradley *et al* 1994, 134

OxA–3044 2460 ±90 BP

δ¹³C: -20.5‰

Sample: West Terminal 101, Sample 8, submitted on 8 August 1990 by R Entwistle

Material: animal bone: *Bos* sp., skull (W Bonner 1990)

Initial comment: from a shallow pit cut into the primary ditch silts, context 27. This feature appeared to have been backfilled after deposition of the skull and was subsequently

sealed by the lower secondary silts, context 5. All sediments at this level were highly calcareous. Cut 33 is an early re-cut sealed by the primary silts.

Objectives: equivalent to OxA-3043 in the adjacent eastern ditch terminal. *See* OxA-3043.

Calibrated date: *1σ:* 780–400 cal BC
                     2σ: 810–380 cal BC

Final comment: R Entwistle (1994), this result was somewhat earlier than expected, indicating a continuing regard for the special significance of the ditch terminals over many centuries (Entwistle in Bradley *et al* 1994, 67)

References: Bradley *et al* 1994, 67

OxA–3130 2810 ±80 BP

δ¹³C: -21.7‰

Sample: 083, Sample 16, submitted on 8 August 1990 by R Entwistle

Material: animal bone (unidentified; tooth fragments) (W Bonner 1990)

Initial comment: recovered from the base of the secondary silts amongst a stone accumulation towards the centre.

Objectives: the rather symmetrical V-shaped form of this ditch represents a putatively later type of linear ditch, possibly Iron Age, and there are a number of examples where demonstrably earlier ditches were re-cut to form this type of profile. The question that most concerns us is whether this selective recutting is part of a continuous process of development in the use of the ditch system, or whether it represents a phase of reuse long after the system as a whole has ceased to function.

Calibrated date: *1σ:* 1060–840 cal BC
                     2σ: 1260–800 cal BC

Final comment: R Entwistle (1994), this unexpectedly early date can only mean that this material was residual, and for that reason other evidence must be relied upon for the dating of the ditch (Entwistle in Bradley *et al* 1994, 60).

References: Bradley *et al* 1994, 60

Wessex Linear Ditches: Windmill Hill linear ditch, Tidworth, Wiltshire

Location: SU 24575113
                      Lat. 51.15.30 N; Long. 01.38.52 W

Project manager: R Entwistle (Reading University), July 1989

Archival body: Devizes Museum

Description: the linear ditch running northwards along the eastern ridge of the Bourne Valley opposite Sidbury Hill. This is a V-shaped ditch 3.4m wide and 1.4m deep with a bank and buried soil surviving on the eastern side.

Objectives: to date the initial construction and subsequent reuse of a well-preserved and coherent layout of linear ditches on Salisbury Plain.

OxA–3047 2130 ±80 BP

δ¹³C: -22.6‰

Sample: 091, Sample 8, submitted on 8 August 1990 by
R Entwistle

Material: animal bone: *Equus* sp., jaw fragments
(W Bonner 1990)

Initial comment: from a shallow, poorly defined pit cut into
the lower secondary silts of the ditch fill. The fill of this
feature, context 8, was a highly calcareous humic silt with
marked calcium carbonate precipitation.

Objectives: although somewhat higher in the ditch
stratigraphy than the human and ox skulls in the Sidbury
Double Linear Ditch sites, East Terminal (100) and West
Terminal (101), this appears to be a further example of the
deliberate placing of a special deposit in a boundary ditch.
Apart from its intrinsic value as the only dating evidence for
this stretch of ditch, it would enable us to determine if these
deposits were broadly synchronous.

Calibrated date: *1σ:* 360–40 cal BC
  2σ: 390 cal BC–cal AD 50

Final comment: R Entwistle (1994), similarly dated events,
such as the burial of this horse skull and the human skull
(OxA-3043) seem to be connected with the reuse of the
boundary system (Entwistle in Bradley *et al* 1994, 68).

References: Bradley *et al* 1994, 68

West Heath Common, West Sussex

Location: SU 786226
  Lat. 50.59.49 N; Long. 00.52.47 W

Project manager: P Drewett (Institute of Archaeology,
  London), 1973–5, 1980, and 1984

Archival body: Chichester District Museum

Description: a Bronze Age barrow cemetery.

Objectives: to date the barrow cemetery.

Laboratory comment: English Heritage (17 June 2009), five
radiocarbon dates were obtained for samples submitted in
1974, and were published in Jordan *et al* 1994, 203-4 (HAR-
645–8, and HAR-1646.) Eleven further dates were published
in Bayliss *et al* (2012, 295–7; HAR-5281–5, HAR-5320–3,
and HAR-7036–7).

References: Bayliss *et al* 2012
  Drewett 1985
  Drewett 1989
  Jordan *et al* 1994
  Walker *et al* 1991a, 88

HAR–1647 1150 ±100 BP

δ¹³C: -26.8‰

Sample: WHCIV-5, submitted in January 1975 by
P L Drewett

Material: charcoal: unidentified

Initial comment: Barrow IV, feature 7, south-west quadrant.

Objectives: to date the hearth cut into the mound.

Calibrated date: *1σ:* cal AD 720–1000
  2σ: cal AD 660–1040

Final comment: P Drewett (14 September 1995), probably a
Saxon feature dug into the side of the barrow mound.

Laboratory comment: AERE Harwell (2 June 1988), this
sample was measured in the miniature gas proportional
counter (Otlet *et al* 1983).

References: Otlet *et al* 1983

West Heslerton, Yorkshire (East Riding)

Location: SE 917765
  Lat. 54.10.33 N; Long. 00.35.42 W

Project manager: D Powlesland (Landscape Research
  Centre), 1978–82, 1985, 1987, 1989–92,
  1995

Description: West Heslerton and its hinterland have been the
subject of continued archaeological research for more than
three decades, including major excavations at Cook's
Quarry, West Heslerton (site 1), which started as a rescue
excavation between 1978 and 1982 and currently are
continuing as the quarry continues to expand. Site 1 proved
to be most important on account of the presence of
extensive deposits of blown sand sealing evidence dating
from the late Mesolithic to early medieval periods, with
the key phases including a late Neolithic and early Bronze
Age barrow cemetery, parts of a late Bronze Age settlement,
and early Anglo-Saxon or Anglian cemetery. Following
the publication of the excavations at site 1, excavation
continued covering sites 2, 6, and 8, between 1984 and
1986, examining most of the remainder of the Anglian
cemetery which had been superimposed on a late Neolithic
and early Bronze Age monument complex. Small-scale
evaluation excavations at sites 20 and 21 in 1984 were
concerned with the sampling within a crop-mark complex,
interpreted as a 'ladder settlement' dating from the middle
Iron Age to post-Roman period. From 1986 until the
end of 1995 work was concentrated on the rescue excavation
of an Anglian settlement (sites 2, 11, 12, and 13), associated
with the previously excavated cemetery but occupied from
the fifth to ninth centuries, a longer duration than the
cemetery which ceased to be used by the mid-seventh
century. The evidence gathered both from excavation and
very intensive aerial and ground-based survey has revealed
the most detailed picture of an archaeological landscape
for its scale in Britain; providing context for the excavations
and an unparalleled insight into the evolution of settlement
covering several thousand hectares.

Objectives: the excavations and the associated dating
programmes at West Heslerton have covered an important
period in the development of radiocarbon dating and its
application to excavated datasets. During the early years of
the project the objectives were simply to secure dates for
material where we were unsure of the date or to assist in
defining the overall chronological sequence. As the precision
of the dates returned has increased and the size of the
samples required has reduced the dating programmes have

been much more precisely targeted. Recently the dating programme has been directed towards two main objectives, the dating of the important prehistoric ceramic assemblage and the dating and sequencing of the vast excavation of the Anglian settlement.

References:	Powlesland *et al* 1986
	Powlesland 1998
	Powlesland and Haughton 1999
	Powlesland and Price 1988
	Powlesland forthcoming

West Heslerton: Foulbridge, North Yorkshire

Location:	SE 918792
	Lat. 54.12.02 N; Long. 00.35.34 W
Project manager:	A T Evans (Ancient Monuments Laboratory), 1990
Archival body:	Hull Museum

Description: a pollen core WH3.

Objectives: to help construct a chronology for the changes seen in the pollen diagram.

References:	Powlesland 1991

GU–5039 7880 ±100 BP

$\delta^{13}C$: -29.7‰

Sample: WH3 RC1, submitted on 1 November 1990 by A T Evans

Material: peat

Initial comment: sample taken from depth 190-193cm from the sediment core.

Objectives: it is hoped that this sample would provide a basal date for the pollen diagram produced from this site.

Calibrated date:	*1σ:* 7030–6600 cal BC
	2σ: 7070–6480 cal BC

Final comment: P Marshall (29 February 2012), this result provides a date for the expansion of deciduous woodland (elm and oak).

GU–5040 3980 ±50 BP

$\delta^{13}C$: -28.9‰

Sample: WH3 RC2, submitted on 1 November 1990 by A T Evans

Material: peat

Initial comment: sample taken from depth 158–161cm from the sediment core, believed to date the elm decline.

Objectives: this sample would provide a date for the first episode of woodland clearance seen in the pollen diagram produced from the site. It is hoped that the clearance episode may be related to the settlement at West Heslerton.

Calibrated date:	*1σ:* 2570–2460 cal BC
	2σ: 2620–2340 cal BC

Final comment: P Marshall (29 February 2012), the radiocarbon date provides a *terminus post quem* for the first clearance episode identified in the pollen diagram. There may be a hiatus in sedimentation below this level.

GU–5041 2750 ±130 BP

$\delta^{13}C$: -28.7‰

Sample: WH3 RC3, submitted on 1 November 1990 by A T Evans

Material: peat

Initial comment: the sample was taken from depth 80–85cm from the sediment core, believed to date the post-elm decline.

Objectives: this sample would provide a date for the second episode of woodland clearance seen in the pollen diagram produced from the site. It is hoped that the clearance episode may be related to the settlement at West Heslerton.

Calibrated date:	*1σ:* 1050–800 cal BC
	2σ: 1270–590 cal BC

Final comment: P Marshall (29 February 2012), this sample dates a major episode of woodland clearance and an increase in grasses, cereal pollen, and clearance indicators.

West Heslerton: Potter Brompton Carr, North Yorkshire

Location:	SE 966787
	Lat. 54.11.41 N; Long. 00.31.09 W
Project manager:	A T Evans (Ancient Monument Laboratory), 1990
Archival body:	Hull Museum

Description: the settlement at Heslerton is situated overlooking the Vale of Pickering, and although this broad valley has now been extensively drained it would, at the time of occupation, have provided an extensive supply of burnable peat.

Objectives: these samples will help to provide a temporal framework for a pollen diagram prepared from the sediment core.

GU–5085 9130 ±70 BP

$\delta^{13}C$: -28.4‰

Sample: PBC 31–33, submitted on 21 January 1991 by A T Evans

Material: peat

Initial comment: this sample was taken from the sediment core at a depth of 31–34cm beneath the current land surface.

Objectives: this sample will help to provide a temporal framework for a pollen diagram prepared from the sediment core. This sample coincides with a fall of *Salix* and *Cyperaceae* pollen and a rise in *Corylus* pollen.

Calibrated date: *1σ:* 8430–8280 cal BC
                      2σ: 8550–8240 cal BC

Final comment: P Marshall (1 March 2012), pollen preservation in the top part of the core was poor and this, together with the degraded nature of the peat, means interpretation of pollen spectra is hampered, as only more robust pollen types have probably survived. Given the result below (GU-5086) is anomalous, this result may have been affected by similar problems.

GU–5086 14150 ±230 BP

δ¹³C: -28.2‰

Sample: PBC 54-57, submitted on 21 January 1991 by A T Evans

Material: peat

Initial comment: this sample was taken from the sediment core at a depth of 54–57cm beneath the current land surface.

Objectives: this sample will help to provide a temporal framework for a pollen diagram prepared from the sediment core. This sample coincides with a fall of numbers of *Betula* pollen, and the beginnings of a rise in *Pinus* pollen.

Calibrated date: *1σ:* 15700–14900 cal BC
                      2σ: 16000–14800 cal BC

Final comment: P Marshall (29 February 2012), this result must be anomalous as this location would probably have been under an ice-sheet at this date.

West Heslerton: Scarp, Yorkshire (North Riding)

Location:	SE 91757510 Lat. 54.09.48 N; Long. 00.35.41 W
Project manager:	M McHugh (University of Newcastle upon Tyne), 1990–1
Archival body:	Hull Museum

Description: samples of charcoal within buried soils and two humose soils were collected from deep colluvial profiles on the north facing chalk scarp directly south of the settlement at West Heslerton (Mesolithic to Anglian).

Objectives: sampling was undertaken as part of an assessment of the palaeoenvironment potential of colluvial soils above the site at West Heslerton. This was to be viewed in the context of related landuse in the wider environs.

Final comment: M McHugh (30 November 1993), while colluviation below the scarp crest (OxA-3152) around the Mesolithic/Neolithic transition might reflect exploitation and/or climatic worsening, at the scarp foot (OxA-2933, OxA-2934, and OxA-2935) it can be linked with expanding landuse and settlement at West Heslerton during the Bronze Age. Other dates from the base of the scarp (OxA-3393 and OxA-3492) suggest that mid-Devensian relics might survive locally.

References: Hedges *et al* 1994, 358–9

OxA–2933 3460 ±80 BP

δ¹³C: -26.3‰

Sample: WHT 21, submitted on 28 January 1991 by M McHugh

Material: charcoal: unidentified

Initial comment: from West Heslerton transect 2 (SE 91425751) taken at a depth of 2.5m from a buried soil found within a deep colluvial profile at the foot of a chalk escarpment. The buried soil is overlain by chalky rubble.

Objectives: this sample represents a presumably early phase of activity which maybe linked with the broader environmental land use project associated with West Heslerton, or with the site itself, since it lies in close proximity with the latter. Like the Scarp Crest samples it defines a base line of activity though in a different topographical location.

Calibrated date: *1σ:* 1890–1680 cal BC
                      2σ: 2020–1530 cal BC

Final comment: M McHugh (30 November 1993), this suggests a middle Bronze Age timescale for the onset of colluviation and perhaps exploitation of the lower scarp slopes.

OxA–2934 3800 ±70 BP

δ¹³C: -27.2‰

Sample: WHT 22, submitted on 28 January 1991 by M McHugh

Material: charcoal: unidentified

Initial comment: from West Heslerton transect 2 (SE 91425751) taken at a depth of 1m within the colluvial soil sequence at the foot of a chalk escarpment. The profile occurs 30m south of OxA-2933.

Objectives: while OxA-2933 represents the base line of datable activity, this sample provides an approximate *terminus ante quem* for major phases of erosion on the scarp slope of the Wolds above the site at West Heslerton.

Calibrated date: *1σ:* 2350–2130 cal BC
                      2σ: 2470–2030 cal BC

Final comment: M McHugh (30 November 1993), the result suggests a middle Bronze Age timescale for the onset of colluviation and perhaps exploitation of the lower scarp slopes. This equates well with a similar dated profile some 80m to the north.

OxA–2935 2800 ±70 BP

δ¹³C: -25.3‰

Sample: WHDH 3, submitted on 28 January 1991 by M McHugh

Material: charcoal: unidentified

Initial comment: from West Heslerton: Devil's Hill (SE 92057565) the sample was found within a buried soil at a depth of 1m within a colluival soil sequence at the foot of the Yorkshire Wolds near Devil's Hill.

Objectives: this sample provides a date for the upper limit of erosive phases on the Scarp face. It should be possible to define an approximate timescale of erosion/stability/activity phases represented by this deep colluvial soil/chalk debris sequence.

Calibrated date: 1σ: 1030–840 cal BC
2σ: 1190–810 cal BC

Final comment: M McHugh (30 November 1993), dating of charcoal taken from the uppermost buried soil within a multiphase colluvial profile suggests a late Bronze Age/early Iron Age timescale for the final major phase of colluviation. This equates well with an expansion of settlement in the area and occupation of the palisaded enclosure at Devil's Hill.

OxA–3152 6690 ±140 BP

δ¹³C: -24.4‰

Sample: WHSC 1, submitted on 24 January 1991 by M McHugh

Material: soil (organic)

Initial comment: from West Heslerton: Scarp Crest (SE 91757510) this material occurs below 3m of colluvium or chalky head on the north facing scarp of the Yorkshire Wolds.

Objectives: the broader environmental project associated with the excavation at West Heslerton has focussed on the identification of materials in the Vale of Pickering and on the chalk escarpment likely to yield relevant palaeoenvironmental information. The best represented buried soils on the scarp face lie deep within the colluvium and must be dated to provide a base line and part of the framework within which other soils and analyses will be considered.

Calibrated date: 1σ: 5730–5480 cal BC
2σ: 5880–5370 cal BC

Final comment: M McHugh (30 November 1993), dating of a humose soil at the base of a profile below the scarp crest suggests a mid to late Mesolithic timescale for soil development and places the onset of colluviation with the Mesolithic/Neolithic transition. Whether this reflects exploitation on the upper escarpment and/or the climatic worsening of that period is unclear at present, though given uncertainties regarding vegetation change on the Yorkshire Wolds (Bush, 1989; Thomas 1989), the soil warrants further study.

Laboratory comment: Oxford Radiocarbon Accelerator Unit (6 September 1991), when we pretreated the soil and removed the humics, we also attempted to extract the humins for dating. However, we found that the soil contained very little in the way of reduced carbon, and so although it was possible to date the humic acids, the humin fraction could not be dated.

References: Bush 1989
Thomas 1989

OxA–3393 33700 ±1000 BP

δ¹³C: -23.0‰

Sample: DHS 3, submitted on 7 October 1991 by M McHugh

Material: charcoal: unidentified

Initial comment: this sample was one of a series of four taken from a colluvial profile adjacent to Devil's Hill (SE 92057565) c 5m south of OxA-2935. The sample was taken from buried soil within chalky colluvium. The two upper samples were not dated as they were too small; the lower sample is OxA-3492.

Objectives: to establish a time scale of erosive phase and therefore agriculture and other activities on the Wolds adjacent to West Heslerton.

Calibrated date: 1σ: 38100–35100 cal BC
2σ: 39300-34500 cal BC

Final comment: M McHugh (30 November 1993), charcoal from within a multiphase colluvial profile at the base of the chalk scarp yielded a surprising date. The charcoal is probably residual, though a date from the base of the profile also equates tentatively with the Upton Warren interstadial complex suggesting that middle Devensian relics probably do survive locally.

OxA–3492 25800 ±500 BP

δ¹³C: -14.2‰

Sample: DHS 4, submitted on 7 October 1991 by M McHugh

Material: soil

Initial comment: from the same profile as OxA-3393 (SE 92057565) for the base of 3.3m colluvial profile at the base of the Wolds escarpment near West Heslerton.

Objectives: this sample will establish the approximate baseline for erosion phases on the Wolds.

Calibrated date: 1σ: 29100–28200 cal BC
2σ: 29400-27500 cal BC

Final comment: M McHugh (30 November 1993), the result for the basal soil horizon suggests development during the later stages of the Upton Warren interstadial complex, though there are certainties associated with dating procedures and additional dates are required for confirmation. Overlying compact chalky rubble may comprise late-middle to late Devensian soliflucted head.

West Heslerton: Yedingham, North Yorkshire

Location: SE 90657712
Lat. 54.10.54 N; Long. 00.36.39 W

Project manager: A Evans (University of Newcastle upon Tyne), 1990

Archival body: Hull Museum

Description: a thin and shallow peat deposit.

Objectives: the samples were submitted for two purposes: to provide dates for pollen derived from the peat deposit and to test the difference in date between samples treated in a number of different ways during chemical pretreatment.

Final comment: M McHugh (1 November 1993), other samples in this series (GU-5002–6 and GU-5020–1, sampled and submitted by D Jordan) were taken from a buried peat on the northern fringes of West Heslerton Carr (SE 9065 7712) and suggest a Loch Lomond stadial/pre-Boreal timescale for early peat accumulation. This correlates well with the date provided by the Yedingham wood sample and with the oldest peats at Seamer and Starr Carrs. Given early post-glacial human activities at the latter and Mesolithic activities at West Heslerton (correlating with later peat accumulation at West Heslerton Carr), buried peats in the eastern Vale may be of some palaeoenvironmental significance.

Final comment: D Jordan (26 November 1993), the first purpose has been met by these results with the caveat that the second purpose yielded disturbingly large differences in date for different chemical fractions. Replicate dates on the same chemical fraction are gratifyingly close.

Laboratory comment: SUERC Radiocarbon Dating Laboratory (AMS), one further sample WH4/2/DJ/2 (GU-5005) was submitted for dating but failed to produce a result as there was insufficient humin.

GU–5002 11420 ±80 BP

$\delta^{13}C$: -28.4‰

Sample: WH4/25-35/AE, submitted on 14 September 1990 by D Jordan

Material: peat (second humic acid fraction)

Initial comment: peat from shallow deposit.

Objectives: to date the lowest 10cm of the peat sequence.

Calibrated date: 1σ: 11200–10700 cal BC
                     2σ: 11500–11100 cal BC

Final comment: D Jordan (26 November 1993), the site is clearly dated as early Flandrian.

Laboratory comment: English Heritage (1 March 2012), the two measurements on the second humic fraction of this sample are statistically inconsistent (T'=13.2; T'(5%)=3.8; ν=1; Ward and Wilson 1978).

References: Ward and Wilson 1978

GU–5003 10480 ±80 BP

$\delta^{13}C$: -28.7‰

Sample: WH4/15-25/AE, submitted on 14 September 1990 by D Jordan

Material: peat (second humic acid fraction)

Initial comment: peat from shallow deposit.

Objectives: to date the upper 10cm of the peat sequence.

Calibrated date: 1σ: 10700–10200 cal BC
                     2σ: 10700–10100 cal BC

Final comment: D Jordan (26 November 1993), this dates the upper 10cm of peat as early Flandrian.

Laboratory comment: English Heritage (1 March 2012), the two measurements on the second humic fraction of this sample are statistically consistent (T'=1.4; T'(5%)=3.8; ν=1; Ward and Wilson 1978).

References: Ward and Wilson 1978

GU–5004 10360 ±60 BP

$\delta^{13}C$: -28.0‰

Sample: WH4/2/DJ/1, submitted on 1 May 1990 by D Jordan

Material: peat (second humic acid fraction)

Initial comment: from a shallow peat deposit; replicate of GU-5003.

Objectives: to compare with GU-5003.

Calibrated date: 1σ: 10450–10120 cal BC
                     2σ: 10570–10030 cal BC

Final comment: D Jordan (26 November 1993), this replicates GU-5003 with which it is in sufficiently close agreement.

Laboratory comment: see GU-5003

GU–5006 11010 ±80 BP

$\delta^{13}C$: -29.1‰

Sample: WH4/1/DJ, submitted on 14 September 1990 by D Jordan

Material: peat (second humic acid fraction)

Initial comment: from shallow peat deposit; a replicate of GU-5002.

Objectives: to compare with GU-5002.

Calibrated date: 1σ: 11500-11200 cal BC
                     2σ: 11500-11100 cal BC

Final comment: D Jordan (26 November 1993), this date replicates GU-5002 in every respect and the results are close enough for confidence.

Laboratory comment: see GU-5002

GU–5020 8390 ±70 BP

$\delta^{13}C$: -27.1‰

Sample: WH4/2/DJ/3, submitted on 14 September 1990 by D Jordan

Material: peat (fulvic acid fraction)

Initial comment: this date was carried out on the same sample as GU-5003 and GU-5004: fulvic acid fraction.

Objectives: to date the upper 10cm of the peat sequence using different pretreatment.

Calibrated date: 1σ: 7540–7360 cal BC
                     2σ: 7590–7300 cal BC

Final comment: D Jordan (26 November 1993), the difference in date is due to a difference in pretreatment which in this case, extracted the fulvic acid fraction. The date differences are disturbing and suggest that the dates on other fractions may also be questionable.

Laboratory comment: English Heritage (1 March 2012), this result on the fulvic acid fraction is statistically significantly younger than the measurements on the second humic acid fraction of this sample (*see* GU-5003-4) (T'=505.4; T'(5%)=6.0; v=2); Ward and Wilson 1978).

References: Ward and Wilson 1978

GU–5021 9830 ±80 BP

δ¹³C: -27.9‰

Sample: WH4/2/DJ/4, submitted on 14 September 1990 by D Jordan

Material: peat (first humic acid fraction)

Initial comment: as GU-5020, this date was carried out using a different chemical fraction but on the same sample material as GU-5003 and GU-5004. This sample represents the first humic acid fraction.

Objectives: to compare with GU-5020.

Calibrated date: 1σ: 9320–9250 cal BC
                       2σ: 9450–9190 cal BC

Final comment: D Jordan (26 November 1993), in this case the date relates to the first humic acid fraction and, again, the discrepancy is disturbing.

Laboratory comment: English Heritage (1 March 2012), this result is also significantly younger (T'=38.0; T'(5%)=6.0; v=2; Ward and Wilson 1978) than the statistically consistent measurements on the second humic acid fraction of this sample (*see* GU-5003-4).

References: Ward and Wilson 1978

GU–5042 10640 ±120 BP

δ¹³C: -27.1‰

Sample: YW1, submitted on 8 November 1990 by M McHugh

Material: wood (waterlogged): unidentified

Initial comment: the sample was taken from Yedingham (NGR: SE 89347965), from within a thin peat horizon buried below *c* 1.5–2.0m of alluvium within a drainage off-shoot of the River Derwent. The wood fragment was made visible by the erosion of the banks. Its origin is not known but it may be redeposited.

Objectives: the sample will give a very approximate date for the upper strata of the Derwent Valley at Yedingham.

Calibrated date: 1σ: 10800–10400 cal BC
                       2σ: 10800–10200 cal BC

Final comment: M McHugh (1 November 1993), the date suggests a late glacial timescale (Loch Lomond stadial/early pre-boreal) and although this correlates well with the oldest organic remains at Seamer and Starr Carrs in the eastern Vale of Pickering, there are contextual uncertainties. These are sustained by pollen analysis of the peat, which indicates agricultural disturbance, though modern (fluvial) contamination is a possibility.

Westhampnett, West Sussex

Location: SU 877054
                      Lat. 50.50.27 N; Long. 00.45.15 W

Project manager: M Allen (Wessex Archaeology), 1992

Archival body: Wessex Archaeology

Description: the 2km long route of the A27 Westhampnett bypass has proved exceptionally rich in archaeological remains. No fewer than five sites were revealed by an archaeological evaluation carried out in November 1991, and these sites were subsequently excavated in 1992 in advance of road construction. The radiocarbon determinations range over a period of 11,000 years with results in the late Quaternary time span, before bristlecone pine calibration is possible, to the middle Bronze Age.

Objectives: to provide a chronological framework for the development and use of this part of the Chichester floodplain.

Final comment: M Allen (2003), as a whole this group of results indicates the surprising longevity (albeit non continuous) of the archaeological occupation of the same location on the West Sussex Coastal Plain. Perhaps the most significant is the presence of an Allerød phase buried soil from which both the radiocarbon and palaeo-environmental results accord well with other sites in southern England. This is one of the first dated occurrences of Allerød phase buried soils and palaeo-environment data from non-chalkland contexts. This evidence enhances our understanding of both the archaeology and quaternary science.

Other dates confirm the long and repeated use of the area over nearly ten millennia. The presence of a late Neolithic radiocarbon date, although not from a feature containing late Neolithic pottery, does confirm the presence of activity in the vicinity as seen by Grooved Ware and Peterborough Ware pottery from the Westhampnett excavations and reported in the vicinity by Drewett (1978; 1980). The middle to later Bronze Age dates provide one of the earliest dated occurrences of a Deverel-Rimbury settlement in Sussex, again perhaps significant that it occurs on the coastal plain rather than the chalkland.

References: Drewett 1978
                      Drewett 1980
                      Fitzpatrick *et al* 2008
                      Fitzpatrick 1997
                      Wessex Archaeology 1992

GU–5307 3510 ±50 BP

δ¹³C: -26.0‰

Sample: W474 49011, submitted on 4 March 1993 by M J Allen

Material: charcoal (*Salix/Populus* sp.): *Quercus* sp.; Pomoideae; *Corylus* sp.; *Prunus* sp. (R Gale 1993)

Initial comment: from a charcoal lens in pit 40218 indicating a single episode of dumping of local waste; from context 40233. The pit also contained secondary series Collared Urns.

Objectives: to date the use of the pit and the activity associated with its use. The layer is very sharp and discrete, representing a single episode of disposal. Though the origin of the charcoal is unknown, it is assumed to be a part of localised contemporary settlement.

Calibrated date: *1σ:* 1910–1750 cal BC
                       2σ: 1960–1690 cal BC

Final comment: M J Allen (2003), the radiocarbon date falls within the date range of secondary series Collared Urns (Longworth 1984).

References: Longworth 1984

GU–5308 3360 ±50 BP

δ¹³C: -28.1‰

Sample: W474 39049, submitted on 4 March 1993 by M J Allen

Material: charcoal: *Quercus* sp.; *Prunus* sp.; *Corylus* sp. (R Gale 1993)

Initial comment: from a small cremation pit surrounding a secondary series Collared Urn. The urn contained no charcoal but was sitting on a layer containing charcoal.

Objectives: to date the cremation, a primary burial within a ring ditch barrow.

Calibrated date: *1σ:* 1740–1600 cal BC
                       2σ: 1760–1510 cal BC

Final comment: M J Allen (2003), this result is relatively late within the general date range of secondary series Collared Urns (Longworth 1984; Burgess 1986), and accords well with the late stylistic affinities of the vessel.

References: Burgess 1986
                     Longworth 1984

GU–5310 9210 ±90 BP

δ¹³C: -29.1‰

Sample: W474 39060 S, submitted on 4 March 1993 by M J Allen

Material: soil (humic ranker) (R I MacPhail 1993)

Initial comment: a combined sample of soil containing struck flints and anthropogenic charcoal from contexts 30353, 30361, and 30362.

Objectives: to date the soil formation as well as the anthropogenic activity and compare with the environmental evidence which includes mollusca, pollen, charcoal, plant remains, and soil micromorphology.

Calibrated date: *1σ:* 8570–8290 cal BC
                       2σ: 8700–8270 cal BC

Final comment: M J Allen (2003), a further radiocarbon determination (AA-11770; 8620 ±105 BP; 7960–7510 cal BC; Reimer *et al* 2004) is statistically significantly different from GU-5310 (T'=18.0; T'(5%)=3.8; ν=1; Ward and Wilson 1978) at 95% confidence, although they are both dates on the humic acid fraction of the same palaeosol. Both results are significantly younger than the determinations on fragments of charcoal from the same soil (*see* OxA-4166, OxA-4167, and AA-11769; 10870 ±80 BP; 11000–10640 cal BC at 95% confidence; Reimer *et al* 2004). This may be explained by the migration downwards of younger humic acids (Dresser 1970). Although Shore (1988) found no significant systematic difference between dates on the humic

acid and humin fractions of acid peats, humic acids are soluble in alkaline environments. The pH of the Allerød soil is 8.0–8.2. A small degree of penetration by younger material would make a relatively large difference to the results because the radiocarbon concentrations in samples of late glacial date are very low. It is worth noting however, that these two results are remarkably close to the spread of the dates from the Mesolithic contexts (OxA-4168; OxA-4170; OxA-4171). Whether this is fortuitous, or is coincidental with warmer temperatures in the early post glacial, and represents renewed pedogenesis, the humic acids from which migrated downwards into the older soil, is undetermined.

References: Dresser 1970
                     Reimer *et al* 2004
                     Shore 1988
                     Ward and Wilson 1978

OxA–4166 10880 ±110 BP

δ¹³C: -24.7‰

Sample: W474 39060, submitted on 4 March 1993 by M J Allen

Material: charcoal: cf *Betula* sp. (R Gale 1993)

Initial comment: context 30361; a sealed palaeosol above cryoturbations and sealed by non organic calcareous marls up to 0.98m thick. The palaeosol is an immature ranker with charcoal and flints (pollen of oak and pine).

Objectives: to date the burning episode which is presumed to be anthropogenic and associated with a single struck flint. The date will provide a chronological framework for human activity and environmental evidence - mollusca, pollen, charcoal, and soil micromorphology.

Calibrated date: *1σ:* 11000–10600 cal BC
                       2σ: 11200–10600 cal BC

Final comment: M J Allen (2003), the three radiocarbon determinations from charcoal within the Allerød phase soil form a consistent group (OxA-4166, OxA-4167, and AA-11769; 10870 ±80 BP; T'=0.1; T'(5%)=6.0; ν=2; Ward and Wilson 1978), suggesting that the soil was formed in the first half of the eleventh millennium cal BC (ie between *c* 11000 and *c* 10500 cal BC using the marine extension of Bard *et al* 1993). These dates also fit well into the existing dates for buried soils as reviewed by Preece (1994).

References: Bard *et al* 1993
                     Bronk Ramsey *et al* 2000b, 249
                     Preece 1994
                     Ward and Wilson 1978

OxA–4167 10840 ±100 BP

δ¹³C: -23.1‰

Sample: W474 39053, submitted on 4 March 1993 by M J Allen

Material: charcoal (cf *Pinus* sp.; cf *Pinus* needle): cf *Betula* sp. (R Gale 1993)

Initial comment: as OxA-4166

Objectives: as OxA-4166

Calibrated date: 1σ: 10900–10600 cal BC
2σ: 11000–10600 cal BC

Final comment: see OxA-4166

References: Bronk Ramsey *et al* 2000b, 249

OxA–4168 9120 ±90 BP

δ¹³C: -22.4‰

Sample: W474 19006H, submitted on 4 March 1993
by M J Allen

Material: plant macrofossils (hazelnuts) (M J Allen 1992)

Initial comment: from a sol lessiv

Objectives: to date the burning of hazelnuts which is assumed
to be a) anthropogenic and b) associated with the extensive
lithic assemblage.

Calibrated date: 1σ: 8450–8270 cal BC
2σ: 8570–8220 cal BC

Final comment: M J Allen (2003), this result is consistent with
the earlier Mesolithic flint assemblage from the soil profile.

References: Bronk Ramsey *et al* 2000b, 249

OxA–4169 4260 ±70 BP

δ¹³C: -25.1‰

Sample: W474 19006C, submitted on 4 March 1993
by M J Allen

Material: charcoal: Pomoideae; *Quercus* sp.; *Corylus* sp.;
Prunus sp. (R Gale 1993)

Initial comment: from a sol lessiv

Objectives: to date the burning and probable Mesolithic
activity to compare with the hazelnuts (OxA-4168) which
are probably directly associated with Mesolithic activity,
rather than the charcoal (OxA-4167) which is possibly
related to activity.

Calibrated date: 1σ: 2920–2870 cal BC
2σ: 3030–2630 cal BC

Final comment: M J Allen (2003), this result is significantly
different from OxA-4168 and the Mesolithic flint assemblage
found within the soil. It was unexpected. This must represent
localised Neolithic activity, for which there is a limited quantity
of Neolithic pottery elsewhere along the Westhampnett bypass
excavations, and Neolithic flints in the immediate vicinity.

References: Bronk Ramsey *et al* 2000b, 249

OxA–4170 8880 ±100 BP

δ¹³C: -24.6‰

Sample: W474 49034 H, submitted on 4 March 1990
by M J Allen

Material: plant macrofossils (hazelnuts) (M J Allen 1992)

Initial comment: from a shallow pit up to 50cm below topsoil,
found with a number of Mesolithic flints and a wider flint
scatter recovered by fieldwalking.

Objectives: to date the burning of the hazelnuts and thus the
Mesolithic activity associated with the flint scatter and to
compare them with that associated with the sol lessiv

Calibrated date: 1σ: 8250–7790 cal BC
2σ: 8290–7610 cal BC

Final comment: M J Allen (2003), this result is statistically
significantly different at 95% confidence from OxA-4171, on
material from the same context (T'=18.7; T'(5%)=3.8; v=1;
Ward and Wilson 1978), although both fall securely within the
earlier Mesolithic.

References: Bronk Ramsey *et al* 2000b, 249
Ward and Wilson 1978

OxA–4171 8300 ±90 BP

δ¹³C: -23.9‰

Sample: W474 49034C, submitted on 4 March 1993
by M J Allen

Material: charcoal: *Quercus* sp.; *Fraxinus* sp.; *Corylus* sp.
(R Gale 1993)

Initial comment: from a shallow pit upto 50cm below the
topsoil, found with a number of Mesolithic flints: from the
same sample as OxA-4170.

Objectives: to date the burning and thus the probable Mesolithic
activity and to compare it with the hazelnuts which are probably
anthropogenic rather than charcoal like this sample, which is
possibly anthropogenic and related to activity.

Calibrated date: 1σ: 7500–7180 cal BC
2σ: 7550–7070 cal BC

Final comment: see OxA-4170

References: Bronk Ramsey *et al* 2000b, 249

OxA–4172 3130 ±80 BP

δ¹³C: -24.5‰

Sample: W474 49020, submitted on 4 March 1993 by
M J Allen

Material: charcoal: *Fraxinus* sp.; *Quercus* sp.; *Prunus* sp.
(R Gale 1993)

Initial comment: from a shallow pit associated with a single
sherd of Peterborough ware. The pit was *c* 30cm deep below
the topsoil.

Objectives: to provide a date for the grooved ware ceramic
tradition and to date the Neolithic activity on the coastal plain.

Calibrated date: 1σ: 1500–1310 cal BC
2σ: 1610–1210 cal BC

Final comment: M J Allen (2003), this result is statistically
indistinguishable at 95% confidence from the others relating
to middle Bronze Age activity on the site (OxA-4174 and
OxA-4175; T'=0.1; T'(5%)=6.0; v=2; Ward and Wilson
1978). This pit must therefore be part of this activity, and
the pottery residual.

References: Bronk Ramsey *et al* 2000b, 249
Ward and Wilson 1978

OxA–4173 3640 ±75 BP

δ¹³C: -24.1‰

Sample: W474 39050, submitted on 4 March 1993 by M J Allen

Material: charcoal: *Prunus* sp.; *Corylus* sp. (R Gale 1993)

Initial comment: from a small localised deposit of burnt material in an otherwise sterile chalk fine gravel-filled barrow ditch; probably very rapidly silted up. The sample was *c* 15cm below the base of the topsoil but all the ditch fills were very clean.

Objectives: the charcoal is directly associated with a very small quantity of cremated bone (0.1g) presumed part of the pyre and thus will date the secondary (cremation) burial in the ditch and can be compared with the primary burial.

Calibrated date: *1σ:* 2140–1900 cal BC
                     2σ: 2210–1770 cal BC

Final comment: M J Allen (2003), *see* GU-5308. Although independently this date would be acceptable for an early Bronze Age barrow, the fact that this result appears to be *c* 300 years earlier than the primary burial, which it was initially assumed to pre-date, is difficult to reconcile, although the two calibrated date ranges do overlap.

References: Bronk Ramsey *et al* 2000b, 249

OxA–4174 3140 ±80 BP

δ¹³C: -23.8‰

Sample: W474 49006, submitted on 4 March 1993 by M J Allen

Material: charcoal: *Fraxinus* sp.; *Quercus* sp.; *Prunus* sp. (R Gale 1993)

Initial comment: from a posthole, part of a posthole arc which was presumably a Bronze Age hut.

Objectives: to date the structure by dating the charcoal in the posthole. Another posthole contained OxA-4175 and a hearth outside the arc which is to be archaeomagnetically dated.

Calibrated date: *1σ:* 1500–1310 cal BC
                     2σ: 1610–1210 cal BC

Final comment: M J Allen (2003), further analysis suggests that this feature was not part of a structure, but a pit showing indications of *in situ* burning and associated with Deverel-Rimbury pottery. The result is consistent with the expected date range of the ceramics.

References: Bronk Ramsey *et al* 2000b, 249

OxA–4175 3110 ±80 BP

δ¹³C: -24.3‰

Sample: W474 49023, submitted on 4 March 1993 by M J Allen

Material: charcoal: Pomoideae; *Quercus* sp.; *Prunus* sp. (R Gale 1993)

Initial comment: from a posthole which was part of a posthole arc, presumably a Bronze Age hut.

Objectives: to date the structure. Another posthole contained charcoal (*see* OxA-4176) and a hearth outside the arc is to be archaeomagnetically dated.

Calibrated date: *1σ:* 1460–1290 cal BC
                     2σ: 1530–1130 cal BC

Final comment: M J Allen (2003), this posthole showed indications of *in situ* burning, although further analysis could not associate it with an identifiable structure. The date is consistent with the expected date range for the ceramics associated with the middle Bronze Age activity on the site.

References: Bronk Ramsey *et al* 2000b, 249

Wetwang Slack, Yorkshire (East Riding)

Location: SE 94055985
                    Lat. 54.01.33 N; Long. 00.33.51 W

Project manager: J Dent (Humberside Archaeology Unit), 1983–87

Archival body: Hull and East Riding Museum

Description: Beaker/Bronze Age cemetery, Iron Age settlement and cemetery, a continuation of the Garton Slack complex.

Objectives: to relate the cultural evidence to a fixed chronological scale.

Laboratory comment: Ancient Monuments Laboratory (1995), ten further dates from this site were funded prior to 1981 and were published in the first volume of Radiocarbon Dates (Jordan *et al* 1994, 206–7). Five further dates from this site were published in Bayliss *et al* (2012, 306–7; HAR-8538–41, and HAR-8543).

References: Bayliss *et al* 2012
                    Dent 1983
                    Hardiman *et al* 1992, 51
                    Jordan *et al* 1994, 206–7
                    Manby *et al* 2003

HAR–9244 3690 ±80 BP

δ¹³C: -26.7‰

Sample: WY8AK, submitted in June 1988 by J Dent

Material: charcoal: unidentified

Initial comment: from a Breaker period grave, the central burial of a ring ditched enclosure. When the oak coffin was re-opened the original inhumation had not decayed and was still partially articulated. It had been rearranged over another body next to which was found a decorated Beaker. The sample was taken from a layer of charcoal presumed to be the collapsed lid, which covered both bodies.

Objectives: to date the monument closely and the decorated Beaker in relation to others in the same extended cemetery (Dent 1983).

Calibrated date: *1σ:* 2200–1950 cal BC
                     2σ: 2300–1880 cal BC

Final comment: J Dent (15 January 2007), the Beaker conforms to Clarke's N/NR group, Lanting's and van der Waals' Step 3, and was a secondary deposition in this primary grave. This group of dates (HAR-9244, HAR-9245, and HAR-9247) is quoted by Manby *et al* (2003, 60–1) "to illustrate the questionable nature of these classifications in the light of high precision radiocarbon dating".

Laboratory comment: English Heritage (1 March 2012), the three radioacarbon measurements on the charred coffin from this grave are statistically consistent (T'=0.4; T'(5%)=6.0; ν=2; Ward and Wilson 1978). The weighted mean (3710 ±50 BP) calibrates to 2280–1950 cal BC at 95% confidence, or 2200–2030 cal BC at 68% confidence (Reimer *et al* 2004).

References: Dent 1983
Hardiman *et al* 1992, 51–2
Manby *et al* 2003
Reimer *et al* 2004
Ward and Wilson 1978

HAR–9245 3680 ±100 BP

δ¹³C: -26.8‰

Sample: WY8AM, submitted in June 1988 by J Dent

Material: charcoal: unidentified

Initial comment: from the central grave of a Beaker period funerary monument. The wood represents part of the charred inner surface of a monoxylous coffin, coming from the upper sides. The coffin contained two burials, the earlier was disturbed by re-opening and was carefully rearranged over the feet of the later crouched inhumation. A decorated Beaker was found with the latter.

Objectives: to date the monument and the Beaker, both being part of the great extended and mostly undated cemetery of round barrows of Garton Slack.

Calibrated date: 1σ: 2210–1920 cal BC
2σ: 2430–1770 cal BC

Final comment: see HAR-9244

Laboratory comment: see HAR-9244

References: Hardiman *et al* 1992, 52
Manby *et al* 2003

HAR–9246 3850 ±100 BP

δ¹³C: -27.4‰

Sample: WY9AL, submitted in June 1988 by J Dent

Material: charcoal: unidentified

Initial comment: from the filling of a secondary grave cut through the circular enclosing ditch of a funerary monument. The grave contained a crouched inhumation with a fine decorated Bell Beaker behind the head.

Objectives: to date the monument and the Beaker.

Calibrated date: 1σ: 2470–2140 cal BC
2σ: 2580–2020 cal BC

Final comment: J Dent (15 January 2007), the Beaker conforms to Clarke's N2 group, Lanting's and van der Waals' Step 3, and was deposited in a grave which cut the enclosing

ditch around the primary grave which furnished three other dates in this series, each of which was later than HAR-9246. This group of dates is quoted by Manby, *et al* (2003, 60–1) "to illustrate the questionable nature of these classifications in the light of high precision radiocarbon dating".

References: Manby *et al* 2003

HAR–9247 3750 ±80 BP

δ¹³C: -26.9‰

Sample: WY8AJ, submitted in June 1988 by J Dent

Material: charcoal (comminuted): unidentified (1.34g); *Quercus* sp., probably sapwood (0.03g, 100%) (R Gale 1999)

Initial comment: found beneath two skeletons in the remains of a wood coffin. A pottery Beaker was found with the second skeleton to be placed in the coffin. The sample is believed to be the charred internal bottom surface of a monoxylous coffin. The grave was central to a circular enclosing ditch.

Objectives: to date the monument and the Beaker.

Calibrated date: 1σ: 2290–2030 cal BC
2σ: 2470–1940 cal BC

Final comment: see HAR-9244

Laboratory comment: see HAR-9244

Laboratory comment: AERE Harwell (30 November 1989), this sample was measured in the miniature gas proportional counter (Otlet *et al* 1983).

References: Hardiman *et al* 1992, 52
Otlet *et al* 1983

Wharram Percy, North Yorkshire

Location: SE 858642
Lat. 54.03.59 N; Long. 00.41.20 W

Project manager: J G Hurst (West Yorkshire Archaeology Service), 1960–70, 1972–8, 1981, 1983–5, 1990

Description: Wharram Percy lies near the north-west scarp of the Yorkshire Wolds, about half-way between York and Scarborough and 10km (7 miles) from the Roman and medieval town of Malton. The main earthworks of the village are situated on the chalk plateau at about 150m above sea level; in the valley is the church of St Martin and the site of the medieval fishpond.

Objectives: the principal objectives of radiocarbon dating at Wharram Percy were to discover whether the phasing sequences proposed for the burials in different areas of the cemetery have chronological integrity, and to put absolute dating onto the phasing structure, and to determine the date of grain processing around the pond.

Final comment: S Wrathmell (6 December 2006), the two areas of greatest chronological uncertainty in the Wharram excavation project were the dating of grain processing activity in the vicinity of the pond, and the phases of burial activity in the churchyard. The radiocarbon dating programme has been successful in establishing chronologies for both. For the churchyard, it underpins a nationally important study of the skeletal material by Simon Mays.

References: Bell and Beresford 1987
Hayfield 1987
Jordan *et al* 1994, 208–9
Mays *et al* 2007
Stamper and Croft 2000
Treen and Atkin 2005

Wharram Percy: site 95, North Yorkshire

Location: SE 858642
Lat. 54.03.59 N; Long. 00.41.20 W

Project manager: J Richards (University of York) (Medieval Village Research Group), 1990

Archival body: Department of the Environment, Medieval Village Research Group, National Monuments Record Centre, Hull City Museums & Art Galleries

Description: a middle Saxon non-ferrous metalworking workshop cut into a Romano-British field boundary ditch.

Objectives: to investigate the origins of the medieval village and identify the nature of the middle Saxon activity.

Final comment: J Richards (6 November 1996), both results have confirmed that the infant burial can be attributed to the early Anglo-Saxon period, probably in the first half of the seventh century AD. The burial must therefore be linked with the building, and may be associated with its construction. Ritual infant burial is known from the Roman period but is unusual for the Anglo-Saxon period (*see* discussion in Milne and Richards 1992, 84–5).

References: Milne and Richards 1992

UtC–1702 1370 ±50 BP

δ¹³C: -21.8‰

Sample: 95/2506, submitted in February 1991 by A Clark

Material: human bone (infant, 39–41 weeks) (S Mays)

Initial comment: an articulated skeleton of a human infant lying just below a trampled surface of ditch fill within a Romano-British ditch, and associated with the skeleton of an animal (UtC-1703).

Objectives: a date should indicate the likely period of deposition of the ditch fills sealed by the burials. It is important to establish if the burials were earlier than the adjacent metal working workshop (Iron Age/Romano-British) or contemporary with it (early/mid Anglo-Saxon) as there was no direct stratigraphic link between the deposits.

Calibrated date: 1σ: cal AD 640–680
2σ: cal AD 590–770

Final comment: J Richards (6 November 1996), the dating result confirms that the infant burial is broadly contemporary with the Anglo-Saxon activity and is not a Romano-British feature (see Mays in Milne and Richards 1992, 79).

References: Milne and Richards 1992, 79

UtC–1703 1450 ±40 BP

δ¹³C: -22.7‰

Sample: 95/2505, submitted in February 1991 by A Clark

Material: animal bone: *Ovis* sp. (S Payne 1991)

Initial comment: partially articulated bones from the skeleton of an animal lying just below the surface of a trampled ditch fill within a Romano-British ditch. Its position appears to have been marked by a flint boulder; and it was adjacent and slightly above the human infant burial (UtC-1702).

Objectives: as UtC-1702

Calibrated date: 1σ: cal AD 570–650
2σ: cal AD 540–660

Final comment: J Richards (6 November 1996), the dating result confirms that the partially articulated animal remains were contemporary with the infant burial and may represent a funerary offering. They highlight the ritual, and possibly pagan, context of the burial.

Final comment: S Payne (14 February 1991), at first sight this group looks like a burial of a sheep which was around a year old, though there is at least one bone from another animal. But the absence of quite large parts of the skeleton and the presence of cut-marks suggest instead that this is more likely to be a dump of partly-butchered bones, possibly in articulated groups, probably mostly from the same animal. The good condition of the bones and the absence of any gnawing marks suggests rapid burial. Making due allowance for age, the bones are fairly small; they would not be out of place in a Roman, Dark Age, or medieval context.

Wharram Percy: South Manor, North Yorkshire

Location: SE 858642
Lat. 54.03.59 N; Long. 00.41.20 W

Project manager: P Stamper (English Heritage), 1985

Archival body: Department of the Environment, Medieval Village Research Group, National Monuments Record Centre, Hull City Museums and Art Galleries

Description: a large area with intensive Saxon and medieval activity.

Objectives: to help clarify the phasing and dating of activities.

Laboratory comment: English Heritage (17 January 2012), two further dates from this site were published in Bayliss *et al* (2012, 309; HAR-5624–5).

References: Bayliss *et al* 2012
Stamper and Croft 2000

GU–5119 1030 ±60 BP

δ¹³C: -24.9‰

Sample: 76/52, submitted in February 1991 by A Clark

Material: charcoal: unidentified

Initial comment: from a penannular gully, possibly from around a straw stack.

Objectives: the site was partly mid-Saxon, and partly early medieval (eleventh/twelfth century AD). Dating of this feature to one or other band will clarify not only its own date but that of several other key features which share the same stratigraphic horizon.

Calibrated date: *1σ:* cal AD 970–1040
   2σ: cal AD 880–1160

Final comment: P Stamper (11 May 1995), GU–5119 and GU–5120 were both taken from a pennanular gully interpreted as a crop stack stand drainage ditch. The dates suggest that this should be placed with the Saxon phase(s), rather than the Norman as provisionally phased. This is a great help, as the site was shallowly stratified, multi-period, and complex.

Laboratory comment: English Heritage (4 March 2012), the two measurements on bulk charcoal from the deposit are statistically indistinguishable (T'=0.8; T'(5%)=3.8; ν=1; Ward and Wilson 1978). Their weighted mean (1064 ±46 BP) calibrates to cal AD 880–1030 at 95% confidence, or cal AD 900–1020 at 68% confidence (Reimer *et al* 2004).

References: Reimer *et al* 2004
   Ward and Wilson 1978

GU–5120 1110 ±70 BP

δ¹³C: -26.4‰

Sample: 76/54, submitted in February 1991 by A Clark

Material: charcoal: unidentified

Initial comment: as GU–5119

Objectives: as GU–5119

Calibrated date: *1σ:* cal AD 870–1020
   2σ: cal AD 720–1040

Final comment: see GU–5119

Laboratory comment: see GU–5119

GU–5121 1380 ±80 BP

δ¹³C: -25.7‰

Sample: 76/146, submitted in February 1991 by A Clark

Material: wood: *Fraxinus* sp., carbonised (D Haddon-Reece 1991)

Initial comment: small planks *c* 100mm × 50mm were found collapsed into a *c* 400mm deep pit. They represent burning wall material which collapsed into the pit and were then sealed. There is little chance of contamination as they were well sealed by the pit fill.

Objectives: as it is reasonable to assume the sample originates from a structural element, of whatever nature, from the mid Saxon occupation site, it will provide a useful comparative date to compare with the other samples from the site from other contexts, especially the smithy. The wood is more mature than other samples submitted, but macroscopic examination suggests the wood may only be of mature coppice age, ie *c* 15 years.

Calibrated date: *1σ:* cal AD 600–690
   2σ: cal AD 540–780

Final comment: P Stamper (11 May 1995), this date which is perfectly plausible, helps to phase the individual feature and far more importantly, to provide a further hard date for the principal, mid-Saxon activity, the dating of which, without radiocarbon dating, would be down to little more than inspired guesswork.

GU–5122 1380 ±50 BP

δ¹³C: -26.0‰

Sample: 76/70, submitted in February 1991 by A Clark

Material: charcoal: unidentified

Initial comment: from the largest of three smithing hearths: a discrete spread of ashy material, charcoal, burnt clay and slag. It was well-sealed by later medieval layers.

Objectives: this site is mainly domestic with large numbers of features and of finds (pot, bone, and small finds). The smithy goes with this activity, and was of some longevity. It is comparable, though on a smaller scale, with that at Ramsbury. It seems likely that this element of the site will be of considerable interest to students of metalworking.

Calibrated date: *1σ:* cal AD 630–670
   2σ: cal AD 580–770

Final comment: P Stamper (11 May 1995), it is considerably earlier than HAR-5624 (1120 ±100 BP; cal AD 670–1160 at 95% confidence; Reimer *et al* 2004), one of the two other samples taken from two other hearths, but more in accord with a third, HAR-5625 (1230 ±70 BP; cal AD 650–980 at 95% confidence; Reimer *et al* 2004). Do these dates indicate long-term industrial/craft activity in this zone or are they, if we take the dates at 2σ range broadly contemporary? Even given these uncertainties, without the radiocarbon dates we would have been hard pressed to be more chronologically specific than Saxon.

References: Reimer *et al* 2004

Wharram Percy: The Dam, North Yorkshire

Location: SE 858642
   Lat. 54.03.59 N; Long. 00.41.20 W

Project manager: formerly J G Hurst (English Heritage) then S Wrathmell (West Yorkshire Archaeology Service), 1981

Archival body: Hull and East Riding Museum

Description: dams and a pond at the southern end of the deserted medieval village.

Objectives: to investigate the sequence of dams, the millpond, and any other utilisation of water from the springs and stream.

Final comment: S Wrathmell (6 December 2006), the results provided a date for the start of grain processing in the area of the pond, as well as dating for some of the earliest associated water channels. There was no datable artefactual material to compare with the radiocarbon determinations; nor were the excavated timbers of sufficient scantling to permit dendrochronological analysis. The radiocarbon dates are, however, entirely credible in terms of their socio-economic context and the dating for later sequences on site.

Laboratory comment: Ancient Monuments Laboratory (2003), two further dates from this site (HAR-1329 and HAR-1337) were funded prior to 1981 and were published in Jordan *et al* (1994, 208). One further sample 811621A (HAR-6840) was submitted for dating but failed to produce a result. Five further dates were published in Bayliss *et al* (2012, 310–11; HAR-4649–2, and HAR-6787).

References: Jordan *et al* 1994, 208
Treen and Atkin 2005

GU–5183 1250 ±60 BP

δ¹³C: -23.6‰

Sample: 30/644, submitted in February 1991 by A Clark

Material: grain (carbonised)

Initial comment: from a dump of carbonised grain and ash on a chalk surface located to the east of the wattle-capped clay bank forming the side of a water channel leading to a probable corn mill site.

Objectives: the relative stratigraphy gives a probable eleventh-century date to the nearest datable level above, from the pond silts. This sample is the only material with potential to date the earliest phase of the dam, associated with milling activities. Was there Saxon activity on the site for three centuries before pond-based milling technology replaced stream-based activity, or is the probability based on contamination of samples from the calcareous environment?

Calibrated date: *1σ:* cal AD 670–880
2σ: cal AD 650–940

Final comment: S Wrathmell (6 December 2006), this sample was statistically consistent with HAR-1329 and HAR-1337 and dates the dump, and the initial dam which contained it, to the ninth or early tenth century. This is consistent with the determinations for earlier and later activity in the stratigraphic sequence.

Laboratory comment: English Heritage (4 March 2012), this result is statistically consistent (T'=0.8; T'(5%)=6.0; ν=2; Ward and Wilson 1978) with two measurements previously undertaken on grain from this deposit (HAR-1329, 1300 ±80 BP and HAR-1337, 1200 ±80 BP). Their weighted mean (1250 ±42 BP) calibrates to cal AD 660–890 (95% confidence; Reimer *et al* 2004), or cal AD 680–810 (68% confidence; Reimer *et al* 2004).

References: Reimer *et al* 2004
Treen and Atkin 2005
Ward and Wilson 1978

Whitwell Quarry Long Cairn (pilot), Derbyshire

Location: SK 532748
Lat. 53.16.02 N; Long. 01.12.08 W

Project manager: I Wall and A Chamberlain (Creswell Heritage Trust), 1989

Archival body: Creswell Heritage Trust

Description: a Neolithic trapezoidal long cairn enclosing two mortuary structures: one structure houses a single inhumation (subsequently enclosed by a circular cairn), while the other linear mortuary structure contains the disarticulated skeletal remains of about 15 individuals.

Objectives: a pilot study to determine whether contamination by water-soluble PVA could be removed successfully by the dating process.

Final comment: P Marshall (19 September 2007), in the light of the re-dating of these samples (*see* below), all three determinations in this series should be considered unreliable. This inaccuracy may relate to the use of the ion exchange method (Hedges and Law 1989) for samples with very low collagen yield (OxA-4176, 5.6mg; OxA-4177, 2.2mg; and OxA-4326; 10.7mg).

References: Chamberlain *et al* 1992
Hedges *et al* 1994, 359–60
Hedges and Law 1989
Vyner and Wall 2011

OxA–4176 5380 ±90 BP

δ¹³C: -20.7‰

Sample: Burial 659, submitted on 15 March 1993 by A Brown

Material: human bone (tibia) (I Wall)

Initial comment: a collective inhumation in phase IV or earlier, sealed by a trapezoidal cairn on limestone. The bone was probably exposed before burial and was damaged by the collapse of the mortuary structure in which it was deposited. *See* OxA-4326 for a further measurement from this phase.

Objectives: to provide a *terminus ante quem* for the closure of the mortuary structure.

Calibrated date: *1σ:* 4340–4050 cal BC
2σ: 4370–3980 cal BC

Final comment: I Wall (9 February 1994), OxA-4176 was an uncontaminated tibia shaft from the mixed burial group.

Laboratory comment: English Heritage (19 September 2007), this measurement is significantly earlier (T'=25.8; T'(5%)=6.0; ν=2; Ward and Wilson 1978) than two, statistically consistent (T'=1.0; T'=3.8; ν=1), replicate measurements subsequently obtained from this skeleton (OxA-14493, 4946 ±32 BP; GrA-27519, 4895 ±40 BP; weighted mean, 4961 ±25 BP, 3795–3660 cal BC at 95% confidence; Reimer *et al* 2004).

References: Reimer *et al* 2004
Ward and Wilson 1978

OxA–4177 5190 ±100 BP

δ¹³C: -20.1‰

Sample: W92A 957, submitted on 15 March 1993 by A Brown

Material: human bone (femur) (I Wall)

Initial comment: from a burial in phase I; the central single inhumation in a possible mortuary structure, within or preceding a round cairn. The bone shows signs of having been exposed prior to burial. The sample had been conserved with water soluble PVA.

Objectives: this burial forms part of the first phase of six on the site, and will form part of a strategy to date the phasing absolutely.

Calibrated date: *1σ:* 4220–3940 cal BC
                      2σ: 4320–3770 cal BC

Final comment: I Wall (9 February 1994), OxA-4177 was from the burial of a female, aged 17 years at the time of death, who was buried alone within the mortuary structure later enclosed by a circular cairn. The left tibia exhibited the earliest known occurrence of a benign osteochondroma in a European skeleton (Chamberlain *et al* 1992).

Laboratory comment: English Heritage (19 September 2007), this measurement is significantly earlier (T′=9.6; T′(5%)=7.8; ν=3; Ward and Wilson 1978) than three, statistically consistent (T′=2.8; T′(5%)=6.0; ν=2), replicate measurements subsequently obtained from this skeleton (OxA-14494, 4961 ±33 BP; GrA-27513, 4875 ±40 BP; and OxA-12763, 4925 ±38 BP; weighted mean, 4927 ±21 BP; 3765–3650 cal BC at 95% confidence; Reimer *et al* 2004).

References: Chamberlain *et al* 1992
                Reimer *et al* 2004
                Ward and Wilson 1978

OxA–4326 5115 ±70 BP

δ¹³C: -20.4‰

Sample: Burial 982, submitted on 15 March 1993 by A Brown

Material: human bone (femur) (I Wall)

Initial comment: from a collective inhumation in phase IV or earlier, sealed by a trapezoidal cairn on limestone. The bone was probably exposed before burial.

Objectives: as OxA-4716, to provide a *terminus ante quem* for the closure of the mortuary structure.

Calibrated date: *1σ:* 3980–3800 cal BC
                      2σ: 4050–3710 cal BC

Final comment: I Wall (9 February 1994), OxA-4326 was an uncontaminated femur shaft from the mixed burial group. This bone had not been consolidated with PVA. The femur lay at the top of the distal pit fill, the distal pit defining the west end to the collective mortuary deposit.

Laboratory comment: English Heritage (19 September 2007), this result is significantly earlier (T′=13.4; T′(5%)=6.0; ν=2; Ward and Wilson 1978) than two, statistically consistent (T′=1.1; T′(5%)=3.8; ν=1), replicate measurements on this skeleton (OxA-14495, 4879 ±32 BP and GrA-27515, 4825 ±40 BP; weighted mean 4858 ±25 BP; 3695–3635 cal BC at 95% confidence; Reimer *et al* 2004).

References: Reimer *et al* 2004
                Ward and Wilson 1978

Wootton-Quarr, Isle of Wight

Location: SZ 5593
                    Lat. 50.44.00 N; Long. 01.13.00 W

Project manager: D L Motkin (Isle of Wight County
                    Council)

Description: the project comprised a survey funded by English Heritage which combined intertidal survey with a study of the hinterland and the offshore zone of this stretch of coast between Wootton Creek and Ryde Pier. Many timber structures were surveyed, ranging from early Neolithic to post-medieval in date. Neolithic trackways were noted at the low water mark below Quarr and Binstead. Prehistoric settlement remains and evidence of a Roman/early medieval/medieval harbour site (incorporating an anchorage, watering place, and stone shipment depot), were also found at Wootton Creek.

Objectives: the project has combined hinterland, intertidal, and offshore survey with a range of environmental analyses including pollen and plant macrofossil analysis, diatom, insect, and sedimentological studies, and radiocarbon and dendrochronological dating. The main objectives of the survey were to provide an overview of the archaeological potential and the sea-level chronology of the Solent, to investigate in detail the Wootton-Quarr coastline chronology (including evidence for prehistoric and later subsistence, trading, and maritime activities), and to develop survey and recording techniques, threat assessment methodologies, and management options for intertidal archaeology.

Final comment: D L Motkin (1993), information obtained from pollen and diatom analysis plus select radiocarbon dating was used to reconstruct the vegetational history of north east Wight and to produce a sea-level curve for the Solent area. The Wootton-Quarr survey has combined hinterland, intertidal, and offshore surveys into a fully integrated assessment of the archaeology of a stretch of coastline. This should assist in the identification of the specific survey, recording, and management needs of this coastal zone.

References: Isle of Wight Council 1994
                Loader *et al* 2002

Wootton-Quarr: 92A, Isle of Wight

Location: SZ 3524089935 to SZ 57785 93210
                    Lat. 50.42.27 N; Long. 01.30.03 W, to
                    Lat. 50.44.06 N; Long. 01.10.52 W

Project manager: F Basford and R Loader (Isle of Wight
                    County Archaeological Centre), 1992

Archival body: Isle of Wight Museum Service

Description: a multi-period site consisting of a palimpsest of post structures on the intertidal shore of the Solent.

Objectives: to provide information on the period and possible function of these timber structures and to assist in the preparation of a Solent area sea-level chronology.

Final comment: D J Tomalin (1993), the Wootton 92A series relates to the palimpsest of post structures. The earliest are small discrete post clusters of early-middle Neolithic date (sites Q24; K19; K20: GU–5251; GU–5257; GU–5259). All are sited around -2m OD and complement a submerged post alignment at the mouth of West Yar (GU–5260). Recurrent features are the long-shore post alignments now dated to later Bronze Age, middle Iron Age, middle Saxon, and medieval (GU–5261; GU–5253; GU–5254 to GU–5256; GU–5250 and GU–5252). Evidence of substantial sea level change is perceived and requires further sampling and definition.

Laboratory comment: English Heritage (4 March 2012), all the waterlogged timbers sampled were whole timbers of slight scantling.

GU–5248 1800 ±50 BP

δ¹³C: -27.8‰

Sample: Wootton 92A 2027 9013, submitted on 22 October 1992 by D L Motkin

Material: wood (waterlogged): *Prunus* sp., wet weight (190g) (R G Scaife 1992)

Initial comment: from intertidal feature Q4. The sample was removed from an apparent layer or accumulation of brushwood within a context of organic silt. It is associated with a timber structure, of which some of the timbers display carpentry work. Roman and medieval pottery has been found on the surface of the organic silt and also on the surface of nearby sand and shingle banks.

Objectives: to provide information on the period and possible function of this timber structure and to assist in the preparation of a Solent area sea-level chronology.

Calibrated date: 1σ: cal AD 130–320
2σ: cal AD 80–380

Final comment: D J Tomalin (1993), the *Prunus* branch from a brushwood platform underlying a Roman tenoned timber structure dated by GU–5258.

GU–5249 630 ±50 BP

δ¹³C: -27.5‰

Sample: Wootton 92A 2027 1000001, submitted on 22 October 1992 by D L Motkin

Material: wood (waterlogged): *Quercus* sp., wet weight (330g) (C Dickson 1992)

Initial comment: from intertidal feature Q12; one of an alignment of stakes in the intertidal zone. It was *in situ* within a context of hard packed sand and shingle and exposed to the marine environment. The post protruded from the silt at -0.03m OD.

Objectives: as GU–5248

Calibrated date: 1σ: cal AD 1280–1400
2σ: cal AD 1270–1420

Final comment: D J Tomalin (1993), a typical oak post taken from a long-shore post alignment. An agreeable medieval date which accords with possible shoreline retreat. The alignment is postulated as the work of the nearby Cistercian community at Quarr Abbey.

GU–5250 610 ±50 BP

δ¹³C: -27.1‰

Sample: Wootton 92A 2027 1000002, submitted on 22 October 1992 by D L Motkin

Material: wood (waterlogged): *Quercus* sp., wet weight (660g) (C Dickson 1992)

Initial comment: from intertidal feature Q11; one of an alignment of stakes in the intertidal zone. It was *in situ* within a context of fine marine silt and exposed to the marine environment. The post protruded from the silt at -1.14m OD.

Objectives: as GU–5248

Calibrated date: 1σ: cal AD 1290–1410
2σ: cal AD 1280–1430

Final comment: D J Tomalin (1993), a typical oak post from a long-shore post alignment which cuts Roman structure Q4. An agreeable medieval date for an alignment which seems to be generally contemporary with the parallel structure Q12 (*see* GU–5249).

GU–5251 5100 ±60 BP

δ¹³C: -27.5‰

Sample: Wootton 92A 2027 1000003, submitted on 22 October 1992 by D L Motkin

Material: wood (waterlogged): *Corylus* sp., wet weight (410g) (C Dickson 1992)

Initial comment: from intertidal feature Q24; one of a cluster of stakes in the intertidal zone. It was *in situ* within a context of fine marine silt and exposed to the marine environment. The post protruded from the silt at -1.89m OD.

Objectives: to provide information on the period and possible function of the stake cluster and to assist in the preparation of a Solent sea-level chronology.

Calibrated date: 1σ: 3970–3800 cal BC
2σ: 4040–3710 cal BC

Final comment: D J Tomalin (1993), a hazel post from a Mesolithic/Neolithic structure composed of four irregularly set posts. Extensive lithic debitage and burnt flint waste is noted in a similar context nearby.

GU–5252 470 ±50 BP

δ¹³C: -26.0‰

Sample: Wootton 92A 2027 1000004, submitted on 22 October 1992 by D L Motkin

Material: wood (waterlogged): *Fraxinus* sp., wet weight (215g) (C Dickson 1992)

Initial comment: from intertidal feature B17; one of an alignment of stakes in the intertidal zone. It was *in situ* within a context of organic silt, and exposed to the marine environment. The post protruded from the silt at -1.71m OD.

Objectives: as GU–5248

Calibrated date: 1σ: cal AD 1410–1450
2σ: cal AD 1400–1490

Final comment: D J Tomalin (1993), an atypical ash post, apparently part of a long-shore post alignment set at mean low water mark. A second post should be sampled to confirm the apparent fifteenth century date of the structure.

Laboratory comment: English Heritage (4 March 2012), a second post was subsequently dated from B17 (GU-5400; 1390 ±50 BP; cal AD 570–690 at 95% confidence; Reimer *et al* 2004), and GU-5252 was consequently re-interpreted as not related to B17.

GU–5253 2270 ±50 BP

δ¹³C: -24.6‰

Sample: Wootton 92A 2027 1000005, submitted on 22 October 1992 by D L Motkin

Material: wood (waterlogged): *Quercus* sp., wet weight (740g) (C Dickson 1992)

Initial comment: from intertidal feature B18; one of an alignment of stakes in the intertidal zone. It was *in situ* within a context of fine marine silt and exposed to the marine environment. The post protruded from the silt at -1.88m OD.

Objectives: as GU-5248

Calibrated date: 1σ: 400–230 cal BC
2σ: 410–200 cal BC

Final comment: D J Tomalin, a typical oak post from a short long-shore alignment lying virtually at mean low water mark. The post dates to the middle Iron Age.

GU–5254 1350 ±50 BP

δ¹³C: -23.6‰

Sample: Wootton 92A 2027 1000006, submitted on 22 October 1992 by D L Motkin

Material: wood (waterlogged): *Quercus* sp., wet weight (850g) (C Dickson 1992)

Initial comment: from intertidal feature K16; one of an alignment of stakes in the intertidal zone. It was *in situ* within the context of organic silt and exposed to the marine environments. The post protruded from the silt at -2.23m OD.

Objectives: as GU-5248

Calibrated date: 1σ: cal AD 640–690
2σ: cal AD 600–780

Final comment: D J Tomalin (1993), an oak member of one of three sampled posts from an extensive middle Saxon long-shore post alignment which approximately follows the present mean low water line. *See also* GU-5255 and GU-5256.

Laboratory comment: English Heritage (4 March 2012), the three measurements on timbers from K16 are statistically consistent (T′=1.1; T′(5%)=3.8; ν=2; Ward and Wilson 1978).

References: Ward and Wilson 1978

GU–5255 1360 ±50 BP

δ¹³C: -26.3‰

Sample: Wootton 92A 2027 1000007, submitted on 22 October 1992 by D L Motkin

Material: wood (waterlogged): *Quercus* sp., wet weight (330g) (C Dickson 1992)

Initial comment: from intertidal feature K16; one of an alignment of stakes in the intertidal zone. It was *in situ* within a context of fine marine silt and exposed to the marine environment. The post protruded from the silt at -2.36m OD.

Objectives: as GU-5248

Calibrated date: 1σ: cal AD 640–680
2σ: cal AD 600–770

Final comment: D J Tomalin (1993), a typical oak post from an extensive middle Saxon long-shore post alignment of at least 600 metres. *See also* GU-5254 and GU-5256.

Laboratory comment: see GU-5254

GU–5256 1420 ±50 BP

δ¹³C: -26.0‰

Sample: Wootton 92A 2027 1000008, submitted on 22 October 1992 by D L Motkin

Material: wood (waterlogged): *Salix* sp., wet weight (275g) (C Dickson 1992)

Initial comment: from intertidal feature Q14-K16; one of an alignment of stakes in the intertidal zone. It was *in situ* within a context of organic silt and exposed to the marine environment. The post protruded from the silt at -2.12m OD.

Objectives: as GU-5248

Calibrated date: 1σ: cal AD 590–660
2σ: cal AD 540–680

Final comment: D J Tomalin (1993), a willow post from the western end of an extensive middle Saxon long-shore post alignment. See also GU-5254 and GU-5255.

Laboratory comment: see GU-5254

GU–5257 4350 ±50 BP

δ¹³C: -26.8‰

Sample: Wootton 92A 2027 1000009, submitted on 22 October 1992 by D L Motkin

Material: wood (waterlogged): *Salix* sp., wet weight (275g) (C Dickson 1992)

Initial comment: from intertidal feature K19; one of a cluster of stakes in the intertidal zone. It was *in situ* within a context of fine marine silt and exposed to the marine environment. The post protruded from the silt at -1.55m OD.

Objectives: as GU-5251

Calibrated date: 1σ: 3030–2900 cal BC
2σ: 3100–2880 cal BC

Final comment: D J Tomalin (1993), a willow post from a small early Neolithic post cluster. The date equates this structure with similar fourth millennium structures which are also sited on the margins of the Quarr palaeochannel (*see* GU-5251 and GU-5259).

GU–5258 1860 ±50 BP

δ¹³C: -26.5‰

Sample: Wootton 92A 2027 1000010, submitted on 22 October 1992 by D L Motkin

Material: wood (waterlogged): *Quercus* sp., wet weight (126g) (R Darrah 1992)

Initial comment: from intertidal feature Q4: from a tenoned timber which was lying horizontally within a complex of stake and other timber components embedded within fine marine silts whose upper layers contain substantial quantities of brushwood and other organic material. This assemblage appears to be the remains of a structure.

Objectives: to provide information on this supposed structure and assist in the preparation of a Solent sea-level chronology.

Calibrated date: *1σ:* cal AD 80–240
                       2σ: cal AD 30–320

Final comment: D J Tomalin (1993), an oak tenoned timber from a collapsed lap-jointed wooden structure on the Holocene fill of the Quarr palaeochannel at a level of -1.23m OD. The date confirms the contemporaneity of this structure with a scatter of Roman artefacts and contributes to the dating of the Solent sea-level change.

GU–5259 4340 ±50 BP

δ¹³C: -27.3‰

Sample: Wootton 92A 2027 1000011, submitted on 22 October 1992 by D L Motkin

Material: wood (waterlogged): *Corylus* sp., wet weight (270g) (C Dickson 1992)

Initial comment: from intertidal feature K20; one of a cluster of stakes in the intertidal zone. It was *in situ* within a context of fine marine silt and exposed to the marine environment. The post protruded from the silt at -1.65m.

Objectives: as GU-5251

Calibrated date: *1σ:* 3020–2900 cal BC
                       2σ: 3100–2880 cal BC

Final comment: D L Tomalin (1993), a hazel post from an early Neolithic post cluster. The date shows general contemporaneity with a similar discrete post cluster on the margins of the Quarr palaeochannel. *See* also GU-5257 and GU-5251.

GU–5260 4220 ±60 BP

δ¹³C: -23.7‰

Sample: Wootton 92A 36106 1000012, submitted on 22 October 1992 by D L Motkin

Material: wood (waterlogged): *Quercus* sp., wet weight (114g) (C Dickson 1992)

Initial comment: from one of a cluster of stakes *in situ* on the seabed below extreme low-water. The eroded tip was sawn off with a hand saw by a shallow water diver. The sample has been shaved back to reveal the good wood.

Objectives: to provide information on the period and possible function of this stake cluster, and to assist in the preparation of the Solent sea-level chronology.

Calibrated date: *1σ:* 2900–2700 cal BC
                       2σ: 2920–2620 cal BC

Final comment: D J Tomalin (1993), a submerged post structure at Yarmouth West. A typical oak post in cross-shore alignment observed below the mean low water mark. The date attests to Neolithic activity near the mouth of the Western Yar river prior to sea-level rise in the western Solent.

GU–5261 2420 ±50 BP

δ¹³C: -25.1‰

Sample: Wootton 92A 1526 1000029, submitted on 22 October 1992 by D L Motkin

Material: wood (waterlogged): *Quercus* sp., wet weight (435g) (C Dickson 1992)

Initial comment: from intertidal feature F34; one of an alignment of stakes in the intertidal zone. It was *in situ* within a context of fine marine silt and exposed to the marine environment. The post protruded from the silt at -1.94m OD.

Objectives: to provide information on period of possible function of this stake alignment and to assist in the preparation of a Solent sea-level chronology.

Calibrated date: *1σ:* 740–400 cal BC
                       2σ: 770–390 cal BC

Final comment: D J Tomalin (1993), a typical oak post at mean low water mark on Fishbourne Beach at the mouth of Wootton Haven. A complementary date for this alignment is GU-5052 from F32.

GU–5262 1990 ±50 BP

δ¹³C: -25.9‰

Sample: Wootton 92A 1526 1000074, submitted on 22 October 1992 by D L Motkin

Material: wood (waterlogged): *Quercus* sp., wet weight (410g) (C Dickson 1992)

Initial comment: from intertidal feature F35; one of an alignment of stakes in the intertidal zone running under the storm beach. The stake protrudes above the surface.

Objectives: to provide information on the period and function of this stake alignment and to assist in the preparation of a Solent sea-level chronology.

Calibrated date: *1σ:* 50 cal BC–cal AD 70
                       2σ: 110 cal BC–cal AD 130

Final comment: D J Tomalin (1993), an oak post from a Roman cross-beach alignment. The structure borders on an extensive strew of Roman anchorage/beach-head artefacts. A complementary date is GU-5263.

Laboratory comment: English Heritage (4 March 2012), the two measurements on posts from this structure are statistically indistinguishable (T'=1.1; T'(5%)=3.8; v=1; Ward and Wilson 1978).

References: Ward and Wilson 1978

GU–5263 1970 ±50 BP

$\delta^{13}C$: -24.7‰

Sample: Wootton 92A 1526 1000075, submitted on 22 October 1992 by D L Motkin

Material: wood (waterlogged): *Quercus* sp., wet weight (840g) (C Dickson 1992)

Initial comment: from one of an alignment of stakes in the intertidal zone running under the storm beach. The stake protrudes above the surface and passes through gravel and sandy silt.

Objectives: as GU-5262

Calibrated date: 1σ: 40 cal BC–cal AD 80
2σ: 90 cal BC–cal AD 130

Final comment: D J Tomalin (1993), an oak post from Roman cross-beach alignment. This structure is adjacent to an extensive strew of Roman anchorage/beach-head artefacts and is complementary with GU-5262.

Laboratory comment: see GU-5262

Wootton-Quarr: 92B, Isle of Wight

Location: *see* individual dates
Lat. ; Long. , see individual dates

Project manager: J Croucher (Isle of Wight County Archaeological Centre), 1992

Archival body: Isle of Wight Museum Service

Description: a multi-period site consisting of a palimpsest of post structures on the intertidal shore of the Solent.

Objectives: to provide information on the period and possible function of this timber structure and to assist in the preparation of a Solent area sea-level chronology.

Final comment: J Hillam (1994), this series was submitted after dendrochronological analysis of the second group of trees from the Wootton Quarr survey project. Many of the trees were dated to produce a 585-year chronology. The three radiocarbon samples were taken from undated tree-ring sequences.

References: Hillam 1991

GU–5298 4100 ±50 BP

$\delta^{13}C$: -24.8‰

Sample: Wootton 92B 1526 1000028, submitted on 2 March 1993 by J Hillam

Material: wood (waterlogged; located at SZ 5584 9314; Lat.50.44.03N; Long. 01.12.32 W): *Quercus* sp. (J Hillam 1993)

Initial comment: this tree lies near the in-shore end of a silted palaeochannel cut into the clays of the beach at Fishbourne. Other nearby trees fell around 2700 BC but this very large tree is in somewhat better condition and may be later. It has only recently been uncovered in the eroding beach. The sample is made up of rings 44–62 from a 138-year ring sequence.

Objectives: to aid dendrochronological dating of this tree as part of a study aimed at investigating marine transgression and deriving a sea-level and environmental chronology of the Solent region; and to assist in producing a dated tree-ring chronology from southern England.

Calibrated date: 1σ: 2860–2570 cal BC
2σ: 2880–2490 cal BC

Final comment: J Hillam (1994), the calibrated dates place this tree-ring sequence off the younger end of the dated tree-ring chronology which spanned the period 3282–2698 BC at the start of the study and now extends to 3463–2694 BC.

GU–5299 4730 ±60 BP

$\delta^{13}C$: -27.8‰

Sample: Wootton 2027 1000021, submitted on 2 March 1993 by J Croucher

Material: wood (waterlogged; located at SZ 5724 9318; Lat. 50.44.04N; Long. 01.11.21W): *Quercus* sp. (J Hillam 1993)

Initial comment: this tree is the westernmost of a group of trees now lying exposed in the intertidal silts at Quarr. The trees lie directly upon a peat deposit which itself overlies, in certain places, deposits of worked and sometimes burnt flint. The trees, recently exposed by erosion, are beginning to erode. This sample is taken from sound wood, and is made up of rings 23–43 from a 260-year ring sequence.

Objectives: as GU-5298

Calibrated date: 1σ: 3640–3370 cal BC
2σ: 3650–3360 cal BC

Final comment: J Hillam (1994), this radiocarbon date places the tree-ring sequence at or off the older end of the current Isle of Wight chronology, 3463–2694 BC. The sequence crossmatches two other undated ring sequences, to produce a 268-year floating master curve. It is hoped that future tree-ring samples will help to link these sequences to the dated chronology.

GU–5300 4620 ±60 BP

$\delta^{13}C$: -23.3‰

Sample: Wootton 92B 2027 1000020, submitted on 2 March 1993 by J Croucher

Material: wood (waterlogged; located at SZ 5729 9318; Lat. 50.44.04N; Long. 01.11.18W): *Quercus* sp. (J Hillam 1993)

Initial comment: this sample was from one of five matching tree-ring sequences which formed a floating tree-ring chronology of 270 years. Rings 29–41 from the trunk of recumbent oak tree 20 from the Quarr-Binstead interfluve.

Objectives: to date the 270-year floating tree-ring chronology, which is made up from five, matching ring sequences.

Calibrated date: *1σ:* 3500–3350 cal BC
                       2σ: 3630–3120 cal BC

Final comment: J Hillam (1994), this sequence has now been linked to the dated chronology from Wootton Quarr to produce a 770-year chronology, 3463–2694 BC. The rings submitted actually date to 3365–3353 BC.

Wootton-Quarr: Wootton Creek, Isle of Wight

Location: SZ 5575393104 to SZ 5593393241
                       Lat. 50.44.03 N; Long. 01.12.36 W, to
                       Lat. 50.44.08 N; Long. 01.12.26 W

Project manager: D L Motkin (Isle of Wight County
                       Archaeological Centre), 1989–90

Archival body: Isle of Wight Museum Service

Description: multi-period intertidal sites have been defined within the vicinity of Wootton Haven on the northern coast of the Isle of Wight.

Objectives: radiocarbon dating may be able to fix the sequences obtained.

Final comment: D J Tomalin (1994), this series identifies episodes of human activity on a submerged land surface and intertidal area at the mouth of Wootton Haven. GU-5051 relates to late Neolithic activity when pegs were set along the central line of a heavily silted header channel. It intimates a contemporary mean high water mark no higher than -1.56m OD. Sample GU-5052 identifies a later Bronze Age post alignment which has yet to be interpreted. The remaining samples in the series provide helpful indicators of late Roman or post-Roman sea-level rise.

GU–5051 3650 ±50 BP

δ¹³C: -29.1‰

Sample: Peg No. 62; 1526.062.0001, submitted on 27 November 1990 by D L Motkin

Material: wood (waterlogged): *Corylus* sp.

Initial comment: from intertidal feature F31; one of 30 surviving pegs in an alignment which runs for some 30 metres along the centre of a silted channel in the intertidal zone of this site on the southern shore of the Solent. The peg was in the fill of the silted channel and was revealed through coastal erosion. The peg has been exposed to marine environment for much of its life, and protruded from the silt at -1.56m OD.

Objectives: the peg was adjacent to a recumbent oak which was felled in 2777 BC (Hillam 1991; 1994), and the event represented by this sample is expected to be later, possibly medieval. The objectives of the dating are to provide information on the period and possible function of the peg alignment and also to provide a *terminus post quem* for the silting of the channel.

Calibrated date: *1σ:* 2130–1940 cal BC
                       2σ: 2200–1890 cal BC

Final comment: D J Tomalin (1994), a typical component of an alignment of late Neolithic hazel pegs set along the axis of a silt-filled header channel. The date provides a *terminus post quem* for sea-level rise from the base level of the channel. Contemporary lithic material has been recovered in close proximity.

References: Hillam 1991
                       Hillam 1994

GU–5052 2600 ±50 BP

δ¹³C: -26.8‰

Sample: Post No. 131; 1526.131.0001, submitted on 27 November 1990 by D L Motkin

Material: wood (waterlogged): *Quercus* sp.

Initial comment: from intertidal feature F32; one of 46 surviving posts in an alignment extending for 90 metres parallel and close to low water mark at this site on the southern shore of the Solent. The post protruded from the silt at -2m OD.

Objectives: to confirm the period of this post alignment and to help elucidate its function. This site has yielded artefacts of all periods from the Mesolithic to the present, however, this sample is thought most likely to be medieval.

Calibrated date: *1σ:* 810–770 cal BC
                       2σ: 840–590 cal BC

Final comment: D J Tomalin (1994), a typical oak post taken from a Bronze Age long-shore post alignment now following approximate mean low water mark. The alignment is 90m long but can be projected to 180m to join a further contemporary segment which is dated by GU-5261 (2420 ±50 BP; cal BC 770–390 at 95% confidence; Reimer *et al* 2004).

References: Reimer *et al* 2004

GU–5053 1140 ±70 BP

δ¹³C: -27.3‰

Sample: Hurdle; 1526..0009, submitted on 27 November 1990 by D L Motkin

Material: wood (waterlogged): unidentified, wet weight (350g)

Initial comment: from intertidal feature F75; from hurdling lying flat in the eroding silt surface near low water mark. It possibly forms part of mole for a medieval fishpond or sea defence work and was found recumbent at -1.98m OD. The hurdling has been exposed to the marine environment.

Objectives: to provide information on fisheries, sea defences, and marine transgression on this part of the multi-period site. The date is probably medieval.

Calibrated date: *1σ:* cal AD 770–990
                       2σ: cal AD 680–1030

Final comment: D J Tomalin (1994), the off-shore mole or artificial bank is attributed to a sea pond cited in the early fourteenth century AD. The assay proffers a middle-late Saxon date for this feature which is unexpectedly early.

GU–5054 2000 ±200 BP

δ¹³C: -27.7‰

Sample: Basketry; 1526..0010, submitted on 27 November 1990 by D L Motkin

Material: organic matter (vegetable fibre; wet weight 55g)

Initial comment: from intertidal context 301 at -0.89m OD; taken from basket fragments buried in a sloping beach of sandy silt. It was taken 4cm below the surface at a point about 0.5m vertically above the foot of the slope. The sample has been exposed to the marine environment.

Objectives: to provide information on the beach use. Datable materials recovered so far from this area of the beach have been mainly Roman, consisting of pottery and coins.

Calibrated date: 1σ: 360 cal BC–cal AD 240
2σ: 420 cal BC–cal AD 430

Final comment: D J Tomalin (1994), scattered Roman ceramics of the first to fourth century AD were found scattered in the estuarine silt together with a quantity of decapitated boss skulls. *Bos* skull GU-5055 complements this date.

Laboratory comment: English Heritage (4 March 2012), this result is statistically consistent with the measurement on a cattle skull from this deposit (GU-5055; T'=1.6; T'(5%)=3.8; ν=1; Ward and Wilson 1978).

Laboratory comment: SUERC Radiocarbon Dating Laboratory (AMS) (6 June 1991), this was a small sample.

References: Ward and Wilson 1978

GU–5055 1740 ±50 BP

δ¹³C: -22.0‰

Sample: Bos skull; 1526.202.2186, submitted on 27 November 1990 by D L Motkin

Material: animal bone: *Bos* sp., skull (1700g)

Initial comment: from intertidal context 301 at -1.05m OD; the sample was recovered from intertidal sandy silt at the mouth of the creek where it was partially exposed by erosion. The sample seems to be from a bone midden, as there were many other skulls and bones. Several of the skulls, including this one, show evidence of slaughter.

Objectives: to establish the period of the bone midden in relation to all the other activities which took place in this multi-period site. It is possible that animals were being slaughtered here in preparation for the export of the carcasses to the British mainland.

Calibrated date: 1σ: cal AD 230–390
2σ: cal AD 130–420

Final comment: D J Tomalin (1994), an acceptable date for one of some twenty decapitated *bos* skulls. Associated is a wide scatter of Roman ceramics and some basketry fragments which offer a complementary date (*see* GU-5054).

Laboratory comment: see GU-5054

Wootton-Quarr: Wootton Creek B, Isle of Wight

Location: SZ 558509931574 to SZ 5594793219
Lat. 50.44.05 N; Long. 01.12.31 W, to
Lat. 50.44.07 N; Long. 01.12.26

Project manager: D L Motkin (Isle of Wight County Archaeological Centre), 1989

Archival body: Isle of Wight Museum Service

Description: a pilot tree-ring study was carried out on six oak timbers from the eroding beach at Wootton Creek.

Objectives: to provide an approximate date for four of the timbers.

Final comment: J Hillam (1994), these samples were submitted during the dendrochronological analysis of the first group of trees from the Wootton Quarr survey project in order to obtain a rough guide to the date of the trees.

References: Hillam 1991

UB–3271 3528 ±37 BP

δ¹³C: -26.7 ±0.2‰

Sample: IOW 182, submitted in January 1990 by J Hillam

Material: wood: *Quercus* sp. (J Hillam 1989)

Initial comment: a slice was taken from post 182 for dendrochronology. This post was one of several *in situ* in the intertidal zone on this part of the eroding beach. The function and period are unknown.

Objectives: to aid tree-ring dating.

Calibrated date: 1σ: 1920–1770 cal BC
2σ: 1960–1740 cal BC

Final comment: J Hillam (15 February 1994), slightly younger than trees 263 (UB-3272) and 603 (UB-3274), this tree is unlikely to be dated by dendrochronology.

Laboratory comment: University of Belfast (28 March 1990), this sample was pretreated using the acid based acid protocol.

UB–3272 3640 ±38 BP

δ¹³C: -26.3 ±0.2‰

Sample: IOW 263, submitted in January 1990 by J Hillam

Material: wood (waterlogged): *Quercus* sp. (J Hillam 1989)

Initial comment: a slice was taken from post 263 for dendrochronology. This post is the second (from south) in a line of four which runs about 1.7m east of the edge of the silted channel. The posts are set upright in clay in the intertidal zone.

Objectives: as UB-3271

Calibrated date: 1σ: 2120–1940 cal BC
2σ: 2140–1890 cal BC

Final comment: J Hillam (15 February 1994), this sample is of a similar date to tree 603 (UB-3274). The tree-ring sequence of 58 rings is probably too short to be dated by dendrochronology.

Laboratory comment: see UB-3271

UB–3273 4357 ±39 BP

$\delta^{13}C$: -25.3 ±0.2‰

Sample: IOW 602, submitted in January 1990 by J Hillam

Material: wood (waterlogged): *Quercus* sp. (J Hillam 1989)

Initial comment: a slice was taken for dendrochronology from a log lying pegged down on the eroding beach partially embedded in silt in the intertidal zone. The visible part of this log was 6.3m long and the sample is in two main parts.

Objectives: to date the activity on this part of the beach.

Calibrated date:　　*1σ:* 3030–2910 cal BC
　　　　　　　　　　2σ: 3100–2890 cal BC

Final comment: J Hillam (15 February 1994), this sample is from a 282-year tree-ring sequence which has since been dated to 3059–2777 cal BC by dendrochronology. The chronology has been consolidated and expanded; it now covers the period 3463–2694 cal BC.

Laboratory comment: see UB-3271

UB–3274 3681 ±38 BP

$\delta^{13}C$: -26.2 ±0.2‰

Sample: IOW 603, submitted in January 1990 by J Hillam

Material: wood (waterlogged): *Quercus* sp. (J Hillam 1989)

Initial comment: a slice was taken for dendrochronology from a log lying on the eroding beach, partially embedded in silt in the intertidal zone. The sample is in two main pieces.

Objectives: as UB-3273

Calibrated date:　　*1σ:* 2140–1980 cal BC
　　　　　　　　　　2σ: 2200–1940 cal BC

Final comment: J Hillam (15 February 1994), although this sample is taken from a 317-year tree-ring sequence, it has not yet been possible to date it by dendrochronology.

Laboratory comment: see UB-3271

Worcester: Deansway, Hereford and Worcester

Location:　　　SO 84905485
　　　　　　　　Lat. 52.11.29 N; Long. 02.13.15 W

Project manager:　C F Mundy (Hereford and Worcester
　　　　　　　　County Council), 1989

Archival body:　Hereford and Worcester County Council,
　　　　　　　　and Worcester Museums

Description: four areas were excavated in advance of construction of a new shopping centre in Worcester. The development site lay west of the High Street, and fronted onto a secondary street (medieval Birdport). The site lay within the area of the Roman 'small town' and within the defended area of the late Anglo-Saxon *burh* and the medieval city walls.

Objectives: to establish the date of a stratigraphically early horse burial, interpreted as Iron Age; to establish a date bracket for the late Roman cemetery on site 4; to date two peripheral burials on other sites, for which stratigraphic/artefactual evidence was slight; to provide dating evidence for parts of the site sequence that were not closely datable by artefacts or stratigraphy; and to resolve the date of seeds preserved in late Anglo-Saxon deposits.

Final comment: H Dalwood (18 September 1996), the dating results have contributed to the original objectives outlined above, and most of the 15 dates have provided useful information: the date of the horse burial is now determined (GU-5012); the date bracket for the late Iron Age cemetery is reasonably well established (OxA-3019, OxA-3020, OxA-3023, and GU-5050); the two peripheral burials now have dates which link them with the cemetery (OxA-3018 and GU-5049); dates on the late Anglo-Saxon pits provide a close date bracket with other evidence (GU-5008 to GU-5010), other attempts to obtain dates on parts of the sequence were less informative (GU-5007 and GU-5011); the dates on seeds show such material can survive for long periods, even without any obvious means of preservation (OxA-3064 to OxA-3066).

References:　　　Baker *et al* 1992
　　　　　　　　Dalwood *et al* 1992

GU–5007 1950 ±50 BP

$\delta^{13}C$: -24.5‰

Sample: 7559, submitted on 1 March 1991 by C F Mundy

Material: charcoal: unidentified

Initial comment: from a large deposit of fine charcoal which infilled depressions in the subsided ditch-fill and which was sealed by a deposit of sand and gravel provisionally identified as a building platform. Both the ditch and the platform are Roman. Although cut by later intrusions, the sample was taken well away from the truncation.

Objectives: the nature of the charcoal deposit, together with the deposits stratigraphically immediately above and below, imply that it was deposited some time after backfilling of the ditch and probably very shortly before the erection of the platform. Whereas artefacts in the ditch backfill provide an indication of date for that activity, the construction of the platform is more difficult and hopefully dating of the sample will clarify this.

Calibrated date:　　*1σ:* cal AD 1–120
　　　　　　　　　　2σ: 50 cal BC–cal AD 140

Final comment: H Dalwood (18 September 1996), the two sigma range is broad, but the sampled deposit is from a phase of occupation of the site dated to the first to second centuries AD; specifically, pre-dating *c* AD 120. Artefacts suggest the deposit dates to the late first century (*terminus post quem*). This date supports the dating of the site sequence at Deansway.

GU–5008 1150 ±60 BP

δ¹³C: -25.0‰

Sample: 6049, submitted on 1 March 1991 by C F Mundy

Material: charcoal: unidentified

Initial comment: taken from a lower fill of a large pit (17109) in which it sealed a deposit of cess which was the primary fill. The pit contained a number of upper fills and all fills above the cess were subject to slumping. This may cause limited contamination but beyond this none noted. The pit was well defined stratigraphically.

Objectives: this sample represents a dump of industrial waste from a phase of industrial activity on site 2 at the west end. The pit into which it was dumped was a cesspit and related to the earliest medieval activity in that part of the site. This was stratigraphically directly above dark earth of a probably Saxon date. Dating of this earliest medieval activity is at present poor due to a poor ceramic assemblage. Dating of this activity and the following industrial phase through samples GU-5008, GU-5009, and GU-5010 is essential to our understanding of the development of early medieval Worcester.

Calibrated date: *1σ:* cal AD 770–980
              2σ: cal AD 690–1020

Final comment: H Dalwood (18 September 1996), although the two sigma range is rather broad, the sampled deposit is interpreted as relating to a documented period of urban development in the late Anglo-Saxon period; specifically, post-dating the establishment of the burh between AD 890 and 905. This date contributes to refining the chronology of this period of urban development, and also helps strengthen the chronological framework for the import of pottery to the town from elsewhere in the Midlands. The reliability of this date is enhanced by other dates from this part of the site sequence (GU-5009 and GU-5010).

GU–5009 1220 ±50 BP

δ¹³C: -25.2‰

Sample: 6053, submitted on 1 March 1991 by C F Mundy

Material: charcoal: unidentified

Initial comment: from a highly charred lump of wood within the bottom cess rich fill of pit 17102.

Objectives: as GU-5008

Calibrated date: *1σ:* cal AD 700–890
              2σ: cal AD 670–950

Final comment: see GU-5008

GU–5010 1030 ±70 BP

δ¹³C: -25.6‰

Sample: 6032, submitted on 1 March 1991 by C F Mundy

Material: charcoal: unidentified

Initial comment: from upper fill of pit (17102) and to a degree affected by slumping.

Objectives: the activity at the pit appears to fall into two phases, an occupational one and a later industrial one. *See* also GU-5008.

Calibrated date: *1σ:* cal AD 900–1040
              2σ: cal AD 880–1170

Final comment: H Dalwood (18 September 1996), the dated sample is stratified above another date in this series (GU-5009). This date contributes to refining the chronology of the late Anglo-Saxon urban development, together with two other dates GU-5008 and GU-5009.

GU–5011 16640 ±120 BP

δ¹³C: -23.6‰

Sample: 4022, submitted on 1 March 1991 by C F Mundy

Material: charcoal: unidentified

Initial comment: a sample was taken of charcoal-rich soil lying on a burnt clay and tile floor surface. The burnt tile and clay floor constitutes part of one of the bronze foundry furnaces.

Objectives: the sample was taken from a furnace structure that had subsided and could not therefore be dated by archaeomagnetism. A separate furnace structure was dated by that method but, failing those, dating for the foundry is vague. The site during the foundry's existence was purely industrial, producing very little domestic debris for dating, and so dating presently relies on insecure typological dating. The foundry is extensive and well-preserved and precise dating will supplement and provide a date frame to help understand the late medieval industry.

Calibrated date: *1σ:* 18100–17600 cal BC
              2σ: 18300–17400 cal BC

Final comment: H Dalwood (18 September 1996), the date obtained was unexpected, in view of the certain medieval dating bracket for the sampled context. No simple explanation can be offered for this anomalous date.

Laboratory comment: English Heritage (4 March 2012), given its anomalously early date, this sample may have contained a component of coal.

GU–5012 2050 ±50 BP

δ¹³C: -15.6‰

Sample: 2058, submitted on 1 March 1991 by C F Mundy

Material: animal bone: *Equus* sp.

Initial comment: selected bone from an articulated horse burial. The burial pit was cut into natural and was sealed by a pebble surface of early Roman date. The horse burial was without any artefactual contents.

Objectives: the horse burial contained no datable artefacts and was cut directly into natural; it could, therefore be any date earlier than the Roman surface that sealed it. The burial is one of several, stratigraphically similar features, virtually all without dating evidence. Dating of the horse burial is important therefore not only to date itself and provide a *terminus post quem* for the laying of the surface that seals it, but also to provide an indication, by extension, of the possible date range of the other stratigraphically similar features.

Calibrated date: *1σ:* 160 cal BC–cal AD 10
                        2σ: 200 cal BC–cal AD 70

Final comment: H Dalwood (18 September 1996), the two sigma date range indicates that the horse burial can probably be dated to the late Iron Age or immediate post-conquest period. Soil micromorphology indicated that pre-Roman landuse of the site was arable fields, and other evidence suggests the Deansway site lay on the periphery of an Iron Age settlement. The dating allows the horse burial to be fairly certainly tied to other evidence for late Iron Age occupation.

GU–5049 1650 ±50 BP

δ¹³C: -23.7‰

Sample: 6712, submitted on 1 March 1991 by C F Mundy

Material: human bone

Initial comment: from crouched inhumation. This was in a severely truncated grave (cut 17651). Stratigraphically the feature was early but due to truncation, cannot be related to any dateable part of the sequence except in that it cut natural, and it was early Roman or prehistoric.

Objectives: there are no associated finds with this inhumation and although the truncating features are datable, no relationship with possibly contemporary stratigraphy survived. Consequently this inhumation could be an early Roman or of a prehistoric date, and the dating may determine the earliest part of the sequence.

Calibrated date: *1σ:* cal AD 340–430
                        2σ: cal AD 250–540

Final comment: H Dalwood (18 September 1996), the two sigma date range was later than anticipated when the sample was submitted, but stratigraphic evidence did not allow a firm date bracket. The date range raises the possibility that this inhumation burial was late Roman rather than early Roman in date, and is broadly contemporary with other inhumation burials date in this series (OxA-3019, OxA-3020, OxA-3023, and GU-5050).

GU–5050 1910 ±50 BP

δ¹³C: -20.0‰

Sample: 9121, submitted on 1 March 1991 by C F Mundy

Material: human bone

Initial comment: selected human bone from inhumation burial (context 21079) identified as grave 12. This is one of an eastern group of burials from site 4. The burial was partly disturbed by a subsequent grave cut that damaged the skull.

Objectives: submitted as 1 of 4 (OxA-3019, OxA-3020, OxA-3023, and GU-5050) from the probable late Roman cemetery on site 4. *See* OxA-3020.

Calibrated date: *1σ:* cal AD 30–140
                        2σ: 40 cal BC–cal AD 240

Final comment: H Dalwood (18 September 1996), the two sigma date range shows that this burial is broadly contemporary with other inhumation burials in the cemetery (see OxA-3019, OxA-3020 and OxA-3023), and confirms

the interpretation that this inhumation formed part of a late Roman cemetery. This date helps establish the period of use of the cemetery, and improves the overall chronology of changing landuse at Deansway.

OxA–3018 1800 ±70 BP

δ¹³C: -20.9‰

Sample: 7569, submitted on 1 March 1991 by C F Mundy

Material: human bone

Initial comment: selected human bone from inhumation burial (context 18210). The grave was found to cut a dark soil deposit which overlay defined Roman contexts (a building platform) but which maybe Roman itself.

Objectives: the burial is stratigraphically later than the building platform and its dating will provide a *terminus ante quem* for the disuse of the platform. Although possibly an outlier from the cemetery identified on site 4, this is not proven and the burial could well be post-Roman. A Saxon date (derived from archaeomagnetic sampling) has already been obtained for an oven on this site, and dating of the burial may further fill in the gap between the Roman and medieval deposits.

Calibrated date: *1σ:* cal AD 120–330
                        2σ: cal AD 60–410

Final comment: H Dalwood (18 September 1996), the dating indicates that the inhumation burial was probably of late Roman date. The possibility (based on the stratigraphic position and other dating evidence) that the burial was post-Roman can now be discounted. Together with other dates in the series (OxA-3019, OxA-3020, and OxA-3023) the period of use of the late Roman cemetery can be established, and the overall chronology of changing landuse at Deansway is improved.

References: Hedges *et al* 1997, 251

OxA–3019 1720 ±70 BP

δ¹³C: -20.4‰

Sample: 9046, submitted on 1 March 1991 by C F Mundy

Material: human bone

Initial comment: selected human bone from an inhumation burial (context 20436). The sample was obtained from grave 4, a north-south orientated grave on site 4. The burial was decapitated, with skull placed at feet. The grave cut an earlier Roman boundary gully on the same alignment.

Objectives: submitted as 1 of 4 (OxA-3019, OxA-3020, OxA-3023 and GU-5050) from ?late Roman cemetery on site 4. *See also* OxA-3020.

Calibrated date: *1σ:* cal AD 230–410
                        2σ: cal AD 130–530

Final comment: H Dalwood (18 September 1996), the burial was crudely dated by stratigraphic and artefactual evidence, and the dating confirms the interpretation that this inhumation formed part of a late Roman cemetery. The date is very close to the date range for OxA-3020. Together with other dates in this series (OxA-3018,

OxA-3020, and OxA-3023) the period of use of the cemetery can be established, and the overall chronology of changing landuse at Deansway is improved.

References: Hedges *et al* 1997, 251

OxA–3020 1710 ±70 BP

δ¹³C: -21.3‰

Sample: 9044, submitted on 1 March 1991 by C F Mundy

Material: human bone

Initial comment: selected human bone from inhumation burial (context 20448). Obtained from grave 2, the only east-west grave excavated on site 4. The grave was sealed by dark earth and cut an earlier Roman ground surface.

Objectives: submitted as one of four (OxA-3019, OxA-3020, OxA-3023, and GU-5050) from the ?late Roman cemetery on site 4. This cemetery is dated by broad stratigraphic criteria, residual material in grave fills, and the typology of the burial site. The duration and disuse of the cemetery requires closer dating, which will have implications for dating of earlier Roman activity on the site, and on the other excavated sites; as well as having general implications for settlement development.

Calibrated date: 1σ: cal AD 240–420
2σ: cal AD 130–540

Final comment: H Dalwood (18 September 1996), the burial was crudely dated from stratigraphic and artefactual evidence, and the dating confirms the supposition that this inhumation burial formed part of a late Roman cemetery. The date is very close to the date range for OxA-3019, and the different orientation of this burial does not appear to be significant. Together with other dates in the series (OxA-3018, OxA-3019, and OxA-3023) the period of use of the cemetery can be established and the overall chronology of changing land use at Deansway is improved.

References: Hedges *et al* 1997, 251

OxA–3023 1510 ±80 BP

δ¹³C: -18.7‰

Sample: 9125, submitted on 1 March 1991 by C F Mundy

Material: human bone

Initial comment: selected human bone from inhumation burial (context 20375). This was an extended north-south inhumation (not decapitated); there was some truncation at head, but most of grave was sealed beneath dark earth. The sample came from grave 1.

Objectives: sample submitted as one of four (OxA-3019, OxA-3020, OxA-3023, and GU-5050) from the ?late Roman cemetery on site 4. The backfill of this grave contained pottery tentatively dated to the fourth century AD. *See* OxA-3020.

Calibrated date: 1σ: cal AD 430–640
2σ: cal AD 390–670

Final comment: H Dalwood (18 September 1996), the burial was crudely dated from stratigraphic and artefactual evidence. The two sigma range places the burial towards

the end of the range of Roman evidence from Worcester: the latest coins date to cal AD 392–394. It had been supposed that this late Roman cemetery was disused by *c* 370 cal AD; this date suggests that a broader date bracket for the cemetery may be appropriate. Together with other dates in the series (OxA-3018, OxA-3019, and OxA-3020) the period of use of the cemetery can be established, and the overall chronology of changing landuse at Deansway is improved.

References: Hedges *et al* 1997, 251

OxA–3064 1150 ±80 BP

δ¹³C: -23.6‰

Sample: 6714, submitted on 1 March 1991 by L Moffett

Material: plant macrofossils (seeds; *Rubus* sp. and *Sambucus nigra*): *Sambucus nigra*; *Rubus* sp. (L Moffett 1991)

Initial comment: seeds taken from a sample of a very well-defined fill of a cesspit. The pit was truncated vertically and horizontally, but was deep (2m+) and well-defined. The sampled fill was from 1m+ into the pit, and was very well-defined. It comprised mainly ash and lime, and sealed the primary cess fill of the pit. It was well-sealed by backfilling with sand, soil, gravel, and further deposits of ash/lime. One of a series of similar features in a reasonably well-defined and stratified phase of activity.

Objectives: the seeds being dated have not been preserved by any of the usual conditions known to preserve archaeological seeds, ie charring, waterlogging, dessication, mineralisation. The contexts chosen for this series have been selected because they were well-sealed and well-dated. If these seeds are modern contaminants then this has important implications for the movement of small artefacts and ecofacts in archaeological deposits. If the seeds are contemporary with the deposits from which they came then this could considerably improve our understanding of how long, and under what conditions, certain seeds can survive.

Calibrated date: 1σ: cal AD 770–990
2σ: cal AD 670–1030

Final comment: L Moffett (1993), OxA-3064, OxA-3065, and OxA-3066 consisted of seed material which was not charred, waterlogged, or visibly mineralised and therefore the seeds were visually indistinguishable from modern seeds. The soil conditions were neither desiccated nor anaerobic and there was no obvious mechanism by which the seeds could have been preserved. The seeds came from contexts which were chosen to be archaeologically well-sealed and well-dated. Since the seeds were of the common disturbed-ground species elder (*Sambucus nigra*) and bramble (*Rubus fruticosus* agg.), one possible and likely explanation was that the seeds were modern intrusions. This would have had implications for the integrity of the archaeological contexts despite their well-sealed appearance. Another possible explanation was that the seeds were archaeological but preserved by some unexplained means. The possibility that some seeds might survive many centuries without an obvious means of preservation has been suspected by archaeobotanists but dating confirmation was needed. The sample dates from this site and also Little Lane, Leicester, are either well-correlated with the archaeological dates, or are earlier than the archaeological dates, confirming that the seeds in these samples are indeed archaeological and have survived in some cases probably over a thousand years of burial.

References: Hedges *et al* 1993, 162–3

OxA–3065 880 ±60 BP

δ¹³C: -24.4‰

Sample: 6713, submitted on 1 March 1991 by L Moffett

Material: plant macrofossils (seeds; *Sambucus nigra*) (L Moffett 1991)

Initial comment: the environmental sample from which this sample derived, was taken from the bottom (primary) fill of a cesspit. This was a well defined fill, approximately 1.5m down the pit, and the sample was taken from well within that fill at an approximate depth of 1.75m from the top of the pit. The feature itself was well-defined and only truncated (vertically) around its top edges, consequently there is very little chance of contamination. The pit was one of a series of cesspits in a reasonably well-defined stratigraphic sequence.

Objectives: as OxA-3064

Calibrated date: *1σ:* cal AD 1040–1220
                      2σ: cal AD 1020–1270

Final comment: see OxA-3064

References: Hedges *et al* 1993, 162–3

OxA–3066 1630 ±70 BP

δ¹³C: -26.0‰ (assumed)

Sample: 6715, submitted on 1 March 1991 by L Moffett

Material: plant macrofossils (seeds; *Rubus* spp.) (L Moffett 1991)

Initial comment: the sample from which the seed sample was taken was of the bottom (primary) fill of a cesspit. This fill was well-defined in a well-defined feature, and the sample was taken 1m from the top of the pit. It is considered very unlikely there was any contamination. The fill was sealed by a dump of ash/lime which was part of the backfilling. The pit was part of a reasonably well-defined and stratified phase of activity.

Objectives: as OxA-3064

Calibrated date: *1σ:* cal AD 340–540
                      2σ: cal AD 240–580

Final comment: see OxA-3064

References: Hedges *et al* 1993, 162–3

Yarnton: Iron Age and Roman, Oxfordshire

Location: *see* individual sites

Project manager: G Hey (Oxford Archaeology), 1989–98

Description: the Yarnton-Cassington project area is situated in the Upper Thames valley, 8km north of Oxford. It lies

on the north bank of the Thames, on the floodplain and the higher second gravel terrace.

Objectives: the primary aim of the scientific dating programme was to date a group of crouched inhumations on the edge of the Iron Age settlement and to understand the sequence of deposits discovered on the adjacent floodplain in relation to the Iron Age and Roman settlement evidence and to landscape change in the area over this period of time.

Final comment: G Hey (12 October 2004), the series of radiocarbon dates for Iron Age and Roman Yarnton has fundamentally changed our perception of Yarnton in the Iron Age period. It has provided middle Iron Age dates for crouched inhumations in a cemetery near to the settlement, a date that could not really have been predicted given the rarity of cemeteries of this date in Britain. The series also demonstrated the extent of Iron Age use of the floodplain, with wooden and stone causeways being constructed, some associated with the ritual deposition of cattle and a small number of metal objects, one of which had been an heirloom since the middle Bronze Age period. In addition, the dates enable landscape and vegetation change to be reconstructed from 700 BC to AD 400.

References: Bell and Hey 1996
                    Hey *et al* 1999
                    Hey *et al* 2011

Yarnton Iron Age and Roman: floodplain section A, Oxfordshire

Location: SP 478110
                      Lat. 51.47.43 N; Long. 01.18.25 W

Project manager: G Hey (Oxford Archaeology)

Archival body: Oxford Archaeology

Description: an area 20m × 20m was excavated across a palaeochannel to the south of a Bronze Age settlement site on the floodplain (Hey 2004, fig. 11.4), revealing a sequence of deposits which dated from the early Holocene to the medieval period. These included channel sediments, wooden structures, and dumps of woodworking debris.

Objectives: the aim of the programme was to date the sequence of deposits in order to understand the chronological relationship between the wooden structures and nearby settlement, and to reconstruct the landscape development of the site as revealed by environmental analysis.

Final comment: G Hey (12 October 2004), although the radiocarbon dates provide support for the hypothesis that there was activity in the adjacent river channel during the life of the middle and late Bronze Age settlement, it is apparent that most of the wooden structures and wood working debris recovered were early Iron Age in date. This is a surprising result, but demonstrates the extensive use of the floodplain during the Iron Age by the inhabitants of the settlement 400m away on the gravel terrace. A useful date was provided for cessation of this activity in this area by the mid to late Iron Age and before the onset of alluviation.

References: Hedges *et al* 1994, 365
                    Hey *et al* 2011
                    Hey 2004

OxA–3644 2585 ±75 BP

δ¹³C: -27.3‰

Sample: YFP CC, submitted on 7 April 1992 by G Hey

Material: wood (waterlogged): *Quercus* sp. (M Robinson)

Initial comment: the sample came from a timber which formed part of a structure jutting out into a plaeochannel. The timber had been driven into a waterlogged deposit (which contained some limestone gravel) and further organic sediments had accumulated against it. It was sealed by a deposit of alluvium. The sample would normally have been waterlogged. The date of this structure is unknown.

Objectives: palaeochannels have been located flowing across the Thames floodplain at Yarnton. The deposits preserved within them are invaluable for providing environmental data related to bankside occupation, use of the channels in the past, changing landscape, and land-use on the floodplain from the early prehistoric periods to the present day. They also have potential for elucidating the alluvial history of the floodplain. Establishing the date of the structure and, by association, the layers within which it was found is critical within this context. Dating will also help in formulating future channel sampling strategies and in assessing the potential of other dating methods (palaeomagnetic and optical) which are being tried.

Calibrated date: 1σ: 820–670 cal BC
                2σ: 900–510 cal BC

Final comment: G Hey (1994), the site has subsequently been excavated and evidence of domestic activity from the early/mid Neolithic to the late Bronze Age has been recorded. The timber was part of a wooden structure, probably a small bridge, which crossed the channel near to the site of late Bronze Age occupation. A date in the late Bronze Age for the timber would thus be consistent with contemporary activity in the channel. Although very little Iron Age material has been found on the floodplain there is an Iron Age site on the adjacent second gravel terrace and use of the floodplain would have continued for agricultural purposes. A date for the structure in the early Iron Age cannot, therefore, be ruled out.

Laboratory comment: Ancient Monuments Laboratory (2002), structure 112 was driven through silts and has produced four statistically inconsistent radiocarbon determinations (OxA-3644, UB-4060, UB-4676, and UB-4677; T'=116.9; T'(5%)=7.8; ν=3; Ward and Wilson 1978). OxA-3644 is slightly earlier than UB-4060 (2465 ±18 BP, 760-415 cal BC at 95% confidence) and UB-4677 (2654 ±16 BP, 830–795 cal BC at 95% confidence; Reimer *et al* 2004), which are statistically consistent (T'=2.9; T'(5%)=3.8; ν=1; Ward and Wilson 1978), and this may also be reused, although there could be an old-wood offset as the part of the oak tree dated is not known. UB-4677 is significantly earlier than the other three posts and is in poor agreement with its stratigraphic position (A=0.0%); it was also probably reused. The structure appears to be early Iron Age in date.

References: Reimer *et al* 2004
                  Ward and Wilson 1978

Yarnton Saxon and medieval, Oxfordshire

Location: SP 4711
                Lat. 54.47.52 N; Long. 01.18.45 W

Project manager: G Hey (Oxford Archaeological Unit), 1990–6

Description: the Oxford Archaeological Unit excavated a series of sites and landscape features of Saxon and medieval date in the ARC Cassington Pit, in the parishes of Yarnton and Cassington between 1990 and 1996. Saxon settlement was found on the three sites on the higher gravel terrace, at Yarnton, Cresswell Field, Yarnton and at Worton. At Yarnton, small-scale settlement of earlier Saxon date comprised sunken-featured buildings with associated pits and one possible post-built structure which suggested a shifting settlement pattern. This was replaced in the late- seventh or early-eighth century AD by occupation with a variety of structure types (timber hall buildings, sunken-featured buildings, a possible granary, and dovecote) organised within a defined area with enclosures, fences, tracks, and paddocks. This settlement appears to have been occupied into the later Saxon period. Only 500m west of the Yarnton middle Saxon settlement, in Cresswell Field, a Saxon timber hall, several sunken-featured buildings, pits, and fencelines were located amongst the features of a densely-occupied Iron Age site. Excavation at Worton, 1.5km west of Yarnton along the gravel terrace, has been much more small-scale and is largely based on evaluation evidence, but elements of early Saxon settlement in the form of sunken-featured buildings and pottery, and middle Saxon settlement (a post-in-trench building) have been found.

Objectives: The main objectives of the excavations were to:
1. investigate the period of transition from the late Roman to the Saxon period
2. understand the choice of Saxon settlement location, its development and changing settlement patterns, and comparing contemporary adjacent sites. Extensive investigation rather than detailed excavation was used to examine these aspects of the archaeological record.
3. reconstruct the landscape in which these settlements were established, understand changing land use strategies from the end of the Roman into the medieval period and assess human impact on the environment. The chronological relationships of different elements of the settlements and landscape were of critical importance in this context, especially given the paucity of pottery and other datable artefacts.

References: Bell and Hey 1996
                 Hey 1991
                 Hey 1994
                 Hey 2004
                 Hey and Muir 1997

Yarnton Saxon and medieval: floodplain channel, Oxfordshire

Location: SP 47361084
                Lat. 51.47.38 N; Long. 01.18.48 W

Project manager: G Hey (Oxford Archaeological Unit)

Archival body: Oxfordshire County Museum Service and Oxford Archaeological Unit

Description: this was a section excavated through a palaeochannel on the floodplain between two sites with Neolithic and Bronze Age features. The channel was once an open watercourse, part of the braided river system of the Thames, but it silted up gradually through time.

Objectives: the objectives of the scientific dating programme for the floodplain channel were:
1. to date the evidence of landscape change which had been retrieved from the sedimentary sequence;
2. to relate this evidence of landscape change to the settlement evidence from the gravel terrace;
3. as part of a post-graduate research programme at Oxford University, to validate the accuracy of OSL dates against an independent archaeological sequence and an independent series of radiocarbon measurements (Rees-Jones 1995).

Final comment: G Hey (2001), the introduction of large quantities of mineral sediment in levels 5 and 6 appears to date to the Roman period. The cessation of this alluviation probably reflects the ending of intensive arable cultivation at the end of the Roman period. The organic deposits, which built up above these sediments are early and middle Saxon in date. The deposition of inorganic alluvium resumed in the later Saxon period, perhaps indicating renewed emphasis on arable agriculture. Over this period of time the evidence from pollen, invertebrate and waterlogged plant remains suggests that the floodplain was used for pasture throughout. There is no suggestion of woodland regeneration, not even the presence of scrub. Roman settlement at Yarnton has been excavated immediately to the west of the Saxon site and fields on the floodplain would have been farmed from here. The deposition of organic material correlates with phases 1 and 2 of the Yarnton Saxon settlement. Although the evidence for early Saxon occupation is slight, it is apparent that there was continued grazing on the floodplain. The onset of alluviation in the later Saxon period is more difficult to relate to particular phases of occupation on the gravel terrace because the dating evidence is too imprecise. The results of the OSL dating programme are in excellent agreement with the independent sequence provided by the stratigraphy and the absolute dating evidence provided by radiocarbon. This method of dating appears to be highly suitable for slowly deposited floodplain sediments, and provides a method for directly dating the deposition of sediments (especially where organic preservation is poor and few samples are available for radiocarbon), but care must be taken for layers, which may have been deposited very rapidly.

References: Hey 2004
Rees-Jones 1995

OxA–4816 1835 ±55 BP

δ¹³C: -27.6‰

Sample: 957b, sample 5, layer 7, submitted in 1992 by J Rees-Jones

Material: plant macrofossils (M Robinson)

Initial comment: from sediment in the channel.

Objectives: to validate OSL dates.

Calibrated date: 1σ: cal AD 80–250
2σ: cal AD 50–340

Final comment: G Hey (2001), the date range for this sample is consistent with the OSL date (957b) of 165 BC–AD 300 (at 68% confidence) obtained from the sediment from which the sample came. The layer is comparatively inorganic silt laid down during flooding at a period of fairly intensive arable agriculture. It was anticipated that this layer would be early Roman in date.

References: Rees-Jones 1995

Yarnton Saxon and medieval: Oxey Mead channel, Oxfordshire

Location: SP 47901095
Lat. 51.47.41 N; Long. 01.18.19 W

Project manager: G Hey (Oxford Archaeological Unit)

Archival body: Oxford Archaeological Unit

Description: four sections were excavated through a palaeochannel on the floodplain north of Oxey Mead, a famous hay meadow on the banks of the Thames. The channel was once an open watercourse, part of the braided river system of the Thames, but it has silted up gradually through time.

Objectives: to date the introduction of hay meadow in this area, as evidenced by invertebrate remains recovered from the sedimentary sequence; and to relate the landscape change to the settlement evidence from the gravel terrace.

Final comment: G Hey (29 January 2001), the objectives of the dating programme were met in that it provided a date for the introduction of the hay meadow at *cal AD 650-850 (OxA-3643;* Hey 2004, fig 13.8). This is most likely to be contemporary with the middle Saxon settlement at Yarnton.

References: Hey 2004

OxA–3643 1190 ±75 BP

δ¹³C: -27.7‰

Sample: YFP CC/1, submitted on 4 April 1992 by G Hey

Material: waterlogged plant macrofossil (flax; *Linum usitatissimum*) (M Robinson 1992)

Initial comment: the flax came from a bundle which was found within a waterlogged organic sediment in a silted-up channel. Some limestone gravel was present. Although the sample was no longer under water it had been saturated at least seasonally. The sample was well-sealed within the layer, and had been placed in the channel as part of the retting process. The layer was overlain by a deposit of alluvium which could either be late Iron Age/Roman or medieval in date.

Objectives: palaeochannels have been located flowing across the Thames floodplain at Yarnton. The deposits preserved within them are invaluable for providing environmental data related to bankside occupation, use of the channels in the past, changing landscape, and land-use on the floodplain. Establishing the date of the deposition/formation of the layers is critical within this context. Dating will also help in formulating future channel sampling strategies and in assessing the potential of other dating methods, palaeomagnetic and optical, which are being tried.

Calibrated date: 1σ: cal AD 710–970

2σ: cal AD 660–1020

Final comment: G Hey (29 January 2001), the mid to late Saxon date for the flax indicates its contemporaneity with the last phase of occupation of the Yarnton excavation site, and enhances our knowledge of the economic activities of this rural community, otherwise mostly deduced from on-site material. Recent work on the floodplain at Yarnton has examined further palaeochannel sections, and current thinking is that during the Saxon period the channels had largely silted up, leaving a series of ponds along their earlier courses, at least during the summer months. The Saxon date for the flax bundle confirms this hypothesis, as re-examination of the section whence it was recovered shows that flax retting was taking place within one of these ponds. The bundle comes from a layer within which there are changes in the character of the invertebrate remains, suggesting the introduction of hay meadow at this time.

Yarnton Saxon and medieval: settlement, halls, Oxfordshire

Location: SP 474113

Lat. 51.47.52 N; Long. 01.18.45 W

Project manager: G Hey (Oxford Archaeological Unit), 1990–1

Archival body: Oxfordshire County Museum Service & Oxford Archaeology

Description: the middle Saxon Yarnton settlement spread over *c* 3ha, and showed evidence of spatial planning. The hall buildings mainly lay in the centre of the site, east of an area of sunken-featured buildings and a granary, and west and north of animal enclosures and a trackway through the settlement.

Objectives: 1. what were the absolute dates between which the settlement was occupied?
2. to what extent were phases chronologically distinct?
3. what was the spatial organisation of major structures in the settlement by phase?
4. was the occupation at Yarnton contemporary with other settlements on the adjacent gravel terrace or did it replace them?

Final comment: G Hey (2001), the estimated date range for the use of the hall buildings was in phases 2 and 3, the middle Saxon phases of the site. The beginning of phase 2/3 is *cal AD 660–780* (at 95% probability; *start_23*; Hey 2004, fig 13.3), and for its end is *cal AD 840–940* (at 95% probability; *end_23*; Hey 2004, fig 13.3). The estimated date range for the end of phase 4 of the Yarnton Saxon settlement is *cal AD 910–1160* (at 95% probability; *last smithy*; Hey 2004, fig 13.4). The phase 2/3 settlement appears to have been occupied for between 90–250 years (at 95% confidence). Twelve of the radiocarbon determinations obtained are regarded as being useful for dating the occupation of the post-built structures. The results suggest that it is unlikely that all the buildings were in use at any one time. Although there are too few measurements to suggest reliably the order in which the buildings were constructed or demolished, general trends can be seen in the estimated dates. For example, it is likely that building B 3348 was

demolished after buildings B 3959 and B 3619 (89% probability), and that its use overlapped with that of building 3620 (over 95% probability).

References: Hey 2004

OxA–3177 1390 ±70 BP

$\delta^{13}C$: -26.0‰ (assumed)

Sample: YWRF CA/1, submitted on 22 March 1991 by G Hey

Material: charcoal: unidentified

Initial comment: from within the postpipe of posthole B3620, part of the construction of the westerly timber hall. The post appeared to have been burnt *in situ* and a lens of burnt gravel was observed adjacent to it. The feature was cut into gravel and not sealed by occupation deposits but the sample came from well within the feature.

Objectives: the sample comes from the remains of a Saxon timber hall. The site seems to have been high-status and is unique in this area. In common with similar sites elsewhere, finds are scarce and not closely datable. A radiocarbon date is vital for dating this phase of the occupation.

Calibrated date: 1σ: cal AD 600–680

2σ: cal AD 540–780

Final comment: G Hey (2001), the original comment on this date was as follows: the four charcoal samples (OxA-3177 to -3180) come from the fill of postholes of two timber halls on the Saxon settlement. Although the two buildings had no physical relationship, the settlement layout suggested they were contemporary. The site lay adjacent to earlier occupation but was, for the most part, spatially discrete. The dates from the westerly hall, OxA-3177 and OxA-3178, are consistent with the expected age range of the settlement. They also accord well with a conventional radiocarbon date (GU-5138; 1390 ±50 BP which calibrates to cal AD 540-780 at 95% confidence; Reimer *et al* 2004) obtained on wood from within a nearby well. However, subsequent radiocarbon determinations have shown that this date is statistically significantly different from dates from this structure which are considered to be reliable. As the wood from which the charcoal derived was not identified, it has been excluded from the calculations of the use and destruction of this building.

References: Hedges *et al* 1993, 162

Reimer *et al* 2004

OxA–3178 1425 ±70 BP

$\delta^{13}C$: -26.0‰ (assumed)

Sample: YWRF CA/2, submitted on 22 March 1991 by G Hey

Material: charcoal: unidentified

Initial comment: from within posthole B3620 from the westerly timber hall. The post was probably burnt *in situ*. The feature was cut into gravel and had not been sealed by occupation deposits, but the same came from well within the feature.

Objectives: as OxA-3177

Calibrated date: 1σ: cal AD 570–670
                         2σ: cal AD 460–770

Final comment: see OxA-3177

References: Hedges *et al* 1993, 162

OxA–3179 3270 ±70 BP

δ¹³C: -26.0‰ (assumed)

Sample: YWRF CA/3, submitted on 22 March 1991 by
G Hey

Material: charcoal: unidentified

Initial comment: OxA-3179 and OxA-3180 both came from a
posthole of the easterly Saxon hall (B 3348). The posts were
probably burnt *in situ*. The feature was cut into gravel and
had not been sealed by occupation deposits, but the samples
came from well within the feature.

Objectives: as OxA-3177

Calibrated date: 1σ: 1630–1450 cal BC
                         2σ: 1740–1410 cal BC

Final comment: G Hey (2001), OxA-3179 is clearly residual.
A small amount of early Bronze Age activity has been
located further east on the site. The charcoal may derive
from this activity or from contemporary tree clearance.

References: Hedges *et al* 1993, 162

OxA–3180 1050 ±70 BP

δ¹³C: -26.0‰ (assumed)

Sample: YWRF CA/4, submitted on 22 March 1991 by
G Hey

Material: charcoal: unidentified

Initial comment: as OxA-3179

Objectives: as OxA-3177

Calibrated date: 1σ: cal AD 890–1030
                         2σ: cal AD 820–1160

Final comment: G Hey (2001), this late date was entirely
unexpected. A small amount of later Saxon material had
been recovered from nearby ditches but there is no evidence
to suggest late Saxon domestic occupation. However, it
should be noted that this building was situated at the eastern
end of a site that had witnessed continuously eastward
shifting occupation from the late Bronze Age, and a later
date for this hall is not implausible. An alternative proposal
is that the date derives from the mixing of contemporary and
intrusive charcoal, the latter being introduced by later,
particularly agricultural, activity. A re-appraisal of this
structure is being undertaken in the post-excavation
assessment. Subsequent radiocarbon dating of this site has
shown that this result is not anomalous. It is also consistent
with other determinations from B 3348 and was used to
calculate the probable period of use and abandonment of the
structure.

References: Hedges *et al* 1993, 162

OxA–3914 1270 ±75 BP

δ¹³C: -22.9‰

Sample: YWRF CA/6, submitted on 29 September 1992
by G Hey

Material: charcoal: unidentified

Initial comment: from the bottom charcoal-packed layer of pit
3693 which was open when an adjacent timber hall, B 3348,
was burned and demolished. The pit would have been
quickly filled with the 0.78m of sandy loam which overlay
this layer. The deposit may have been partially waterlogged
in the past but modern drainage has dried out the ground.

Objectives: to help establish a date for the end of this phase of
occupation, and in particular the destruction of a Saxon hall.

Calibrated date: 1σ: cal AD 660–870
                         2σ: cal AD 640–950

Final comment: G Hey (2001), although the charcoal from
which the determination came was not identified, the result
was not statistically different from others associated with B
3348. It seems to be compatible with the expected date of
destruction of the hall building.

References: Bronk Ramsey *et al* 2002, 50–1

Yarnton Saxon and medieval: settlement, other features, Oxfordshire

Location: SP 474113
                         Lat. 51.47.52 N; Long. 01.18.45 W

Project manager: G Hey (Oxford Archaeological Unit),
                         1990–1

Archival body: Oxfordshire Museum Service and Oxford
                         Archaeology, Oxfordshire Museum
                         Service

Description: a characteristic of the Yarnton middle Saxon
settlement was the wide range of archaeological features
present, that included not only timber halls and sunken-
featured buildings, but also small post-built structures,
wells/waterholes, pits, and a smithy.

Objectives: this element of the dating programme aimed to
understand the chronological and spatial development of the
site by submitting samples from a range of these features.
The period of use of certain crops and the associations of
environmental and economic evidence from the waterholes
was also addressed by this suite of determinations.

Final comment: G Hey (2001), the waterholes were situated in
the south-east of the settlement. A wooden object waterlogged
in the bottom of 3029 was made of oak and it seems likely that
the result has a significant age-at-death offset, and so is older
than the date of manufacture of the object. For this reason the
result is not useful for dating the waterhole. Two samples of
charred cereals from the adjacent waterhole 3043 produced an
estimated date range for this feature of *cal AD 770–900*
(*last_3043*; Hey 2004, fig 13.3). Two samples, one of cereal,
and one of unidentified charcoal from hearth 3666 of smithy
3926, suggested an estimated date range of *cal AD 910–1160*
(*smithy*; Hey 2004, fig 13.4) for the use of the smithy.

References: Hey 1991
                         Hey 2004

GU–5138 1390 ±50 BP

δ¹³C: -28.2‰

Sample: YWRF CB/1, submitted on 22 March 1991
by G Hey

Material: wood (waterlogged): *Quercus* sp., mature
(J Watson 1991)

Initial comment: from part of a waterlogged wooden object
resembling a ladder found in the bottom of a ?Saxon
waterhole which was cut into sandy loam and gravel, context
3029/A/9. The feature was not sealed but the 1.2m of
deposit which overlay the object would have been deposited
rapidly

Objectives: the sample is associated with the occupation of a
Saxon site. The site seems to have been high-status and is
unique in this area but, in common with similar sites
elsewhere, finds are scarce and not closely datable. A
radiocarbon date is vital for dating this phase of occupation.

Calibrated date: *1σ:* cal AD 610–670
                        2σ: cal AD 570–690

Final comment: G Hey (2001), although this object was
constructed partly of alder or hazel, a piece of mature oak
was unfortunately submitted for radiocarbon dating. This has
produced a date which is too old to belong to an object in
use in the middle Saxon settlement.

OxA–3915 1040 ±65 BP

δ¹³C: -23.1‰

Sample: YWRF CA/7, submitted on 29 September 1992
by G Hey

Material: charcoal: unidentified

Initial comment: from an area of burning adjacent to a ?Saxon
smithy. Although the top of this deposit lay beneath the
modern ploughsoil the sample was removed from 0.10m
below the top of the layer and there is no reason to believe it
was disturbed.

Objectives: the sample is associated with the occupation of a
Saxon site. The site seems to have been high-status and is
unique in this area but, in common with similar sites
elsewhere, finds are scarce and not closely datable. A
radiocarbon date is vital for dating this phase of occupation.

Calibrated date: *1σ:* cal AD 900–1030
                        2σ: cal AD 880–1160

Final comment: G Hey (2001), although the wood charcoal
which provided this sample was not identified, the result was
not statistically significantly different from another sample
from the smithy (OxA-5467; 1055 ±55 BP; cal AD
880–1120 at 95% confidence; Reimer *et al* 2004). It was
within the expected date range for a structure known to be
stratigraphically later than most other features on the site.

References: Bronk Ramsey *et al* 2002, 50–1
                   Reimer *et al* 2004

Bibliography

Adams, M, 1996 Excavation of a pre-Conquest cemetery at Addingham, West Yorkshire, *Medieval Archaeol*, **40**, 151–91

Ainslie, R, and Wallis, J, 1987 Excavations on the Cursus at Drayton, Oxon, *Oxeniensia*, **52**, 4–6

Allen, M J, 1988 *Archaeological and environmental aspects of colluviation in south-east England*, BAR Int Ser, **410**, Oxford: Brit Archaeol Rep

Allen, M J, 1995 Before Stonehenge: Mesolithic human activity in a wildwood landscape, in *Stonehenge in its landscape: twentieth-century excavations* (eds R M J Cleal, K E Walker, R Montague, and M J Allen), Engl Heritage Archaeol Rep, **10**, 470–473 London: Engl Heritage

Allen, M J, and Bayliss, A, 1995 Appendix 2: the radiocarbon dating programme, in *Stonehenge in its landscape: twentieth century excavations* (eds R M J Cleal, K E Walker, and R Montague), Engl Heritage Archaeol Rep, **10**, 511–35, London: Engl Heritage

Ambers, J, Bowman, S G E, Garwood, P, Hedges, R, and Houseley, R, 1999 Appendix 1: Radiocarbon dating, in *Excavations at Barrow Hills, Radley, Oxfordshire, Vol. 1* (A Barclay and C Halpin), Thames Valley Landscapes Monogr, **11**, 330–9 Oxford: Oxford Univ Comm Archaeol

Anderson, J, 1988 A dig in the ribs [palaeopathology of Ailcy Hill, Ripon inhumations], *Bull York Archaeol Trust*, **13**, 24–32

Ashbee, P, 1978 Amesbury Barrow 51, Excavations 1960, *Wiltshire Archaeol Natur Hist Mag*, **70/71**, 1–60

Ashbee, P, 1979–80 Amesbury Barrow 39, Excavations 1960, *Wiltshire Archaeol Natur Hist Mag*, **74/75**, 3–34

Ashbee, P, 1984 The excavation of Amesbury barrows 58, 61a, 61, 72, *Wiltshire Archaeol Natur Hist Mag*, **79**, 39–91

Ashbee, P, 1992 Amesbury Barrows 61 and 62: a Radiocarbon Postscript, *Wiltshire Archaeol Natur Hist Mag*, **85**, 140–1

Ashbee, P, with Bayliss, A, 2005 The Snail Down Radiocarbon Dates, in *The Bronze Age barrow cemetery and related earthworks on Snail Down, in the parishes of Collingbourne Ducis and Collingbourne Kingston, Wiltshire, excavations 1953, 1955, and 1957* (N Thomas), Wiltshire Archaeol Soc Monogr, **3**, 253–8

Ashmore, P, 1999 Radiocarbon dating: avoiding errors by avoiding mixed samples, *Antiquity*, **73**, 124–30

Ashwin, T, and Bates, S, 2000 *Excavations on the Norwich Southern Bypass, 1989–91, part 1: excavations at Bixley, Caistor St Edmund, Trowse, Cringleford and Little Melton*, E Anglian Archaeol Rep, **91**, Dereham: Norfolk Museums Service

Audouy, M, and Chapman, A, 2009 *Rounds: the origin and growth of a midland village AD 450–1500: excavations in north Raunds, Northamptonshire 1977–87*, Oxford: Oxbow Books

Austin, D, 1980 Barnard Castle, Co Durham. Second interim report: excavation in the inner ward 1976–8, the later medieval period, *J Brit Archaeol Ass*, **133**, 86–96

Avery, M, 1982 The Neolithic causewayed enclosure, Abingdon, in *Settlement patterns and the Oxford region: excavations at the Abingdon causewayed enclosure and other sites* (H J Case and A W R Whittle), CBA Res Rep, **44**, 10–50 London: CBA

Baillie, M G L, 1990 Checking back on an assemblage of published radiocarbon dates, *Radiocarbon*, **32**, 361–6

Baker, N, Dalwood, H, Holt, R, Mundy, C, and Taylor, G, 1992 From Roman to medieval Worcester: development and planning in the Anglo-Saxon city, *Antiquity*, **66**, 65–74

Balkwill, N D, and Silvester, R J, 1976 Earthworks on Sourton Down, near Okehampton, *Proc Devon Archaeol Soc*, **34**, 86–9

Barclay, A, and Halpin, C, 1999 *Excavations at Barrow Hills, Radley, Oxfordshire. Volume 1: the Neolithic and Bronze Age monument complex*, Thames Valley Landscapes Monogr, **11**, Oxford: Oxford Univ Comm Archaeol

Barclay, A, Gray, M, and Lambrick, G, 1995 *Excavations at the Devil's Quoits, Stanton Harcourt, Oxfordshire, 1972–3 and 1988*, Thames Valley Landscapes: the Windrush Valley, **3**, Oxford: Oxford Univ Comm Archaeol

Barclay, A, Lambrick, G, Moore, J, and Robinson, M, 2003 *Lines in the landscape. Cursus monuments in the Upper Thames Valley: excavations at the Drayton and Lechlade cursuses*, Thames Valley Landscapes Monogr, **15**, Oxford: Oxford Univ School Archaeol

Bard, E, Arnold, M, Fairbanks, R G, and Hamelin, B, 1993 ^{230}Th-^{234}U and ^{14}C ages obtained by mass spectrometry on corals, *Radiocarbon*, **35**, 191–200

Barnatt, J, 1986 Bronze Age remains on the East Moors of the Peak District, *Derbyshire Archaeol J*, **106**, 18–101

Barnatt, J, 1987 Bronze Age settlement on the gritstone East Moors of the Peak District of Derbyshire and South Yorkshire, *Proc Prehist Soc*, **53**, 393–418

Barnatt, J, 1989 *Peak District Barrow Survey* **9:2**, unpubl rep, Peak District National Park

Barnatt, J, 1994 Excavations of a Bronze Age unenclosed cemetery, cairns, and field boundaries at Eaglestone Flat, Curbar, Derbyshire, 1984, 1989–1990, *Proc Prehist Soc*, **60**, 287–370

Barnatt, J, 1995 Neolithic and Bronze Age radiocarbon dates from the Peak District: a review, *Derbyshire Archaeol J*, **115**, 5–19

Barnatt, J, and Collis, J, 1996 *Barrows in the Peak District: recent research*, Sheffield: J R Collis

Barnes, B, 1975 *Palaeoecological studies of the Late Quaternary Period in the North West Lancashire Lowlands*, unpubl PhD thesis, Univ Lancaster

Bayliss, A, 2005 Radiocarbon Dating, in *Stonea and the Roman Fens* (T Malim), 94–6, Oxford: Tempus

Bayliss, A, 2009 Rolling out Revolution: using radiocarbon dating in archaeology, *Radiocarbon*, **51**, 123–47

Bayliss, A, and Atkins, C, 2011 Chapter 15: Specialist Studies 1, Interpreting Chronology, in *St Peter's, Barton-upon-Humber, Lincolnshire: a parish church and its community. Volume 1: History, Archaeology and Architecture, Part 2* (W Rodwell with C Atkins), 753–88, Oxford: Oxbow Books

Bayliss, A, and Bronk Ramsey, C, 2004 Pragmatic Bayesians: a decade integrating radiocarbon dates into chronological models, in *Tools for constructing chronologies: tools for crossing disciplinary boundaries* (eds C E Buck and A R Millard), 25–41, London: Springer

Bayliss, A, and Hey, G, 2004 Chapter 13: Scientific dating, in *Yarnton Saxon and Medieval Settlement and Landscape* (G Hey), Thames Valley Landscape Monogr, **20**, 255–66

Bayliss, A, and Hey, G, 2011 Absolute Chronology, in *Yarnton: Iron Age and Romano-British settlement and landscape* (G Hey, P Booth, and J Timby), Thames Valley Landscapes, **35**, 333–43, Oxford: Oxford Archaeol

Bayliss, A, and Orton, C, 1994 Strategic consideration in dating, or 'How many dates do I need?', *Inst Archaeol Bull*, **31**, 151–65

Bayliss, A, and Pryor, F, 2001 Radiocarbon and absolute chronology, in *The Flag Fen Basin: archaeology and environment of a Fenland landscape* (F Pryor), Engl Heritage Archaeol Rep, 390–9

Bayliss, A, Barclay, A, Lambrick, G, and Robinson, M, 2003 Radiocarbon determinations, in *Cursus monuments in the upper Thames valley: excavations at the Drayton and Lechlade cursuses* (eds A J Barclay, G Lambrick, J Moore, and M Robinson), Thames Valley Landscapes Monogr, **15**, 180–5

Bayliss, A, Bronk Ramsey, C, van der Plicht, J, and Whittle, A, 2007 Bradshaw and Bayes: towards a timetable for the Neolithic, *Cambridge Archaeol J*, **17(1) suppl**, 1–28

Bayliss, A, Cook, G T, McCormac, F G, and Pettitt, P, 2002 The radiocarbon determinations, in *Downland Settlement and Landuse: the archaeology of the Brighton Bypass* (ed D Rudling), UCL Fld Archaeol Unit Monogr, **1**, 239–48, London: Archetype and Engl Heritage

Bayliss, A, Groves, C, McCormac, F G, Bronk Ramsey, C, Baillie, M G L, Brown, D, Cook, G G, and Switsur, R, 2004a Dating, in *The Dover Bronze Age Boat* (ed P Clark), 250–2, Swindon: Engl Heritage

Bayliss, A, Healy, F, Bronk Ramsey, C, McCormac, F G, Cook, G T, and Harding, J, 2011 Absolute chronology, in *The Raunds Area Project: a Neolithic and Bronze Age landscape in Northamptonshire. Volume 2. Supplementary Studies* (eds J Harding and F Healy), 866–85, Swindon: Engl Heritage

Bayliss, A, Healy, F, Bronk Ramsey, C, McCormac, F, and Mercer, R, 2008 Interpreting chronology, in *Hambledon Hill, Dorset, England. Excavation and Survey of a Neolithic Monument Complex and its Surrounding Landscape (English Heritage Archaeological Report)* (R Mercer and F Healy), 378–411, Swindon: Engl Heritage

Bayliss, A, Hedges, R, Otlet, R, Switsur, R, and Walker, A J, 2012 *Radiocarbon dates from samples funded by English Heritage between 1981 and 1988*, Swindon: Engl Heritage

Bayliss, A, McCormac, F G, van der Plicht, J, 2004b An illustrated guide to measuring radiocarbon from archaeological samples, *Physics Education*, **39**, 137–44

Bayliss, A, Pettitt, P, and Malim, T, 1996 The radiocarbon determinations, in The Cambridgeshire Dykes and Worsted Street (ed T Malim), *Proc Cantab Antiq Soc*, **85**, 95–8

Beazley, O, 2001 Chapter 1: Excavations in St Martin-at-Palace Church, 1987, in *Two medieval churches in Norfolk* (O Beazley and B Ayers), E Anglian Archaeol Rep, **96**, 1–63 Dereham: Norfolk Museums and Archaeol Service

Bell, C, and Hey, G, 1996 Yarnton Cresswell Field, *S Midlands Archaeol*, **26**, 63

Bell, M, 1990 *Brean Down excavation 1983–1987*, Engl Heritage Archaeol Rep, **15**, London: Engl Heritage

Bell, M G, 1983 Valley sediments as evidence of prehistoric land-use on the South Downs, *Proc Prehist Soc*, **49**, 119–50

Bell, R D, and Beresford, M W, 1987 *Wharram: a study of settlement on the Yorkshire Wolds, 3: Wharram Percy: the church of St Martin*, Soc Medieval Archaeol Monogr Ser, **11**, London: Soc Medieval Archaeol

Bellamy, P S, 1991 The excavation of Fordington Farm round barrow, *Proc Dorset Natur Hist Archaeol Soc*, **113**, 107–132

Best, E M, 1964 Excavation of three barrows on the Ridgeway, Bincombe, *Proc Dorset Natur Hist Archaeol Soc*, **86**, 102–103

Bewley, R H, 1960 Excavations on two crop-marks sites in the Solway plain, Cumbria. Ewanrigg settlement and Swarthy Hill 1986–1988, *Trans Cumberland Westmorland Antiq Archaeol Soc*, **92**, 23–47

Bewley, R H, Longworth, I H, Browne, S, Huntley, J P, and Varndell, G, 1992 Excavation of a Bronze Age cemetery at Ewanrigg, Maryport, Cumbria, *Proc Prehist Soc*, **58**, 325–54

Bidwell, P T, and Holbrook, N, 1989 *Hadrian's Wall Bridges*, Engl Heritage Archaeol Rep, **9**, London: Engl Heritage

Blaauw, M, and Christen, J A, 2005 Radiocarbon peat chronologies and environmental change, *Applied Statistics*, **54**, 805–16

Blair, J, 1988 Thornbury, Binsey: a probable defensive enclosure associated with Saint Frideswide, *Oxoniensia*, **53**, 3–20

Blake, B, 1960 Excavations of native (Iron Age) sites in Cumberland, 1956–8, *Trans Cumberland Westmorland Antiq Archaeol Soc*, **59**, 1–15

Blockley, K, and Blockley, P, 1989 Excavations at Bigberry, near Canterbury, 1981, *Archaeol Cantiana*, **107**, 239–51

van de Borg, K, Alderiesten, C, Houston, C M, De Jong, A F M, and Van Zwol, N A, 1987 Accelerator Mass Spectrometry with ^{14}C and ^{10}Be in Utrecht, *Nuclear Methods and Instruments in Physics B*, **29**, 143–5

Bowman, S, 1990 *Interpreting the Past: Radiocarbon dating*, London: Brit Museum

Bradley, R, 1992 The excavations of an oval barrow beside the Abingdon causewayed enclosure, Oxfordshire, *Proc Prehist Soc*, **58**, 127–43

Bradley, R, and Edmonds, M, 1993 *Interpreting the axe trade: production and exchange in the Neolithic*, Cambridge: Cambridge Univ Press

Bradley, R, Chowne, P, Cleal, R M J, Healy, F, and Kinnes, I, 1992 *Excavations on Redgate Hill, Hunstanton, Norfolk, and at Tattershall Thorpe, Lincolnshire*, E Anglian Archaeol, **57**, Dereham: Norfolk Fld Archaeol Division

Bradley, R, Entwistle, R, and Raymond, F, 1994 *Prehistoric land divisions on Salisbury Plain: the work of the Wessex Linear Ditches Project*, Engl Heritage Archaeol Rep, **2**, London: Engl Heritage

Bradley, R, Lobb, S, Richards, J, and Robinson, M, 1980 Two late Bronze Age settlements on the Kennet Gravels: excavations at Aldermaston Wharf and Knight's Farm, Burghfield, Berkshire, *Proc Prehist Soc*, **46**, 217–95

Branch, N, 1988 *Pollen and preliminary plant macrofossil analysis of peat columns from Lindow Moss, Cheshire*, Anc Mon Lab Rep, **111/88**

Brindley, A L, Lanting, J N, and Mook, W G, 1990 Radiocarbon dates from Irish fiadh and other burnt mounds, *J Ir Archaeol*, **5**, 25–33

Brock, F, Higham, T, Ditchfield, P, and Bronk Ramsey, C, 2010 Current pretreatment methods for AMS radiocarbon dating at the Oxford Radiocarbon Accelerator Unit (ORAU), *Radiocarbon*, **52**, 103–12

Bronk Ramsey, C, 1995 Radiocarbon calibration and analysis of stratigraphy, *Radiocarbon*, **36**, 425–30

Bronk Ramsey, C, 1998 Probability and dating, *Radiocarbon*, **40**, 461–74

Bronk Ramsey, C, 2001 Development of the radiocarbon calibration program OxCal, *Radiocarbon*, **43**, 355–63

Bronk Ramsey, C, 2008 Deposition models for chronological records, *Quat Sci Rev*, **27**, 42–60

Bronk Ramsey, C, 2009 Bayesian analysis of radiocarbon dates, *Radiocarbon*, **51**, 37–60

Bronk Ramsey, C, Higham, T F G, Owen, D C, Pike, A W G, and Hedges, R E M, 2002 Radiocarbon Dates from the Oxford AMS System: Archaeometry Datelist 31, *Archaeometry*, **44**, 1–149

Bronk Ramsey, C, Pettitt, P B, Hedges, R E M, Hodgins, G W L, and Owen, D C, 2000a Radiocarbon dates from the Oxford AMS system: Archaeometry datelist 30, *Archaeometry*, **42**, 459–79

Bronk Ramsey, C, Pettitt, P B, Hedges, R E M, Hodgins, G W L, and Owen, D C, 2000b Radiocarbon dates from the Oxford AMS system: Archaeometry datelist 29, *Archaeometry*, **42**, 243–54

Bronk, C R, and Hedges, R E M, 1990 A gaseous ion source for routine AMS radiocarbon dating, *Nuclear Instruments and Methods in Physics B*, **52**, 322–6

Brooks, H, 1989 The Stansted project: a report on the second and third years' work, *Essex J*, **24**, 6–10

Brooks, H, and Bedwin, O, 1989 *Archaeology at the airport: the Stansted Archaeological Project 1985–89*, Chelmsford: Essex County Council

Brown, F, Howard-Davis, C, Brennand, M, Boyle, A, Evans, T, O'Connor, S, Spence, A, Heawood, R, and Lupton, A, 2007 *The archaeology of the A1 (M) Darrington to Dishforth DBFO road scheme*, Lancaster Imprints, **12**, Lancaster: Oxford Archaeol North

Brown, N, and Kinnes, I, 1995 Ardleigh reconsidered: Deverel-Rimbury pottery in Essex, in *Unbaked urns of rudely shape: essays on British and Irish pottery for Ian Longworth* (ed G Varndell), Oxbow Monogr, **55**, 123–44, Oxford: Oxbow

Buck, C E, Kenworthy, J B, Litton, C D, and Smith, A F M, 1991 Combining archaeological and radiocarbon information: a Bayesian approach to calibration, *Antiquity*, **65**, 808–21

Buck, C E, Litton, C D, and Smith, A F M, 1992 Calibration of radiocarbon results pertaining to related archaeological events, *J Archaeol Sci*, **19**, 497–512

Buck, C E, Cavanagh, W G, and Litton, C D, 1996 *Bayesian Approach to Interpreting Archaeological Data*, Chichester: Wiley

Buck, C E, Litton, C D, and Scott, E M, 1994a Making the most of radiocarbon dating: some statistical considerations, *Antiquity*, **68**, 252–63

Buck, C E, Christen, J A, Kenworthy, J B, and Litton, C D, 1994b Estimating the duration of archaeological activity using ^{14}C determinations, *Oxford J Archaeol*, **13**, 229–40

Burgess, C, 1986 Urnes of no small variety: Collared Urns reviewed, *Proc Prehist Soc*, **52**, 339–51

Burleigh, R, Hewson, A, and Meeks, N, 1976 British Museum natural radiocarbon measurements VIII, *Radiocarbon*, **18**, 16–42

Bush, M B, 1989 Early Mesolithic disturbance: a force of the landscape, *J Archaeol Sci*, **15**, 453–62

Butterworth, C A, and Lobb, S J, 1992 *Excavations in the Burghfield Area, Berkshire: developments in the Bronze Age and Saxon landscapes*, Wessex Archaeol Rep, **1**, Salisbury: Wessex Archaeol

Calkin, J B, 1967 Some records of barrow excavations re-examined, *Proc Dorset Natur Hist Antiq Fld Club*, **88**, 128–48

Callow, W J, and Hassall, G I, 1970 National Physical Laboratory radiocarbon measurements VII, *Radiocarbon*, **12**, 181–6

Cardwell, P, 1990 St Giles Hospital, Brompton-on-Swale, North Yorkshire, *Bull CBA Churches Comm*, **27**, 14–7

Cardwell, P, 1995 Excavation of the hospital of St Giles by Brompton Bridge, North Yorkshire, *Archaeol J*, **152**, 109–245

Cardwell, P, and Speed, G, 1996 Prehistoric occupation at St Giles by Brompton Bridge, North Yorkshire, *Durham Archaeol J*, **12**, 27–40

Carr, R, 1992 The Middle-Saxon settlement at Staunch Meadow, Brandon, Suffolk - a final update, *The Quarterly: J Norfolk Archaeol Res Group*, **5**, 16–22

Carr, R D, Tester, A, and Murphy, P, 1988 The middle Saxon settlement at Staunch Meadow, Brandon, *Antiquity*, **62**, 371–7

Chamberlain, A T, Roberts, S, and Romanowski, C, 1992 Osteochondroma in a British Neolithic skeleton, *Br J Hosp Med*, **47**, 51–53

Chambers, F M, and Jones, M K, 1984 Antiquity of rye in Britain: status of 'Bronze Age' records unclear, *Antiquity*, **58**, 219–24

Chapman, A, 2010 *West Cotton, Raunds: a study of medieval settlement dynamics AD 450-1450: excavation of a deserted medieval hamlet in Northamptonshire, 1985-89*, Oxford: Oxbow Books

Chowne, P, and Copson, C, 1989 *Fordingham Farm round barrow*, unpubl interim rep, Trust of Wessex Archaeol

Christen, J A, and Litton, C D, 1995 A Bayesian approach to wiggle-matching, *J Archaeol Sci*, **22**, 719–25

Christen, J A, Clymo, R S, and Litton, C D, 1995 A Bayesian approach to the use of ¹⁴C dates in the estimation of the age of peat, *Radiocarbon*, **37**, 431–42

Clark, P, 1992 The prehistoric boat at Dover: an interim note, *NewsWARP*, **12**, 19–21

Clark, P, 2004a *The Dover Bronze Age Boat*, Swindon: Engl Heritage

Clark, P, 2004b *The Dover Bronze Age boat in context: society and water transport in prehistoric Europe*, Oxford: Oxbow Books

Clark, P, and Keeley, H, 1997 The Dover Bronze Age boat - palaeoenvironmental assessment and updated project design for analysis, July 1997, unpubl rep, Canterbury Archaeol Trust

Clark, R M, 1975 A calibration curve for radiocarbon dates, *Antiquity*, **49**, 251–66

Clarke, D L, 1970 *Beaker pottery of Great Britain and Ireland*, Cambridge: Cambridge Univ Press

Clarke, P, 1991 Brightlingsea, *Curr Archaeol*, **11**, 272–3

Clay, P, 1986 A watching brief and salvage excavations at Hemington Fields, Castle Donington, *Leicestershire Archaeol Hist Soc Trans*, **60**, 80–1

Clay, P, 1992a An Iron Age farmstead at Grove Farm, Enderby, Leicestershire, *Trans Leicestershire Archaeol Hist Soc*, **66**, 1–82

Clay, P, 1992b A Norman mill dam at Hemington Fields, Castle Donington, Leicestershire, in *Alluvial Archaeology in Britain: Proceeding of a Conference sponsored by the RMC Group plc 3–5 January 1991, British Museum* (eds S Needham and M G Macklin), Oxbow Monogr, **27**, 163–8, Oxford: Oxbow Books

Clay, P, 1998 Neolithic/Early Bronze Age pit circles and their environs at Oakham, Rutland, *Proc Prehist Soc*, **64**, 293–330

Clay, P, and Salisbury, C R, 1991 A Norman mill dam and other sites at Hemington Fields, Castle Donington, Leicestershire, *Archaeol J*, **147**, 276–307

Cleal, R, Walker, K E, Montague, R, and Allen, M J, 1995 *Stonehenge in its landscape: twentieth-century excavations*, Engl Heritage Archaeol Rep, **10**, London: Engl Heritage

Coles, B J, and Dobson, M J, 1989 Calibration of radiocarbon dates from the Somerset Levels, *Somerset Levels Pap*, **15**, 64–9

Coles, J M, and Orme, B J, 1976 The Sweet Track, railway site, *Somerset Levels Pap*, **2**, 34–65

Coles, J M, and Orme, B J, 1979 The Sweet Track: drove site, *Somerset Levels Pap*, **5**, 43–64

Coles, J M, and Orme, B J, 1981 The Sweet Track 1980, *Somerset Levels Pap*, **7**, 6–12

Coles, J M, and Orme, B J, 1984 Ten excavations along the Sweet Track (3200 BC), *Somerset Levels Pap*, **10**, 5–45

Corfield, M, 1993 The first cross-channel ferry?, *Engl Heritage Conserv Bull*, **19**, 8–9

Corfield, M, 1994 Launch of Bronze Age boat appeal, *Perspective*, **6**, 2–3

Cowell, R W, and Innes, J B, 1994 *North West Wetlands Survey 1: the wetlands of Merseyside*, Lancaster Imprints, **2**, Lancaster: Lancaster Univ Archaeol Unit

Cracknell, S, 1996 *Roman Alcester series, volume 2. Roman Alcester: defences and defended area, Gateway Supermarket and Gas House Lane*, CBA Res Rep, **106**, York: CBA

Cracknell, S, and Hingley, R, 1993–4 Park Farm, Barford: excavation of a prehistoric settlement site, 1988, *Trans Birmingham Warwickshire Archaeol Soc*, **98**, 1–30

Crawford, O G S, 1933 An English hill-top town, *Antiquity*, **7**, 347–50

Creighton, J, 1990 *Excavations at Hawling Road*, unpubl rep

Cromarty, A M, Barclay, A, Lambrick, G, and Robinson, M, 2006 *Late Bronze Age ritual and habitation on a Thames eyot at Whitecross Farm, Wallingford: the archaeology of the Wallingford bypass, 1986–92*, Thames Valley Landscapes Monogr, **22**, Oxford: Oxford Univ Comm Archaeol

Crompton, E, 1953 Grow the soil to grow the grass, some pedological aspects of marginal land improvement, *Agriculture*, **60**, 301–38

Dalwood, C H, Buteux, V A, and Jackson, R A, 1992 Interim report on excavations at Deansway, Worcester, 1989–89, *Trans Worcestershire Archaeol Soc*, **13**, 121–8

Davies, S M, Bellamy, P S, Heaton, M J, and Woodward, P J, 2002 *Excavations at Alington Avenue, Fordington, Dorchester, Dorset 1984–87*, Dorset Natur Hist and Archaeol Soc Monogr, **15**, Dorchester: Dorset Natur Hist Archaeol Soc

Davies, S M, Stacey, L C, and Woodward, P J, 1986 Excavations at Alington Avenue, Fordington, Dorchester, 1984/5: Interim report, *Dorset Archaeol Natur Hist Soc Proc*, **107**, 101–10

Davis, S, 1993 A barrow full of cattle skulls, *Antiquity*, **67**, 12–22

Dent, J S, 1983 A summary of the excavations carried out in Garton and Wetwang Slack 1964–80, *E Riding Archaeol*, **7**, 1–14

Dent, J S, 1983 A summary of the excavations carried out in Garton and Wetwang Slack, *E Riding Archaeol*, **7**, 1–12

Dix, B, 1987 The Raunds Area project: second interim report, *Northamptonshire Archaeol*, **21**, 3–30

Dresser, Q, 1970 *A study of sampling and pretreatments of materials for radiocarbon dating*, unpubl PhD thesis, Queens Univ Belfast

Drewett, P, 1978 Neolithic Sussex, in *Archaeology in Sussex to AD 1500* (ed P Drewett), CBA Res Rep, **29**, 23–9 London: CBA

Drewett, P, 1980 Neolithic pottery in Sussex, *Sussex Archaeol Collect*, **118**, 23–30

Drewett, P, 1989 Anthropogenic soil erosion in prehistoric Sussex: excavations at West Heath and Ferring, 1984, *Sussex Archaeol Collect*, **127**, 11–29

Drewett, P L, 1985 The excavation of Barrows V–IX at West Heath, Harting, 1980, *Sussex Archaeol Collect*, **123**, 35–60

Drinkall, G, and Foreman, M, 1998 *The Anglo-Saxon cemetery at Castledyke South, Barton-on-Humber*, Sheffield Excavation Rep, **6**, Sheffield: Sheffield Academic Press

Edwards, K J, and Hirons, R K, 1982 Date of blanket peat initiation and rates of spread - a problem in research design, *Quat Newsletter*, **36**, 32–7

Ellis, P, 1993 *Beeston Castle, Cheshire, a report on the excavations 1968–85 by Laurence Keen and Peter Hough*, Engl Heritage Archaeol Rep, **23**, London: Engl Heritage

Evans, C, and Hodder, I, 2006a *A woodland archaeology: the Haddenham Project*, MacDonald Inst Archaeol Res, **1**, Cambridge: MacDonald Inst Archaeol Res

Evans, C, and Hodder, I, 2006b *Marshland communities and cultural landscape: The Haddenham Project*, MacDonald Inst Archaeol Res, **2**, Cambridge: MacDonald Inst Archaeol Res

Evans, C, Pollard, J, and Knight, M, 1999 Life in woods: tree-throws, 'settlement', and forest cognition, *Oxford J Archaeol*, **18**, 241–54

Evans, J G, 1971 Habitat change on the calcareous soils of Britain: the impact of Neolithic man, in *Economy and settlement in Neolithic and early Bronze Age and Europe* (ed D D A Simpson), 27–73, Leicester: Leicester Univ Press

Evans, J G, 1972 *Land snails in archaeology*, London: Seminar Press

Farley, M, 1986 Aylesbury: Iron Age hillfort to medieval town, *Curr Archaeol*, **101**, 187–9

Farrar, R, 1951 Archaeological fieldwork in Dorset in 1951, *Proc Dorset Nat Hist Arch Soc*, **73**, 85–115

Filmer-Sankey, W, and Pestell, T, 2001 *Snape Anglo-Saxon cemetery: excavations and surveys 1824–1992*, E Anglian Archaeol Rep, **95**, Ipswich: Suffolk County Council Archaeol Service

Filmer-Sankey, W, Cameron, E, Carnegie, S, and Pestell, T, 1991 *Snape Anglo-Saxon cemetery (SNP 007) 1991 Excavation Assessment Report*, unpubl rep, Suffolk Archaeol Unit for Engl Heritage

Fitzpatrick, A P, 1997 *Archaeological excavations on the route of the A27 Westhampnett bypass, West Sussex, 1992, volume 2: the Late Iron Age, Romano-British, and Anglo-Saxon cemeteries*, Wessex Archaeol Rep, **12**, Salisbury: Trust Wessex Archaeol

Fitzpatrick, A P, Powell, A B, and Allen, M J, 2008 *Archaeological excavations on the route of the A27 Westhampnett Bypass, West Sussex, 1992, volume 1: Late Upper Palaeolithic-Anglo-Saxon*, Wessex Archaeol Rep, **21**, Salisbury: Wessex Archaeol

French, C , and Pryor, F, 2005 *Archaeology and Environment of the Etton Landscape*, E Anglian Archaeol Rep, **109**, Peterborough: Fenland Archaeol Trust

French, C A I, 1988 The south-west fen dyke survey project, in Special section: survey, environment and excavation in the English Fenland, (eds D Hall and C Chippindale), *Antiquity*, **62**, 346–7

French, C A I, and Pryor, F M M, 1993 *The south-west fen dyke survey project 1982–86*, E Anglian Archaeol Rep, **59**, Peterborough: Fenland Archaeol Trust

Frere, S S, Hassall, M W C, and Tomlin, R S O, 1988 Roman Britain in 1987, *Britannia*, **19**, 447–8

Gaimster, D R M, Margeson, S, and Barry, T, 1989 Medieval Britain and Ireland in 1988, *Medieval Archaeol*, **33**, 215–17

Garton, D, 1987 Buxton, *Current Archaeol*, **9**, 250–3

Garton, D, 1991 Neolithic settlement in the Peak District: perspective and prospects, in *Recent developments in the archaeology of the Peak District* (eds R Hodges and K Smith), 3–21, Sheffield: Univ Sheffield

Garwood, P, 1999 *Grooved Ware in Britain and Ireland*, Neolithic Studies Group Seminar Pap, **3**, Oxford: Oxbow Books

Gear, A, and Turner, J, 1992 *Changing patterns of landuse during the late Holocene on Stainmore, northern Pennines*, unpubl typescript rep, Durham Univ

Gelfand, A E, and Smith, A F M, 1990 Sampling approaches to calculating marginal densities, *J Amer Stat Assoc*, **85**, 398–409

Gerloff, S, 1975 *The early Bronze Age daggers of Great Britain and a reconsideration of the Wessex Culture*, Prähistorishe Bronzefunde, **6**, Munich: C H Beck

Gibson, A, and Kinnes, I, 1997 On the urns of a dilemma: radiocarbon and the Peterborough Ware problem, *Oxford J Archaeol*, **16**, 65–72

Gillespie, R, Gowlett, J A J, Hall, E T, Hedges, R E M, and Perry, C, 1985 Radiocarbon dates from the Oxford AMS system: Archaeometry datelist 2, *Archaeometry*, **27**, 237–46

Gillespie, R, Hedges, R E M, and White, N R, 1983 The Oxford radiocarbon accelerator facility, *Radiocarbon*, **25**, 729–37

Gillespie, R, Hedges, R E M, and Wand, J O, 1984 Radiocarbon dating of bone by Accelerator Mass Spectrometry, *J Archaeol Sci*, **11**, 165–70

Gillespie, R, Hedges, R E M, and Humm, M J, 1986 Routine AMS dating of bone and shell proteins, *Radiocarbon*, **28**, 451–6

Griffith, F M, 1984 Archaeological investigations at Colliford Reservoir, Bodmin Moor, 1977–8, *Cornish Archaeol*, **23**, 49–139

Griffiths, S, 2011 *Chronological modelling of the Mesolithic/Neolithic transition in the North and Midlands of England*, unpubl PhD thesis, Cardiff Univ

Grinsell, L V, and Sherwin, G A, 1941 Isle of Wight barrows, *Proc Isle Wight Natur Hist Archaeol Soc*, **3**, 179–222

Halkon, P, and Millett, M, 1999 *Rural settlement and industry: studies in the Iron Age and Roman archaeology of lowland East Yorkshire*, Yorkshire Archaeol Rep, **4**, Leeds: Yorkshire Archaeol Soc, Roman Antiquities Section

Hall, D, Wells, C E, and Huckerby, E, 1995 *North West Wetlands Survey 2: the Wetlands of Greater Manchester*, Lancaster Imprints, **3**, Lancaster: Lancaster Univ Archaeol Unit

Hall, R, 1987 Ripon yarns 2: return to the Hill [Ailcy Hill, Ripon], *Bull York Archaeol Trust*, **12**, 15–22

Hall, R A, and Whyman, M, 1996 Settlement and monasticism at Ripon, North Yorkshire, from the 7th to 11th centuries AD, *Medieval Archaeol*, **40**, 62–150

Hall, R, and Whyman, M, 1986 Ripon yarns…getting to the root of the problem, *Bull York Archaeol Trust*, **11**, 29–37

Harcourt, R A, 1971 Animal bones from Durrington Walls, in *Durrington Walls excavations 1966–1968* (G J Wainwright and I H Longworth), Rep Res Comm Soc Antiq, **39**, 338–50 London: Soc Antiq London

Hardiman, M A, Fairchild, J E, and Longworth, G, 1992 Harwell radiocarbon measurements XI, *Radiocarbon*, **34**, 47–70

Harding, A F, and Lee, G E, 1987 *Henge monuments and related sites of Great Britian: air photographic evidence and catalogue*, BAR Brit Ser, **175**, Oxford: BAR

Harding, A F, and Ostoja-Zagorski, J, 1994 Prehistoric and early medieval activity on Danby Rigg, North Yorkshire, *Archaeol J*, **151**, 6–97

Harding, J, and Healy, F, 2007 *The Raunds Area Project: a Neolithic and Bronze Age landscape in Northamptonshire. Volume 1*, Swindon: Engl Heritage

Harding, J, and Healy, F, 2011 *The Raunds Area Project: a Neolithic and Bronze Age landscape in Northamptonshire. Volume 2. Supplementary Studies*, Swindon: Engl Heritage

Haslett, J, and Parnell, A C, 2008 A simple monotone process with application to radiocarbon-dated depth chronologies, *Applied Statistics*, **57**, 399–418

Havis, R, and Brooks, H, 2004 *Excavations at Stansted Airport, 1986–91*, E Anglian Archaeol Rep, **107**, Chelmsford: Essex County Council

Hayfield, C, 1987 *An archaeological survey of the Parish of Wharram Percy*, BAR Brit Ser, **172**, Oxford: BAR

Healy, F, 2004 Hambledon Hill and its implications, in *Monuments and Material Culture. Papers in Honour of an Avebury Archaeologist: Isobel Smith* (eds R Cleal and J Pollard), 15–38, East Knoyle: Hobnob Press

Healy, F, Harding, J, and Bayliss, A, 2007 Chapter 3: the development of the monuments, in *The Raunds Area Project: a Neolithic and Bronze Age landscape in Northamptonshire* (J Harding and F Healy), 37–198, Swindon: Engl Heritage

Hedges, R E M, 1981 Radiocarbon dating with an accelerator: review and preview, *Archaeometry*, **23**, 1–18

Hedges, R E M, and Law, I H, 1989 The radiocarbon dating of bone, *Applied Geochemistry*, **4**, 249–53

Hedges, R E M, and Van Klinken, G J, 1992 A review of current approaches to the pretreatment of bone for radiocarbon dating by AMS, *Radiocarbon*, **34**, 279–91

Hedges, R E M, Bronk, C R and Housley, R A 1989 The Oxford Accelerator Mass Spectrometry facility: technical developments in routine dating, *Archaeometry*, **31**, 99–113

Hedges, R E M, Housley, R A, Bronk Ramsey, C, and van Klinken, G J, 1993 Radiocarbon dates from the Oxford AMS system: Archaeometry datelist 16, *Archaeometry*, **35**, 147–67

Hedges, R E M, Housley, R A, Bronk Ramsey, C, and van Klinken, G J, 1994 Radiocarbon dates from the Oxford AMS system: Archaeometry datelist 18, *Archaeometry*, **36**, 337–74

Hedges, R E M, Housley, R A, Bronk Ramsey, C, and Van Klinken, G J, 1995 Radiocarbon dates from the Oxford AMS system: Archaeometry datelist 20, *Archaeometry*, **37**, 417–30

Hedges, R E M, Housley, R A, Bronk, C R, and van Klinken, G J, 1990 Radiocarbon dates from the Oxford AMS system: Archaeometry datelist 11, *Archaeometry*, **32**, 211–37

Hedges, R E M, Housley, R A, Bronk, C R, and van Klinken, G J, 1991a Radiocarbon dates from the Oxford AMS system: Archaeometry datelist 12, *Archaeometry*, **33**, 121–34

Hedges, R E M, Housley, R A, Bronk, C R, and van Klinken, G J, 1991b Radiocarbon dates from the Oxford AMS system: Archaeometry datelist 13, *Archaeometry*, **33**, 279–96

Hedges, R E M, Housley, R A, Bronk, C R, and van Klinken, G J, 1992 Radiocarbon dates from the Oxford AMS system: Archaeometry datelist 14, *Archaeometry*, **34**, 141–59

Hedges, R E M, Pettitt, P B, Bronk Ramsey, C, and Van Klinken, G J, 1996 Radiocarbon dates from the Oxford AMS system: Archaeometry datelist 22, *Archaeometry*, **38**, 391–415

Hedges, R E M, Pettitt, P B, Bronk Ramsey, C, and Van Klinken, G J, 1997 Radiocarbon dates from the Oxford AMS system: Archaeometry datelist 23, *Archaeometry*, **39**, 247–62

Heighway, C M, 1978 Excavations at Gloucester: fourth interim report, St Oswald's Priory 1975–6, *Antiq J*, **58**, 103–32

Heighway, C M, 1980 Excavations at Gloucester: 5th interim report: St Oswald's Priory 1977–8, *Antiq J*, **60**, 207–26

Heighway, C M, and Bryant, R M, 1999 *The Saxon Minster and medieval priory of St Oswald at Gloucester*, CBA Res Rep, **117**, York: CBA

Hey, G, 1991 Yarnton Worton Rectory Farm, *S Midlands Archaeol*, **21**, 86–92

Hey, G, 1994 Yarnton Cassington evaluation, *S Midlands Archaeol*, **24**, 49–52

Hey, G, 2004 *Yarnton: Saxon and medieval settlement and landscape: results of excavations 1990–1996*, Thames Valley Landscapes Monogr, **20**, Oxford: Oxford Univ School of Archaeol

Hey, G, and Muir, J, 1997 Cassington Worton Rectory Farm, *S Midlands Archaeol*, **27**, 55–8

Hey, G, Bayliss, A, and Boyle, A, 1999 Iron Age inhumation burials at Yarnton, Oxfordshire, *Antiquity*, **73**, 551–62

Hey, G, Booth, P, and Timby, J, 2011 *Yarnton: Iron Age and Romano-British settlement and landscape*, Thames Valley Landscapes Monogr, **35**, Oxford: Oxford Univ School Archaeol

Hillam, J, 1991 *The dating of oak timbers from Wootton Creek, Fishbourne, Isle of Wight - an interim report*, Ancient Monuments Lab Rep, **47/91**, London: Engl Heritage

Hillam, J, 1994 *The dating of oak timbers from the Wootton Quarr Survey, Isle of Wight*, Anc Mon Lab Rep, **10/1994**

Hillam, J, Groves, C M, Brown, D M, Baillie, M G L, Coles, J M, and Coles, B J, 1990 Dendrochronology of the English Neolithic, *Antiquity*, **64**, 210–20

Hillam, J, Morgan, R A, and Tyers, I, 1987 Sapwood estimates and the dating of short ring sequences, in *Applications of tree-ring studies* (ed R G W Ward), BAR Int Ser, **333**, 165–85, Oxford: BAR

Hodgkinson, D, Huckerby, E, Middleton, R, and Wells, C E, 2000 *North West Wetlands Survey 6: the lowland wetlands of Cumbria*, Lancaster Imprints, **8**, Lancaster: Lancaster Univ Archaeol Unit

Hoskins, W G, 1972 *A new survey of England: Devon*, new edn, Newton Abbot: David and Charles

Hough, P R, 1984 Beeston Castle, *Curr Archaeol*, **91**, 245–9

Howard-Davis, C, Stocks, C, and Innes, J B, 1988 *Peat and the past: a survey and assessment of the prehistory of the lowland wetlands of north-west England*, Lancaster: Lancaster Univ

Hughes, G, and Woodward, A, 1995 Part 1: a ring ditch and Neolithic pit complex at Meole Brace, Shrewsbury, in Excavations at Meole Brace 1990 and at Bromfield 1981–1991, *Shropshire Hist Archaeol*, **70**, 1–21

Hurst, J D, 1991 Major Saxon discoveries at Droitwich - excavations at the Upwich brine pit, *Curr Archaeol*, **126**, 252–5

Hurst, J D, 1997 *A multi-period salt production site at Droitwich: excavations at Upwich*, CBA Res Rep, **107**, York: CBA

Innes, J B, 1988 *Report on pollen analysis from Midgeholme Moss, Birdoswald, Cumbria*, unpubl report, Uni Liverpool

International Study Group, 1982 An inter-laboratory comparison of radiocarbon measurements in tree-rings, *Nature*, **298**, 619–23

Isle of Wight Council, 1994 *The Wootton-Quarr Survey: a summary of the field assessment. Draft 1*, Newport, Isle of Wight

Jackson, D A, 1994 Excavation of the hillfort defences at Hunsbury, Northampton, in 1952 and 1988, *Northamptonshire Archaeol*, **25**, 5–20

Jarvis, K, 1982 *Excavations in Christchurch 1969–80*, Dorset Natur Hist Archaeol Soc Monogr Ser, **5**, Dorset: Dorset Natur Hist Archaeol Soc

Jones, P, 1990a Neolithic Field Monuments and Occupation at Staines Road Farm, Shepperton, *Surrey Archaeol Soc Bull*, **252**, 6–8

Jones, P, 1990b Staines Road Farm: cropmark, *Surrey Archaeol Soc Bull*, **247**, 6

Jones, P, 2008 *A Neolithic ring ditch and later prehistoric features at Staines Road Farm, Shepperton*, SpoilHeap Monogr, **1**, SpoilHeap Publications

Jordan, D, Haddon-Reece, D, and Bayliss, A, 1994 *Radiocarbon dates from samples funded by English Heritage and dated before 1981*, London: Engl Heritage

Kerney, M P, 1977 A proposed zonation scheme for late-glacial and post-glacial deposit using land mollusca, *J Archaeol Sci*, **4**, 387–90

King, M, 1993 Bronze Age boat found at Dover, *Kent Archaeol Rev*, **111**, 21–3

Kinnes, I, 1979 *Round barrows and ring ditches in British Neolithic*, Brit Mus Occas Pap, **7**, London: Brit Mus

Kinnes, I, Gibson, A, Ambers, J, Bowman, S, Leese, M, and Boast, R, 1991 Radiocarbon dating and British Beakers: the British Museum programme, *Scott Archaeol Rev*, **8**, 35–78

Kromer, B, and Becker, B, 1993 German oak and pine ^{14}C calibration, 7200–9400 BC, *Radiocarbon*, **35**, 125–36

Kromer, B, Ambers, J, Baillie, M G L, Damon, P E, Hessaimer, V, Hoffman, J, Jöris, O, Levin, I, Manning, S W, McCormac, F G, van der Plicht, J, Spurk, M, Stuiver, M, and Weninger, B, 1996 Report: summary of the workshop "Aspects of high-precision radiocarbon calibration", *Radiocarbon*, **38**, 607–10

Kromer, B, Rhein, M, Bruns, M, Schoch-Fischer, B, Münnich, K-O, Stuiver, M, and Becker, B, 1986 Radiocarbon calibration data for the 6th to the 8th millennia BC, *Radiocarbon*, **28**, 954–60

Kromer, B, Manning, S W, Kuniholm, P I, Newton, M W, Spurk, M, and Levin, I, 2001 Regional ^{14}CO$_2$ offsets in the troposphere: magnitude, mechanisms, and consequences, *Science*, **294**, 2529–32

Kromer, B, Manning, S, Friedrich, M, Talamo, S, and Trano, N, 2010 ^{14}C calibration in the 2nd and 1st millennia BC Eastern Mediterranean Radiocarbon Comparison Project (EMRCP), *Radiocarbon*, **52**, 875–86

Kueppers, L M, Southon, J, Baer, P, and Harte, J, 2004 Dead wood biomass and turnover time, measured by radiocarbon, along a subalpine elevation gradient, *Oecologia*, **141**, 641–51

Lamb, H H, 1977 British quaternary studies: recent advances, in *The late quaternary history of the climate of the British Isles* (ed F W Shotton), 59–67, Oxford: Oxford Univ Press

Lambrick, G, 1992a Alluvial archaeology of the Holocene in the Upper Thames basin 1971–1991: a review, in *Alluvial archaeology in Britain* (eds S Needham and S Macklin), Oxbow Monogr, **27**, 209–26, Oxford: Oxbow Books

Lambrick, G, 1992b The development of late prehistoric and Roman farming on the Thames gravels, in *Developing landscapes of lowland Britain. The archaeology of the British gravels: a review* (eds M Fulford and E Nichols), Soc Antiq London Occas Pap, **14**, 78–105, London: Soc Antiq London

Lanting, J N, Aerts-Bijma, A T, and van der Plicht, J, 2001 Dating of cremated bones, *Radiocarbon*, **43**, 249–54

Law, I A, and Hedges, R E M, 1989 A semiautomated pretreatment system and the pretreatment of older and contaminated samples, *Radiocarbon*, **31**, 247–53

Lawrence, L, 1993 The prehistoric boat at Dover, *Kent Archaeol Soc News*, **24**,

Lawson, A J, 1980 The evidence for later Bronze Age settlement in Norfolk, in *Settlement and society in the British later Bronze Age* (J Barrett and R Bradley), BAR British Ser, **83**, 271–94 Oxford: Brit Archaeol Rep

Leach, P J, 1991 The Roman site at Fosse Lane, Shepton Mallet: an interim report of the 1990 archaeological investigations, *Proc Somerset Archaeol Natur Hist*, **134**, 47–55

Leach, P, and Evans, C J, 2001 *Fosse Lane, Shepton Mallet, 1990: excavation of a Romano-British roadside settlement in Somerset*, Britannia Monogr Ser, **18**, London: Soc for the Promotion of Roman Studies

Leah, M D, 1997 *North west wetlands survey 4: the wetlands of Cheshire*, Lancaster Imprints, **5**, Lancaster: Lancaster Univ Archaeol Unit

Leah, M D, Wells, C E, Stamper, P, Huckerby, E, and Welch, C, 1996 *The wetlands of Shropshire and Staffordshire*, North West Wetlands Survey, **5**, Lancaster: Lancaster Univ Archaeol Soc

Lewis, G D, 1966 Some radiocarbon dates for the Peak District, *Derbyshire Archaeol J*, **86**, 115–6

Liddle, P, 1987 Archaeology in Leicestershire and Rutland 1986, *Trans Leicestershire Archaeol and Hist Soc*, **61**, 87–91

Lindley, D V, 1985 *Making decisions*, 2nd edn, London: Wiley

Linick, T W, Jull, A J T, Toolin, L J, and Donahue, O J, 1986 Operation of the NSF Arizona Accelerator facility for radioisotope analysis and results from selective collaborative research projects, *Radiocarbon*, **28**, 522–33

Linick, T W, Suess, H E, and Becker, B, 1985 La Jolla measurements of radiocarbon in south German oak tree-ring chronologies, *Radiocarbon*, **27**, 20–32

Loader, R, Westmore, I, and Tomalin, D, 2002 *Time and tide: an archaeological survey of the Wootton-Quarr coast*, Newport, Isle of Wight: Isle of Wight Council

Lobb, S, 1992 Excavations at Shortheath Lane, Abbotts Farm, Sulhamstead, in *Excavations in the Burghfield Area, Berkshire: developments in the Bronze Age and Saxon periods* (C A Butterworth and S Lobb), Wessex Archaeol Rep, **1**, 72–8 Salisbury: Wessex Archaeol

Lobb, S J, and Morris, E L, 1994 Investigations of Bronze Age and Iron Age features at Riseley Farm, Swallowfield, *Berkshire Archaeol J*, **74**, 37–68

Locock, M, Trett, B, and Lawler, M, 2000 Further late prehistoric features on the foreshore at Chapeltump, Magor, Monmouthshire: Chapeltump II and the Upton trackway, *Studia Celtica*, **34**, 17–48

Longin, R, 1971 New method of collagen extraction for radiocarbon dating, *Nature*, **230**, 241–2

Longworth, I H, 1984 *Collared urns of the Bronze Age in Great Britain and Ireland*, Cambridge: Cambridge Univ Press

Losco-Bradley, P M, and Salisbury, C R, 1988 Saxon and Norman Fish Weir at Colwick, Nottinghamshire, in *Medieval fish, fisheries and fishponds in England* (ed M Aston), BAR Brit Ser, **182**, 329–51 Oxford: BAR

Machin, M L, 1971 Further excavations of the enclosure at Swine Sty, Big Moor, Baslow, *Trans Hunter Archaeol Soc*, **10**, 5–13

Machin, M L, and Beswick, P, 1975 Further excavations of the enclosure at Swine Sty, Big Moor, Baslow and report on the shale industry at Swine Sty, *Trans Hunter Archaeol Soc*, **10**, 204–11

Mackreth, D, 1984 Recent Work on Monastic Peterborough, *Durobrivae*, **9**, 18–21

Mackreth, D F, 1983a Peterborough, cathedral cloisters, in Archaeology in Northamptonshire 1982, (ed A E Brown), *Northamptonshire Archaeol*, **18**, 177

Mackreth, D F, 1983b Peterborough, Cathedral, in Medieval Britain and Ireland in 1982, (eds S M Youngs, J Clark, and T B Barry), *Medieval Archaeol*, **27**, 168–9

Macphail, R I, and Goldberg, P, 1990 The micromorphology of tree subsoil hollows: their significance to soil science and archaeology, in *Soil Micromorphology: a basic and applied science* (L A Douglas), Developments in Soil Science, **19**, 425–9 Amsterdam: Elsevier

Malim, T, 1993 An investigation of multi-period cropmarks at Manor Farm, Harston, *Proc Cambridge Antiq Soc*, **82**, 11–54

Malim, T, 1996 New evidence on the Cambridgeshire Dykes and Worsted Street Roman road, *Proc Cambridge Antiq Soc*, **1996**, 27–122

Malim, T, 2005 *Stonea and the Roman Fens*, Stroud: Tempus

Manby, T G, Moorhouse, S, and Ottaway, P, 2003 *The archaeology of Yorkshire: an assessment at the beginning of the 21st century*, Yorkshire Archaeol Soc Occas Pap, **3**, Leeds: Yorkshire Archaeol Soc

Mann, W B, 1983 An international reference material for radiocarbon dating, *Radiocarbon*, **25**, 519–27

Marshall P D, 2004 Radiocarbon determinations, in *Trethurgy: excavations at Trethurgy Round, St Austell: community and status in Roman and post-Roman Cornwall* (H Quinnell), 161–5

Marshall, P D, 2006 Phasing and chronology, in *Marshland communities and cultural landscapes from the Bronze Age to present day: the Haddenham project, volume 2*, (C Evans and I Hodder), 267–9, Cambridge: McDonald Instit Archaeol Res

Marshall, P, Bayliss, A, Wall, I, Bronk Ramsey, C, and van der Plicht, J, 2011 Radiocarbon dating, in A Neolithic cairn at Whitwell, Derbyshire (B Vyner and I Wall), *Derbyshire Archaeol J*, **131**, 30–40

Martin, E A, 1988 Swales Fen, Suffolk: a Bronze Age cooking pit?, *Antiquity*, **62**, 358–9

Martin, E A, and Murphy, P, 1988 West Row Fen, Suffolk: a Bronze Age fen-edge settlement site, *Antiquity*, **62**, 353–8

Mays, S, 1991 *The medieval burials from the Blackfriars Friary, School Street, Ipswich, Suffolk (excavated 1983–85)*, Anc Mon Lab Rep, **16/91**, London: Engl Heritage

Mays, S, Crane-Kramer, G, and Bayliss, A, 2002 Two probable cases of treponemal disease of Medieval date from England, *American J Physical Anthropology*, **120**, 133–43

Mays, S, Harding, C, and Heighway, C, 2007 *Wharram: a study of settlement on the Yorkshire Wolds, 11: the churchyard,* York Univ Archaeol Pub, **13**, York: York Univ Dept Archaeol

McAvoy, F, 1991 Godmanchester, Cambridgeshire, *Conserv Bull,* **14**, 16–8

McCormac, F G, Baillie, M, Pilcher, J, and Kalin, R, 1995 Location-dependent differences in the ¹⁴C content of wood, *Radiocarbon,* **37**, 395–407

McDonnell, R R J, 1985 *Archaeological survey of the Somerset Claylands: report on survey work, 1984–85,* unpubl rep, Somerset County Council

McDonnell, R R J, 1986 *Archaeological survey of the Somerset Claylands: report on survey work, 1985–86,* unpubl rep, Somerset County Council

Meadows, J, Farley, M, Jones, G, Bronk Ramsey, C, and Cook, G 2012 *Iron Age ritual, a hillfort and evidence for a minster at Aylesbury, Buckinghamshire,* Oxford: Oxbow Books

Mercer, J, 1988 Hambledon Hill, Dorset, England, in *Enclosures and defences in the Neolithic of western Europe* (eds C Burgess, P Topping, C Mordant, and M Maddison), BAR Int Ser, **403**, 89–106 Oxford: Brit Archaeol Rep

Mercer, J, 1999 The origins of warfare in the British Isles, in *Ancient Warfare* (eds J Carman and A Harding), 143–56, Stroud: Sutton Publishing Ltd

Mercer, R, 1986 *Excavation of a Neolithic enclosure at Helman Tor, Lanlivery, Cornwall, 1986: interim report,* Dept Archaeol, Univ Edinburgh, Project Pap, **4**

Mercer, R J, 1980 *Hambledon Hill: a Neolithic landscape,* Edinburgh: Edinburgh Univ Press

Mercer, R J, 1985 A Neolithic fortress and funerary center, *Sci American,* **252/3**, 76–83

Mercer, R, and Healy, F, 2008 *Hambledon Hill, Dorset, England: excavation and survey of a Neolithic monument and its surrounding landscape,* Swindon: Engl Heritage

Middleton, R, 1991 North West Wetlands Survey radiocarbon dates for 1990/91, in *North West Wetlands Survey Annual Report,* 51–2, Lancaster: Lancaster Univ Archaeol Unit

Middleton, R, 1992 *Three animal excavations in Cumbria: North West Wetlands Survey Annual Report 1992,* unpubl rep, for Engl Heritage

Middleton, R, Wells, C E, and Huckerby, E, 1995 *The wetlands of North Lancashire,* North West Wetlands Survey, **3**, Lancaster: Lancaster Univ Archaeol Unit

Milne, G, and Richards, J D, 1992 *Wharram: a study of settlement on the Yorkshire Wolds, 7: two Anglo-Saxon buildings and associated finds,* Univ York Archaeol Pub, **9**, York: Univ York, Department of Archaeol

Moffett, L C, 1991 *Plant economy at Burton Dassett, a deserted medieval village in south Warwickshire,* Anc Mon Lab Rep, **111/91**, London: Engl Heritage

Mook, W G, 1986 Business meeting: Recommendations/Resolutions adopted by the Twelfth International Radiocarbon Conference, *Radiocarbon,* **28**, 799

Mook, W G, and Waterbolk, H T, 1985 *Radiocarbon Dating,* Handbook for Archaeologists, **3**, Strasbourg: European Science Foundation

Mook, W G, and van der Plicht, J, 1999 Reporting ¹⁴C activities and concentrations, *Radiocarbon,* **41**, 227–40

Mullin, D, 2001 Remembering, forgetting, and the invention of tradition: burial and natural places in the English early Bronze Age, *Antiquity,* **75**, 533–7

Murphy, P, 1988 *The Stumble (Site 28A, Blackwater Estuary, Essex): carbonised Neolithic plant remains,* Ancient Monuments Lab Rep, **157/1988**, London: Engl Heritage

Murphy, P, 1989 Carbonised Neolithic plant remains from The Stumble, an intertidal site in the Blackwater Estuary, Essex, England, *Circaea,* **6**, 21–38

Naylor, J C, and Smith, A F M, 1988 An archaeological inference problem, *J American Statistical Assoc,* **83**, 588–95

Needham, S P, 1996 Chronology and periodisation in the British Bronze Age, *Acta Archaeologica,* **67**, 121–40

Neve, J, 1999 *Dendrochronology of the Flag Fen Basin,* Anc Mon Lab Rep, **58/1999**, London: Engl Heritage

Noakes, J E, Kim, S M, and Stipp, J J, 1965 Chemical and counting advances in Liquid Scintillation Age dating, in *Proceedings of the sixth international conference on radiocarbon and tritium dating* (eds E A Olsson and R M Chatters), 68–92, Washington DC

Nowakowski, J A, 1991 Trethellan Farm: excavation of a lowland Bronze Age settlement and Iron Age cemetery, *Cornish Archaeol,* **30**, 52–242

Oldfield, F, and Statham, D C, 1965 Stratigraphy and Pollen Analysis on Cockerham and Pilling Mosses, North Lancashire, *Memoirs Proc Manchester Lit Phil Soc,* **107**, 1–16

Olsson, I U, 1970 The use of Oxalic acid as a Standard, in *Radiocarbon variations and absolute chronology, Nobel symposium, 12th proceedings* (ed I U Olsson), 17, New York: Wiley

Olsson, I U, 1979 The importance of the pretreatment of wood and charcoal samples, in *Radiocarbon Dating: Proceedings of the 9th International Radiocarbon Conference,* 135–46, Los Angeles and San Diego: Univ California Press

Orme, B J, 1982 The use of radiocarbon dates from the Somerset Levels, *Somerset Levels Pap,* **8**, 9–25

Oswald, A, Dyer, C, and Barber, M, 2001 *The creation of monuments: Neolithic causewayed enclosures in the British Isles,* Swindon: Engl Heritage

Otlet, R L, 1977 Harwell radiocarbon measurements II, *Radiocarbon,* **19**, 400–23

Otlet, R L, 1979 An assessment of laboratory errors in liquid scintillation methods of ¹⁴C dating, in *Proceedings of the ninth International Radiocarbon Conference* (eds R Berger and H E Suess), 256–67, Univ California Press

Otlet, R L, and Evans, G V, 1983 Progress in the application of miniature gas counters to radiocarbon dating of small samples, in *Proceedings of the First International Symposium ¹⁴C and Archaeology* (eds W G Mook and H T Waterbok), *PACT,* **8**, 213–22, Strasbourg: Council of Europe

Otlet, R L, and Polach, H A, 1990 Improvements in the precision of radiocarbon dating through recent developments in liquid scintillation counters, *Proceedings of the Second International Symposium: ¹⁴C and Archaeology* (eds W G Mook and H T Waterbolk), *PACT*, **29**, 225–38, Strasbourg (Council of Europe)

Otlet, R L, and Slade, B S, 1974 Harwell radiocarbon measurements I, *Radiocarbon*, **16**, 178–91

Otlet, R L, and Warchal, R M, 1978 Liquid scintillation counting of low-level ¹⁴C dating, *Liquid Scintillation Counting*, **5**, 210–18

Otlet, R L, Huxtable, G, and Sanderson, D C W, 1986 The development of practical systems for ¹⁴C measurement in small samples using miniature counters, *Radiocarbon*, **28**, 603–14

Otlet, R L, Huxtable, G, Evans, G V, Humphreys, D G, Short, T D, and Conchie, S J, 1983 Development and operation of the Harwell small counter facility for the measurement of ¹⁴C in very small samples, *Radiocarbon*, **25**, 565–75

Otlet, R L, Walker, A J, Hewson, A D, and Burleigh, R, 1980 ¹⁴C interlaboratory comparison in the UK: experiment design, preparation, and preliminary results, *Radiocarbon*, **22**, 936–46

Owen, E, and Frost, M, 2000 *The Dover Bronze Age boat gallery guide*, Dover: Dover District Council

Palmer, R, 1976a Interrupted ditch enclosures in Britain: the use of aerial photography for comparative studies, *Proc Prehist Soc*, **42**, 161–86

Parfitt, K, 1993a The Dover boat, *Curr Archaeol*, **12**, 4–8

Parfitt, K, 1993b *Dover Bronze Age boat*, Canterbury: Canterbury Archaeol Trust

Parfitt, K, and Bates, M, 1993 The discovery of the Dover Bronze Age boat, *Rescue News*, **59**, 3

Parnell, A C, Haslett, J, Allen, J R M, Buck, C E, and Huntley, B, 2008 A flexible approach to assessing synchroneity of past events using Bayesian reconstructions of sedimentation history, *Quat Sci Rev*, **27**, 1872–85

Parry, C, 1998 Excavations near Birdlip, Cowley, Gloucestershire, 1987–8, *Trans Bristol Glos Archaeol Soc*, **116**, 25–92

Parry, C, and Rawes, B, 1989 Cowley, Birdlip Bypass, in Archaeological Review No 13, *Trans Bristol and Glos Archaeol Soc*, **107**, 254

Parry, S, 2006 *Raunds Area Survey: an archaeological study of the landscape of Raunds, Northamptonshire 1985–94*, Oxford: Oxbow Books

Pearson, G W, 1979 Precise ¹⁴C measurement by liquid scintillation counting, *Radiocarbon*, **21**, 1–21

Pearson, G W, 1984 *The development of high-precision ¹⁴C measurement and its application to archaeological time-scale problems*, unpubl PhD thesis, Queen's Univ Belfast

Pearson, G W, 1986 Precise calendrical dating of known growth-period samples, using a 'curve-fitting' technique, *Radiocarbon*, **28**, 292–9

Pearson, G W, 1987 How to cope with calibration, *Antiquity*, **61**, 98–103

Pearson, G W, and McCormac, F G, 2003 Radiocarbon dating, in *Haughmond Abbey, Shropshire* (T Pearson), Archaeol Investigation Rep Ser, **AI/10/2003**, 360 York: Engl Heritage

Pearson, G W, and Stuiver, M, 1986 High-precision calibration of the radiocarbon timescale, AD 500–2500 BC, *Radiocarbon*, **28**, 839–62

Pearson, G W, Becker, B, and Qua, F, 1993 High-precision ¹⁴C measurements of German and Irish oaks to show the natural ¹⁴C variations from 7890 to 5000 BC, *Radiocarbon*, **35**, 93–104

Pearson, G W, Pilcher, J R, Baillie, M G L, Corbett, D M, and Qua, F, 1986 High-precision ¹⁴C measurement of Irish oaks to show the natural ¹⁴C variations from AD 1840 to 5210 BC, *Radiocarbon*, **28**, 911–34

Pearson, T, 2003 *Haughmond Abbey, Shropshire*, Archaeol Investigation Rep Ser, **AI/10/2003**, York: Engl Heritage

Pennington, W, 1975 The effect of man on the environment in North-West England: the use of absolute pollen diagrams, in *The effect of man on the landscape: the Highland Zone* (eds J G Evans, S Limbrey, and H Cleere), CBA Res Rep, **11**, 74–86 CBA

Piggott, S, 1973a The Wessex Culture, in *The history of Wiltshire* (ed E Crittall), Victoria County History of Wiltshire, **1 (2)**, 352–75, Oxford: Clarendon Press

Piggott, S, 1973b The final phase on bronze technology, in *The history of Wiltshire* (ed E Crittall), Victoria County History of Wiltshire, **1 (2)**, 376–407, Oxford: Clarendon Press

Pilcher, J R, Hall, V A, and McCormac, F G, 1995 Dates of Holocene Icelandic volcanic eruptions from tephra layers in Irish peats, *The Holocene*, **5**, 103-10

Polach, H A, 1972, Cross checking of the NBS oxalic acid and secondary laboratory radiocarbon dating standards, *Proceedings of the 8th International Radiocarbon Dating Conference, Lower Hutt, New Zealand* (eds Rafter, T A and Grant-Taylor, T) 688–717, Royal Soc New Zealand, Wellington

Powlesland, D, 1991 *Archaeological excavations 1987-90: an interim report on the Anglo-Saxon village at west Heslerton, North Yorkshire*, Medieval Settlement Res Group Annual Rep, **5**

Powlesland, D J, 1998 West Heslerton - the Anglian settlement: assessment of potential for analysis and updated project design, *Internet Archaeol*, **5**, http://intarch.ac.uk/journal/issue5/westhes_index.html

Powlesland, D J, 2003b *25 years of archaeological research on the sands and gravels of Heslerton*, Yedingham: Landscape Res Centre

Powlesland, D J, forthcoming *West Heslerton: the excavation of the Anglian settlement*, Yedingham: Landscape Res Centre

Powlesland, D J, and Price, J, 1988 Approaches to the excavation and interpretation of the Romano-British landscape in the Vale of Pickering, in *Recent research in Roman Yorkshire: studies in honour of Mary Kitson Clarke* (ed P R Wilson), BAR, **193**, 139–51 Oxford: BAR

Powlesland, D J, Haughton, C A, and Hanson, J H, 1986 Excavations at Heslerton, North Yorkshire 1978–82, *Archaeol J*, **143**, 53–173

Powlesland, D, and Haughton, C, 1999 *West Heslerton: the Anglian cemetery*, Landscape Res Centre Monogr, **1**, Yedingham: Landscape Res Centre

PPG16 1990 *Planning Policy Guidance: Archaeology and Planning*, Department of the Environment

Preece, R C, 1994 Radiocarbon dates from the 'Allerød Soil' in Kent, *Proc Geol Ass*, **105**, 111–23

Pryor, F, 1992 Introduction to current research at Flag Fen, Peterborough, *Antiquity*, **66**, 439

Pryor, F, 2001 *The Flag Fen basin: archaeology and environment of a fenland landscape*, Engl Heritage Archaeol Rep, London: Engl Heritage

Quinnell, H, 1992 Radiocarbon dating, in Excavations at a Romano-British round: Reawla, Gwinear, Cornwall, *Cornish Archaeol*, **31**, 92–4

Quinnell, H, 2004 *Trethurgy: excavations at Trethurgy Round, St Austell: community and status in Roman and post-Roman Cornwall*, Truro: Cornwall County Council

Rahtz, P, Hirst, S, and Wright, S M, 2000 *Cannington Cemetery Excavations 1962–3 of prehistoric, Roman, post-Roman, and later features at Cannington Park Quarry, near Bridgwater, Somerset*, Britannia Monogr Ser, **17**, London: Society for the Promotion of Roman Studies

Ralph, E K, Michael, H N, and Han, M C, 1973 Radiocarbon dates and reality, *MASCA Newsletter*, **9**, 1–20

Ratcliffe, J, 1991 *Autumn 1990*, Fieldwork in Scilly, Truro: Cornwall Archaeol Unit

Ratcliffe, J, and Straker, V, 1996 *The early environment of Scilly: palaeoenvironmental assessment of cliff-face and intertidal deposits, 1989–1993*, Truro: Cornwall County Council, Cornwall Archaeol Unit

RCHME, 1970 *An inventory of the historical monuments in the county of Dorset, part 3: 2, South-east*, Roy Comm Hist Monuments Engl

RCHME, 1979 *Long Barrows in Hampshire and the Isle of Wight*, London: HMSO

Rees-Jones, J, 1995 *Optical dating of selected archaeological sediments*, unpubl DPhil thesis, Univ of Oxford

Reimer, P J, Baillie, M G L, Bard, E, Bayliss, A, Beck, J W, Bertrand, C J H, Blackwell, P G, Buck, C E, Burr, G S, Cutler, K B, Damon, P E, Edwards, R L, Fairbanks, R G, Friedrich, M, Guilderson, T P, Hogg, A G, Hughen, K A, Kromer, B, McCormac, F G, Manning, S, Bronk Ramsey, C, Reimer, R W, Remmele, S, Southon, J R, Stuiver, M, Talamo, S, Taylor, F W, van der Plicht, J, and Weyhenmeyer, C E, 2004 IntCal04 Terrestrial Radiocarbon Age Calibration, 0–26 cal kyr BP, *Radiocarbon*, **46**, 1029–58

Reimer, P J, Baillie, M G L, Bard, E, Bayliss, A, Beck, J W, Blackwell, P G, Bronk Ramsey, C, Buck, C E, Burr, G S, Edwards, R L, Friedrich, M, Grootes, P M, Guilderson, T P, Hajdas, I, Heaton, T J, Hogg, A G, Hughen, K A, Kaiser, K F, Kromer, B, McCormac, F G, Manning, S W, Reimer, R W, Richards, D A, Southon, J R, Talamo, S, Turney, C S M,

van der Plicht, J, and Weyhenmeyer, C E, 2009 IntCal09 and Marine09 radiocarbon age calibration curves, 0–50,0000 Years cal BP, *Radiocarbon*, **51**, 1111–50

Richardson, G G S, and Preston, F L, 1969 Excavations at Swine Sty, Big Moor, Baslow, 1967, *Trans Hunter Archaeol Soc*, **9**, 261–3

Roberts, I, Stead, I M, Rush, P, Sitch, B J, McHugh, M, and Milles, A, 2005 Excavation of the Henge Bank and Ditch, 1991: a summary report, in *Ferrybridge Henge: the ritual landscape: Archaeological investigations at the site of the Holmfield Interchange of the A1 motorway* (ed I Roberts), Yorkshire Archaeol Ser, **10**, 223–235 Leeds: Archaeol Services WYAS

Robertson-Mackay, R, 1987 The Neolithic causewayed enclosure at Staines, Surrey: excavations 1961–63, *Proc Prehist Soc*, **53**, 23–128

Robinson, B, 1992 *Excavations at Brent Ditch 1992 - an interim report*, unpubl rep, Cambridgeshire County Council Archaeol Section

Rodwell, W, 2001 *The archaeology of Wells Cathedral: excavations and structural studies, 1978-93*, Engl Heritage Archaeol Rep, **21**, London: Engl Heritage

Rodwell, W J, 1982 From Mausoleum to Minster: the early development of Wells Cathedral, in *The Early Church in Western Britain and Ireland: studies presented to C A Ralegh Radford arising from a conference organised in his honour by the Devon Archaeological Society and Exeter City Museum* (ed S Pearce), BAR Brit Ser, **102**, 49–59 Oxford: BAR

Rodwell, W J, 1987 *Wells Cathedral: excavations and discoveries*, 3rd Ed, Somerset: Friends of Wells Cathedral

Rodwell, W, and Atkins, C, 2011 *St Peter's, Barton-upon-Humber, Lincolnshire: a parish church and its community. Volume 1: history, archaeology and architecture*, Oxford: Oxbow Books

Rodwell, W, and Rodwell, K A, 1982 St Peter's Church, Barton-upon-Humber: excavation and structural study 1978–81, *Antiq J*, **62**, 283–315

Rose, P, 1992a Stannon and King Arthur's Hall, Bodmin Moor, in Recent work by the Cornwall Archaeological Unit, *Cornish Archaeol*, **31**, 166–7

Rose, P, 1992b *Archaeological investigations of a water pipeline adjacent to King Arthur's Hall and Stannon, Bodmin Moor, Cornwall*, unpubl rep, Cornwall Archaeol Unit

Rozanski, K, 1991 *Report on the International Atomic Energy Agency consultants' group meeting on C-14 reference materials for radiocarbon laboratories, February 18-20, 1991, Vienna, Austria*, unpubl report, Vienna: IAEA

Rozanski, K, Stichler, W, Gonfiantini, R, Scott, E M, Beukens, R P, Kromer, B, and van der Plicht, J, 1992 The IAEA ¹⁴C intercomparison exercise 1990, *Radiocarbon*, **34**, 506–19

Rudling, D, 2001 Chanctonbury Ring revisited: the excavations of 1988–1991, *Sussex Archaeol Collect*, **139**, 75–121

Rudling, D, 2002 *Downland settlement and land-use: the archaeology of the Brighton Bypass*, UCL Fld Archaeol Unit Monogr, **1**, Institute of Archaeol, Univ College London

Russel, A D, 1990 Two Beaker burials from Chilbolton, Hampshire, *Proc Prehist Soc*, **56**, 153–72

Salisbury, C R, 1980 The Trent, the story of a river, *Curr Archaeol*, **74**, 88–91

Salisbury, C R, 1984 Flandrian courses of the River Trent at Colwick, Nottinghamshire, *Mercian Geologist*, **9**, 189–207

Salisbury, C R, 1991 Primitive British fishweirs, in *Waterfront archaeology: proceedings of the third international conference on waterfront archaeology held at Bristol 23–26 September 1988* (eds G L Good, R H Jones, and M W Ponsford), CBA Res Rep, **74**, 76–87, London: CBA

Salisbury, C R, 1992 The archaeological evidence for palaeochannels in the Trent Valley, in *Alluvial Archaeology in Britain: Proceeding of a Conference sponsored by the RMC Group plc 3–5 January 1991, British Museum* (eds S Needham and M G Macklin), Oxbow Monogr, **27**, 155–62, Oxford: Oxbow Books

Salisbury, C R, 1995 The excavation of Hemington Fields, *Curr Archaeol*, **145**, 34–5

Salisbury, C R, 1996 Hemington Fields - a Medieval landscape, *Newswarp*, **19**, 24–32

Scaife, R, 2004 Pollen analysis, in *Gravelly Guy, Stanton Harcourt: the development of a prehistoric and Romano-British landscape* (eds G Lambrick and T Allen), Thames Valley Landscapes Monogr, **21**, 417–9, Oxford: Oxford Univ School of Archaeol

Scott, E M, Aitchison, T C, Harkness, D D, Cook, G T, and Baxter, M S, 1990 An overview of all three stages of the international radiocarbon intercomparison, *Radiocarbon*, **32**, 309–19

Scott, E M, 2003 The Third International Radiocarbon Intercomparison (TIRI) and the Fourth International Radiocarbon Intercomparision (FIRI) 1990 – 2002: results, analyses, and conclusions, *Radiocarbon*, **45**, 135–408

Shore, J S, 1988 *The radiocarbon dating of peat fractions in relation to pollen analysis*, unpubl PhD thesis, Univ Leeds

Shotton, F W, and Williams, R E G, 1971 Birmingham University radiocarbon dates V, *Radiocarbon*, **13**, 141–56

Simmons, I G, and Innes, J B, 1987 Mid-Holocene adaptations and later Mesolithic forest disturbance in northern England, *J Archaeol Sci*, **14**, 385–403

Slack, C, 1993 The discovery and recovery of the Dover Bronze Age boat, *Conserv News*, **1993**, 14–6

Slota Jr, P J, Jull, A J T, Linick, T W and Toolin, L J, 1987 Preparation of small samples for ^{14}C accelerator targets by catalytic reduction of CO, *Radiocarbon*, **29**, 303–6

Smith, G H, 1991 Pave Lane triple ditched Iron Age enclosure, Chetwynd Aston, Shropshire, 1990, *W Midlands Archaeol*, **34**, 35–45

Smith, R J C, 1997 *Excavations along the route of the Dorchester by-pass, Dorset (1986–8)*, Wessex Archaeol Rep, **11**, Salisbury: Trust for Wessex Archaeol

Stamper, P A, and Croft, R A, 2000 *Wharram: a study of settlement on the Yorkshire Wolds, 8: the south manor area*, York Univ Archaeol Pub, **10**, York: Univ York, Dept Archaeol

Stanford, S C, 1982 Bromfield, Shropshire - Neolithic, Beaker, and Bronze Age sites 1966–79, *Proc Prehist Soc*, **48**, 279–320

Stanford, S C, 1985 Bromfield excavations - from Neolithic to Saxon times, *Trans Shropshire Archaeol Soc*, **64**, 1–7

Stanford, S C, 1995 A Cornovian Farm and Saxon cemetery at Bromfield, Shropshire, *Trans Shropshire Archaeol Soc*, **70**, 95–170

Stenhouse, M J, and Baxter, M S, 1983 ^{14}C dating reproducibility: evidence from routine dating of archaeological samples, *PACT*, **8**, 147–61

Straker, V, 1986 *Roadford Reservoir, Devon - potential for environmental archaeology*, unpubl rep, for Devon County Council

Stuiver, M, and Kra, R S, 1986 Editorial comment, *Radiocarbon*, **28(2B)**, ii

Stuiver, M, and Pearson, G W, 1986 High-precision calibration of the radiocarbon timescale, AD 1950–2500 BC, *Radiocarbon*, **28**, 805–38

Stuiver, M, and Polach, H A, 1977 Reporting of ^{14}C data, *Radiocarbon*, **19**, 355–63

Stuiver, M, and Reimer, P J, 1986 A computer program for radiocarbon age calculation, *Radiocarbon*, **28**, 1022–30

Stuiver, M, and Reimer, P J, 1993 Extended ^{14}C data base and revised CALIB 3.0 ^{14}C age calibration program, *Radiocarbon*, **35**, 215–30

Stuiver, M, Kromer, B, Becker, B, and Ferguson, C W, 1986 Radiocarbon age calibration back to 13,300 years BP and ^{14}C age-matching of German oak and US bristlecone pine chronologies, *Radiocarbon*, **28**, 969–79

Stuiver, M, Reimer, P J, Bard, E, Burr, G S, Hughen, K A, Kromer, B, McCormac, G, van der Plicht, J, and Spurk, M, 1998a INTCAL 98 radiocarbon age calibration 24,000–0 cal BP, *Radiocarbon*, **40**, 1041–84

Stuiver, M, Reimer, P J, and Braziunas, T T, 1998b High-precision radiocarbon age calibration for terrestrial and marine samples, *Radiocarbon*, **40**, 1127–51

Suess, H E, 1967 Bristlecone pine calibration of the radiocarbon time scale from 4100 BC to 1500 BC, in *Radiocarbon dating and methods of low level counting*, 143–51, Vienna: IAEA

Switsur, R, 1972 Combustion bombs for radiocarbon dating, in *Proceedings of the 8th International ^{14}C Conference, Vol 1, B11–B23*, 11–23, Wellington: Royal Soc New Zealand

Switsur, V R, Burleigh, R, Meeks, N, and Cleland, J M, 1974 A new sample combustion bomb for radiocarbon dating, *International J Applied Radiation and Isotopes*, **25**, 113–7

Tamers, M A, 1965 Routine carbon-14 dating using liquid scintillation techniques, in *Radiocarbon and tritium dating: proceedings of the sixth international conference on radiocarbon and tritium dating* (eds R M Chatters and E A Olson), 53–67, Washington D C

Taylor, M P, Macklin, M G, and Hudson-Edwards, K, 2000

River sedimentation and fluvial response to Holocene environmental change in the Yorkshire Ouse Basin, northern England, *The Holocene*, **10**, 201–12

Taylor, M, and French, C, 1985 Desiccation and destruction: the immediate effects of de-watering at Etton, *Oxford J Archaeol*, **4**, 139–55

Thomas, K D, 1989 Vegetation of the British chalklands in the Flandrian period: a response to Bush, *J Archaeol Sci*, **15**, 549–53

Thomas, N, 2005 *Snail Down, Wiltshire. The Bronze Age Barrow Cemetery and Related Earthworks, in the parishes of Collingbourne Ducis and Collingbourne Kingston: Excavations, 1953, 1955 and 1957*, Wiltshire Archaeol Natur Hist Soc Monogr, **3**, Devizes: Wiltshire Archaeol Natur Hist Soc

Thorley, A, 1981 Pollen analytical evidence relating to the vegetation history of the Chalk, *J Biogeogr*, **8**, 93–106

Tomalin, R S O, 1973 The Roman aqueduct at Bowes, Yorkshire N R, *Yorkshire Archaeol J*, **45**, 181–4

Tooley, M J, 1978 *Sea-level changes, North West England during the Flandrian stage*, Oxford: Oxford Univ Press

Tooley, M J, Middleton, R, and Innes, J B, forthcoming *The wetlands of south-west Lancashire*, Lancaster: Lancaster Univ

Treen, C, and Atkin, A, 2005 *Wharram: a study of settlement on the Yorkshire Wolds, 10: water resources and their management*, York Univ Archaeol Publ, **12**, York: Univ York, Dept Archaeol

Turner, J, and Hodgson, J, 1981 Studies in the vegetation history of the north Pennines, *J Ecol*, **69**, 171–88

Tyers, I, 2001 *The tree-ring analysis of coffin timbers excavated at the church of St Peter, Barton on Humber, North Lincolnshire*, Centre for Archaeol, **48/2001**, pp?

Vyner, B, 2001 *Stainmore: the archaeology of a north Pennine Pass*, Tees Archaeol Monogr Ser, **1**, Hartlepool and London: Tees Archaeol and Engl Heritage

Vyner, B, and Wall, I, 2011 A Neolithic cairn at Whitwell, Derbyshire, *Derbyshire Archaeol J*, **131**, 1–132

Wainwright, G J, 1979 *Mount Pleasant, Dorset: Excavations 1970–71*, Soc Antiq Res Rep, **37**, London: Soc Antiq

Wait, G A, 1991 *Fleam Dyke, 1991 - Interim Report: report no 49*, unpubl rep, Cambridgeshire Archaeol

Walker, A J, and Otlet, R L, 1988 Harwell radiocarbon measurements VI, *Radiocarbon*, **30**, 297–317

Walker, A J, Williams, N, and Otlet, R L, 1990 Harwell radiocarbon measurements VIII, *Radiocarbon*, **32**, 165–96

Walker, A J, Young, A W, and Otlet, R L, 1991a Harwell radiocarbon measurements X, *Radiocarbon*, **33**, 87–113

Walker, A J, Young, A W, Keyzor, R S, and Otlet, R L, 1991b Harwell radiocarbon measurements IX, *Radiocarbon*, **33**, 79–86

Wallis, S, 1989 A multi-period site at Slough House Farm, Great Totham parish, *Essex J*, **24**, 39–43

Wallis, S, and Waughman, M, 1998 *Archaeology and the landscape in the Lower Blackwater Valley*, E Anglian Archaeol Rep, **82**, Chelmsford: Essex County Council Archaeol Section

Wand, J O, Gillespie, R, and Hedges, R E M, 1984 Sample preparation for accelerator-based radiocarbon dating. *J Archaeol Sci*, **11**, 159–63

Ward, G K, and Wilson, S R, 1978 Procedures for comparing and combining radiocarbon age determinations: a critique, *Archaeometry*, **20**, 19–31

Waterbolk, H T, 1971 Working with radiocarbon dates, *Proc Prehist Soc*, **37**, 15–33

Waughman, M, 1989 Chigborough Farm, Goldhanger: The first season's excavation of an early settlement, *Essex J*, **24**, 15–8

Webster, L E, and Cherry, J, 1980 Medieval Britain in 1979, *Medieval Archaeol*, **24**, 218–64

Weddell, P J, and Reed, S J, 1997 Excavations at Sourton Down, Okehampton 1986-1991: Roman Broad deserted medieval hamlet and other landscape features, *Devon Archaeol Soc Proc*, **55**, 39–147

Weddell, P J, Reed, S, and Simpson, S J, 1993 Excavations of the Exeter-Dorchester Roman Road at the River Yarty and the Roman fort ditch and settlement site at Woodbury, near Axminster, *Proc Devon Archaeol Soc*, **51**, 33–133

Welch, C M, 1997 A Bronze Age 'burnt mound' at Milwich, *Staffordshire Archaeol Hist Soc Trans*, **36**, 1–15

Welch, D, 1984 Studies in grazing of heather moorland in north-east Scotland: II response of heather, *J Applied Ecology*, **21**, 197–207

Wells, C, Huckerby, E, and Hall, V, 1997 Mid and late holocene vegetation history and tephra studies at Fenton Cottage, Lancaster, UK, *Vegetation Hist Archaeobotany*, **6**, 153–66

Wessex Archaeology, 1992 *Westhampnett from the Ice Age to the Romans*, Salisbury: Wessex Archaeol

Whittle, A, Healy, F, and Bayliss, A, 2011 *Gathering time: dating the early Neolithic enclosures of southern Britain and Ireland*, Oxford: Oxbow Books

Whitwell, B, 1990 Excavation of the Anglian Cemetery Castledyke South, Barton-on-Humber, in Archaeology in Lincolnshire and South Humberside 1989–90, (ed N Field), *Lincolnshire Hist Archaeol*, **25**, 51–3

Wilkinson, K, Barber, L, and Bennell, M, 2002 The examination of six dry valleys in the Brighton area: the changing environment, in *Downland settlement and land-use: the archaeology of the Brighton Bypass* (D Rudling), UCL Fld Archaeol Monogr, **1**, 203–38 London: Archetype

Wilkinson, T J, 1987 *Archaeological investigations at Bradwell on Sea 1987: a preliminary report*, unpubl rep, Essex County Council

Wilkinson, T J, and Murphy, P, 1988 *The Hullbridge basic survey interim report*, unpubl rep 8, Essex County Council

Wilkinson, T J, and Murphy, P, 1995 *The archaeology of the Essex coast, volume 1: the Hullbridge survey*, E Anglian Archaeol Rep, **71**, Chelmsford: Essex County Council Archaeol Section

Williams, P, and Newman, R, 2006 *Market Lavington,*

Wiltshire, and Anglo-Saxon cemetery and settlement: excavations at Grove Farm, 1986–90, Wessex Archaeol Rep, **19**, Salisbury: Wessex Archaeol

Williams, R J, and Zeepvat, R J, 1994 *Bancroft: a late Bronze Age/Iron Age settlement, Roman villa and temple mausoleum*, Buckinghamshire Archaeol Soc Monogr Ser, 7, Aylesbury: Buckinghamshire Archaeol Soc

Willis, E H, Tauber, H, and Munnich, K O, 1960 Variations in the atmospheric radiocarbon concentration over the past 1300 years, *Radiocarbon*, **2**, 1–4

Wilmott, T, 1997 *Birdoswald excavations of a Roman fort on Hadrian's Wall and its successor settlements 1987–92*, Engl Heritage Archaeol Rep, **14**, London: Engl Heritage

Wiltshire, P J, and Bayliss, A, 2006 The Easterton Brook palaeochannel, in *Market Lavington, Wiltshire: an Anglo-Saxon cemetery and settlement* (P Williams and R Newman), Wessex Archaeol Rep, **19**, 118–21

Windell, D, Chapman, A, and Woodiwiss, J, 1990 *From barrows to bypass: excavations at West Cotton, Raunds, Northamptonshire 1985–1989*, Northampton: Northamptonshire Archaeol Unit

Woodward, P J, 1988 Pictures of the Neolithic: discoveries from the Flagstones House excavations, Dorchester, Dorset, *Antiquity*, **62**, 266–74

Woodward, P J, and Smith, R J C, 1987 Survey and excavation along the route of the southern Dorchester bypass 1986–1987 - an interim note, *Proc Dorset Natur Hist Archaeol Soc*, **109**, 84

Wymer, J J, 1996 Barrow Excavations in Norfolk 1984–88, *E Anglian Archaeol*, 77, 58–89

Yates, T G S, 1986 *The selection of non-marine mollusc shells for radiocarbon dating*, unpubl PhD thesis, Univ College London

Younger, P L, and McHugh, M, 1995 Peat development, sand cones and palaeohydrogeology of a spring-fed mire in East Yorkshire, *The Holocene*, **5**, 59–67

Index of laboratory codes

General Index

Page numbers in **bold** refer to illustrations, page numbers in *italic* refer to tables

North Cave, Yorkshire (East Riding) 118–19
North Furzton, Buckinghamshire 119
North West Wetlands Survey 120
 Bonds Farm, Lancashire *xxii*, 120
 Brook Farm, Lancashire 120–1
 Chat Moss, Greater Manchester 121–2
 Cumbria 132–6
 Ditton Brook, Merseyside 122–3
 Fenton Cottage, Lancashire 122–7
 Greater Manchester 121–2
 Ince Blundell, Merseyside 127
 Knowsley Park, Merseyside *xxii*, 128–9
 Lancashire 120–1, 122–7, 130–2, 136–9
 Merseyside 122–3, 127–9
 Peel, Lancashire 130
 Queensway, Lancashire 130
 Rawcliffe 1, Lancashire 131
 Rawcliffe 2, Lancashire 132
 Solway Cow, Cumbria *xxii*, 132–3
 Solway Moss, Cumbria 133–5
 Solway Sheep, Cumbria 135–6
 Stafford's Dyke, Lancashire 136
 Winmarleigh Moss, Lancashire 136–9
North Yorkshire *xxii*, 54, 166–7, 212, 212–13, 214–16,
  220–1, 221, 221–2, 222–3
Northamptonshire 94–5, 162–3, 149–50, 150–3, 153–4,
  154–5, 155–6, 156–7, 157–8, 159, 159–60, 161,
  162, 163–5
Northumberland, Chesters bridge abutment 52
Norwich: southern bypass, Norfolk 139–41
Norwich: St Martin-at-Palace Norfolk 141–2
Nowakowski, J A 195–9

Oakham, Leicestershire 142–3
offsets xix, **xx**
O'Hara, P 165–6
O'Neill, F 143–4
organic matter
 A66 Stainmore Pass: Vale House Farm 10
 Fenton Cottage 124
 Solway Cow *xxii*, 133
 Solway Sheep *xxii*, 135
 Stonea Camp 187
 Wootton-Quarr: Wootton Creek 230
Orton Longueville, Cambridgeshire 143–4
Oxford Radiocarbon Accelerator Unit **viii**, xv, **xv**, xvii, 15,
  19, 37, 41, 76, 87, 143, 146, 149, 181, 214
Oxfordshire ix, 28–9, 54–6, 61–2, 62–4, 77, 77–8, 78,
  78–80, 145–9, 202–3, 235, 235–6, 236, 236–7, 237–8,
  238–9, 239–40

Palmer, N 46–7
Palmer, N J 89–90
Parry, C 29–30
Parry, G 68–9
Parry, S 158
Payne, S 221
Pearl Wood linear ditch, Tidworth, Wessex Linear Ditches,
  Wiltshire 209
Pearson, G **xvi**
Pearson, T 1–2, 168–71
peat *ix*, **x**, xii, xiv–xvi, *xxi*, *xxii*, xxv, 3–4, 4, 5, 6–7, 8, 8–9, 9,
  10, 21, 25–7, 30, 31, 32–3, 33–4, 49, 51, 60, 61, 70,
  94, 99, 100–1, 101–2, 107–8, 112–13, 114, 121, 106,
  122–7, 127, 128, 130, 131, 132, 133–5, 135–6, 136,

  136–9, 154–5, 169–70, 179, 180–1, 184–5, 212,
  212–3, 214–6
Peel, Lancashire, North West Wetlands Survey 130
Pestell, T 178
Peterborough: Cathedral Cloisters, Cambridgeshire 144–5
Pettitt, P 37–8
Pilcher, J **xvi**
pit-ring, Raunds prehistoric: South Stanwick 155–6
plant macrofossil 12, 103, 151, 218, 234–5, 237
plant macrofossil, carbonised **x**, xv, *xxi, xxii*, 20–1, 47, 56–7,
  93, 109, 148, 150, 152
plant macrofossil, waterlogged **x**, xii, 59, 60, 62, 75, 77–8,
  80–1, 81, 157, 163, 237–8
pollen 3, 6–7, 7–8, 21, 30, 31, 32–3, 33–4, 106, 107–8, 113,
  114, 122–3, 128–9, 132, 133–5, 154–5, 212, 212–3,
  214–16
pond barrows 147, 149
Potter Brompton Carr, West Heslerton, North Yorkshire
  212–13
pottery 29–30, 39, 40, 42, 43, 45, 49, 50, 51, 53–4, 56, 62,
  64, 68, 78, 79, 85, 87, 93, 95, 95–6, 97–8, 98–9, 109,
  111–12, 115, 116, 118–19, 119, 139–41, 145, 151,
  160, 162, 163, 164, 165–6, 167, 172–3, 176–7, 177,
  182, 183, 186, 188, 190, 191, 192, 193, 197, 200,
  207, 209, 216, 218, 219, 220, 225, 230, 232
Powlesland, D 211–12
Price, J 201–2
protein fraction dating xiii
Pryor, F 71
PVA, water soluble 223, 224

quality assurance xviii–xix, *xix*, **xx**, *xxi–xxii*, xxii–xxiv,
  xxiii, xxiv
Queensway, Lancashire, North West Wetlands Survey 130
Quinnell, H 165–6, 199–201

radiocarbon dates
 calibration xvii–xviii, **xviii**
 conventions for quoting xvii
Radley: Barrow Hills, Oxfordshire ix, 145–9
Ratcliffe, J 98–102, 172–3
Raunds, Northamptonshire
 Burystead 162–3
 West Cotton, medieval activity 163–5
Raunds Area Project 149–50, 162–3
Raunds prehistoric, Northamptonshire 149–50
 Irthlingborough skulls 153–4
 peat profile 154–5
 South Stanwick 155–6
 Stanwick, Redlands Farm 156–7
 West Cotton, barrow 6 157–8
 West Cotton, long enclosure 159
 West Cotton, long mound 159–60
 West Cotton, palaeochannel and riverine structure 161
 West Cotton, turf mound 162
Ravock, Durham
 field system, site B 9
 field system, site D 9
 oval enclosure 9–10
Rawcliffe 1, Lancashire, North West Wetlands Survey 131
Rawcliffe 2, Lancashire 132
RCHME 84
Reawla, Cornwall 165–6
Reed, S 1, 14, 168–71
reforestation, Fenton Cottage 123–4